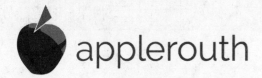

D1191751

Applerouth
1768 Century Blvd Suite B
Atlanta, GA 30345
Email: info@applerouth.com

Director: Richard Vigneault
Writers: Jed Applerouth, Sarah Fletcher, Matt Kiesner, Emma Vigneault, Richard Vigneault
Contributing Writers: Desirina Boskovich, Marshall Findlay, Jenn Gaulding, William Konop, Michael Payne
Contributing Editors: John Cadenhead, Kayla Edgett, Marshall Findlay, Bess Kaye, Matt Kiesner, William Konop, Angela Pirko

Layout Design: Tina Motway, Richard Vigneault
Interior Illustrations: Azekeal McNees, Tina Motway

July 2016

Version 1.1

Manufactured in the United States of America.

Special Thanks

A shout-out to the people who made this book possible.

Thanks to our content-creators:

- **Sarah Fletcher**, for uploading her math genius into our brains.
- **Matthew Kiesner**, for his insane passage-finding skills and his prodigious essay-writing prowess.
- **Marshall Findlay** and **William Konop**, for writing more math practice problems than anyone thought humanly possible.
- **Natalie Henderson**, for *taking* more math practice problems than anyone thought possible.
- **Our Reading team:**
  Emma Vigneault, Matthew Kiesner, and Jenn Gaulding
- **Our Writing team:**
  Emma Vigneault and Matthew Kiesner
- **Our Math team:**
  Richard Vigneault, Sarah Fletcher, Marshall Findlay, and William Konop
- **Our Essay team:**
  Emma Vigneault, Matthew Kiesner, Desirina Boskovich, and Michael Payne

Thanks to our design and graphics team:

- **Tina Motway**, for her infallible taste and dedication.
- **Zeke McNees**, for his unbridled enthusiasm and fantastic attitude.
- **Tobi Motway**, for all the hard work he put in this year.
- **Our lead designers:** Tina Motway and Richard Vigneault
- **Our illustration team:** Azekeal McNees and Tina Motway
- **Our book technology supervisor:** Ryan Paulsen

Thanks to our editing team:

John Cadenhead, Kayla Edgett, Marshall Findlay, Natalie Henderson, Bess Kaye, Matthew Kiesner, William Konop, Will Lewis, Angela Pirko

Thanks to all our tutors, whose insights, dedication, and love for their students are our most valuable resources.

Contents

Writing

Day 1

Day 2

Day 3

Day 4

Day 5

Day 6

Math

Day 7

Day 8

Day 9

Day 10

Day 11

Day 12

Day 20

Practice Test

Day 21

Day 22

Answer Key

Day 23

Letter from Jed

Every year over a million students partake in the time-honored ritual of taking the SAT. If you are reading this book, then your time has come to join the ranks and see just how high you can raise your score.

The SAT, like any other test, can be studied and mastered. Succeeding on the SAT does not require the waving of a magic wand. It requires a combination of effort and the proper tools. We've worked hard to create the ultimate SAT preparation tool. And now it's in your hands.

We kept several principles in mind when we designed this book:

- Keep things simple and clear.

- Break things into smaller steps and build on them.

- Keep things visually interesting.

- Use humor whenever possible: it's okay to laugh while learning!

This book is comprehensive. We've analyzed every aspect of the new SAT to bring you the strategies included in this book. Use it well, and hit the scores you need to get into the schools of your dreams. If you are looking for additional information or resources to help you along the way, please check us out online at www.applerouth.com.

Thanks and good luck!

Jed Applerouth

SAT FAQs

You probably have a lot of questions about the new SAT. We've answered some Frequently Asked Questions below, but you can always go to applerouth.com for more information.

What is the SAT?

The SAT is the mother of all standardized tests. It has undergone numerous changes since it first came on the scene in the 1920s when it was created to identify students who would thrive in a university setting. In March 2005, the SAT went from a total score of 1600 to 2400, adding the Writing section, which included grammar and an essay that was previously administered as a SAT Subject Test.

In March 2016, the College Board redesigned the SAT. The total score dropped back down to 1600, with the Writing and Reading sections now combined into an Evidence-Based Reading and Writing score. The essay is now optional, just like the ACT, and does not affect any other score. The College Board also scrapped the sentence completions and shifted the math section away from geometry and instead focused on algebra and data representations.

Why did the SAT change?

There are two answers to this question. First, the College Board designed the new SAT to align better with the Common Core and similar standards, and test math that better matched what students would be learning in school. The second answer is that more and more students were turning to the ACT and the College Board feared that if they did not retool, the SAT would become obsolete.

Does the SAT have a guessing penalty?

Nope! They scrapped the guessing penalty as part of the changes implemented with the March 2016 test. **Students should answer all questions in a section, even if it's just a guess.**

How does the SAT differ from the ACT?

In all honesty, the redesigned SAT mirrors the ACT in many ways. The SAT Writing and Language section is nearly identical to the ACT English section. The SAT Reading section dropped the advanced vocabulary and now focuses on medium length passages similar to the ACT. Finally, The SAT gave up its guessing penalty, so now students should answer all questions, just like on the ACT.

However, there are still noticeable differences between the two tests. The SAT does not have a Science section like the ACT has; instead, the SAT integrated data analysis into all sections. This means that both the Reading and the Writing and Language sections have figures and tables attached to some passages.

In math, the ACT focuses equally on Geometry, Algebra, and Arithmetic, with a handful of Trig and Pre-Calc concepts thrown in. The redesigned SAT dropped nearly all of its Geometry and instead focuses on Algebra and the way it can be used to model and understand real-world situations.

Another big difference between the SAT and ACT math section is the SAT's No Calculator section. Here the College Board wants to test students' abilities to crunch numbers, graph, factor, and FOIL without the help of a calculator. Finally, the ACT math section is entirely multiple choice, while the new SAT contains grid-in problems at the end of each math section.

Overall, the biggest difference between the tests may be in terms of time. The ACT is a fast-paced test, forcing students to move quickly from question to question. On the ACT **Reading** section, students only have 53 seconds per question, while the **SAT gives 75 seconds per question**. On the **Math** section, the ACT gives 60 seconds per question, while the **SAT gives 83 seconds.** A major factor in choosing the ACT or SAT may be how a student manages time.

For an in-depth illustrated comparison of the ACT and the new SAT, visit **www.applerouth.com/testcomparison.**

What do colleges really think about the SAT?

As a whole, colleges seem ready to hang back and see how the redesigned SAT pans out. As of now, no college has shown a preference towards either the SAT or ACT. This may change as colleges will eventually be able to track long-term success and graduation rates after a few years.

How important is my SAT score?

For most students, their SAT score is profoundly important to the college admissions process. After considering your GPA and academic schedule strength, most colleges look to your SAT score next. Other aspects of your application—recommendations, admissions essays, and activities—are subordinate to your score on the SAT. Strong scores can open the door to bettercolleges and universities, and increase the chance to win valuable scholarships.

Why do colleges put so much weight on the SAT?

Colleges want to ensure that the students they pick for their incoming classes will be able to succeed academically. To make better picks, admissions officers first look to high school GPA: the single best predictor of success in college. But a 3.2 cumulative GPA at one school means something completely different from a 3.2 at another school, even one right down the street. Colleges need another efficient measure that is standardized, the same for all students; that's where the SAT fits in. It turns out students with stronger SAT scores tend to achieve stronger grades in college. A strong SAT score increases the confidence of admissions officers that you have what it takes to succeed in college.

What does the SAT test?

The SAT tests one thing: your ability to take the SAT. It is not an IQ test, and it certainly does not test any innate aptitude. In fact, especially in the math sections, the new SAT focuses on content you have learned in school rather than tricky problems seemingly designed to confuse. Given enough time, energy, and dedication to the process of preparing for this test, a student can see a dramatic increase in his or her test score.

What do the scores actually mean?

The new SAT has more scores than ever before. Here's a breakdown of the scores you'll receive when you take the real test:

Score	Details	Range
Total score	The total sore is the sum of the two section scores.	400-1600
2 Section Scores	Math Evidence-Based Reading and Writing	200-800
3 Test Scores	Reading Writing Math (Calc and No-Calc)	10-40
2 Cross-Test Scores	Analysis in History/Social Studies Analysis in Science	10-40
7 Subscores	Command of Evidence Words in Context Expression of Ideas Standard of English Conventions Heart of Algebra Passport to Advanced Math Probability and Data Analysis	10-40
3 Essay Scores	Reading Analysis Writing	2-8

The terminology is a bit confusing, so let us explain what all these scores mean. The **3 Test Scores** are your scores for the different sections of the test: Reading, Writing and Language, and Math. The Math Test Score is a combination of your scores on the No Calculator and Calculator sections; you will not receive separate scores for these two sections.

The **2 Section Scores** are a combination of the Test Scores. To get the total Evidence-Based Reading and Writing Score, College Board adds your Reading Test Score and Writing Test Score, then multiplies by 10. To get your Math Score, College Board simply multiplies your Math Test Score by 20. The Total Score is the sum of the two Section Scores.

The **2 Cross-Test Scores** come from questions on all sections of the test that fall under the topics of Analysis in History/Social Science or Analysis in Science. For example, the questions attached to the Science passages in the Reading section count towards your Analysis in Science score, while the questions about Data Analysis on the math sections count towards your Analysis in History/Social Science score.

The **7 Subscores** reflect your performance on certain question types. Some only apply to one section (e.g. Expression of Ideas is a Writing subscore only), some apply across sections (e.g. Words in Context shows up in the Reading and Writing sections).

Reading and Writing Subscores:

- **Command of Evidence** questions test your ability to use evidence to support your answer. These questions might ask you to choose a section of the passage that supports a previous answer, or require you to analyze a graphic as it relates to the passage.

- **Words in Context** questions ask you to choose the appropriate word in the context of a larger passage.

Writing Subscores:

- **Expression of Ideas** test your ability to edit and revise for content, logic, and use of language.

- **Standard English Conventions** questions require you to edit passages for grammar and syntax errors.

Math Subscores:

- **Heart of Algebra** questions test your understanding of functions and linear equations: calculating slope, interpreting what slope means in context, balancing equations.

- **Passport to Advanced Math** questions test similar skills as Heart of Algebra questions, but as they relate to non-linear equations: exponents bigger than one, factoring of quadratics.

- **Probability and Data Analysis** is relatively new ground for the SAT. Probability, percentages, and unit conversion are tested here, but so are drawing conclusions from study results, understanding the importance of sample size, and other statistics-related topics.

What score do I need to get into a particular college?

More competitive schools require more competitive scores. To find out the average score for incoming students for a particular school, visit the school's web site or contact its admissions office. The College Board's website, www.collegeboard.com, has a great tool which allows you to enter the name of a school, click on "Applying" on the left, go to the "SAT & ACT Scores" tab and see the breakdown of SAT scores for admitted freshmen. In order to submit a highly competitive application, you should aim for an SAT score in the top 25% for each school to which you are applying.

Additionally, you can create an account at **www.applerouth.com** to build your very own **personalized college tracker**. Click "Add College" and enter the names of colleges in which you are interested. Check back as you improve your score to see where you fall in each school's desired SAT score range.

How much can I improve my SAT score?

Most students have the potential to significantly improve their SAT scores. On average, our privately-tutored students move up 14 percentiles on the SAT, meaning a student starting in the 70th percentile usually ends up in the 84th percentile: that's a big jump! Some achieve much greater gains, and we've even seen increases of over 60 percentiles. What differentiates the most successful students from those who are less successful is their level of dedication, motivation, and the amount of time they invest in the process. If you invest 100 hours toward achieving a higher score, your chance of picking up 300 points is much greater than if you invest 20 hours. The more time you invest, the more homework you complete, and the more practice tests you complete under timed conditions, the better you will tend to do on the SAT.

How much time do I need to spend on this process?

This completely depends on your introductory score and your ultimate goal. If you need to pick up a mere 20 points, you may need only a handful of hours of preparation. If you are shooting for an increase of 80 or 100 points, your investment will need to be much more substantial. On average, if you are shooting for a gain of 60 points or greater, you will need to invest 50-60 hours in this process. Some students need much less preparation, and some need more. However, everyone must put in the time to drill problems and complete timed sections and tests. Each practice test takes roughly three hours, and you will want to complete at least four of them to get ready for the official test.

Considering how important your SAT score is to your college application, 50-60 hours is really a modest investment. Remember, for most college admissions offices, SAT score is second in importance only to your GPA. However, at some larger state schools, SAT and GPA receive almost equal weight. It takes roughly 4,000 hours of class time to generate a high school GPA and only 60 hours to attain a competitive SAT score. Dedicating time to your SAT score is the single most efficient way to improve your odds of gaining admission to a competitive college.

How often should I take the SAT?

You should always check with the specific colleges you're applying to for their requirements, but here are our recommendations. Generally, three times should be adequate to achieve your optimal score, but there is usually no penalty for taking the SAT as many times as you need to achieve the score you seek. An increasing number of schools will "superscore" your tests and create a composite SAT score, combining the highest section scores from different administrations to create your "Super" score.

Because SATs vary in difficulty from one administration to the next, it's in your best interest to take this test multiple times until you reach your target score. Just as there are easier and harder tests, students have good and bad days. Even when you are fully prepared, certain factors beyond your control can influence your score: were the passages easy or hard for you? How effectively did you guess? Did you make careless errors? There is some luck involved, and the more frequently you take the SAT, the more you minimize the "luck" component.

The more you take this test, the more comfortable and confident you become. You eventually move into a zone where you know what to expect and achieve a level of mastery of the testing process. As students move from their first to their second SAT, they tend to achieve their biggest score increases. Students generally see smaller gains through their third SAT.

Should I set goals for each test I take?

Absolutely! Always keep your ultimate goal in mind, and view each test as a stepping stone towards this goal. Set distinct section goals for each test you plan to take. Say, for example, your introductory score is a 540 reading and 520 math, giving you a total score of 1060, and you want to hit a total of 1200. Set short term goals for each test you plan to take, and write them down. "In October my goal is 560 reading and 550 math. In December my goal is 580 reading and 570 math. My goal for June is 610 Reading and 590 math." As you write your goals, enumerate the steps you will take to achieve them, such as practicing with your Applerouth Guide to the SAT and taking mock tests. **Setting and attaining short term goals has a positive impact on your sense of confidence and your level of motivation.** Use these short term goals to help you attain your ultimate goal.

When should I take the SAT?

Fall and winter of junior year are ideal times to take the first SAT. The December or January SAT is a natural first test. For students who are enrolled in Algebra II as juniors, we generally recommend January as the first official SAT; this gives them a semester to hone their Algebra II skills. The majority of our students, having finished Algebra II as sophomores, are ready to jump in at the beginning of junior year.

Keep your schedule in mind! If you have a major time commitment in the fall, wait until the winter to start your prep. It is quite common to prep intensely and take two SATs back to back. Once you've knocked out a test or two, it's fine to take breaks and come back for one later in the year.

Many of our students see their greatest gains on the June SAT. This has to do with our students' growing familiarity and comfort with the test as well as their freedom from academic and extracurricular obligations. Once school is out, students can really focus on the June SAT.

Ideally students will take the SAT two to three times their junior year. SATs administered during the fall of their senior year are available as back-ups. The October, November, and December tests of senior year will all count for regular admissions. The October test is generally the last SAT that will count for Early Decision / Early action.

How do I register for the SAT?

Log in to www.collegeboard.org. Click "Sign up/Log in" and create an account. Follow the instructions. Make sure to sign up early to secure a spot at a preferred location. The good locations can fill up quickly.

What do I need to take to the SAT?

- A few No. 2 pencils (no mechanical pencils)
- Your registration information, printed from the computer
- Your driver's license or other form of photo ID
- A digital watch or one with a second hand
- Your graphing calculator and extra batteries (for a list of approved calculators, go to www.sat.collegeboard.org/register/calculator-policy)
- Snacks and water
- Layers of clothing, in the event you are in a cold or hot room

When can I expect my scores to be available?

The scores for the March 2016 and May 2016 tests will be delayed until June. This is because the College Board wants to be able to compare results across a large sample of students to calibrate the scores properly. Previously, scores were available online 17 days after test day, but we don't know if that will hold true after June.

How do I report my SAT scores to schools?

When you sign up for an SAT administration, you can select up to four schools to receive your SAT scores free of charge. You can send your scores to additional schools for a fee. After the test, you can log onto your College Board My SAT account to send your scores to schools.

Do I have to send all of my SAT scores?

College Board allows you to send particular scores and withhold others. If a college superscores the SAT, it is in your best interest to send all tests which contain a personal best on any section. Keep in mind, some colleges require that you send all of your scores. That will be made clear during the application process.

What is extended time? Do I need it? Can I get it?

Some students with diagnosed disabilities are allowed to take the SAT with accommodations such as extended time. Only a licensed psychologist can make the diagnosis of whether a student needs extended time to compensate for a learning disability. In most cases, before the College Board will consider granting extended time or any other accommodation, your high school must acknowledge your disability and grant you the accommodation for it.

Do I need additional SAT prep materials to supplement this book?

We encourage our students to get as much practice as possible! The College Board offers three options for practice. They released four full-length practice tests, which students can print out and take as mock tests. The College Board also published The Official SAT Study Guide, which contains the same tests in book form. These tests are excellent tools to help you practice your pacing and time-management skills. Secondly, the College Board has released a Daily Practice app for Apple and Android phones. The third option is from Khan Academy, which offers free practice to students who create an account.

Structure of the SAT

Let's look at the overall structure of the Redesigned SAT.

The SAT consists of 4 timed sections: Reading, English, Math–No Calculator, and Math–Calculator. A fifth section, the Essay, is optional. The order of the sections on the SAT is the same on every test:

1 **READING**

The Reading section consists of **five passages** designed to test your reading comprehension skills. You will be given one passage each about Literature, Politics, and Social Science, and two passages about Natural Science. Two of the passages come with charts, tables, or graphs. You have **65 minutes** to answer **52 multiple choice questions**.

2 **WRITING AND LANGUAGE**

The Writing section consists of **four passages** designed to test your grammatical and rhetorical skills. One or two passages come with charts, tables, or graphs. You have **35 minutes** to answer **44 multiple choice questions.**

3 **MATH–NO CALCULATOR**

The Math–No Calculator section consists of 20 questions, most of which test your ability to solve and manipulate algebraic equations. You have **25 minutes** to answer **15 multiple choice questions and 5 grid-in questions.**

MATH–CALCULATOR

The Math–Calculator section consists of 38 questions that test your ability to solve Algebra and Data Analysis problems in real-world contexts. You have **55 minutes** to answer **30 multiple choice questions and 8 grid-in questions.**

If you sign up for the SAT with the optional **Essay**, you will be given **50 minutes** to read a passage and write an essay that analyzes the author's argument and the passage's persuasive and stylistic elements.

Pacing and Practice

Time is a precious resource on the SAT. Learn how to spend it wisely with these good habits that will help you stay on pace.

TIP

Be sure to bring your own watch, in case the clock is placed behind you or if there is no clock in the testing room.

Keep your Eye on the Clock

To skillfully manage your pacing, you must develop a habit of regularly **checking in with the clock.** You don't want to go 15 minutes without looking at the clock, then realize "WOW, I am way behind schedule!"

A far more effective strategy is to check in with the clock every few questions to ensure that you are pacing well and smartly allocating your time. This will help you cut down on "OMG!" moments.

Actively Read

When you skillfully read the questions and **<u>underline</u> key content** with your pencil, you are able to answer the questions more quickly. Passively reading followed by re-reading is a major time sink.

Play to your Strengths

Depending on your score goal, you might be better off skipping questions, or even whole passages, that are tough for you and focusing on the ones that you know you can get right. You don't have to take each question in order; leave the hardest questions and passages for last so you can use most of your time to really nail the stuff you know.

Guessing

If you don't know the answer to a question, don't forget to bubble in a guess! There is no penalty for guessing, so you have a 25% chance of getting a point when you randomly bubble in.

Stay on Task

Every question type has a step-by-step strategy, which we will outline for you. **Get started on the first step right away.** Stick with the steps; don't stray from the path.

Don't Spin Your Wheels

Once you have skillfully narrowed down your answer choices, it's time to **pick one and move on**. There's no time for wheel spinning or second guessing! In the immortal words of Jay Z, we're "on to the next one."

Now that you know the four good timing habits, to push your timing even further, you need to shift from the "macro" to the "micro" level. It's time to focus on timing intervals: the number of seconds you spend on each question.

Learn Your Intervals

If you divide the amount of time allotted for a complete section by the number of questions in a section, you arrive at the average time allowed per question.

Section	Minutes	Questions	Seconds per Question
Reading	65	52	75 (including reading time)
Writing	35	44	48 (including reading time)
Math–No Calc	25	20	75
Math–Calc	55	38	87

It's important that you learn to manage these intervals and identify your areas of timing strength and weakness.

Timing Drills: The Art of Getting Faster

The best way to increase your speed on the SAT is to conduct **timing drills.** Once you've identified the section that is giving you the biggest timing challenge, it's time to drill.

Determine your natural pace

Get a timer (most smartphones or watches will do fine) and find a quiet room. Start the timer and complete a full section, without breaks, to determine your natural speed.

Let's say you complete a timed Math–No Calc section, and it takes you 30 minutes, rather than 25, to answer all the questions. So you are **five minutes over the limit.** Let's find out where you're spending that extra time.

Determine where the time is going

Try another Math–No Calc section, but this time work with the clock and record how long it takes you to do **each problem.** Then analyze the results.

Problem	Seconds	Correct
1	60	Yes
2	55	Yes
3	130	No
4	75	Yes
5	152	No

TIP

It's common for students to miss the problems on which they spend the most time!

Where are you spending your time? Are you **spinning your wheels** and spending 2-3 minutes on certain problems? Are you getting these time-intensive problems right?

If you see that you're missing these problems, you can feel confident that guessing and moving on when you come to a challenging question **will not hurt your score.** Similarly, when you get to a problem that you know will take some serious time, **mark it** and **come back to it later!**

Set new timing targets

TIP

Improving your speed is not about thinking faster or being smarter, it's just about getting comfortable with a faster pace.

Establish new timing "ceilings" for each question: the time at which you will force yourself to guess and move on. If you were previously averaging 100 seconds/question, set a new limit of 90 seconds/question.

Conduct a timing drill at this accelerated pace. How did you do? Were you able to increase your pace without sacrificing accuracy? If you were too aggressive too quickly, bring it back a step. Try 95 seconds/question, and keep on drilling!

The Importance of Practice Tests

No SAT prep program would be complete without **timed practice tests.** Timed tests allow you to practice your time management skills while also testing your knowledge of each subject. They also help you build mental endurance ,self-regulation strategies, and self-motivation techniques.

In this book is **1 complete SAT practice test.** This is a fabulous tool to help you prepare for the actual SAT. There are also 4 tests available for free on the College Board website. Take one timed test early in your study schedule to help identify areas that need improvement, and use the second test to monitor your progress closer to the test.

In addition to the practice test, you will find complete passages in the Reading and Writing chapters, and complete Math sections in the Math chapter. If you take your first practice test and identify a particular section that poses a timing challenge, use these sections for timing drills. Remember, it takes practice to get used to a new pace. So bust out that stopwatch, smart phone, or sundial, and get to it!

How to Use This Book

This book is divided into the key sections of the SAT: Reading, Writing, Math, and essay. Each chapter contains strategies, illustrated explanations, and practice sections.

TIP

It's a good idea to flip through a chapter that you've already read and review the Tips and Notes.

Tips and Notes

As you make your way through the book, you will notice a **variety of call-outs** in the margins. These highlight material that you will want to remember and provide you with additional strategies and tricks.

EXAMPLES and SOLUTIONS

A large portion of this book is dedicated to working through example problems to show you the best way to approach the material. Give every example a shot before you read the solution. Then, check your work and answer against the solution, reading for tips that will help you solve future problems.

Portals

In every section of the book, you'll find portals in the margins, leading you to other pages in the book that might help you understand or practice a topic. These are designed to help you **make connections** between different concepts to boost your understanding of each.

Peppers

Problems marked with peppers are the most difficult problems in our book and on the SAT. Unless you are aiming for a **near-perfect score,** you can skip these problems, as you'll get more payoff for your time spent on other topics.

Exercises

Some chapters have exercises, interactive practice designed to bridge the gap between learning a concept and putting it into practice on an example problem. Look for the **pencil icon** to build up your learning!

Practice Problems

This book has over 500 different practice problems—not including the practice test and examples—that are modeled after real SAT passages and problems. After completing each chapter, complete the practice problems attached and **be sure to check your answers!**

Ways to Study

There is no single, "right" way to prepare for the SAT. You should consider your own unique strengths and weaknesses when deciding on the study plan that will work best for you. Let's look at two approaches to SAT prep:

① The Comprehensive Review

Each week complete a series of lessons and practice problems from each of the three sections: Reading, Writing, and Math. In week 1, you may tackle Basic Algebra in Math, All About Clauses in Writing, and Active Reading in Reading. This balanced approach will keep you moving forward on all fronts as you prepare to take on all the sections of the SAT.

② Isolate and Focus

Take a practice test. Determine your individual areas of weakness. Use the book to focus on the areas where you are weakest. If your Reading score is low, put your energy there. If you are grappling with Accomplish a Task questions, go there first. You can use your mock tests as feedback to guide your preparation.

Don't Cram: Spread out your SAT Review

Memory researchers have found that packing all of your review into long sessions is not nearly as effective as spacing your study over multiple, shorter sessions. Each time you review a concept, you strengthen and "reinforce" it, etching the material deeper into your brain, so it will be there when you need it on test day!

Review the Next Day

As soon as you learn a new concept in this book, review it within **24 hours** to help **lock it into your memory**. Researchers have found that this practice dramatically increases your ability to recall what you have learned on test day!

Reading Intro

Here's what you can expect to see on the SAT Reading section.

The SAT Reading section assesses your ability to quickly read large blocks of text (and a few graphs), recall specific details, make inferences, and find evidence for your answers. Before we dive into the strategies that will help you ace this section, let's learn about the types of passages and questions you'll see on the test.

Passage Types

The Reading section is divided into 5 parts: 4 long passages and 1 pair of shorter comparison passages, with 10-11 questions attached to each part. On each test you will find:

 One **Literature** passage telling a story. It could be from the 1800s, the 2000s, or any time in between; the older passages usually have harder vocabulary and are more difficult for some students.

 One **Social Science** passage (or a pair of comparison passages) about economics, psychology, or sociology. This passage will often be about population trends or new technology, and will always come with an attached chart, table, or graph.

 One **Politics** passage (or a pair of comparison passages), usually focused on American politics, that could date as far back as the 1700s. Again, many students will find older passages more difficult to understand.

 Two **Natural Science** passages (or one long passage and one pair of comparison passages) about biology, chemistry, physics, or Earth science. One of these will come with an attached chart, table, or graph. One is usually informative, and the other recounts an experiment or study.

TIP

Skipping tougher passages and coming back later is encouraged, but make sure you're bubbling in your answers on the correct question!

Leave Tough Passages for Last

Some of the passages will be easy to understand; some will sound very old-timey and might leave you scratching your head. Here's a **secret**: you don't have to do the passages in order! If you love Science, but English class gives you a headache, leave the Literature passage for last so you don't burn out at the beginning of the test. Do you love reading about American History, but can't stay awake in your Biology class? Start with the Politics passage and come back to the science passages after you've finished the rest of the test.

Question Types

The questions on the Reading section are all trying to get at one thing: did you understand what you read? You'll see 4 question types on the test:

- **Content and Analysis** questions ask you to find key information in the passage, analyze rhetorical strategies used by the author, or describe the overall structure and purpose of the passage.

- **Vocabulary in Context** questions ask for the correct meaning of a word in the context of the passage.

- **Evidence-Based Questions** almost always come in pairs; the first is a regular Content and Analysis question, and the second asks for the lines in the passage that *prove* the first answer is correct.

- **Charts, Tables, and Graphs** questions require you to combine information from the passage with data from a figure, such as a table or a line graph.

Balancing your Time

On average, you have **13 minutes** to move through each of the five passages and knock out all the accompanying questions. That's a lot of time! This test is an *open-book test*: all the answers to the questions are right there in the passages. So take your time to **actively read**, marking up the passage as you go. When you get to the questions, you'll use your active reading to locate key parts of the passage, eliminate wrong answers, and **prove** the right answer.

Building Habits

The Reading section is different from the Math and Writing sections of the test. There are no rules to memorize or formulas to cram into your brain. Instead, we'll be building better **habits**. You'll learn reading habits that make it easier for you to understand the passage, answering habits that help you eliminate wrong answers and find evidence for the right answer, and habits that keep you from spending too much time on one question. But like all habits, these won't simply appear overnight.

The Importance of Practice

The sure-fire way to improve your Reading score is to practice, practice, practice. When you first try out the strategies in this section, they might slow you down or feel awkward at first. When you're tired, you might forget and slip into old habits. But over time, passage-by-passage, you'll be turning those new strategies into good, solid habits. Eventually, the strategies will become second nature; as a result, you'll actually **become** a better reader and test-taker. So let's get started!

Reading Strategy

On a basic level, every Reading question can be solved the same way.

1 **ACTIVELY READ THE PASSAGE**

Actively reading the passage is the first and **most important** step to answering the questions. With this foundation, answering the questions is a breeze!

2 **ACTIVELY READ AND PARAPHRASE THE QUESTION**

Before you can answer a question, you have to know what it's asking. To check your understanding, put the question into your own words.

3 **SEARCH THE PASSAGE FOR EVIDENCE THAT ANSWERS THE QUESTION**

Use your active reading to find the answer in the passage. If the question contained a line reference, begin your search there, always remembering to **read in context!**

4 **USE THROWAWAYS TO ELIMINATE WRONG ANSWER CHOICES**

Focusing on individual "throwaway" words, cross out answer choices that are not supported by the passage. Find your right answer through the magical process of elimination.

5 **FOLLOW QUESTION-SPECIFIC STRATEGIES**

Lots of questions have specific strategies that will help you tackle them. Go through the strategies step-by-step to nail these questions every time.

Active Reading

When students struggle with the Reading section, it is often because they are used to reading passively. This is a sure-fire way to struggle on SAT Reading!

Glucose

It's in food. Your body needs it to do things like read, think, answer questions, and keep from falling out of a desk and into a coma.

PLEASE do not skip breakfast on test day. And bring a snack!

Passive Reading: To Blur is Human

Does this sound familiar? You get all fired up to start scanning a long reading comprehension passage. In the back of your mind, you start to worry about how much time you have, then you realize you're hungry (like **really** hungry), and then your eyes start to glaze over, and the passage starts to look like this:

> It is highly doubtful that the Allied forces would have won World War II without the help of Polish mathematician **Marian** Rejewski. At age fourteen, Rejews
> secret   Soon his
> full-time **occupation** was decoding the German **Enigma machine. Combining** his usage of pure mathematics with **informatio**n p   **Rejewski succeeded** in decoding the Enigma, and consequently, the Allied forces were able to **intercept German intelligence transmissions for six years.** Historian Da
>   ng **achievement "elevates him to the pantheon of the greatest cryptanalysts of all time." On the** 100th an   rsary of **his birthday, a sculpted memorial was** presented to his **hometown** of Bydgo   , **Poland.**

As a result, you have to waste time re-reading chunks of the passage to answer the questions. All this leaves you feeling rushed and frustrated.

The Drawbacks of Passive Reading

- **Blurred understanding** of the passage
- Likely to **miss key information**
- **Waste time** searching for answers

Active Reading: To Underline is Divine

When you read actively, you wisely trade all that re-reading for some **quick pencil movements** early on. The key is to invest your time on the front end so that you can breeze through the questions later on.

When your hand is busy, your brain is more active. You retain more information, making it easier to answer questions from memory. When you do need to go back and check the passage, your active reading serves as a handy outline and map, guiding you to the area of the passage where you'll find the correct answer. You can spot an active reader just by glancing at her test:

Do you have time for this?

YES! These simple pencil movements add mere seconds to your reading time, but they save you precious minutes when answering questions.

The better question is: **"Can you afford NOT to do this?"**

> *WWII*
> It is highly <u>doubtful</u> that the <u>Allied forces</u> would have <u>won World War II</u> without the help of <u>Polish mathematician</u> Marian <u>Rejewski</u>. At age <u>fourteen</u>, <u>Rejewski</u> enrolled in a <u>secret cryptology course</u> for German speakers. Soon his full-time occupation was <u>decoding</u> the German <u>Enigma machine</u>. *Enigma* ☆ <u>Combining</u> his usage of pure <u>mathematics</u> with information provided by <u>French intelligence</u>, Rejewski <u>succeeded</u> in <u>decoding</u> the Enigma, and (consequently,) the Allied forces were able to intercept German intelligence transmissions for six years. *Kahn* <u>Historian David Kahn</u> says that Rejewski's stunning achievement "elevates him to the <u>pantheon of the greatest cryptanalysts of all time</u>." On the 100th anniversary of his birthday, a sculpted <u>memorial</u> was presented to his hometown of Bydgoszcz, <u>Poland</u>.

Underlines, circles, notes, and stars cover the passage. As a result, you can quickly answer easy questions, have help finding the answer to tough ones, and are far too busy killing it to be stressed. On the next few pages, we'll dive into each of the four components of active reading: **underlining** key information, taking **notes** in the margin, **circling** logic words, and **starring** main ideas.

The Benefits of Active Reading

- ✛ Check **understanding** as you read
- ✛ Easier to **find key information**
- ✛ **Less time searching** for answers

1 Underline Key Ideas

Most information in a passage plays only a supporting role, and some is simply there to distract you. You only need to underline content that conveys the main points and key ideas of each paragraph. In general, you will underline roughly 20 to 30 percent of the words in a passage.

Read the following passage, underlining key facts as you go.

It is highly doubtful that the Allied forces would have won World War II without the help of Polish mathematician Marian Rejewski. At age fourteen, Rejewski enrolled in a secret cryptology course for German speakers. Soon his full-time occupation was decoding the German Enigma machine. Combining his usage of pure mathematics with information provided by French intelligence, Rejewski succeeded in decoding the Enigma, and consequently, the Allied forces were able to intercept German intelligence transmissions for six years. Historian David Kahn says that Rejewski's stunning achievement "elevates him to the pantheon of the greatest cryptanalysts of all time." On the 100th anniversary of his birthday, a sculpted memorial was presented to his hometown of Bydgoszcz, Poland.

Compare your active reading with the sample on the previous page. They don't need to be exactly the same, but you should be underlining a similar amount of words overall (about 30% of the total passage).

The Benefits:

Underlining as you read helps raise your score in two ways. First, it makes it easier to come back to certain parts of the passage when answering questions. If a question asks about "German speakers," you can quickly scan only your underlined words for "German" to spot the relevant part of the passage. Second, and more importantly, the act of deciding what is and isn't worth underlining helps you condense the passage down to just the important pieces. This effectively shrinks the passage so it's juuuust small enough to fit inside your short-term memory.

notes = good

2 Take Notes in the Margin

A responsible active reader takes quick, 1-to-4 word notes in the margin next to each paragraph and major idea. These notes summarize the focus of the passage at that point, making it immensely easier to see the flow of the passage just by scanning the margins. Whereas underlining helps you focus on the really important content in each sentence, margin notes help you see the flow of ideas throughout the passage.

Write a margin note for each paragraph in the blank provided.

_____ Brick by brick, six-year-old Alice is building a magical kingdom. Imagining fairy-tale turrets and fire-breathing dragons, wicked sorcerers and gallant heroes, she's creating an enchanting world. Although she isn't aware of it, this fantasy will have important repercussions in her adult life: it is helping her take her first steps towards her capacity for abstract thought and creativity.

_____ Minutes later, Alice has abandoned the kingdom in favor of wrestling with her brother—or, according to educational psychologists, developing her capacity for strong emotional attachments. When she bosses him around as 'his teacher,' she's practicing how to regulate her emotions through pretence. When they settle down with a board game, she's learning about rules and turn-taking. "Play in all its rich variety is one of the highest achievements of the human species," says Dr. David Whitebread from Cambridge's Faculty of Education. "It underpins how we develop as intellectual, problem-solving, emotional adults and is crucial to our success as a highly adaptable species."

_____ Recognizing the importance of play is not new: over two millennia ago, Plato extolled its virtues as a means of developing skills for adult life, and ideas about play-based learning have been developing since the 19th century. But we live in changing times, and Whitebread is mindful of a worldwide decline in play. "Over half the world's population live in cities. Play is curtailed by perceptions of risk to do with traffic, crime, abduction, and germs, and by the emphasis on 'earlier is better' in academic learning. The opportunities for free play, which I experienced almost every day of my childhood, are becoming increasingly scarce. Today, play is often a scheduled and supervised activity."

3 Circle Key Words

If you circle key words that are likely to come up later in the questions, you will make it that much easier to find correct answers. There are different types of words to focus on depending on the **type of passage** you are reading. For example, questions on a literature passage will often ask you about different characters, their descriptions, and their motives. Circling those character names when they first show up will make it much easier for you to highlight parts of the passage that are likely to be important later on!

On **Narrative** passages, focus on character names & descriptions, as well as words indicating how the different characters *feel* about each other or events around them.

On **Informative** passages, focus on dates, names, and the order of events for historical topics. For more scientific passages, circle new terms & their definitions – particularly ones that are new to you.

On **Argumentative** passages, where the author is arguing a particular point, circle the author's thesis, as well as any counter-arguments from an opposing side.

Many authors, regardless of passage type, signal that a main point is coming by using a "logic word" like **but**, **however**, **therefore**, and **although.** When you see logic words like those in the table below, circle them! This will help you spot *shifts in the author's argument* and identify the logical flow of the passage as a whole.

LOGIC WORDS	
Conclusion	**Logical Shift**
Thus	But
Consequently	However
Therefore	Although
Because	Nevertheless
Hence	Nonetheless

4 Star Main Ideas

Finally, when the author lays out what feels like the essence of his or her argument, put a star next to it in the margins. When you get to questions asking for the main idea, let these stars guide you home!

The Importance of Practice

If you are not used to reading actively, the process may slow you down at first. That's okay—it's normal! You will naturally speed up as you practice over the course of several weeks, and you'll be able to practice throughout this entire chapter.

Before we dive into strategies for answering the questions, let's try reading actively with a full-length SAT passage. Before you start, find a clock, watch, or timer app and record how long it takes you to actively read the passage below. Eventually, we'll be aiming to spend just around 7 minutes reading each passage on the test. For now, though, your only goals are to get comfortable reading actively and to find out how much you'll need to speed up or slow down over the course of your practice.

LET'S RECAP!

Active Reading is the most effective tool you have for increasing your SAT Reading score. Using your pencil while you read keeps you alert, makes it easier to find answers to each question, and speeds you up!

The four components of active reading are:

- **Underline** key ideas
- Take **notes** in the margin
- **Circle** key words
- **Star** main ideas

Reading Practice Passage 1
TO STAY ON PACE, YOUR TIMING GOAL IS 13 MINUTES

DIRECTIONS

Each passage or pair of passages below is followed by a number of questions. After reading each passage or pair, choose the best answer to each question based on what is stated or implied in the passage or passages and in any accompanying graphics (such as a table or graph).

Questions 1-10 are based on the following passage.

This passage is from H. C. McNeile, "A Question of Personality." Originally published in 1921.

The personally conducted tour round Frenton's Steel Works paused, as usual, on reaching the show piece of the entertainment. The mighty hammer, operated
Line with such consummate ease by the movement of a
5 single lever, though smaller than its more celebrated brother at Woolwich Arsenal, never failed to get a round of applause from the fascinated onlookers. There was something almost frightening about the deadly precision with which it worked, and the uncanny
10 accuracy of the man who controlled it. This time it would crash downwards delivering a blow which shook the ground: next time it would repeat the performance, only to stop just as the spectators were bracing themselves for the shock—stop with such mathematical
15 exactitude that the glass of a watch beneath it would be cracked but the works would not be damaged.

For years now, personally conducted tours had come round Frenton's works. Old Frenton was always delighted when his friends asked him if they might
20 take their house-parties round: he regarded it as a compliment to himself. For he had made the works, watched them grow and expand till now they were known throughout the civilized world. They were just part of him, the fruit of his brain—born of labour and
25 hard work and nurtured on the hard-headed business capacity of the rugged old Yorkshireman. He was a

millionaire now, many times over, but he could still recall the day when sixpence extra a day had meant the difference between chronic penury and affluence.
30 And in those far-off days there had come a second resolve into his mind to keep the first and ever present one company. That first one had been with him ever since he could remember anything—the resolve, to succeed; the second one became no less deep rooted.
35 When he did succeed he'd pay his men such wages that there would never be any question of sixpence a day making a difference. The labourer was worthy of his hire: out of the sweat of his own brow John Frenton had evolved that philosophy for himself…
40   And right loyally he had stuck to it. When success came, and with it more and more, till waking one morning he realized that the big jump had been taken, and that henceforth Frenton's would be one of the powers in the steel world, he did not forget. He paid
45 his men well—almost lavishly: all he asked was that they should work in a similar spirit. And he did more. From the memories of twenty years before he recalled the difference between the two partners for whom he had then been working. One of them had never been
50 seen in the works save as an aloof being from another world, regarding his automatons with an uninterested but searching eye: the other had known every one of his men by name, and had treated them as his own personal friends. And yet his eye was just as searching…
55 But—what a difference: what an enormous difference!
    And so John Frenton had learned and profited by the example which stared him in the face: things

CONTINUE ➤

might perhaps be different today if more employers had learned that lesson too. To him every man he
60 employed was a personal friend: again all he asked was that they should regard him likewise…

"Boys," he had said to them on one occasion, when a spirit of unrest had been abroad in the neighbouring works, "if you've got any grievance,
65 there's only one thing I ask. Come and get it off your chests to me: don't get muttering and grousing about it in corners, if I can remedy it, I will: if I can't I'll tell you why. Anyway, a talk will clear the air…"

1

The primary purpose of the passage is to

A) detail the precision of an impressive mechanical hammer.

B) vividly capture the details of a tour of a factory.

C) highlight the economic disparity amongst the workers in the factory.

D) provide a character analysis of a successful factory owner.

2

As used in line 8 "deadly" most nearly means

A) fierce.

B) exact.

C) overwhelming.

D) toxic.

3

The author mentions "the glass of a watch" (line 15) in order to

A) express the accuracy of the rhythm of the hammer.

B) show the degree of control capable when implementing the hammer.

C) suggest the that the watch was sturdy and well-made.

D) satirize the display of strength typically personified by the hammer.

4

The "difference" (line 55) refers to the difference between

A) hard-working employees and lazy employees.

B) generous employers and miserly employers.

C) distant employers and friendly employers.

D) loyal employees and disloyal employees.

CONTINUE

5

Which choice provides the best evidence for the answer to the previous question?

A) Line 40 ("And right…it")
B) Lines 40-44 ("When…forget")
C) Lines 44-46 ("He paid…spirit")
D) Lines 49-54 ("One…just as searching")

6

The reference to "more employers" (line 58) suggests

A) John Frenton considers himself more enlightened than many other factory owners.
B) a fierce competition among employers for the best workers.
C) other factories, including Woolwich Arsenal, are having labor difficulties.
D) that good paying jobs have become relatively scarce in factories at that time.

7

As used in line 63 "abroad" most nearly means

A) developing.
B) sailing.
C) distant.
D) shunned.

8

John Frenton would best be described as

A) jovial yet demanding.
B) miserly and controlling.
C) hardworking and generous.
D) frivolous and lighthearted.

9

Which of the following best describes John Frenton's philosophy towards his workers?

A) He considers them friends and loves to have them take tours of his factory.
B) He pays high wages so he can employ the best workers in the region in order to gain advantage against other factories.
C) He expects honest talk from his workers and strives to treat them fairly.
D) He pays his men far too much and is unconcerned that he may head toward bankruptcy.

10

Which choice provides the best evidence for the answer to the previous question?

A) Line 18-21 ("Old … himself")
B) Line 23-26 ("They … Yorkshireman")
C) Line 40-44 ("When … forget")
D) Line 62-68 (""Boys," … why")

STOP

If you finish before time is called, you may check your work on this section only.
Do not turn to any other section.

Active Reading

This passage is from H. C. McNeile, "A Question of Personality." Originally published in 1921.

factory tour — The personally conducted tour round Frenton's Steel Works paused, as usual, on reaching the show piece of the entertainment. The mighty hammer, operated
Line with such consummate ease by the movement of a
5 single lever, though smaller than its more celebrated brother at Woolwich Arsenal, never failed to get a round of applause from the fascinated onlookers. There was something almost frightening about the deadly precision with which it worked, and the uncanny
10 accuracy of the man who controlled it. This time it
hammer would crash downwards delivering a blow which shook the ground: next time it would repeat the performance, only to stop just as the spectators were bracing themselves for the shock—stop with such mathematical
15 exactitude that the glass of a watch beneath it would be cracked but the works would not be damaged.

For years now, personally conducted tours had come round Frenton's works. Old Frenton was always
Frenton delighted when his friends asked him if they might
20 take their house-parties round: he regarded it as a compliment to himself. For he had made the works, watched them grow and expand till now they were known throughout the civilized world. They were just part of him, the fruit of his brain—born of labour and
25 hard work and nurtured on the hard-headed business capacity of the rugged old Yorkshireman. He was a millionaire now, many times over, but he could still
past recall the day when sixpence extra a day had meant the difference between chronic penury and affluence.
30 And in those far-off days there had come a second resolve into his mind to keep the first and ever present one company. That first one had been with him ever since he could remember anything—the resolve, to *2 resolves* succeed; the second one became no less deep rooted.
35 When he did succeed he'd pay his men such wages *generous pay* that there would never be any question of sixpence a day making a difference. The labourer was worthy of his hire: out of the sweat of his own brow John Frenton had evolved that philosophy for himself…

40 And right loyally he had stuck to it. When success came, and with it more and more, till waking one morning he realized that the big jump had been taken, and that henceforth Frenton's would be one of the powers in the steel world, he did not forget. He paid
45 his men well—almost lavishly: all he asked was that they should work in a similar spirit. And he did more. From the memories of twenty years before he recalled the difference between the two partners for whom he *old bosses* had then been working. One of them had never been
bad 50 seen in the works save as an aloof being from another world, regarding his automatons with an uninterested but searching eye: the other had known every one of his
good men by name, and had treated them as his own personal friends. And yet his eye was just as searching…
55 But—what a difference: what an enormous difference!

And so John Frenton had learned and profited by the example which stared him in the face: things might perhaps be different today if more employers had learned that lesson too. To him every man he *workers = F's friends*
60 employed was a personal friend: again all he asked was that they should regard him likewise…

"Boys," he had said to them on one occasion, when a spirit of unrest had been abroad in the neighbouring works, "if you've got any grievance, *communication*
65 there's only one thing I ask. Come and get it off your chests to me: don't get muttering and grousing about it in corners, if I can remedy it, I will: if I can't I'll tell you why. Anyway, a talk will clear the air…"

Explanations

Answers & explanations for "A Question of Personality"

1. The primary purpose of the passage is to:

   A) detail the precision of an impressive mechanical hammer.
   B) vividly capture the details of a tour of a factory.
   C) highlight the economic disparity amongst the workers in the factory.
   (D) provide a character analysis of a successful factory owner.

> We need to think about the passage as a **whole**. It starts with a description of a factory tour, but then spends the rest of the passage telling us about the owner, **Frenton**. Choices A and B are only in the first paragraph, and choice C only shows up at the end of the passage. **Choice D** is all about **Frenton**, so it's our right answer.

2. As used in line 8 "deadly" most nearly means

   A) fierce.
   (B) exact.
   C) overwhelming.
   D) toxic.

> We need to look at the word in context:
>
> > *"There was something almost frightening about the **deadly** precision with which it worked, and the uncanny accuracy of the man who controlled it."*
>
> The author did not use "deadly" literally, since no one is in danger. Later in the paragraph on lines 14-15, the author describes the hammer as having **"mathematical exactitude."** This is our strongest clue for this question. If we swap "deadly" for **choice B**, "exact," the sentence keeps its meaning.

> *"There was something almost frightening about the **exact** precision with which it worked, and the uncanny accuracy of the man who controlled it."*

3. The author mentions "the glass of a watch" (line 15) in order to

   A) express the accuracy of the ~~rhythm~~ of the hammer.
   B) show the degree of control capable when implementing the hammer.
   C) suggest the that the watch was ~~sturdy and well-made~~.
   D) ~~satirize~~ the display of strength typically personified by the ~~hammer~~.

First let's look at the phrase in context:

> *"This time it would crash downwards delivering a blow which shook the ground: next time it would repeat the performance, only to stop just as the spectators were bracing themselves for the shock—stop with such **mathematical exactitude** that the glass of a watch beneath it would be cracked but the works would not be damaged."*

The sentence describes the amount of control the operator has over the hammer, which is a perfect match for **choice B**.

4. The "difference" (line 55) refers to the difference between

   A) hard-working employees and lazy employees.
   B) generous employers and miserly employers.
   C) distant employers and friendly employers.
   D) loyal employees and disloyal employees.

5. Which choice provides the best evidence for the answer to the previous question?

   A) Line 40 ("And right...it")
   B) Lines 40-44 ("When...forget")
   C) Lines 44-46 ("He paid...spirit")
   D) Lines 49-54 ("One...just as searching")

We can use the lines in Q5 to find the answer to Q4. We need to find the quote that talks about a **difference**; only **choice D**, lines 49-54, is about the difference between two things:

> "**One of them** had never been seen in the works save as an aloof being from another world, regarding his automatons with an uninterested but searching eye: **the other** had known every one of his men by name, and had treated them as his own personal friends. And yet his eye was just as searching"

So one of Frenton's old employers was **"aloof"** and **"disinterested,"** and the other treated employees like **"personal friends."** That's a perfect match for **choice C** in Q4.

6. The reference to "more employers" (line 58) suggests

(A) John Frenton considers himself more enlightened than many other factory owners.
B) a ~~fierce competition~~ among employers for the best workers.
C) other factories, including ~~Woolwich Arsenal~~, are having labor difficulties.
D) that good paying jobs have ~~become relatively scarce~~ in factories at that time.

First, let's look at the phrase in context:

> "And so John Frenton had learned and profited by the example which stared him in the face: things might perhaps be different today if more employers had learned that lesson too. To him every man he employed was a personal friend: again all he asked was that they should regard him likewise..."

We can paraphrase this as "Frenton thinks he has come up with a smart business practice and that other employers should also try." **Choice A** matches the lines and our paraphrase.

7. As used in line 63 "abroad" most nearly means

(A) developing.
B) sailing.
C) distant.
D) shunned.

We need to look at the word in context first:

*"Boys," he had said to them on one occasion, when a spirit of unrest had been **abroad** in the neighbouring works, "if you've got any grievance, there's only one thing I ask. Come and get it off your chests to me."*

"Abroad" refers to the "spirit of unrest," so we need a word that means "**around**" or "**growing**." "**Developing**" matches "growing," and it fits well in the sentence. **Choice A** is correct.

*"Boys," he had said to them on one occasion, when a spirit of unrest had been **developing** in the neighbouring works, "if you've got any grievance, there's only one thing I ask. Come and get it off your chests to me."*

8. John Frenton would best be described as

A) jovial yet ~~demanding~~.
B) ~~miserly~~ and ~~controlling~~.
(C) hardworking and generous.
D) ~~frivolous~~ and lighthearted.

This question is a bit tricky, as we really have to be critical of the words in the answer choices. A and D both have one word that's supported by the passage, and one that isn't. Choice B is completely wrong. Only **Choice C** is completely supported by lines 44-45:

"He paid his men well–almost lavishly: all he asked was that they should work in a similar spirit."

9. Which of the following best describes John Frenton's philosophy towards his workers?

   A) He considers them friends and loves to have them ~~take tours of his factory~~.
   B) He pays high wages so he can employ the best workers in the region in order to ~~gain advantage~~ against other factories.
   C) He expects honest talk from his workers and strives to treat them fairly.
   D) He pays his men far ~~too much~~ and is unconcerned that he may head toward bankruptcy.

10. Which choice provides the best evidence for the answer to the previous question?

   A) Line 18-21 ("Old Frenton … himself.")
   B) Line 23-26 ("They … Yorkshireman.")
   C) Line 40-44 ("When … forget.")
   D) Line 62-68 ("'Boys,' … why.")

We can answer Questions 9 and 10 together by using Q10's choices to find evidence for Q9. Looking at the lines in Q10, only **choice D** is about how Frenton treats laborers.

> *"Boys," he had said to them on one occasion, when a spirit of unrest had been abroad in the neighbouring works, "if you've got any grievance, there's only one thing I ask. Come and get it off your chests to me."*

The quote says he wants his workers to talk directly to him and not complain about issues behind his back.

Now we need to find an answer to Q9 that matches this quote. In **choice C**, "honest talk" matches "Come and get it off your chests," so C is correct.

Throwaways

*The essence of a wrong answer lies in a word or series of words that is not supported by evidence from the passage. We call these words **throwaways**, and they make the entire choice flat-out wrong!*

The Anatomy of a Wrong Answer

Most of the words in a wrong answer choice sound pretty great. This makes sense: if every word was totally out of left field, spotting the correct answer would be too easy. Instead, the test-writers take an otherwise great answer and change one or two words to make it wrong. For example, consider this question about the previous chapter:

> 1. **The primary purpose of the Active Reading chapter is to:**
>
>   (A) encourage students to use their pencils more when reading.

A is correct because *every single word* in the choice accurately reflects the last chapter on Active Reading. Now, we can make a number of wrong answer choices simply by inserting a *single* "throwaway" word:

> B) encourage ⬚teachers⬚ to use their pencils more when reading.
>
> C) ⬚force⬚ students to use their pencils more when reading.
>
> D) encourage students to use their pencils ⬚less⬚ when reading.

Notice how most words in the wrong answers look great. However, when even one word is off, the whole choice must be incorrect. The test-writers hope you'll be so distracted by the good that you won't notice the bad.

Box 'em

Throughout this chapter, whenever you spot a throwaway, draw a box around it.

Alternate Strategy:

After putting it into a box, put that box inside of another box, then mail that box to yourself, and, when it arrives, *SMASH IT WITH A HAMMER.*

Time Saver!

Many students get stuck debating between two answers that both sound pretty great. They waste time trying to "feel out" which one is more correct.

By instead focusing on throwaways, you make the Reading section feel more concrete and move from question to question MUCH faster.

Strategy: Goin' Huntin'

To avoid falling into the test-writers' trap, we're going to become a hunter of throwaways. Be on high alert for words that sink an answer choice. Answer the questions below by scanning the answer choices for throwaways. When you find one, do the following:

(1) Draw a box around the throwaway(s)

(2) Cross off that choice. It's wrong.

EXAMPLES 1 & 2

It is highly doubtful that the Allied forces would have won World War II without the help of Polish mathematician Marian Rejewski. At age fourteen, Rejewski enrolled in a
Line secret cryptology course for German speakers. Soon his full-
5 time occupation was decoding the German Enigma machine. Combining his usage of pure mathematics with information provided by French intelligence, Rejewski succeeded in decoding the Enigma, and consequently, the Allied forces were able to intercept German intelligence transmissions for six
10 years. Historian David Kahn says that Rejewski's stunning achievement "elevates him to the pantheon of the greatest cryptanalysts of all time." On the 100th anniversary of his birthday, a sculpted memorial was presented to his hometown of Bydgoszcz, Poland.

1. The author most likely mentions historian David Kahn (line 10) in order to

   A) introduce a lighthearted digression.
   B) offer evidence to support a prior claim.
   C) offer an anecdote revealing the flaw in a popular misconception.
   D) suggest the value perceived in a historical event.

2. The primary purpose of the passage is to

A) explain how the Enigma machine was decoded.
B) illustrate the principles of cryptology.
C) highlight the contribution of a noted mathematician to the war effort.
D) provide insight into the motivations of a renowned cryptanalyst.

TIP

Put each question into your own words, then read that paraphrase before each choice. For example:

"The author mentions the historian to introduce a lighthearted digression."

SOLUTION

1. The author most likely mentions historian David Kahn (line 10) in order to

~~A)~~ introduce a 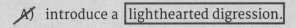lighthearted digression.

There's nothing funny here, so **lighthearted** is a throwaway. And we haven't changed topics at all, so **digression** is also a throwaway!

~~B)~~ offer evidence to support a prior claim.

What **evidence** is Kahn bringing to the table? He's simply saying the event was important; that's not evidence.

~~C)~~ offer an 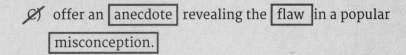anecdote revealing the flaw in a popular misconception.

There are a number of throwaways in this question, but **anecdote** is the easiest to see. There's no personal story here.

(D)) suggest the value perceived in a historical event.

Nothing outlandish here! **D** is the best choice!

Paraphrase

"The author wrote this passage to…"

SOLUTION

2. The primary purpose of the passage is to

A) explain how the Enigma machine was decoded.

Did you learn how the machine worked? Could you build one now? The words **explain how** are throwaways.

B) illustrate the principles of cryptology.

Quick—name the **principles** of cryptology. Can you do it? Don't beat yourself up; they weren't in the passage!

C) highlight the contribution of a noted mathematician to the war effort.

Nothing glaringly wrong with this answer; let's move on.

D) provide insight into the motivations of a renowned cryptanalyst.

The passage doesn't say **why** Rejewski helped.

EXAMPLES 3 & 4

Coleman Hawkins, one of the first great saxophonists of the Harlem Renaissance, was a consistently modern improviser who possessed an encyclopedic knowledge of music. Hawkins was
Line a giant of the jazz scene for more than forty years. His musical
5 odyssey began in front of the keys of a piano at the age of five; he moved on to the cello before settling on the tenor saxophone. In the 1920s and 30s, the saxophone was primarily considered a novelty instrument used in marching bands. However, Hawkins saw a greater potential for this instrument. His lyrical tones
10 and innovative style helped usher in a new age of avant-garde jazz known as Bebop and placed the saxophone at the center of the new jazz aesthetic. Succeeding generations of saxophonists, whose members included Sonny Rollins, Lester Young, and John Coltrane, acknowledged the profound influence that "Hawk"
15 had on their musical styles.

3. The passage supports which of the following statements about Hawkins?

    A) He broke new ground for jazz saxophonists.
    B) His innovative lyrics helped usher in a new musical era.
    C) His music earned international acclaim for many decades.
    D) His modernist style alienated more traditional musicians.

4. The author references Hawkins' "odyssey" (line 5) in order to

    A) enumerate the steps he took to develop his saxophone technique.
    B) suggest the many challenges he faced in his musical training.
    C) convey appreciation for artists' journey of self-expression.
    D) highlight Hawkins' experience with multiple instruments before starting his saxophone career.

Paraphrase

"The passage says that…"

SOLUTION

3. The passage supports which of the following statements about Hawkins?

    (A)) He broke new ground for jazz saxophonists.

No throwaway here: each word has support in the passage.

    B̶) His innovative lyrics helped usher in a new musical era.

The passage says he has a "lyrical tone", but we never read about Hawkins writing out actual lyrics. He was a sax player!

    C̶) His music earned international acclaim for many decades.

He was definitely acclaimed. But there's no mention of **international** acclaim. Don't assume anything you can't find evidence for in the passage!

    D̶) His modernist style alienated more traditional musicians.

This COULD be true, but nowhere in the passage do we read about a negative reaction to Hawkins.

Paraphrase

"The point of the fourth line is to…"

SOLUTION

4. The author references Hawkins' "odyssey" (line 5) in order to

~~A)~~ enumerate the steps he took to develop his saxophone technique.

These lines list the instruments he tried **before** saxophone.

~~B)~~ suggest the many challenges he faced in his musical training.

Didn't see anything in this line about **challenges** he faced.

~~C)~~ convey appreciation for artists' journey of self-expression.

This choice is trying to sound smart to hide the fact that "journey of self-expression" is not mentioned in the passage.

(D)) highlight Hawkins' experience with multiple instruments before starting his saxophone career.

We read all of that! Hawkins played piano, then cello, then finally got stuck on saxophone! No throwaways here.

EXAMPLES 5 & 6

Walter Alvarez, the fourth in a line of eminent and successful scientists, was practically destined for distinction in the world of science. Even with his pedigree, no one could have predicted
Line the magnitude of his contributions to the study of dinosaurs.
5 Alvarez ventured into the field of geology and discovered a significant amount of iridium in the layer of the Earth's crust containing the last fossilized remains of many dinosaur species. Because iridium commonly appears in asteroids, Alvarez concluded that an asteroid must have driven the dinosaurs to
10 extinction. His theory is now the most widely-believed answer to the most widespread of questions: what killed the dinosaurs?

5. The author primarily references Alvarez's "pedigree" (line 3) in order to

   A) illustrate the level of fame attained by prominent scientists.
   B) suggest his tendency toward progressive ideas.
   C) show that he was entrenched in the scientific theories of the day.
   D) imply that Alvarez was almost certain to achieve scientific renown.

6. The statement in lines 10-11 ("His… dinosaurs?") serves primarily to underscore the

   A) popular appeal of a theory.
   B) impressionability of the public.
   C) general public's fascination with dinosaurs.
   D) level of celebrity achieved by scientists.

SOLUTION

5. The author primarily references Alvarez's "pedigree" (line 3) in order to

~~A)~~ illustrate the |level of fame| attained by prominent scientists.

~~B)~~ suggest his tendency toward |progressive ideas.|

~~C)~~ show that he was |entrenched| in the scientific theories of the day.

(D)) imply that Alvarez was almost certain to achieve scientific renown.

SOLUTION

6. The statement in lines 10–11 ("His… dinosaurs?") serves primarily to underscore the

(A)) popular appeal of a theory.

~~B)~~ |impressionability| of the public.

~~C)~~ |general public's fascination| with dinosaurs.

~~D)~~ level of |celebrity| achieved by scientists.

Evidence

When throw-aways alone can't finish the job, turn to evidence. Evidence consists of words from the passage that match words in the answer choices.

Wrong answers always contain throwaways, but what do right answers look like? Every single right answer **lacks throwaways** and **contains evidence** linking it directly to the passage.

The Reading Courtroom

When you're assessing answer choices, you are like a judge in a courtroom. Each choice makes its case, and you decide which backs up its claim with sufficient evidence from the passage. The only reason to choose an answer choice is if it has a direct link to a word, phrase, or sentence from the passage. Sometimes, choices are ripped directly from the passage; usually, evidence takes the more subtle form of **synonyms**.

Assumptions

Be very careful not to make assumptions and talk yourself into an answer that isn't backed up by evidence. If you can't point to the exact word or phrase that serves as evidence for an answer choice, that choice is wrong!

The Great Synonym Hunt

To find evidence, start with the words in the remaining answer choices, and begin the wonderful game of **Word Match** or **Synonym Hunt**. If you can't point to specific words that support an answer choice, you've got no proof. Cross out that sorry excuse for an answer choice!

Matching Words

When you are hunting for synonyms, use your pencil to help make a match between words in the question and words in the passage.

> The parakeet would not be caged. He was as rambunctious as a red-footed mongoose, as feral as a ginger-fed jackrabbit, and he was the bane of the existence of Marvin, the beleaguered janitor of Humperdink's Insane Clown Academy.
>
> 1. The author characterizes the parakeet as
>
>   A) an undomesticated nuisance.

In the example above, **feral** is *evidence* for **undomesticated** and **bane** is *evidence* for **nuisance**. Practice hunting for matching words in the following examples.

EXAMPLES 1 & 2

Although it is in our nature to be superstitious, cultural and environmental factors clearly influence how superstitious an individual actually is. For example, when we feel we are losing
Line control over our lives, we tend to become more superstitious.
5 One study found that people living in high-risk areas of the Middle East, such as Tel Aviv, are much more likely to carry a lucky charm than are other people. Nobody is immune. "We can all shift our supernatural inclination depending on the circumstances," says Bruce Hood, cognitive psychologist from
10 the University of Bristol.

1. The author supports his argument by

   A) quoting an authority with whom he disagrees.
   B) exploring a controversial scientific theory.
   C) presenting the findings of a study.
   D) disproving an alternate hypothesis.

2. The actions of the people in Tel Aviv (lines 5-7) primarily suggest that

   A) certain groups of people are inherently superstitious.
   B) environmental factors impact our level of superstitious behavior.
   C) the collective power of superstition is reinforced by heightened anxiety.
   D) people who feel frightened rely more on supernatural interventions.

SOLUTION

Although it is in our nature to be superstitious, cultural and environmental factors clearly influence how superstitious an individual actually is. For example, when we feel we are losing
Line control over our lives, we tend to become more superstitious.
5 One study found that people living in high-risk areas of the Middle East, such as Tel Aviv, are much more likely to carry a lucky charm than are other people. Nobody is immune. "We can all shift our supernatural inclination depending on the circumstances," says Bruce Hood, cognitive psychologist from
10 the University of Bristol.

Paraphrase

"The author backs up his argument by…"

1. The author supports his argument by

   A) quoting an authority with whom he disagrees.

A psychologist is an **authority**. I see a quote! But there's nothing about agreement or disagreement.

   B) exploring a controversial scientific theory.

No direct evidence for **controversy**.

   C) presenting the findings of a study.

Findings matches **found**, and *study* matches **study**!

   D) disproving an alternate hypothesis.

The author does not bring up any alternative explanation or hypothesis.

63

Paraphrase

"We learn from the Tel Aviv folks that…"

SOLUTION

Although it is in our nature to be superstitious, cultural and environmental factors clearly influence how superstitious an individual actually is. For example, when we feel we are losing
Line control over our lives, we tend to become more superstitious.
5 One study found that people living in high-risk areas of the Middle East, such as Tel Aviv, are much more likely to carry a lucky charm than are other people. Nobody is immune. "We can all shift our supernatural inclination depending on the circumstances," says Bruce Hood, cognitive psychologist from
10 the University of Bristol.

2. The actions of the people in Tel Aviv (lines 5-7) primarily suggest that

A) certain groups of people are inherently superstitious.

The author writes that we are **all** superstitious by nature, not just certain groups.

B) environmental factors impact our level of superstitious behavior.

These phrases are taken directly from the passage.

C) the collective power of superstition is reinforced by heightened anxiety.

Watch your assumptions! We can't connect either of these phrases to specific words in the passage.

D) people who feel frightened rely more on supernatural interventions.

These words seem on topic, but frightened has no direct synonym in the passage. It's an assumption.

EXAMPLES 3 & 4

At a time when natural resources such as oil, coal, and natural gas are being depleted at an alarming rate, "alternative energy" seem to be the magic words at the tip of everyone's
Line tongue. One of the most exciting proposals for generating
5 renewable energy comes from an old idea: the solar updraft tower. Conceived in 1903, the solar tower, designed like a giant chimney, draws heated air into openings at its base. Once inside the hollow tower, the heated air rises, accelerating to speeds of 35 mph. As the air rushes upward, dozens of wind turbines
10 turn, generating electricity. A solar updraft tower as high as 1,000 meters with a diameter as large as 7 kilometers could eventually power as many as 200,000 typical households.

3. The phrase "magic words" (lines 3) most directly emphasizes the

   A) unsubstantiated belief in a proposed solution.
   B) inevitability of an ecological crisis.
   C) ability of language to capture the public's attention.
   D) perceived appeal of a solution.

4. The last sentence of the passage (lines 10-12) serves to

   A) convey the importance of a problem.
   B) highlight the potential benefits of an invention.
   C) speculate about the likelihood of an outcome.
   D) defend a widely accepted practice.

Paraphrase

"From the phrase 'magic words' we learn about the…"

SOLUTION

At a time when natural resources such as oil, coal, and natural gas are being depleted at an alarming rate, "alternative energy"
Line seem to be the magic words at the tip of everyone's tongue. One
5 of the most exciting (proposals) for generating renewable energy comes from an old idea: the solar updraft tower. Conceived in 1903, the solar tower, designed like a giant chimney, draws heated air into openings at its base. Once inside the hollow tower, the heated air rises, accelerating to speeds of 35 mph. As
10 the air rushes upward, dozens of wind turbines turn, generating electricity. A solar updraft tower as high as 1,000 meters with a diameter as large as 7 kilometers could eventually power as many as 200,000 typical households.

3. The phrase "magic words" (lines 3) most directly emphasizes the

A) unsubstantiated belief in a proposed solution.

The passage does not say whether the proposal is substantiated.

B) inevitability of an ecological crisis.

No evidence that there is a crisis afoot, even if you believe that's the case. Watch your assumptions.

C) ability of language to capture the public's attention.

Though the public is talking, we have no evidence that it's **language** that is responsible for capturing its attention.

D) perceived appeal of a solution.

This is the *least* wrong answer. Nothing brazenly wrong. It's the best of our options.

SOLUTION

At a time when natural resources such as oil, coal, and natural gas are being depleted at an alarming rate, "alternative energy"
Line seem to be the magic words at the tip of everyone's tongue. One
5 of the most exciting proposals for generating renewable energy comes from an old idea: the solar updraft tower. Conceived in 1903, the solar tower, designed like a giant chimney, draws heated air into openings at its base. Once inside the hollow tower, the heated air rises, accelerating to speeds of 35 mph. As
10 the air rushes upward, dozens of wind turbines turn, generating electricity. A solar updraft tower as high as 1,000 meters with a diameter as large as 7 kilometers could eventually power as many as 200,000 typical households.

4. The last sentence of the passage (lines 10-12) serves to

    A) convey the importance of a problem.

This is not about a problem but about a proposed **solution**.

    B) highlight the potential benefits of an invention.

Bingo—this is perfect! Exactly what the passage says.

    C) speculate about the likelihood of an outcome.

We are not speculating about the **probability** of this taking place, just what might happen.

    D) defend a widely accepted practice.

We are not **defending** anything, nor is the practice widely accepted.

Paraphrase

"The last sentence is there to..."

Reading Practice Passage 2
TO STAY ON PACE, YOUR TIMING GOAL IS 13 MINUTES

DIRECTIONS

Each passage or pair of passages below is followed by a number of questions. After reading each passage or pair, choose the best answer to each question based on what is stated or implied in the passage or passages and in any accompanying graphics (such as a table or graph).

Questions 1-10 are based on the following passage.

This passage is adapted from Holly MacDonald's "The Revival of the Peanut" written in 2010.

Peanuts have undergone a strong revival in the 21st century, seen as a potent, cost-effective source of protein and heart-healthy monounsaturated fats. With
Line so many nutritional benefits, peanuts have found a
5 variety of culinary uses beyond the "PB & J" childhood sandwich staple, used in everything from Asian stir fry dishes to African peanut soups to fruit smoothies. As the Food & Drug Administration (FDA) cracks down on trans fats–partially hydrogenated oils known for
10 their shelf stability and connection to heart disease– peanut oil looks to be more popular than ever on both supermarket shelves and in restaurant deep fryers.

Unfortunately, not everyone is overjoyed with the proliferation of peanut-based products. Approximately
15 0.6% of Americans suffer from a peanut allergy, making any food containing peanuts certainly hazardous if not outright fatal. Allergic reactions to peanuts can range from rashes and hives to anaphylaxis. The latter is a life-threatening condition where exposure to the
20 allergen leads to throat-swelling, which can cut off the supply of oxygen to the lungs in extreme cases. Obviously the best approach for someone with a peanut allergy would also be the most simple: don't eat peanuts! While certainly pragmatic advice, exposure to peanuts
25 can occur through the use of peanuts and peanut byproducts in a variety of hard-to-forecast routes. For example, in a school cafeteria, a cook could make a peanut butter sandwich on a counter and then make a bologna sandwich immediately after for a child with
30 a peanut allergy. If the counter and the cook's hands and utensils were not properly cleaned, it is entirely possible that some trace amount of peanut butter could end up on the bologna sandwich, triggering an allergic reaction in a child with an acute sensitivity to peanuts.

35 Thankfully, the FDA has been making great strides to inform consumers about potential allergens in food. Food manufacturers must clearly label common allergens and also acknowledge potential cross-contamination when food is processed on
40 the same equipment or even in the same facility. The concern over cross-contamination has led to the banning of peanuts as a mid-flight snack on airlines and in many schools that worry about the legal ramifications of a lunchtime misstep.

45 While these precautions certainly help to reduce accidental exposure to allergens, scientists at North Carolina A & T State University have come up with a different way to combat allergic reactions to peanuts. A person with a peanut allergy is not allergic to the entire
50 peanut, as peanuts are made up of the same organic compounds as most other foods, and the human body itself. Scientists have discovered the two primary culprits in peanuts that cause allergic reactions: proteins Ara h 1 and Ara h 2. Without these two proteins, the
55 rest of the content of the peanut will likely not cause a reaction. This is why foods cooked in peanut oil do not cause allergic reactions, since Ara h 1 and Ara h

CONTINUE

2 are stripped away during the refining process. The scientists, led by Dr. Jianmei Yu, began to look for
60 ways to not only remove the allergen, but also retain the nutrition and consistency of whole peanuts.

The solution proved to be surprisingly simple. Using a mixture of two food-safe enzymes, trypsin and alpha chymotrypsin, and the application of
65 ultrasound, the offending allergens were removed from roasted peanuts to the point that their presence could no longer be detected. Even better for a peanut fan, the taste and texture of the post-treatment peanuts were identical to untreated ones. Initial
70 studies, using a pin prick method to determine an allergic reaction, have proven promising, and the University has partnered with biotech firm Algrn to produce hypoallergenic peanuts for the consumer market. The hope is that this patented process
75 can eventually be adapted to remove allergens in other foods, including tree nuts and soybeans.

The current indicators all point to success; however, there are some lingering questions. Assuming that the FDA approved the process as safe, only universal
80 compliance to hypoallergenic standards would lead to total peace of mind for someone with a peanut allergy. Is the complete processing of the domestic and international peanut crop to hypoallergenic standards feasible? How would this additional
85 processing affect the price and profitability of growing and preparing peanuts? While Algrn certainly has humanitarian ideals, the company also looks to profit from the patented process it purchased from the university. It may be advisable for Algrn to target
90 institutional sales from schools and theme parks looking to reduce liability while still offering choice.

Perhaps the most unpredictable reaction will come from peanut allergy sufferers themselves. After a lifetime of fearing peanuts, would a peanut
95 allergy sufferer welcome eating a hypoallergenic peanut? The person's hesitance, or even outright refusal, is quite understandable when a food foe becomes a food friend overnight.

1

The author refers to "PB & J" on line 5 in order to

A) show how children prefer simpler foods.

B) exemplify traditional uses of peanut butter.

C) recommend new uses of peanut butter in foods.

D) suggest that new uses of peanut butter have become more popular than traditional uses.

2

As used in line 26, "routes" most nearly means

A) scenarios.

B) conspiracies.

C) attacks.

D) favors.

3

In lines 26-34, the hypothetical example serves to

A) denounce careless conditions within cafeterias.

B) show why people with peanut allergies must be careful about what they choose to eat.

C) highlight how easily cross-contamination can occur.

D) acknowledge that cross-contamination of foods is unavoidable in a commercial kitchen.

4

The third paragraph (lines 35-44) suggests that the author believes that the precautions taken towards preventing allergic reactions are

A) reasonable.

B) overbearing.

C) unwarranted.

D) infallible.

CONTINUE ➔

5

In line 58, "refining" most nearly means

A) polishing.
B) mixing.
C) boiling.
D) extracting.

6

The passage asserts that regular peanuts and hypoallergenic peanuts

A) have the same taste and texture.
B) are both in high demand.
C) cost the same amount to produce.
D) are both dangerous for those with peanut allergies.

7

Which choice provides the best evidence for the answer to the previous question?

A) Lines 56-58 ("This … process")
B) Lines 67-69 ("Even … ones")
C) Lines 84-86 ("How … peanuts")
D) Lines 94-96 ("After … hypoallergenic peanut")

8

What function does the sixth paragraph (lines 77-91) serve in the passage as a whole?

A) It advocates for greater testing before hypoallergenic peanuts are available to purchase.
B) It admits that hypoallergenic peanuts will likely not be a commercial success.
C) It addresses some practical concerns about the production and distribution of hypoallergenic peanuts.
D) It forecasts a commercial backlash against hypoallergenic peanuts since few people will want to eat them.

9

The passage supports which of the following statements about Algrn?

A) They are concerned about the safety of the allergen removal process.
B) They plan on exploiting a serious medical problem for their own profit.
C) They hope to be able to remove allergens from the North American food supply.
D) They need to balance economic realities with the desire to improve people's health.

10

Which choice provides the best evidence for the answer to the previous question?

A) Lines 69-74 ("Initial … market")
B) Lines 74-76 ("The hope … soybeans")
C) Lines 86-89 ("While … university")
D) Lines 89-91 ("It … choice")

STOP

If you finish before time is called, you may check your work on this section only.
Do not turn to any other section.

Active Reading

This passage is adapted from Holly MacDonald's "The Revival of the Peanut" written in 2010.

Peanuts have undergone a strong revival in the 21st century, seen as a potent, cost-effective source of protein and heart-healthy monounsaturated fats. With
Line so many nutritional benefits, peanuts have found a
5 variety of culinary uses beyond the "PB & J" childhood sandwich staple, used in everything from Asian stir fry dishes to African peanut soups to fruit smoothies. As the Food & Drug Administration (FDA) cracks down on trans fats–partially hydrogenated oils known for
10 their shelf stability and connection to heart disease– peanut oil looks to be more popular than ever on both supermarket shelves and in restaurant deep fryers.

Unfortunately not everyone is overjoyed with the proliferation of peanut-based products. Approximately
15 0.6% of Americans suffer from a peanut allergy, making any food containing peanuts certainly hazardous if not outright fatal. Allergic reactions to peanuts can range from rashes and hives to anaphylaxis. The latter is a life-threatening condition where exposure to the
20 allergen leads to throat-swelling, which can cut off the supply of oxygen to the lungs in extreme cases. Obviously the best approach for someone with a peanut allergy would also be the most simple: don't eat peanuts! While certainly pragmatic advice, exposure to peanuts
25 can occur through the use of peanuts and peanut byproducts in a variety of hard-to-forecast routes. For example, in a school cafeteria, a cook could make a peanut butter sandwich on a counter and then make a bologna sandwich immediately after for a child with
30 a peanut allergy. If the counter and the cook's hands and utensils were not properly cleaned, it is entirely possible that some trace amount of peanut butter could end up on the bologna sandwich, triggering an allergic reaction in a child with an acute sensitivity to peanuts.
35 Thankfully, the FDA has been making great strides to inform consumers about potential allergens in food. Food manufacturers must clearly label common allergens and also acknowledge potential cross-contamination when food is processed on

40 the same equipment or even in the same facility. The concern over cross-contamination has led to the banning of peanuts as a mid-flight snack on airlines and in many schools that worry about the legal ramifications of a lunchtime misstep.
45 While these precautions certainly help to reduce accidental exposure to allergens, scientists at North Carolina A & T State University have come up with a different way to combat allergic reactions to peanuts. A person with a peanut allergy is not allergic to the entire
50 peanut, as peanuts are made up of the same organic compounds as most other foods, and the human body itself. Scientist have discovered the two primary culprits in peanuts that cause allergic reactions: proteins Ara h 1 and Ara h 2. Without these two proteins, the rest
55 of the content of the peanut will likely not cause a reaction. This is why foods cooked in peanut oil do not cause allergic reactions, since Ara h 1 and Ara h 2 are stripped away during the refining process. The scientists, led by Dr. Jianmei Yu, began to look for
60 ways to not only remove the allergen, but also retain the nutrition and consistency of whole peanuts.

The solution proved to be surprisingly simple. Using a mixture of two food-safe enzymes, trypsin and alpha chymotrypsin, and the application of
65 ultrasound, the offending allergens were removed from roasted peanuts to the point that their presence could no longer be detected. Even better for a peanut fan, the taste and texture of the post-treatment peanuts were identical to untreated ones. Initial
70 studies, using a pin prick method to determine an allergic reaction, have proven promising, and the University has partnered with biotech firm Algrn to produce hypoallergenic peanuts for the consumer market. The hope is that that this patented process
75 can eventually be adapted to remove allergens in other foods, including tree nuts and soybeans.

The current indicators all point to success however, there are some lingering questions. Assuming that the FDA approved the process as safe, only universal
80 compliance to hypoallergenic standards would lead to total peace of mind for someone with a peanut allergy. Is the complete processing of the domestic

CONTINUE ▶

and international <u>peanut crop</u> to <u>hypoallergenic</u>
<u>standards feasible</u>? How would this additional
85 processing affect the <u>price</u> and <u>profitability</u> of growing
and preparing peanuts? While Algrn certainly has

$$ <u>humanitarian ideals</u>, the company also looks to <u>profit</u>
from the patented process they purchased from the
university. It may be <u>advisable</u> for Algrn to <u>target</u>
90 institutional sales from <u>schools</u> and <u>theme parks</u>
looking to <u>reduce liability</u> while still offering <u>choice</u>.

Perhaps the most unpredictable reaction will
come from <u>peanut allergy sufferers</u> themselves.

ppl w/
allergy

After a <u>lifetime</u> of <u>fearing</u> peanuts, would a peanut
95 allergy sufferer <u>welcome</u> eating a <u>hypoallergenic</u>
peanut? The person's <u>hesitance</u>, or even outright
refusal, is quite <u>understandable</u> when a food
<u>foe</u> becomes a food <u>friend</u> overnight.

Explanations

Answers & explanations for "The Revival of the Peanut"

....

1. The author refers to "PB & J" in line 5 in order to

   A) show how children ~~prefer~~ simpler foods.
   B) exemplify traditional uses of peanut butter.
   C) ~~recommend~~ new uses of peanut butter in foods.
   D) suggest that new uses of peanut butter have become ~~more popular~~ than traditional uses.

> Let's read in context to find out what "PB&J" is doing in the sentence:
>
> > *"With so many nutritional benefits, peanuts have found a variety of culinary uses beyond the **"PB&J" childhood sandwich staple**, used in everything from Asian stir fry dishes to African peanut soups to fruit smoothies."*
>
> Here, PB&J is a childhood staple, and it's contrasted with more new and exciting uses of peanut butter. In **choice B**, "traditional uses" matches "childhood staple."

2. As used in line 26, "routes" most nearly means

   A) scenarios.
   B) conspiracies.
   C) attacks.
   D) favors.

> First, let's read in context:
>
> > *"While certainly pragmatic advice, exposure to peanuts can occur through the use of peanuts and peanut byproducts in a variety of hard-to-forecast **routes**."*

The sentence describes how people might be exposed to peanuts, in a variety of routes, or "**ways**." **Choice A**, "scenarios" fits the meaning of the sentence, while the other words all change the meaning.

> *"While certainly pragmatic advice, exposure to peanuts can occur through the use of peanuts and peanut byproducts in a variety of hard-to-forecast **scenarios**."*

3. In lines 26-34, the hypothetical example serves to

A) ~~chastise~~ careless conditions within cafeterias.
B) show why people with peanut allergies must be careful about ~~what they choose to eat~~.
C) highlight how easily cross-contamination can occur.
D) acknowledge that cross-contamination of foods is ~~unavoidable~~ in a commercial kitchen.

As always, we need to read in context to figure out what the example is doing in the paragraph:

> *"While certainly pragmatic advice, exposure to peanuts can occur through the use of peanuts and peanut byproducts in a variety of hard-to-forecast routes. **For example**, in a school cafeteria, a cook could make a peanut butter sandwich on a counter and then make a bologna sandwich immediately after for a child with a peanut allergy. If the counter and the cook's hands and utensils were not properly cleaned, it is entirely possible that some trace amount of peanut butter could end up on the bologna sandwich, triggering an allergic reaction to a child with an acute sensitivity to peanuts."*

If we read in context, we see that the hypothetical is an example of one of those "hard-to-forecast routes" through which someone might be exposed to peanuts. The example shows how you could be accidentally exposed to peanuts if your food is prepared on a surface that touched peanuts; **choice C** is a perfect match!

4. The third paragraph (lines 35-44) suggests that the author believes that the precautions taken towards preventing allergic reactions are

(A) reasonable.
B) overbearing.
C) unwarranted.
D) infallible.

The paragraph begins:

> "**Thankfully**, the FDA has been making great strides to inform consumers about potential allergens in food."

We're looking for a positive word to describe the author's attitude toward these precautions. Choice D, "infallible," is **too** positive, since there's no evidence that the author thinks the precautions are perfect and incapable of mistakes. **Choice A**, "reasonable," is a much better match to the passage.

5. In line 58, "refining" most nearly means

A) polishing.
B) mixing.
C) boiling.
(D) extracting.

First, let's read the word in context:

> "This is why foods cooked in peanut oil do not cause allergic reactions, since ARa h 1 and Ara h 2 are stripped away during the **refining** process."

"Refining" describes process, and the process is that of turning peanuts into peanut oil. Only **choice D**, "extracting," makes sense in the context of turning peanuts into oil.

> "This is why foods cooked in peanut oil do not cause allergic reactions, since ARa h 1 and Ara h 2 are stripped away during the **extracting** process."

6. The passage asserts that regular peanuts and hypoallergenic peanuts

   (A) have the same taste and texture.
   B) are both in high demand.
   C) cost the same amount to produce.
   D) are both dangerous for those with peanut allergies.

7. Which choice provides the best evidence for the answer to the previous question?

   A) Lines 56-58 ("This ... process")
   (B) Lines 67-69 ("Even ... ones")
   C) Lines 84-86 ("How ... peanuts")
   D) Lines 94-96 ("After ... hypoallergenic peanut")

> Let's look at this pair of questions together, and use Q7 to solve Q6. According to Q6, we're looking for what's true about both regular and hypoallergenic peanuts. Now, let's evaluate the line references in Q7, looking for the choice that references both peanut types. Only **choice B** in Q7 mentions both kinds of peanuts, and it tells us that their "taste and texture" are "identical." In Q6, **choice A** matches those lines perfectly.

8. What function does the sixth paragraph (lines 77-91) serve in the passage as a whole?

   A) It ~~advocates~~ for ~~greater testing~~ before hypoallergenic peanuts are available to purchase.
   B) It admits that hypoallergenic peanuts will likely ~~not be a commercial success~~.
   (C) It addresses some practical concerns about the production and distribution of hypoallergenic peanuts.
   D) It forecasts a ~~commercial backlash~~ against hypoallergenic peanuts since few people will want to eat them.

> There are lots of question marks in paragraph 6, and my active reading note for paragraph 6 says "still questions." These questions are all about the nitty-gritty details of making and selling these new peanuts. **Choice C** is the only answer that matches the passage!

9. The passage supports which of the following statements about Algrn?

   A) They are ~~concerned~~ about the safety of the allergen removal process.
   B) They plan on ~~exploiting~~ a serious medical problem for their own profit.
   C) They hope to soon be able to remove allergens from the ~~North American food supply~~.
   (D) They need to balance economic realities with the desire to improve people's health.

10. Which choice provides the best evidence for the answer to the previous question?

   A) Lines 69-74 ("Initial ... market")
   B) Lines 74-76 ("The hope ... soybeans")
   (C) Lines 86-89 ("While ... university")
   D) Lines 89-91 ("It ... choice")

Let's work these problems together; Q9 asks us about Algrn, so let's look at Q10's answer choices to find lines that tell us about Algrn. A, C, and D all mention Algrn, so now we must cross-reference Q9's answer choices and find a match. **Choice D** in Q9 matches **choice C** in Q10: "balance economic realities" matches "looks to profit" and "desire to improve people's health" matches "humanitarian ideals."

Evidence-Based Questions

At least 4 questions per passage will be EBQs. Luckily, these questions lead you straight to the answer in the passage!

On the test, you'll encounter pairs of questions that, approached with the right strategy, can be easy points on the Reading section! "Evidence-Based Question" pairs, or "EBQs" for short, are most easily spotted by the **second question** in the pair. You'll see answer choices that are full of line references and quotations, tipping you off that it's connected to the previous question.

1

The central idea of the first paragraph (lines 1–12) is that

A) sharks are terrors of the sea that must be stopped.
B) jokes should not be attempted by the faint of heart.
C) you are a monster, but we like you anyways.
D) snapping is an activity enjoyed by all ages.

2

Which choice provides the best evidence for the answer to the previous question?

A) Lines 1–2 ("Sharks…help!!")
B) Lines 3–4 ("You…monster")
C) Lines 6–8 ("Oh…snap")
D) Lines 9–11 ("Funny…jokes?")

After reading the passage, scan the questions for evidence-based questions.

Anatomy of EBQs

Evidence-based questions are **connected**, and we can use that to our advantage. We're more likely to get both correct if we use the right strategy. Before we dive in, let's get to know each member of this duo.

The 1st question asks you something about the passage.

The central idea of the first paragraph (lines 1–12) is that

A) sharks are terrors of the sea that must be stopped.
B) jokes should not be attempted by the faint of heart.
C) you are a monster, but we like you anyways.
D) snapping is an activity enjoyed by all ages.

The 2nd asks for evidence that *proves* your previous answer.

Which choice provides the best evidence for the answer to the previous question?

A) Lines 1–2 ("Sharks...help!!")
B) Lines 3–4 ("You...monster")
C) Lines 6–8 ("Aw...shucks")
D) Lines 9–11 ("Funny...jokes?")

BOGO!

EBQs are 2 for the price of 1; if you get one right, you're very likely to get the other right as well!

Good News, Everybody!

Here's the good news: these questions make the Reading test significantly easier! If you treat EBQs not as two separate questions, but as **a single unit** with two steps, you can breeze through them on your way to an amazing Reading score.

Strategy

To see the strategy for EBQs, follow along with the example below. First, actively read the short passage, taking notes, underlining, circling, and starring. After that, we'll jump into the questions.

> The following passage was adapted from a letter that Susan B. Anthony, a 19th Century civil rights activist, wrote to her brother, Kansas resident Daniel Read Anthony, in 1859. At that time, Kansas was preparing to enter the Union as a state and was in the midst of a debate regarding slavery and civil rights.

Even the smallest human right denied, is large. The fact that the ruling class withhold this right is prima facie* evidence that they deem it of importance for good or for evil. In either case, therefore, the
Line human being is outraged. It, perchance, may matter but little whether
5 Kansas be governed by a constitution made by her bona fide settlers or by people of another State or by Congress; but for Kansas to be denied the right to make her own constitution and laws is an outrage not to be tolerated. So the constitution and laws of a State and nation may be just as considerate of woman's needs and wants as if framed
10 by herself, yet for man to deny her the right to a voice in making and administering them, is paralleled only by the Lecompton usurpation**. For any human being or class of human beings, whether black, white, male or female, tamely to submit to the denial of their right to self-government shows that the instinct of liberty has been blotted out.
15 You blunder on this question of woman's rights just where thousands of others do. You believe woman unlike man in her nature; that conditions of life which any man of spirit would sooner die than accept are not only endurable to woman but are needful to her fullest enjoyment. Make her position in church, State, marriage,
20 your own; everywhere your equality ignored, everywhere made to feel another empowered by law and time-honored custom to prescribe the privileges to be enjoyed and the duties to be discharged by you; and then if you can imagine yourself to be content and happy, judge your mother and sisters and all women to be.
25 It was not because the three-penny tax on tea was so exorbitant that our Revolutionary fathers fought and died, but to establish the principle that such taxation was unjust. It is the same with this woman's revolution; though every law were as just to woman as to man, the principle that one class may usurp the power to
30 legislate for another is unjust, and all who are now in the struggle from love of principle would still work on until the establishment of the grand and immutable truth, "All governments derive their just powers from the consent of the governed."***

* Prima Facie is a Latin expression meaning "at first sight."

** The Lecompton Constitution was proposed by the proslavery legislature in Kansas, but rejected by the voters.

*** Anthony is paraphrasing from the Declaration of Independence

1. Anthony indicates that the women's revolution and the American revolution are similar in that they both

   A) were centered on the principle of justice.
   B) were caused by righteous indignation.
   C) were primarily orchestrated by members of the upper class.
   D) are consistent with the ideals in the Constitution.

2. Which quote provides the best evidence for the previous question?

   A) Lines 3–4 ("In either ... outraged")
   B) Lines 8–11 ("So ... usurpation")
   C) Lines 12–14 ("For ... blotted out")
   D) lines 25–28 ("It ... revolution")

Once you spot an EBQ pair, it's time to implement the **strategy**:

1 Actively Read & Summarize Q1

1. Anthony indicates that the women's revolution and the American revolution are similar in that they both

   A) were centered on the principle of justice.
   B) were caused by righteous indignation.
   C) were primarily orchestrated by members of the upper class.
   D) are consistent with the ideals in the Constitution.

What do women's and American revolutions have in common?

TIP

If you **immediately** remember the answer (or know exactly where to find it in the passage), then you can go ahead and answer Q1.

However, on longer passages, it is often easier to **let Q2 guide you** to the answer!

Use your active reading to **summarize**, in a few words, what Q1 is asking. Here, we need to find lines from the passage about "what the women's and American revolutions have in common."

Rather than go hunting for the right answer, we can use Q2 to help us answer Q1. So, with our summary of Q1 in-hand, let's **skip to Q2** and let it guide us to the answer.

2 Use Q2 to find lines that answer Q1.

One of Q2's answer choices points you to the **evidence** you need to answer Q1. So let's start by checking for lines that are **on topic**. This is where our summary comes in handy! For each choice, ask:

"are these lines about the American and women's revolutions?"

Context

Use margin notes and active reading to help understand the context for each choice.

2. Which quote provides the best evidence for the previous question?

    A) Lines 3-4 (*In either case, therefore, the human being is outraged.*)

No mention of **revolutions** here.

    B) Lines 8-11 (*So the constitution and laws of a State and nation may be just as considerate of woman's needs and wants as if framed by herself, yet for man to deny her the right to a voice in making and administering them, is paralleled only by the Lecompton usurpation.*)

This relates the women's revolution to the **Lecompton usurpation**, but not the **American revolution**.

    C) Lines 12-14 (*For any human being or class of human beings, whether black, white, male or female, tamely to submit to the denial of their right to self-government shows that the instinct of liberty has been blotted out.*)

This sounds related to the revolutions, but doesn't directly reference them.

    D) Lines 25-28 (*It was not because the three-penny tax on tea was so exorbitant that our Revolutionary fathers fought and died, but to establish the principle that such taxation was unjust. It is the same with this woman's revolution;*)

Great! This choice mentions **both** revolutions, and that last sentence directly **compares** them.

Choice D is the best match for the topic of Q1.
Now we can use these lines to **go back and answer Q1**!

3 Match Q2's answer with Q1's choices.

Now that we know where to find the **evidence** for Q1, picking the correct answer choice should be easy. We know the correct answer should be supported by evidence from lines 23-25, which tells us the American and women's revolutions were fought:

"to establish the **principle** that such taxation was **unjust**."

A) centered on the **principle** of <u>justice</u>.

B) were caused by righteous indignation.

C) were primarily orchestrated by members of the upper class.

D) are consistent with the ideals in the Constitution.

The words "principle" and "justice" perfectly match our evidence from Q2! So the answer to Q1 is A, and the answer to Q2 is D. We're done!

The Onesie

Occasionally, the SAT will get lazy and combine Q1 and Q2 into a single question, making your life even easier:

3. Which of the following statements in the passage supports the conclusion that dogs are better than cats?

   A) Lines 8-11 (Dogs...rule)
   B) Lines 34-35 (Cats...drool)
   C) Lines 50-51 (Just...kidding)
   D) Lines 87-89 (Wink...wink)

With only one question to deal with, we can skip step 3 in the process completely. Simply read the lines in context, looking for the choice that answers the question.

Back-Up Plan

Very rarely (seriously, it hardly ever happens), you'll get to Step 2 of the strategy and find that more than one choice in Q2 could provide evidence for Q1. If you stumble upon one of these rare questions, you just need to adjust Step 3 a bit. Rather than matching a single Q2 choice to a single Q1 choice, you can **cross-reference** the answer choices to both questions, finding the two that match. Only **one** quotation in Q2 will have a great match in Q1!

LET'S RECAP!

Evidence-Based Questions usually come in pairs. Q1 asks a question about the passage, and Q2 asks for evidence that proves your answer. Think of these as two parts of a single question and use the lines as a roadmap to your answer! Here are your steps:

1) **Actively read Q1**

2) **Use Q2 answer choices to find lines that answer Q1**

3) **Match Q2 answer with Q1 choices**

Vocabulary in Context

You'll find one or two VIC questions attached to every passage. These are some of the easiest points on the test, so practice the strategy and get those points!

When you see the words "most nearly means," you know you've found a VIC question. The SAT writers won't ask you to define crazy three-syllable words; in fact, the VIC words are usually common words with multiple meanings. Here's what they look like:

1. As used in line 35, "raised" most nearly means,

   A) built.
   B) lifted.
   C) increased.
   D) nurtured.

As you can see, all of our answer choices are possible definitions of "raised," so we need some more information. When in doubt, go back to the passage! We need to read these words in **context** to figure out which is correct. Here are your step-by-step instructions:

TIP

We'll say it again: when in doubt, go back to the passage! That's where all the answers are.

① **Find the line** mentioned in the question, and read one sentence up and one sentence down.

② **Plug in each answer choice**, reading in context.

③ **Pick the choice that makes sense!**

Let's give it a whirl:

EXAMPLE 1

Lithium-oxygen, or lithium-air, batteries have been touted as the 'ultimate' battery due to their theoretical energy density, which is ten times that of a lithium-ion battery. Such a high
Line energy density would be comparable to that of gasoline—and
5 would enable an electric car with a battery that is a fifth the cost and a fifth the weight of those currently on the market to drive from London to Edinburgh on a single charge. Scientists have developed a working laboratory demonstrator of a lithium-oxygen battery which has very high energy density, is more than
10 90% efficient, and, to date, can be recharged more than 2,000 times. Their work presents potential solutions to several of the problems holding back the development of these devices.

1. As used in line 8, "developed" most nearly means,

    A) grown
    B) matured
    C) created
    D) unfolded

SOLUTION

(1) **Find the line** mentioned in the question, and read one sentence up and one sentence down.

*Such a high energy density would be comparable to that of gasoline—and would enable an electric car with a battery that is a fifth the cost and a fifth the weight of those currently on the market to drive from London to Edinburgh on a single charge. Scientists have **developed** a working laboratory demonstrator of a lithium-oxygen battery which has very high energy density, is more than 90% efficient, and, to date, can be recharged more than 2,000 times. Their work presents potential solutions to several of the problems holding back the development of these devices.*

② **Plug in each answer choice**, reading in context.

A) Scientists have **grown** a working laboratory demonstrator of a lithium-oxygen battery which has very high energy density, is more than 90% efficient, and, to date, can be recharged more than 2,000 times.

Can scientists grow batteries? I doubt it.

B) Scientists have **matured** a working laboratory demonstrator of a lithium-oxygen battery which has very high energy density, is more than 90% efficient, and, to date, can be recharged more than 2,000 times.

Wow, a fully-grown mature battery! This doesn't make sense.

C) Scientists have **created** a working laboratory demonstrator of a lithium-oxygen battery which has very high energy density, is more than 90% efficient, and, to date, can be recharged more than 2,000 times.

Now **that** makes sense. The scientists created a battery!

D) Scientists have **unfolded** a working laboratory demonstrator of a lithium-oxygen battery which has very high energy density, is more than 90% efficient, and, to date, can be recharged more than 2,000 times.

I don't know how you would fold **or** unfold a battery!

③ **Pick the choice that makes sense!**

In context, only **choice C** makes any sense. Let's choose **C**.

Reading Graphs

The science passages contain questions that require you to combine your reading of the passage with information in charts, tables, or graphs.

Go Figure!

The Natural and Social Science passages often include a chart, table, or graph that illustrates data relevant to the passage. For example, you might read a scientific report on temperature trends in the Himalayas, and then see a line graph of yearly temperatures. The exact type of figure changes passage-to-passage, so it's helpful to step back from any one particular figure and focus on what they all have in common, and how those similarities will help you answer the questions.

On the Reading section, graph-reading questions ask you to combine information from the passage with information from the figures. To do this, you want to ask some key questions about the figures:

(1) What **groups** are being compared?

(2) How are the groups being **measured**?

(3) What **conclusions** can we draw?

The First Rule of Graph Club

Before we dive into any of the above questions, we should emphasize one, all-helpful rule: **read the titles of the figures!** Seriously, there is no faster way to get a sense of what you're looking at than to read the title of the graph or figure. After all, when someone *wrote* that title, they had to consider the groups, the measurements, and the conclusions all at once!

TIP

TIP

There can be, and in fact often are, more than two groups. A line graph plotting temperatures for each month of the year would be comparing **12 different groups**.

What *groups* are being compared?

Graphs and tables are fantastic ways of illustrating how different groups are, well, different! The first thing you want to identify in a figure is what exactly those different groups are. If we're comparing temperatures in June with temperatures in December, then "June" and "December" would be our groups. If we're comparing reaction times between male and female mice, then "male mice" and "female mice" would be our groups.

In **tables**, you can spot the groups by looking at the **row/column labels**. In the table below, we're comparing "Swallowtails", "Monarchs", and "Other", as well as "Shady Grove" and "Johnson Park":

Number of Butterflies

Groups →	Shady Grove	Johnson Park
Swallowtails	12	6
Monarchs	18	10
Other	7	5

In **graphs**, you can often spot groups in **the legend** or on the **x-axis**. In the bar graph below, we're comparing "untreated" and "treated" peaches, as well as "open air" and "laboratory" locations:

Effect of Treatment on Peach Diameter

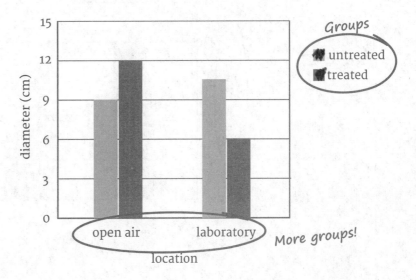

89

How are the groups being measured?

Once you've identified the groups being compared, the next step is to identify how those groups are being measured. If we're comparing temperatures for June and December, then temperature (in °C or °F) is our measurement.

In **tables**, the best place to look for measurements is in the title or in header cells. In the table below, the title tells us that the data reflects the "number of butterflies" of each type and in each location:

measurement

Number of Butterflies

	Shady Grove	Johnson Park
Swallowtails	12	6
Monarchs	18	10
Other	7	5

In **graphs**, the best place to look for measurements is in the **axis labels** – particularly the *y-axis label*. In the graph below, just glancing at the y-axis label tells us the peaches are being compared by a measurement of their diameters, in centimeters.

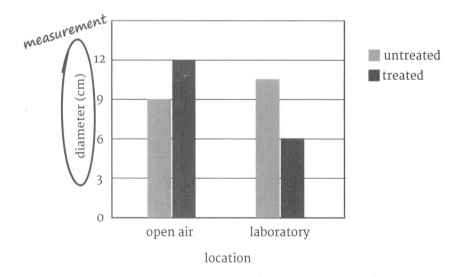

Effect of Treatment on Peach Diameter

What conclusions can we draw?

The last step is the most important one: identify what conclusions can be drawn from the figure. This often boils down to simply noticing which group scores higher or lower on the measurement, or if there is an overall upward or downward trend. For conclusions, the best place to look is in the **meat of the graph itself**: What trends are in the data? Where are the highest and lowest points? Is one group consistently higher than another? If not, why not?

In **tables**, look for rows or columns (groups) that consistently contain bigger values than the other rows or columns. In the table below, we can conclude that there are more butterflies in Shady Grove than in Johnson Park, and more Monarchs than other types of butterflies:

Number of Butterflies

	Shady Grove	Johnson Park
Swallowtails	12	6
Monarchs	18	10
Other	7	5

Biggest row (Monarchs)

Biggest column (Shady Grove)

In **graphs**, look for groups that measure higher or lower than other groups, or for general trends in the data. In the graph below, we can conclude that untreated peaches are smaller in open air than in the laboratory, while treated peaches are just the opposite. We can also conclude from the peak in the graph that treated, open air peaches are the biggest in diameter:

Effect of Treatment on Peach Diameter

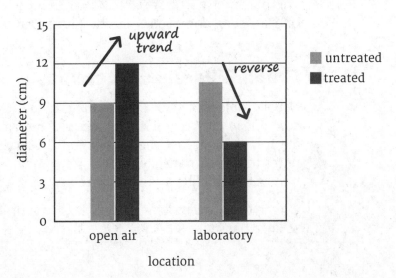

Strategy: Let the Question Guide You

You don't need to understand the graph until you **need** to understand the graph. When you finish actively reading a passage with figures, don't spend time deciphering their content just yet; instead, head right to the questions. There are multiple conclusions you could draw and observations you could make about a figure, but only one or two of them will actually come up!

It's much easier (and faster) to wait until a question asks you about a table or graph. Those questions will have key words that point you to a specific group or data point on the graph, which lets you narrow your focus and more quickly find the answer. For example, a question might ask of our butterfly table:

> "The table provides support for which of the following statements about Swallowtail butterflies?"

In that case, we would know to focus our attention to the **Swallowtail** row in the table:

Number of Butterflies

		Shady Grove	Johnson Park
Focus	Swallowtails	12	6
	Monarchs	18	10
	Other	7	5

This becomes particularly helpful when the figures contain large amounts of distracting data. So remember: **let the question guide your focus!**

Graph & Passage Questions

Usually, at least one of the graph reading questions will require you to combine what the graph tells you with information in the passage. As always, you'll answer these questions by relying on your **active reading** notes to find & match key words from the question. The only difference here is that you'll make a "pit stop" at the graph.

On the next several pages, we'll get some practice with a graph-equipped science passage.

Reading Practice Passage 3
TO STAY ON PACE, YOUR TIMING GOAL IS 13 MINUTES

Each passage or pair of passages below is followed by a number of questions. After reading each passage or pair, choose the best answer to each question based on what is stated or implied in the passage or passages and in any accompanying graphics (such as a table or graph).

Questions 1-11 are based on the following passage.

This passage is adapted from Mary Hoff, "What's Behind the Spread of White Syndrome in Great Barrier Reef Corals?" © 2007 Public Library of Science.

Coral reefs, among Earth's richest ecosystems, traditionally teem with an abundance of life. The tiny corals that form the foundation of the community
Line are microcosms themselves, sheltering single-celled
5 algae that feed the community with energy from the sun. The three-dimensional physical space they create with their skeletons supports an astounding array of other animals, from sponges to sharks.

But in recent years, corals have been dying in
10 droves. Scientists suspect a variety of factors, ranging from accidental damage from fishing activity to the effects of polluted runoff from land. One threat that appears to be growing dramatically in Australia's famed Great Barrier Reef is white syndrome, a mystery-riddled
15 disease that is spreading rapidly, leaving stripes of dead corals like ribbons of death in its wake. But why?

Global warming seems a likely suspect for several reasons. Past epidemiological studies across a broad range of life forms have shown that stress—
20 including the stress of changing environmental conditions—often increases disease susceptibility. As temperatures rise, pathogens can reproduce more quickly. The fact that coral diseases seem to spread faster in summer also provides support for the
25 notion that warmer temperatures may be involved.

In hope of improving understanding of the spread of white syndrome, John Bruno, Amy Melendy, and colleagues conducted a regional-scale longitudinal study of the hypothesized link between
30 warm temperature deviations and the presence of white syndrome, considering the density of coral cover as an additional variable of interest.

To quantify temperature fluctuations, the researchers used a high-resolution dataset on ocean
35 surface temperature provided by the United States National Oceanic and Atmospheric Association and the University of Miami. They used the dataset to calculate weekly sea surface temperature anomalies (WSSTAs)—instances in which temperature was higher by 1°C or
40 more from mean records for that week—for 48 reefs within the Great Barrier Reef. To evaluate the extent of white syndrome and coral cover, the researchers used data collected by the Australian Institute of Marine Science Long-term Monitoring Program on 48 reefs
45 from a 1,500-kilometer stretch of the Great Barrier Reef from 1998 to 2004 at a depth of 6 to 9 meters. Divers counted the number of infected colonies on each reef. Coral cover, the amount of the bottom with living corals, was measured from videos taken of the reefs.

50 The researchers then evaluated the relationship between the occurrence of white syndrome and three variables: number of WSSTAs occurring during the previous 52 weeks, coral cover, and the interaction between the two. They found that the third variable
55 showed a statistically significant correlation with number of white syndrome cases, indicating that

CONTINUE

the presence of both conditions—temperature
anomalies and high coral cover—creates the
conditions in which white syndrome outbreaks are
60 most likely to occur. In other words, WSSTAs were
a necessary but not sufficient condition for white
syndrome outbreaks, whereas the combination
of heat stress and a dense colony was deadly.

What does this mean for corals and the ecosystem
65 they support? If global warming increases the
incidence of warm temperature anomalies in tropical
oceans in the years ahead, these results suggest
that corals in high-cover areas will be increasingly
vulnerable to white disease. If the effect is large
70 enough, the tightly woven web of life within coral
reefs could begin to unravel, potentially transforming
habitats that were once among the planet's richest
ecosystems into underwater wastelands.

This strong evidence for a link among a
75 warming ocean, coral density, and white syndrome
provides a rich foundation for further work to
understand the spread of coral disease in the Great
Barrier Reef. It also provides valuable insights
into marine epidemiology that could be of much
80 value in investigating and potentially mitigating
other devastating global-warming-related disease
outbreaks in the world's vast and vulnerable oceans.

1

The main purpose of the passage is to discuss how coral
reefs are dying from

A) a rapidly spreading disease.
B) chemical runoff from land.
C) disturbance due to fishing activity.
D) climate change alone.

2

Which choice provides the best evidence for the answer
to the previous question?

A) Lines 2-6 ("The tiny … sun")
B) Lines 10-12 ("Scientists … land")
C) Lines 12-16 ("One … wake")
D) Lines 17-18 ("Global … reasons")

3

In line 7, "supports" most nearly means

A) bears weight.
B) encourages.
C) props up.
D) sustains.

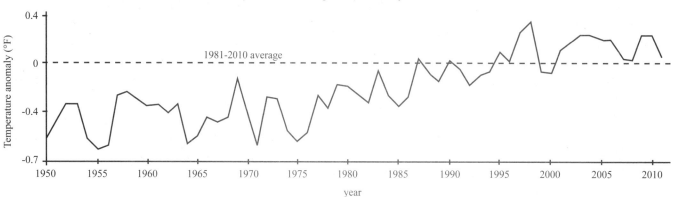

Yearly sea surface temperature anomaly 1950-2011

CONTINUE

4

According to the passage, the number of coral colonies affected by white syndrome was determined by

A) a dataset provided by Bruno, Melendy, and team.
B) divers who tallied and recorded their observations.
C) high-resolution technology directed towards a specific locale.
D) a cooperative effort between scientists from many nations.

5

Which choice provides the best evidence for the answer to the previous question?

A) Lines 33-37 ("To quantify ... Miami")
B) Lines 37-41 ("They ... Great Barrier Reef")
C) Lines 46-47 ("Divers ... reef")
D) Lines 48-49 ("Coral ... reefs")

6

The use of the words "If," "suggest," and "potentially" in the seventh paragraph (lines 64-74) serves to emphasize that

A) Bruno, et al., continue to analyze information that will predict the fate of coral reefs.
B) the information obtained by the United States National Oceanic and Atmospheric Association is most likely inaccurate.
C) the future of marine ecosystems is still uncertain.
D) current theories on changes in the Great Barrier Reef are based on verifiable data.

7

In line 74, "strong" most nearly means

A) meaningful.
B) mighty.
C) thriving.
D) aggressive.

8

According to the data in the figure, the greatest above-average temperature variation occurred around what year?

A) 1955
B) 1969
C) 1987
D) 1998

9

Which statement is best supported by the information provided in the figure?

A) After 2010, weekly sea surface temperature anomalies will decrease.
B) The steady increase in sea surface temperature over the past five decades suggests an increase in the amount of coral cover on ocean floors.
C) Before 2000, the yearly sea surface temperature was always below the 1981-2010 average.
D) Since 2001, the yearly sea surface temperature has always been above the 1981-2010 average.

10

Based on the information in the passage and the figure, a white syndrome outbreak most likely occurred during

A) 1955 in a reef with high coral cover.
B) 1955 in a reef with low coral cover.
C) 2010 in a reef with high coral cover.
D) 2010 in a reef with low coral cover.

11

Which choice provides the best evidence for the answer to the previous question?

A) Lines 23-25 ("The fact ... involved")
B) Lines 50-54 ("The researchers ... two")
C) Lines 54-60 ("They ... occur")
D) Lines 69-73 ("If the ... wastelands")

STOP

Active Reading

This passage is adapted from Mary Hoff, "What's Behind the Spread of White Syndrome in Great Barrier Reef Corals?" © 2007 Public Library of Science.

Coral reefs, among Earth's richest ecosystems, traditionally teem with an abundance of life. The tiny corals that form the foundation of the community
Line are microcosms themselves, sheltering single-celled
5 algae that feed the community with energy from the sun. The three-dimensional physical space they create with their skeletons supports an astounding array of other animals, from sponges to sharks. But in recent years, corals have been dying in
10 droves. Scientists suspect a variety of factors, ranging from accidental damage from fishing activity to the effects of polluted runoff from land. One threat that appears to be growing dramatically in Australia's famed Great Barrier Reef is white syndrome, a mystery-riddled
15 disease that is spreading rapidly, leaving stripes of dead corals like ribbons of death in its wake. But why?

Global warming seems a likely suspect for several reasons. Past epidemiological studies across a broad range of life forms have shown that stress—
20 including the stress of changing environmental conditions—often increases disease susceptibility. As temperatures rise, pathogens can reproduce more quickly. The fact that coral diseases seem to spread faster in summer also provides support for the
25 notion that warmer temperatures may be involved.

In hope of improving understanding of the spread of white syndrome, John Bruno, Amy Melendy, and colleagues conducted a regional-scale longitudinal study of the hypothesized link between
30 warm temperature deviations and the presence of white syndrome, considering the density of coral cover as an additional variable of interest.

To quantify temperature fluctuations, the researchers used a high-resolution dataset on ocean
35 surface temperature provided by the United States National Oceanic and Atmospheric Association and the University of Miami. They used the dataset to calculate weekly sea surface temperature anomalies (WSSTAs)— instances in which temperature was higher by 1°C or

40 more from mean records for that week—for 48 reefs within the Great Barrier Reef. To evaluate the extent of white syndrome and coral cover, the researchers used data collected by the Australian Institute of Marine Science Long-term Monitoring Program on 48 reefs
45 from a 1,500-kilometer stretch of the Great Barrier Reef from 1998 to 2004 at a depth of 6 to 9 meters. Divers counted the number of infected colonies on each reef. Coral cover, the amount of the bottom with living corals, was measured from videos taken of the reefs.
50 The researchers then evaluated the relationship between the occurrence of white syndrome and three variables: number of WSSTAs occurring during the previous 52 weeks, coral cover, and the interaction between the two. They found that the third variable
55 showed a statistically significant correlation with number of white syndrome cases, indicating that the presence of both conditions—temperature anomalies and high coral cover—creates the conditions in which white syndrome outbreaks are
60 most likely to occur. In other words, WSSTAs were a necessary but not sufficient condition for white syndrome outbreaks, whereas the combination of heat stress and a dense colony was deadly.

What does this mean for corals and the ecosystem
65 they support? If global warming increases the incidence of warm temperature anomalies in tropical oceans in the years ahead, these results suggest that corals in high-cover areas will be increasingly vulnerable to white disease. If the effect is large
70 enough, the tightly woven web of life within coral reefs could begin to unravel, potentially transforming habitats that were once among the planet's richest ecosystems into underwater wastelands.

This strong evidence for a link among a
75 warming ocean, coral density, and white syndrome provides a rich foundation for further work to understand the spread of coral disease in the Great Barrier Reef. It also provides valuable insights into marine epidemiology that could be of much
80 value in investigating and potentially mitigating other devastating global-warming–related disease outbreaks in the world's vast and vulnerable oceans.

Explanations

Answers & explanations for "What's Behind the Spread of White Syndrome in Great Barrier Reef Corals?"

1. The main purpose of the passage is to discuss how coral reefs are dying from

   (A) a rapidly spreading disease.
   B) chemical runoff from land.
   C) disturbance due to fishing activity.
   D) climate change alone.

2. Which choice provides the best evidence for the answer to the previous question?

   A) Lines 2–6 ("The tiny … sun")
   B) Lines 10–12 ("Scientists … land")
   (C) Lines 12–16 ("One … wake")
   D) Lines 17–18 ("Global … reasons")

Let's try our brand new EBQ strategy! According to Q1, we need a quote that explicitly mentions the cause of the coral's demise. Looking at the four options, only **choice C**, lines 12-16, mentions coral reefs dying:

> *"One threat that appears to be growing dramatically in Australia's famed Great Barrier Reef is white syndrome, **a mystery-riddled disease** that is spreading rapidly, leaving stripes of **dead corals** like ribbons of death in its wake."*

Now we need a match for "mystery-riddled disease that is spreading rapidly" in Q1's answer choices. **Choice A** is perfect!

3. In line 7, "supports" most nearly means

    A) bears weight.
    B) encourages.
    C) props up.
    (D) sustains.

First, we need to look at the word in context:

> *"The three-dimensional physical space they create with their skeletons **supports** an astounding array of other animals, from sponges to sharks."*

If we plug "**sustains**" into the sentence, the meaning stays the same. **Choice D** is correct!

> *"The three-dimensional physical space they create with their skeletons **sustains** an astounding array of other animals, from sponges to sharks."*

4. According to the passage, the number of coral colonies affected by white syndrome was determined by

    A) a dataset provided by Bruno, Melendy, and team.
    (B) divers who tallied and recorded their observations.
    C) high-resolution technology directed towards a specific locale.
    D) a cooperative effort between scientists from many nations.

5. Which choice provides the best evidence for the answer to the previous question?

    A) Lines 33-37 ("To quantify ... Miami")
    B) Lines 37-41 ("They ... Great Barrier Reef")
    (C) Lines 46-47 ("Divers ... reef")
    D) Lines 48-49 ("Coral ... reefs")

We can use our EBQ strategy to evaluate the quotes in Q5 to find the answer to both questions. We need to find the quote that tells us how they determine the number of coral colonies affected by white syndrome. **Choice C**, lines 46-47, clearly tells us that the scientists used data collected by divers. In Q4, **choice B** tells us that "divers" collected the data.

6. The use of the words "If," "suggest," and "potentially" in the seventh paragraph (lines 64–74) serves to emphasize that

A) Bruno, et al. continue to analyze information that will predict the fate of ~~coral reefs~~.
B) the information obtained by the United States National Oceanic and Atmospheric Association is most likely ~~inaccurate~~.
C) the future of marine ecosystems is still uncertain.
D) current theories on changes in ~~the Great Barrier Reef~~ are based on verifiable data.

The seventh paragraph extends the scope from the coral reefs to the entire marine ecosystem. The words listed modify the statements to acknowledge that the negative outcome *could* happen. **Choice C** gives us a great match: "uncertain" matches "if," "suggest," and "potentially."

7. In line 74, "strong" most nearly means

A) meaningful.
B) mighty.
C) thriving.
D) aggressive.

First, we need to read the word in context:

*"This **strong** evidence for a link among a warming ocean, coral density, and white syndrome provides a rich foundation for further work to understand the spread of coral disease in the Great Barrier Reef."*

"Strong" modifies the evidence, so we need to pick an answer that would logically modify evidence. Only "**meaningful**" makes sense as a modifier for evidence. **Choice A** is correct.

*"This **meaningful** evidence for a link among a warming ocean, coral density, and white syndrome provides a rich foundation for further work to understand the spread of coral disease in the Great Barrier Reef."*

8. According to the data in the figure, the greatest above-average temperature variation occurred around what year?

   A) 1955
   B) 1969
   C) 1987
   D) 1998

> All we have to do is look for the **tallest peak** above the average temperature variation. Although it's difficult to determine the exact year of the peak, if we look at the answer choices, only **1998** is close, so **choice D** must be answer!

9. Which statement is best supported by the information provided in the figure?

    A) After 2010, weekly sea surface temperature anomalies will decrease.
    B) The steady increase in sea surface temperature over the past five decades suggests an increase in the amount of coral cover on ocean floors.
    C) Before 2000, the yearly sea surface temperature was always below the 1981–2010 average.
   D) Since 2001, the yearly sea surface temperature has always been above the 1981–2010 average.

> For this question, we need to evaluate each answer choice and see which one most closely matches the information in the figure. Choice A is an assumption; the graph shows that the surface temperature anomaly is decreasing after 2010, but will it continue to decrease? We can't predict the future, so we can't choose A.
>
> Choice B is also an assumption; there has been an increase over the past 50 years, but we **cannot** say that there has also been an increase in coral cover. Coral cover could be increasing, but we don't know that based on this graph.
>
> Choice C is incorrect because the line is above the 1981-2010 average from 1994-1999.
>
> Only **choice D** is supported by the figure; after 2001, the line stays above the 1981-2010 average.

10. Based on the information in the passage and the figure, a white syndrome outbreak most likely occurred during

   A) 1955 in a reef with high coral cover.
   B) 1955 in a reef with low coral cover.
   C) 2010 in a reef with high coral cover.
   D) 2010 in a reef with low coral cover.

11. Which choice provides the best evidence for the answer to the previous question?

   A) Lines 23-25 ("The fact ... involved")
   B) Lines 50-54 ("The researchers ... two")
   C) Lines 54-60 ("They ... occur")
   D) Lines 69-73 ("If the ... wastelands")

Using our EBQ strategy will help us answer this paired set. Let's look at Q11's choices to find a quote that mentions white syndrome outbreak. **Choice C**, lines 53-58, says:

> *"They found that the third variable showed a statistically significant correlation with number of white syndrome cases, indicating that the presence of both conditions—temperature anomalies and high coral cover—creates the conditions in which white syndrome outbreaks are most likely to occur."*

Now let's find a match in Q10. We know we need high coral cover, so we can cross off B and D. But what about temperature anomalies?

Lines 36-39 tell us that temperature anomalies are "instances in which temperature was **higher** by 1°C or more from mean records for that week." 1955 (choice A) had a temperature anomaly **lower** than average, and 2010 (choice C) had a temperature anomaly **higher** than average. **Choice C**, high coral cover and 2010, a year with higher temperature anomaly, fits the passage and the figure.

Literature

Let's get some practice with a Literature passage.

Remember, you can save the hardest passage for last so you don't waste time and energy. Each question is worth the same, so focus on the easy points first!

The Literature passage, often the first on the test, is a **narrative** that could be from olden times or nowadays. We've seen passages from the 1800s with fancy words like "hitherto," but we've also seen contemporary passages. You may have even read the passage before in school; famous authors like Jane Austen and Charlotte Bronte have shown up on the test.

Tips for Active Reading

In Literature passages, your focus should be on **characters**: their feelings, their actions, how they are perceived, and how they change. **Circle** the name of each new character so you can easily find them when you're looking for evidence. When you finish the passage, ask yourself: Did the characters end in a different place than they started? What was their emotional journey?

Literature Passage
TO STAY ON PACE, YOUR TIMING GOAL IS 13 MINUTES

Each passage or pair of passages below is followed by a number of questions. After reading each passage or pair, choose the best answer to each question based on what is stated or implied in the passage or passages and in any accompanying graphics (such as a table or graph).

Questions 1-10 are based on the following passage.

The passage is adapted from Mark Twain, *A Dog's Tale*, originally published in 1903.

My father was a St. Bernard, my mother was a collie, but I am a Presbyterian. This is what my mother told me, I do not know these nice distinctions myself. To
Line me they are only fine large words meaning nothing.
5 My mother had a fondness for such; she liked to say them, and see other dogs look surprised and envious, as wondering how she got so much education. But, indeed, it was not real education; it was only show: she got the words by listening in the dining-room and
10 drawing-room when there was company, and by going with the children to Sunday-school and listening there; and whenever she heard a large word she said it over to herself many times, and so was able to keep it until there was a gathering of dogs in the neighborhood,
15 then she would rattle it off, and surprise and distress them all, from pocket-pup to mastiff, which rewarded her for all her trouble. When she told the meaning of a big word they were all so taken up with admiration that it never occurred to any dog to doubt if it was
20 the right one; and that was natural, because, for one thing, she answered up so promptly that it seemed like a dictionary speaking, and for another thing, where could they find out whether it was right or not? for she was the only cultivated dog there was.
25 By and by, when I was older, she brought home the

word Unintellectual, one time, and worked it pretty hard all the week at different gatherings, making much unhappiness and despondency; and it was at this time that I noticed that during that week she was asked for
30 the meaning at eight different assemblages, and flashed out a fresh definition every time, which showed me that she had more presence of mind than culture, though I said nothing, of course. She had one word which she always kept on hand, and ready, like a life-preserver, a
35 kind of emergency word to strap on when she was likely to get washed overboard in a sudden way—that was the word Synonymous. When she happened to fetch out a long word which had had its day weeks before and its prepared meanings gone to her dump-pile, if there was
40 a stranger there of course it knocked him groggy for a couple of minutes, then he would come to, and by that time she would be away down wind on another tack, and not expecting anything; so when he'd hail and ask her to cash in, I (the only dog on the inside of her game)
45 could see her canvas flicker a moment—but only just a moment—then it would belly out taut and full, and she would say, as calm as a summer's day, "It's synonymous with supererogation," or some godless long reptile of a word like that, and go placidly about and skim away
50 on the next tack, perfectly comfortable, you know, and leave that stranger looking profane and embarrassed, and the initiated slatting the floor with their tails in unison and their faces transfigured with a holy joy.
And it was the same with phrases. She would drag
55 home a whole phrase, if it had a grand sound, and

CONTINUE

play it six nights and two matinees, and explain it a
new way every time—which she had to, for all she
cared for was the phrase; she wasn't interested in what
it meant, and knew those dogs hadn't wit enough to
60 catch her, anyway. Yes, she was a daisy! She got so she
wasn't afraid of anything, she had such confidence in
the ignorance of those creatures. She even brought
anecdotes that she had heard the family and the
dinner-guests laugh and shout over; and as a rule
65 she got the nub of one chestnut hitched onto another
chestnut, where, of course, it didn't fit and hadn't any
point; and when she delivered the nub she fell over and
rolled on the floor and laughed and barked in the most
insane way, while I could see that she was wondering
70 to herself why it didn't seem as funny as it did when
she first heard it. But no harm was done; the others
rolled and barked too, privately ashamed of themselves
for not seeing the point, and never suspecting that the
fault was not with them and there wasn't any to see.

1

The passage as a whole is best characterized as

A) a reflection on canine social hierarchy.
B) an examination of a mother's efforts to educate
   her son.
C) a defense of a mother's fondness for language.
D) a memoir of a mother's unique use of words.

2

As used in line 4, "fine" most nearly means

A) fancy.
B) acceptable.
C) delicate.
D) sincere.

3

Which most resembles the "education" mentioned in
line 8?

A) A piano player learns to play a concerto by listening
   to other musicians instead of by learning to read
   music.
B) An artist practices forging master paintings to
   develop his skill.
C) A culinary student watches cooking shows to
   develop new recipes.
D) A chemistry student memorizes the periodic table
   to impress his teachers without understanding its
   purpose.

4

The phrase "had more presence of mind than culture"
(line 32) suggests which of the following about the
narrator's mother?

A) She is very intelligent but is plagued by poor
   memory.
B) She compensates for her lack of knowledge with
   quick thinking.
C) Her personal charm is diminished by her lack of
   sophistication.
D) Her imposing intellect prevents her from
   participating in canine culture.

5

The narrator's mother uses the word "synonymous" in
order to

A) rescue herself from a potentially embarrassing
   situation.
B) amuse strangers with her lack of knowledge.
C) entertain her son with extraordinary words.
D) confuse her fellow dogs by recycling her vocabulary.

CONTINUE ➡

6

Which choice provides the best evidence for the answer to the previous question?

A) Lines 33-37 ("She … Synonymous")

B) Lines 37-41 ("When … minutes")

C) Lines 43-46 ("so when … just a moment")

D) Lines 47-53 (" 'It's synonymous … joy")

7

Lines 54-56 ("She would … matinees") mainly serve to

A) demonstrate that the mother presents her phrases in a highly dramatic fashion.

B) suggest that the mother uses her phrases to impress whenever possible.

C) show that the mother is more cultured than her audience.

D) indicate that the mother enjoys the challenge of creating new definitions for her phrases.

8

The narrator's attitude toward his mother is primarily one of

A) incredulity.

B) appreciation.

C) ambivalence.

D) criticism.

9

Which choice provides the best evidence for the answer to the previous question?

A) Lines 2-3 ("This … myself.")

B) Lines 7-8 ("But … show")

C) Lines 25-28 ("By and by … despondency")

D) Line 60 ("Yes … daisy")

10

The narrator indicates that the mother's use of anecdotes is

A) affected by her inability to remember them correctly.

B) appreciated by the other dogs.

C) a source of joy for the narrator.

D) confusing for strangers but admired by her friends.

STOP

If you finish before time is called, you may check your work on this section only.

Do not turn to any other section.

Explanations

Answers & explanations for the "A Dog's Tale" Passage.

1. The passage as a whole is best characterized as...

   A) a reflection on canine ~~social hierarchy~~
   B) an examination of a mother's efforts to ~~educate~~ her son
   C) a ~~defense~~ of a mother's fondness for language
   (D) a memoir of a mother's unique use of words

   The story is about a dog **remembering** his mother and her unusual use of vocabulary, so we'll need an answer that best matches that description. "Memoir" in **Choice D** is perfect, so that's our answer!

2. As used in line 4, "fine" most nearly means

   (A) fancy
   B) acceptable
   C) delicate
   D) sincere

   Let's look at the word in context:

   > "I do not know these nice distinctions myself. To me they are only **fine** large words meaning nothing."

   We want a word that parallels "nice" in the previous sentence, and that also captures the context of how the author's mother uses words to impress others. "Fancy" best captures this context when we plug it in:

   > "I do not know these nice distinctions myself. To me they are only **fancy** large words meaning nothing."

   Choice A is correct.

3. Which most resembles the "education" mentioned in line 8?

   A) A piano player learns to play a concerto by listening to other musicians instead of by learning to read music
   B) An artist practices forging master paintings to develop his skill
   C) A culinary student watches cooking shows to develop new recipes
   (D) A chemistry student memorizes the periodic table to impress his teachers without understanding its purpose

> The key is that she "learns" words without learning their proper meaning, so we need to find an analogous situation in the answers. It doesn't matter if the subject matter is different.
>
> **Choice D** is best. The student knows the symbols and the numbers, but doesn't **understand** how they relate to chemistry. This is similar to how the narrator's mother uses words.

4. The phrase "had more presence of mind than culture" (line 32) suggests which of the following about the narrator's mother?

   A) She is very intelligent but is plagued by ~~poor memory~~.
   (B) She compensates for her lack of knowledge with quick thinking.
   C) Her personal charm is ~~diminished~~ by her lack of sophistication.
   D) Her imposing intellect ~~prevents~~ her from participating in canine culture.

> First let's look at the phrase in context:
>
> *"...and it was at this time that I noticed that during that week she was asked for the meaning at eight different assemblages, and flashed out a fresh definition every time, which showed me that she had more presence of mind than culture, though I said nothing, of course."*
>
> It seems like the narrator's mother doesn't know the definition of the word, but she's good at bluffing her way through the situation. In choice B, "quick thinking" matches "flashed out a fresh definition," while "lack of knowledge" matches our paraphrase. **Choice B** is correct!

5. The narrator's mother uses the word "synonymous" in order to

   A) rescue herself from a potentially embarrassing situation.
   B) amuse strangers with her lack of knowledge.
   C) entertain her son with extraordinary words.
   D) confuse her fellow dogs by recycling her vocabulary.

6. Which choice provides the best evidence for the answer to the previous question?

   A) Lines 33–37 ("She … Synonymous")
   B) Lines 37–41 ("When … minutes")
   C) Lines 43–46 ("so when … just a moment")
   D) Lines 47–53 (" 'It's synonymous … joy")

   Let's check Q6 quotes and find the quote that shows **how** she uses the word "synonymous." Lines 33-37, **choice A**, tell us that she uses the word Synonym "like a life-preserver." In Q6, choice A says she uses synonymous to **rescue** herself; life-preservers are used for rescue, so we found our match.

7. Lines 54–56 ("She would … matinees") mainly serves to

   A) demonstrate that the mother presents her phrases in a highly ~~dramatic fashion~~.
   B) suggest that the mother uses her phrases to impress whenever possible.
   C) show that the mother is ~~more cultured~~ than her audience.
   D) indicate that the mother enjoys the challenge of creating ~~new definitions~~ for her phrases.

First, let's review the whole sentence in context:

"And it was the same with phrases. She would drag home a whole phrase, if it had a grand sound, and play it six nights and two matinees, and explain it a new way every time—which she had to, for all she cared for was the phrase; she wasn't interested in what it meant, and knew those dogs hadn't wit enough to catch her, anyway."

The phrase "play it six nights and two matinees" implies that she uses a favorite phrase **many times**, since she "explains it a new way every time." **Choice B** tells us she uses the phrase "**whenever possible.**"

8. The narrator's attitude toward his mother is primarily one of

   A) incredulity.
   B) appreciation.
   C) ambivalence.
   D) criticism.

9. Which choice provides the best evidence for the answer to the previous question?

   A) Lines 2–3 ("This … myself.")
   B) Lines 7–8 ("But … show")
   C) Lines 25–28 ("By and by … despondency")
   D) Line 60 ("Yes … daisy!")

Let's evaluate Q9's quotes and pick the one that most clearly expresses the **narrator's opinion of his mother**. **Choice D** tells us that the narrator views his mom as "a daisy," which is certainly positive. **Choice B** in Q8 is the only positive choice, so it's correct!

10. The narrator indicates that the mother's use of anecdotes is

(A) affected by her inability to remember them correctly.
B) ~~appreciated~~ by the other dogs.
C) a source of joy for ~~the narrator~~.
D) ~~confusing for strangers~~ but admired by her friends.

The narrator mentions anecdotes on lines 62-74:

*"She even brought **anecdotes** that she had heard the family and the dinner-guests laugh and shout over; and as a rule **she got the nub of one chestnut hitched onto another chestnut**, where, of course, it didn't fit and hadn't any point; and when she delivered the nub she fell over and rolled on the floor and laughed and barked in the most insane way, while I could see that **she was wondering to herself why it didn't seem as funny as it did when she first heard it**. But no harm was one; the others rolled and barked too, privately ashamed of themselves for not seeing the point, and never suspecting that the fault was not with them and there wasn't any to see."*

When the narrator talks about "nubs" and "chestnuts," he's talking about the set-ups and punchlines in his mother's anecdotes. The mother mixes up her jokes, so that when she finally delivers them to the other dogs, they don't make any sense. **Choice A** tells us that she can't remember them correctly, which matches the passage perfectly.

Politics

Let's get some practice with a Politics passage.

Remember, you can save the hardest passage for last so you don't waste time and energy. Each question is worth the same, so focus on the easy points first!

The Politics passage is often the hardest on the whole test. You might see an excerpt from a book or essay, a political speech, or even a letter. Passages can date from the 1960s all the way to pre-Revolutionary War; the writers are often American, but we've seen other countries represented as well. The older the passage, the more difficult it will be for modern readers, so don't hesitate to leave this passage for last! More than likely, you'll have heard of the authors in English or U.S. History classes; use that to your advantage! If you've read Henry David Thoreau and know that he is famous for simple living and civil disobedience, keep that in mind while you read. Knowing the perspective of the writer will help you understand his or her point, especially on the really tough passages.

Don't forget: always read the intro text above the passage, especially on the Politics passage. It often contains crucial information that will help you understand the paragraphs to come. Make note of the date the passage was written to put it in historical context. A passage about slavery written in 1860 will have a different perspective than one written in 1800!

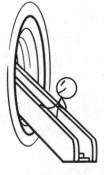

PORTAL

For more examples of persuasive arguments, check out the Essay chapter on page 694.

Tips for Active Reading

Politics passages are usually going to be **persuasive arguments**: the author is trying to persuade you to come around to his or her point of view. Focus on the author's **thesis** and make sure you know his or her argument by the end of the passage. An argument can be like a roller coaster; there are twists and turns, ups and downs. **Circle** logic words to track the author's argument and follow the structure of the passage. When you finish the passage, ask yourself: What was the author's thesis? What is the problem the author wants to address? What is the proposed solution?

Politics Passage

TO STAY ON PACE, YOUR TIMING GOAL IS 13 MINUTES

DIRECTIONS

Each passage or pair of passages below is followed by a number of questions. After reading each passage or pair, choose the best answer to each question based on what is stated or implied in the passage or passages and in any accompanying graphics (such as a table or graph).

Questions 1-10 are based on the following passage.

This passage is adapted from Elizabeth Cady Stanton, Susan B. Anthony, and Matilda Joslyn Gage, *History of Women's Suffrage, Volume 1*. Originally published in 1881.

The prolonged slavery of woman is the darkest page in human history. A survey of the condition of woman through those barbarous periods, when physical force
Line governed the world, when the motto, "might makes
5 right," was the law, enables one to account for the origin of woman's subjection to man without referring the fact to the general inferiority of the sex, or Nature's law.

One of the greatest minds of the century has thrown a ray of light on this gloomy picture by tracing
10 the origin of woman's slavery to the same principle of selfishness and love of power in man that has thus far dominated all weaker nations and classes. This brings hope of final emancipation, for as all nations and classes are gradually, one after another, asserting and
15 maintaining their independence, the path is clear for woman to follow. The slavish instinct of an oppressed class has led her to toil patiently through the ages, giving all and asking little, cheerfully sharing with man all perils and privations by land and sea, that husband
20 and sons might attain honor and success. Justice and freedom for herself is her latest and highest demand.

Another writer asserts that the tyranny of man over woman has its roots, after all, in his nobler feelings; his love, his chivalry, and his desire to protect

25 woman in the barbarous periods of pillage and war. But wherever the roots may be traced, the results at this hour are equally disastrous to woman. Her best interests and happiness do not seem to have been consulted in the arrangements made for her
30 protection. But if a chivalrous desire to protect woman has always been the mainspring of man's dominion over her, it should have prompted him to place in her hands the same weapons of defense he has found to be most effective against wrong and oppression.

35 It is often asserted that as woman has always been man's slave—subject—inferior—dependent, under all forms of government and religion, slavery must be her normal condition. This might have some weight had not the vast majority of men also
40 been enslaved for centuries to kings and popes, and orders of nobility, who, in the progress of civilization, have reached complete equality. And did we not also see the great changes in woman's condition, the marvelous transformation in her character, from
45 a drudge in the fields to a leader of thought in the literary circles of France, England, and America!

Woman's steady march onward, and her growing desire for a broader outlook, prove that she has not reached her normal condition, and that society has not
50 yet conceded all that is necessary for its attainment.

Moreover, woman's discontent increases in exact proportion to her development. Instead of a feeling of gratitude for rights accorded, the wisest are indignant at the assumption of any legal disability based on
55 sex, and their feelings in this matter are a surer test

CONTINUE ▶

of what her nature demands than the feelings and prejudices of the sex claiming to be superior.

The broader demand for political rights has not commanded the thought its merits and dignity should
60 have secured. While complaining of many wrongs and oppressions, women themselves did not see that the political disability of sex was the cause of all their special grievances, and that to secure equality anywhere, it must be recognized everywhere. Like
65 all disenfranchised classes, they begun by asking to have certain wrongs redressed, and not by asserting their own right to make laws for themselves.

Overburdened with cares in the isolated home, women had not the time, education, opportunity, and
70 pecuniary independence to put their thoughts clearly and concisely into propositions, nor the courage to compare their opinions with one another, nor to publish them, to any great extent, to the world.

1

The authors suggest that one explanation for the oppression of women comes from

A) a natural inequality between men and women.
B) a miscommunication regarding cultural ideals.
C) a leftover notion of protection from an earlier era.
D) an unwillingness for either side to compromise.

2

Which choice provides the best evidence for the answer in the previous question?

A) Lines 12-16 ("This … follow")
B) Lines 22-25 ("Another … war")
C) Lines 38-42 ("This … equality")
D) Lines 64-67 ("Like … themselves")

3

The reference to a "final emancipation" acknowledges

A) the end of the abolitionist movement.
B) a universal desire for rights.
C) that women have led the charge for civil rights.
D) the civil rights era had come to a conclusion.

4

On line 45, "drudge" most nearly means

A) burden.
B) trowel.
C) laborer.
D) crop.

5

From information in the passage, the "normal condition" on line 49 implies

A) there is an underlying desire to oppress others.
B) that gender equality should be the natural order in society.
C) that most women at the time lacked worldly experience.
D) when gender equality happens, it will lead to many financial rewards.

6

The seventh paragraph (lines 58-67) is primarily concerned with

A) encouraging women to participate politically.
B) suggesting that political disempowerment is the root of oppression.
C) refuting the claim that women are politically uninformed.
D) chastising women for not engaging in political activism.

7

On line 59, "thought" most nearly means

A) assumption.
B) idea.
C) imagination.
D) consideration.

8

On line 68, "overburdened with cares" most strongly suggests that

A) domestic responsibilities have impacted activism.
B) emotional responses to inequality are less effective.
C) the expected in-home duties are far too strenuous for most women.
D) fighting for rights is often less important than completing day-to-day obligations.

9

The authors relate which of the following paradoxes regarding women's rights?

A) Women are more subjugated now than during earlier barbaric times.
B) With more rights having been gained, women now desire more direction from male authority.
C) The recent gains made in women's rights have only intensified the desire for equality.
D) Activists have disobeyed unjust laws in order to indirectly change those laws.

10

Which choice provides the best evidence for the answer in the previous question?

A) Lines 2-7 ("A survey … Nature's law")
B) Lines 16-20 ("The slavish … success")
C) Lines 52-57 ("Instead … superior")
D) Lines 64-67 (" Like … themselves")

STOP
If you finish before time is called, you may check your work on this section only.
Do not turn to any other section.

Explanations

Answers & explanations for "History of Women's Suffrage"

1. The authors suggest that one explanation for the oppression of women comes from

   A) a natural inequality between men and women.
   B) a miscommunication regarding cultural ideals.
   C) a leftover notion of protection from an earlier era.
   D) an unwillingness for either side to compromise.

2. Which choice provides the best evidence for the answer in the previous question?

   A) Lines 12–16 ("This ... follow")
   B) Lines 22–25 ("Another ... war")
   C) Lines 38–42 ("This ... equality")
   D) Lines 64–67 ("Like ... themselves")

We need to answer Questions 1 and 2 together. Q1 gives us the clue that we're looking for "one explanation of the oppression of women." In Q2, **choice B**, lines 22-25, mentions the **roots** of oppression coming from **nobler feelings** from **barbarous periods**.

Now we can match that with an answer choice in Q1. **Choice C** is great! Oppression is leftover from an earlier, more barbarous age.

3. The reference to a "final emancipation" acknowledges

   A) the end of the abolitionist movement.
   B) a universal desire for rights.
   C) that women have led the charge for civil rights.
   D) the civil rights era had come to a conclusion.

Let's look at the phrase in context:

*"This brings hope of **final emancipation**, for as all nations and classes are gradually, one after another, asserting and maintaining their independence, the path is clear for woman to follow."*

The sentence talks about **all nations and classes**, so we need an answer that includes everybody. **Choice B** is perfect. "Universal" certainly includes everyone!

4. On line 45, "drudge" most nearly means

A) burden.
B) trowel.
C) laborer.
D) crop.

Let's look at the word in context:

*"And did we not also see the great changes in woman's condition, the marvelous transformation in her character, from a **drudge** in the fields to a leader of thought in the literary circles of France, England, and America!"*

We want a word that replaces "drudge" in the context. "Laborer" works best in context, since drudge must represent a person.

*"... from a **laborer** in the fields to a leader of thought in the literary circles of France, England, and America!"*

Choice C is correct.

5. From information in the passage, the "normal condition" on line 49 implies

A) there is an underlying ~~desire to oppress others~~.
B) that gender equality should be the natural order in society.
C) that most women at the time ~~lacked worldly experience~~.
D) when gender equality happens, it will lead to many ~~financial rewards~~.

First, let's look at the phrase "normal condition" in context:

> "Woman's steady march onward, and her growing desire for a broader outlook, prove that she has not reached her **normal condition**, and that society has not yet conceded all that is necessary for its attainment."

The **desire** for more rights proves that the only normal condition is complete equality. **Choice B** is spot on! **Gender equality** should be the **normal condition**.

6. The seventh paragraph (lines 58–67) is primarily concerned with

    A) ~~encouraging~~ women to participate politically.
    B) suggesting that political disempowerment is the root of oppression.
    C) ~~refuting~~ the claim that women are politically uninformed.
    D) ~~chastising~~ women for not engaging in political activism.

The seventh paragraph states that "**political** disability of sex was the **cause** of all their special **grievances**." This means we need an answer that addresses the relationship between political power and oppression. **Choice B** is the best. "Political disempowerment" has led to the inequality.

7. On line 59, "thought" most nearly means

    A) assumption.
    B) idea.
    C) imagination.
    D) consideration.

Let's look at word in context:

> "The broader demand for political rights has not commanded the **thought** its merits and dignity should have secured."

117

The authors use "thought" to mean "to think over," or ponder. Let's plug in "consideration," which is the closest to our guess:

*"The broader demand for political rights has not commanded the **consideration** its merits and dignity should have secured."*

Choice D is correct!

8. On line 68, "overburdened with cares" most strongly suggests that

(A) domestic responsibilities have impacted activism.
B) ~~emotional responses~~ to inequality are less effective.
C) the expected in-home duties are ~~far too strenuous~~ for most women.
D) fighting for rights is often ~~less important~~ than completing day-to-day obligations.

First, let's look at the phrase in context:

*"**Overburdened with cares** in the isolated home, women had not the time, education, opportunity, and pecuniary independence to put their thoughts clearly and concisely into propositions, nor the courage to compare their opinions with one another, nor to publish them, to any great extent, to the world."*

This sentence details how women's in-home responsibilities affect their ability to express their desire for rights outside the home. **"Cares"** refers to duties in the home.

Choice A is a match! Taking care of the family has impacted the fight for rights.

9. The authors relate which of the following paradoxes regarding women's rights?

   A) Women are more subjugated now than during earlier barbaric times.
   B) With more rights having been gained, women now desire more direction from male authority.
   C) The recent gains made in women's rights have only intensified the desire for equality.
   D) Activists have disobeyed unjust laws in order to indirectly change those laws.

10. Which choice provides the best evidence for the answer in the previous question?

    A) Lines 2–7 ("A survey … Nature's law")
    B) Lines 16–20 ("The slavish … success")
    C) Lines 52–57 ("Instead … superior")
    D) Lines 64–67 (" Like … themselves")

We need to answer Questions 9 and 10 together. Q9 tells us to look for a "**paradox,**" or a statement that seems contradictory, about women's rights. In Q10's answer choices, only **choice C**, lines 52-57, contain a paradox. They say that "Instead of a feeling of **gratitude**," women feel "**indignant** at the assumption of any legal disability based on sex." So we need an answer for Q9 that shows that women are still **indignant**, instead of gracious.

Choice C is perfect. Yes, there have been gains, but those gains only have created the desire for more equality.

Natural Science

Let's get some practice with a Natural Science passage.

PORTAL

To learn more about designing studies and experiments, go to the Study Design chapter on page 636.

You'll see two Natural Science passages on the test: one will be **informative**, and one will describe an **experiment or study** and its results. In the informative passage, you will learn more about a topic in biology, physics, or chemistry such as genetics, evolution, or even space.

In the experiment/study passage, you'll read about scientists and researchers testing a **hypothesis** by conducting an **experiment**, then analyzing the **results**. Let's dive into a sample experiment to learn what these terms mean:

> Jeb and Cassandra have a **hypothesis**: plants can grow just as tall under sun lamps as they can under real sunlight. To test their hypothesis, they come up with an **experiment**: Jeb plants some roses in his kitchen and puts them under a sun lamp. Cassandra plants some roses in her garden where they will get plenty of real sunlight. They use the same amount of water, fertilizer, treatments, etc. on their plants, so their central **assumption** is that any difference in the height of the flowers will be due to the different sources of light. After a month, they look at the **results**: Cassandra's flowers are two inches taller than Jeb's flowers! Since the plants grown in sunlight grew taller than those under the sun lamp, the experiment did **not** support their hypothesis.

It is much easier to remember what happened in a scientific passage like this if you understand these few, primary components of the study or experiment. Make sure you understand *what* the scientists wanted to test (**hypothesis**), *how* they tested it (**experiment**), *why* they assumed that experiment would tell them what they wanted to know (**assumptions**), and what their **results** were.

TIP

Always read the intro text above the passage, especially on the Science passage; it often defines science terms or explains difficult concepts referenced in the passage.

Tips for Active Reading

For an **informative** passage, the regular Active Reading steps will serve you well. Take margin notes, underline important words, star main ideas, and circle logic words to follow the author's thought process. When you finish the passage, ask yourself:

> What was the main **topic** of the passage?
>
> Were different **perspectives** considered?
>
> Did the author come to a **conclusion**?

For an **experiment/study** passage, use stars to highlight the hypothesis, experiment or study design, and the results. If there's a word or concept that's new to you, circle it and underline its definition. When you finish the passage, ask yourself:

> What **question** were the researchers trying to answer?
>
> What **assumptions** did they make in setting up the study?
>
> How did they test their **hypothesis**?
>
> What were their **conclusions**?

Natural Science (Informative) Passage
TO STAY ON PACE, YOUR TIMING GOAL IS 13 MINUTES

Questions 1-10 are based on the following passage.

This passage is adapted from "Natural Biodiversity Breaks Yield Barriers," © 2004 Public Library of Science.

The birth of agriculture, some 10,000 years ago in the Middle East's Fertile Crescent, revolutionized human culture and society. Refined farming techniques
Line led to increased yields and freed humans from the
5 demands of constant foraging. Along with that freedom came social complexity, division of labor, improved standards of living, and a measure of leisure time. Agriculture also led to overpopulation followed by starvation, conflict over fertile farming
10 land, and environmental damage. For the Maya and other civilizations, such consequences proved fatal.

Many consumer and environmental groups believe that modern industrial agricultural practices like factory farming of animals and genetic engineering
15 of crops threaten to bring similar ruin. But with 6 billion people living on the planet—a figure that's expected to increase 50% in just 50 years—many plant scientists believe that feeding a burgeoning population will require the tools of biotechnology. Plant
20 breeders face the daunting challenge of developing high-yielding, nutritious crops that will improve the global quality of life without harming the environment or appropriating dwindling natural habitats for agricultural production. A major roadblock to feeding

25 the world is a continuing decline in the genetic diversity of agricultural crops, which has in turn limited their yield improvement. (Domestication often involves inbreeding, which by definition restricts the gene pool.) Now Amit Gur and Dani Zamir of Hebrew University
30 report a way to lift these productivity barriers by tapping into the natural diversity of wild plants.

Traditional plant breeders improve the quality and yield of crops by crossing plants with desired traits to create a new, hopefully improved, hybrid strain. But
35 traditional breeding is limited by the available gene pool of a cultivated plant species and eventually hits a wall—reshuffling the same genetic variation can boost yield only so much. With the advent of biotechnology, plant scientists were buoyed by the prospect of
40 improving plants through genetic modification. But aside from a few successes with introducing single-gene herbicide- and pest-resistant traits, most plant traits have proved too complex to repay the incorporation of a single transgene—that is, a gene taken from
45 a different species—with the hoped-for response. Biotech-based investigations and applications in plant science have also been hampered by consumer reaction against genetically modified organisms.

Faced with these limitations, Gur and Zamir
50 tried another approach—a back-to-nature approach. "Natural biodiversity is an unexploited sustainable resource that can enrich the genetic basis of cultivated plants," they explain in the report. Wild plants, as distant cousins of cultivated plants, can be seen

CONTINUE ➡

55 as a "huge natural mutagenesis* resource" with
novel gene variants that can increase productivity,
quality, and adaptability. Not only that, the genetic
material of wild plants—every gene and regulatory
element—has already been refined and tested by over
60 a billion years of evolution and natural selection.

To identify genomic regions in wild tomato
species that affect yield, Gur and Zamir created a
population of hybrid crosses of a wild tomato species
and a cultivated tomato species; each line had a
65 single genomic region from the wild tomato inserted
into the cultivated plant. Rather than introducing a
single wild tomato gene into the cultivated plants, the
authors used a "pyramided" strategy that combined
three independent yield-enhancing genomic regions
70 from the wild species into the new plant line. Plants
were grown over three seasons, during which they
were exposed to different environments, including
drought. By combining traditional phenotyping
techniques—which characterize the plant's physical
75 traits based on its genetic makeup—with genetic
marker analysis, the authors identified a number of
wild tomato genomic regions that increased yield.

Their results demonstrate that an approach based on
biodiversity—which takes advantage of the rich genetic
80 variation inherent in wild relatives of cultivated crops—
can produce varieties that outperform a commercially
available hybrid tomato in both yield and drought
resistance. Gur and Zamir attribute the improved
performance to their unique pyramiding strategy.
85 Their hybrid model—applying the tools of modern
genomics to traditional plant breeding—offers plant
breeders a powerful approach to improving the quality
and yield of cultivated plants by taking advantage
of the inherent biodiversity of the natural world.

* the process by which genetic mutations occur

1

As identified in the passage, a major barrier to feeding
the human population is

A) the limited gene pool within the crops that have
been cultivated for agriculture.
B) genetically modified organisms do not grow at a
rate that can sustain the rapidly increasing human
population.
C) the plants that are used as food have particularly
complex genes.
D) consumers are skeptical of genetically engineered
crops.

2

Which choice provides the best answer to the previous
question?

A) Lines 15-19 ("But … biotechnology")
B) Lines 24-27 ("A major … improvement")
C) Lines 40-45 ("But … response")
D) Lines 46-48 ("Biotech-based … organisms")

3

As used in line 3, "refined" most nearly means

A) cultured.
B) purified.
C) improved.
D) aerated.

4

As used in line 33, "crossing" most nearly means

A) hindering.
B) transversing.
C) intersecting.
D) interbreeding.

CONTINUE

5

In the fourth paragraph (lines 49-60), the author indicates that wild plants

A) share the same genetic material as cultivated plants.
B) have limited and diminishing gene pools.
C) contain useful genetic material.
D) are overused in agriculture.

6

The main purpose of the fifth paragraph (lines 61-77) is to

A) summarize the results of an experiment.
B) predict the outcome to a scientific question.
C) explain a methodology.
D) critique a claim.

7

As presented in the passage, the practice of crossing plants to improve crops is best described as

A) a revolutionary and impactful discovery.
B) an established though recently modernized strategy.
C) a sustainable and unexploited breakthrough.
D) a potentially costly yet liberating convenience.

8

Which choice provides the best evidence for the answer to the previous question?

A) Lines 5-8 ("Along … time")
B) Lines 38-40 ("With … modification")
C) Lines 51-53 ("'Natural … report")
D) Lines 85-89 ("Their … world")

9

The final sentence of the passage (lines 85-89) serves to

A) define the limits of current research on crop vitality.
B) show the potential significance of the research presented.
C) address the lack of crop diversity across multiple cultures.
D) downplay the scientists' accomplishments by showing their narrow scope of influence.

10

The passage acknowledges that scientific research on crops can be negatively affected by

A) the amount of diversity found within wild plant species.
B) the use of single-gene herbicides and pest-resistant traits.
C) the public's perception of genetically modified organisms.
D) the unpredictable yields due to unforeseen droughts.

STOP

If you finish before time is called, you may check your work on this section only.
Do not turn to any other section.

Explanations

Answers & explanations for the Natural Biodiversity Passage.

1. As identified in the passage, a major barrier to feeding the human population is

   (A) the limited gene pool within the crops that have been cultivated for agriculture.
   B) genetically modified organisms do not grow at a rate that can sustain the rapidly increasing human population.
   C) the plants that are used as food have particularly complex genes.
   D) consumers are skeptical of genetically engineered crops.

2. Which choice provides the best answer to the previous question?

   A) Lines 15-19 ("But ... biotechnology")
   (B) Lines 24-27 ("A major ... improvement")
   C) Lines 40-45 ("But ... response")
   D) Lines 46-48 ("Biotech-based ... organisms")

   We need to answer questions 1 and 2 together. The clue in Q1 is "major barrier," so we need to look for a quote from Q2 that relates. Clearly **choice B** is best, since "major barrier" and "major roadblock" are certainly synonyms. The roadblock is the "decline in the genetic diversity of agricultural crops." **Choice A** in Q1 perfectly matches, since "limited gene pool" is the same as a "decline in genetic diversity."

3. As used in line 3, "refined" most nearly means

   A) cultured.
   B) purified.
   (C) improved.
   D) aerated.

First let's look at the word in context:

> "**Refined** *farming techniques led to increased yields and freed humans from the demands of constant foraging.*"

"Increased yields" are a good thing, so we need a word that means the same thing as "better." Of the choices given, "improved" is the best match. Let's test it in the sentence.

> "**Improved** *farming techniques led to increased yields and freed humans from the demands of constant foraging.*"

Choice C is correct.

4. As used in line 33, "crossing" most nearly means

A) hindering.
B) transversing.
C) intersecting.
D) interbreeding.

First let's look at the word in context:

> "*Traditional plant breeders improve the quality and yield of crops by* **crossing** *plants with desired traits to create a new, hopefully improved, hybrid strain.*"

The context is about plant breeding, so we need a word that's about breeding. "Interbreeding" looks like a good match. Let's try it in context:

> "*Traditional plant breeders improve the quality and yield of crops by* **interbreeding** *plants with desired traits to create a new, hopefully improved, hybrid strain.*"

Choice D is best.

5. In the fourth paragraph (lines 49–60), the author indicates that wild plants

 A) share the ~~same~~ genetic material as cultivated plants.
 B) have ~~limited~~ and diminishing gene pools.
 C) contain useful genetic material.
 D) are ~~overused~~ in agriculture.

> Looking over the fourth paragraph, it discusses "a back-to-nature approach," using **wild plants** to **add** to genetic **diversity**. The scientists are confident that this will work, since wild plant DNA "has already been refined and tested by over a billion years of evolution and natural selection."
>
> **Choice C** is the best. The genetic materials of wild plants has been **refined and tested** already, so that makes the scientists' research easier!

6. The main purpose of the fifth paragraph (lines 61–77) is to

 A) summarize the ~~results~~ of an experiment.
 B) ~~predict~~ the outcome to a scientific question.
 C) explain a methodology.
 D) ~~critique~~ a claim.

> The fifth paragraph explains an experiment done on tomatoes. The researchers used "a 'pyramided' strategy," which helped them to determine which strain had the highest yield.
>
> **Choice C** works best. A methodology is the analysis of a process, and that's exactly what the fifth paragraph is!

7. As presented in the passage, the practice of crossing plants to improve crops is best described as

A) a revolutionary and impactful discovery.
B) an established though recently modernized strategy.
C) a sustainable and unexploited breakthrough.
D) a potentially costly yet liberating convenience.

8. Which choice provides the best evidence for the answer to the previous question?

A) Lines 5-8 ("Along ... time")
B) Lines 38-40 ("With ... modification")
C) Lines 51-53 ("'Natural ... report")
D) Lines 85-89 ("Their ... world")

We need to answer questions 7 and 8 together. Q7 tells us to find a quote about "the practice of crossing plants." In Q8, **choice D** offers a quote that matches:

> *"Their hybrid model—applying the tools of modern genomics to traditional plant breeding—offers plant breeders a powerful approach to improving the quality and yield of cultivated plants by taking advantage of the inherent biodiversity of the natural world."*

Choice B in Q7 is a match for that quote. Crossing plants has been done for a long time ("traditional") but now uses "modern genomics."

---

9. The final sentence of the passage (lines 85-89) serves to

A) define the limits of current research on crop vitality.
B) show the potential significance of the research presented.
C) address the lack of crop diversity across multiple cultures.
D) downplay the scientists' accomplishments by showing their narrow scope of influence.

First, let's look at the sentence:

> *"It's a strategy that may well apply to rice, wheat, and other vital staples of the world's food supply."*

The last sentence shows the **value** of the research, as it could be used to grow more important crops like rice and wheat.

Choice B is spot on! If the research can be used on vital crops, then that will be really important.

10. The passage acknowledges that scientific research on crops can be negatively affected by

    A) the amount of diversity found within wild plant species.
    B) the use of single-gene herbicides and pest-resistant traits.
    C) the public's perception of genetically modified organisms.
    D) the unpredictable yields due to unforeseen droughts.

The clue in the question is "negatively affected." Looking over the passage, lines 46-48 says:

> *"Biotech-based investigations and applications in plant science have also been **hampered** by **consumer reaction** against **genetically modified organisms**."*

"Hampered" is a very close match to "negatively affected." **Choice C** is the winner. People do not want to buy genetically modified organisms, so that affects the research.

Natural Science (Study) Passage
TO STAY ON PACE, YOUR TIMING GOAL IS 13 MINUTES

DIRECTIONS

Each passage or pair of passages below is followed by a number of questions. After reading each passage or pair, choose the best answer to each question based on what is stated or implied in the passage or passages and in any accompanying graphics (such as a table or graph).

Questions 1-11 are based on the following passage.

This passage is adapted from Liza Gross, "Math and Fossils Resolve a Debate on Dinosaur Metabolism." © 2006 Public Library of Science.

Of the many mysteries surrounding the life history of dinosaurs, one of the more enduring is how such gigantic organisms—some reaching 42
Line feet tall and weighing 90 tons—regulated their body
5 temperature. For many years, scientists had assumed that dinosaurs, which evolved from reptiles, were also cold blooded (ectotherms), with a slow metabolism that required the sun's heat to thermoregulate. But, in the late 1960s, the notion emerged that dinosaurs,
10 like mammals and birds, might have been warm blooded (endotherms) with relatively constant, high body temperatures that were internally regulated like their avian descendants (and mammals).

Still others argued that while most dinosaurs had
15 a metabolism similar to contemporary reptiles, the large dinosaurs managed a higher, more-constant body temperature through thermal inertia, which is how modern alligators, Galapagos tortoises, and Komodo dragons retain heat. Thermal inertia
20 allows the body to approach homeothermy, or constant body temperature, when the ratio of body mass to surface area is high enough. If this "inertial homeothermy" hypothesis is correct, dinosaur body temperature should increase with body size.

25　　In a new study, James Gillooly, Andrew Allen, and Eric Charnov revisit—and resolve—this debate. The researchers used a model that provided estimates of dinosaur body temperature based on developmental growth trajectories inferred from juvenile and adult
30 fossil bones of the same species. The model predicts that dinosaur body temperature did increase with body mass, and that large dinosaurs had body temperatures similar to those of modern birds and mammals (95-110°F), while smaller dinosaurs'
35 temperatures were more like contemporary reptiles. These results suggest that the large dinosaurs (but not the smaller ones) had relatively constant body temperatures maintained through thermal inertia.

Gillooly et al. compiled data from eight dinosaur
40 species from the early Jurassic and late Cretaceous periods that ranged in size from 30 pounds to 28 tons. The growth trajectories, taken from the published research papers, were determined by using bone histology (microscopic study) and body size
45 estimates to estimate the maximum growth rate and mass at the time of maximum growth. The recent availability of these data, the researchers explain, along with advances in understanding how body size and temperature affect growth, allowed them to use
50 a novel mathematical model to estimate dinosaur body temperatures. The researchers modified the model to estimate the body temperature of each dinosaur species, based on its estimated maximum growth rate and mass at the time of maximum

CONTINUE ➤

55 growth. The model shows that body temperature
   increases with body size for seven dinosaur species.
      The model shows that dinosaur body temperature
   increased with body size, from roughly 77 °F at 26
   pounds to 105.8 °F at 14 tons. These results, the
60 researchers explain, suggest that the body temperatures
   of the smaller dinosaurs (77 °F) were close to the
   environmental temperature—just as occurs for modern
   smaller reptiles—which meant they acquired heat
   from external sources (in addition to the internal
65 heat generated by metabolism). The results also
   suggest that body temperature rose as an individual
   dinosaur grew, increasing by about 37.4 °F for species
   weighing about 661 pounds as adults and nearly
   68 °F for those reaching about 27 tons (*Apatosaurus*
70 *excelsus*). Predicted body temperature for the largest
   dinosaur (*Sauroposeidon proteles* at about 60 tons)
   was about 118 °F—just past the limit for most
   animals, suggesting that body temperature may have
   prevented dinosaurs from becoming even bigger.
75   Gillooly et al. demonstrate the validity of these
   results by showing that the model successfully predicts
   documented increases in body temperature with
   size for existing crocodiles. Altogether, these results
   indicate that dinosaurs were reptiles and that their body
80 temperature increased with body size—providing strong
   evidence for the inertial homeothermy hypothesis.

1

The first paragraph serves primarily to

A) recount different explanations to answer a
   longstanding question.
B) prove that all dinosaurs were cold blooded.
C) emphasize how scientific ideas change over time.
D) suggest that dinosaurs and birds share a common
   ancestor.

2

In line 9, "notion" most nearly means

A) article.
B) indication.
C) concept.
D) sentiment.

3

In line 50, "novel" most nearly means

A) innovative.
B) peculiar.
C) literary.
D) rare.

Species	Mass (tons)		Body Temperature (°F)
	Min	Max	
A huinculensis	50	90	116
S. giganteus	9.9	22.5	108
S. aegyptiacus	7	20.9	105
T. prorsus	9	10.9	101
S. ungulatus	3.8	7	99

CONTINUE

4

The main purpose of the final sentence in the fourth paragraph ("The model shows that body temperature increases with body size for seven dinosaur species.") is to

A) dispute the assumptions made by a breakthrough mathematical model.

B) define a complex term.

C) suggest a further course of study.

D) summarize the findings from an analyzed data set.

5

The passage suggests that organisms achieve homeothermy when

A) the ratio of body mass to surface area is large.

B) juveniles become adults.

C) large animals migrate to warmer climates.

D) body size decreases.

6

Which choice provides the best evidence for the answer to the previous question?

A) Lines 5-8 ("For … thermoregulate")

B) Lines 19-22 ("Thermal … enough")

C) Lines 36-38 ("These … inertia")

D) Lines 65-70 ("The results … excelsus)")

7

Gillooly, et al., demonstrate confidence in their findings because

A) contemporary alligators, Galapagos tortoises, and Komodo dragons are cold blooded.

B) small dinosaurs have fluctuating body temperatures.

C) their mathematical model correctly predicts body mass and temperature measurements gathered from crocodiles.

D) thermal inertia allows large dinosaurs to maintain higher and more constant body temperatures.

8

Which choice provides the best evidence for the answer to the previous question?

A) Lines 14-19 ("Still … heat")

B) Lines 36-38 ("These … inertia")

C) Lines 75-78 ("Gillooly … crocodiles")

D) Lines 78-81 ("Altogether … hypothesis")

9

Do the data in the figure support the hypothesis of inertial homeothermy?

A) Yes, because as mass decreases, body temperature decreases.

B) Yes, because as mass decreases, body temperature increases.

C) No, because as mass decreases, body temperature decreases.

D) No, because as mass decreases, body temperature increases.

CONTINUE ➤

10

Based on the table, which species of dinosaur had the least variation in body mass?

A) *A. huinculensis*

B) *S. aegyptiacus*

C) *T. prorsus*

D) *S. ungulatus*

11

Which concept is supported by the passage and by information in the table?

A) Large dinosaurs had body temperatures similar to modern warm-blooded animals.

B) Dinosaurs could not grow larger than 20 tons due to producing excessive heat.

C) Body temperatures of extinct species can be deduced by examining fossils under the microscope.

D) Dinosaurs had a range of body temperatures similar to those of living reptiles.

STOP

If you finish before time is called, you may check your work on this section only.

Do not turn to any other section.

Explanations

Answers & explanations for "Math and Fossils Resolve a Debate on Dinosaur Metabolism."

1. The first paragraph serves primarily to

   A) recount different explanations to answer a longstanding question.
   B) prove that all dinosaurs were cold blooded.
   C) emphasize how scientific ideas change over time.
   D) suggest that dinosaurs and birds share a common ancestor.

   The first paragraph questions how dinosaurs "regulated their body temperatures" and it offers several different theories; they could be ectotherms or endotherms.

   Choice A is a match!

2. In line 9, "notion" most nearly means

   A) article.
   B) indication.
   C) concept.
   D) sentiment.

   Let's look at the word in context:

   *"But, in the late 1960s, the **notion** emerged that dinosaurs, like mammals and birds, might have been warm blooded (endotherms) with relatively constant, high body temperatures that were internally regulated like their avian descendants (and mammals)."*

In this context, "notion" means the same as "idea." Of the choices, "concept" is the closest to "idea." Let's plug the answer choice to make sure it works:

> "But, in the late 1960s, the **concept** emerged that dinosaurs, like mammals and birds, might have been warm blooded (endotherms) with relatively constant, high body temperatures that were internally regulated like their avian descendants (and mammals)."

Choice C is correct.

3. In line 50, "novel" most nearly means

A) innovative.
B) peculiar.
C) literary.
D) rare.

It's important that we look at the word in context:

> "The recent availability of these data, the researchers explain, along with advances in understanding how body size and temperature affect growth, allowed them to use a **novel** mathematical model to estimate dinosaur body temperatures."

"Novel" means new, so of the choices, "innovative" is the closest match. Let's plug it back in to the sentence to make sure it works.

> "The recent availability of these data, the researchers explain, along with advances in understanding how body size and temperature affect growth, allowed them to use an **innovative** mathematical model to estimate dinosaur body temperatures."

Choice A is best.

4. The main purpose of the final sentence in the fourth paragraph ("The model shows that body temperature increases with body size for seven dinosaur species.") is to

A) dispute the assumptions made by a breakthrough mathematical model.
B) define a complex term.
C) suggest a further course of study.
D) summarize the findings from an analyzed data set.

The fourth paragraph describes how the researchers collected data, and how they used the data to draw conclusions. The final sentence says:

"The model shows that body temperature increases with body size for seven dinosaur species."

This sentences **sums up** what they found when they analyzed all the data they collected. **Choice D** is a perfect match.

5. The passage suggests that organisms achieve homeothermy when

A) the ratio of surface area to body mass is large.
B) juveniles become adults.
C) large animals migrate to warmer climates.
D) body size decreases.

6. Which choice provides the best evidence for the answer to the previous question?

A) Lines 5–8 ("For ... thermoregulate")
B) Lines 19–22 ("Thermal ... enough")
C) Lines 36–38 ("These ... inertia")
D) Lines 65–70 ("The results ... excelsus)")

We need to answer questions 5 and 6 together. Q5 gives us the clue that we need to find evidence about how dinosaurs get close to a constant body temperature. In Q6, the lines in **choice B** give us the answer:

> *"Thermal inertia allows the body to approach homeothermy, or constant body temperature, when the ratio of body mass to surface area is high enough."*

Also, the very next sentence begins with "inertial homeothermy hypothesis!" Now we need to find a match in Q5. **Choice A** perfectly sums up the evidence in lines 19-22.

7. Gillooly, et al., demonstrate confidence in their findings because

   A) contemporary alligators, Galapagos tortoises, and Komodo dragons are cold blooded.
   B) small dinosaurs have fluctuating body temperatures.
   C) their mathematical model correctly predicts body mass and temperature measurements gathered from crocodiles.
   D) thermal inertia allows large dinosaurs to maintain higher and more constant body temperatures.

8. Which choice provides the best evidence for the answer to the previous question?

   A) Lines 14-19 ("Still ... heat")
   B) Lines 36-38 ("These ... inertia")
   C) Lines 75-78 ("Gillooly ... crocodiles")
   D) Lines 78-81 ("Altogether ... hypothesis")

We need to answer questions 7 and 8 together. The clue in Q7 is that we're looking for what Gillooly et al. think. **Choice C** in question 8 starts off with Gillooly et al., so we know we found our answer to 8. The sentence says that they "successfully predicted" body temperatures by studying crocodiles.

Choice C is best for Q7 as it's the only answer choice that mentions crocodiles.

9. Do the data in the figure support the hypothesis of inertial homeothermy?

    (A) Yes, because as mass decreases, body temperature decreases.
    B) Yes, because as mass decreases, body temperature increases.
    C) No, because as mass decreases, body temperature decreases.
    D) No, because as mass decreases, body temperature increases.

First we need to look to the passage for a definition of inertial homeothermy:

> "If this "inertial homeothermy" hypothesis is correct, dinosaur body temperature should increase with body size."

Looking at the figure, the **higher** the body temperature, the **larger** the body size and vice versa.

Choice A works best; if the body size increases as the temperature increases, then body size **decreases** as temperature **decreases**.

10. Based on the table, which species of dinosaur had the least variation in body mass?

    A) *Argentinosaurus huinculensis*
    B) *Spinosaurus aegyptiacus*
    (C) *Triceratops prorsus*
    D) *Stegosaurus ungulatus*

All we have to do is read the table for this one. The least variation can be discovered by seeing which had the smallest range of body masses.

Choice C is correct, because the body mass range of a *triceratops prorsus*, 9 to 10.9 tons, varies the least out of the four ranges given.

11. Which concept is supported by the passage and by information in the table?

(A) Large dinosaurs had body temperatures similar to modern warm-blooded animals.

B) Dinosaurs could not grow larger than 20 tons due to producing excessive heat.

C) Body temperatures of extinct species can be deduced by examining fossils under the microscope.

D) Dinosaurs had a range of body temperatures similar to those of living reptiles.

Looking at the table, the range of body temperatures goes from 99° to 116°F. The passage states on lines 33-34 that modern birds and mammals have temperatures that range from 95-110°F. That means that the dinosaurs in the table were as **warm** as **modern warm-blooded animals**. All the dinosaurs in the table are at least 3.8 tons: those are some **large** dinosaurs!

Choice A is the most supported by the passage and table.

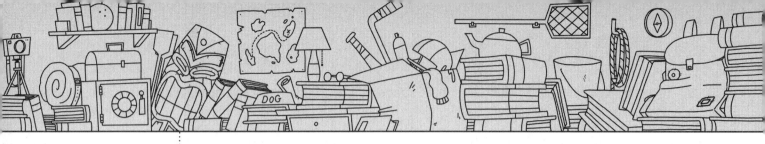

Social Science

Let's get some practice with a Social Science passage.

The Social Science passage is an **informative** passage that pulls from fields like economics, psychology, sociology: passages often deal with topics related to technology and modern society. You'll learn about population trends, fancy tech solutions, and fascinating psychological phenomena. These passages always come with a chart, table, or graph.

Tips for Active Reading

For an informative passage, the regular Active Reading steps will serve you well. Take margin notes, underline important words, star main ideas, and circle logic words to follow the author's path. If there's a word or concept that's new to you, circle it and underline its definition. When you finish the passage, ask yourself: What was the main topic of the passage? Were different perspectives considered? Did the author come to a conclusion?

Social Science Passage

TO STAY ON PACE, YOUR TIMING GOAL IS 13 MINUTES

DIRECTIONS

Each passage or pair of passages below is followed by a number of questions. After reading each passage or pair, choose the best answer to each question based on what is stated or implied in the passage or passages and in any accompanying graphics (such as a table or graph).

Questions 1-11 are based on the following passage.

This passage is adapted from Cindi Lightballoon, "Cleaning our Cities' Air." Originally published in 2013.

An unavoidable byproduct of human communities is waste. As societies developed from nomadic wandering to year-round residences, the waste of society remained.
Line The initial solutions were simple: bury it, burn it,
5 or dump it in a body of water. By the Middle Ages, waste management in cities had become a legitimate problem, as denizens would loft all household waste out onto the street. The slurry of muck necessitated the invention of "stepping stones" so that pedestrians could
10 travel relatively unslathered in the unhygienic slop.

The industrialization of Western cities forced the development of proper sewers and waste treatment, since the increased density of cities made earlier lax policies towards waste management unbearable.
15 While solid and liquid waste now had proper channels for disposal, a new problem–air pollution–began impacting cities. London's famous pea-soup thick fog was mostly a result of the predominant practice of burning coal during the Industrial Revolution.
20 Thankfully the urban use of coal is behind us, but air pollution from the burning of gasoline and other fossil fuels still affects the quality of city life. While regulation of fossil fuel-burning engines and wider availability of alternative energy sources imply
25 progress, the quality of air in major cities still negatively impacts the respiratory health of many citizens. These approaches focus on the polluters; however, Dutch designer Daan Roosegaarde has offered a revolutionary means of actually cleaning the air itself.

30 The idea is fairly simple: place a large air purifier within a city to clean polluted air. Instead of using traditional filters, which can only pick up large particles, Roosegaarde's 7 meters high smog-free tower uses air ionisers, which negatively charge air molecules. The
35 charged impurities in the air then attach to electrified metal plates; the process uses the same principle of static electricity that makes socks fresh from the dryer cling to each other. Air ionisers are nothing new and small models designed for home use were heavily
40 marketed in the 1990s and early 2000s. While these models did remove some air pollutants, the ionization process also created ozone (O_3), which is a harmful pollutant itself. Roosegaarde claims that his smog-free tower uses only ozone-free ion technology, and
45 can clean 30,000 cubic meters of air an hour using only 1,400 watts of energy, which is more energy efficient than an average household clothes dryer.

Any ionic air purifier will need the metal collection plates frequently cleaned, and Roosegaarde has come up
50 with an ingenious use for the dust particles. Instead of disposing of them by conventional solid waste methods, Roosegaarde has developed a means to compress the dust into small gems. These gems, which look similar to black obsidian, are then placed in jewelry and sold
55 to consumers who know that their purchase helps fund

CONTINUE

the air purifiers. The jewelry's minimalist design, a black cube made from the compressed pollutants encased in a clear lucite cube, simply expresses the project's idealism.

Roosegaarde's Smog-Free Project is still in
60 its nascency, but has gained support via online crowdfunding. A fully-functional prototype premiered in Rotterdam, Netherlands and that same prototype was later sold to the city of Beijing, China. Beijing has an unfortunate reputation for air pollution, a byproduct
65 of its own rapid industrialization that occurred over the last two decades. Beijing officials are well-aware of how the poor air quality affects the city's international prestige and have implemented a plan to remove the smog by 2017. This plan will likely mean more sales
70 for Roosegaarde and further opportunities for people concerned with how to manage a city's air-based waste.

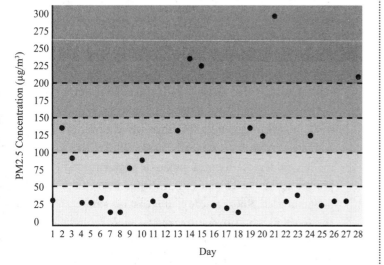

PM2.5* Concentration in Beijing, China at 12:00pm during February 2015
Data collected from the US Embassy in Beijing, US State Department

PM2.5 Concentration	Air Quality
0-50 $\mu g/m^3$	Good
51-100 $\mu g/m^3$	Moderate
101-150 $\mu g/m^3$	Unhealthy for sensitive groups**
151-200 $\mu g/m^3$	Unhealthy
201-300 $\mu g/m^3$	Very Unhealthy

*Particulate matter less than 2.5 micrometers
**People with heart or lung disease, the elderly, or children

---

1

In the context of the passage as a whole, the first sentence

A) criticizes the amount of waste modern society creates.
B) suggests the need for a permanent solution.
C) addresses a systemic problem.
D) provides a premise that will be refuted later.

2

In line 7, "loft" most nearly means

A) extend.
B) amass.
C) fling.
D) raise.

3

In line 12, "proper" most nearly means

A) respectable.
B) peculiar.
C) refined.
D) suitable.

CONTINUE ➡

4

The passage mentions "pea-soup thick fog" in lines 17-18 in order to

A) give an example of a quality that made London famous.
B) visually represent an environmental problem.
C) detail how much cleaner London's air is today.
D) warn readers against the use of coal as a fuel source.

5

The purpose of the third paragraph (lines 20-29) is to

A) introduce the idea of air pollution.
B) transition from a persistent problem to a proposed solution.
C) present the current danger air pollution presents to city dwellers.
D) explain why cities have moved away from using coal as a source of energy.

6

Unlike other air purifiers, Roosegaarde's smog-free tower

A) was originally intended to create and market jewelry.
B) is the first machine to use ionization to improve air quality.
C) cleans air without creating ozone.
D) can clean a city's air in just a few hours.

7

Which choice provides the best evidence for the answer to the previous question?

A) Lines 34-36 ("The charged … plates")
B) Lines 40-44 ("While … technology")
C) Lines 50-53 ("Instead … gems")
D) Lines 61-63 ("A fully-functional … China")

8

The passage implies that the shape of the jewelry made from compressed air pollutants is

A) symbolic of the purpose of the air purifier.
B) simplistic and likely not very appealing to many consumers.
C) miniscule and not intended to draw attention.
D) more ornate than functional.

9

The author would likely respond to the information in the graph by stating it

A) supports the assessment that Beijing's air quality is the worst in the world.
B) shows that Beijing's air quality is often unhealthy and a solution is necessary.
C) reveals that pollution in Beijing is gradually decreasing due to Roosegaarde's air purifier.
D) predicts that Roosegaarde's air purifier will be an inadequate solution to the level of pollution in Beijing.

10

Which choice provides the best evidence for the answer to the previous question?

A) Lines 20-22 ("Thankfully … life.")

B) Lines 23-26 ("While … citizens.")

C) Lines 59-61 ("Roosegaarde's … crowdfunding.")

D) Lines 66-69 ("Beijing … 2017.")

11

According to the graph, air quality becomes unhealthy for elderly citizens when the PM2.5 concentration exceeds

A) 50 μg/m³.

B) 100 μg/m³.

C) 150 μg/m³.

D) 300 μg/m³.

STOP

If you finish before time is called, you may check your work on this section only.
Do not turn to any other section.

Explanations

Answers & explanations for the "Cleaning our Cities' Air" Passage.

1. In the context of the passage as a whole, the first sentence

    A) criticizes the amount of waste ~~modern~~ society creates.
    B) suggests the need for a ~~permanent~~ solution.
    C) addresses a systemic problem.
    D) provides a premise that will be ~~refuted later~~.

> The passage is all about pollution and how to fix it. The first sentence says waste, which includes pollution, is "an unavoidable byproduct of human communities," which means that cities will always make waste. A "systemic problem" cannot be avoided, so **C** is the right answer.

2. In line 7, "loft" most nearly means

    A) extend.
    B) amass.
    C) fling.
    D) raise.

> Let's look at the word in context:
>
> > *"By the Middle Ages, waste management in cities had become a legitimate problem, as denizens would **loft** all household waste out onto the street."*
>
> In this sentence, a good synonym would be "**throw**." "Fling," **choice C**, is closest to "throw," so that's our answer.
>
> > *"By the Middle Ages, waste management in cities had become a legitimate problem, as denizens would **fling** all household waste out onto the street."*

145

3. In line 12, "proper" most nearly means

A) respectable.
B) peculiar.
C) refined.
D) suitable.

> We need to look at the word in context:
>
> > *"The industrialization of Western cities forced the development of **proper** sewers and waste treatment, since the increased density of cities made earlier lax policies towards waste management unbearable."*
>
> We could replace "proper" with "**adequate**" and it would have the same meaning. "Suitable" means the same thing as "adequate" in this sentence, so **D** must be our answer.
>
> > *"The industrialization of Western cities forced the development of **suitable** sewers and waste treatment, since the increased density of cities made earlier lax policies towards waste management unbearable."*

4. The passage mentions "pea-soup thick fog" in lines 17-18 in order to

A) give an example of a quality that ~~made London famous~~.
B) visually represent an environmental problem.
C) detail how much cleaner London's air is ~~today~~.
D) ~~warn~~ readers against the use of coal as a fuel source.

> First let's read in context:
>
> > *"London's famous **pea-soup thick fog** was mostly a result of the predominant practice of burning coal during the Industrial Revolution."*
>
> Why did the author include this descriptive phrase? It helps us to **imagine the effect** air pollution had on the environment. **Choice C** works best: the burning of coal was an "environmental problem," and "pea-soup thick fog" gives the reader a visual, so this answer works!

5. The purpose of the third paragraph (lines 20-29) is to

    A) introduce the ~~idea~~ of air pollution.
    B) transition from a persistent problem to a proposed solution.
    C) present the ~~current danger~~ air pollution presents to city dwellers.
    D) explain ~~why~~ cities have moved away from using coal as a source of energy.

> Paragraph 3 moves from "the burning of gasoline and other fossil fuels" to "a revolutionary means of actually cleaning the air itself." So we're shifting from the problems of pollution to Roosegaarde's new method of mitigating that pollution. **Choice B** is perfect: the first two paragraphs talk about pollution as a problem and the third paragraph transitions to Roosegaarde's solution!

6. Unlike other air purifiers, Roosegaarde's smog-free tower

    A) was originally intended to create and market jewelry.
    B) is the first machine to use ionization to improve air quality.
    C) cleans air without creating ozone.
    D) can clean a city's air in just a few hours.

7. Which choice provides the best evidence for the answer to the previous question?

    A) Lines 34-36 ("The charged ... plates")
    B) Lines 40-44 ("While ... technology")
    C) Lines 50-53 ("Instead ... gems")
    D) Lines 61-63 ("A fully-functional ... China")

> Let's use our EBQ strategy: according to Q6, we need a quote that tells us the **difference** between other air purifiers and Roosegaarde's. Only **choice B**, lines 40-44, talk about that difference:
>
> > "While **these models** did remove some air pollutants, the ionization process also created ozone (O_3), which is a harmful pollutant itself. Roosegaarde claims that **his smog-free tower** uses only ozone-free technology..."

147

So other air purifiers created ozone, but Roosegaarde's doesn't. That's a perfect match to **choice C** in Q6.

8. The passage implies that the shape of the jewelry made from compressed air pollutants is

    (A) symbolic of the purpose of the air purifier.
    B) simplistic and likely ~~not very appealing~~ to many consumers.
    C) ~~miniscule~~ and not intended to draw attention.
    D) more ~~ornate~~ than functional.

The passage discusses the look of the jewelry on lines 56-58:

> "The jewelry's minimalist design, a black cube made from the compressed pollutants encased in a clear lucite cube, simply expresses the project's idealism."

The key phrases are "**minimalist design**" and "**expresses the project's idealism**," so we need an answer that includes these concepts. In **choice A**, "symbolic of the purpose" matches "expresses the project's idealism," so it's the best answer.

9. The author would likely respond to the information in the graph by stating it

    A) supports the assessment that Beijing's air quality is the ~~worst~~ in the world.
    (B) shows that Beijing's air quality is often unhealthy and a solution is necessary.
    C) reveals that pollution in Beijing is gradually ~~decreasing due~~ to Roosegaarde's air purifier.
    D) predicts that Roosegaarde's air purifier will be an ~~inadequate~~ solution to the level of pollution in Beijing.

10. Which choice provides the best evidence for the answer to the previous question?

    A) Lines 20-22 ("Thankfully ... life.")
    B) Lines 23-26 ("While ... citizens.")
    C) Lines 59-61 ("Roosegaarde's ... crowdfunding.")
    (D) Lines 66-69 ("Beijing ... 2017.")

Looking at the graph, it shows that far too often the air in Beijing is unhealthy. Let's check our lines to find a choice that relates to Beijing's unhealthy air: only **choice D**, lines 66-69, are specifically about Beijing:

> "**Beijing** officials are well-aware of how the **poor air quality** affects the city's international prestige and have implemented a plan to remove the smog by 2017."

In Q9, the choice that most closely relates to the evidence in lines 66-69 is **choice B**, since "Beijing's air quality is often unhealthy" matches "well-aware of how the poor air quality affects the city's international prestige," and "a solution is necessary" matches "have implemented a plan to remove the smog."

11. According to the graph, air quality becomes unhealthy for elderly citizens when the PM2.5 concentration exceeds

    A) 50 µg/m³.
    (B) 100 µg/m³.
    C) 150 µg/m³.
    D) 300 µg/m³.

This question is all about decoding the figure. We need to find where the concentration becomes unhealthy for the elderly. The table tells us that a 101 µg/m³ concentration of PM2.5 is unhealthy for sensitive groups. However, if we follow the footnote, it confirms that sensitive groups includes the elderly. That means **B** is our answer!

Comparison

Let's get some practice with a comparison passage.

There is one pair of comparison passages on every test, but they could be from Social Science, Natural Science, or Politics. Whatever the topic, there is a specific strategy for tackling these passages:

① Actively read the intro text and Passage 1
The intro text often contains crucial information about both authors' perspectives, so don't skip it!

② Answer questions that only deal with Passage 1
You'll find a mix of all question types; follow your strategies as you normally would.

③ Actively read Passage 2
Don't forget those margin notes!

④ Write down the relationship between the passages
This is the most important step! There will always be a question asking for the **relationship** between the two passages, so you might as well answer it now. If the two authors met in a coffee shop, what would they say to each other?

- That's completely wrong!
- Wow, I never knew that.
- I sort of agree, but not quite.
- That's a great idea, but I have an even better one!

⑤ Answer questions that only deal with Passage 2
Again, you'll find a mix of all question types; follow your strategies as usual.

⑥ Answer questions that deal with both passages.
Use that relationship-of-the-passages note to answer the questions that ask you to compare the two passages.

Comparison Passage

TO STAY ON PACE, YOUR TIMING GOAL IS 13 MINUTES

DIRECTIONS

Each passage or pair of passages below is followed by a number of questions. After reading each passage or pair, choose the best answer to each question based on what is stated or implied in the passage or passages and in any accompanying graphics (such as a table or graph).

Questions 1-11 are based on the following passages.

Passage 1 is adapted from Ahmed Habibi, "The History of the Automobile." Originally published in 2014. Passage 2 is adapted from Sophia Valdez, "Google's Mountain View Experiment." Originally published in 2015.

Passage 1

Coined in the late 19th Century, "automobile," a linguistic mashup of the Greek root for self and the Latin root for movable, clearly defined the
Line new motorized vehicle. Simply put, an automobile
5 was a carriage that did not require a horse or similar animal to power its movement.

Automotive technology has made astounding leaps since those nascent days, yet the root "auto" still proves prescriptive. Many of the technological
10 improvements made to cars over the years–automatic transmissions, cruise control, antilock brakes, traction control–have given greater control to the car itself. Although some drivers prefer the precise control of a manual transmission, most
15 would rather have the convenience and simplicity of a vehicle with semi-automated controls.

Indeed, the future of the automobile points toward complete automation of the driving process, as several companies test the practicality and safety of self-
20 driving cars. Using a combination of GPS, cameras, microphones, and motion sensors, self-driving cars are

beginning to navigate our highways and cities. Unlike a human driver, who can only see in one direction at a time, a self driving car perceives the entire environment
25 around the vehicle. It is impossible for a self-driving car to cut off another vehicle since it has no "blind spots" and can only make decisions deemed safe for all.

The easiest task for a self-driving car is maintaining its lane and staying on the road. Since 2009, Google,
30 an early pioneer of self-driving cars, has had self-driving vehicles capable of navigating congestion-free highways. Highways are predictable, with no cross-traffic to consider. The greatest challenge for self-driving cars has been navigating city streets and
35 their erratic inhabitants. In a perfect world, self-driving cars would politely transverse the roads, yielding and stopping along the route as needed. The problems so far have been entirely human-based, as a self-driving car must account for jaywalking pedestrians and
40 hurried, irritable drivers. Google has permission to test its self-driving cars on the streets of Mountain View, California, as long as a "safety driver" is aboard to monitor the car's behavior and performance.

Researchers are optimistic about the future
45 of self-driving cars, although some questions still maintain. Will drivers embrace computerized chauffeurs? Will the government and insurance companies create policies that will expedite or restrict the access to self-driving cars? How will self-driving
50 cars affect roadway safety? There are still many unknowns, but our nation's commuter traffic may look dramatically different in the coming decades.

CONTINUE ▶

Passage 2

Owning a self-driving car is an appealing idea, but as with many previous endeavours into "mad
55 science," it's important that we keep a healthy level of skepticism, which seems to be lacking in most media coverage. No doubt, some drivers will blithely turn over their keys and trust in the vehicle's perceptive abilities. Others may go as far as to proclaim human-
60 driven cars a danger we need to evolve past. Before we can accept such bold statements as fact, we must inquire about how the artificial intelligence in these cars process information, determine risk, and make choices. Given a situation between endangering a
65 pedestrian and endangering the passenger, how should a self-driving car react? Do we trust a computer to make a split-second decision between life and death?

Proponents of self-driving cars admit that the primary hurdle has been navigating the disorder of an
70 average city street. Can we program a car to prepare for every possible hazard? Google certainly believes it will and is now testing its self-driving cars on the roads of Mountain View, CA. While the bustling suburb offers plenty of human interactions, its geographic
75 location avoids many real-world hazards. Located within "Silicon Valley," Mountain View is quite flat (its name refers to its view *of* a mountain, not the view *from* atop a mountain) and does not offer the narrow sightlines found on curvy, inclined roads. Coastal
80 California also has some of the best weather in the nation and snow and ice are meteorological aberrations in the region. How will a self-driving car traverse the icy roads of a Midwest winter? Will the cameras still work when faced with the blinding reflection
85 of a snowbank glistening on a cold, sunny day?

Undoubtedly, more research must occur before we roll the self-driving car onto the diverse roads of the nation. Assuming this hurdle is satisfactorily met, another question arises: will most Americans want a
90 self-driving car? The freedom of the open road is deeply ingrained in American ideology and getting a driver's license is an important rite of passage for most young Americans. Will citizens want a computerized nanny to shuttle them from place to place? Will citizens accept

95 self-driving cars and the accompanying loss of agency, or will they reject automation and embrace control? The unintended consequence of homogenizing our country's traffic could spell the end of the frontier spirit that defined the development and prosperity of our nation.

1

As used in line 1, "coined" most nearly means

A) valued.
B) created.
C) pressed.
D) placed.

2

In context of the passage as a whole, the first paragraph of Passage 1 (lines 1-6) serves to

A) begin a discussion on the complex origins of common words.
B) highlight the significance the automobile has had on the development of the modern world.
C) explain how early automobiles were just carriages with a motor.
D) introduce a topic by revealing the origin of a word.

CONTINUE

3

Why does the author include the list in lines 10-12 ("automatic ... traction control")?

A) The list shows how the development of self-driving cars relates to previous technological improvements.

B) The list demonstrates how much safer cars have become.

C) The list distances self-driving cars from their technological ancestors.

D) The list offers many features made obsolete by self-driving cars.

4

The author of Passage 1 would most likely respond to lines 90-93 in Passage 2 ("The freedom ... young Americans") with

A) agreement that many citizens could share this sentiment.

B) resentment that few citizens will embrace technological progress.

C) begrudging acceptance that few will ever buy self-driving cars.

D) protest regarding the generalization of American culture.

5

Which choice provides the best evidence for the answer to the previous question?

A) Lines 17-20 ("The future ... cars")

B) Lines 25-27 ("It is ... all")

C) Lines 40-43 ("Google ... performance")

D) Lines 44-47 ("Researchers ... chauffeurs")

6

The questions in lines 64-67 ("Given ... death") help to

A) define difficult situations that could challenge the artificial intelligence of the vehicle.

B) show the clear danger that self-driving cars present.

C) expose the limits of current artificial intelligence.

D) dramatize a likely scenario if self-driving cars become popular.

7

Passage 2 discusses Mountain View, California in order to

A) show why the city is an ideal testing location for self-driving cars.

B) clear up a common misconception about the name of the city.

C) analyze the city's merits and drawbacks as a testing site for self-driving cars.

D) suggest that the city is too lenient in allowing Google to test self-driving cars on its streets.

8

As used in line 98, "spell" most nearly means

A) structure.

B) arrange.

C) signal.

D) correct.

9

Opposed to the attitude of the author of Passage 1, the author of Passage 2 views self-driving cars with greater

A) enthusiasm.

B) reservation.

C) contempt.

D) indifference.

10

Which choice provides the best evidence for the answer to the previous question?

A) Lines 57-59 ("No doubt... abilities")

B) Lines 59-60 ("Others ... past")

C) Lines 71-73 ("Google ... Mountain View, CA")

D) Lines 86-88 ("Undoubtedly ... nation")

11

With which of the following statements would both authors would most likely agree?

A) Self-driving cars will likely never become the dominant form of transportation.

B) There are still many questions surrounding the use of self-driving cars.

C) The use of self-driving cars would affect national identity.

D) Self-driving cars can learn how to navigate different terrain and weather conditions.

STOP

If you finish before time is called, you may check your work on this section only.
Do not turn to any other section.

Explanations

Answers & explanations for the comparison passages.

1. As used in line 1, "coined" most nearly means

   A) valued.
   (B)) created.
   C) pressed.
   D) placed.

   > We need to start by looking at the word in context:
   >
   > > "**Coined** *in the late 19th Century, "automobile," a linguistic mashup of the Greek root for self and the Latin root for movable, clearly defined the new motorized vehicle."*
   >
   > We need a word that means "invented." Looking at the answers, **choice B** looks best. Let's make sure by testing "created" in the sentence:
   >
   > > "**Created** *in the late 19th Century, "automobile," a linguistic mashup of the Greek root for self and the Latin root for movable, clearly defined the new motorized vehicle."*
   >
   > Perfect! **Choice B** is correct.

2. In context of the passage as a whole, the first paragraph of Passage 1 (lines 1-6) serves to

   A) begin a discussion on the complex origins of common ~~words~~.
   B) highlight the significance the automobile has had on the ~~development of the modern world~~.
   C) ~~explain~~ how early automobiles were just carriages with a motor.
   (D)) introduce a topic by revealing the origin of a word.

The first paragraph describes where the word **automobile** came from and why it was created to describe "**the new motorized vehicles**." While this is the focus of the first paragraph, it's important to recognize that this is not the main topic of discussion in Passage 1.

Choice D works great! It introduces the topic, self-driving cars, by looking at the origin of the word "automobiles."

3. Why does the author include the list on lines 10-12 ("automatic ... traction control")?

A) The list shows how the development of self-driving cars relates to previous technological improvements.
B) The list demonstrates how ~~much safer~~ cars have become.
C) The list ~~distances~~ self-driving cars from their technological ancestors.
D) The list offers many features made ~~obsolete~~ by self-driving cars.

First, let's look at the phrase in context:

"Many of the technological improvements made to cars over the years–automatic transmissions, cruise control, antilock brakes, traction control–have given greater control to the car itself."

The list is about how "**improvements**" give "**greater control to the car itself**." Since Passage 1 is about the development of self-driving cars, this list shows that cars have gradually become more and more autonomous.

Choice A is a match! The first two paragraphs relate automobiles' past to the future of self-driving cars and this list supports the connection.

4. The author of Passage 1 would most likely respond to lines 90–93 in Passage 2 ("The freedom ... young Americans") with

   (A) agreement that many citizens could share this sentiment.
   B) resentment that few citizens will embrace technological progress.
   C) begrudging acceptance that few will ever buy self-driving cars.
   D) protest regarding the generalization of American culture.

5. Which choice provides the best evidence for the answer to the previous question?

   A) Lines 17–20 ("The future ... cars")
   B) Lines 25–27 ("It is ... all")
   C) Lines 40–43 ("Google ... performance")
   (D) Lines 44–47 ("Researchers ... chauffeurs")

We'll need to answer questions 4 and 5 together. First we'll need to look at what Passage 2 says:

> *"The freedom of the open road is deeply ingrained in American ideology and getting a driver's license is an important rite of passage for most young Americans."*

This sentence is about how learning to drive is part of American culture. Now we need to look for evidence used in Q5 that relates to how Americans would respond to no longer having to get a driver's license. **Choice D** is the only one that relates, as Passage 1 ponders if Americans will "embrace computerized chauffeurs?"

For Q4, **choice A** is the best answer, because the author of Passage 1 admits that drivers could dislike self-driving cars and would prefer to stick with the "rite" of getting a driver's license.

6. The questions in lines 64–67 ("Given ... death") help to

   (A) define difficult situations that could challenge the artificial intelligence of the vehicle.
   B) show the clear danger that self-driving cars present.
   C) expose the limits of current artificial intelligence.
   D) dramatize a likely scenario if self-driving cars become popular.

Let's look at the questions in the passage:

> "Given a situation between endangering a pedestrian and endangering the passenger, how should a self-driving car react? Do we trust a computer to make a split-second decision between life and death?"

The author suggests some tricky situations that might mix up the car's AI. **Choice A** is the best, since these hypotheticals could happen, while the other answers take these examples as facts.

7. Passage 2 discusses Mountain View, California in order to

A) show why the city is an ~~ideal testing location~~ for self-driving cars.
B) clear up a ~~common misconception~~ about the name of the city.
C) analyze the city's merits and drawbacks as a testing site for self-driving cars.
D) suggest that the city is ~~too lenient~~ in allowing Google to test self-driving cars on its streets.

Passage 2 discusses Mountain View, California on lines 75-79:

> "Located within "Silicon Valley," Mountain View is quite flat (its name refers to its view of a mountain, not the view from atop a mountain) and does not offer the narrow sightlines found on curvy, inclined roads."

The author's point is that Mountain View is flat, which is good, but that flatness does not challenge the car's AI.

Choice C works great! Testing self-driving cars in Mountain View has both a good side (flat) and a bad side (no curvy roads).

8. As used in line 98, "spell" most nearly means

A) structure.
B) arrange.
C) signal.
D) correct.

Let's look at the word in context:

*"The unintended consequence of homogenizing our country's traffic could **spell** the end of the frontier spirit that defined the development and prosperity of our nation."*

In this sentence spell means "indicate." Looking at the options, "signal" is the closest to "indicate." Let's plug "signal" into the sentence:

*"The unintended consequence of homogenizing our country's traffic could **signal** the end of the frontier spirit that defined the development and prosperity of our nation."*

Choice C is correct.

9. Opposed to the attitude of the author of Passage 1, the author of Passage 2 views self-driving cars with greater

A) enthusiasm.
B) reservation.
C) contempt.
D) indifference.

10. Which choice provides the best evidence for the answer to the previous question?

A) Lines 57-59 ("No doubt... abilities")
B) Lines 59-60 ("Others ... past")
C) Lines 71-73 ("Google ... Mountain View, CA")
D) Lines 86-88 ("Undoubtedly ... nation")

We need to answer Questions 9 and 10 together. Q9 asks how the tone of Passage 2's author is different than that of Passage 1. Now we can look over the evidence in Q10 and see which one best expresses the author's opinion. Of the options, only **choice D** states the author's opinion of self-driving cars:

> *"Undoubtedly, **more research** must occur before we roll out the self-driving car onto the diverse roads of the nation."*

Suggesting "more research" needs to be done is more **cautious** than the "optimistic" opinion expressed on line ? of Passage 1. The best answer for Question 9 must be **choice B**, since the author of Passage 2 is not ready to commit to a self-driving car.

11. With which of the following statements would both authors would most likely agree?

    A)   Self-driving cars will likely ~~never~~ become the dominant form of transportation.

    (B))   There are still many questions surrounding the use of self-driving cars.

    C)   The use of self-driving cars would ~~affect~~ national identity.

    D)   Self-driving cars ~~can learn~~ how to navigate different terrain and weather conditions.

We need to think about where the two authors agree. The easiest way to answer this is to evaluate the answer choices. Choice A is not supported by either passage. Choice C is only supported by Passage 2 (lines 90-91, *"The freedom of the open road is deeply ingrained in American ideology"*). Choice D is not addressed in Passage 1, and Passage 2 is uncertain of the AI's ability.

Choice B is the most supported. Passage 1 stated in lines 45-46 that "some questions still maintain," and Passage 2 said in line 86 that "more research must occur," so both author agree there should be more research.

Reading for Recall

Reading for recall is a skill. Believe it or not, there are things you can do to drastically improve your reading comprehension and recall.

Pinball Reading

For many students, reading can be a frustrating endeavor. They bounce back and forth between the questions and the passage, never feeling like they have a real grasp of what's going on.

They feel rushed, inefficient, and **frustrated**. And they wonder how other students can keep all that information in their heads.

Students struggle on Reading when they read **passively**. Their eyes scan the page like a paint brush, passing over each word without fully processing the meaning underneath. When it comes time to answer questions on the text, they are not able to recall key information and must go back to read yet again.

"What did I just read?"

Skillful Reading

Students perform much better on Reading when they read actively. They work with the passage; they use their pencil, they paraphrase, and they engage their imagination. As a result, when it comes time to answer questions on the text, they are able to recall enough information to quickly move toward the right answer.

Let's look in more detail at the different levels of Reading for Recall:

① Use your pencil

You already know this as Active Reading: your hand is moving, underlining, starring, and notating. The reason this is effective is you are making choices, prioritizing the text, and establishing a hierarchy. This "analysis in action" aids recall.

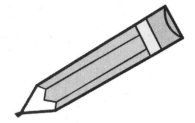

② Paraphrase

It's easier to remember your own words.

Hard phrase to remember:

"The collective efforts of the anguished artists yielded few enduring results."

Easy phrase to remember:

The artists achieved nothing.

When you translate the author's language into your own, you make the phrases "stickier" for your mind. Simplify and personalize: it's like Velcro for the brain.

③ Engage your imagination

If you've ever read a book you loved or heard a friend tell a riveting story, you've let your imagination loose and pictured a story as it unfolded. This is incredibly beneficial for remembering the story later. Images are the stickiest things of all. If you bring your imagination to the test room, watch your reading score rise.

If you improve in any of these three areas, your ability to recall text will improve, and your score will increase. If you work all three at once, you can unleash your inner SAT Reading Beast!

Using your pencil + Paraphrasing + Imagining = BEAST MODE

Reading Styles

All great readers actively engage with the passage, but not all readers have the same reading style. To maximize your score, find the style that works best for you.

Let's look at three readers and see what strategies they use to recall the text.

Reader 1: Picture Patterson

Patterson is a super-visual reader. He remembers pictures better than words. Since the ACT doesn't have any pictures, he makes his own mental images to help remember what he reads.

When he hears the word cow, he doesn't just think "cow: bovine, milk-giving mammal" or see the word COW, he actually imagines a cow. He will likely be able to tell you what color the cow is!

Let's see how Patterson would approach the following passage:

> My father was a St. Bernard, my mother was a Collie, but I am a transcendentalist. This is what my mother told me, I do not know these nice distinctions myself. To me they are only fine large words meaning nothing. My mother had a fondness for such words; she liked to say them, and see other dogs look surprised and envious, wondering how she got so much education. But, indeed, it was not real education; it was only show: she got the words by listening in the dining-room and drawing-room when there was company, and by going with the children to Sunday-school and listening there.

Picture Patterson's Approach:

My father was a St. Bernard, my mother was a Collie, but I am a transcendentalist.

This is what my mother told me, I do not know these nice distinctions myself. To me they are only fine large words meaning nothing. My mother had a fondness for such words; she liked to say them, and see other dogs look surprised and envious, wondering how she got so much education.

But, indeed, it was not real education; it was only show: she got the words by listening in the dining-room and drawing-room when there was company,

and by going with the children to Sunday-school and listening there.

Do you like Patterson's approach? If you pictured things in a similar way, you might be a Picture Patterson kind of reader. Breaking out this skill on the test may be your pathway to a higher score. If you're a Picture Patterson, feed your imagination!

Reader 2: Movie Melissa

Melissa has a cinematic imagination. When she reads about a field, she pictures herself in the field, she can smell the grass, feel the texture of the flowers: she brings it to life.

Melissa doesn't picture static images like Patterson. Instead she pictures an unfolding narrative in which she's the star, or at least the best supporting actress. Making a movie in her mind helps her recall the sequence of information from the passage.

Let's see how Melissa tackles the following passage.

Once upon a time, when the most advanced piece of technology in the typical office was a fax machine, "work" was somewhere you went—typically from 9-5, dressed in a suit and a tie. There was a clear delineation between "work" and "home," and that boundary helped most people define a balance between productivity and play. Now, "work" is no longer a place you go, but something you do. It can be done from anywhere—and typically is.

It's time that our cities and our public spaces began responding to these social changes. Stuffy, outdated office parks full of empty cubicles should give way to more flexible spaces that invite productivity without demanding it. Desks need not be replaced entirely, but should give way to couches, countertops, and comfortable chairs. Communal areas and conference rooms should be granted more space in the office, since increasingly people are coming in expressly for meetings. Coffee shops should be supplemented with productivity centers where nomadic workers can stop for an hour or an afternoon for a small fee. Parks should offer WiFi. And the kind of technology you'd typically find in an office—from high-res scanners to high-speed printers—should be available on every corner.

Not only would these changes assist nomadic workers in attaining greater productivity on a daily basis, they'd make things easier on those who still do the 9-5, by cutting down on traffic and congestion, and making the freelancers and contractors they collaborate with easier to reach.

Movie Melissa's Approach:

Once upon a time, when the most advanced piece of technology in the typical office was a fax machine, "work" was somewhere you went—typically from 9-5, dressed in a suit and a tie. There was a clear delineation between "work" and "home," and that boundary helped most people define a balance between productivity and play.

Now, "work" is no longer a place you go, but something you do. It can be done from anywhere—and typically is.

It's time that our cities and our public spaces began responding to these social changes. Stuffy, outdated office parks full of empty cubicles...

167

...should give way to more flexible spaces that invite productivity without demanding it. Desks need not be replaced entirely, but should give way to couches, countertops, and comfortable chairs. Communal areas and conference rooms should be granted more space in the office, since increasingly people are coming in expressly for meetings.

Coffee shops should be supplemented with productivity centers where nomadic workers can stop for an hour or an afternoon for a small fee. Parks should offer WiFi. And the kind of technology you'd typically find in an office—from high-res scanners to high-speed printers—should be available on every corner.

Not only would these changes assist nomadic workers in attaining greater productivity on a daily basis, they'd make things easier on those who still do the 9-5, by cutting down on traffic and congestion, and making the freelancers and contractors they collaborate with easier to reach.

Reader 3: Paraphrase Paul

Paul is not really a visual guy. He's more of a word guy. He's all about **logic**, ideas and keeping things simple.

"I'm your father!"

"Dada!"

When his friends tell him, "Paul, we've deliberated amongst ourselves and come to the conclusion that we want to travel to the House of Pies," he responds, "You're hungry. Got it."

Paul was **born** to paraphrase. He's been doing it since he was a baby.

Read the following passage and practice your active reading skills. On the next page, Paul will show you how he breaks a passage down into his own words.

The one good thing society can do for the artist is to leave him alone. Give him liberty. The more completely the artist is freed from the pressure of public taste and opinion, from the hope of rewards and the menace of morals, from the fear of absolute starvation or punishment, and from the prospect of wealth or popular consideration, the better for him and the better for art, and therefore the better for everyone.

Liberate the artist: here is something that those powerful and important people who are always assuring us that they would do anything for art can do. They might begin the work of encouragement by disestablishing and disendowing art; by withdrawing funding from art schools, and confiscating the moneys misused by the Royal Academy.

The case of the schools is urgent. Art schools do nothing but harm, because they must do something. Art is not to be learned; at any rate it is not to be taught. All that the drawing-master can teach is the craft of imitation. In schools there must be a criterion of excellence and that criterion cannot be an artistic one; the drawing-master sets up the only criterion he is capable of using—fidelity to the model.

Paraphrase Paul's Approach:

The one good thing society can do for the artist is to leave him alone.

Leave artists alone.

Give him liberty. The more completely the artist is freed from the pressure of public taste and opinion, from the hope of rewards and the menace of morals, from the fear of absolute starvation or punishment, and from the prospect of wealth or popular consideration, the better for him and the better for art, and therefore the better for everyone.

Leave alone = better art, happier people.

Liberate the artist: here is something that those powerful and important people who are always assuring us that they would do anything for art can do. They might begin the work of encouragement by disestablishing and disendowing art; by withdrawing funding from art schools, and confiscating the moneys misused by the Royal Academy.

Cut $$ from art schools.

The case of the schools is urgent. Art schools do nothing but harm, because they must do something. Art is not to be learned; at any rate it is not to be taught.

Art can't be taught.

All that the drawing-master can teach is the craft of imitation. In schools there must be a criterion of excellence and that criterion cannot be an artistic one; the drawing-master sets up the only criterion he is capable of using—fidelity to the model.

Teachers turn artists into imposters.

Okay, easy. Leave artists alone to get better art. Cut schools. Teachers make imposters. Got it.

Translating As You Read

Patterson, Melissa, and Paul each have their own unique approach to reading a passage. All three students, however, have one crucial thing in common: they **translate what they read into their own language.** This language is easier for them to understand as they read, and easier to remember when they get to the questions.

The SAT rewards each of them with a **higher Reading score!**

Find Your Style

It's your turn. Use the next passage to practice translating into your own language. Whether that means picturing like Patterson, imagining like Melissa, or paraphrasing like Paul (or your own unique blend), take a few minutes to find what works for **you**.

Engage more with the passage, and your recall (and score) **will** improve.

Practice:

The new guy, Zeke, had started at the coffee shop ten days ago, and things were different since he arrived. It was hard to put into words. But the machines kept malfunctioning, the faucet would suddenly turn scalding when it was supposed to run cold, and the milk kept mysteriously going bad. It was like a force field; everything around Zeke went strange.

Space to draw or write

_____

The customers could feel it too. They didn't stay as long; they shifted awkwardly in their seats, gulped their drinks, and left. Students complained that their laptops were acting up – turning on, turning off, blue screen of death... that kind of thing. We didn't mind that so much. No one wanted a bunch of table-hogging kids who bought a cup of joe for $1.85, then parked themselves in prime real estate for three hours.

_____

Zeke himself was totally average: the surfer type, slightly built with broad shoulders and skinny legs. He was tan, with shoulder-length yellow hair, bleached by the sun. He tended to look away when he spoke to you, fidgeting with the edge of his striped hoodie, digging into the pocket of his khaki shorts. He was nice, but it was hard to draw him out. "So tell me about yourself, Zeke," I asked him one day when the shop was slow. Zeke shook his head. "I don't know, nothing much to tell," he mumbled, then slunk away to clean out the espresso machine.

I'd been working at the coffee shop for two years, so I was an old pro; I knew all the regulars (and their drinks). I also knew that our cranky old espresso machine broke down once a month like clockwork; until Zeke showed up. Then it started breaking down every other day.

Odd sorts started coming into the shop. They wore long, dingy coats that almost touched the floor, and long, dingy hair that lay limp and greasy on their shoulders. Their faces were pale and shiny, as if overly scrubbed, and they didn't say much. They counted their money very carefully, fingering each coin as if trying to remember it. They bought drinks but didn't drink them.

But that wasn't the strangest thing about them. The strangest thing was this: I saw them come in all the time. But I never once saw one of them leave. They'd go into the bathroom. Then they'd just disappear. You probably think I'm crazy, but I know what I saw. Finally I decided I was going to investigate. For some reason the odd sorts—I'd begun calling them "irregulars"—always came in when we were extra busy, so for a while it was hard to find the time. They'd sneak into the bathroom when I was busy with a customer, then next thing I knew their table was empty and they were gone.

But finally I caught one. He was my father's age. He wore an oversized tan trench coat; it was tattered, with faded stains like coffee and mustard. He wore a childlike expression, lost and vacant. I saw him go into the men's room; I ran over to the door and waited outside, arms crossed. Several minutes passed, then several more. I banged on the door, but no one answered. Then I heard a strange swelling of music, like smooth jazz mixed with the scary music they play at the beginning of a horror movie mixed with old radio announcements in loud cheerful tones. I heard a muffled scream. I banged on the door again, then tried the knob. It opened freely. There was no one inside.

Zeke walked up behind me and cleared his throat. "Something VERY weird is going on," I said. He rubbed his ear thoughtfully, then brushed his long hair out of his eyes for the nineteenth time that day. "The espresso machine is broken again," he said, and walked away.

List of Grammar Rules/Topics

Writing Overview

In the Writing and Language section of the SAT, you will play the role of editor-in-chief, correcting grammar errors and improving the flow and content of 4 less-than-perfect passages.

Structure

You will have 35 minutes to read and edit 4 passages with 11 questions each, for a total of 44 questions. You will see one passage each about Careers, History/Social Studies, Humanities, and Science. One or two of the passages will also come with a graph or chart related to the topic. These passages range from easy to medium comprehension level: no AP Literature or Ye Olde English dictionary required.

Content

There are **two** question types on the SAT Writing section. Every question you'll see belongs to one of these types.

 STANDARD ENGLISH CONVENTIONS 20/44 (45%)

Standard English Conventions is a fancy way to say **grammar rules**. These questions ask you to revise sentences so that they follow all the grammar rules you're about to learn! You'll see rogue commas, crazy clauses, and misplaced modifiers. Once you know the rules, you'll be able to identify and fix errors quickly.

 EXPRESSION OF IDEAS: 24/44 (55%)

Lots of questions test how well you can express ideas: using the right words in the right place to communicate an idea. These questions ask you to revise the passage for content, organization, and logic. To answer these questions, you will need to think bigger! Broaden your focus to include surrounding sentences and paragraphs to understand the flow and content of the passage.

Strategy

You could take on each question as if it were a brand new, never-before-seen error that you must figure out. But that's the hard way! The table of contents list on the previous page tells you almost every kind of question you will ever see on this section. So use it as a guide to outsmart the test writers! Now, we're not suggesting that you memorize all 18 items on the list and go through them one by one for every question. Instead, use **context clues** in the question text *and* answer choices to quickly deduce what kind of error you've got on your hands.

Here is your step-by-step guide to conquering these questions:

> (1) **Spot the topic**
>
> (2) **Remember the rule**
>
> (3) **Apply the rule**

Let's see the steps in action!

Recent research by several historians <u>question</u> the long–held belief that Marie Antoinette once said, "Let them eat cake."

A) NO CHANGE
B) questioning
C) questions
D) have questioned

1 Spot the topic

The underlined word is a **verb**, and the answer choices are different forms of the same verb. The two topics dealing with verbs are **Subject-Verb Agreement** and **Tense Switch**!

2 Remember the rule

I'll check for agreement first. I think I remember the rule from that chapter: The verb and subject must both be **singular** or **plural**. Our verb is plural, but the subject "research" is singular. There's the error!

3 Apply the rule

I need to find a **singular** verb to match the **singular** subject. "Questions" is singular, so I'll try reading it into the sentence:

> Recent research by several historians questions the long-held belief that Marie Antoinette once said, "Let them eat cake."

Sounds good! I'll choose **C**.

And that's all there is to it! If you can keep that small list of rules in your head and cross-reference it with questions using context clues, you will be able to predict the test writers' moves and stay one step ahead of them.

Comma Basics

To ace the SAT, you need to know what commas can and can't do in a sentence.

A comma's main job is to separate different ideas in a single sentence. Before we dive into the specifics of comma rules, let's learn some comma basics.

Listening for Comma Errors

Commas live where you naturally break in your speech, so you can actually hear correct comma placement. That simple fact means that if you pause when you see a comma, and it still sounds right, then it's likely in the right spot! Let's try it. Read the following sentences aloud. Each time you come to a comma, greatly exaggerate the pause before moving on. When there's no comma, blaze ahead without stopping.

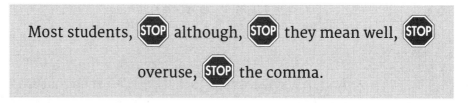

Now that's just plain silly. Did you notice your ear getting frustrated at having to constantly stop and start? Extra commas interrupt an idea before it's finished! What if we removed all the commas?

Most students although they mean well overuse the comma.

Notice how you started to feel rushed and a bit jumbled by the end of the sentence? There were too many ideas and not enough commas keeping them separate.

Now let's try to separate our ideas with commas:

> Most students, although they mean well, overuse
>
> the comma.

Perfect! This sounds right, and that's because we have two ideas at play in this sentence:

1) Most students overuse the comma.

2) They (the students) mean well.

Commas allow us to put these two related ideas in the same sentence. Practice using commas to separate ideas, remembering to use your ear to double check your answer!

EXAMPLE 1

Recent showings by two local artists <u>suggest, that</u> Raleigh's art scene is experiencing a renaissance.

SOLUTION

The comma after "suggest" sounds strange to my ear, and that's because it is breaking up one idea; the showings suggest that Raleigh's art scene is experiencing a renaissance.

Recent showings by two local artists **<u>suggest that</u>** Raleigh's art scene is experiencing a renaissance.

EXAMPLE 2

Some <u>horses, which I had never paid much attention to began</u> stampeding through Aunt Bessie's kitchen.

As written, this sentence sounds rushed. That's because we need a pause to separate our two ideas:

1) Some horses began stampeding through Bessie's kitchen
2) I had never paid much attention to those pesky horses

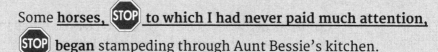

Notice that in our last example, we are sticking the second idea **into** the first idea, and using commas to keep them separate. When you have an idea in the middle of another idea, you need to be careful with your commas!

Slipping Ideas Out of a Sentence

If you stick a supporting clause in the middle of a sentence with commas on either end, you must be able to **slip the clause out** while keeping the primary idea intact. We call these clauses **nonessential**, as they are not essential to the meaning of the sentence. Nonessential clauses **always** need commas around them. Here's an example of slipping out the clause:

Most students, although they mean well, overuse the comma.

Most students, although they mean well, overuse the comma.

although they mean well

⟶ Most students overuse the comma. ⟵

Without the nonessential clause, the sentence still gets its idea across: **most students overuse the comma.**

The SAT will often open a nonessential clause with a comma, but forget to close it! It's your job to remember to finish what they started.

EXAMPLE 3

My new iPhone <u>23—my dearest friend and most trusty companion, just</u> took out a third mortgage on my house despite our previous agreement that it would always check with me before completing any major transactions.

Dashes vs. Commas:

The SAT treats commas and dashes identically, so the same rules apply to both. But be careful! If you open with a comma, you have to close with a comma. If you open with a dash, close with a dash! **Never start with a comma and end with a dash, or vice-versa!**

SOLUTION

"My dearest friend and most trusty companion" is a **nonessential** idea. The sentence still makes sense if we slip it out. So we need to grease up the edges with some punctuation. We can use commas or dashes, but not both. If you open with a dash, stick with it to the end!

My new iPhone <u>23—my dearest friend and most trusty companion—just</u> took out a third mortgage on my house despite our previous agreement that it would always check with me before completing any major transactions.

EXAMPLE 4

The next afternoon, using her <u>sandwich, as bait</u> she was able to lure the mouse out of the cupboard.

SOLUTION

The original sentence is all jumbled because our **comma** is in the wrong place. If we slip out the nonessential clause, we get this:

The next afternoon as bait she was able to lure the mouse out of the cupboard.

Is *the afternoon* the bait? Is *she* the bait? I don't think so. The **sandwich** is bait, so it belongs inside the commas.

The next afternoon, using her <u>**sandwich as bait,**</u> she was able to lure the mouse out of the cupboard.

Quiz

Identify the error (if present) in each of the following sentences.

1. Flying horses, in her opinion were prettier and more intimidating than turtles that knew karate.

2. What had started as a dare during recess had quickly escalated into the town's first annual Hog Olympics.

3. Sally came home, from the salon, with freshly manicured nails and a tightly curled perm that brought back all the glory of the eighties.

4. For as long as he could remember, Johnny had wanted to become a private detective, when he grew up investigating crimes in the fashion of the heroes of film noir.

5. Clancy's over-investment in dryer lint companies, forced him to fire his housekeeper when the stock market took a spill.

Answers

1. Flying horses, in her opinion, were prettier and more intimidating than turtles that knew karate.

2. *Correct!*

3. Sally came home, from the salon, with freshly manicured nails and a tightly curled perm that brought back all the glory of the eighties.

4. For as long as he could remember, Johnny had wanted to become a private detective, when he grew up, investigating crimes in the fashion of the heroes of film noir.

5. Clancy's over-investment in dryer lint companies, forced him to fire his housekeeper when the stock market took a spill.

Practice Problems

Select the answer choice that produces the best sentence

1

Modern artist Man Ray, widely known for his stylized <u>photography also</u> directed several short films.

A) NO CHANGE
B) photography, he also
C) photography; also
D) photography, also

2

Although the use of synthetic materials continues to flourish, textile manufacturers, fashion <u>designers, and</u> many consumers agree that cotton offers a cost-effective range of applications, from rugged denim to soft undergarments.

A) NO CHANGE
B) designers: and
C) designers, and,
D) designers; and

3

Edmond Thomas Quinn—an American sculptor and <u>painter, is best known</u> for his bronze of *Edwin Booth as Hamlet*, which was placed in New York City's Gramercy Park in 1919.

A) NO CHANGE
B) painter is best known
C) painter; is best known
D) painter—is best known

4

Jeffrey <u>Sconce, an associate professor of communications at Northwestern University</u> has written several articles that analyze the appeal of watching really terrible movies.

A) NO CHANGE
B) Sconce, an associate professor of communications, at Northwestern University,
C) Sconce, an associate professor of communications at Northwestern University,
D) Sconce an associate, professor of communications at Northwestern University

5

Unlike traditional trail mix, Hutchinson's recipe includes many exotic <u>ingredients, such as</u> dried jicama, juniper berries, and salted cod.

A) NO CHANGE
B) ingredients such as:
C) ingredients, such as,
D) ingredients, such as:

6

While on a college visit to Stanford University, I discovered a garden filled with <u>sculptor, August Rodin's bronze</u> statues nestled among the campus's many buildings.

A) NO CHANGE
B) sculptor August Rodin's bronze
C) sculptor, August Rodin's, bronze
D) sculptor August Rodin's, bronze

7

Napoleon III, largely responsible for modernizing Paris, was captured at the end of the Franco-Prussian war and eventually exiled, <u>or banished from</u> France for the rest of his life.

A) NO CHANGE
B) or, banished from
C) or banished, from
D) or banished from,

Incorporating singing, dancing, and playing the piano into their performances, the Hilton Sisters, a pair of conjoined twins, wanted to offer their audience a show that extended beyond their physical uniqueness.

A) NO CHANGE
B) performances, the Hilton Sisters;
C) performances; the Hilton Sisters,
D) performances, the Hilton Sisters

9

For each scene, a film composer arranges the audio elements—the rhythms, melodies, and tonalities, and enhances the mood to draw the audience into the cinematic experience.

A) NO CHANGE
B) elements: the rhythms, melodies, and tonalities,
C) elements, the rhythms, melodies, and tonalities—
D) elements—the rhythms, melodies, and tonalities—

Louise became famous at Wagstaff School for her boisterous personality, elaborate pranks and, pink bunny hat.

A) NO CHANGE
B) elaborate pranks, and pink bunny hat.
C) elaborate pranks, and pink, bunny hat.
D) elaborate pranks, and pink, bunny, hat.

All About Clauses

Clauses are the building blocks of sentences. They come in two varieties: independent and dependent.

Independent vs. Dependent

An independent clause can stand on its own (independently) as a complete thought. If you plop a period at the end of an independent clause, you have a sentence. For example:

> The pigs flew.

Pigs is our subject, **flew** is our verb, and this clause is a complete thought. It gives a pretty clear picture of what's happening! How about this one:

> Tina was surprised.

Again, this independent clause can stand on its own as a sentence. It gives us a complete thought to imagine.

The pigs flew.   Tina was surprised.

A **dependent** clause is an incomplete thought. Take a look:

> Since the pigs flew

...then what? What happened next? This dependent clause sounds unfinished because it is an incomplete thought. We still have a subject: **pigs**. We still have a verb: **flew**. But "since" tells us that there's more to come. To make a complete sentence, we could attach it to an independent clause:

> Since the pigs flew, I haven't looked at bacon the same.
> *dependent*   *independent*

TIP

A dependent clause DEPENDS on another clause to make a sentence.

Determine whether each clause is independent (I) or dependent (D) and circle the correct corresponding letter.

1.	Sharonda, whose parents are both dentists	I	**(D)**
2.	The rain fell through the window	I	D
3.	Sweeping the dust under the rug	I	D
4.	Since my dog is amazing at performing tricks	I	D
5.	The train whistle wakes me up every night	I	D
6.	Jeffrey's amazing sculpting skills that had been kept secret for so long	I	D
7.	Running a marathon is almost impossible	I	D
8.	Unfortunately, I got stuck in traffic	I	D
9.	When I got back from vacation	I	D
10.	Fragments, which are always incorrect	I	D

Answers: 2. I, 3. D, 4. D, 5. I, 6. D, 7. I, 8. I, 9. D, 10. D

Fragments

When we incorrectly plop a period at the end of a dependent clause, we make a **fragment**, or an incomplete sentence. The SAT writers create fragments by dropping one of these fragment makers into a perfectly good sentence.

Fragment Makers	
which	since
when	if
who	and
that	-ing verb

To get rid of fragments, you usually need to delete the fragment maker. Let's see this in action!

EXAMPLE 1

John Cage's <u>music, which was</u> powerfully influenced by the soundscape of modern life.

We have our subject (music) and we have our verb (was), but that pesky **which** is turning our independent clause into a dependent one, leaving us with a fragment. Delete the fragment maker, and we're left with a complete sentence!

John Cage's **<u>music was</u>** powerfully influenced by the soundscape of modern life.

EXAMPLE 2

Since art classes in elementary schools are central to cultivating creativity, art education <u>deserving continuing</u> support.

 SOLUTION

Let's look at our clauses:

Since art classes in elementary schools are central to cultivating creativity, *(dependent)*

art education deserving continuing support. *(dependent)*

To make a complete sentence, **one** clause must be independent. The first clause is locked in, so we need to turn the second dependent clause into an independent one.

The subject is "education," but we're missing a main verb. An -ing verb isn't strong enough to be our main verb, so we're left with a fragment. Change the -ing to a regular present tense verb, and voila: complete sentence!

Since art classes in elementary schools are central to cultivating creativity, art education <u>**deserves**</u> continuing support.

Separating Clauses with Punctuation

Now that we can identify independent and dependent clauses, we need to learn how to separate them with punctuation. We'll take each punctuation choice you'll see on the test and tell you what it **can** and **cannot** separate.

Semicolon

The semicolon has one primary job; it separates two independent clauses. Authors sometimes choose to use a semicolon instead of a period when they want to show a close connection between two adjoining ideas.

 Semicolons are great; I use them all the time!
independent　　　　　　*independent*

TIP

You'll never be asked to choose between a semicolon and a period on the test; they have the same job. If you see two answer choices that are exactly the same **except for** a period and semicolon switch, you know they are both wrong.

You can check semicolons on the test by asking "Would a period work here?" If the answer is "no," then you cannot use a semicolon either. Because semicolons, like periods, are "full-stop" punctuation, they can **never** separate a dependent and an independent clause.

> ✗ Since semicolons are great; I use them all the time!
>   *dependent*   *independent*

Colon

The colon is an expert at making introductions. It always follows an independent clause, but it can introduce pretty much anything!

- <u>An Independent Clause</u>
  There was only one explanation: Aliens had replaced my parents with highly embarrassing body doubles.

- <u>A Dependent Clause</u>
  Wilhelmina's travels were extensive: trips to every major capital in Europe and Asia.

- <u>A List</u>
  I have three hobbies: snorkeling, wombat training, and Thomas Edison impersonating.

Commas

Commas are great at separating independent and dependent clauses, and vice versa:

> When I heard we were going to Disneyworld for spring break,
>   *dependent*
> I nearly lost my mind in blissful delirium.
>   *independent*

> The Tower of Terror was my favorite ride,
> *independent*
>
> which isn't surprising given my love of elevators.
> *dependent*

TIP

If you go to Disney World, **go on the Tower of Terror ride**. That won't raise your SAT score, we just heartily recommend it.

Comma Splice

There is one thing a comma can **never** do: separate two independent clauses. This results in the dreaded *comma splice*:

> The pigs flew, Tina was surprised.

That comma is too weak to separate the pig and Tina. So what can we do about it? There are **four** equally good ways to fix a comma splice: make one clause dependent, replace the comma with a period, replace it with a semicolon, or replace it with a colon. Let's look at how each option fixes a comma splice.

① Replace the comma with a period

Since independent clauses are so close to sentences already, why not give them what they want and put periods at the end of each?

> The pigs flew. Tina was surprised.

A bit boring, but it gets the point across and uses punctuation correctly! But what if we wanted to emphasize that these clauses are connected?

② Replace the comma with a semicolon

Semicolons are masters of separating two independent clauses. That's all they do! By changing the comma to a semi, we fix the comma splice while still showing the relationship between the two sentences:

> The pigs flew; Tina was surprised.

③ Make one clause dependent

If we're going to use a comma, we have to turn one of the complete thoughts into an *incomplete* thought. To do this, we can add a conjunction or a fragment maker:

> The pigs flew, **so** Tina was surprised.
>
> **Since** the pigs flew, Tina was surprised.
>
> **When** the pigs flew, Tina was surprised.

Another way to turn a complete thought into an incomplete one is to get rid of the subject and change the verb into an -ing.

> ✗ The pigs flew through the sky, it surprised Tina.
>
> ✓ **Flying** through the sky, the pigs surprised Tina.

④ Replace the comma with a colon...

...but **ONLY** if it follows the colon rules. Remember, colons must follow an independent clause, and they are best at making **introductions**. We'd need to do some rewriting:

> There's one thing that was more memorable than the pigs' flight through the air: the look of shock on Tina's face.

Separate the clauses below with a comma, colon, or semicolon. The first two are completed for you.

1. The flying squirrel had not eaten in two days **;** it was famished.

2. If you've ever had an unfortunate run-in with superglue **,** then you know the stuff is simply impossible to unstick.

3. The clown impersonator seemed to inspire my little sister Annie **,** who raided our mom's makeup cabinet, stacked our mattresses, and bounced all night long.

4. Abraham Lincoln is revered by many for the role he played in ending slavery **;** most people are surprised to learn that he was also a seasoned vampire hunter.

5. When I was a child growing up in New Canaan **,** my parents and I spent our summers on the coast.

6. There is another factor to consider when choosing which car to purchase **:** the cupholder situation.

7. This year, the president of the PTA will be chosen by committee **,** which will include parents, teachers, and school administrators.

8. In the midwest, the weather in April is completely unpredictable **;** daily temperatures range from balmy to below freezing.

9. Its red light blinking insistently **,** the answer machine announced a new message.

10. The basket overflowed with various kinds of fruit **:** apples, oranges, bananas, and grapes.

Answers: Commas – 2, 3, 5, 7, 9; Semicolons – 4, 8; Colons – 6, 10

Now, it's time to put it all together. Try these test problems, and don't forget to

(1) Check your clauses

- Are they dependent or independent?

(2) Remember your punctuation rules

- Commas **cannot** separate independent clauses

- **Only** semicolons and periods can separate independent clauses

- Colons **introduce** a dependent clause, an independent clause, or a list

EXAMPLE 3

Students and teachers alike are happy with the language of the new Honor Code, <u>this is</u> a set of rules or guidelines that prohibits cheating, among other offenses.

A) NO CHANGE
B) it is
C) this was
D) which is

SOLUTION

That comma is separating two clauses, so let's make sure we're not dealing with a comma splice.

subject   *verb*

Students and teachers alike are happy with the language of the new Honor Code,

(independent)

subject   *verb*

this is a set of rules or guidelines that prohibits cheating, among other offenses.

(independent)

A comma can **never** separate two independent clauses. The comma is locked in, so we need to make the second clause **dependent** by either adding a fragment maker or getting rid of the subject. B and C replace "this is" with different subject/verb combinations. Only **D** deletes the subject and adds a fragment maker: **which**.

Students and teachers alike are happy with the language of the new Honor Code, **which is** a set of rules or guidelines that prohibits cheating, among other offenses.

EXAMPLE 4

Stopping to smell the flowers and enjoy the <u>sunshine;</u> Little Red Riding Hood dawdled away the afternoon and left her grandmother in the lurch.

A) NO CHANGE
B) sunshine:
C) sunshine, and
D) sunshine,

SOLUTION

Let's check our clauses!

Stopping to smell the flowers and enjoy the <u>sunshine;</u>
(dependent)

Little Red Riding Hood dawdled away the afternoon and left her grandmother in the lurch.
(independent)

Semicolons can only separate two **independent** clauses, so A has to go. B replaces the semi with a colon, but colons can only follow **independent** clauses. C gives us a comma, which is a step in the right direction! Commas are perfect for separating dependent and independent clauses. However, the connector **and** is not logical here.

D just replaces the semi with a comma. Simple and correct!

Stopping to smell the flowers and enjoy the <u>**sunshine,**</u> Little Red Riding Hood dawdled away the afternoon and left her grandmother in the lurch.

Quiz

Identify the error (if present) in each of the following sentences.

1. Maura, a veritable recluse, has a terrible sense of style, when she does leave the house, she wears only ancient flannel pajamas.

2. There's just one thing you need to know about bears, don't get between them and honey.

3. It was a beautiful day: for a picnic.

4. Singing the sweetest notes I've ever heard; the nightingale outside my window woke me up this morning.

5. Santiago is originally from North Dakota, but because he is fluent in Spanish, everyone assumes he was born in South America.

Answers

1. Maura, a veritable recluse, has a terrible sense of style; when she does leave the house, she wears only ancient flannel pajamas. .

2. There's just one thing you need to know about bears: don't get between them and honey.

3. It was a beautiful day/for a picnic.

4. Singing the sweetest notes I've ever heard, the nightingale outside my window woke me up this morning.

5. *Correct!*

Practice Problems

Select the answer choice that produces the best sentence

1

Giethoorn in the Netherlands does not have any car <u>traffic, the</u> city is built around canals, and residents use boats and pedestrian bridges to move from place to place.

A) NO CHANGE
B) traffic; the
C) traffic; since the
D) traffic the

2

Since I just got my degree in agricultural <u>management. I</u> am looking for an internship at a farming co-op to gain experience.

A) NO CHANGE
B) management, I
C) management; I
D) management, but

3

That the governor used public funds for the illegal transaction <u>which</u> makes it all the worse.

A) NO CHANGE
B) and
C) that
D) DELETE the underlined portion

4

Over the course of the summer, I began to appreciate the unique backgrounds of the members of my adult kickball <u>team, two</u> doctors, three attorneys, two airplane mechanics, a professional saxophone player, and a massage therapist.

A) NO CHANGE
B) team: two
C) team; two
D) team two

5

Avocados and bananas share a surprising similarity, both are a climacteric fruit that matures on the plant, but does not ripen until removed from the plant.

A) NO CHANGE
B) similarity: both, are
C) similarity, but both are
D) similarity: both are

6

The Ilen School in Limerick, Ireland provides training in a traditional and often forgotten craft students, build traditional Irish boats—including the Gandelow, Currach, and Dory—with simple woodworking tools in order to teach carpentry skills and pride in one's work and culture.

A) NO CHANGE
B) craft—students
C) craft: students
D) craft students

7

Al "Bubba" Baker, a former professional football player. He patented a process to remove the bones from barbequed ribs and now runs a successful restaurant and mail-order business.

A) NO ERROR
B) player: he
C) player,
D) player; he

8

Built in the late 1600s, Castillo de San Marcos is the oldest fort still standing in the United States, its stone structure is surrounded by a now-dry moat.

A) NO CHANGE
B) States, it's
C) States. Its
D) States. It's

9

From the lively streets of downtown Bangkok to the suburbs of the city of Atlanta to the cobblestone alleys of <u>Paris. These cities</u> across the globe are embracing the food truck trend.

A) NO CHANGE
B) Paris. Cities
C) Paris, cities
D) Paris; these cities

10

Carbon dating works by measuring a specimen's level of radiocarbon, <u>it is</u> a radioactive isotope of carbon.

A) NO CHANGE
B) being
C) that is
D) DELETE the underlined portion

Writing Practice Passage 1
TO STAY ON PACE, YOUR TIMING GOAL IS 8.5 MINUTES

DIRECTIONS

Each passage below is accompanied by a number of questions. For some questions, you will consider how the passage might be revised to improve the expression of ideas. For other questions, you will consider how the passage might be edited to correct errors in sentence structure, usage, or punctuation. Each passage or a question may be accompanied by one or more graphics (such as a table or graph) that you will consider as you make revising and editing decisions.

Some questions will direct you to an underlined portion of the passage. Other questions will direct you to a location in a passage or ask you to think about the passage as a whole. After reading each passage, choose the answer to each question that most effectively improves the quality of writing in the passage or that makes the passage conform to the conventions of standard written English. Many questions include a "NO CHANGE" option. Choose that option if you think the best choice is to leave the relevant portion of the passage as it is.

Questions 1–11 are based on the following passage.

The Wonderful World of Dirt

Consider what resides in dirt. At the most visible level, we have insects, **1** earthworms, plants, and small vertebrate creatures. Then we have slender worms in the nematode family, and spiders, centipedes, millipedes, and other creatures in the arthropod family. Also present—though too tiny to **2** see, are the multitudes of fungi, bacteria, protozoa, algae, and other microscopic organisms. A single tablespoon of soil can contain as many as 50 billion microbes. Life **3** that abounds at every size, and each creature has its own role to play in producing healthy soil with the nutrients to support flourishing plant life.

1
A) NO CHANGE
B) earthworms; plants, and small
C) earthworms: plants, and small
D) earthworms plants, and, small

2
A) NO CHANGE
B) see:
C) see—
D) see

3
A) NO CHANGE
B) which
C) it
D) DELETE the underlined portion

CONTINUE

One key aspect of this process is the nitrogen cycle. Nitrogen is one of the main elements that plants and other living organisms require to [4] thrive, it plays a role in producing the building blocks of life, or proteins, amino acids, and nucleic acids. Since nitrogen is stored in organic matter (organisms that were once alive, and may be living still), this organic matter must be broken down to release the nitrogen. Enter the superheroes known as [5] "The Decomposers:" they are bacteria, fungi, and worms. These creatures assist with the process of decomposition, using biochemical compounds to break down complex matter.

Certain plants have developed mutually beneficial relationships with these bacteria, assisting in supplying nitrogen to the soil. These [6] plants known as nitrogen fixers, can chiefly be found in the legume family: soy beans, clover, alfalfa, and more. Their roots offer a delightful habitat for bacteria called Rhizobia, [7] they are particularly enthusiastic nitrogen processors. They get busy transforming nitrogen into a form that their friends the clover roots can use. When the plant dies, all the nitrogen it accumulated is returned to the soil, now in a form that's easily available to other plants. This is just one of the many symbiotic [8] relationships, that can be observed in the complex web of life beneath the ground.

[4]

A) NO CHANGE
B) thrive; it
C) thrive. While it
D) thrive, therefore it

[5]

A) NO CHANGE
B) "The Decomposers;" they are
C) "The Decomposers:"
D) "The Decomposers,"

[6]

A) NO CHANGE
B) plants, known as nitrogen fixers,
C) plants, known as nitrogen fixers
D) plants, known, as nitrogen fixers,

[7]

A) NO CHANGE
B) that being
C) those are
D) DELETE the underlined portion

[8]

A) NO CHANGE
B) relationships that, can
C) relationships, that, can
D) relationships that can

CONTINUE

Another crucial element in soil **9** is carbon. If you were paying attention in chemistry class, you know that carbon is special: it's the basis of all known life. That includes microorganisms in the soil, which require carbon to live. This is why it's important that nitrogen and carbon remain in balance in the soil. In the presence of excess nitrogen, soil organisms will increase rapidly in numbers and go on a feeding **10** frenzy. Extracting all the carbon from the soil and exhaling it in the form of carbon dioxide, which enters the atmosphere as a greenhouse gas. When they've extracted all the available carbon, they'll suffer population collapse and quickly die off, leaving the soil bereft of helpful organisms. Nature-friendly gardeners avoid this problem by staying away from nitrogen-heavy chemical fertilizers. Instead, they fertilize with a mixture of organic material—such as dead leaves, grass clippings, and decomposing vegetable and fruit **11** scraps, they contains carbon and nitrogen in life-supporting ratios.

9

A) NO CHANGE
B) is: carbon.
C) is, carbon.
D) is; carbon.

10

A) NO CHANGE
B) frenzy; extracting
C) frenzy, extracting
D) frenzy, they extract

11

A) NO CHANGE
B) scraps—which
C) scraps—they
D) scraps, which

STOP
If you finish before time is called, you may check your work on this section only.
Do not turn to any other section.

Tense Switch

What happens in Vegas stays in Vegas. Likewise, what happened in the past should stay in the past.

TIP

Be on the lookout for context clues that point you to the correct tense. Words like "Fifty years ago…" are probably going to be followed by past tense verbs!

The test-writers create "tense switch" errors by switching a verb's tense from one that makes sense with the rest of the sentence to one that does not make sense with the rest of the sentence.

Not surprisingly, the best way to fix one of these errors is to look at the rest of the sentence! Most of the time, there's a second verb that is in the correct tense. Your job is to find that verb and match the tense.

EXAMPLE 1

The Mayan empire, after enduring for more than six hundred years, collapsed when overpopulation, climate change, and drought <u>limit</u> its ability to sustain its population.

A) NO CHANGE
B) will limit
C) have limited
D) limited

SOLUTION

We have a verb underlined and a bunch of tense options in the answer choices: this is definitely a verb tense problem! To figure out which tense is correct, we need to find another verb in the sentence:

The Mayan empire, after enduring for more than six hundred

years (collapsed) when overpopulation, climate change, and
past

drought <u>limit</u> its ability to sustain its population.
present

209

> "Collapsed" is in the past tense, but "limit" is in the present. To best match these tenses, we need to pick choice **D**.
>
> The Mayan empire, after enduring for more than six hundred years, collapsed when overpopulation, climate change, and drought **limited** its ability to sustain its population.

EXAMPLE 2

Most babies, upon seeing Beyoncé's *Single Ladies* video, <u>did begin</u> to dance uncontrollably, but few are able to nail the hand gestures and fewer still can hit those high notes.

A) NO CHANGE
B) does begin
C) have begun
D) do begin

TIP

Google "baby dancing to Beyonce" on your next break. It's a very real, if pointless, baby phenomenon.

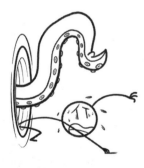

PORTAL

Many questions test tense switch and subject-verb agreement at the same time. Head to page 215 for practice matching your subjects and verbs.

SOLUTION

This question deals with both verb tense and subject-verb agreement; you'll see that a lot on the SAT. First, let's find other verbs in the sentence and note their tenses:

> Most babies, upon seeing Beyoncé's *Single Ladies* video,
>
> <u>did begin</u> to dance uncontrollably, but few (are able) to nail the
> *past*   *present*
> hand gestures and fewer still (can hit) those high notes.
>   *present*

"did begin" is in the **past** tense, but the rest of the sentence is in the **present** tense. There's no reason to use past tense here, so we can cross off A and C.

Now we have a choice between a singular verb, "does begin," and a plural verb, "do begin." What is the subject of this verb? **Babies**, which is plural! We can cross off B and choose **D**!

> Most babies, upon seeing Beyoncé's Single Ladies video, **do begin** to dance uncontrollably, but few are able to nail the hand gestures and fewer still can hit those high notes.

Quiz

Identify the error (if present) in each of the following sentences.

1. By the time she was 15 years old, Leann Rimes is one of the most successful country-western singers in the United States.

2. The world's first astronauts were not only brave beyond compare, but are also some of the world's nicest people.

3. Although Jane Austen wrote *Pride and Prejudice* more than a century ago, it is still one of the best-selling and most-loved novels in the world.

4. Now that the spring sun is warming the ground, the daffodils were emerging in full force.

5. After studying astrophysics for sixteen consecutive hours, Bart worried that he would forget how to spell his name on the actual exam because his brain turns to ooze.

Answers

1. By the time she was 15 years old, Leann Rimes *was* one of the most successful country-western singers in the United States.

2. The world's first astronauts were not only brave beyond compare, but *were* also some of the world's nicest people.

3. *Correct!*

4. Now that the spring sun is warming the ground, the daffodils *are* emerging in full force.

5. After studying astrophysics for sixteen consecutive hours, Bart worried that he would forget how to spell his name on the actual exam because his brain *had turned* to ooze.

Practice Problems

Select the answer choice that produces the best sentence.

1

Storing bananas in the refrigerator delays ripening and spoiling but <u>will increase</u> how quickly bananas grow mushy.

A) NO CHANGE
B) would increase
C) has increased
D) increases

2

Life-size reproductions of 1970s disco divas and 1980s glam rockers made entirely out of ice <u>were</u> often the focus of Esmeralda's elaborate music-themed parties.

A) NO CHANGE
B) was
C) being
D) has been

3

When Bobbi Rae hogtied her calf in less than 30 seconds last summer, she <u>had been</u> the first woman to win first prize at the Effingham County Annual Hog-tying Festival.

A) NO CHANGE
B) became
C) had become
D) has been

4

Miguel believes that aliens are attempting to make contact with humans, which <u>causing</u> him to talk on his homemade ham radio every night.

A) NO CHANGE
B) caused
C) causes
D) is causing

5

The Mayan Empire, after thriving for centuries, finally ended when the last remnants of its people <u>are absorbed</u> into the Toltec society long before the Spanish arrived in Latin America.

A) NO CHANGE
B) is absorbed
C) were absorbed
D) was absorbed

6

Gertie <u>has proved</u> that a petite, 100-pound woman can eat more than a 6-foot-tall quarterback can when she won the pie-eating contest at last year's county fair.

A) NO CHANGE
B) proved
C) proves
D) will prove

7

In the famous European fairytale known today as *Cinderella*, an overworked scullery maid receives a fancy gown from her fairy godmother to wear to the royal ball, dances with the handsome prince until midnight, and <u>was shocked</u> to find him on her doorstep the next day holding her lost shoe.

A) NO CHANGE
B) shocked
C) will be shocked
D) is shocked

8

Most high school juniors are not as well-versed in the ancient art of karate as I <u>was,</u> but they also don't have Mr. Miyagi as a teacher.

A) NO CHANGE
B) have,
C) will,
D) am,

9

It was time to replace the old building's many broken windows, which <u>had fallen</u> prey to stray baseballs, rambunctious vandals, and falling sticks.

A) NO CHANGE
B) will fall
C) fall
D) having fallen

10

There <u>were</u> a few paths you can explore when you visit the Atlanta Botanical Gardens.

A) NO CHANGE
B) are
C) was
D) is

Subject-Verb Agreement

If the subject of your sentence is plural, then the verb must also be plural. If the subject is singular, then the verb must be singular. If a verb is underlined, check that subject!

....

Subject after the verb

Usually, your ear notices when a sentence's subject and verb don't match:

> "I cooks an omelette!"

That sounds pretty bad. If every problem were this easy, it would be pointless testing subject-verb agreement on the SAT. One way the test-writers attempt to trick your ear is to place the subject **after** the verb.

EXAMPLE 1

Over the misty mountaintops <u>glide</u> the majestic grey eagle.

SOLUTION

Notice that, although there is an error here, the sentence doesn't **sound** all that incorrect. Why is that? Since "glide" (a plural verb) follows "mountaintops" (a plural noun), your ear is tricked. But mountaintops don't glide! The **eagle** is doing the gliding— that's our subject! Let's flip the sentence to see this clearly:

The majestic grey eagle **glide** over the misty mountaintops.

That's not right! It's harder to miss when you place the subject next to the verb. Our original sentence *should* read:

Over the misty mountaintops <u>**glides**</u> the majestic grey eagle.

TIP

Remember: the SUBJECT of a sentence is the noun or pronoun that does the verb's action. When you see the verb "run," ask yourself "who is running?"

EXAMPLE 2

Despite the prevalence in Latin American culture of macabre folktales about El Chupacabra, <u>only recently have</u> physical evidence in the form of cave paintings been discovered in the mountains of Peru.

SOLUTION

The key to answering these problems correctly is to identify the subject (**evidence**) and match it with the verb (**has**).

Despite the prevalence in Latin American culture of macabre folktales about El Chupacabra, <u>only recently **has**</u> physical evidence in the form of cave painting been discovered in the mountains of Peru.

Quiz

Identify the error (if present) in each of the following sentences.

1. Even though whipped cream and chocolate syrup are great, there are nothing like maraschino cherries on an ice cream sundae!

2. Soaring gracefully over the icy waters of Lake Champlain are a flock of geese, honking like a New York City cab driver in the middle of rush hour.

3. Deep beneath the earth's crust is buried immense treasures in the form of fossils, lost artifacts, and relics from long-dead cities.

4. Frolicking merrily through the peppermint forest of bubble gum trees is a band of cuddly, animated forest friends, all of whom make you desperately wish you had never agreed to babysit your three-year-old niece.

5. Of the myriad explanations Herbie gave to explain how his underwear ended up atop a street light at the end of the cul-de-sac, there were only one that remotely resembled the truth.

Answers

1. Even though whipped cream and chocolate syrup are great, there *is* nothing like maraschino cherries on an ice cream sundae!

2. Soaring gracefully over the icy waters of Lake Champlain *is* a flock of geese, honking like a New York City cab driver in the middle of rush hour.

3. Deep beneath the earth's crust *are* buried immense treasures in the form of fossils, lost artifacts, and relics from long-dead cities.

4. *Correct!* Band is singular and so is the verb.

5. Of the myriad explanations Herbie gave to explain how his underwear ended up atop a street light at the end of the cul-de-sac, there *was* only one that remotely resembled the truth.

Subject and Verb Separated

The second way that the SAT complicates subject/verb agreement is by separating the subject and the verb in a sentence. The test writers are hoping all those distracting words will trick your ear. To counter this, **cross out distractors** between the subject and verb.

EXAMPLE 3

The relationship between the clownfish and the sea anemone are truly symbiotic, for both receive protection from predators.

SOLUTION

Did you hear the error? If not, it might be due to that prepositional phrase between the subject and verb. Cross it out!

The relationship ~~between the clownfish and the sea anemone~~
      subject
is truly symbiotic, for both receive protection from predators.
verb

Now we see that **relationship** is our singular subject which requires a singular verb: **is**.

<u>The relationship between the clownfish and the sea anemone</u> **is** truly symbiotic, for both receive protection from predators.

EXAMPLE 4

The library near the town's fast food restaurants <u>have</u> more books than all of the others combined.

SOLUTION

The SAT writers are trying to trick you again! They put a plural word right next to our verb. **Restaurants** is NOT our subject!

The <u>library</u> ~~near the town's fast food restaurants~~ <u>have</u> more
   subject   *verb*
books than all of the others combined.

Library have? That's not right! Library *has*.

The library near the town's fast food restaurants **has** more books than all of the others combined.

Either/Or...Neither/Nor

If you have two singular subjects joined by either or neither, you need a singular verb to match.

EXAMPLE 5

Neither Sara nor Tracy <u>want</u> to babysit on Saturday.

SOLUTION

Sara is singular and **Tracy** is too! So when they are joined by a neither/nor, we have to use a singular verb. A great strategy here is simply to replace the entire either/or or neither/nor phrase with the singular pronoun **he**, **she**, or **it**.

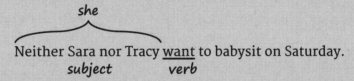

she

Neither Sara nor Tracy <u>want</u> to babysit on Saturday.
subject   *verb*

The mistake students make is to say "neither of them want." You can't lump those girls together! It's **neither Tracy wants nor Sara wants**.

Neither Sara nor Tracy <u>wants</u> to babysit on Saturday.

Tricky Words

Some words seem plural but are actually singular! When one of these words is the **subject**, the verb should be **singular**. Check out the table below for some common examples.

Singular Subjects	
anybody, anyone	group, family, audience, team, club
amount, number	nobody, no one
each	none
everybody, everyone	nothing, everything

both

The word **both** is always plural! It always implies two subjects!

Quiz

Identify the error (if present) in each of the following sentences.

1. The welcoming ceremony on the planet of the purple-skinned aliens reveal interesting details about their preferred forms of entertainment.

2. Whipped up by the wind, the waves rolling in against the rocky beach points to a storm off the coast.

3. If one of those sad, frowning clowns are walking around this town, I don't know what I'll do.

4. One of the ancient city's favorite attractions, the Cloisters, is known for an austere, stony beauty.

5. It turned out that my delicious bowl of oat and honey clusters have actually been tainted with raisins all along.

Answers

1. The welcoming **ceremony** ~~on the planet of the purple-skinned aliens~~ *reveals* interesting details about their preferred forms of entertainment.

2. Whipped up by the wind, the **waves** ~~rolling in against the rocky beach~~ *point* to a storm off the coast.

3. If **one** ~~of those sad, frowning clowns~~ *is* walking around this town, I don't know what I'll do.

4. *Correct!*

5. It turned out that my delicious **bowl** ~~of oat and honey clusters~~ *has* actually been tainted with raisins all along.

Practice Problems

Select the answer choice that produces the best sentence.

1

Nico, the world's most prolific writer of haiku poems, <u>are</u> inspired by his bonsai trees and model train collection.

A) NO CHANGE
B) is
C) being
D) DELETE the underlined portion.

2

Although the fishermen of the Red Reef <u>prefers</u> salmon to walleye, experts concur that walleye is the more delicious of the two fish.

A) NO CHANGE
B) prefer
C) preferring
D) has a greater preference for

3

The Da Vinci Code, the fourth of Dan Brown's byzantine and suspenseful thrillers, soon <u>were</u> the nation's most popular novel.

A) NO CHANGE
B) were recognized as
C) were seen as
D) was

4

The President, who recently authorized the Mutant Registration acts, <u>were</u> indicted for racketeering charges early this morning.

A) NO CHANGE
B) was
C) being
D) having been

5

The presentation by my esteemed colleagues <u>disregard</u> my extensive research on the subject.

A) NO CHANGE
B) disregarding
C) disregards
D) have disregarded

6

The old radio, as it plays a succession of the past decade's greatest hits, <u>take</u> us back to the past.

A) NO CHANGE
B) takes
C) are taking
D) have taken

7

Tonight at Lucy Lou's Watering Hole, the band Hot Sandal, the reigning band of the Tri-City's famous regional battle of the bands, <u>is playing</u>.

A) NO CHANGE
B) are playing
C) play
D) are going to be playing

8

The dusty old books that line the many shelves of the quiet library <u>is</u> filled with useful information on hunting vampires.

A) NO CHANGE
B) are
C) being
D) that is

9

My favorite restaurant in all of Lubbock, Texas <u>are going to be launching</u> a brand new taco.

A) NO CHANGE
B) is going to launch
C) having launched
D) are launching

10

Roger, who loves to remind us that "good fences make good neighbors," <u>mend</u> the fences on a regular basis.

A) NO CHANGE
B) are mending
C) have mended
D) mends

Pronoun Error

A pronoun is a word that takes the place of a noun. Pronouns can either be subjects or objects in a sentence.

Subject vs. Object Pronouns

Subjects are the doers in sentences; they **act**. Things happen to objects; they are **acted upon**. For example:

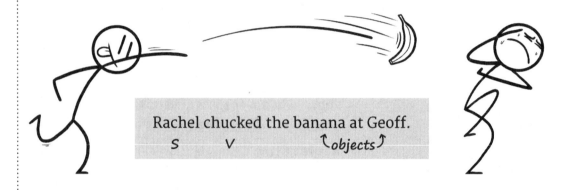

Rachel chucked the banana at Geoff.
S   V   ⌐objects⌐

Rachel is the subject; she is the one **acting** in the sentence. The banana and Geoff are objects; they are being **acted upon**. Now, let's replace Rachel, banana, and Geoff with pronouns.

She chucked it at him.
S   V   ⌐objects⌐

We would never say "her" chucked it to him, because "**her**" is an **object pronoun**. Similarly, we would never say "She chucked it at **he**" since you can never use a subject pronoun to replace an object in a sentence.

TIP

Prepositional phrases contain (1) prepositions and (2) **objects** of a preposition.

If your pronoun is the object of a preposition, it *must* be an **object pronoun**.

TIP

Never use an object pronoun to replace a subject, or a subject pronoun to replace an object.

Here's a handy chart in case you forget which pronouns are which:

Subject	Object
I	Me
You	You
He, She, It, Who	Him, Her, It, Whom
We	Us
They	Them

chuckers ... *receivers*

EXAMPLE 1

Our tour guide for the day was a friendly young woman <u>whom</u>, after showing us around the main academic buildings on campus, showed us some of her own favorite landmarks.

SOLUTION

Whom is an object pronoun – but is it being acted upon in the sentence? Looks like "whom" refers to the tour guide, and she is acting all over the place! She **shows** us the buildings, plus her favorite landmarks. We should replace whom with the subject pronoun **who**.

Our tour guide for the day was a friendly young woman <u>**who**</u>, after showing us around the main academic buildings on campus, showed us some of her own favorite landmarks.

The (Not-So) Difficult Case of I vs. Me

You might notice that people often aren't sure when to say "I" and when to say "me." But the rules are the same as with any other subject and object pronoun. **I** is a subject, and **me** is an object.

I do things. Things happen to **me**.
subject ... *object*

Remember: if the pronoun is the object of a preposition, **"me"** is correct.

EXAMPLE 2

In appreciation of all the hard work we did designing the set, the cast of *You're a Good Man, Charlie Brown* <u>threw a party for Joyce, Steve, and I</u>.

Let's cross out Joyce and Steve, and let our ears do all the work:

In appreciation of all the hard work we did designing the set, the cast of *You're a Good Man, Charlie Brown* <u>threw a party for ~~Joyce, Steve, and~~ I</u>.

The cast threw a party for **I**? That doesn't sound right! That's because "I" isn't doing the action in the sentence. The **cast** threw the party, not "I." We need the **object** pronoun **me**.

In appreciation of all the hard work we did designing the set, the cast of *You're a Good Man, Charlie Brown* <u>threw a party for Joyce, Steve, and **me**</u>.

Pronoun-Antecedent Agreement

A pronoun's antecedent is the word or words the pronoun replaces. If the antecedent is singular, the pronoun must be too: Emmylou chucked **the banana** to him becomes Emmylou chucked **it** to him. The SAT likes to trick you by using words that sound plural, but are really singular. Be on the lookout for pronouns that do not agree with their antecedents!

EXAMPLE 3

Every member of the football team <u>shaved their head</u> when the team won the game against its biggest rival.

TIP

When the SAT gives you a long list of names including "I" or "me", cross out everything but the pronoun. It will make it easier for your ear to guide you!

SOLUTION

Did every member shave **their** head? Do they share one head? **Every** is a singular word, so we can't use the plural pronoun **their** to replace it. We need the singular pronoun **his** or **her**.

Every member of the football team shaved his head when the team won the game against its biggest rival.

EXAMPLE 4

Because the U.S. Army anticipated only a brief engagement in Falluja, they only had enough supplies for 24 days of combat.

SOLUTION

The U.S. Army is a singular entity, a thing, an it. **It** takes the place of a singular noun.

Because the U.S. Army anticipated only a brief engagement in Falluja, **it** only had enough supplies for 24 days of combat.

EXAMPLE 5

Meteorologists have been studying comets for years, but they have only recently realized how varied in composition they can be.

SOLUTION

"They" is a plural pronoun, so it must have a plural antecedent. But here's the problem: we have **two** plural nouns in the sentence! Does "they" refer to the meteorologists, or the comets? Pronouns are handy, but not if they make the sentence more confusing. If it's unclear which word is the antecedent to your pronoun, ditch the pronoun altogether and repeat the noun.

Meteorologists have been studying comets for years, but they have only recently realized how varied in composition **comets** can be.

Sneaky Singular Words

Remember this list of singular words that seem plural:

anybody, anyone	nothing, everything
everybody, everyone	nobody, no one
each	none
either, neither	amount, number
group, family	audience, team, club

Quiz

Identify the error (if present) in each of the following sentences.

1. Over the course of the 40-week academic calendar, roughly three dozen students will take its turn as Most Popular Kid of the Third Grade.

2. Marjorie gained unlikely celebrity for her "Bouncing On Air" initiative, in which she trained adults whom had never learned to pogo properly.

3. The students in Ms. Odewabe's underwater basket weaving class have discovered working together heightens its creativity.

4. According to our calculations, Millie and me have spent more than $427 on our collection of super bouncy balls.

5. Just between you and I, Albie's new girlfriend is a compulsive liar: I saw that self-righteous vegetarian stuffing her face at Fat Matt's Rib Shack on Tuesday.

Answers

1. Over the course of the 40-week academic calendar, roughly three dozen students will take *their* turn as Most Popular Kid of the Third Grade.

2. Marjorie gained unlikely celebrity for her "Bouncing On Air" initiative, in which she trained adults *who* had never learned to pogo properly.

3. The students in Ms. Odewabe's underwater basket weaving class have discovered working together heightens *their* creativity.

4. According to our calculations, *Millie and I* have spent more than $427 on our collection of super bouncy balls.

5. Just between *you and me*, Albie's new girlfriend is a compulsive liar: I saw that self-righteous vegetarian stuffing her face at Fat Matt's Rib Shack on Tuesday.

Practice Problems

Select the answer choice that produces the best sentence.

....

1

Some of the biggest proponents of the myth that 2012 would bring the Mayan Apocalypse were those <u>whom believed</u> that an alien planet named Nibiru crosses paths with Earth every 3,600 years.

A) NO CHANGE
B) whom believes
C) who believed
D) who believes

2

Medical students are required to dissect human bodies—known as cadavers—during <u>one's</u> first year, usually in an anatomy lab.

A) NO CHANGE
B) their
C) his or her
D) our

3

When one of the many priceless paintings in the collection <u>were damaged, it</u> had to be taken to an art restoration expert.

A) NO CHANGE
B) were damaged, they
C) was damaged, it
D) was damaged, they

4

The Elephant Sanctuary hosts volunteers once a month; while <u>it is</u> not guaranteed contact with the animals, volunteers might get a glimpse of an elephant in her natural habitat.

A)   NO CHANGE
B)   one is
C)   he or she is
D)   they are

5

The bear's winter hideout—a warm, dry cave lined with a bed of leaves—keeps <u>them</u> safe during the snowy months of hibernation.

A)   NO CHANGE
B)   it
C)   one
D)   those

6

After that fateful night, a tense curtain fell between <u>my father and me</u>, one that was not lifted until many awkward dinners had passed.

A)   NO CHANGE
B)   my father and I
C)   my father and myself
D)   I and my father

7

Lesotho, famous for <u>their</u> beautiful mountainous landscape, joined 41 others countries in 2008 by signing the UN Convention on the Rights of Persons with Disabilities.

A) their
B) one's
C) it's
D) its

8

Music education—including band, orchestra, choir, and individual music lessons—promotes learning in other subjects, as <u>they help</u> children practice skills they will use in math and English class.

A) they help
B) they are helping
C) it helps
D) it will help

Writing Practice Passage 2
TO STAY ON PACE, YOUR TIMING GOAL IS 8.5 MINUTES

DIRECTIONS

Each passage below is accompanied by a number of questions. For some questions, you will consider how the passage might be revised to improve the expression of ideas. For other questions, you will consider how the passage might be edited to correct errors in sentence structure, usage, or punctuation. Each passage or a question may be accompanied by one or more graphics (such as a table or graph) that you will consider as you make revising and editing decisions.

Some questions will direct you to an underlined portion of the passage. Other questions will direct you to a location in a passage or ask you to think about the passage as a whole. After reading each passage, choose the answer to each question that most effectively improves the quality of writing in the passage or that makes the passage conform to the conventions of standard written English. Many questions include a "NO CHANGE" option. Choose that option if you think the best choice is to leave the relevant portion of the passage as it is.

Questions 1-11 are based on the following passage.

The Changing Roles of Women in Comics

Comics and graphic novels, though long considered commercial and lowbrow, nevertheless **1** possesses a uniquely American essence in their tales of heroism and their stylized depictions of daring exploits. At one time, they were a leading medium in science fiction and fantasy; then they fell out of favor. Now, the superhero stories that defined the classics of the genre **2** are being revived through "reboot" movies with fast-paced action scenes and dazzling set pieces. Meanwhile, with **3** there interest piqued by the movies, readers are returning to the genre, but many of them are looking for something beyond the same old, same old.

1
A) NO CHANGE
B) possess
C) possessed
D) will possess

2
A) NO CHANGE
B) is being revived
C) have been revived
D) were revived

3
A) NO CHANGE
B) their
C) they're
D) its

CONTINUE

233

Throughout comics' history, one factor has remained fairly constant: this has always been a boys' game. Comic books have mostly featured male heroes (Superman and Batman, anyone?), relegating any female characters to supporting roles. The majority of creators have also always been men, dating back to earlier parts of the 20th century when the creative fields were particularly unwelcoming to women.

Today, the lion's share of the comics industry is split by two major companies, Marvel and DC. While Marvel tends to stick to spandex-clad superheroes and more old-fashioned [4] fare, and DC has made some efforts to expand into more innovative, diverse territory. But even as [5] they shift focus, DC has not avoided missteps. In a 2011 major branding campaign titled "New 52," the company cancelled all [6] its existing comic book titles and launched 52 new titles. Some featured old favorites, while others introduced unfamiliar heroes. Executives hoped to present a fresh image and draw in a larger and more diverse audience. But the plan backfired when fans objected to the fact that the company was now working with even fewer female creators than before (the percentage dropped from 12% to just 1% of their overall staff). The backlash against this regressive decision manifested in protest activities around San Diego Comic [7] Con; the largest gathering of comic fans in the world. Fans launched a petition calling on the company to hire more female creators and presented a list of more than 120 female editors, artists, and writers—all with plenty of accomplishments and experience under their belts— [8] who DC could consider hiring for future projects. In response, [9] they delivered an official statement stating "We hear you," adding "we want these adventures to resonate in the real world, reflecting the experiences of our diverse readership."

[4]
A) NO CHANGE
B) fare; and
C) fare;
D) fare,

[5]
A) NO CHANGE
B) they will shift
C) it shifts
D) it shifted

[6]
A) NO CHANGE
B) it's
C) one's
D) their

[7]
A) NO CHANGE
B) Con, it is the
C) Con, the
D) Con. The

[8]
A) NO CHANGE
B) whose
C) whom
D) who,

[9]
A) NO CHANGE
B) it delivers
C) they will deliver
D) the company delivered

CONTINUE ➡

But while female comics creators may have been snubbed by the big two firms, **10** there is plenty of female creators thriving with indie companies. Some of the most groundbreaking and lauded works to emerge in recent years are so off the well-trod ground of superheroes, that some people might not think of them as comics at all. For example, Marjane Satrapi's autobiographical novel *Persepolis*, an innovative and gripping work depicting her Iranian childhood and teenage **11** years received international acclaim and was adapted into an Academy award-nominated animated film in 2007.

10

A) NO CHANGE
B) there are
C) there will be
D) there being

11

A) NO CHANGE
B) years, received
C) years, receives
D) years—received

STOP

If you finish before time is called, you may check your work on this section only. Do not turn to any other section.

Possession

Who owns what? The key to possession is understanding the apostrophe and where it fits.

Possessive Nouns

In most cases, you simply add an **'s** to a noun to show ownership. However, when you do this to a word that already ends in an **s**, like **dogs's**, it looks and sounds terrible. So, the rulers of the English language decided you can just say **dogs'**. If you have a plural or singular noun that already ends in an **s**, simply pop in an apostrophe after the **s** to show ownership.

The dog's bone.

The dogs' bone.

When you see a noun followed by an apostrophe on the test, just ask yourself two questions:

1. **Does this noun own something?**

2. **Should the noun be singular or plural?**

EXAMPLE 1

Georgia's minimum sentences are defined by the <u>states criminal laws</u>, which are in turn determined by the legislature.

A) NO CHANGE
B) states' criminal laws'
C) state's criminal laws
D) state's criminal law's

SOLUTION

We're dealing with **two** possible possessions, so let's take them one at a time by asking our two questions:

   1) Does "**states**" own anything in the sentence?

Yes! It owns the **criminal laws**, so we need either *state's* or *states'* to show ownership. That lets us cross off A.

   2) Should "**states**" be singular or plural?

Georgia is only one state, so we need a singular possessive— **state's**. That lets us cross off B.

To help us choose between C and D, we need only ask one question: Does "laws" own anything in the sentence? Nope! So we don't need any apostrophe here. That leaves **C** as the only choice that gets it right:

Georgia's minimum sentences are defined by the <u>**state's criminal laws**</u>, which are in turn determined by the legislature.

Possessive Pronouns

The SAT wants to make sure you know when to use a possessive pronoun and when to use a *contraction*. Possessive pronouns like *its*, *your*, *whose*, and *their* **do not use** an apostrophe. If you see an apostrophe, you've got a contraction on your hands!

Check out the handy-dandy table below to help you keep your possessives and contractions straight.

Possessive	Contraction
its	it's (it is)
their	they're (they are)
your	you're (you are)
whose	who's (who is)

EXAMPLE 2

The French horn players have long suspected that the flautists fill their horns with Gatorade before the halftime shows, ruining <u>they're</u> melodious music.

A)   NO CHANGE
B)   their
C)   there
D)   it's

They're has an apostrophe, so it's a *contraction*. Do we want to say "ruining they are melodious music?" That's nonsense! We need to show **ownership**, since the French horn players own the melodious music. That means we need to use **their**, the possessive pronoun. The answer is **B**:

The French horn players have long suspected that the flautists fill their horns with Gatorade before the halftime show, ruining **<u>their</u>** melodious music.

PORTAL

Possession questions often get thrown in with **Pronoun Error** questions. For a refresher on pronoun rules, turn to page 224.

EXAMPLE 3

Despite <u>its</u> long history as a haunted house, the Shrieking Shack has become the most popular venue for high school proms.

A) NO CHANGE
B) it's
C) their
D) they're

Does "it" own anything? Yes, it owns the "long history!" **Its** shows ownership... but so does **their**. How do we know which to choose? Remember your Pronoun rules: singular pronouns refer to singular nouns, and plural pronouns refer to plural nouns. **It** refers to the **Shrieking Shack**; the shack has a long history as a haunted house. Since the antecedent is singular, we need a **singular** pronoun. Our answer is **A**!

Despite <u>its</u> long history as a haunted house, the Shrieking Shack has become the most popular venue for high school proms.

Quiz

Identify the error (if present) in each of the following sentences.

1. Because of there teachers severe case of the Mondays, the students watched the seminal film *Bring It On* during English class today.

2. It is Jacob's responsibility to clean the microscope's lenses' once a week.

3. Scientific studies have expanded our knowledge about the brains' ability to heal itself after a traumatic injury.

4. Known for their distinctive tuxedos, penguins are the cutest animals in Antarctica.

5. When your at the end of you're rope, try eating your weight in peanut butter and jelly sandwiches.

Answers

1. Because of *their teacher's* severe case of the Mondays, the students watched the seminal film *Bring It On* during English class today.

2. It is Jacob's responsibility to clean the microscope's *lenses* once a week.

3. Scientific studies have expanded our knowledge about the *brain's* ability to heal itself after a traumatic injury.

4. *Correct!*

5. When *you're* at the end of *your* rope, try eating your weight in peanut butter and jelly sandwiches.

Practice Problems

Select the answer choice that produces the best sentence.

1

On <u>Baghdads</u> busiest commercial avenue, I encountered people driving in shiny BMWs and riding on donkeys.

A) NO CHANGE
B) Baghdads'
C) Baghdad's
D) Badghdad its

2

<u>Babies</u> first attempts at speech often generate excited responses from adults, but that's no excuse for my aunt's behavior this weekend.

A) NO CHANGE
B) Baby's
C) Babys
D) Babies'

3

Carrie, one of <u>Stephen King's most famous novels</u>, is the story of a high school misfit with unusual abilities.

A) NO CHANGE
B) Stephen Kings most famous novels
C) Stephen King's most famous novel's
D) Stephen King's most famous novels'

4

Over a casual game of cards, the astronauts reminisced fondly about <u>their many adventure's</u> back in the old days.

A) NO CHANGE
B) there many adventures'
C) their many adventures
D) they're many adventures

5

Everyone claims that the old house at the end of the block is haunted, but <u>its reluctant to give up its</u> secrets.

A) NO CHANGE
B) it's reluctant to give up it's
C) its reluctant to give up it's
D) it's reluctant to give up its

6

After dinner, I heard one of <u>my guest's comment</u>, "That was the most delicious peach cobbler I've ever tasted!"

A) NO CHANGE
B) my guests' comment,
C) my guests comment,
D) my guests had commented,

7

Like brass, <u>it's</u> closest metallic counterpart, bronze is primarily made of copper, with the addition of 12% tin to increase durability.

A) NO CHANGE
B) its
C) their
D) there

8

The runaway greenhouse effect may have led to devastating results on Venus, creating so much heat that <u>they're</u> oceans boiled and evaporated.

A) NO CHANGE
B) their
C) it's
D) its

9

Fully aware of <u>their</u> potential for disaster, Karen decided against incorporating brown and black food coloring into her cake.

A) NO CHANGE
B) they're
C) there
D) its

10

Guidance counselors recommend considering class size, location, and financial aid opportunities when <u>your picking</u> a college or university.

A) NO CHANGE
B) you're picking
C) your pick
D) you're choosing to pick

Parallelism

To keep your sentences flowing, use parallelism! Stick with the same structure in a list, and only compare similar things.

Parallel Lists

All items in a list must be the same part of speech, whether they are nouns, adjectives, adverbs, or verbs. If your list contains only verbs, each verb must be the same tense.

EXAMPLE 1

A talented and versatile artist, Steve Martin has <u>been a comedian, a playwright, and directed</u> several Hollywood films.

SOLUTION

Let's take a closer look at this list:

… Steve Martin has <u>been a comedian, a playwright, and directed</u>
                        noun   *noun*   *verb*
several Hollywood films.

Obey your parallel structure rules: when you see a list, make sure all the items are the same part of speech. We need to change that pesky **verb** into a **noun** to maintain parallelism!

A talented and versatile artist, Steve Martin has <u>been a comedian,</u>
                                                                noun

<u>a playwright, and **a director of**</u> several Hollywood films.
noun   *noun*

Parallel Structure

What if our list gets more complicated? Many times, items in lists are more than one word, like "in the treehouse" or "changing her name." In that case, your job is to match the **structure** of each item. Does each item in your list start with a preposition? Keep the same structure for the next item, and cut out any words that don't fit into the structure.

EXAMPLE 2

By the Cenozoic era, mammals had proliferated throughout the newly-formed grasslands, swinging from trees, walking through fields, and <u>they were tunneling</u> under the ground.

SOLUTION

First, let's check the structure of the first two list items:

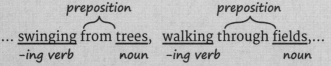

... <u>swinging</u> from <u>trees</u>, <u>walking</u> through <u>fields</u>,...

The last item should keep the structure **parallel**, so we can get rid of "they were." It doesn't fit the list's structure!

By the Cenozoic era, mammals had proliferated throughout the newly-formed grasslands, swinging from trees, walking through fields, and **tunneling** under the ground.

KEEP IT PARALLEL

Parallel Comparisons

While it's often said that you can't compare apples and oranges, it's fair game on the SAT! You can always compare similar things: a fruit to a fruit, a person to a person, or a country to a country. You can **not** compare a fruit to a country. The SAT writers will try to trick you into comparing two things that are not similar at all. Here's an example:

EXAMPLE 3

Because they often used their work as a means of social or political protest rather than as an exercise in aesthetics, many 20th century artists <u>differed from earlier times</u>.

A) NO CHANGE
B) differing from earlier times
C) differed from that in earlier times
D) differed from artists of earlier times

SOLUTION

What are we comparing in this sentence? Take a look:

...many 20th century <u>artists</u> differed from <u>earlier times</u>
          people   *time period*

Artists from one time period may be different from artists from another time period; for example, Impressionists were very different from Cubists. We could also compare one time period to another; the Middle Ages differed from the Renaissance. Both of those are **parallel comparisons.** But we **cannot** compare artists to time periods. Those are very different things! A and B both compare artists to times, so we can cross them out.

C gives us a singular pronoun "that," but the antecedent is the plural "artists." Only **D** compares artists to artists with no other errors.

Because they often used their work as a means of social or political protest rather than as an exercise in aesthetics, many 20th century artists **differed from artists of earlier times**.

EXAMPLE 4

Students at the University of Chicago often use Internet databases for research because these databases are easier to use than <u>those who use</u> traditional print sources.

A) NO CHANGE
B) the use of
C) using
D) DELETE the underlined portion

SOLUTION

Let's check our comparison!

...these <u>databases</u> are easier to use than <u>those</u> who use traditional
thing   **vs.**   *people*
print sources.

Comparing things to people is not parallel! Because "databases" is a thing, we need a choice that compares it to another thing. We can cross out both A (thing vs. person) and C (thing vs. verb). Choice B creates a confusing redundancy: "databases are easier to use than the use of traditional print sources..."

We can communicate the same idea in a much less awkward way if we just DELETE the underlined portion. That way, we're comparing databases (thing) to sources (thing). Let's go with choice **D**:

Students at the University of Chicago often use Internet databases for research because these databases are easier to use than traditional print sources.

Quiz

Identify the error (if present) in each of the following sentences.

1. My roommate, a librarian with a passion for organization, believes she can create a cataloging system as complex as Melvil Dewey.

2. My mother thinks Larry and his brother Daryl are great catches because they are hard workers, good drivers, and dance beautifully.

3. The Sumatran tiger, the smallest subspecies of tiger in the world, is critically endangered because of illegal poaching, its habitat being destroyed, and low birth rates.

4. Geraldine's blind date was the funniest man she'd ever met, and her favorite hobbies, knitting and skydiving, were similar to him.

5. Many of our university's philosophy students are believers in political anarchy, rebel against contemporary conventions, and the power of individual thought.

Answers:

1. My roommate, a librarian with a passion for organization, believes she can create a cataloging system as complex as *Melvil Dewey's system.*

2. My mother thinks Larry and his brother Daryl are great catches because they are hard workers, good drivers, and *beautiful dancers.*

3. The Sumatran tiger, the smallest subspecies of tiger in the world, is critically endangered because of illegal poaching, *habitat destruction*, and low birth rates.

4. Geraldine's blind date was the funniest man she'd ever met, and her favorite hobbies, knitting and skydiving, were similar to *his (hobbies).*

5. Many of our university's philosophy students are believers in political anarchy, *rebellion* against contemporary conventions, and the power of individual thought.

Practice Problems

Select the answer choice that produces the best sentence.

1

Sacagawea was an integral part of Lewis and Clark's expedition; she served as the group's Shoshone interpreter, advised on local edible plants, and <u>she provided</u> invaluable knowledge of Western geography, leading the men through a previously unknown pass in the Rocky Mountains.

A) NO CHANGE
B) provided
C) providing
D) provides

2

Because of the injury to her head, Suzanne could neither <u>play ice hockey</u> nor be a dancer.

A) NO CHANGE
B) have been an ice hockey player
C) be playing ice hockey
D) be an ice hockey player

3

Eliana's car is covered with stickers, with a "Hogwarts School of Witchcraft and Wizardry" sticker below the antenna, an "I Hate Mondays" sticker next to the windshield wiper, and <u>an "I Love Corgis" sticker in the middle of the bumper.</u>

A) NO CHANGE
B) an "I Love Corgis" sticker is in the middle of the bumper.
C) the bumper has an "I Love Corgis" sticker in the middle.
D) the bumper, in the middle of it, has an "I Love Corgis" sticker.

4

My biology teacher firmly believes that Rosalyn Franklin's work, unlike <u>collaborators Francis Crick and James Watson</u>, was integral to discovering the structure of DNA.

A) NO CHANGE
B) that of collaborators Francis Crick and James Watson
C) those of collaborators Francis Crick and James Watson
D) these of collaborators Francis Crick and James Watson

5

To become an expert fly fisherman, you must learn to cast a line, read the water, and <u>tying</u> a fly to use as bait.

A) NO CHANGE
B) to tie
C) how to tie
D) tie

6

When it comes to buying asparagus, the greenest, <u>thick, and longest</u> stalks are usually the best.

A) NO CHANGE
B) thickest, and they are the longest
C) thickest, and longest
D) thickest, and long

7

Mr. Sideburns' mutant powers allow him to regenerate his health, use super-human force, and <u>he reads people's minds.</u>

A) NO CHANGE
B) he will read people's minds.
C) reading people's minds.
D) read people's minds.

8

Street artist Invader's handiwork can be seen all over the streets of Paris: on the sides of buildings, on highway overpasses, and even <u>located on</u> the iconic blue street signs.

A) NO CHANGE
B) on
C) it is located on
D) DELETE the underlined portion.

9

Since I learned to play the drums, I have been scaring off neighborhood dogs who are terrified of the noises coming from my basement, as well as <u>freaked</u> out neighbors.

A) NO CHANGE
B) freak
C) freaking
D) have freaked

10

In the world of soccer, there is no story more inspirational than <u>Brazil's national hero, Pelé.</u>

A) NO CHANGE

B) Pelé, who is Brazil's national hero.

C) that of Brazil's national hero, Pelé.

D) Brazil's national hero, being Pelé.

Misplaced Modifier

Some phrases act as adjectives, describing—or modifying—the closest noun or pronoun in the sentence. If the modifier is next to the wrong noun or pronoun, the sentence can get a bit silly.

When a modifier is misplaced, strange things can happen. Your job is to figure out which noun or pronoun the modifier should be modifying, and put the phrase next to that noun or pronoun.

EXAMPLE 1

Ripping through her street, Emily was terrified of the tornado.

SOLUTION

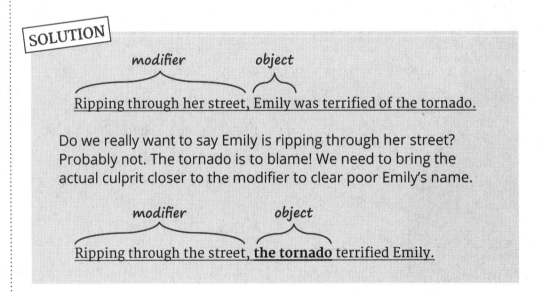

        modifier   object

Ripping through her street, Emily was terrified of the tornado.

Do we really want to say Emily is ripping through her street? Probably not. The tornado is to blame! We need to bring the actual culprit closer to the modifier to clear poor Emily's name.

        modifier   object

Ripping through the street, **the tornado** terrified Emily.

TIP

First, identify the modifier and see if it is acting appropriately. If not, look for the word that **should** be next to the modifier.

EXAMPLE 2

Timmy found his stray gerbil cleaning his room.

SOLUTION

How did Timmy train his gerbil to clean his room? That *would* be impressive, but it's much more likely that **Timmy**, not his gerbil, was cleaning his room. Remember, place your modifier **next** to the noun doing the action.

While cleaning his room, Timmy found his stray gerbil.

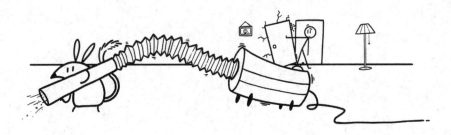

EXAMPLE 3

Loved for their small size and chipper dispositions, more and more people are breeding Chiweenies, which are Chihuahua and Dachshund mixes.

SOLUTION

It has been said that owners begin to look like their pets after they have lived together for many years. Even so, it's doubtful the **people** that breed these dogs are loved for their small size and chipper dispositions. More likely, the modifier was meant to refer to the little **Chiweenies** themselves.

More and more people are breeding Chiweenies, Chihuahua and Dachshund mixes, loved for their small size and chipper dispositions.

253

EXAMPLE 4

Flying out the window, Naomi spotted her errant parrot.

Do we even need to address this? Unless Naomi is secretly Supergirl from Krypton, it was the errant parrot that was flying out the window.

Naomi spotted her errant parrot flying out the window.

Quiz

Identify the error (if present) in each of the following sentences.

1. Leaning too closely to her birthday candles, Eunice's hair burst into flames.

2. Last Halloween, our dentist passed out toothbrushes dressed as Napoleon Bonaparte instead of candy.

3. Harold tripped over his pet turtle dancing across his room.

4. The spy plane spotted our secret hideout flying through the sky.

5. Running through the woods to escape Sasquatch, the brambles tore Ida's skirt.

Answers

1. *Eunice's hair burst into flames while she was leaning too closely to her birthday candles.*

2. Last Halloween, our dentist, *dressed as Napoleon Bonaparte, passed out toothbrushes instead of candy.*

3. *Dancing across his room*, Harold tripped over his pet turtle.

4. *Flying through the sky*, the spy plane spotted our secret hideout.

5. *The brambles tore Ida's skirt as she was running through the woods to escape Sasquatch.*

Practice Problems

Select the answer choice that produces the best sentence.

1

Prized for their rarity, collectors will pay thousands
of dollars for Baccarat perfume bottles designed by
Salvador Dali.

A) NO CHANGE
B) Collectors will pay thousands of dollars, prized for their
   rarity, for Baccarat perfume bottles designed by
   Salvador Dali.
C) Designed by Salvador Dali, collectors will pay
   thousands of dollars for Baccarat perfume bottles,
   prized for their rarity.
D) Collectors will pay thousands of dollars for Baccarat
   perfume bottles, prized for their rarity and designed by
   Salvador Dali.

2

Finding his sister's diary fascinating, all the pages were
read thoroughly by Horatio.

A) NO CHANGE
B) Horatio thoroughly read all the pages.
C) thoroughly all the pages were read by Horatio.
D) its pages were all read thoroughly by Horatio.

3

We believe we have found Amelia Earhart's crashed
Lockheed 10E exploring the Pacific Ocean off the coast of
New Britain Island near New Guinea.

A) NO CHANGE
B) While exploring the Pacific Ocean, we believe we have
   found Amelia Earhart's crashed Lockheed 10E
C) Exploring the Pacific Ocean, Amelia Earhart's crashed
   Lockheed 10E was, we believe, found
D) Amelia Earhart's crashed Lockheed 10E was found, we
   believe, exploring the Pacific Ocean

4

Soaked in rum and set aflame, diners were impressed by the exotic bananas foster served at the popular Florida restaurant.

A) NO CHANGE
B) Diners were impressed, soaked in rum and set aflame, by the exotic bananas foster served
C) The exotic bananas foster impressed diners, soaked in rum and set aflame
D) Soaked in rum and set aflame, the exotic bananas foster impressed diners

5

Enjoying the spring day, the laundry was hung out to dry as the maid sang folk songs from her childhood.

A) NO CHANGE
B) the maid hung the laundry out to dry and
C) the maid hanging laundry out to dry and
D) the laundry being hung out to dry by the maid who

Writing Practice Passage 3
TO STAY ON PACE, YOUR TIMING GOAL IS 8.5 MINUTES

DIRECTIONS

Each passage below is accompanied by a number of questions. For some questions, you will consider how the passage might be revised to improve the expression of ideas. For other questions, you will consider how the passage might be edited to correct errors in sentence structure, usage, or punctuation. Each passage or a question may be accompanied by one or more graphics (such as a table or graph) that you will consider as you make revising and editing decisions.

Some questions will direct you to an underlined portion of the passage. Other questions will direct you to a location in a passage or ask you to think about the passage as a whole. After reading each passage, choose the answer to each question that most effectively improves the quality of writing in the passage or that makes the passage conform to the conventions of standard written English. Many questions include a "NO CHANGE" option. Choose that option if you think the best choice is to leave the relevant portion of the passage as it is.

Questions 1-11 are based on the following passage.

The Jungle

The Jungle, published in 1905, tells the story of Lithuanian immigrant Jurgis Rudkus and his young wife Ona. **1** The newlyweds settle in Chicago where Jurgis gets a job at the meatpacking plant, full of ambition and hope for the future. But their dreams are dashed by one misfortune after another; swindlers and predatory lenders take advantage of their naive attitude and lack of literacy, plunging them further into poverty. Jurgis' job is grueling and unsafe, and he cannot provide enough to support the family. Eventually, after sinking completely into disillusionment and despair, Jurgis discovers the socialist movement and **2** he finds new purpose.

1

A) NO CHANGE
B) The newlyweds settle in Chicago where Jurgis, getting a job at the meatpacking plant, full of ambition and hope for the future.
C) The newlyweds settle in Chicago, full of ambition and hope for the future, where Jurgis gets a job at the meatpacking plant.
D) Full of ambition and hope for the future, the newlyweds settle in Chicago where Jurgis gets a job at the meatpacking plant.

2

A) NO CHANGE
B) finds
C) finding
D) found

CONTINUE ▶

The Jungle was primarily a work of political persuasion. [3] Its author, Upton Sinclair, hoped to write a book that would illustrate in vivid imagery the flaws of capitalism. Sinclair wanted to expose the plight of the impoverished in his society. Believing that the capitalist impulse of profit at all costs made life unbearable for those at the bottom of the heap, [4] the book was envisioned as a compelling argument for socialism.

However, despite Sinclair's impassioned plea on behalf of the poor, it was actually his description of the slaughterhouse that made the strongest impression on the public. His seven weeks of undercover research had provided him with some memorable horror stories. *The Jungle* included revolting descriptions of rats being ground into sausage, offal being swept off the floor and made into tinned lunchmeat, and rusty nails and dirty water [5] were dumped into the grinder. Instead of being appalled at the sordid lives and [6] mistreating cruelty of workers, the American readership was outraged by the thought of tainted meat in their grocery stores. As Sinclair himself ruefully described it, "I aimed at the public's heart, and by accident I hit it in the stomach."

3

A) NO CHANGE
B) It's
C) Their
D) There

4

A) NO CHANGE
B) the book is envisioned
C) he envisioned the book
D) and he envisioned the book

5

A) NO CHANGE
B) which were dumped
C) being dumped
D) that were being dumped

6

A) NO CHANGE
B) cruelly mistreat
C) cruel mistreating
D) cruel mistreatment

CONTINUE

The book reached readers at the height of a protracted political battle about the [7] government's responsibilities' to regulate food and medicine. Better food standards, according to the U.S. Bureau of Chemistry, [8] was necessary for public health. Others in the food industry claimed such regulations would restrict the economy and significantly diminish profits. Then-President Theodore Roosevelt read *The Jungle* and found himself as disgusted as his constituents. He decided to send two men to inspect the meatpacking plants and investigate Sinclair's allegations, instructing them to keep [9] their findings confidential. Their report substantiated nearly all of Sinclair's allegations. Despite [10] Roosevelts desires to keep the findings private, the public clamored to see the report and demanded immediate action. That summer, Congress passed the Pure Food and Drug Act of 1906, making the sale of adulterated or misbranded foods and medicines illegal. The legislation also established new regulatory powers for the Bureau of Chemistry, [11] in 1930 it became known as the Food and Drug Administration.

7

A) NO CHANGE
B) government's responsibilities
C) governments' responsibility's
D) governments responsibilities

8

A) NO CHANGE
B) is
C) were
D) had been

9

A) NO CHANGE
B) their finding's
C) there finding's
D) there findings

10

A) NO CHANGE
B) Roosevelts desire's
C) Roosevelts' desires'
D) Roosevelt's desire

11

A) NO CHANGE
B) in 1930, it, became
C) which in 1930 became
D) which, in 1930 became,

STOP

If you finish before time is called, you may check your work on this section only.
Do not turn to any other section.

Redundancy

Redundancy errors involve saying the same thing several times or unnecessarily defining an obvious idea.

Repetition Redundancy

Often, the SAT writers will unnecessarily repeat or rephrase an idea. When you are solving redundancy questions, cross off answer choices that repeat information already given in the sentence.

Cross off the redundant word or phrase in the following sentences. The first two are done for you.

1. I studied ~~and prepared~~ for the test.

2. Initially this product was ~~first~~ offered in May.

3. I do my annual taxes every year.

4. It was a confusingly bewildering outcome.

5. Frequently, underprepared students often do poorly on exams.

6. The queen offered renewed inspiration all over again.

7. There was a recent increase in migration over the last few years.

8. At a future date, the winners will later receive confirmation.

9. Over many months, as time went by, my puppy grew.

Answers: *3. annual/every year 4. confusingly/bewildering 5. frequently/often 6. renewed/all over again 7. recent/over the last few years 8. at a future date/ later 9. over many months/as time went by*

delete

Note the power of DELETE!

In redundancy problems, when **DELETE** is a choice, it is almost always the correct answer!

EXAMPLE 1

The results of the soil tests indicated a chemical problem that threatened to postpone <u>and delay</u> the construction of the building.

A) NO CHANGE
B) to a later date
C) by delaying
D) DELETE the underlined portion

SOLUTION

Three of the four choices fail to fix the redundancy in the sentence. We don't need a synonym of postpone such as **later**, **delay** or **delaying**. The correct answer is the shortest and simplest option: **D**

The results of the soil tests indicated a chemical problem that threatened to postpone the construction of the building.

EXAMPLE 2

The choreographers decided that their work needed to <u>reflect and show the multiple, numerous</u> abilities of the ensemble dance troupe.

A) NO CHANGE
B) reflect and show the multiple
C) mirror and reflect the numerous
D) reflect the numerous

SOLUTION

This question gives us not one, but **two** redundancies! We can eliminate answer choices that fail to fix either one of our redundancies. This actually makes it much easier for us. The only choice that trims the fat on both ends is **choice D:**

The choreographers decided that their work needed to **reflect the numerous** abilities of the ensemble dance troupe.

Definition Redundancy

Frequently, the SAT will give you a word and then define it, creating a redundancy. Again, your job is simply to get rid of the redundancy. Once is enough!

Cross off the redundant word or phrase in the following sentences. The first one is done for you.

1. The criminal, ~~who had broken the law,~~ was tried in court.

2. I am looking for my canine dog.

3. I was trapped in a congested traffic jam.

4. She used an artificial preservative that was not natural.

5. He traversed the lush, sloping hill.

Answers: 2. canine/dog 3. congested 4. artificial/that was not natural 5. sloping

EXAMPLE 3

Billy walked up onto the <u>grass-covered lawn</u>.

A) NO CHANGE
B) mowed, grass-covered lawn
C) grass-covered, lawn
D) lawn

Lawns, by definition, are grass-covered, so choices A, B, and C are all redundant. That means choice **D is our answer:**

Billy walked up onto the <u>lawn</u>.

EXAMPLE 4

My new job opportunity <u>may or may not offer</u> valuable training and connections to enhance my career development.

A) NO CHANGE
B) might offer
C) could provide important and
D) might indeed provide one with

SOLUTION

In this case, our trickiest answer choice is C. It solves for the may or may not redundancy but opens up a brand new redundancy with **important** and **valuable**. Sneaky! And incorrect. Our correct answer is short and sweet: **B**.

My new job opportunity <u>**might offer**</u> valuable training and connections to enhance my career development.

Quiz

Identify the error (if present) in each of the following sentences.

1. I stopped at the bank, a local financial institution, to withdraw some cash for my date.

2. For years, Melinda refused to go to bed; she'd yell and shout and raise her voice while beating her fists on the pillow.

3. The eccentric neighbor turned out to be writing a novel that was a book about a fisherman who catches a magical fish.

4. The dream involved a terrifying figure, who was very frightening, looking in my windows repeatedly.

5. By the time he was 7, Samuel was actually very tall for his age and not short.

Answers

1. I stopped at the *local bank* to withdraw some cash for my date.

2. For years, Melinda refused to go to bed; she'd *yell* while beating her fists on the pillow.

3. The eccentric neighbor turned out to be writing *a novel* about a fisherman who catches a magical fish.

4. The dream involved a *terrifying figure* looking in my windows repeatedly.

5. By the time he was 7, Samuel was actually very *tall* for his age.

Practice Problems

Select the answer choice that produces the best sentence.

1

I was seated next to him at a friend's wedding; he seemed pleased that I'd read his <u>book of which he was the author.</u>

A) NO CHANGE
B) book by him.
C) book that he'd written.
D) book.

2

This little dog is such a good boy that I believe he should get a <u>treat to have.</u>

A) NO CHANGE
B) treat that he would enjoy.
C) treat that would be enjoyable for him.
D) treat.

3

He wrote a letter in which he <u>explained</u> that he would do everything he could to help.

A) NO CHANGE
B) carefully made clear and explained
C) put into words and explained
D) communicated a clarifying explanation

4

<u>At first to begin with, Marshall</u> believed that he'd discovered the hamburger of which he'd dreamed for so long.

A) NO CHANGE
B) At first, Marshall
C) At first in the beginning, Marshall
D) At first, Marshall initially

5

She told the <u>class of students</u> that she was impressed with all of its good ideas.

A) NO CHANGE
B) class of pupils
C) class
D) class of learners

6

Houseplants aren't for everyone, but during the winter <u>a collection of multiple</u> vibrant green plants can create a more cheerful environment.

A) NO CHANGE
B) a collection of various assorted
C) a collection of several different
D) a collection of

7

Griselda decided she'd had enough; it was time to begin <u>demanding</u> better treatment.

A) NO CHANGE
B) demanding and requesting
C) requiring and insisting upon
D) insistently requesting her demand for

8

When the casting list was posted, Terry was devastated to discover <u>the information that</u> his name was missing.

A) NO CHANGE
B) that
C) the fact that
D) the piece of news that

Prepositions

A.k.a "Because we said so."

Some questions simply test common use of prepositions. For example:

> - **We DO say:** "Working nights and weekends is not consistent with my beliefs."
> - **We DON'T say:** "Working nights and weekends is not consistent to my beliefs."

The reason the correct answers are correct boils down to *"Because that's just how it's said,"* which, let's face it, is just about the worst explanation parents or teachers can give a well-intentioned student such as yourself.

But here's some good news: If you like to read books, articles, blogs, comics, or all of the above, these questions will be pretty easy. And if you are not a big reader... well, there aren't many of these on the test anyway, and you've still heard and seen these expressions your whole life.

Either way, your job here is simply to **trust your ear**. You've heard the *correct* preposition more than you've heard any of the *wrong* ones, so the correct answer is usually the one that sounds the best.

TIP

Try whispering the different choices to yourself. Pick the choice that feels the most natural.

EXAMPLE 1

My neighbor Ben Dover will never forgive his parents <u>about</u> their terrible choice in naming him.

A) NO CHANGE
B) with
C) from
D) for

SOLUTION

If you read this sentence out loud, your ear should tell you something is wrong with the preposition. The word **forgive** is always paired with the preposition **for**. That's just the way it is!

My neighbor Ben Dover will never forgive his parents <u>for</u> their terrible choice in naming him.

EXAMPLE 2

Many urban condominiums favor an open floor plan as a means <u>through</u> maximizing liveable space in an otherwise small area.

A) NO CHANGE
B) from
C) of
D) DELETE the underlined portion of the sentence.

SOLUTION

Once again, your ears should be burning right about now! Open floor plans could be a means **of** maximizing space. They could even be a means **to** maximize space. But they can never be a means *through* maximizing space.

Many urban condominiums favor an open floor plan as a means <u>of</u> maximizing liveable space in an otherwise small area.

Here are some common verb/preposition pairs you might see on the test. You don't need to memorize these to answer the questions correctly; instead, trust your ear and go with the most familiar pairing.

verb	preposition
abide	by
accuse	of
agree	to/with/on/upon
apologize	for
apply	to/for
approve	of
argue	with/about/over
arrive	at
believe	in
blame	for
care	about/for
charge	for/with
compare	with/to
complain	about/of/to
consist	of
contribute	to
count	upon/on
cover	with
decide	upon/on
depend	upon/on
differ	about/from/over/with
discriminate	against
distinguish	from/between
dream	of/about
escape	from

verb	preposition
excel	in
excuse	for
forget	about
forgive	for
hide	from
hope	for
insist	upon/on
object	to
participate	in
prevent	from
prohibit	from
protect	against/from
provide	for/with
recover	from
rely	upon/on
rescue	from
respond	to/with
stare	at
stop	from
subscribe	to
substitute	for
succeed	in
thank	for
vote	for/on/against
wait	for/on
worry	about

Quiz

Identify the error (if present) in each of the following sentences.

1. Born in the South, Dixie has suffered with terrible teasing about her accent by her fellow classmates in New York.

2. After further investigation, it appears that Samson falsely accused Delilah with chopping off his luscious locks.

3. Three weeks after his parents suspended his allowance and in desperate need of funds, Rigoberto finally realized he needed a summer job and applied at Ed's World of Twinkies.

4. Despite the objections of their families to their union, Tyrone and Pamela succeeded with getting married in a private ceremony last month.

5. Ten years in the making, his new skyscraper is both a response to a dramatic change in popular aesthetics and to his critics' dislike with his earlier buildings.

Answers

1. Born in the South, Dixie has suffered *from* terrible teasing about her accent by her fellow classmates in New York.

2. After further investigation, it appears that Samson falsely accused Delilah *of* chopping off his luscious locks.

3. Three weeks after his parents suspended his allowance and in desperate need of funds, Rigoberto finally realized he needed a summer job and applied *to* Ed's World of Twinkies.

4. Despite the objections of their families to their union, Tyrone and Pamela succeeded *in* getting married in a private ceremony last month.

5. Ten years in the making, his new skyscraper is both a response to a dramatic change in popular aesthetics and to his critics' dislike *of* his earlier buildings.

Practice Problems

Select the answer choice that produces the best sentence.

1

My younger brother's opinions on everything differ so greatly <u>with</u> mine that it is hard to believe we are even related.

A) NO CHANGE
B) to
C) from
D) against

2

Tired of his neighbor's cats invading his property and falling asleep inside his garage, Orlando finally succeeded <u>in</u> keeping them away by gluing a strongly-worded note to an unlucky orange tabby.

A) NO CHANGE
B) with
C) to
D) at

3

The term "silkscreening" comes from a 19th century technique <u>for which</u> specific parts of a screen of porous fiber, silk or polyester, are blocked off with non-permeable material to create a stencil to be inked onto cloth or paper.

A) NO CHANGE
B) whereby
C) to which
D) on which

4

After a heated argument between the vegetarians and the omnivores at the table, we agreed everyone should have the <u>right for ordering</u> what he or she desires.

A) NO CHANGE
B) right of ordering
C) right to order
D) right ordering

5

Hester hid her favorite book of household wizardry spells in the freezer, where she would have easy access <u>of</u> it whenever she ran into any complications in the kitchen.

A) NO CHANGE
B) by
C) with
D) to

6

Citrus fruits are well known for their high levels of Vitamin C, but many other fruits, including bell peppers and strawberries, can serve <u>to be</u> excellent sources of Vitamin C.

A) NO CHANGE
B) from
C) as
D) like

7

While visiting the Waitomo Caves in New Zealand, the tour guide told a Maori folk tale <u>when</u> the origin of the caves' famous glowworms.

A) NO CHANGE
B) about
C) for
D) to

8

Participants in taste tests found only minor differences <u>to</u> Diet Coke and Coke Zero.

A) NO CHANGE
B) between
C) than
D) from

9

My grandmother's sweet potato pie recipe pales <u>in</u> comparison to Abdul's, probably because he doubles the sugar.

A) NO CHANGE
B) with
C) by
D) to

10

Zoltan's sunny disposition is inconsistent <u>to</u> the neo-gothic clothing he wears to the mall.

A) NO CHANGE
B) about
C) against
D) with

Vocabulary in Context

When it comes to vocabulary on the SAT, context is everything! Choose the word that best fits the context of the sentence.

TIP

Think about where you might have heard the word before to give you a clue. For example, you might have heard "decreed" in an episode of *Game of Thrones*, or "apprehended" on *Law and Order*.

These context clues can point you in the right direction!

Sometimes, you'll encounter answer choices filled with words that can have similar meanings. Your job is to pick the word that matches the context of the sentence. To choose the best word:

(1) Read it into the sentence to see if it fits the context

(2) Look for the most precise match to the context of the sentence

(3) When in doubt, **use your ear**!

EXAMPLE 1

Dozens of soft lamps <u>elucidated</u> the interior of the newly designed Nexxus Gallery, creating an ambience that enabled viewers to experience a heightened intimacy with each work of art.

A) NO CHANGE
B) enlightened
C) irradiated
D) illuminated

SOLUTION

We have a bunch of words that all sound similar and have relatively similar meanings. Let's plug each answer choice back into the **context** of our sentence.

A)   The lamps <u>elucidated</u> the interior.

Elucidate means to make an idea clear, which doesn't fit the context perfectly. But it does have the root **luc**, which has to do with light. Let's keep it for now.

B)   The lamps <u>enlightened</u> the interior.

Enlightened obviously has the word light in it, but in most cases, enlightened has to do with learning and education. "Enlighten me!" Let's go ahead and eliminate B.

C)   The lamps <u>irradiated</u> the interior.

Are we talking about Marie Curie? Radioactive particles? I don't think our intention is to irradiate the gallery. Let's eliminate C.

D)   The lamps <u>illuminated</u> the interior.

This sounds spot on! Let's not eliminate illuminate.

We are left with **elucidate** and **illuminate**. We know that illuminate works, but we are unsure about elucidate. Always choose a *good* answer over a *possibly* good one. **D** is our answer.

Dozens of soft lamps **<u>illuminated</u>** the interior of the newly designed Nexxus Gallery, creating an ambience that enabled viewers to experience a heightened intimacy with each work of art.

EXAMPLE 2

Harrison's research reveals a(n) <u>vicious</u> cycle: when teachers and peers label a student as "deviant," the resulting stigma further isolates the child, making it more likely he or she will act out in class.

A) NO CHANGE
B) violent
C) unprincipled
D) malevolent

SOLUTION

Again, all the answer choices have similar meanings, so let's plug in and use context.

A) Harrison's research reveals a <u>vicious</u> cycle.

The phrase "vicious cycle" is very familiar and sounds great to my ear. A vicious cycle is a chain of events that continually makes a situation worse. That describes what's happening in this sentence perfectly!

B) Harrison's research reveals a <u>violent</u> cycle.

Violent is a very strong word, and there's no hint of violence in the sentence. This doesn't fit.

C) Harrison's research reveals an <u>unprincipled</u> cycle.

Unprincipled means immoral or dishonest; this situation is certainly bad, but there's no immorality here.

D) Harrison's research reveals a <u>malevolent</u> cycle

Malevolent might remind you of Maleficent, the evil sorceress in Sleeping Beauty. This word means super-duper evil, which doesn't fit this sentence.

Choice A creates a familiar phrase that perfectly describes what's happening in our sentence. **A** it is!

Harrison's research reveals a **<u>vicious</u>** cycle: when teachers and peers label a student as "deviant," the resulting stigma further isolates the child, making it more likely he or she will act out in class.

TIP

ALWAYS read the word back into the sentence and check for familiar phrases. If a pairing of words sounds right to your ear, that's a great sign!

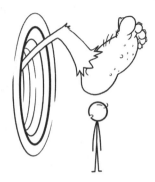

PORTAL

For common possession & contraction flips, check out the Possession chapter on page 236.

Common Flips

The SAT will sometimes ask you to choose between two words that sound the same but have completely different meanings. Here are some words to memorize so you don't fall for that trap!

Common Flips	
Effect	noun; the consequence of an action
	Example: The Hallelujah Chorus has a profound **effect** on me.
Affect	verb; to make a difference to
	Example: How much you study for the SAT **affects** your score.
Excess	more than necessary, left over
	Example: After knitting my Doctor Who scarf, I gave the **excess** yarn to my brother.
Access	to approach or enter
	Example: Jacob **accessed** the secret hard drive with his amazing hacking skills.
Then	at that time *or* after that
	Example: First, I ditched my **then**-babysitter, Rita. **Then**, I stayed up until dawn watching all fourteen *Land Before Time* movies.
Than	used in comparisons
	Example: Although he'll eat both, Marius loves Red Vines much more **than** he loves Twizzlers.
Principle	a fundamental truth or belief
	Example: Jogging on Fridays goes against all my **principles** as a strict Pastafarian.
Principal	first in order of importance
	Example: The **principal** difference between us is that you love Celine Dion, while I can't stand her.
Cite	to quote as evidence
	Example: Elijah **cited** all quotations in his history paper.
Site	an area to build something *or* a website
	Example: I learned about the **site** for *Glass-Blown Ornament Shack's* new storefront by reading the blog on their **site**.
Sight	the ability to see *or* something you can see.
	Example: "What a **sight**!" she exclaimed when I revealed my Spongebob Squarepants tattoo.

Quiz

Identify the error (if present) in each of the following sentences.

1. No one could have guessed the affect the new robot would have on the household.

2. After a long day at the office, nothing tastes better then a big plate of bacon.

3. Peanut butter is a perfect compliment to jelly.

4. My gym teacher is no longer excepting handwritten doctor's notes as an excuse to avoid running the mile.

5. Access to the pool is restricted due to a suspicious floating object.

Answers

1. No one could have guessed the *effect* the new robot would have on the household.

2. After a long day at the office, nothing tastes better *than* a big plate of bacon.

3. Peanut butter is a perfect *complement* to jelly.

4. My gym teacher is no longer *accepting* handwritten doctor's notes as an excuse to avoid running the mile.

5. *Correct!*

Practice Problems

Select the answer choice that produces the best sentence.

1

Stefan couldn't wait for his friends to taste the new teriyaki sauce he'd <u>coined</u>.

A) NO CHANGE
B) invented
C) fabricated
D) instituted

2

As the full moon draws near, werewolves benefit from <u>aggravated</u> sensory abilities.

A) NO CHANGE
B) heightened
C) raised
D) lifted

3

During the third Martian war, many young women <u>opposed</u> bravely in the dusty red trenches.

A) NO CHANGE
B) campaigned
C) repressed
D) fought

4

The angry <u>contest</u> in the grocery store produce section began when two old ladies happened to reach for the same grapefruit at the identical moment.

A) NO CHANGE
B) dispute
C) challenge
D) difference

5

The tropical flowers at the botanical garden bloomed delightfully in a <u>realistic</u> display.

A) NO CHANGE
B) lurid
C) garish
D) vivid

Matching Tone

Occasionally, the test writers will ask you to fix language that is either too informal or too formal when compared to the rest of the passage.

Whenever you are given a few different ways of saying the same thing, ask yourself: which choice matches the tone of the rest of the passage? Is this passage casual (like a blog post) or more formal (like a newspaper editorial)?

CONTEXT

When dealing with a matching tone question, be sure to read the whole paragraph for context. That way, you can more easily get a feel for that passage's "dress code."

EXAMPLE 1

When he announced his intention to join the famed and highly exclusive Moscow Ballet, there was a great deal of debate regarding whether a US-born dancer <u>could hack it</u>; following his first performance, however, international critics warmed greatly to Webster's portrayal of the Swan King in Tchaikovsky's *Swan Lake*.

A) NO CHANGE
B) was up to snuff;
C) could succeed in that environment;
D) could hang with the Russians;

In this case, we need to look at the level of formality of the passage. It looks fairly straightforward and buttoned up. Up to snuff, hang with the Russians, and could not hack it: all of these are examples of **informal** language. To match the tone of the rest of the sentences, we need to stick with the most **formal**, boring language provided: **C** is our answer!

EXAMPLE 2

My great grandmother Nancy's recipes have made their way through the generations of our family. She never wrote down her recipes, preferring to add a dash of salt here, a sprinkling of parsley there, <u>refining her concoctions extemporaneously</u>. To preserve them, my grandmother Patsy begged her to dictate each step to her and wrote down her every move. Years later, my father typed them up on his brand-new Macintosh II. Now, I write a cooking blog where I share her well-worn recipes with the Internet masses.

A) NO CHANGE
B) improving each dish instinctively
C) feeling it out on the fly
D) enhancing each creation with spontaneity

SOLUTION

This language sounds way **too formal** for the tone of the passage! D also sounds too fancy in context. But don't go too far in the opposite direction either; "feeling it out" and "on the fly" are both casual idioms that don't fit the passage. **B** is not too formal, not too casual—it's just right!

Quiz

Identify the error (if present) in each of the following sentences.

1. Tucker and Dale were so delighted to have their own hunting cabin that they barely noticed how busted up it was.

2. The new university president was one cool cat, impressing the entire campus with his numerous accolades.

3. From the grinding noises emanating from the organ room, it was evident that the ancient instrument was fixing to break down.

4. The kids couldn't wait for the circus to come to town, bringing with it the promise of a real blast.

5. From sunrise to sunset, they put in some elbow grease to bring in the crops before they were blighted by the harsh winds of winter.

Answers

1. Tucker and Dale were so delighted to have their own hunting cabin that they barely noticed how *dilapidated* it was.

2. The new university president was *accomplished*, impressing the entire campus with his numerous accolades.

3. From the grinding noises emanating from the organ room, it was evident that the ancient instrument was *about to* break down.

4. The kids couldn't wait for the circus to come to town, bringing with it the promise of a *good time*.

5. From sunrise to sunset, they *labored* to bring in the crops before they were blighted by the harsh winds of winter.

Writing Practice Passage 4
TO STAY ON PACE, YOUR TIMING GOAL IS 8.5 MINUTES

DIRECTIONS

Each passage below is accompanied by a number of questions. For some questions, you will consider how the passage might be revised to improve the expression of ideas. For other questions, you will consider how the passage might be edited to correct errors in sentence structure, usage, or punctuation. Each passage or a question may be accompanied by one or more graphics (such as a table or graph) that you will consider as you make revising and editing decisions.

Some questions will direct you to an underlined portion of the passage. Other questions will direct you to a location in a passage or ask you to think about the passage as a whole. After reading each passage, choose the answer to each question that most effectively improves the quality of writing in the passage or that makes the passage conform to the conventions of standard written English. Many questions include a "NO CHANGE" option. Choose that option if you think the best choice is to leave the relevant portion of the passage as it is.

Questions 1-11 are based on the following passage.

The Gila "Monster"

Biodiversity, the incredible variety of species on Earth, is **1** compulsory for human life. Consider the Gila monster: a large, stocky lizard, significantly bigger than most of its North American brethren. One of the few venomous lizards in the world, it is one of only three venomous species found in all of the Americas. The overall effect creates a tough-looking lizard, worthy of the name "monster." But despite its moniker, fearsome **2** visual appearance, and venomous bite, the Gila monster actually poses very little threat to humans. In fact, humans are benefitting from the Gila monster's unique defenses.

1

A) NO CHANGE
B) acute in
C) essential to
D) unalterable with

2

A) NO CHANGE
B) appearance,
C) appearance to the eye,
D) visual appearance to the eye,

Its sturdy build makes it cumbersome and slow-moving, yet the Gila monster's stout physique does [3] give it a leg up in the desert: the thick tail can store fat and its slow metabolism allows the Gila monster to survive for long periods without a meal. Unlike venomous snakes, Gila monsters lack the ability to [4] inject their venom as snakes do. Instead, a Gila monster must allow the venom to enter its victim's wounds through exposure to saliva by chewing. The venom causes pain and an overall feeling of sickness, but there have been no human fatalities [5] from Gila monster bites recorded in the last 75 years.

Recent medical interest in Gila monster venom has not focused on its [6] negative effects, but rather its potential to improve human health. Gila monster venom contains a hormone called extendin-4, which is similar to a human hormone, glucagon-like peptide-1 analog (GLP1), found in the human digestive tract. GLP-1 assists in the production of insulin to combat peaks in a human's blood sugar level. Extendin-4 has shown to work better than GLP-1, as [7] it's effects last longer. Scientists have been able to recreate extendin-4, calling the synthetic hormone "exenatide."

3
A) NO CHANGE
B) give it a shot
C) give it an advantage
D) ensure its advantaged position

4
A) NO CHANGE
B) inject their venom.
C) inject their venom like their cousins the snakes.
D) inject their venom into their victims.

5
A) NO CHANGE
B) about
C) around
D) with

6
Which choice best maintains the tone of the passage?
A) NO CHANGE
B) evil
C) awful
D) malevolent

7
A) NO CHANGE
B) it's affects
C) its affects
D) its effects

CONTINUE →

In 2005, the Food and Drug Administration approved exenatide for use in managing type-2 diabetes. Type-2 diabetes, also referred to as adult-onset diabetes, is a complication commonly associated **8** to obesity; it occurs when cells stop responding to the body's production of insulin. Exenatide not only helps produce insulin, but also creates a feeling of fullness in the stomach that **9** can help and assist with weight loss. Dr. John Buse, the lead researcher in the exenatide study is excited "that patients that continue exenatide injections continue to lose a bit of weight while maintaining blood sugar control, even in their third year of therapy."

A discovery such as this **10** points: to the global need to maintain biodiversity. Who knows what other molecular miracles are hiding in the creatures inhabiting remote regions of our world? The surprising fact that the venom of the near-threatened Gila monster can help improve human lives dramatically **11** emphasize the benefits of conservation and research.

8

A) NO CHANGE
B) through
C) with
D) DELETE the underlined portion.

9

A) NO CHANGE
B) can help
C) can help, even assist,
D) is known to help and even assist

10

A) NO CHANGE
B) points,
C) points;
D) points

11

A) NO CHANGE
B) emphasizes
C) emphasized
D) emphasizing

STOP

If you finish before time is called, you may check your work on this section only.
Do not turn to any other section.

Illogical Connectors

When you're linking two ideas with a connecting word or phrase, make sure you're making a logical connection.

Some connectors link similar ideas: and, so, similarly, thus. Other connectors link opposite ideas: however, although, despite, even though. This distinction is crucial on the test, so let's first get some practice spotting similar and opposite relationships.

Connect the ideas below with a = for similar or a ≠ for opposites. The first two have been completed for you.

1. Most people thought that Auntie Gladys, with her thick cockney accent, was born in London's East End, **≠** she had never even left Kansas!

2. My little brother realized too late that his plastic superhero did not have the power of flight; **=** , we watched the red and blue figure plummet into our mother's beet garden two floors below.

3. Four out of five doctors agree that Colgate is the best toothpaste. ___, Dr. Fluffington prefers brushing his teeth with a mixture of baking soda and sea salt.

4. Katniss and Elmer's meticulously planned outdoor wedding had to be moved inside at the last minute, ___ it started to rain.

5. According to the review of Guillermo's new novel, the plot was muddled and confusing, ___ the book was redeemed by its insightful character development.

6. The unseasonably warm winter caused significant thawing in the California mountains. ___, more counties than usual are under flash flood warnings.

7. Abjit diligently trained for eight months, ▮ he was able to finish all 26 miles of the Boston Marathon.

8. Many people believe that Napoleon was unusually short; ▮, he was 5'7", above average for men at that time.

9. The author Bram Stoker is most famous for his novel *Dracula*, which is set in the Romanian region of Transylvania. ▮, Stoker never travelled to Eastern Europe, spending most of his life in Ireland and England.

10. Globally, public health campaigns reporting the ill effects of tobacco smoke are having positive effects; ▮, in 2005, Bhutan became the first country to outlaw the sale and use of tobacco products.

Answers: 3. ≠ 4. = 5. ≠ 6. = 7. = 8. ≠ 9. ≠ 10. =

So, when you see answer choices full of connecting words, follow these steps to choose the most logical answer:

① Determine the relationship
Figure out the relationship between the ideas; are they similar or opposite?

② Eliminate illogical choices
If the ideas are similar, cross off all opposite connectors, and vice versa.

③ Plug 'em in
Plug in any remaining choices into the sentence, focusing on the meaning of each connector. You're looking for the most logical and specific connection!

EXAMPLE 1

There was one thing Wilhelmina knew for sure about lobsters: stay away from the pincers. <u>Therefore,</u> when a large lobster attempted to share her beach towel, she vacated the area in a hurry.

A) NO CHANGE
B) Conversely,
C) Nonetheless,
D) Despite this,

Let's take this problem one step at a time.

① Determine the relationship

In our first sentence, Wilhelmina learns to stay away from lobsters. In our second sentence, she follows through on that great advice and stays away from some lobsters. We're definitely dealing with similar ideas.

② Eliminate illogical choices

Any connectors that link opposite ideas have to go. That means we can cross off B, C, and D, which are all opposite connectors. That just leaves us with A! We can skip step 3 and circle **A**, our correct answer.

There was one thing Wilhelmina knew for sure about lobsters: stay away from the pincers. **<u>Therefore,</u>** when a large lobster attempted to share her beach towel, she vacated the area in a hurry.

EXAMPLE 2

Jane's obsession with great apes began at an early age. <u>Finally</u>, she insisted on celebrating her fifth birthday by dressing up like an orangutan and trying to communicate with her furry friends at the zoo.

A) NO CHANGE
B) Similarly,
C) For example,
D) Although,

SOLUTION

① Determine the relationship

Are these ideas similar or opposite? Jane's ape obsession and her orangutan birthday party are **similar**.

② Eliminate illogical choices

We can cross off any connectors that link **opposite** ideas. D is out!

③ Plug 'em in

We're left with three connectors that all link similar ideas. Let's try each one to find the most logical connection:

A) Jane's obsession with great apes began at an early age. **<u>Finally,</u>** she insisted on celebrating her fifth birthday by dressing up like an orangutan and trying to communicate with her furry friends at the zoo.

There's nothing final about a 5-year-old's birthday party. This one is out.

B) Jane's obsession with great apes began at an early age. **<u>Similarly,</u>** she insisted on celebrating her fifth birthday by dressing up like an orangutan and trying to communicate with her furry friends at the zoo.

These two ideas are certainly similar. This connection is okay, but I think we can get more specific. Let's keep it around for now.

C) Jane's obsession with great apes began at an early age. **For example,** she insisted on celebrating her fifth birthday by dressing up like an orangutan and trying to communicate with her furry friends at the zoo.

Jane's fifth birthday at the zoo is an **example** of her early ape obsession. This connector makes a tight, logical connection between these ideas. **C** is correct!

Sometimes, the SAT will try to force a connection where there is none to be found. Don't try to connect unrelated ideas; instead, just delete the connector.

EXAMPLE 3

At my brother's graduation party, we all chowed down on delicious Mexican food from Los Hermanos Taqueria. <u>Despite this,</u> the perfectly seasoned salsa was the first item to run out.

A) NO CHANGE
B) Given that,
C) Furthermore,
D) DELETE the underlined portion and begin the sentence with a capital letter.

These ideas are similar, but none of these connectors fit! If there's no logical connection, **delete** the connector.

At my brother's graduation party, we all chowed down on delicious Mexican food from Los Hermanos Taqueria. The perfectly-seasoned salsa was the first item to run out.

In order to make logical connections, you must be familiar with the connectors you'll see on the SAT. In the table below, you'll find some of the most common connectors and how they are used.

Function	Similar (=)	Opposite (≠)
Showing Logic	Thus Consequently Therefore Hence So Because	However Despite Nevertheless Nonetheless Regardless Although Yet But
Extending Ideas	Additionally In addition Furthermore Moreover Likewise Also	Alternatively On one hand On the other hand In contrast
Giving Examples	For example For instance In fact	
Showing Time	Thereafter Subsequently Next Previously Finally	
Summarizing Ideas	In short In broad terms In other words	

Practice Problems

Select the answer choice that produces the best sentence.

1

In the movie *Titanic*, actress Kate Winslet speaks with a convincing blue-blooded American accent, <u>and</u> she was born in Reading, England.

A) NO CHANGE
B) so
C) as
D) although

2

Francois' entire fraternity was looking forward to spring break and its annual camping trip in the Arctic tundra. <u>In contrast,</u> the trip was canceled at the last minute, due to inclement weather.

A) NO CHANGE
B) Otherwise,
C) Consequently,
D) However,

3

Santa's elves were livid when they heard about the mandatory overtime scheduled for the week before Christmas; <u>in contrast,</u> there were discussions of a strike or some other form of organized protest.

A) NO CHANGE
B) finally,
C) on the other hand,
D) DELETE the underlined portion.

4

When a skunk infiltrated the St. Hildegards' wood pile, Samuel St. Hildegard dearly hoped someone else would be chosen to chase it away. <u>Consequently,</u> it was he who drew the shortest straw.

A) NO CHANGE
B) Thereafter,
C) Unfortunately,
D) In fact,

5

After stuffing himself with crab cakes, Jackson had little desire to go swimming with his cousin as he'd promised. <u>Accordingly,</u> he stripped down to his swim trunks and dived in.

A) NO CHANGE
B) Nevertheless,
C) Alternatively,
D) In broad terms,

6

While traditional wisdom says it is dangerous to wake a sleepwalker, <u>but</u> there is no scientific evidence to support that claim.

A) NO CHANGE
B) and
C) for
D) DELETE the underlined portion.

7

As a childhood star, Roberto was loved for his gap-toothed smile and first-grade witticisms. <u>However,</u> his successful adult career has benefited from his easy grin and juvenile sense of humor.

A) NO CHANGE
B) Conversely,
C) On the other hand,
D) Likewise,

8

Twin sisters Mela and Milla drew a line down the middle of their bedroom, dividing it perfectly in half. <u>Indeed,</u> they still found themselves mired in disputes over cleaning duties.

A) NO CHANGE
B) In fact,
C) Even so,
D) DELETE the underlined portion.

9

As I reached the fifteenth floor of the Hearst building, the elevator lost power, trapping me inside with the reporter for more than twelve hours. <u>Therefore,</u> the meeting was uneventful.

A) NO CHANGE
B) Instead,
C) Furthermore,
D) Otherwise,

10

Windbreaker, the golden retriever, loved going on summer vacations with his people, <u>especially since</u> they were always rolling down the windows to air out the car; he loved sticking his nose in the breeze.

A) NO CHANGE
B) notwithstanding the fact that
C) and for example
D) in addition

Combining Sentences

When the test asks you to combine two sentences, look for logical combinations that eliminate redundancies and keep the paragraph flowing.

When it comes to combining sentence questions, you will see an easy version and a hard version. Let's tackle the easy version first.

The Easy Version: Short and Sweet

If the underlined portion only encompasses where the two sentences meet, you've got an **easy** combining sentences question on your hands. Your job is to:

(1) Eliminate redundancies
get rid of repeated words or unnecessary pronouns

(2) Keep it short
the right answer is usually the shortest answer

Let's see this strategy in action:

EXAMPLE 1

Yesterday, I noticed the leaves changing color on the tree in my front <u>yard. This reminds</u> me how much I hate raking leaves.

Which choice most effectively combines the two sentences at the underlined portion?

A) yard and these leaves remind
B) yard, and this change reminds
C) yard, and such changes remind
D) yard, reminding

SOLUTION

All of the choices combine the sentences, and none of them are grammatically incorrect. But only **one** follows our two rules for Easy Combining Sentences questions:

① Eliminate redundancies

Choices A, B, and C have redundant words that appear in the previous sentence. We already know we're talking about "changes" and "leaves," so why waste time repeating ourselves?

② Keep it short

The shortest answer is **D**, and it happens to be correct!

Yesterday, I noticed the leaves changing color on the tree in my front **yard, reminding** me how much I hate raking leaves.

EXAMPLE 2

The month of July is named for Julius <u>Caesar. Caesar</u> played an integral role in the rise of the Roman Empire.

A) NO CHANGE
B) Caesar, who
C) Caesar, but he
D) Caesar, and he

SOLUTION

① Eliminate redundancies

Besides failing to combine the two sentences, choice A is the most redundant answer to ever exist. It's just one word repeated. Remember, once is enough!

Choices C and D don't repeat the word "Caesar", but they use the pronoun "he" as a replacement for "Caesar." That's just as bad! Unnecessary pronouns are big clues that the answer is redundant.

② Keep it short

The shortest answer is **B**, and what do you know, it's also the correct answer!

The month of July is named for Julius **Caesar, who** played an integral role in the rise of the Roman Empire.

The Hard Version

When the underlined portion stretches to two full sentences, you have found yourself a **hard** combining sentences question. Don't panic! These questions just require you to wade through some confusing, awkward-sounding wrong answers to find the logical right answer. Take a look:

EXAMPLE 3

During the Civil War, Sarah Josepha Hale wrote a series of letters urging President Lincoln to formalize New England's yearly Pilgrims' Harvest Festival into a national holiday. The result was the holiday dedicated to stuffing one's face with turkey and mashed potatoes while watching football and extolling the virtues of pumpkin pie. It was Thanksgiving Day.

Which choice most effectively combines the underlined sentences?

A) The result was Thanksgiving Day, the holiday dedicated to stuffing one's face with turkey and mashed potatoes while watching football and extolling the virtues of pumpkin pie.
B) The result was the holiday, Thanksgiving Day, dedicated to stuffing one's face with turkey and mashed potatoes while watching football and extolling the virtues of pumpkin pie.
C) The holiday dedicated to stuffing one's face with turkey and mashed potatoes while watching football and extolling the virtues of pumpkin pie was the result, Thanksgiving Day.
D) A holiday stuffing one's face with turkey and mashed potatoes resulted, and one watches football and extols the virtues of pumpkin pie; it was Thanksgiving Day.

TIP

Remember your two passage rules: any changes you make MUST

1) Stay on topic

2) Transition smoothly between ideas

SOLUTION

Let's take each answer choice one at a time:

 A) The result was Thanksgiving Day, the holiday dedicated to stuffing one's face with turkey and mashed potatoes while watching football and extolling the virtues of pumpkin pie.

This option is logical and sounds good to my ear. The subject is **Thanksgiving Day**, which is the focus of the entire sentence. That's a great sign!

 B) The result was the holiday, Thanksgiving Day, dedicated to stuffing one's face with turkey and mashed potatoes while watching football and extolling the virtues of pumpkin pie.

Why is **Thanksgiving Day** breaking up the idea? There's no reason to interrupt the phrase here, and it sounds **awkward**!

 C) The holiday dedicated to stuffing one's face with turkey and mashed potatoes while watching football and extolling the virtues of pumpkin pie was the result, Thanksgiving Day.

Thanksgiving Day is the focus of our sentence, but it's not the subject. It doesn't show up until the very end! This isn't the best choice.

D) A holiday stuffing one's face with turkey and mashed potatoes resulted, and one watches football and extols the virtues of pumpkin pie; it was Thanksgiving Day.

So many unnecessary pronouns here. Stuffing one's face... one watches... it was Thanksgiving Day. With all those extra pronouns, this is not the most efficient and logical sentence.

Very often, the right combination will provide a **logical transition** that **keeps the flow** between paragraphs or sentences. Remember, the SAT absolutely loves a good transition, so be on the lookout for answers that keep things flowing!

EXAMPLE 4

For a 10-year-old, there is no greater joy than having some extra money in your pocket to spend on the diversion of your choice. In this uncertain economy, more and more kids are turning to lemonade stands for those discretionary funds, as one afternoon's work can net as much as ten dollars!

Lemonade stands are also environmentally sustainable apart from generating much-needed income. They typically release a level of carbon dioxide that falls well below international emission limits for food production. An increasing number of lemonade entrepreneurs are also using locally-grown organic lemons, further reducing their carbon footprint.

Which choice most effectively combines the underlined sentences?

A) The environmental sustainability of lemonade stands, apart from generating much-needed income, typically releases a level of carbon dioxide that falls well below international emission limits for food production.

B) Apart from generating much-needed income, lemonade stands are also environmentally sustainable, typically releasing a level of carbon dioxide that falls well below international emission limits for food production.

C) Lemonade stands typically release a level of carbon dioxide that falls well below international emission limits for food production, which generate much-needed income and are environmentally sustainable.

D) Typically releasing a level of carbon dioxide that falls well below international emission limits for food production, lemonade stands generate much-needed income and are environmentally sustainable.

SOLUTION

Once again, let's look at each combination:

 A) The environmental sustainability of lemonade stands, apart from generating much-needed income, typically releases a level of carbon dioxide that falls well below international emission limits for food production.

If we cross out the junk between the subject and verb of our sentence, we get:

The environmental sustainability ~~of lemonade stands, apart from generating much-needed income,~~ typically releases a level of carbon dioxide that falls well below international emission limits for food production.

That doesn't make sense! The **lemonade stands** release carbon dioxide, not the environmental sustainability.

B) Apart from generating much-needed income, lemonade stands are also environmentally sustainable, typically releasing a level of carbon dioxide that falls well below international emission limits for food production.

What a great transition! The previous paragraph is all about **income**, which we see at the beginning of this sentence, and "environmentally sustainable" is directly followed by more information on **how** they are sustainable.

 C) Lemonade stands typically release a level of carbon dioxide that falls well below international emission limits for food production, which generate much-needed income and are environmentally sustainable.

This rewording suggests that the *emission limits* (not the lemonade stands) generate income. That doesn't match the meaning of the original sentences.

 D) Typically releasing a level of carbon dioxide that falls well below international emission limits for food production, lemonade stands generate much-needed income and are environmentally sustainable.

Compare this answer choice to choice **B** to see the power of **good transitions**. By hiding "lemonade stands generate much-needed income" in the middle of the sentence, we interrupt the transition from a discussion about income to one about environmental impact. It also makes "environmentally sustainable" sound like an afterthought rather than the main focus of the sentence.

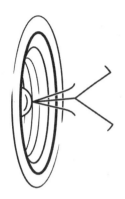

PORTAL

The key to good transitions and combinations is to group similar ideas together. To see what can go wrong when ideas are out of order, check out the Misplaced Modifiers chapter on page 252.

LET'S RECAP!

Bad sentence combinations are

- redundant
- illogical
- awkward to your ear
- confusing
- grammatically incorrect

Good sentence combinations have

- logical construction (they make sense!)
- no unnecessary words (especially pronouns)
- good transitions between ideas, sentences, and paragraphs
- proper emphasis on the main idea of the sentence

Order/Placement

Order/Placement questions ask you to move a sentence or a paragraph to its proper place in a passage. The key is to focus on linking words.

Focus on Linking Words

To answer Order/Placement questions, you will need to pay close attention to the logical connections between paragraphs and sentences. Events have to proceed logically; you cannot make an omelet before you buy the eggs! Similarly, you must introduce a pronoun before you use it; you cannot say "his car was fast" before you identify who "he" is.

No sentence is an island. Every sentence is linked to the preceding and following sentences by related words which we call "linking words." Let's take a look at two simple sentences:

> I trust my dog.
>
> She wouldn't steal.

PORTAL

In this sentence, "dog" is the **antecedent** of the pronoun "she." We talked about pronouns and antecedents in the **Pronoun Error** chapter on page 224.

There is a **link** between these two sentences that makes them flow logically. We understand who "she" is in the second sentence because it connects with "my dog" in the first sentence:

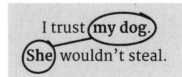

Focusing on linking words will help make Order/Placement problems more concrete on the test. Let's look a little closer at how key words can connect each sentence in a paragraph.

Make it Click

When the sentences are in the right order, they fit together like a puzzle:

She and **my dog** are **linking words** that give the sentences their proper order. When you are working with Order/Placement questions, think of the entire paragraph as a series of linked puzzle pieces, with key words telling you where each sentence belongs:

> I awoke profoundly **hungry**. So I perused the **fridge**, but all I could find was marshmallow cream. I heaped that **marshmallowy goodness** onto a roll and took a bite. Finally I had found a **meal** that suited my refined palate.

One sentence flows logically to the next, thanks to all the linking words! If you move the sentences around, the logical order is disturbed:

> Finally I had found a **meal** that suited my refined palate. I heaped that **marshmallowy goodness** onto a roll and took a bite. I awoke profoundly **hungry**. So I perused the **fridge**, but all I could find was marshmallow cream.

Notice how reading the sentences out of order raises a lot of questions. What **meal**? Which **marshmallowy goodness**? Why are you **hungry** when you just ate? When the sentences are put back in the right order, these linking words click right in place.

EXAMPLE 1

[1] Born in Dublin in 1874, Ernest Shackleton displayed an early passion for exploration and adventure. [2] As a child he was a voracious reader, which only fueled his far-flung imagination and spirit. [3] Before long he was renting skiffs and voyaging deep into the icy waters of the North Atlantic. [4] By 1909 he had led the first expedition to pinpoint the approximate location of the South Magnetic Pole, deep in the heart of the Antarctic. [5] He went on to lead one of the most daring expeditions in history, and today he is celebrated as a model of leadership. [6] These trips increased his confidence and contributed to his growing celebrity, leading to his first commission of an Antarctic bound vessel.

For the sake of the logic and coherence of the preceding paragraph, Sentence 6 should be placed:

A) where it is now.
B) after Sentence 2.
C) after Sentence 3.
D) after Sentence 4.

 SOLUTION

First, let's look at the **linking words** in sentence 6.

The sentence seems to assume that we know what **"these trips"** refers to, so we need to place Sentence 6 **after** a sentence that discusses **trips**. We also see "leading to his first commission," so we need to place our sentence somewhere *before* Shackleton leads a crew into the Antarctic. Let's look at our choices:

A) Hm... I like **expeditions**, but these happened **after** Shackleton had his "first commission." The chronology is off here. Lose A.

B) Sentence 2 talks about reading, not taking trips.

C) Sentence 3 talks about **early voyages**, which could be our **linking word** for "these trips!" This might be a winner.

D) Sentence 4 mentions one expedition, but "these trips" is plural!

The linking words lead us to the best choice! **C** is our answer.

LET'S RECAP!

To answer Order/Placement questions, remember to:

1) Focus on **linking words**

2) Listen to your **ear**

Writing Practice Passage 5
TO STAY ON PACE, YOUR TIMING GOAL IS 8.5 MINUTES

DIRECTIONS

Each passage below is accompanied by a number of questions. For some questions, you will consider how the passage might be revised to improve the expression of ideas. For other questions, you will consider how the passage might be edited to correct errors in sentence structure, usage, or punctuation. Each passage or a question may be accompanied by one or more graphics (such as a table or graph) that you will consider as you make revising and editing decisions.

Some questions will direct you to an underlined portion of the passage. Other questions will direct you to a location in a passage or ask you to think about the passage as a whole. After reading each passage, choose the answer to each question that most effectively improves the quality of writing in the passage or that makes the passage conform to the conventions of standard written English. Many questions include a "NO CHANGE" option. Choose that option if you think the best choice is to leave the relevant portion of the passage as it is.

Questions 1-11 are based on the following passage.

Synesthesia: Secondary Sensing

Have you ever tasted a picture? Or seen the color of a sound? These questions may seem like whimsical contradictions worthy of *Alice in Wonderland*, **1** therefore some people do experience the world in this way. They have a neurological condition called **2** synesthesia. This is when an experience from one sensory pathway also triggers a second sensory experience.

1

A) NO CHANGE
B) and
C) but
D) alternatively

2

Which choice most effectively combines the two sentences at the underlined portion?

A) synesthesia, in which
B) synesthesia, and this is when
C) synesthesia, and this condition occurs when
D) synesthesia and that occurs if

CONTINUE

Imagine [3] one is in the kitchen and a grandmother is removing [4] cookies that were very recently baked fresh from the oven; this event would register through multiple sensory pathways. You would *see* the grandmother leaning down to remove the baking sheet from the oven. You would *hear* the oven door creak as it opens, and perhaps the sizzling of melted chocolate on the baking sheet. If you were standing close enough to the oven, you would *feel* the gust of hot air escaping the oven. You would certainly *smell* the cookies as they left the oven. [5] Still warm and soft from the oven, hopefully you would be able to *taste* the cookies.

[3]

A) NO CHANGE
B) one was
C) you were
D) you are

[4]

A) NO CHANGE
B) freshly baked cookies
C) cookies that are just freshly baked
D) oven-baked freshly made cookies

[5]

A) NO CHANGE
B) Hopefully you would be able to *taste* the cookies, still warm and soft from the oven.
C) Hopefully you would be able, still warm and soft from the oven, be able to *taste* the cookies.
D) You would be able, hopefully, to be able to *taste*, still warm and soft from the oven, the cookies.

Now imagine that you are looking at a photograph of a grandmother removing cookies from an oven. While a photograph only provides visual sensory stimulation, **6** but you could use previous experiences to recall what your other senses would experience if the photo were real. **7** This addition of secondary sensory experiences comes involuntarily to a person with synesthesia. The secondary sensory information does not cancel out the primary experience.

There are two main types of synesthesia: projecting and associative. With projecting synesthesia, the person will actually experience the sensory effect. **8** Moreover, a person may see the sound of an oboe as yellow circles. Someone with associative synesthesia would not see the color yellow, but would strongly associate the sound of the oboe with the color yellow.

6

A) NO CHANGE
B) and
C) yet
D) DELETE the underlined portion.

7

Which choice most effectively combines the two sentences at the underlined portion?

A) To a person with synesthesia, the addition of secondary sensory experiences comes involuntarily, and this does not cancel out the primary sensory experience.

B) A person with synesthesia does not cancel out the primary sensory experience, but the addition of secondary sensory experiences comes involuntarily.

C) This addition of secondary sensory experiences—which does not cancel out the primary sensory experience—comes involuntarily to a person with synesthesia.

D) The primary sensory experience, which does not cancel out with the addition of secondary sensory experiences, comes involuntarily to a person with synesthesia.

8

A) NO CHANGE
B) For example,
C) Therefore,
D) Regardless,

[1] One of the most common variants of synesthesia is grapheme-color synesthesia, where a person relates numbers and letters to specific colors. [2] Even when presented 9 with black lettering on a white back-ground, a grapheme-color synesthete will see the letters and numbers as shaded. [3] This can lead to some learning difficulties, as certain spellings or math concepts may "clash" with a person's internal color conception, making the number and/or letter combination appear ugly and therefore not correct. [4] Another relatively common form is chromesthesia synesthesia, which connects sounds to colors. [5] Each individual has unique color associations for different pitches and timbres, but most associate higher pitches with bright colors and 10 darker colors with low pitches. 11

9

A) NO CHANGE
B) to
C) by
D) at

10

A) NO CHANGE
B) dark colors with lower pitches.
C) low pitches with darker colors.
D) lower pitches with dark colors.

11

To improve the cohesion of the paragraph, the author wants to add the following sentence:

> Within the two main categories, there are multiple sub-types of synesthesia.

The sentence would most logically be placed

A) before sentence 1.
B) after sentence 2.
C) after sentence 3.
D) after sentence 5.

STOP

If you finish before time is called, you may check your work on this section only.
Do not turn to any other section.

Add and Delete

The SAT writers will frequently propose adding a new sentence to the passage, or deleting the existing one. First, you need to pick "yes" or "no," and then choose the best reason for your response.

Yes or No?

Add and Delete questions tend to follow the same pattern. You'll be told that the writer is considering making an addition, and the answer choices will often look something like this:

> At this point, the writer is considering adding the following sentence. "Scooby-Doo can never seem to get enough scooby snacks." Should the writer make this addition here?
>
> A) Yes (for a good reason).
> B) Yes (for a bad reason).
> C) No (for a good reason).
> D) No (for a bad reason).

Notice that both A and C have good reasons attached, even though only one can be the correct answer! To avoid being lured into a wrong choice, **answer "Yes" or "No" yourself** before looking at the choices.

So, how do you make that choice? Well, anything you add to the passage must follow these two rules:

> **① Stay on topic**
> **② Transition smoothly between ideas**

Most of the time, the decision hinges on whether the addition would distract from the main point of the paragraph. If the sentence is off-topic or goes off on a tangent, it breaks the flow of ideas.

Let's look at some common reasons to say "yes" or "no":

Add sentence if it:	Do NOT add sentence if it:
introduces an idea in the passage	blurs the focus of the paragraph
transitions between two paragraphs	interrupts the flow of an idea
supports existing ideas	adds unnecessary/off-topic details

EXAMPLE 1

Once I returned home from my semester abroad, I heard through the grapevine that Dooley's Cafe, my favorite eatery, was under new management and had undergone many significant changes. **1** The restaurant had added a second counter, which greatly reduced wait time. Though the quesadillas were gone now, the new Bagel-Blast Jell-O Supreme was actually quite tasty. The prices had come down on certain items, including my old standby: lava-drenched, peanut drizzle flatbread. The owners had also upgraded the seating to include more than just the bean bag chairs of old. Finally, my back wouldn't hurt after lunch!

At this point, the writer is considering adding the following statement:

I expected the changes would all be for the worst, but pleasantly, they weren't.

Should the writer make this addition here?

A) Yes, because it provides an example of the phenomenon introduced in the preceding sentence.
B) Yes, because it provides a logical transition between the preceding sentence and the rest of the paragraph.
C) No, because it blurs the focus of the paragraph by adding an irrelevant detail.
D) No, because it fails to indicate why Dooley's Cafe is the narrator's favorite eatery.

TIP

Adding a sentence or phrase that transitions between ideas is almost always a good idea!

SOLUTION

① Choose Yes or No

Remember, our job is to **stay on topic** and **maintain the flow** of the paragraph. If we make the addition, the paragraph flows like this:

> When I came back I learned Dooley's had **changed**...
> The **changes** were surprisingly pleasant...
> There was **less** wait time, **tasty** dishes, and **better** seating.

Are we **on topic**?

We lead by talking about change, mention the changes in our added sentence, and then enumerate the changes. We are clearly on topic!

Is there a **smooth transition**?

The addition helps us transition from the first sentence to the specific examples. This sentence looks like a winner! We can cross off answers C and D.

② Pick the best reason

Here are the two reasons we have to choose from:

A) Yes, because it provides an **example of the phenomenon** introduced in the preceding sentence.

B) Yes, because it provides a **logical transition** between the preceding sentence and the rest of the paragraph.

Do you see any **examples** in the added sentence? Nope! It's just the narrator's opinion! A gets the Yes/No correct but gives a bad reason. **B** is the winner!

EXAMPLE 2

Washington, DC has earned the distinction of being the city in which a driver is most likely to have an auto accident. To help reduce the rate of accidents, legislators banned drivers' use of cell phones. Studies showed that drivers were distracted while using cell phones and were just as likely to have an accident as individuals who were driving while intoxicated. The first year following the passing of the legislation, the number of accidents dropped by 25 percent.

At this point, the writer is considering adding the following sentence.

Some cities restrict texting while driving as an alternative to a complete cell phone ban.

Should the writer make this addition here?

A) Yes, because it provides an explanation of the terms used in the preceding sentence.
B) Yes, because it suggests a method that could have prevented the event described later in the paragraph.
C) No, because it contradicts the the point made earlier that the city banned cell phone usage.
D) No, because it blurs the focus of the paragraph by supplying irrelevant information.

SOLUTION

① Choose Yes or No

Are we on topic? The paragraph focuses exclusively on **Washington, DC**. Does info about other cities support our point? No! We have a clear distraction here, so we need a **No** answer.

② Pick the best reason

Let's check out our reasons:

C) No, because it contradicts the point made earlier that the city banned cell phone usage.

The **city** of Washington, DC isn't even mentioned in the addition, so this one's flat out wrong!

D) No, because it blurs the focus of the paragraph by supplying irrelevant information.

Bingo! Info about other cities is **irrelevant** to this paragraph all about DC. **D** is correct!

Sometimes, the test writers will ask you if you should **delete** or **keep** a sentence or phrase. Again, choose the **Yes/No** by asking yourself "Does this stay on topic?" and "Does this transition smoothly?" Delete anything that **blurs the focus** of the paragraph, and keep anything that **transitions smoothly** between paragraphs or ideas.

EXAMPLE 3

Last month, a new tenant took over the apartment above my own. I met him in the mail room and learned that his name was Heisenberg. He had eyes like the Indian Ocean and a pony tail that flowed majestically. We chatted about German philosophy and exchanged strudel recipes before going our separate ways. I didn't hear from him for a few weeks and had almost forgotten that he was living above me! Then, he installed a new hardwood floor in his apartment—<u>and boy did he love to dance.</u>

Sunday afternoon, my chandelier was shaking to Nicki Minaj. Monday evening my picture frames were pulsating to Carrie Underwood. I knew that I needed to say something to protect my eardrums, but I didn't want to interfere with his groove.

The writer is considering deleting the underlined portion. Should the writer make this change?

A) Yes, because it does not provide a transition from the topic of the previous paragraph.
B) Yes, because it distracts from the main argument of the passage.
C) No, because it provides more detail about the narrator's disposition.
D) No, because it sets up the events of the next paragraph.

SOLUTION

① Choose Yes or No

If we delete the underlined portion, the passage flows like this:

> He installed a **hardwood floor**...
> My chandelier was shaking to **Nicki Minaj**.

What just happened? How in the world did we get from hardwood floors to shaking chandeliers? Without that underlined portion, the passage **does not transition smoothly**. Let's add it back in and see what happens:

> He installed a **hardwood floor**...
> He loves to **dance**...
> My chandelier was shaking to **Nicki Minaj**.

There's our logical transition! The fact that Heisenberg loves to dance on his hardwood floor **transitions** between these two paragraphs. We can cross off A and B.

② Pick the best reason

Our reasons are:

C) No, because if provides more detail about the narrator's disposition.

This has nothing to do with the narrator; Heisenberg is the one who loves to dance.

D) No, because it sets up the events of the next paragraph.

Perfect! This phrase is essential to understanding the chandelier-shaking that follows. **D** it is!

EXAMPLE 4

The works of Christo and Jeanne Claude involve wrapping enormous objects in fabric and creating architectural landscapes that evoke the imagination. One of their most celebrated art projects involved wrapping the sharp exterior of the German parliament building, the Reichstag, in metallic, billowing fabric. <u>The Reichstag was built in the center of Berlin and opened in 1894.</u> More than a hundred mountain climbers and assistants accomplished the enormous task of wrapping the building. For nearly two weeks the center of Germany's government became an art piece that drew in tens of thousands of curious visitors.

The writer is considering deleting the underlined sentence. Should the sentence be kept or deleted?

A) Kept, because it provides a detail that supports the main argument of the paragraph.
B) Kept, because it introduces the importance of the Reichstag.
C) Deleted, because it interrupts the paragraph with a loosely related detail.
D) Deleted, because it does not reveal the architect of the Reichstag.

SOLUTION

① Choose Keep or Delete

The words are different, but the idea is the same!

Are we **on topic**?

The underlined sentence is about the **history** of the **Reichstag**. The paragraph mentions the Reichstag, but only in reference to Christo and Jeanne Claude's **art piece**. This seems off-topic.

Is there a **smooth transition**?

Let's delete the sentence and see if we lose a transition:

One of their **art projects** involved **wrapping** the Reichstag… Mountain climbers accomplished the task of wrapping the building.

That's a smooth transition! Let's delete the sentence and cross off A and B.

② Pick the best reason

C) Deleted, because it interrupts the paragraph with a loosely related detail.

That's exactly what is going on. We don't need to interrupt our talk about modern art with historical facts!

D) Deleted, because it does not reveal the architect of the Reichstag.

Who cares? The paragraph is not about the architect of the building; it's about the art. This reason doesn't work. **C** is correct!

Accomplish a Task

Often, the SAT writers will ask you to choose a sentence or phrase that best accomplishes a specific task.

The answer choices for Accomplish a Task questions will all be grammatically correct, and a few might even contain some really interesting facts! But only **one** will accomplish the **task** that you'll find in the question prompt. The golden rule for this question type is simple: **Underline your task!** The correct answer will have **specific words** that help accomplish that underlined task. Here are some examples of tasks you might see on the test:

- Give another supporting example
- Reflect the point made earlier in the paragraph
- Provide evidence to support a point
- Introduce the next paragraph
- Conclude the passage

Some of these tasks only require you to understand a sentence or two, some require you to connect two whole paragraphs, and one even requires you to understand the passage as a whole. Whatever your task, your job is to find **specific words** in the correct answer choice that match the task and/or the passage. Let's take a look at some examples!

EXAMPLE 1

There was much speculation regarding Hughes' whereabouts: perhaps he had left the country and was living incognito, or perhaps he was hiding in one of his many properties scattered throughout the nation.

At this point, the writer wants to develop further the idea from the preceding sentence. Which choice most effectively accomplishes this goal?

A) His airline designs led to widespread innovation in the fledgling airline industry.
B) Many have questioned his political motives and speculated about his involvement with national elections.
C) Still another theory was that Hughes had gone into protective custody and was living in a bunker underneath Sandusky, Ohio.
D) Many missing persons turn up of their own accord after years of absence.

SOLUTION

First, let's find and underline our task:

Which choice would best <u>develop the idea in the preceding sentence</u>?

All we care about is the point from the previous sentence, which is that folks were **speculating about Hughes' location**.

Let's go through our choices, looking for specific words that match this idea.

 His airline designs led to widespread innovation in the fledgling airline industry.

Airline industry? That's way off-topic.

 Many have questioned his political motives and speculated about his involvement with national elections.

Speculation matches the sentence, but **political motives** doesn't match our task.

C) Still another theory was that Hughes had gone into protective custody and was living in a bunker underneath Sandusky, Ohio.

Theory is related to **speculation**, and **Sandusky** is a location where we might find **Hughes**. This matches!

~~D)~~ Many missing persons turn up of their own accord after years of absence.

Missing persons is related to Hughes' disappearance, but this is too vague. Be on the lookout for answers that are related to your task, but are not specific enough.

Some of these options are interesting and even on-topic. However, only one choice accomplishes our task: **C is our answer**.

EXAMPLE 2

The term "aerotropolis" -- a combination of the words "airport" and "metropolis" -- was originally coined in 1939 by Nicholas DeSantis, a commercial artist from New York City. A 1939 article in the magazine Popular Science, titled "Skyscraper Airport for City of Tomorrow," outlines DeSantis' bold proposal: a 200-story skyscraper of homes and offices, topped by an expansive airfield. This arrangement would allow commuters from the suburbs to jet to work in their private planes. DeSantis' detailed drawings depict luxury accommodations at a vast scale, accompanied by plenty of explanations of how his fanciful future city might function.

2 <u>Of course, this hypothetical aerotropolis never quite took off.</u> Today, most airports are built at the periphery of cities, only accessible via lengthy drives or subway rides. But contemporary thinkers are envisioning a new, updated take on the aerotropolis. In this modern imagining, an aerotropolis is any urban center with the airport at its heart -- a structure that more effectively connects the city to the global network and international marketplace.

Which choice most effectively links the first paragraph with the ideas that follow?

A) NO CHANGE
B) The earliest "airports" were grassy fields where small planes could approach at any angle, depending on the direction of the wind.
C) At the Changi International Airport in Singapore, travelers are pampered with free foot massages, a movie theater, and a rooftop swimming pool.
D) Naturally, the idea of an aerotropolis was met with praise from those in the field of aeronautics.

PORTAL

Don't forget the two golden rules of Expression of Ideas questions:

1. Stay on topic

2. Transition smoothly between ideas.

For a refresher, go to the Add & Delete chapter on page 312.

Our task is to <u>link the first paragraph with the ideas that follow.</u> This means the right answer will have **specific matches** to **both** paragraphs! Actively read both paragraphs to get a quick summary for what each is about. Here's what we came up with:

> Paragraph 1: original "aerotropolis" idea
> Paragraph 2: modern "aerotropolis" idea

It looks like the first paragraph tells us DeSantis' original aerotropolis idea, and the second tells us how people think of an aerotropolis today. An answer that links both paragraphs should be about that **change** in the definition of **aerotropolis**. Let's go to our answer choices and find a match!

 A) Of course, this hypothetical aerotropolis never quite took off.

Aerotropolis? Check. **Change**? "Hypothetical" and "never took off" tell us that the original idea didn't work. This perfectly sets up the following paragraph about today's airports and the new definition of aerotropolis. This one matches!

 B) The earliest "airports" were grassy fields where small planes could approach at any angle, depending on the direction of the wind.

There's no mention of **aerotropolis** in this answer, so we can cross it off.

 C) At the Changi International Airport in Singapore, travelers are pampered with free foot massages, a movie theater, and a rooftop swimming pool.

Again, I don't see a match for **aerotropolis** anywhere in this answer. It's out!

 D) Naturally, the idea of an aerotropolis was met with praise from those in the field of aeronautics.

Aerotropolis? Check. **Change**? Not so much. This sentence also talks about **praise** from the field of **aeronautics**. There are no matches for those words in the second paragraph, so this does not provide a good transition.

EXAMPLE 3

The Maya were a Mesoamerican civilization that thrived between 250 and 900 A.D, in the region that is now Central and South America. Though the modern Maya still inhabit these regions, their ancient ancestors hold a special fascination for many throughout the world. One item of particular interest is the Mayan calendar. Though a complex and brilliant masterpiece in its own right, the Mayan calendar has received a massive amount of media attention based on an unfortunate and baseless rumor that it predicted the end of the world... which was supposedly slated to occur at the end of 2012.

These speculations appear to date back to the 1900s. But the idea gained new ground in the 1970s, when New Age writers began exploring 2012's significance. **3** While no scientific data supported it, the rumor picked up even more steam, as people enjoyed sharing information, engaging in discussions, and forming communities related to conspiracy theories and unexplained phenomena. In 2002, the popular TV show "The X-Files" added fuel to the fire with the fictional revelation that extraterrestrials would arrive to colonize the Earth on 12/21/12.

Which choice most effectively sets up the list given at the end of the sentence?

A)   NO CHANGE
B)   As the alleged apocalypse drew closer,
C)   Then, in the age of the internet,
D)   As the belief became more popular,

SOLUTION

Our answer should set up the list at the end of the sentence, so let's start there!

...as people enjoyed **sharing information**, **engaging in discussions**, and **forming communities** related to conspiracy theories and unexplained phenomena...

Which answer has a match for this list? Only choice **C**! The **internet** is the perfect vehicle for sharing information, engaging in discussions, and forming communities. None of the other choices have **specific** links to the list.

LET'S RECAP!

Accomplish a Task questions ask you to choose the answer that best matches the task you are given. To nail these questions:

1) **Underline the task** so you don't get confused by the wrong answers that sound good, but don't match the task.

2) **Match specific words** in the answer choices to your task. This may require you to dive deeper into the sentence, the paragraph, or even the whole passage.

Describing Data

Some Writing passages contain bar graphs, line graphs, or other figures.

Chart Basics

Some questions will refer you to a bar or line graph that shows data relevant to the topic of the passage. Your job is to rewrite a sentence so that it **accurately describes the data** in that graph. That's it! There are no additional grammar rules to memorize or errors to watch out for when answering these questions.

When you come across a graph question, use a **process of elimination** strategy to spot the correct answer:

(1) Locate the graph in the passage.

(2) Check each choice with the graph.

(3) Eliminate choices that do not accurately describe the **groups** or **trends** in the data

Three of the choices will just flat-out get the data wrong. They'll say Group A was bigger than Group B when it's the reverse, or they'll say a particular value increased when, in fact, it decreased. There's no gray area here: a choice either gets it right or wrong.

The First Rule of Graph Club

Before we look at an example, we should emphasize one, all-helpful rule: **read the titles of the figures!** Seriously, there is no faster way to get a sense of what you're looking at than to read the title of the graph or figure. After all, when someone *wrote* that title, their job was to describe the main purpose of the graph. So let's use that to our advantage!

PORTAL

Graph questions are easier here than when they show up in the Reading section.

For a deeper dive into the different components of charts, tables, and graphs, head to the Reading Graphs chapter on page 88.

EXAMPLE 1

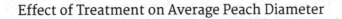

Effect of Treatment on Average Peach Diameter

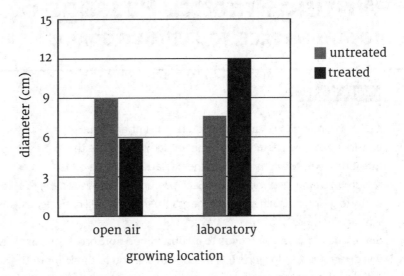

Which choice offers an accurate interpretation of the data in the chart?

A) peaches will grow to at least 10 cm if left to grow untreated in the open air.
B) treated peaches that are grown in the laboratory weigh, on average, 3 kg more than untreated peaches grown in the open air.
C) if left untreated, peaches grow larger in open air than they do in the laboratory.
D) peach diameter increases with treatment for both open air and lab-grown peaches.

SOLUTION

Let's compare each answer choice with the chart, eliminating wrong choices as we go:

A) The light grey bar in the left group shows us untreated, open air peaches. That bar only goes to 9cm, **not** 10cm.

B) Careful! this chart says nothing about weight in **kilograms**. This choice misreads the left axis label.

C) Yep! This one is correct – the light grey bar (untreated) is taller in the open air group than in the laboratory group.

D) Nope, diameter **decreased** with treatment for open air peaches. This one's wrong too.

Writing Practice Passage 6
TO STAY ON PACE, YOUR TIMING GOAL IS 8.5 MINUTES

DIRECTIONS

Each passage below is accompanied by a number of questions. For some questions, you will consider how the passage might be revised to improve the expression of ideas. For other questions, you will consider how the passage might be edited to correct errors in sentence structure, usage, or punctuation. Each passage or a question may be accompanied by one or more graphics (such as a table or graph) that you will consider as you make revising and editing decisions.

Some questions will direct you to an underlined portion of the passage. Other questions will direct you to a location in a passage or ask you to think about the passage as a whole. After reading each passage, choose the answer to each question that most effectively improves the quality of writing in the passage or that makes the passage conform to the conventions of standard written English. Many questions include a "NO CHANGE" option. Choose that option if you think the best choice is to leave the relevant portion of the passage as it is.

Questions 1-11 are based on the following passage.

The Many Lives of Yogurt

What comes to mind when you hear the word "yogurt"? You probably think of a sweet dairy product in fruity **1** flavors like strawberry or peach, conveniently packaged for breakfast on-the-go. But while that may be yogurt's most commonly found form in today's American grocery store, many different varieties of yogurt **2** has existed during its 5,000-year history.

1

A) NO CHANGE
B) flavors like, strawberry or peach,
C) flavors like strawberry, or peach
D) flavors, like strawberry, or peach

2

A) NO CHANGE
B) had existed
C) have existed
D) exist

CONTINUE ➡

[1]These wandering tribes might have accidentally created yogurt by carrying fresh milk in pouches made from sheep stomachs, [3] a Neolithic substitute for the glass bottle. [2] Some food historians believe that yogurt was discovered as early as the Neolithic era when nomadic herdsmen began domesticating milk-producing animals, the ancestors of today's cows, sheep, and goats. [3]Or perhaps it was in the ancient lands of Mesopotamia that yogurt made its first appearance. [4] [4] Conversely, there is evidence that yogurt played an important role in the diets of people throughout the world, even before recorded history. [5]

Which choice provides a potential explanation for how the yogurt was created?

A) NO CHANGE
B) which contain a milk-curdling enzyme.
C) the custom at the time.
D) which were used to transport liquids during travel.

4

A) NO CHANGE
B) Either way,
C) Because,
D) Therefore

To make this paragraph most logical, sentence 1 should be placed

A) where it is now.
B) after sentence 2.
C) after sentence 3.
D) after sentence 4.

The first true description of yogurt was provided around 1000 A.D. by a Turkish author named Mahmud of Kashgar. [6] Not only to include an entry for yogurt, one of the first encyclopedias was written by him, firmly establishing its place in Turkish history.

[7] Iranians enjoy sour kefir yogurt in dishes such as ashe-mast, a warm soup made from yogurt, lentils and spinach. In Eastern European and Balkan countries such as Albania, Bulgaria and Serbia, yogurt is served as a cold soup seasoned with cucumbers and dill—a light and refreshing dish. A similar dish, tzatziki, is a popular condiment in Greece, served alongside pita sandwiches and grilled meat. In South Asia, a yogurt-based sauce called raita—made with cucumbers, onions, mint, and cumin—makes a delicious complement to spicy curries. [8]

6

A) NO CHANGE
B) Not only did he create one of the first encyclopedias, he also included an entry for yogurt,
C) One of the first encyclopedias was created by him, but it included an entry for yogurt,
D) Not only did it have an entry for yogurt, but he also wrote one of the first encyclopedias,

---

7

Which of the following sentences would most effectively transition between the two paragraphs?

A) In the ensuing centuries, yogurt's popularity has remained strong in cuisines throughout the world.
B) Americans typically expect yogurt to be served sweet, but this is not the case everywhere.
C) In many recipes, yogurt is accompanied by cucumber.
D) In modern times, refrigeration technology affects the way people consume dairy products.

8

At this point, the writer is considering adding the following sentence.

> Curries of many varieties are popular throughout this region.

Should the writer make this addition here?

A) Yes, because it highlights the global role yogurt has played in cuisine.
B) Yes, because it explains yogurt's popularity in South Asia.
C) No, because it interrupts the flow of the passage with irrelevant information.
D) No, because it contradicts the previous sentence's claim about curry.

CONTINUE ►

9 To some extent, yogurt's popularity is due in part to its considerable nutritional value; it is full of protein, calcium, and vitamins. **10** It also contains probiotics, live microorganisms that are thought to boost immune response. Whatever the reason, yogurt has become more popular than ever in the past decade; in 2006, Americans purchased **11** over 5 billion pounds of yogurt. Perhaps the history of yogurt is just beginning.

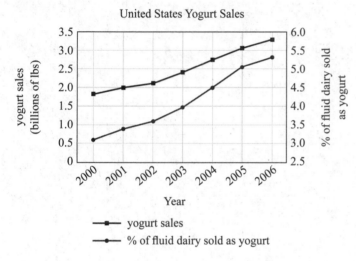

United States Yogurt Sales

Year

■— yogurt sales
●— % of fluid dairy sold as yogurt

9

A) NO CHANGE
B) Yogurt's popularity is due in part
C) To some extent, yogurt's popularity is partly due
D) Yogurt's popularity is somewhat due in part

10

The writer is considering deleting the underlined sentence. Should the sentence be kept or deleted?

A) Kept, because it provides evidence that supports the claim made in the previous sentence.
B) Kept, because it provides a transition between the preceding and following ideas.
C) Deleted, because it blurs the focus of the paragraph.
D) Deleted, because it repeats information that has already been provided.

11

Which choice offers an accurate interpretation of the data in the graph?

A) NO CHANGE
B) over 5% of all yogurt sold globally.
C) under 6% of all dairy products sold as yogurt.
D) over 3 billion pounds of yogurt.

STOP

If you finish before time is called, you may check your work on this section only.
Do not turn to any other section.

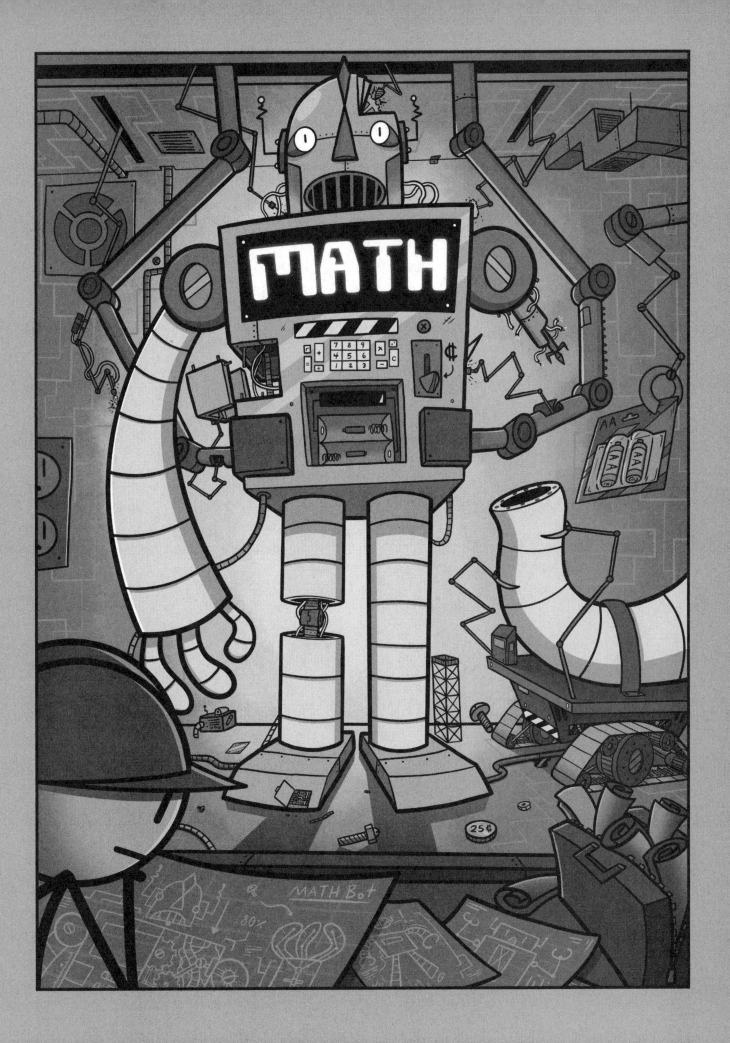

Math Intro

Before we dive in, let's take a broad view of how we'll raise your Math score.

All is one

Slope, rates of change, balanced manipulations, factoring... many seemingly different ideas are just two sides of the same coin.

The more connections you make between ideas, the better your math fluency... and the easier the SAT will seem!

Making Connections

Math tests can be daunting – particularly when you feel like you've fallen behind. Even equipped with a study guide, you might still feel anxious just scanning the table of contents. Though there are a lot of chapters, you'll start to notice something as we move through these pages: there really aren't THAT many different ideas covered on the SAT...

Sure, there are (for example) graphing questions that require you to calculate **slopes**, and there are word problems that require you to calculate & compare **prices-per-unit**... and, yes, there are data analysis questions that ask you to find **lines of best fit** in a scatterplot.

These questions certainly *look* different at first, and they do have their own unique strategies and quirks. But, the more you practice, the more you realize that these questions are all kind of getting at the same idea, **rates of change**, just from slightly different angles.

You'll also start to notice that basic skills you learn early on, such as making **balanced changes** to an equation to get it in a more helpful form, keep popping up again and again, in solution after solution. The reason is that SAT math has become a highly focused test. It tests a few core ideas, mostly algebraic ones, over and over.

What does this mean for you?

It means that every time you master one topic, you're improving on past *and* future topics. It means that every time you make the connection between two seemingly disconnected topics (such as factors of a function and *x*-intercepts on a graph), you're instantly better at both.

And, most importantly, it means you CAN do this. No matter what your experience with math has been so far, there are **significant** score gains to be had by focusing on some key skills. So buckle up, get curious, flip back and forth to connect different ideas, and above all: keep practicing!

Section 3: Non-Calculator Section

25 Minutes,   20 Questions

The third section of the SAT is the non-calculator math section, which primarily focuses on your ability to manipulate algebraic equations. Even if you could use your calculator, you likely wouldn't use it as you'll be mostly moving around variables and solving systems of equations.

This section can be tough to finish within the time limit. Technically, you have just over a minute to answer each question. However, not all questions are created equal! The last five questions are grid-ins rather than multiple choice. While the questions generally get tougher as you go, some of the hardest questions on the test come **just before** the grid-ins, which start easy and quickly get tough again. That means you might want to **skip questions 13–15** and nab some easier grid-in points if you're tight on time.

Section 4: Calculator Section

55 Minutes,   38 Questions

The fourth section of the SAT is the calculator math section, and it is full of **word problems** that test your algebra and arithmetic skills in the context of real-world situations. You'll come across a boat-load of "Data Analysis" questions that test your ability to pull data from **charts, tables,** and **graphs**, to work with percentages and proportions, and to calculate basic statistics like mean, median, and range.

You have over twice as long to work your way through this section. While this provides you with a bit more breathing room than you have on the fast-paced non-calculator section, you will want to use that time to **actively read** all those wordy questions. Remember, just because you can use your calculator on this section doesn't mean you can afford to let your pencil rest! Careful work is still the name of the game.

Avoiding Traps

Test writers are crafty. For each math problem, they anticipate calculation errors that you are likely to make if you are stressed, rushed, or otherwise not keeping careful work. They'll figure out the answer you would get with that error and *make it* one of the answer choices! Avoid these traps by **writing out each step of your work**.

Secret to Math

The ultra-rare, super-genius, never-heard-that-before secret is...

Workin' It

SAT Math questions should progress logically. You're given an equation or some information that is precisely what you need to start working towards an answer. Tragically, each year, thousands of points are lost by students around the world who refuse to write out their work. Rather than copy down a given equation and start from there, they jump to the first step of the work, making a small calculation error in the process. *Don't let this be you!* Write out each step of your math work: you'll make fewer mistakes and can check your work if you get stuck along the way.

UNIT | Algebra Basics

Chapters

Key Skills

In this chapter, we'll learn the basics of manipulating equations. This skill will help us as we move into the equation of a line and some advanced algebra in the factoring & foiling section.

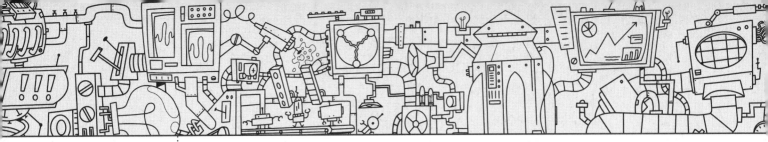

Basic Algebra

The key to manipulating algebraic equations is to make careful, balanced changes. As long as you play by the rules, you can do whatever you want!

Keep it Balanced

Solving basic algebra problems is just a balancing act. The test writers will give you an algebra equation, like:

$$2x - 7 = -21$$

...and then they'll ask you to "solve for *x*." Which really just means that we need to strategically add, subtract, multiply, or divide until "*x*" is alone on one side of the equation.

But here's the key: we have to keep the equation **balanced**. Anything we do to the left side of the equal sign we must also do to the right side... otherwise, we throw off the balance and change the equation:

Balanced!

$$2x - 7 = -21$$
$$+7 \quad +7$$
$$2x = -14$$

Not Balanced!

$$2x - 7 = -21$$
$$+7$$
$$2x = -21$$

On the right, we made the mistake of only adding 7 to one side of the equation. We can tell at a glance that something's wrong... after all, how can $2x = -21$ when $2x - 7 = 21$? To avoid this, remember to always make step-by-step, **balanced changes** to each side of the equation.

TIP

In this example, if we add 7 to the left side of the equation and NOT to the right side, it disrupts the balance and **changes the equation.**

Clean Work is Happy Work

Making balanced changes is the most basic algebra skill we can cover. But in the rush of the test, it's often these basic skills that suffer. It's not just "careless" students who make "careless errors" – they can result from focusing so much on the tougher topics that you forget to actually work out the simpler steps. As a result, you forget to distribute a negative or you make a basic error of substitution. To avoid these errors, get in the habit of writing out careful, step-by-step work.

Follow the step-by-step instructions to complete the solution below.

If $5x - 6 = 54$, then $x = ?$	
1. *Rewrite equation*	
2. *Add 6 to both sides*	
3. *Write the result*	
4. *Divide both sides by 5*	
5. *Write the result*	

Answers: **1)** $5x - 6 = 54$ **2)** $5x - 6 + 6 = 54 + 6$ **3)** $5x = 60$ **4)** $5x \div 5 = 60 \div 5$ **5)** $x = 12$

The Freedom to Tinker

Here's the first, key thing to understand about solving algebra problems on the SAT. As long as you follow the rule of making balanced changes to each side (as well as those pesky rules about not dividing by zero, etc.) you are **free** to manipulate the equation as you see fit. If you feel like adding 1,000,000 and then subtracting 1,000,000 to each side before starting the exercise above, you'd be totally free to do that! We wouldn't recommend it, but, hey, you're the boss. *Experimentation* is a skill that can be a huge help on tougher problems.

TIP

These problems may seem a little basic, but the skills behind them are **important**!

Basic Algebra skills and a little balanced experimentation here and there are the keys to solving even the toughest algebra problems on the test.

Solve for *x* in the problems below.

Equation	*x* = ?
1. $12x + 12 = 12$	
2. $3x - 7 = 14$	
3. $2x + 3 = 4x - 8$	
4. $-13x = -3x + 30$	
5. $15x - 10 = 12x + 11$	

Scratch Work

Answers: **1)** 0 **2)** 7 **3)** 11/2 **4)** –3 **5)** 7

EXAMPLE 1

What value of x satisfies the equation $\frac{13}{15}x - \frac{8}{15}x = \frac{3}{5} + \frac{3}{20}$?

TIP

When you have fractional coefficients, you add and subtract them following normal fraction rules.

SOLUTION

Start by combining like terms on the left. Both terms have the same denominators and one x, so let's combine and simplify:

(1) *combine* $\qquad \frac{5}{15}x = \frac{3}{5} + \frac{3}{20}$

(2) *simplify* $\qquad \frac{1}{3}x = \frac{3}{5} + \frac{3}{20}$

Now clean up the right side. We have two constants.
To combine these fractions, we need a common denominator:

(3) *find C.D.* $\qquad \frac{1}{3}x = \frac{3}{5} + \frac{3}{20} \Rightarrow \frac{12}{20} + \frac{3}{20} \Rightarrow \frac{15}{20} \Rightarrow \frac{3}{4}$

so... $\qquad \frac{1}{3}x = \frac{3}{4}$

Finally, make balanced changes to isolate x. To get x by itself, we need to get rid of that fraction by multiplying *both sides* by 3.

(4) *balance* $\qquad (\times 3)\,\frac{1}{3}x = \frac{3}{4}\,(\times 3)$

voila! $\qquad x = \boxed{\frac{9}{4}}$

EXAMPLE 2

If $\frac{4m + 2}{m - 7} = 9$ what is the value of m?

TIP

It's completely okay (and often necessary) to multiply both sides of an equation by an **expression**, such as $(m - 7)$, rather than just a variable or constant.

Remember, you can do anything you want to the equation as long as you keep it balanced!

SOLUTION

First, look at the left side. We have a fraction with the variable we're looking for, m, in both the numerator and denominator. That's messy. Let's get rid of the fraction by multiplying **both sides** of the equation by the denominator, then make more balanced changes until m is all by itself.

① *Multiply by* **(m − 7)** $(m - 7)\frac{4m + 2}{m - 7} = 9\,(m - 7)$

$$4m + 2 = 9m - 63$$

② *Subtract* **(4m)** $4m - 4m + 2 = 9m - 4m - 63$

$$2 = 5m - 63$$

③ *Add* **(63)** $2 + 63 = 5m - 63 + 63$

$$65 = 5m$$

④ *Divide by* **(5)** $5\overline{)65} = 5\overline{)5m}$

...booyah! $\boxed{13} = m$

PORTAL

Balancing and substitution form the very **heart** of algebra. You'll use these basic skills to solve even the toughest systems of equations problems.

Don't believe us? Turn to page 494 to see for yourself!

Substitution: Rename and Plug-in

Whenever you are given (or discover through work) another "name" for a variable, you can **plug in** that new name anywhere the variable appears. For example, if we have the equation:

$$5k + a = 26$$

...and we learn that **$k = 2$**, we can go back and **substitute** in 2 anywhere we see k, and that will help us move forward in the problem:

$$5(2) + a = 26$$
$$10 + a = 26$$
$$10 - 10 + a = 26 - 10$$
$$a = 16$$

For now we are focusing on replacing a variable with a number, but this also works if you are told that **$k = a - 2$**. In this case, we just replace every k with an (**$a - 2$**):

$$5(a - 2) + a = 26$$
$$5a - 10 + a = 26$$
$$6a - 10 = 26$$
$$6a - 10 + 10 = 26 + 10$$
$$6a = 36$$
$$a = 6$$

The name's k, but YOU can call me (a − 2)!

Parentheses

Please use them! We've seen far too many students forget to place parentheses before they substitute, only to accidentally forget a negative and miss easy points.

Solve for *d* by following each step below.

$3a - b - c = d$ If $a = -2$, $b = -5$, and $c = 1$, then $d = ?$	
1. *Rewrite equation*	$3a - b - c$
2. *Substitute for a*	
3. *Substitute for b*	
4. *Substitute for c*	
5. *Simplify*	
6. *Solve*	$d =$

Substitute the given values to solve each problem below.

$a = 3$ $b = 4$ $c = -2$
7. $2a + 7 =$
8. $b - 2c =$
9. $2a + 3b - 4c =$
10. $a^2 + 2a + c =$
11. $ab - bc + ac =$

Answers: **1)** $3a - b - c = d$ **2)** $3(-2) - b - c$ **3)** $3(-2) - (-5) - c$ **4)** $3(-2) - (-5) - (1)$ **5)** $-6 + 5 - 1$ **6)** -2

7) 13 **8)** 8 **9)** 26 **10)** 13 **11)** 14

Practice Problems

Use your new skills to answer each question.

1

If $\frac{m}{m+n} = \frac{5}{7}$, what is the value of $\frac{3n}{m}$?

A) $\frac{10}{7}$

B) $\frac{6}{5}$

C) $\frac{1}{2}$

D) $\frac{15}{2}$

2

$$\frac{4}{7}x - \frac{1}{2} = \frac{2}{7}x + \frac{13}{14}$$

What is the value of x in the equation above?

3

If $a = kb$ where k is a constant and $a = 12$ when $b = 15$, what is the value of a when $b = 12$?

A) $\frac{4}{5}$

B) $\frac{5}{4}$

C) $9\frac{3}{5}$

D) 12

4

If 7 less than 5 times a number is two more than twice that number, what is the result when the number is added to 8 ?

A) $\frac{5}{7}$

B) 3

C) 11

D) 17

5

If $\frac{2}{3}x = 6y$, and x and y are non-zero numbers, what is the value of $\frac{x-y}{y}$?

A) 9

B) 8

C) 3

D) $-\frac{8}{9}$

6

Which of the following is a solution to the inequality $4x - 6 \geq 5x - 2$?

A) -1
B) -2
C) -3
D) -4

7

If the points (5, 20) and (3, a) are solutions for the equation $y = kx$, where k is a constant, what is the value of a ?

A) 5
B) 6
C) 12
D) 19

8

If $\frac{10}{4-n}$ = $-c$, what is the value of n when c = 10 ?

A) −5
B) −3
C) 3
D) 5

9

If $\frac{1}{2}(n - 12) = -5$, what is the value of $4n + 5$?

A) 2
B) 6
C) 13
D) 14

10

If $6x + 1$ is 3 more than $3x + 13$, what is the value of 8 subtracted from 4 times x ?

A) 12
B) −5
C) −20
D) −28

$$3(3x + 13) = 6x + 1$$

$$9x + 39 = 6x + 1$$
$$-9x \quad -1 \quad -9x \quad -1$$
$$39 = -3x$$

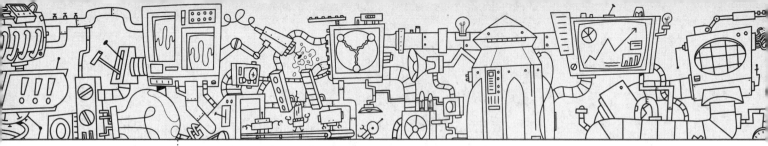

Exponents & Algebra

The next "level" of basic algebra questions throws basic exponent rules into the mix. Combine your knowledge of exponent rules with your balancing skills to answer these questions.

Exponent Rules	
When you **multiply** like bases, **add** exponents.	$x^2 \cdot x^3 = x^5$
When you **divide** like bases, **subtract** exponents.	$x^6 \div x^2 = x^4$
When you raise a **power to a power, multiply** exponents.	$(x^2)^5 = x^{10}$
When you have a **negative exponent**, take the **reciprocal**.	$x^{-2} = \frac{1}{x^2}$
When you have a **fractional exponent**, make it a **root**.	$x^{\frac{1}{2}} = \sqrt{x}$
Any number **raised to zero** is equal to **one**.	$x^0 = 1$

Rule Recap

Take a gander at the table above to make sure you're brushed up on the basic exponent rules. We'll be focusing in this chapter on the intersection of these rules and making balanced changes to algebraic equations.

Combining Like Terms

The simplest questions that test these exponent rules are basic algebra questions that require you to **combine like terms**. After all, "like terms" just means "terms with the same variable and exponent." Remember: we can combine $x + 2x$, and we can combine $x^2 + 2x^2$, but we can NOT combine $x + x^2$. Got it? Good. Let's get some practice.

like terms (n.)

Any terms with the same variable and exponent. For example:

· $2a$ and $3a$

· $6a^5$ and $8a^5$

NOT $3a$ and $3a^2$

EXAMPLE 1

$$4x^2 + 7x - 12$$
$$-2x^2 + 3x - 5$$

What is the sum of the two given polynomials?

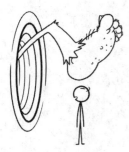

PORTAL

If you can't wait, you'll find more **systems of equations** than you can handle on page 491.

SOLUTION

This is a "systems of equations" problem, which we'll dive into in a later chapter. To add these polynomials, we'll need to **combine like terms** (terms where the variables *and exponents* are the same). In this problem, the like terms are conveniently aligned vertically! Let's combine like terms:

$$
\begin{array}{ccc}
4x^2 & +\ 7x & -\ 12 \\
+\ (-2x^2) & +\ (+\ 3x) & +\ (-5) \\
\hline
2x^2 & +\ 10x & -\ 17
\end{array}
$$

And that's it! By adding the like terms in each column, we get our answer: **$2x^2 + 10x - 17$.**

EXAMPLE 2

$$(4x^2 - 11x + 3) - 3(x^2 + 4x - 5)$$

If the expression above is rewritten in the form $ax^2 + bx + c$, where a, b, and c are constants, which of the following is the value of $b + c$?

A) −35
B) −11
C) −5
D) 41

Watch Signs!

Most students who miss this problem either forget to distribute the negative in **–3** or miss that **b** must be *negative* 23, not just 23. Can you see why that is?

If you made one of these errors, what precautions could you take to avoid making the same mistake again?

Before we can combine like terms in this problem, we have to take care of the parentheses (remember your order of operations!). The parentheses around **(4x² – 11x + 3)** are just grouping them, so we can safely remove them without changing anything. But before we can combine like terms, we first need to distribute the **–3** across **(x² + 4x – 5)**:

(1) *distribute* $-3 (x^2 + 4x - 5) = -3x^2 - 12x + 15$

Now we can put it together and find like terms.

(2) *combine like terms* $\dfrac{4x^2 - 11x + 3 - 3x^2 - 12x + 15}{x^2 - 23x + 18}$

We have now rewritten the original expression in the exact form we need! If we stack them, we can figure out what a, b, and c are.

(3) *stack & spot*
$$x^2 - 23x + 18$$
$$ax^2 + bx + c$$

$a = 1$
$b = -23$
$c = 18$

If we match patterns between these two expressions, we see that **a = 1**, **b = –23**, and **c = 18**. Now we just need to find **b + c**

(4) *add!* $b + c = -23 + 18 = \boxed{-5}$

C

EXAMPLE 3

$$2(a^2 + 2ab - 8ab^2) - (2a^2 + 3ab - 5ab^2)$$

Which of the following is equivalent to the above expression?

A) $3a^2 + 5ab - 13ab^2$
B) $ab - 11ab^2$
C) $ab - 21ab^2$
D) $4a^2 - ab - 3ab^2$

TIP

"Which of the following is equivalent to..."

is just SAT speak for:

"Simplify that junk up there and see what you get."

NOTE

Anytime a term has no coefficient, there is secretly a 1 hidden there. That's why **a = 1** in the previous question.

That's also why here you multiply each term by **−1** when you see a minus sign outside of the parentheses.

SOLUTION

When you first look at this problem, the terms with multiple letters might look complicated. But they don't actually make it any harder! The first step is the same as the last problem – **distribute across the parentheses**, being careful with negative signs.

$$2\,(a^2 + 2ab - 8ab^2) - 1(2a^2 + 3ab - 5ab^2)$$

$$2a^2 + 4ab - 16ab^2 \quad - 2a^2 - 3ab + 5ab^2$$

Now we need to combine like terms. This is just pattern matching.

$$(2-2)a^2 + (4-3)ab + (-16+5)ab^2$$

$$= 0a^2 + 1ab - 11ab^2$$

$$= \boxed{ab - 11ab^2}$$

B

EXAMPLE 4

For $i = \sqrt{-1}$, what is the sum of $(18 - 6i) + (-15 + 13i)$?

A) $33 + 7i$
B) $3 - 7i$
C) $10i$
D) $3 + 7i$

TIP

Don't panic if you see an unfamiliar (or rusty) topic on the test! As in this problem, many topics are there simply to "dress up" what is otherwise just a basic algebra problem.

SOLUTION

This problem is technically working with complex numbers, but you don't have to know a thing about them to solve it! The parentheses here are just for grouping, so we can remove them and, you guessed it, combine like terms:

$$18 - 6i - 15 + 13i$$

$$= (18 - 15) + (-6 + 13)i$$

$$= \boxed{3 + 7i}$$

D

Working with Fractional Exponents (a.k.a. Roots)

Square roots, cube roots, and fractional exponents are messy. The test writers have a tendency to make basic algebra problems tougher by trapping variables inside a square-root-prison. Most of the time, your job is simply to break them out of that prison: get the root to one side, square (or cube) both sides, and go about your merry balancing business.

EXAMPLE 5

$$\sqrt{3q^2 + 13} + p = 0$$

If $q < 0$ and $p = -11$ in the equation above, what is the value of q ?

A) 6
B) −6
C) −5
D) −7

SOLUTION A

First, take stock of what you know. We are told that $q < 0$ and $p = -11$. It's not immediately obvious why we need to know q is less than 0, but we should keep it in mind as we go. Let's start by plugging in **−11** for p:

(1) *plug-in* $\sqrt{3q^2 + 13} + (-11) = 0$

Now isolate and clear the square root. We want to solve for q, but it is currently trapped under a root. Let's break it free:

(2) *isolate* $\sqrt{3q^2 + 13} - 11 + 11 = 0 + 11$

$\sqrt{3q^2 + 13} = 11$

(3) *square both sides* $(\sqrt{3q^2 + 13})^2 = (11)^2$

$3q^2 + 13 = 121$

Now we need to **solve for q**, so let's get q² alone on one side...

continue →

④ *isolate q* $3q^2 + 13 - \mathbf{13} = 121 - \mathbf{13}$

$$3q^2 = 108$$

$$(\tfrac{1}{3})3q^2 = 108(\tfrac{1}{3})$$

$$q^2 = 36$$

Now take the square root of both sides. But we have to remember to consider both the positive and negative roots!

⑤ *square root* $\sqrt{q^2} = \sqrt{36}$

$$q = \pm 6$$

These are both possible answer choices. But remember what they told us at the beginning! If $q < 0$, then +6 doesn't work as an answer. That leaves us with $q = -6$ **(B).**

OPTION: Working Backwards

Alternatively, let's try **working backwards** to solve this problem. Plug each answer choice in for q in the original equation and see which choice comes out equaling 11:

A) $\sqrt{3(6)^2 + 13} = \sqrt{3(36) + 13} = \sqrt{108 + 13} = \sqrt{121} = 11$ ✔

B) $\sqrt{3(-6)^2 + 13} = \sqrt{3(36) + 13} = \sqrt{108 + 13} = \sqrt{121} = 11$ ✔

C) $\sqrt{3(-5)^2 + 13} = \sqrt{3(25) + 13} = \sqrt{75 + 13} = \sqrt{88} \approx 9.3$ ✘

D) $\sqrt{3(-7)^2 + 13} = \sqrt{3(49) + 13} = \sqrt{147 + 13} = \sqrt{160} \approx 12.6$ ✘

Both A and B work, but since we're told that $q < 0$ the answer must be B! Quick and easy!

B

TIP

Always cross out answer choices that do not follow the rules set out in the problem.

We're told that $q < 0$, so we know choice A is wrong right away!

EXAMPLE 6

If $r = 2\sqrt[3]{5}$ and $3r = \sqrt[3]{5s}$, what is the value of s?

SOLUTION

We are told that $r = 2\sqrt[3]{5}$, so the first thing we do is plug in:

 plug in for r $\qquad\qquad 3(2\sqrt[3]{5}) = \sqrt[3]{5s}$

$\qquad\qquad\qquad\qquad\qquad\qquad 6\sqrt[3]{5} = \sqrt[3]{5s}$

From here we have **two options** for how to solve for s.

Option A: We see cube roots on both sides and both sides are connected by multiplication, making it easy to **cube both sides**.

(2A) *cube both sides* $\qquad\qquad (6\sqrt[3]{5})^3 = (\sqrt[3]{5s})^3$

$\qquad\qquad\qquad\qquad\qquad\qquad (216)(5) = 5s$

(3A) *divide by 5* $\qquad\qquad\qquad\boxed{216} = s$

Option B: We can **split cube roots** across multiplication if it makes it easier for us to reach our goal:

(2B) *split the cube root* $\qquad\qquad 6\sqrt[3]{5} = \sqrt[3]{5s}$

$\qquad\qquad\qquad\qquad\qquad\qquad 6\sqrt[3]{5} = (\sqrt[3]{5})(\sqrt[3]{s})$

(3B) *divide by* $(\sqrt[3]{5})$ $\qquad\qquad 6 = \sqrt[3]{s}$

(4B) *cube both sides* $\qquad\qquad (6)^3 = (\sqrt[3]{s})^3$

$\qquad\qquad\qquad\qquad\qquad\qquad\boxed{216} = s$

TIP

Remember your fractional exponent rules:

$$x^{\frac{1}{n}} = \sqrt[n]{x}$$

356

Working With Like Bases

When basic algebra problems get tougher, they usually involve the use of **substitution** and **exponent rules**. As usual, your job involves combining like terms and making balanced manipulations to reach your goal. However, sometimes you'll need to first create "like bases" before you can combine terms. Remember, we can always substitute one term for an equivalent one, so we could change **27** to **3³**, or **25** to **5²** if it helps us out. Let's look at an example where this helps.

EXAMPLE 7

If $4x - 2y = 7$, what is the value of $\dfrac{16^x}{4^y}$?

A) $2^{3.5}$
B) 2^7
C) 4^7
D) 4^{14}

SOLUTION

First of all, we know that we are going to *somehow* use the info that $4x - 2y = 7$ to help us evaluate that complicated fraction. Let's keep that in mind as we work this problem.

Since x and y are both in exponents, let's try to combine terms by **finding a like base**. We could replace 16 with 4^2 and work from there, or we could notice that **16 = 2⁴** and **4 = 2²**. That ends up being easier, so let's try that:

① *find like bases* $\qquad \dfrac{16^x}{4^y} = \dfrac{(2^4)^x}{(2^2)^y}$

② *simplify* $\qquad \dfrac{16^x}{4^y} = \dfrac{(2^4)^x}{(2^2)^y} = \dfrac{2^{4x}}{2^{2y}} = 2^{4x-2y}$

Aha! Notice anything familiar? We were told that **$4x - 2y = 7$**, so...

③ *put it all together!* $\qquad \dfrac{16^x}{4^y} = 2^{4x-2y} = \boxed{2^7}$

B

The Hardest Exponent Question

Let's take a look at a question that attempts to use just about every exponent rule in the book. While this question is one of the hardest exponent problems you might come across, the solution involves the same manipulation skills you've been practicing. Give it a shot, keeping in mind that they won't come much harder than this!

EXAMPLE 8

$$\left(\frac{27}{a^6b^{12}}\right)^{-\frac{2}{3}} (12a^5b)^{\frac{1}{2}}$$

Which of the following is equivalent to the above expression?

A) $\dfrac{2a^8b^{12}\sqrt{3ab}}{27}$

B) $\dfrac{2a^8b^{12}\sqrt{3ab}}{3}$

C) $\dfrac{12a^6b^8\sqrt{b}}{9}$

D) $\dfrac{2a^6b^8\sqrt{3ab}}{9}$

Disclaimer

This question is based on the hardest exponent question we could find on the test. It is quite a time sink and should only be attempted if you're going for a near-perfect score on the math test.

If you're NOT going for a perfect score, you'd be better off skipping this one on the test and spending some time on other problems. After all, it's only worth one point!

SOLUTION

Take it one piece at a time. Let's focus on the first term:

(1) *rewrite first term* $\qquad \left(\frac{27}{a^6b^{12}}\right)^{-\frac{2}{3}} = ?$

(2) *flip fraction to clear negative exponent* $\qquad \left(\frac{27}{a^6b^{12}}\right)^{-\frac{2}{3}} = \left(\frac{a^6b^{12}}{27}\right)^{\frac{2}{3}}$

Now that looks nasty, but take it one piece at a time. We can **distribute the exponent** to each term in the fraction.

continue ➝

When we distribute the exponent, the top terms simplify cleanly into new exponents:

③ *distribute exponent* $(\frac{a^6 b^{12}}{27})^{\frac{2}{3}} = (\frac{a^{6 \cdot 2/3} b^{12 \cdot 2/3}}{27^{2/3}})$

④ *simplify numerator* $= (\frac{a^4 b^8}{27^{2/3}})$

To **simplify the denominator**, take the cubed root and square it. The cubed root of 27 is 3, and 3 squared is 9:

⑤ *simplify denominator* $(\frac{a^4 b^8}{27^{2/3}}) = (\frac{a^4 b^8}{9})$

Now we can focus on the second term. Since the exponent is just 1/2, we can just take the square root and pull out any squares.

⑥ *rewrite second term* $(12a^5 b)^{\frac{1}{2}} = \ ?$

⑦ *distribute exponent* $(12a^5 b)^{\frac{1}{2}} = \sqrt{12a^5 b}$

⑧ *simplify square root* $\sqrt{12a^5 b} = 2a^2 \sqrt{3ab}$

And at long last, we can **multiply the first and second terms**:

⑨ *rewrite new terms* $\frac{a^4 b^8}{9} \times 2a^2 \sqrt{3ab}$

⑩ *combine* $= \boxed{\frac{2a^6 b^8 \sqrt{3ab}}{9}}$

D

Practice Problems

Select the best answer choice for each equation.

1

$$3(x^2 - 2x + 4) - 2(x - 7)$$

Which of the following expressions is equivalent to the one shown above?

A) $x^2 - 9x + 4$
B) $x^2 - 3x - 3$
C) $3x^2 - 8x + 26$
D) $3x^2 - 3$

2

$$3a^2 - 6a + 7$$
$$7a^2 + 9a - 13$$

Which of the following is equivalent to the sum of the two expressions above?

A) $10a^2 + 15a - 6$
B) $10a^2 + 3a + 6$
C) $10a^2 + 15a + 20$
D) $10a^2 + 3a - 6$

3

$$(3 + 2i) - (-5 - 3i)$$

Given that $i = \sqrt{-1}$, which of the following expressions is equivalent to the one shown above?

A) $8 + 5i$
B) $8 - i$
C) $-2 + 5i$
D) $-2 - i$

4

$$f(x) = 3x^2 - 2x + 4$$
$$g(x) = -x^2 + 7x - 2$$

For the functions given above, $f(x) + g(x) = h(x)$. If $h(x)$ is given by the equation $h(x) = ax^2 + bx + c$, where a, b, and c are constants, what is the value of ab?

A) -20
B) -10
C) 0
D) 10

5

$$2(ab^2 + a^2b + ab) - (4ab - 3a^2b - 2ab^2)$$

Which of the following expressions is equivalent to the expression above?

A) $-2a^2b - 2ab^2 - ab$
B) $-2ab - 2a^2b - ab^2$
C) $4ab^2 + 5a^2b - 2ab$
D) $-ab + 3a^2b - 3ab^2$

6

Which of the following is equal to the sum of $5a^5 + 3a^3 - 7$ and $-2a^4 - 4a^3 - 5a^2 + a$?

A) $3a^5 - 2a^3 - 6$
B) $5a^5 - 2a^4 + 3a^2 - 7$
C) $5a^5 - 2a^4 + 7a^3 - 5a^2 - 7a$
D) $5a^5 - 2a^4 - a^3 - 5a^2 + a - 7$

7

If $\sqrt{108}$ is equal to $2x\sqrt{3}$, and x is greater than zero, what is the value of x?

A) 3
B) 18
C) 27
D) 54

8

$$2\sqrt{9a^3b^4c}$$

Which of the following is equivalent to the expression above?

A) $6ab^2\sqrt{ac}$

B) $\sqrt{18ab^2c}$

C) $18abc\sqrt{a^2b^3}$

D) $6a^2b^2\sqrt{ac}$

9

If $\sqrt{ab} = \sqrt{bc}$, $\sqrt{ac} = \sqrt{4c^4}$, and a, b, and c are greater than zero, what is the value of c?

A) $\dfrac{1}{4}$

B) $\dfrac{1}{2}$

C) 2

D) 4

Applied Algebra

The non-calculator section tests the very same basic algebra skills we've practiced so far in the form of scientific word problems. Your job is to look past the science jargon and focus on making balanced manipulations.

Look Ahead

These wordy algebra questions are typical of the non-calculator section, which focuses on the connection between algebra and real-world situations.

Here, we do not need to "understand" this equation: we just need to use algebra skills to shuffle it around. Later, in the Modeling chapter, we'll see problems that DO require a deeper understanding – only with much easier, everyday contexts.

Alphabet Soup

Algebra word problems can look a bit like alphabet soup at first glance. You will be given a scientific context and presented with an equation involving a (potentially) large number of variables. After all that setup, you will simply rearrange the equation and solve for a different variable than the one that's given. The only thing you need the paragraph for is to know what the different variables stand for.

As a warm-up, let's practice solving for different variables. The algebra rules you have practiced work just as well with a bunch of variables as they did when there were just one or two!

Fill in the blanks to complete the solution below.

If $s = 654 + 5.7t$, then $t = ?$	
1. *Rewrite equation*	
2. *Subtract to isolate t*	$s - (\quad) = 654 - (\quad) + 5.7t$
3. *Write the result*	$= 5.7t$
4. *Divide*	$=$
5. *Write the result*	$= t$

Answers: **(1)** $s = 654 + 5.7t$ **(2)** $654, 654$ **(3)** $s - 654$ **(4)** $(s - 654) \div 5.7 = 5.7t \div 5.7$ **(5)** $(s - 654) \div 5.7 = t$

Chemiwhat?

This equation comes from Chemistry, but (mercifully) you don't need to know a *thing* about Chemistry to solve these problems. They are just basic algebra problems in disguise.

DISCLAIMER:
We are in no way knocking Chemistry – it's actually pretty awesome when you get into it.

TIP

Variables won't always be the first letter of the word they represent, so it's always smart to check the paragraph!

EXAMPLE 1

$$PV = nRT$$

For an ideal gas, the pressure P, volume V, number of moles n, and temperature T are related by the above equation through the proportionality constant R. Which of the following equations lets you solve for the temperature if you know the other variables?

A) $\quad T = \dfrac{nR}{PV}$

B) $\quad T = PVnR$

C) $\quad T = \dfrac{1}{PVnR}$

D) $\quad T = \dfrac{PV}{nR}$

SOLUTION

First, **identify what you're solving for**: temperature.

Next, scan the paragraph (or just glance at the answer choices) to **find the variable** that represents temperature: T. So really, the problem is as simple as "solve the equation for T." We might not fully comprehend what happens to gassy moles under pressure, but we can *definitely* solve for T:

① *rewrite the equation* $\qquad PV = nRT$ ← *our focus!*

② *isolate T* $\qquad (\frac{1}{nR})PV = nRT(\frac{1}{nR})$

③ *celebrate. ya done.* $\qquad \boxed{\dfrac{PV}{nR} = T}$

D

EXAMPLE 2

$$P = \frac{S - E}{S}$$

A company uses the above equation to determine what profit ratio P they get when they make S dollars worth of sales and have E dollars in expenses. Which of the following equations would allow the company to determine how much it needs to make in sales to reach a target profit ratio if expenses are fixed ?

A) $S = \frac{E}{1 - P}$

B) $S = \frac{P - 1}{E}$

C) $S = \frac{1 - P}{E}$

D) $S = \frac{P - E}{P}$

This Guy

Just keeps on balancin'.

SOLUTION

The first step is always to **determine what you are solving for**. In this case, we are asked for **sales**, which is represented by S.

 GOAL: solve for S $P = \frac{S - E}{S}$

Unfortunately, our target variable (S) is in both the top *and bottom* of the fraction. That's trouble. So let's multiply both sides by S to **get rid of that fraction** and go from there:

(1) *clear denominator* $(S)\, P = \frac{S - E}{S}\,(S)$

$SP = S - E$

(2) *gather the S's* $SP - (S) = S - (S) - E$

$SP - S = -E$

(3) *factor out an S* $S(P - 1) = -E$

(4) *solve for S* $S = \frac{-E}{P - 1}$ or $\boxed{\frac{E}{1 - P}}$ **A**

EXAMPLE 3

$$E = \tfrac{1}{2}mv^2 + mgh$$

Conservation of energy tells us that the total energy E of a pendulum of mass m is constant at every point in its swing. The above equation shows how that energy is split between kinetic and potential energy at any given point, in terms of the pendulum's velocity v, its height h above the lowest point in its swing, and the gravitational constant g. Which of the following equations gives the height of the pendulum in terms of the other variables ?

A) $\quad h = \dfrac{E - \tfrac{1}{2}v^2}{g}$

B) $\quad h = E - \tfrac{1}{2}mv^2 - mg$

C) $\quad h = \dfrac{E}{mg} - \dfrac{v^2}{2g}$

D) $\quad h = \dfrac{E - v^2}{mg}$

SOLUTION

The first thing we need to do is **formulate the first law of thermodynamics** for a compressible, closed system:

(!) *just kidding* $\qquad\qquad we = jk$

We defintely don't have to do that. While that *is* an impressive paragraph of physics goodness up there, we're just here to rearrange some formulas and go home. Our goal is to make balanced changes until height, **h**, is alone on one side:

(1) *rewrite equation* $\qquad\qquad E = \tfrac{1}{2}mv^2 + mgh$

(2) *subtract* $\qquad\qquad E - \tfrac{1}{2}mv^2 = mgh$

(3) *divide* $\qquad\qquad \dfrac{E - \tfrac{1}{2}mv^2}{mg} = h$

Hmm... we got **h** alone on one side but the equation doesn't match any of the answer choices! Our work is good so far, though, so there **must** be a way to simplify our equation...

continue $\longrightarrow$

Work with confidence!

If you carefully write out each step of your work, you can quickly check to see that you're on the right track when you hit a slight roadblock. That way, you can focus on finding a way **forward**.

So, now we have a new goal:

 GOAL: simplify $\qquad h = \dfrac{E - \frac{1}{2}mv^2}{mg}$

What could we do to simplify? Well, one idea is to try **splitting the fraction**... so why not, let's try it:

4 *split the fraction* $\qquad h = \dfrac{E}{mg} - \dfrac{\frac{1}{2}mv^2}{mg}$

5 *cancel the m's* $\qquad h = \dfrac{E}{mg} - \dfrac{\frac{1}{2}\cancel{m}v^2}{\cancel{m}g}$

$$h = \dfrac{E}{mg} - \dfrac{\frac{1}{2}v^2}{g}$$

This looks familiar! Our equation is looking a lot like choice C:

C) $\quad h = \dfrac{E}{mg} - \dfrac{v^2}{2g} \qquad \longleftrightarrow \qquad h = \dfrac{E}{mg} - \dfrac{\frac{1}{2}v^2}{g}$

The only difference is a **2** in the denominator instead of a **1/2** in the numerator... and that's the same thing!

Think about it: we could write **1/2** as **2⁻¹**... and then drop the 2 to the denominator. Which means... **C is the correct answer!**

C

EXAMPLE 4

$$G = -RT\ln K$$

The standard change of Gibbs free energy for a system at equilibrium is described by the above equation in terms of the temperature T, the equilibrium constant K, and a proportionality constant R. Which of the following expresses the temperature in terms of the other quantities?

A) $T = \dfrac{G - \ln K}{-R}$

B) $T = \dfrac{G - \ln K}{-R}$

C) $T = \dfrac{G}{-R\ln K}$

D) $T = G + R - \ln K$

SOLUTION

The first step is to **determine what we're asked to solve for**. In this case, we are looking for **temperature**, again denoted by T. In our equation, $G = -RT\ln K$, we notice that T is being multiplied by "$\ln K$". This is the "natural log" function, but that doesn't matter and we don't need to know what that is to solve this problem! We can treat the whole expression ($\ln K$) as a single chunk. Since that chunk is being multiplied to T, we can just divide both sides by **(−R)** and by **($\ln K$)** to isolate T:

our focus!

1. *rewrite equation* $G = -RT\ln K$

2. *divide by (−R)* $\dfrac{G}{-R} = T\ln K$

3. *divide by ($\ln K$)* $\dfrac{G}{-R\ln K} = T$

C

Practice Problems

Select the best answer choice for each question.

1

$$\frac{1}{T} = \frac{1}{R} + \frac{1}{S}$$

When two resistors are in parallel in a circuit, their combined resistance T is the reciprocal of the sum of the reciprocals of the resistance of the two individual resistors R and S as shown in the equation above. Which of the following equations gives the resistance S needs to have if we know the resistance of R and the desired combined resistance?

A) $S = \dfrac{T(R)}{R - T}$

B) $S = \dfrac{T(R)}{T - R}$

C) $S = R + T$

D) $S = \dfrac{T - R}{R(T)}$

2

$$V = IR$$
$$P = IV$$

When we are looking at an ideal circuit, the above equation explains the relationship between the voltage V, current I, resistance R, and power P. Which of the following equations gives an expression for the resistance of the circuit in terms of the voltage and power?

A) $R = \dfrac{V}{P}$

B) $R = \dfrac{V^2}{P}$

C) $R = \dfrac{P}{V^2}$

D) $R = \dfrac{P}{V}$

3

$$F = -\frac{G(m_1 + m_2)}{r^2}$$

The gravitational force F between two objects a distance r apart with masses m_1 and m_2 respectively is shown in the equation above. G is a gravitational constant. Which of the following expressions gives the mass of the first object in terms of the other values?

A) $m_1 = \frac{FGm_2}{r^2}$

B) $m_1 = -\frac{FGm_2}{r^2}$

C) $m_1 = \frac{Fr^2}{G} + m_2$

D) $m_1 = -\frac{Fr^2}{G} - m_2$

4

$$\delta = \frac{1}{\sqrt{1 - (\frac{v}{c})^2}}$$

The Lorentz factor δ is important for a number of calculations in relativistic mechanics. In the above equation, v is the relative velocity of the object and c is the speed of light. Which of the following equations would let us find the relative velocity of the object if we knew the Lorentz factor?

A) $v = c\sqrt{1 - \frac{1}{\delta^2}}$

B) $v = c - \frac{c}{\delta}$

C) $v = c^2 - \frac{c^2}{\delta^2}$

D) $v = c\sqrt{\delta^2 - 1}$

5

$$n_1\sin(\Theta_1) = n_2\sin(\Theta_2)$$

When a ray of light passes between materials, it refracts. Snell's law, given above, describes the relationship between the angle of incidence Θ_1 in a material with index of refraction n_1 and the angle of refraction Θ_2 in a material with index of refraction n_2. A scientist knows the angle of incidence and index of refraction of the first material. If they want to find the necessary index of refraction to attain a specific angle of refraction in the second material, which of the following equations should they use?

A) $n_2 = n_1\sin(\Theta_1) - \sin(\Theta_2)$

B) $n_2 = \dfrac{\sin(\Theta_1)}{n_1\sin(\Theta_2)}$

C) $n_2 = \dfrac{n_1\sin(\Theta_1)}{\sin(\Theta_2)}$

D) $n_2 = \dfrac{n_1\Theta_1}{\Theta_2}$

6

$$v^2 = v_0^2 + 2a(x - k)$$

The above equation gives the square of the velocity v of a car given its initial velocity v_0, constant acceleration a, current position x and starting position k. Which of the following equations would allow you to solve for the starting position of the car if you knew its current position, acceleration, and current velocity?

A) $k = \dfrac{v_0^2 - v^2 - x}{2a}$

B) $k = v^2 - v_0^2 - 2ax$

C) $k = \dfrac{v^2 - v_0^2}{2ax}$

D) $k = x - \dfrac{v^2 - v_0^2}{2a}$

Questions 7-8 refer to the following information:

The real cash flow, R, in dollars, from a bank deposit after one year is given by $R = \frac{N}{1+I}$, where R is the real cash flow in dollars, N is the nominal cash flow in dollars, and I is the rate of inflation.

7

Which of the following equations gives the rate of inflation in terms of real and nominal cash flow?

A) $I = \frac{N}{R} - 1$

B) $I = \frac{R-1}{N}$

C) $I = \frac{N}{R+1}$

D) $I = \frac{R}{N} + 1$

8

If the nominal cash flow of a bank deposit was $35, but the real cash flow for that deposit was $34, what was the inflation rate for that year, rounded to the nearest percent?

A) 1%
B) 2%
C) 3%
D) 4%

Questions 9-10 refer to the following information:

$$t = \sqrt{\frac{2h}{9.81}}$$

The time t it takes, in seconds, for an object to hit the ground after getting dropped from rest at a height h, in meters, is given by the equation above.

9

Which of the following equations gives the height from which the object was dropped in terms of the time it took for the object to hit the ground?

A) $h = \sqrt{\frac{9.81t}{2}}$

B) $h = \frac{2t^2}{9.81}$

C) $h = \frac{9.81t^2}{2}$

D) $h = (9.81)(2)t^2$

10

Francesca dropped a pebble into a river while standing on a bridge 20 meters above the river. Approximately how long will it take for the pebble to leave Francesca's hand and land in the river?

A) 2 seconds
B) 4 seconds
C) 8 seconds
D) 16 seconds

Questions 11–13 refer to the following information:

$$\$2{,}750 + \$37E = B$$

The total operating budget for a certain manager each year is given by the equation above, where E represents the number of employees the manager oversees and B represents the total operating budget in dollars.

11

Which of the following expressions gives the number of employees in terms of the total operating budget?

A) $E = \dfrac{2750 - B}{37}$

B) $E = \dfrac{2750 + B}{37}$

C) $E = \dfrac{B - 2750}{37}$

D) $E = \dfrac{B + 2750}{37}$

12

If the manager has an operating budget of \$17,550, how many employees does the manager have?

A) 300
B) 350
C) 400
D) 450

13

What is the meaning of \$2,750 in the equation?

A) The manager has an operating budget of \$2,750.
B) The manager can spend \$2,750 per employee.
C) The manager must spend \$2,750 each year.
D) The manager has at least \$2,750 for the operating budget.

UNIT | Lines & Functions

Chapters

Key Skills

In this unit, we'll learn about the connection between basic algebra, linear equations, and their illustrations, **graphs**. We'll also practice thinking of equations and graphs as **functions** built on inputs and outputs.

Equation of a Line

In this chapter we are learning the definition of slope, how to recognize the equation of a line, and what it means when lines are perpendicular and parallel.

Graphs are Illustrations

Every line on a graph is attached to a certain mathematical equation that tells you how to find points on that line. You can think of the graph of a line as simply an **illustration** of all the possible solutions to an equation. We can illustrate "$y = 2x + 1$" or "$y = -2x + 1$" just like we can illustrate "Marian Rejewski" or "Tobi the dog."

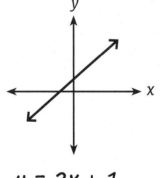

Marian Rejewski

$y = 2x + 1$

$y = -2x + 1$

Tobi the Dog

Slope-Intercept Form

Before we can illustrate a linear equation, however, it helps to put the equation in what we call the **slope-intercept form**.

$$y = mx + b$$

We call it the slope-intercept form because that's exactly what it tells us about the line. Just by looking at an equation in this form, we can see the line's **slope (m)** and it's **y-intercept (b)**. And if you know these two things, you know exactly how to draw the line!

ⓑ y-intercept

Every line drawing's gotta start somewhere, and there's no better place than the point where the line crosses the y-axis, a.k.a. the **y-intercept**. This is the point where x is zero.

Ⓜ slope

Once we know our y-intercept, we need to know our slope. The slope of a line is the relationship between two of its points. It tells us whether the line goes uphill or downhill, and just how steep of a hill we're talking. A **positive** slope runs uphill from left to right, while a **negative** slope runs downhill from left to right.

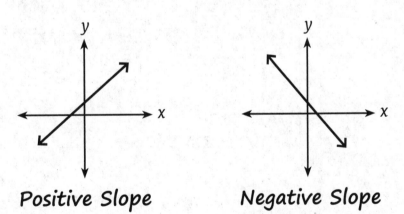

Positive Slope   Negative Slope

Sidenote: Special Slopes

Sometimes, instead of a slope, you have a flat ground or a sheer cliff. When a line is a flat, horizontal line, it has a **slope of zero**. When a line is a straight, vertical line, its slope is **undefined**.

Reading Slope-Intercept Form

Before we try some test problems, let's get used to reading the slope intercept form. The table below contains a number of linear equations. For problems 1-5, make sure the equation is in the $y = mx + b$ form and determine the slope (m) and y-intercept (b). For problems 6-8, you are told the slope and y-intercept of a line and must write its equation in slope-intercept form.

TIP

Equations will not always be in slope-intercept form.

Whenever a line's equation is not in the form **y = mx + b**, rearrange it!

Fill in the empty entries in the table below.

Equation	m	b
1. $y = -5x + 4$	-5	
2. $y = \frac{2}{7}x - 3$		
3. $6 = 3x - y$		
4. $-32 = -8x + 4y$		
5. $8x + y = 0$		
6.	$\frac{1}{3}$	7
7.	-4	2
8.	$\frac{5}{13}$	-4

Answers: **1)** $m = -5$, $b = 4$ **2)** $m = 2/7$, $b = -3$ **3)** $m = 3$, $b = -6$ **4)** $m = 2$, $b = -8$ **5)** $m = -8$, $b = 0$
6) $y = (1/3)x + 7$ **7)** $y = -4x + 2$ **8)** $y = (5/13)x - 4$

Calculating Slope

We calculate slope as **rise over run**, or change in y over change in x:

$$\text{Slope } (m) = \frac{rise}{run} = \frac{y_2 - y_1}{x_2 - x_1}$$

If you're given two points on a line—(x_1, y_1) and (x_2, y_2)—you can find the slope just by plugging them into the slope formula above.

Find the slope of the lines containing the following pairs of points.

Points		Slope
1. $(2, 7)\,(9, 3)$	$\dfrac{y_2 - y_1}{x_2 - x_1} = \dfrac{3 - 7}{9 - 2} =$	$-\dfrac{4}{7}$
2. $(10, -8)\,(6, 7)$		
3. $(2, 4)\,(1, 9)$		
4. $(-7, 0)\,(-9, -10)$		
5. $(-45, 2)\,(31, -21)$		
6. $(3, a)\,(4, 7)$		
7. $(s, t)(0, 5)$		
8. $(-2, 15)(x, 6)$		

Answers: 1) $-\dfrac{4}{7}$ 2) $-\dfrac{15}{4}$ 3) -5 4) 5 5) $-\dfrac{23}{76}$

6) $7 - a$ 7) $-\dfrac{5 - t}{s}$ 8) $\dfrac{-9}{x + 2}$

EXAMPLE 1

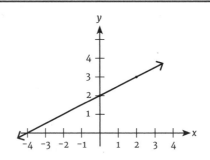

Which of the following represents the relationship between x and y?

A) $x = 2y$

B) $y = 2x + 2$

C) $y = 2x + \frac{1}{2}$

D) $y = \frac{1}{2}x + 2$

SOLUTION

Asking for the relationship between x and y is another way of asking for the equation of the line. Imagine that you wanted to text information about this line to your friend so they could recreate it. You could accomplish that in just three questions:

🖊 *Where does the line cross the y-axis?* (0 , 2)

🖊 *Is the line going uphill or downhill?* uphill

🖊 *How much does the line go up for every unit it goes over?* 1/2

So our y-intercept (b) is **2**, and our slope (m) is **positive** $\frac{1}{2}$. We can plug that into the slope-intercept equation to find our answer:

① *write line equation* $y = mx + b$

② *plug-in* $y = \frac{1}{2}x + 2$

D

Finding Slope

We can find the slope by looking at the graph or by plugging two points on the graph, **(–4, 0)** and **(0, 2)**, into the slope formula:

$$m = \frac{2-0}{0-(-4)} = \frac{2}{4} = \frac{1}{2}$$

EXAMPLE 2

A line in the xy-plane passes through the origin and has a slope of $\frac{2}{3}$. Which of the following points lies on the line?

A) $(2, 3)$
B) $(3, 2)$
C) $(4, 6)$
D) $(-2, 3)$

SOLUTION

In this problem, they give us a slope of $m = \frac{2}{3}$. They don't come right out and say "the y-intercept is...", but they do tell us that the line **passes through the origin**, or point $(0, 0)$. That's a y-intercept! So $b = 0$. Now, we can write the equation of this line:

(1) *write line equation* $y = mx + b$

(2) *plug-in* $y = \frac{2}{3}x$

Now we can find a point on this line in many ways.

Option 1: Test Points
First, let's try a trick that works in multiple situations: **test points with our equation**. Since we have the equation of the line, we can plug each point from the answer choices into our equation. If plugging in the given x-value gives the given y-value, then that point is on the line!

(A) *Try (2, 3)* $y = \frac{2}{3}(2) = \frac{4}{3} \neq 3$ ✗

(B) *Try (3, 2)* $y = \frac{2}{3}(3) = 2$ ✓

Bingo! By testing points, we can see that point $(3, 2)$ is on the line.

Option 2: Draw and Plot
There's another way to find a point on this line. Since we have a point $(0, 0)$ and we know that the slope goes **up 2** and **right 3,** we can **draw the line** and find our own points one-by-one.

continue →

TIP

Once you know the equation of a line, you can do **almost** anything! Find that equation!

TIP

There are two things you need to know to draw a line:

1) one point
2) the slope

Anytime you know these two things, you can start at the point and use the slope to find more points.

So let's use what we know about slope to **find our own points**:

(1) *start at y-intercept*

(2) *move up 2, right 3*

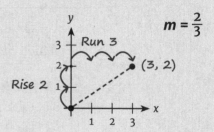

And voila! The first point we find in this way happens to be our answer: (3, 2).

Option 3: Adding with Slope
We could do this same general idea without even drawing a graph. By applying "rise 2, run 3", you can generate as many points as you fancy:

(1) *first point*   (0, 0)

 ⟩ +3, +2

(2) *second point*   **(3, 2)**

 ⟩ +3, +2

(3) *third point*   (6, 4)

 ⟩ +3, +2

(4) *fourth point...*   (9, 6)

We could keep going forever! But we won't. We can just add points until we see one that is an answer choice, so we can stop at **(3, 2).**

B

EXAMPLE 3

The graph of the linear function f has intercepts at $(a, 0)$ and $(0, b)$ in the xy-plane. If $ab < 0$, which of the following must be true about the slope of the graph of f?

A) It is positive
B) It is negative
C) It equals zero
D) There is not enough information to say.

SOLUTION

This problem is a litte bit abstract, but don't let that scare you. Let's pick out what we have to work with:

- The function is "linear", so it's **a line**.

- The graph has both an x-intercept $(a, 0)$ and a y-intercept $(0, b)$. The fact that the question gives us points on the xy-plane suggests that **drawing a sketch** might be helpful.

- $ab < 0$

This last bit tells us that either a or b (but not both!) is negative. Which means, if we're **sketching a line**, there are two different ways we could draw our points:

① *if a were positive...*
then b would be negative.

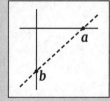

② *if a were negative...*
then b would be positive.

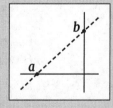

If you imagine "sliding" any of these points toward or away from zero, the steepness of the slope changes, but the fact that it's *positive* never does. Therefore, the answer is **A**— and we just **proved** that if only one of the intercepts is positive, the **slope** must be positive! That's pretty cool.

A

NOTE

Neither a nor b could be 0, because then ab wouldn't be less than zero... it'd just be zero.

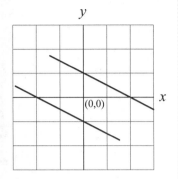

Parallel Lines

Any two lines that are **parallel** have the same exact slope. Which, of course, also means that any two lines with the same slope are parallel! On the test, if you see two equations with the same "m", then you know they must be parallel lines.

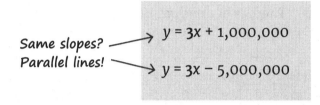

Same slopes?
Parallel lines!

$y = 3x + 1{,}000{,}000$

$y = 3x - 5{,}000{,}000$

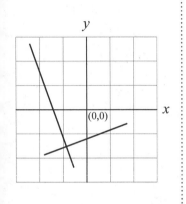

Perpendicular Lines

Two lines that are perpendicular (meet at a 90° angle) have slopes that are **negative reciprocals** of one another. To find the **negative reciprocal** of a fraction:

(1) *Flip the fraction* $\quad \frac{1}{2} \quad \frac{2}{1}$

(2) *Flip the sign* $\quad +\frac{2}{1} \quad -\frac{2}{1}$

So if a line has a slope of $\frac{1}{5}$, then a perpendicular line has a slope of **−5**.

And if a line has a slop of **−6**, then a perpendicular line has a slope of $\frac{1}{6}$.

opposite slopes?
perpendicular lines!

$y = \frac{1}{2}x + 1{,}000{,}000$

$y = -2x - 5{,}000{,}000$

EXAMPLE 4

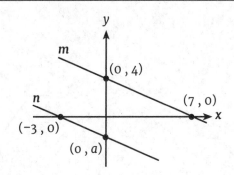

In the xy-plane above, line m is parallel to line n. What is the value of a ?

A) 21

B) $-\dfrac{4}{7}$

C) $-\dfrac{21}{4}$

D) $-\dfrac{12}{7}$

SOLUTION

Here's a tip: if you see parallel lines in a coordinate plane, there is a good chance you are going to be working with **slope**– especially since there are two points marked on each line. So let's find the slope of each line:

1 *find* **slope** *of line m* $slope_m = \dfrac{0-4}{7-0} = -\dfrac{4}{7}$

2 *find* **slope** *of line n* $slope_n = \dfrac{a-0}{0-(-3)} = \dfrac{a}{3}$

And since our lines are **parallel**, we know that these slopes must really be the **exact same**. So...

3 *set slopes equal to each other* $slope_m = slope_n$

$$-\dfrac{4}{7} = \dfrac{a}{3}$$

4 *cross multiply* $-12 = 7a$

5 *solve for a* $\boxed{-\dfrac{12}{7}} = a$

D

TIP

Whenever you use the slope formula, make sure your negatives are straight:

$$-\dfrac{4}{7} \neq \dfrac{-4}{-7}$$

EXAMPLE 5

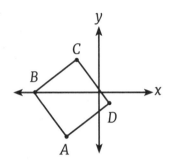

In the xy-plane above, $ABCD$ is a square. The coordinates of points A and B are $(-3, -4)$ and $(-6, 0)$, respectively. Which of the following is the equation of the line that passes through points A and D?

A) $y = -\frac{4}{3}x - \frac{7}{4}$

B) $y = \frac{3}{4}x - \frac{7}{4}$

C) $y = -\frac{3}{4}x - \frac{7}{4}$

D) $y = \frac{3}{4}x + \frac{4}{7}$

SOLUTION

Let's start by **going over what we know**. We know that $ABCD$ is a square, which means each side is *perpendicular* to its adjoining sides. That may help later, so let's keep it in mind.

We also know we are looking for the **equation of a line** that passes through points A and D. So before we do anything else, let's just jot down the slope-intercept form to start us off:

① *write slope-intercept form* $\qquad y = mx + b$

Okay! To fill out this equation, we'll need to find the **slope (m)** of line $\overline{AD}$. To do that, we need two points on the line. We don't have that... but we *do* have two points on line $\overline{BA}$: **(-3, -4)** and **(-6, 0)**. Since we can, let's go ahead and find the slope of $\overline{BA}$.

② *find slope of $\overline{BA}$* $\qquad m_{BA} = \frac{y_2 - y_1}{x_2 - x_1} = \frac{-4 - 0}{-3 - (-6)} = -\frac{4}{3}$

continue →

Aha! And remember how we know that line $\overline{AD}$ is *perpendicular* to line $\overline{BA}$? That means their slopes are **negative reciprocals** of each other! If the slope of line $\overline{BA}$ is $-\frac{4}{3}$, then the slope of our line is $\frac{3}{4}$. Let's update our equation:

③ *update equation* $\qquad\qquad\qquad$ $y = \frac{3}{4}x + b$

Now we just need to find **b**. We can do that with our old trick: plugging in a point we know to be on the line... Let's use point **A (–3, –4)** to help us find **b:**

④ *plug in (–3, –4)* $\qquad\qquad$ $y = \frac{3}{4}x + b$

$$-4 = \frac{3}{4}(-3) + b$$

$$-4 = -\frac{9}{4} + b$$

⑤ *solve for b* $\qquad\qquad\qquad$ $-\frac{16}{4} + \frac{9}{4} = b$

$$-\frac{7}{4} = b$$

At last, we have the last piece of the line equation! Let's plug **m** and **b** back into the equation for our answer:

⑥ *finalize equation* $\qquad\qquad$ $y = mx + b$

$$y = \frac{3}{4}x - \frac{7}{4}$$

B

389

Practice Problems

Use your new skills to answer each question.

1

A line in the *xy*-plane passes through the origin and the point (2, 3). Which of the following is the slope of the line?

A) $\frac{2}{3}$

B) $\frac{3}{2}$

C) 2

D) 3

rise / run

2

The line *y = mx* − 7, where *m* is a constant, is graphed in the *xy*-plane. If the line contains the point (6, −3), what is the value of *m* ?

$-3 = 6m - 7$
$+7 \qquad +7$

$4 = 6m$

$\frac{4}{6} = m$

$\frac{2}{3} = m$

3

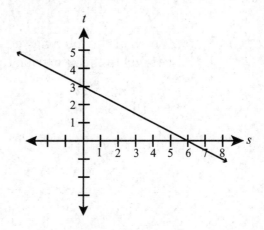

Which of the following represents the relationship between s and t?

A) $t = 3s - \frac{1}{2}$

B) $t = -\frac{1}{2}s + 3$

C) $s = 2t + 3$

D) $s = -\frac{1}{2}t + 3$

$s = 6$

$t = 0$

$s = 3$

$t = 1$

4

The graph of a particular line contains the points $(-1, -3)$ and $(1, 3)$. What is the equation of the line?

A) $y = x + 3$

B) $y = x$

C) $y = 3x$

D) $y = 3x + 1$

5

$$y = \frac{5}{3}x - 2$$

Which of the following equations represents a line that is parallel to the line given by the equation above?

A) $5x - 3y = 12$
B) $2y - 6x = 5$
C) $5y - 3x = 12$
D) $3x - 5y = 6$

6

$$ax + 6y = 3$$
$$bx + 5y = 2$$

If the system of equations above is parallel, which of the following must be a true statement?

A) $5b = 6a$
B) $5a = 6b$
C) $a + b = 11$
D) $ab = 30$

7

$$7x + 3y = 4$$
$$-14x + ny = 10$$

The two equations above are parallel and n is a constant. If $(1, c)$ is a solution to the second equation, what is the value of c?

A) -4

B) $-\frac{2}{3}$

C) 0

D) 4

8

The graph of the linear function f passes through the quadrants I, II, and IV. Which of the following is true about the slope of the function f?

A) The slope is undefined.
B) The slope is positive.
C) The slope is negative.
D) There is not enough information provided.

9

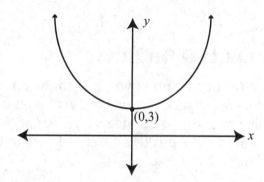

The graph of $f(x)$ is shown above. If $g(x)$ is a non-vertical linear function which intersects $f(x)$ at exactly one point, which of the following must be true?

A) The slope of $g(x)$ is 0.
B) The slope of $g(x)$ is undefined.
C) $g(x) = 3$
D) The y intercept of $g(x)$ is less than or equal to 3.

10

The line $2ax - by = 2$, where a and b are constants, is graphed in the xy-plane. If the line contains the point $(2, -4)$, what is the slope of the line in terms of b?

A) $-b$

B) $2b$

C) $b + \frac{2}{b}$

D) $\frac{1 - 2b}{b}$

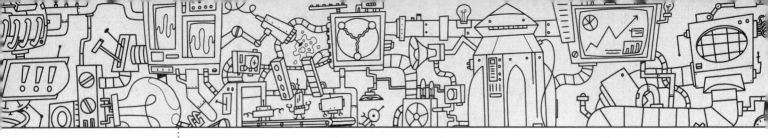

Function Machines

In this chapter, we become familiar with function notation in all of its forms and get used to working with the MACHINE.

Inputs & Outputs

A function is something that **takes an input** and **returns an output**. In the last chapter, we worked with lines and their equations, which actually illustrate this exact idea. A line equation can be thought of as a function that lets you **put IN** an *x*-coordinate to **get OUT** the *y*-coordinate at that point on the line.

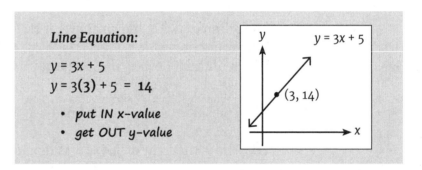

Line Equation:

$y = 3x + 5$
$y = 3(3) + 5 = 14$

- *put IN x-value*
- *get OUT y-value*

So we can think of the line equation as a perfectly built **function** for finding points on a line. As we dive deeper, however, we sometimes want to graph multiple lines at once, or work with equations where the graph isn't particularly relevant. For those reasons, it helps to use a different notation that emphasizes the connection between inputs and outputs.

And that's where **function notation** comes in!

Function Notation & The Machine

Instead of writing an equation in terms of y, we can write in terms of $f(x)$:

line equation	$y = 3x + 5$
function notation	$f(x) = 3x + 5$

Reading $f(x)$

We read $f(x) = 3x + 5$ as:

"f of x is three times x plus five."

f on its own is NOT a variable, and those parentheses do NOT mean multiplication.

Function notation makes it clear that the left side of the equation **depends** on what you plug in for x on the right side. You can think of the (x) on the left as the input chute for the **function machine**. Anything you plug into the chute for x replaces the x's on the right. If you plug in a different input, you'll get a different output:

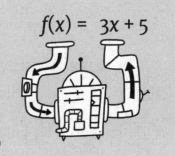

Function Machine:

$f(2) = 3(2) + 5 = 11$
$f(-4) = 3(-4) + 5 = -7$
$f(90) = 3(90) + 5 = 270$

- put IN value for x
- get OUT a value for f(x)

$f(x) = 3x + 5$

EXAMPLE 1

If $f(x) = -4x + 3$, what is $f(-2a)$ equal to?

A) $8a + 3$
B) $-8a + 3$
C) $-2a - 1$
D) $8ax + 3$

TIP

It's a good, nay, a GREAT idea to keep the parentheses whenever you make a substitution.

SOLUTION

Any time you see an equation whose left side is a letter followed by another letter in parentheses, such as $f(x)$, you should assume you are working with a function. In this problem we have a function $f(x)$ to evaluate when $x = -2a$. This means we need to replace each x on the right hand side with $(-2a)$:

① *Copy equation* $f(x) = -4x + 3$

② *Plug in $(-2a)$ for x* $f(-2a) = -4(-2a) + 3$

③ *Simplify* $f(-2a) = \boxed{8a + 3}$

A

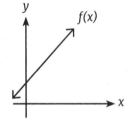

NOTE

When we plot all of the input-output pairs of function $f(x)$ in a graph, we call that line (or parabola) simply "$f(x)$".

Functions and Graphs

Function equations and graphs of those equations are two sides of the same coin. As we saw earlier, we can think of the equation of a line as a specific type of function machine that gives us a y-coordinate when we plug in an x-coordinate. As we plug more and more x-coordinates into that function machine, we collect points on that line. We can talk about those points in terms of xy-coordinates or in terms of function notation:

> If point $(2, 3)$ is on the graph of $f(x)$, then $f(2) = 3$.
>
> If point $(0, 4)$ is on the graph of $g(x)$, then $g(0) = 4$.

In the next few examples, we'll see how we can be flexible with our understanding of functions as both machines and graphs to solve a number of different types of problems.

EXAMPLE 2

z	1	2	3	4
$g(z)$	3	1	−1	−3

The table above shows some values of the linear function g. Which of the following defines g ?

A) $g(z) = z + 2$

B) $g(z) = 3z − 2$

C) $g(z) = −2z + 5$

D) $g(z) = −\frac{1}{2}z + 5$

SOLUTION

We can solve this problem in a couple of different ways. We can think of the function graphically and use our equation of a line skills... or we can think of the function like a machine, and do some plugging and chugging.

Option 1: Thinking with Graphs
We are told that $g(z)$ is a **linear** function. This is just a fancy way of telling us that the graph of $g(z)$ is a **line**... and each column in the table tells us the coordinates of points on that line:

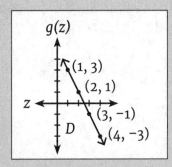

To find the equation of this line, we'll need a slope. We can find that by using any two points on this graph, such as (1, 3) and (2, 1):

① *find slope of $g(z)$*   slope $= \dfrac{1-3}{2-1} = -\dfrac{2}{1}$

So the **slope** of the line equation is **-2.** If we look at our answer choices, we see that only **choice C** has the correct slope!

continue →

Option 2: Thinking with Functions
Alternatively, we could work backwards to solve this problem. Each column in the table tells us what we should get OUT of the correct equation for different inputs. In the correct equation, $g(1) = 3$, $g(2) = 1$, $g(3) = -1$, and $g(4) = -3$. Just like we can "test" line equations by plugging in points, we can also test each answer choice by plugging in z values from the table. The only choice that works with **every value in the table** is choice C:

C) $g(z) = -2z + 5$

$g(1) = -2(1) + 5 = 3$ ✓

$g(2) = -2(2) + 5 = 3$ ✓

$g(3) = -2(3) + 5 = -1$ ✓

$g(4) = -2(4) + 5 = -3$ ✓

C

EXAMPLE 3

$$h(x) = \frac{5}{2}x + k$$

In the function defined above, k is a constant. If $h(-4) = 3$, what is the value of $h(2)$?

A) -2
B) -7
C) 13
D) 18

SOLUTION

Our goal is to find $h(2)$. To do that, we'll first need to figure out what k is. Luckily, we're given that **$h(-4) = 3$**. We can plug in this solution in order to **find k**.

① *Copy equation* $\qquad\qquad\qquad h(x) = \frac{5}{2}x + k$

② *Plug-in $h(-4) = 3$* $\qquad\qquad 3 = \frac{5}{2}(-4) + k$

③ *Solve for k* $\qquad\qquad\qquad 3 = -10 + k$

$\qquad\qquad\qquad\qquad\qquad\qquad 13 = k$

So now that we know what k is, we can **find $h(2)$**:

④ *Update equation* $\qquad\qquad h(x) = \frac{5}{2}x + 13$

⑤ *Plug-in $h(2)$* $\qquad\qquad\quad h(2) = \frac{5}{2}(2) + 13$

⑥ *Simplify* $\qquad\qquad\qquad\quad h(2) = 5 + 13$

$\qquad\qquad\qquad\qquad\qquad\qquad h(2) = ⑱$ **D**

EXAMPLE 4

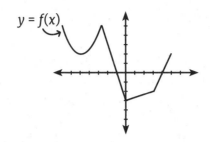

The complete graph of the function f is shown in the xy-plane above. For which of the following values of x is $f(x) > x$?

I. $x = -5$
II. $x = -1$
III. $x = 5$

A) I only
B) I and II only
C) II and III only
D) I, II, and III

SOLUTION

This problem might look complicated at first, but it's really just asking us to **find the points on the line** at $x = -5$, $x = -1$, and $x = 5$. So let's find the y-value for each one:

(I) $(-5, 2)$

(II) $(-1, 0)$

(III) $(5, 2)$

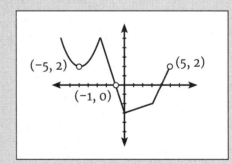

Our three points are **(–5, 2)**, **(–1, 0)**, and **(5, 2)**.

We're asked for which of these points is **$f(x) > x$**. We know that here $f(x) = y$, so we just need to find the choices where the y-coordinate is greater than the x-coordinate. Since **2 > –5** and **0 > –1**, choices I and II are correct. III doesn't work because **2 < 5**.

That means **choice B is the answer!**   **B**

Compound Functions

Sometimes you'll come across functions-within-functions. These are simply **multistep function problems** where you need to *focus on the inside function first* and work your way out.

EXAMPLE 5

A function f satisfies f(2) = 4 and f(5) = 7. A function g satisfies g(5) = 2 and g(7) = 3. What is f(g(5)) ?

A) 2
B) 3
C) 4
D) 7

SOLUTION

We want to evaluate f(g(5)), so let's **start with the inside function**, g(5). We are told that g(5) = 2, so we can substitute 2 in:

1 *substitute* $f(g(5)) = ?$

$f(2) = ?$

Once we resolve the inside function, we see that what's left is just f(2), which the problem tells us is **equal to 4**!

C

Getting Flexible

Let's get flexible with function notation by working through a few exercises. Once you get used to the idea of functions as machines, you'll be able to apply that idea of inputs and outputs no matter the context.

✏️ **Use the table** to answer the questions below.

x	♥	💣	◑	✳	☆
$f(x)$	☺	⚡	💬	☹	♥

1. What is $f(\text{💣})$? _____

2. What is $f(\text{✳})$? _____

3. If $f(a) = \text{💬}$, what is a? _____

4. If $f(k) = \text{☹}$, what is k? _____

5. What is $f(f(\text{☆}))$? _____

✏️ **Use the graphs** to find or estimate information about each function.

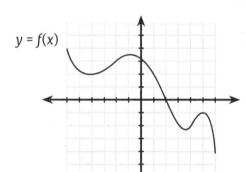

$y = f(x)$

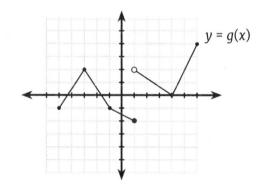

$y = g(x)$

6. What is $f(-4)$? _____

7. What is $g(-1)$? _____

8. What is $f(4)$? _____

9. What is $g(1)$? _____

10. What is $g(4)$? _____

11. If $f(a) = 3$ and $-3 < a < 0$, what is a? _____

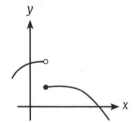

NOTE

Whenever you see two points for the same x-value, a hollow circle (O) is NOT considered a point on the line, while a solid point (●) is.

Answers: 1) ⚡ 2) ☹ 3) ◑ 4) ✳ 5) ☺ 6) 2 7) −1 8) −2 9) −2 10) 0 11) −2

Use the functions to complete the problems below. The first one has already been completed for you because we are generous!

$f(x) = 3x - 4$ $\qquad$ $g(x) = x^2 - 2x + 7$ $\qquad$ $h(x) = -x + 5$
1. $f(100) =$ $\;$ $3(100) - 4 = 296$
2. $g(-3) =$
3. $h(17) =$
4. $f(x + 5) =$
5. $h(2x - 3) =$
6. $g(-7a) =$
7. $f(2) + f(4) =$
8. $h(f(4)) =$

Answers: **1)** 296 $\quad$ **2)** 22 $\quad$ **3)** -12 $\quad$ **4)** $3x + 11$ $\quad$ **5)** $-2x + 8$ $\quad$ **6)** $49a^2 + 14a + 7$ $\quad$ **7)** 10 $\quad$ **8)** -3

Practice Problems

Use your new skills to answer each question.

1

If $f(x - 2) = 3x^2 - 5x + 4$, what does $f(-3)$ equal?

A) 46
B) 12
C) 2
D) –3

2

$$f(x) = 3x^2 + bx$$

For the function f defined above, b is a constant and $f(2) = 18$. What is the value of $f(-2)$?

A) –6
B) 0
C) 6
D) 3

3

A function satisfies $g(1) = -2$ and $g(3) = 4$. If the function is linear, which of the following defines g?

A) $g(x) = x - 3$
B) $g(x) = 2x - 4$
C) $g(x) = 3x - 5$
D) $g(x) = 4x - 6$

4

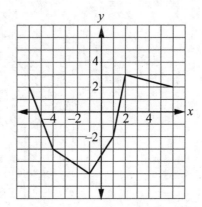

The complete graph of the function *g* is shown in the *xy*-plane above. If $g(a)$ gives the maximum value of the graph, what is the value of *a* ?

A) 3
B) 2
C) −1
D) −5

5

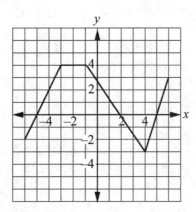

The complete graph of the function f is shown in the *xy*-plane above. Which of the following is equal to 4?

I. $f(-2.5)$
II. $f(-1)$
III. $f(4)$

A) I only
B) II and III only
C) I and II only
D) I, II and III

6

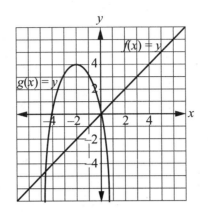

Graphs of functions f and g are shown in the xy-plane above. For which of the following values of x does $f(x) + g(x) = 0$?

A) −5
B) −3
C) −2
D) 1

7

If $f(x) = -7x - 4$, what is $f(-5x)$ equal to?

A) $35x^2 - 4$
B) $-35x - 4$
C) $35x - 4$
D) $35x^2 + 20x$

8

A function f satisfies $f(2) = 3$ and $f(4) = 5$. A function g satisfies $g(3) = 4$ and $g(6) = 2$. What is the value of $f(g(3))$?

A) 2
B) 3
C) 4
D) 5

9

x	2	3	4
f(x)	3	7	11

The table above shows values for the function f. If the function is linear, which of the following defines f?

A) $f(x) = -2x + 7$
B) $f(x) = 3x - 3$
C) $f(x) = 4x$
D) $f(x) = 4x - 5$

10

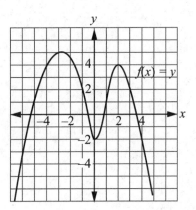

The graph above is a representation of the function $f(x)$. If $f(3) = f(b)$, which of the following could be b?

A) −2
B) −1
C) 1
D) 2

UNIT | Polynomials

Chapters

Key Skills

In this chapter, we'll learn how we can use the distributive property and factoring to work with **non-linear functions** (a.k.a., equations with x^2 and larger exponents).

Just as basic algebra helped us work with the equation of a line, the skills we learn in this chapter will help us to understand the graphs of parabolic equations.

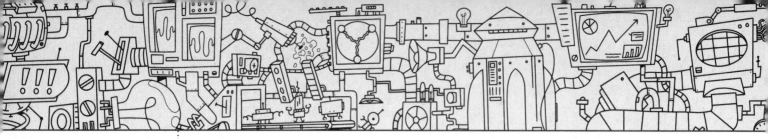

Factoring Basics

We're now moving beyond basic algebra into the slightly more complicated, but extremely predictable, world of factoring polynomials. Before we dive in, let's review some factoring basics.

Distributive Property

One of our tools for working with algebraic expressions is the distributive property. When we use parentheses as a shorthand for multiplication, this property tells us what to do.

*The outside term gets multiplied (distributed) to **every term** inside.*

Factors & Factoring

factoring (v.)

Rewriting an expression as the product of its components, or "factors".

Now, since we multiplied **3** and **(2x – 5)** to get 6x – 15, we say 3 and (2x – 5) are each *factors* of 6x – 15, in the same way that **3** and **5** are *factors* of 15. When we "factor" an expression, like 6x – 15, or a number, like 15, we are just working in the opposite direction from before:

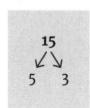

*Factors work the same whether they are **expressions** or **integers**.*

Factoring Polynomials

In this unit, we'll be distributing and factoring with *polynomials*. We'll start off simple, then try tougher and tougher problems. If you understand how we can go from an expression, like 6x – 15, to its factors, then you already understand the core concept behind even the toughest problems. So before we dive in, let's review the steps:

polynomial (n.)

An expression with **many** ("poly-") **terms** ("-nomial"), especially the sum of several terms that contain different powers of the same variable(s):

e.g., $x^2 - 3x + 7$

① *look at the expression* $6x - 15$

② *see that 3 is a factor of both 6x and −15* $6x - 15$ $(3)(2x) - (3)(5)$

③ *"factor out" a 3* $3(2x - 5)$

Fill in the blanks to complete the solutions below.

1. *distribute*	$2x(3x^2 + 4x + 5)$ =
2. *think...*	The common term in $12x^2 + 15x + 3$ is _____.
3. *factor*	$12x^2 + 15x + 3$ =
4. *distribute*	$7(2a + 3b + c)$ =
5. *factor*	$20ab + 28a^2 + 8a$ =

Answers: **(1)** $6x^3 + 8x^2 + 10x$ **(2)** 3 **(3)** $3(4x^2 + 5x + 1)$ **(4)** $14a + 21b + 7c$ **(5)** $4a(5b + 7a + 2)$

Multiplying Expressions

Sometimes we need to multiply two **expressions** together, such as:

$$(x + 3)(x - 2) = ?$$

The Distributive Property still applies! We need to multiply **every term** in the first expression with **every term** in the second expression. While this might look new and complicated when you first see it, it's actually as simple as doing **two** distributions and adding them together:

$$(x + 3)(x - 2) = x(x - 2) + 3(x - 2)$$

If we rewrite the multiplication this way, we can see how plain ol' distribution gives us the answer:

$$x(x - 2) + 3(x - 2)$$
$$x^2 - 2x + 3x - 6$$
$$\boxed{x^2 + x - 6}$$

NOTE

If the first term had been **(x − 3)** instead of (x + 3), then we would be **subtracting** the two distributions:

$$x(x - 2) - 3(x - 2)$$

And *then* we'd have to remember to **distribute the negative** along with the 3.

Pencil Skills

And that's it! So what's the main difference between multiplying two expressions and standard, one-term distribution? Simply the number of steps involved. But we need to be careful! When we're working so many steps at once, the chances of making an error (such as forgetting to distribute a negative) increases.

To help us avoid such errors, we will need to carefully write out each step. Luckily, we have one or two tricks to help us cleanly multiply two expressions together: the **FOIL Method** and the **Box Method**.

Careful Work is Key!

FOIL Method

In school you likely learned the FOIL method for multiplying two expressions. FOIL stands for First-Outer-Inner-Last, and it simply gives us an order in which to carry out these four multiplications:

1 *First terms* $(x + 3)(x - 2) = x^2$

2 *Outer terms* $(x + 3)(x - 2) = x^2 - 2x$

3 *Inner terms* $(x + 3)(x - 2) = x^2 - 2x + 3x$

4 *Last terms* $(x + 3)(x - 2) = x^2 - 2x + 3x - 6$

$(x + 3)(x - 2) = \boxed{x^2 + x - 6}$

Visualizing with the Box Method

We can also visualize this multiplication using the **box method**. To use the box method with two binomials, we draw a two-by-two box, labeling the columns with the terms from one factor and the rows with the terms from the other. Then, for each cell, multiply the row label by the column label. Once you're done, add up each result:

1 *Draw box*

2 *Label box*

3 *Fill-in products*

4 *Add products*

$(x + 3) \times (x - 2)$

	x	$+ 3$
x	x^2	$3x$
$- 2$	$-2x$	-6

$= x^2 + 3x + (-2x) + (-6)$

$= \boxed{x^2 + x - 6}$

FOIL the given factors to complete the table below.

Factors	F	O	I	L
1. $(2x + 1)(x + 5)$ =	$2x^2$ +	$10x$ +	x +	5
2. $(x + 3)(x - 7)$ =	+	+	+	
3. $(a + 2)(2a + 3)$ =	+	+	+	
4. $(t - 1)(t - 8)$ =	+	+	+	
5. $(3x + 2)(x - 5)$ =	+	+	+	
6. $(2a + 2)(3a - 1)$ =	+	+	+	
7. $(x + y)(x - y)$ =	+	+	+	
8. $(x + 4)(x - 4)$ =	+	+	+	

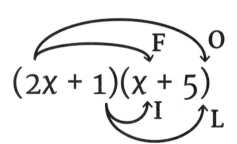

$$(2x + 1)(x + 5)$$

Answers: **1)** $2x^2 + 10x + x + 5$ **2)** $x^2 - 7x + 3x - 21$ **3)** $2a^2 + 3a + 4a + 6$ **4)** $t^2 - 8t - t + 8$

5) $3x^2 - 15x + 2x - 10$ **6)** $6a^2 - 2a + 6a - 2$ **7)** $x^2 - xy + xy - y^2$ **8)** $x^2 - 4x + 4x - 16$

EXAMPLE 1

$$5(3s + 1)(2s - 1)$$

Which of the following is equivalent to the above expression?

A) $20s$
B) $30s^2 - 5$
C) $30s^2 - 5s - 5$
D) $150s^2 - 25s + 25$

SOLUTION

In this problem we have 3 expressions multiplied together. When we multiply 3 numbers, say 2, 3, and 4, we know that it doesn't matter what order they are multiplied in. For example:

$$2(3 \times 4) = 4(3 \times 2)$$

The same is true when we multiply expressions. That means we can work this problem in whichever way is easiest for us. Let's start by multiplying the two binomials together:

1 *FOIL the binomials* $(3s + 1)(2s - 1) = 6s^2 + 2s - 3s - 1$

$$= 6s^2 - s - 1$$

Now we can multiply the result by 5, remembering to distribute:

2 *multiply by 5* $5(6s^2 - s - 1) = 30s^2 - 5s - 5$

C

TIP

Studies show that looking at a drawing of a dragon can increase cognitive ability.

This is a pretty dry chapter, so here, have a dragon!

Factoring Quadratics

Often, you will be asked to **solve** a quadratic equation, or find some value to make a quadratic "true". For example, a question might ask for a value of "x" that satisfies the equation:

$$x^2 + 2x - 8 = 0$$

Remember how we could factor expressions by applying the distributive property in reverse? To solve the quadratic, we can **FOIL** in reverse. The trick is to set up the factors and think backwards from the quadratic. Let's start by focusing on the **first** term. What two "first" terms would multiply to equal x^2? Two x's would work!

$$(\; ? \quad)(\; ? \quad) = (x^2) + 2x - 8$$

$$(x \quad)(x \quad) = x^2 + 2x - 8$$

Next, we need to look at the middle *and* end terms of the quadratic. We need two numbers that **multiply to –8** and **add to +2**. The best way to do that is to list the factors of –8, keeping an eye out for two that combine to equal positive 2. Once we find a match, we drop them into our factors:

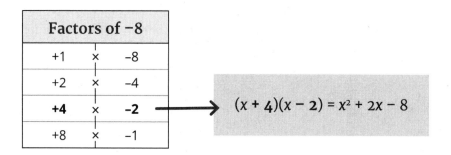

Factors of −8		
+1	×	−8
+2	×	−4
+4	×	**−2**
+8	×	−1

$$(x + 4)(x - 2) = x^2 + 2x - 8$$

Now that we have our factors, we can easily see the solutions to the original equation. Remember, our original equation was equal to zero. Which means we just need values for x that **make either factor zero**:

$$(x + 4)(x - 2) = 0$$

$$x = -4, +2$$

INTERACTIVE EXAMPLE

Factor: $x^2 + 3x - 18 = ($ $)($ $)$

Q1) What are the **first** terms of the factors?

S1) To end up with an x^2, the first terms must simply be x:

$$x^2 + 3x - 18 = (x \quad)(x \quad)$$

Q2) To end up with **negative** 18 as a constant, what must the **signs** be in the two factors?

    A) both are positives
    B) both are negatives
    C) one is positive, one is negative

S2) If the "Last" terms in our factors multiply to be a negative, like –18, then one must be negative and the other positive:

    A̶) (positive #)(positive #) = positive number
    B̶) (negative #)(negative #) = positive number
    Ⓒ) (positive #)(negative #) = **negative** number

INTERACTIVE EXAMPLE (continued)

Factor: $x^2 + 3x - 18 = (x + \quad)(x - \quad)$

Q3) What are the **factors of −18**?

S3) Let's write out the different factors of −18:

Factors of −18					
+ 1 × − 18	+ 2 × − 9	+ 3 × − 6	+ 6 × − 3	+ 9 × − 2	+ 18 × − 1

Q4) Which pair of factors of −18 will give us a +3*x* as a middle term?

Think

If the original polynomial had "−3x" as its middle term instead of "+3x", what would the factors be?

S4) We need factors of −18 that add up to positive 3. Looking at our table of factors, it looks like +6 and −3 are our best bet:

Factors of −18					
+ 1 × − 18	+ 2 × − 9	+ 3 × − 6	**+ 6** × **− 3**	+ 9 × − 2	+ 18 × − 1

Which means our finished factors are:

$$x^2 + 3x - 18 = (x + 6)(x - 3)$$

TIP

Any time you come across a quadratic, factoring is a good option to consider! In this problem, a glance at the answer choices tells us that we should **definitely** try factoring!

EXAMPLE 2

$$3n^2 - 6n - 45$$

Which of the following is equivalent to the above expression?

A) $(n - 3)(n + 5)$
B) $3(n + 3)(n - 5)$
C) $3(n - 3)(n + 5)$
D) $(n - 15)(3n + 3)$

SOLUTION

The answer choices hint to us that we need to factor the original expression. A good place to start is to **look for a common factor**:

  1 *identify any common factor* $3n^2 - 6n - 45$
                                    multiples of 3!

  2 *factor out* **(3)** $3(n^2 - 2n - 15)$

Now to **factor the quadratic** in the parentheses. Since the coefficient of n^2 is **1**, the first term in each factor will just be *n*:

  3 *set up the first term* $(n^2 - 2n - 15) = 3(n\quad)(n\quad)$

Next, we need to **factor the –15** at the end. To end up with a negative, we know that one factor *must* be negative:

  4 *place signs* $3(n^2 - 2n - 15) = 3(n -\quad)(n +\quad)$

Next, we need two numbers that **multiply to 15**. Our options are:

  5 *factor* **15** $3(n^2 - 2n - 15)$ $3(n - 15)(n + 1)$
                                              or
                                          $3(n + 3)(n - 5)$

Of these two options, only **–5** and **+3** also **add to –2**. So...

  6 *bring it home!* $3n^2 - 6n - 45 = 3(n + 3)(n - 5)$

B

419

EXAMPLE 3

$$3t^2 - 13t = 10$$

What is a value of t that satisfies the above equation?

SOLUTION

Anytime you are asked to *solve* a quadratic equation, a good first step is to **move everything to one side** of the equation.

(1) *gather to one side* $3t^2 - 13t - 10 = 0$

If we factor the polynomial on the left, we will end up with the product of two things that equal zero.

(2) *prepare to factor!* $(\quad)(\quad) = 0$

Now it's time to factor. First, **determine the first terms**. We see a coefficient of 3 in front of the t^2. Since there is no common term to factor out, that means our first terms must be **$3t$** and **t**:

(3) *Write first terms* $(3t\quad)(t\quad) = 0$

Next, we need to find two "Last" terms that multiply to –10. So let's **factor –10**.

(4) *factor –10*

Factors of –10		
+1	×	–10
+2	×	–5
+5	×	–2
+10	×	–1

continue →

Now, notice that none of these pairs of factors add up to –13. That's because we have a "3" coefficient in our first term that will multiply with one of those factors:

$$(3t + a)(t - b)$$

We'll need to **play around with different options** to find the one that works. However, since we know that we will end up with **negative 13**, it's a good bet that the *negative* factor is the one getting multiplied by 3. Let's multiply our negative factors by 3 and see which row combines to –13:

+1	–10
+2	–5
+5	–2
+10	–1

(×3)

+1	–30
+2	**–15**
+5	–6
+10	–3

Aha! If we use **+2** and **–5**, and make sure the –5 gets multiplied by the 3t term, we end up with **–13t** as our middle term.

⑤ *Finish the factors*　　　$3t^2 - 13t - 10 = 0$

$$(3t + 2)(t - 5) = 0$$

At long last, we can determine our *t*-values! If these two factors multiply to equal **zero**, then we need values for *t* that turn either one to zero.

⑥ *Find t-values*　　　$(3t + 2)(t - 5) = 0$

$$t = -\frac{2}{3}, \text{ or } 5$$

Factoring with the Box Method

The box method can be particularly useful when dealing with problems like Example 3 on the previous page, where the coefficient of one of your first terms is not simply 1. Let's look at how a step-by-step box method can help us solve for *x* in the following equation:

Factor: $6x^2 - 11x - 10 = 0$

① *Create a box and place* **6x²** *in the top left and* **−10** *in bottom right.*

6x²	
	−10

② *Multiply these to get* −60x². 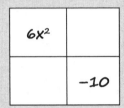 $6x^2 \times -10 = -60x^2$

③ *Find two factors of* −60x² *that add up to the middle term,* −11x. *Here, that is* **−15x** *and* **4x**. *Put them in the open boxes.*

6x²	−15x
4x	−10

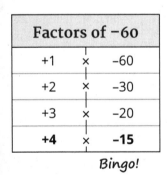

Factors of −60

+1	×	−60
+2	×	−30
+3	×	−20
+4	×	**−15**

Bingo!

④ *Factor out common terms from each row and each column:*

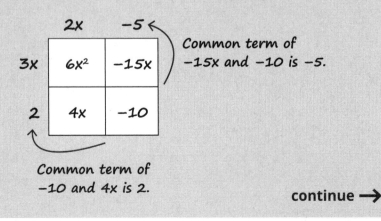

Common term of −15x and −10 is −5.

Common term of −10 and 4x is 2.

TIP

When factoring out a common term, **take the sign of the closer box**.

Here, for example, the "−5" takes the sign of "−15x" and the "2" takes the sign of "4x".

continue →

⑤ *Take the **sum of the common factors** for the columns and for the rows to find your two polynomial factors!*

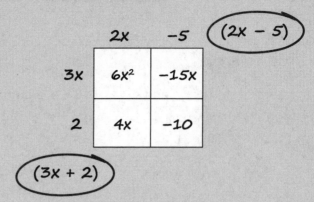

$6x^2 - 11x - 10 = \boxed{(2x - 5)(3x + 2)}$

Thanks box method!

Remember

When factoring out a common term, **take the sign of the closer box**.

HINT

If there are no common terms, factor out a **1** or **–1**.

 Your Turn

Use the box method to factor the polynomials below. You can also choose to draw a dragon in the margin if you need a little boost.

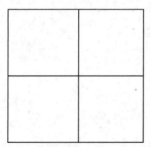

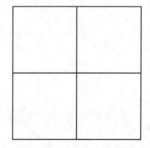

1. *factor:* $3x^2 - x - 30$

2. *factor:* $6x^2 - 7x + 2$

Answers: *See next page.*

Practice Problems

Use your new skills to answer each question.

1

If $s > 0$ and $s^2 + 3s - 28 = 0$, what is the value of s?

A) -7
B) 3
C) 4
D) 7

2

$$4(3x^2 + 6)(5x^2 + 1)$$

Which of the following is equivalent to the expression above?

A) $60x^4 + 24$
B) $32x^4 + 28$
C) $60x^4 + 132x^2 + 24$
D) $216x^4$

3

$$12x^2 + 2x - 24$$

Which of the following is equivalent to the expression above?

A) $2(3x - 4)(2x + 3)$
B) $(4x - 3)(3x + 8)$
C) $12(x - 2)(x + 1)$
D) $12(x - 1)(x + 2)$

4

If $(x + 4)(x - 2) = (x + 1)^2 + b$, what is the value of b?

A) 8
B) -7
C) -8
D) -9

Answers for previous page: **1)** $(3x - 10)(x + 3)$ **2)** $(3x - 2)(2x - 1)$

5

$$\frac{1}{x+b} + \frac{1}{x-b} = \frac{2x}{x^2-9}$$

Given the equation above, where $b < 0$ and $|x| \neq b$, what is the value of b ?

A) -1
B) -3
C) -6
D) -9

6

If $20x^2 - 23x - 21$ factors as $(ax + b)(cx - d)$ where $a, b, c,$ and d are all positive numbers, what is c ?

7

$$(x-6)(x+1) + 10$$

Which of the following is equivalent to the expression above?

A) $x^2 + 5x + 16$
B) $(x+5)^2 + 10$
C) $(x+4)(x+1)$
D) $(x-4)(x-1)$

8

What is the product of all values of k that satisfy $4k^2 - 3k = 7$?

A) -7

B) $-\frac{7}{4}$

C) $-\frac{4}{7}$

D) $\frac{7}{4}$

9

If $x > 3$, which of the following is equivalent to $\dfrac{1}{\dfrac{1}{x+3} - \dfrac{1}{x+4}}$?

A) $x^2 + 7x + 12$

B) $\dfrac{1}{x^2 - 7x - 12}$

C) $\dfrac{2x + 7}{x^2 - 7x - 12}$

D) $\dfrac{x^2 - 7x - 12}{2x + 1}$

10

If $t > 0$ and $t^2 - 25 = 0$, what is the value of t ?

Pattern Matching

In this chapter, we'll practice manipulating equations until they match a given pattern. We'll then use that pattern to determine unknown values.

Pattern Matching

Occasionally, you are asked to find multiple unknowns using a single equation. The trick to discovering their values is **pattern matching**. For example, say we are asked find *a*, *b*, and *c*, in the following equation:

$$5x^2 + 3x + 7 = ax^2 + bx + c$$

It would actually be impossible for us to "solve" for each of these unknown variables... but we don't need to! Notice how each side follows the exact same **pattern**:

same pattern!
$$ax^2 + bx + c$$
$$5x^2 + 3x + 7$$

There's an x^2 with a coefficient (5 or *a*), an *x* with a coefficient (3 or *b*), and a constant at the end (7 or *c*). Since they are in the same form, we can simply match *a*, *b*, and *c* with the numbers on the left!

$$a = 5, \quad b = 3, \quad c = 7$$

Before we look at some test questions, let's get some practice using pattern matching to figure stuff out!

Use pattern matching to complete the table below. You may need to rearrange the equation first! Use the bottom of the page for work.

Equation	a	b	c
1. $8x^2 + 2x - 15 = ax^2 + bx + c$	8		
2. $5x^2 - 7x + 12 = ax^2 + bx + c$			
3. $99x^2 - \frac{1}{99}x + 5 = ax^2 + bx - c$			
4. $-x^2 - x = ax^2 + bx + c$			
5. $7x^2 + \frac{1}{3}x + 4 = ax^2 + \frac{1}{b}x + c$			
6. $x^2 + 2x - bx + 2 = ax^2 + c$			
7. $3x^2 + 6 = ax^2 + bx + 3x + c$			
8. $3x^2 - 17x - 5 = ax^2 + bx + 3x + c$			

Scratch Work

Answers: **1)** 8, 2, –15 **2)** 5, –7, 12 **3)** 99, $-\frac{1}{99}$, –5 **4)** –1, –1, 0 **5)** 7, 3, 4 **6)** 1, 2, 2

7) 3, –3, 6 **8)** 3, –20, –5

EXAMPLE 1

$$3x(2x - 3) + 2(4x + 5) = ax^2 + bx + c$$

In the equation above, a, b, and c are constants. If the equation is true for all values of x, what is the value of b?

TIP

Anytime you see "**true for all values of x**...", it's likely you are dealing with a simple pattern matching problem.

SOLUTION

Our goal is to **simplify the left side** of the equation until it matches the pattern on the right side. So let's start by distributing:

(1) *copy the left side* $3x(2x - 3) + 2(4x + 5)$

(2) *distribute* $6x^2 - 9x + 8x + 10$

(3) *simplify* $6x^2 - x + 10$

Now we have both sides of the equation in a matching pattern. We want the value of b, which is the coefficient of x on the right side. That means our answer is the **coefficient of** x on the left:

(4) *match pattern* $6x^2 - x + 10 = ax^2 + bx + c$

$6x^2 - (1)x + 10 = ax^2 + bx + c$

So b must equal **–1**.

429

EXAMPLE 2

$$\frac{30x^2 - 52x - 12}{kx + 7} = -6x + 2 - \frac{26}{kx + 7}$$

The above equation is true for all values of $x \neq -\frac{7}{k}$, where k is a constant. What is the value of k ?

A) −6

B) −5

C) 5

D) $\frac{52}{6}$

SOLUTION

Since we see "for all values of x" (except the one that makes the fraction undefined), we are likely dealing with a pattern matching problem. The two sides look nothing alike, though, so we'll need to do some simplifying. Since they make things tricky, let's start by **moving the fractions to one side** and combining:

$$\frac{30x^2 - 52x - 12}{kx + 7} = -6x + 2 - \frac{26}{kx + 7}$$

$$\frac{30x^2 - 52x - 12}{kx + 7} + \frac{26}{kx + 7} = -6x + 2$$

$$\frac{30x^2 - 52x + 14}{kx + 7} = -6x + 2$$

Now we can multiply both sides by the denominator, **$kx + 7$**, in order to **clear those pesky fractions**:

$$(kx + 7)\frac{30x^2 - 52x + 14}{kx + 7} = (-6x + 2)(kx + 7)$$

$$30x^2 - 52x + 14 = -6kx^2 - 42x + 2kx + 14$$

Now we *almost* have an exact pattern match. The only problem is we have **two** x terms on the right... but we can fix that!

continue ➡

Let's **move −42x to the left side**. It'll be happier there anyway

$$30x^2 - 52x + 14 \;=\; -6kx^2 - 42x + 2kx + 14$$

$$30x^2 - 10x + 14 \;=\; -6kx^2 + 2kx + 14$$

match!

Now we're talking! Both sides of the equation now follow the same $ax^2 + bx + c$ pattern. To solve for k, we can either match the x^2 coefficients or the x coefficients. Either way gives us the answer:

$$30x^2 \;=\; -6kx^2$$
$$30 \;=\; -6k$$
$$-5 \;=\; k$$

$$-10x \;=\; 2kx$$
$$-10 \;=\; 2k$$
$$-5 \;=\; k$$

(B)

Bonus Solution: Picking Numbers

We're told that the equation is true "for all values of x." This is often a big sign that we make things easier for ourselves by **picking numbers**. If it's true for all values of x, then it should be true for $x = 1$. Try plugging 1 in for x right from the start, and simplify until you find k. This technique is not always useable, but when it is, it can save you a lot of time and heartache.

EXAMPLE 3

If $(mx + 3)(nx - 5) = -6x^2 + rx - 15$ is true for all values of x and $m + n = 1$, what are the two possible values of r ?

A) −15 and −6
B) −2 and 3
C) −10 and 9
D) −21 and 19

SOLUTION

We're told that the equation is "true for all values of x", and we have way too many unknowns: these are signs that we need to use pattern matching! To do that, we'll need to FOIL the left side:

(**1**) *rewrite the left side* $\qquad (mx + 3)(nx - 5)$

(**2**) *FOIL* $\qquad mnx^2 - 5mx + 3nx - 15$

Let's pause here and look for a pattern that can help us:

$$\boxed{mnx^2} - 5mx + 3nx - 15 = \boxed{-6x^2} + rx - 15$$

If we focus on the x^2 **coefficients**, we can see that $mn = -6$. Let's combine that with what we already know about m and n:

$$mn = -6$$
$$m + n = 1$$

Later, we'll talk formally about how to solve "systems of equations" like this, but for now we can just look at it. We need **two numbers** that **multiply to –6** and **add to 1**.

If we play around with it, we find that **m = 3** and **n = –2** would work. Let's try plugging that into our equation and do some pattern matching:

$$(3)(-2)x^2 - 5(3)x + 3(-2)x - 15 = -6x^2 + rx - 15$$

$$-6x^2 - 15x - 6x - 15 = -6x^2 + rx - 15$$

$$-6x^2 - 21x - 15 = -6x^2 + rx - 15$$

match!

Bingo! Now that we have a **pattern match**, we see that **r = – 21**. If we check the answer choices, we see that we don't even need to find a second possible value: only **choice D** has –21 in it!

D

EXAMPLE 4

What is the sum of all values of x that satisfy $3x^2 - 18x + 21 = 0$?

A) 6
B) –6
C) $3\sqrt{6}$
D) $6\sqrt{3}$

SOLUTION

This looks like it's asking us to solve a quadratic. The first thing to try when solving a quadratic is always **factoring.** All of the coefficients are multiples of 3, so we can **pull 3 out**:

① *copy equation* $3x^2 - 18x + 21$

② *factor out 3* $3(x^2 - 6x + 7)$

Now, ordinarily, we would just factor the quadratic and get two answers. But there's a problem. We would need to find two numbers that multiply to 7 and add to –6. But our only choices are 1 and 7 (which add to 8) or –1 and –7 (which add to –8). So neither option works! This doesn't mean there are no solutions... just no solutions that are **whole numbers**.

We can solve *this* problem in two different ways: the "hard work" way or the "hard thinking" way.

Option A: "Hard Work" Way
Since we can't factor this quadratic, we'll have to turn to our old, bulky friend: **the quadratic formula**.

A3 *quadratic formula* $(x^2 - 6x + 7)$ $x = \dfrac{-b \pm \sqrt{b^2 - 4ac}}{2a}$

$a = 1,\ b = -6,\ c = 7$ $x = \dfrac{6 \pm \sqrt{(-6)^2 - 4(7)}}{2(1)}$

$x = \dfrac{6 \pm \sqrt{8}}{2}$

$x = \dfrac{6 \pm 2\sqrt{2}}{2}$

$x = 3 \pm \sqrt{2}$

continue →

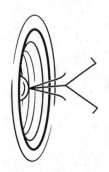

PORTAL

Forget the quadratic formula? Flip to page 449 for a reminder.

433

Now we have two solutions: $(3 + \sqrt{2})$ and $(3 - \sqrt{2})$. Since the question asks for the sum of all solutions, we just add these:

(A4) *add solutions* $\qquad 3 + \sqrt{2} \ + 3 - \sqrt{2} = \boxed{6}$

Option B: "Hard Thinking" Way

Let's think about this a little bit abstractly. We wish we could factor $x^2 - 6x + 7$ to find the solutions. Let's pretend we can do that and use variables to stand in for the factors. Say our solutions to the quadratic were *r* and *s*. What would that look like?

(B) *pretend to factor* $\qquad x^2 - 6x + 7 = (x - r)(x - s)$

$$x^2 - 6x + 7 = x^2 - rx - sx + rs$$

$$x^2 - 6x + 7 = x^2 - (r + s)x + rs$$

Now we can do some pattern matching! For this factoring to work out, it must be true that those last two terms, *r* and *s*, multiply to equal 7... and **add to equal 6**. Otherwise, FOILing wouldn't produce the right quadratic! So:

$$r + s = 6$$

And look! This is exactly what the question asked for. If "*r*" and "*s*" are the solutions to this quadratic, then we've shown just from how factoring works that the solutions must add to equal 6!

A

Practice Problems

Use your new skills to answer each question.

1

$$4x(7x + 2) + 5(x - 4) = ax^2 + bx + c$$

In the equation above, a, b, and c are constants. If the equation is true for all values of x, what is the value of b ?

A) −20
B) 5
C) 8
D) 13

2

$$\frac{2y^2 + 11y + 12}{y + 4} = ay + b$$

In the equation above, a, b, and c are constants. If the equation is true for all values of y, what is the value of a ?

A) $-\frac{3}{2}$

B) 2

C) 3

D) 11

3

If $(ax - 3)(2x + b) = -2(5x^2 + 8x + 3)$ for all values of x, what is the value of ab ?

A) −16
B) −10
C) 10
D) 15

4

What is the sum of all values of x that satisfy
$3x^2 + 17x - 2 = 0$?

A) -2

B) $-\frac{2}{3}$

C) $-\frac{17}{3}$

D) 17

5

The equation $\frac{15x^2 + 21x - 32}{ax - 3} = 3x + 6 - \frac{14}{ax - 3}$ is true for all

values of $x \neq \frac{3}{a}$, where a is a constant. What is the value of a ?

A) 3
B) 5
C) 14
D) 15

6

The equation $\dfrac{x^2 + 8x - 9}{x - b} = x + 3 - \dfrac{24}{x - b}$ is true for all values of

$x \neq b$, where b is a constant. What is the value of b?

A) -5

B) $\dfrac{11}{3}$

C) 5

D) 8

7

$$(x - 3)(x - 2)(x + 4) = ax^3 + bx^2 + cx + 24$$

The above expression is true for all values of x. What is the value of c?

A) -1
B) -14
C) 14
D) 24

8

The expression $6ax + b(x + a) = 14x + 4$ is true for all values of x. If $a \neq b$, what is the value of a?

A) $\dfrac{1}{3}$

B) 3

C) $\dfrac{7}{3}$

D) 12

The expression $(3x + 2y)(x - 4y) = ax^2 + bxy + cy^2$ is true for all values of x and y. What is the value of b ?

A) −10
B) −8
C) −2
D) 14

Advanced Factoring

a.k.a. *"Jumping through hoops before we can factor like normal."*

We have seen that when we want to find **solutions** to a quadratic equation, it's useful to move everything to one side and factor. Occasionally, you'll run into situations that make this more difficult – for example, when there's an x^3 in the equation. These situations look impossible at first, but there's an important thing to remember:

> Nothing is impossible!

We **can** and **will** get around these obstacles! We just need to use a clever trick or two to make factoring easier.

Factoring by Grouping

Let's look at a technique that is particularly useful for handling cubics. Say we were asked to find a **real solution** to the following equation:

$$x^3 - 3x^2 + 5x - 15 = 0$$

As usual, when we see a polynomial equal to zero, our instinct should be to **factor the polynomial**. Unfortunately, our usual method for factoring quadratics doesn't work when there's an x^3 involved...

The first step is to **be confident**: there *must* be a way to simplify this cubic somehow so that we can factor like normal... we just need to jump through a hoop or two first.

Usually, the first step to factoring is to **factor out a common term**. Is there a term common to every single term in this equation? No! But... what if we **break this equation into two groups:**

$$x^3 - 3x^2 + 5x - 15 = 0$$

$$\underbrace{(x^3 - 3x^2)}_{\text{group 1}} + \underbrace{(5x - 15)}_{\text{group 2}} = 0$$

Now, are there common terms *within each group*? Yes! We can factor out an x^2 from the first group and a 5 from the second group:

$$\overset{\text{factor}}{x^2}(x - 3) + 5(x - 3) = 0$$

Do you notice anything about the equation now? We have a new "common term" **(x – 3)** that we can factor out:

$$\overset{\text{factor}}{(x - 3)}(x^2 + 5) = 0$$

Now, magically, we have factored our original equation! From these factors, we can see that one real solution for the equation is **x = 3**. Remember: nothing is impossible on the test. If it looks like you can't factor because of a large exponent, try grouping!

Factoring by Grouping

When you are asked to solve a cubic polynomial, try this:

(1) *copy equation* $x^3 + 10x^2 + 5x + 50 = 0$

(2) *create groups* $(x^3 + 10x^2) + (5x + 50) = 0$

(3) *factor out like terms* $x^2(x + 10) + 5(x + 10) = 0$

(4) *factor out expression* $(x + 10)(x^2 + 5) = 0$

Separate each equation into two groups and factor out common terms.

Equation	Group 1	Group 2
1. $x^3 - 3x^2 + 5x - 15$	$x^2(x - 3)$	$5(x - 3)$
2. $a^3 + 7a^2 + 5a + 35$		
3. $2x^3 - 9x^2 + 6x - 27$		
4. $21x^3 - 3x^2 - 28x + 4$		
5. $x^3 + 4x^2 - 9x - 36$		
6. $ap + al + np + nl$		

Now **factor the equations** into two factors.

Equation	Factors
7. $x^3 - 3x^2 + 5x - 15$	$(x - 3)(x^2 + 5)$
8. $a^3 + 7a^2 + 5a + 35$	
9. $2x^3 - 9x^2 + 6x - 27$	
10. $21x^3 - 3x^2 - 28x + 4$	
11. $x^3 + 4x^2 - 9x - 36$	
12. $ap + al + np + nl$	

Answers: *See next page.*

Factoring with Even Exponents

Let's look at another situation that may look too hard to factor at first:

$$x^6 + 2x^3 + 1 = 0$$

The x^6 term might look scary, but this is actually a polynomial you know how to solve! Notice that $x^6 = x^3 \cdot x^3$. To make this problem simpler, we could make up our own variable. Let's say $\boldsymbol{z = x^3}$. Then we could rewrite this equation and factor it like normal:

$$z^2 + 2z + 1 = 0$$
$$(z + 1)(z + 1) = 0$$

Now that we're done factoring, we can just substitute $\boldsymbol{x^3}$ back in for $\boldsymbol{z}$:

$$(x^3 + 1)(x^3 + 1) = 0$$

Of course, you don't have to substitute every time you encounter one of these problems once you get used to the pattern. The most common thing to watch for is a polynomial with 3 terms where the larger exponent is double the smaller:

$$x^6 + 2x^3 + 1 = (x^3 + 1)(x^3 + 1)$$
$$x^4 - 8x^2 + 6 = (x^2 - 3)(x^2 - 2)$$
$$x^{12} + 8x^6 - 48 = (x^6 + 12)(x^6 - 4)$$

Answers: **1)** $x^2(x - 3) + 5(x - 3)$ **2)** $a^2(a + 7) + 5(a + 7)$ **3)** $x^2(2x - 9) + 3(2x - 9)$ **4)** $3x^2(7x - 1) - 4(7x - 1)$

5) $x^2(x + 4) - 9(x + 4)$ **6)** $a(p + l) + n(p + l)$ **7)** $(x - 3)(x^2 + 5)$ **8)** $(a + 7)(a^2 + 5)$

9) $(2x - 9)(x^2 + 3)$ **10)** $(7x - 1)(3x^2 - 4)$ **11)** $(x + 4)(x^2 - 9)$ **12)** $(p + l)(a + n)$

EXAMPLE 1

$$2u^4 + 7u^2v^2 + 3v^4$$

Which of the following is equivalent to the expression shown above?

A) $(2u^3 + 3v^2)(u^2 + 3v^2)$
B) $(2u + v^3)(u^3 + 3v)$
C) $(2u + v)(u^3 + 3v^3)$
D) $(2u^2 + v^2)(u^2 + 3v^2)$

Workin' Backwards

If this tricky factoring gives you trouble, you can **work backwards** by FOILing out each answer choice. The correct choice will work out to be the given equation!

You could also use the **box method** to factor here!

 SOLUTION

Looking at the answer choices, they clearly want us to **factor the expression.** Notice that we have terms with u^4, v^4, and u^2v^2.

Since $(u^2)^2 = u^4$ and $(v^2)^2 = v^4$, we want to think about u^2 and v^2 as our base variables.

$$2u^4 + 7u^2v^2 + 3v^4 = (\_u^2 + \_v^2)(\_u^2 + \_v^2)$$

This is the only setup that would give us the correct variables after FOILing. So all we need to do now is **find the coefficients**. The only factors of 2 are 2 and 1, so let's put that in:

$$2u^4 + 7u^2v^2 + 3v^4 = (2u^2 + \_v^2)(u^2 + \_v^2)$$

Now we just need to find the final coefficients. We want to end up with a 3, so the only possible factors are **3** and **1**. We can't just put them in any order, however. Since we want to end up with a 7 as our middle term, we need to place these coefficients so that the 3 gets multiplied by the 2 when we FOIL:

$$2u^4 + 7u^2v^2 + 3v^4 = (2u^2 + v^2)(u^2 + 3v^2)$$

And that's it! **Our answer is D!**   **D**

EXAMPLE 2

$$x^3(x^2 - 13) = -36x$$

If $x > 0$, what is one possible value of x that satisfies the equation above?

TIP

When we factor out an *x* from the whole expression, it tells us that one possible solution to the equation is *x = 0*.

However, since the question tells us that *x > 0*, we can ignore that factor here.

SOLUTION

Looking for a "value of x that satisfies the equation" just means that we need to solve the polynomial. Which means our first step is to **move everything to one side**.

1 *copy equation* $x^3(x^2 - 13) = -36x$

2 *move to one side* $x^3(x^2 - 13) + \mathbf{36x} = 0$

3 *simplify* $x^5 - 13x^3 + 36x = 0$

Next, as always, we want to **pull out any common factors**:

4 *pull out common term* $x(x^4 - 13x^2 + 36) = 0$

Now we just need to **factor $(x^4 - 13x^2 + 36)$**. Since $x^4 = (x^2)^2$, we can factor like normal, using x^2 as our base variable:

5 *factor* $x^4 - 13x^2 + 36 = 0$

       $(x^2 - 9)(x^2 - 4) = 0$

6 *solve* $x^2 = 9$

       $x^2 = 4$

       $x = 3$

       $x = 2$

continue →

Bonus: Difference of Squares
We could actually keep factoring to see these solutions factored out if we notice that each factor is a **difference of squares**:

Notice: *Difference of Squares* $(x^2 - y^2) = (x + y)(x - y)$

(8) *factor again* $(x^2 - 9)(x^2 - 4) = 0$

$(x + 3)(x - 3)(x + 2)(x - 2) = 0$

$x = -3, 3 \quad x = -2, 2$

Since we're told that $x > 0$, we know that the two possible values for x are **2** and **3**.

Practice Problems

Use your new skills to answer each question.

1

$$x^3 + 5x^2 - 4x - 20 = 0$$

For what positive real value of x is the equation above true?

[handwritten work:] $x^2(x+5) - 4(x+5)$

$x^2 - 4 = 0 \quad x+5$

$x = 2$

2

$$x^5 = 7x^3 + 18x$$

If $x > 0$, what is the integer solution to the equation above?

[handwritten work:] $0 = -x^5 + 7x^3 + 18x$

$x(-x^4 + 7x^2 + 18)$

$-x(x^4 - 7x^2 - 18) \quad x^2(x^2+2) - 9(x^2+2)$

$-x(x^4 + 2x^2 - 9x^2 - 18) \qquad x^2 - 9 = 0 \quad x^2 + 2 = 0$

$x = 3$

3

$$f(x) = x^3 - 7x^2 + 3x - 21$$

The function $f(x)$ is defined above. What is the x-coordinate where it crosses the x-axis?

4

$$x^2(x^2 + 4) = 21$$

For what negative real value of x is the equation above true?

A) -21
B) -7
C) -3
D) $-\sqrt{3}$

5

$$x^5 + 7x^3 - 8x^2 - 56 = 0$$

For what real value of x is the equation above true?

A) −3
B) −2
C) 2
D) 3

6

$$4x^3 + 4x^2 - 9x = 9$$

For what positive value of x is the equation above true?

A) 4

B) $\dfrac{9}{4}$

C) $\dfrac{3}{2}$

D) 1

7

$$4x^4 + 12x^2y^2 + 9y^4$$

Which of the following expressions is equivalent to the expression shown above?

A) $(2x^2 + 3y^2)^2$
B) $(2x + 3y)^4$
C) $(4x^2 + 9y^2)^2$
D) $(4x + 9y)^4$

$$f(x) = 3x^3 - 12x^2 + 9x$$
$$g(x) = x^2 - 4x + 3$$

HINT

Before diving into some complicated factoring, look for a **relationship** between $f(x)$ and $g(x)$. The answer choices provide a clue.

The polynomials $f(x)$ and $g(x)$ are defined above. Which of the following polynomials is divisible by $3x - 2$?

A) $p(x) = f(x) + g(x)$
B) $q(x) = 3f(x) - 2g(x)$
C) $r(x) = f(x) - 2g(x)$
D) $s(x) = -2f(x) + 3g(x)$

$$g(x) = 2x^3 + 10x^2 + 12x$$
$$h(x) = x^2 + 5x + 6$$

For the polynomials $g(x)$ and $h(x)$ defined above, which of the following polynomials is divisible by $6x + 4$?

A) $k(x) = g(x) + h(x)$
B) $m(x) = 6g(x) + 4h(x)$
C) $n(x) = 3g(x) + 4h(x)$
D) $p(x) = 4g(x) + 6h(x)$

The Unfactorables

On rare occasions, factoring simply won't solve the problem. This can happen when the solutions aren't nice, rational numbers. In this chapter, we're going to look at what you can do when factoring just isn't helping.

Quadratic Formula

If the test asks you to **solve** a quadratic equation and you see that there are **square roots in the answer choices**, don't bother trying to factor. The question is practically *begging* you to use the quadratic formula.

Quadratic Formula
The solutions to a quadratic in the form $ax^2 + bx + c$...

$$x = \frac{-b \pm \sqrt{b^2 - 4ac}}{2a}$$

TIP: It's a good idea to fully write out the formula whenever you use it.

EXAMPLE: Solve $x^2 + 6x + 2 = 0$ using the quadratic formula.

(1) *copy quadratic formula*

$$x = \frac{-b \pm \sqrt{b^2 - 4ac}}{2a}$$

(2) *substitute* $a = 1,\ b = 6,\ c = 2$

$$x = \frac{-6 \pm \sqrt{(6)^2 - 4(1)(2)}}{2(1)}$$

(3) *simplify*

$$x = \frac{-6 \pm \sqrt{28}}{2}$$

$$x = \frac{-6 \pm 2\sqrt{7}}{2}$$

(4) *voila!*

$$x = \boxed{-3 \pm \sqrt{7}}$$

EXAMPLE 1

$$x^2 - \frac{2m}{3}x = \frac{n}{3}$$

In the quadratic equation above, m and n are constants. What are the solutions for x?

A) $-\frac{2m}{3} \pm \dfrac{\sqrt{(2/3)m^2 + (4/3)n}}{2}$

B) $\dfrac{m}{3} \pm \sqrt{\frac{1}{9}m^2 + \frac{n}{3}}$

C) $1, -\dfrac{1}{3}$

D) $\dfrac{2m}{3} \pm \dfrac{\sqrt{m^2 + (1/3)n}}{3}$

The answer choices on this one are a huge sign that we need to use the quadratic formula. Let's start by writing out the formula:

(1) *copy quadratic formula* $\qquad x = \dfrac{-b \pm \sqrt{b^2 - 4ac}}{2a}$

Now, we need our original equation to be in form $ax^2 + bx + c = 0$

(2) *set equation equal to zero* $\qquad x^2 - \dfrac{2m}{3}x - \dfrac{n}{3} = 0$

So it looks like $a = 1$, $b = -\dfrac{2m}{3}$, and $c = -\dfrac{n}{3}$. Let's plug those in:

(3) *plug into QF* $\qquad x = \dfrac{-b \pm \sqrt{b^2 - 4ac}}{2a}$

$$x = \dfrac{\frac{2}{3}m \pm \sqrt{(-\frac{2}{3}m)^2 - 4(1)(-\frac{n}{3})}}{2(1)}$$

(4) *simplify* $\qquad x = \dfrac{\frac{2}{3}m \pm \sqrt{\frac{4}{9}m^2 + 4(\frac{n}{3})}}{2}$

continue →

This doesn't quite look like any of the answer choices, which means we need to do some tricky simplifying:

⑤ *keep simplifying*

$$x = \frac{\frac{2}{3}m \pm \sqrt{\frac{4}{9}m^2 + 4(\frac{n}{3})}}{2}$$

factor out a 4 under the root

$$x = \frac{\frac{2}{3}m \pm \sqrt{4(\frac{1}{9}m^2 + \frac{n}{3})}}{2}$$

take square root of 4

$$x = \frac{\frac{2}{3}m \pm 2\sqrt{\frac{1}{9}m^2 + \frac{n}{3}}}{2}$$

divide both terms by 2

$$x = \frac{1}{3}m \pm \sqrt{\frac{1}{9}m^2 + \frac{n}{3}}$$

B

THINK

Can you figure out WHY the discriminant tells us the number of real solutions?

Here's a hint: it has to do with that plus or minus symbol, and the fact that you can't talk about the square root of negative numbers without using imaginary numbers (i).

The Discriminant

In the quadratic formula, the stuff beneath the square root ($b^2 - 4ac$) is called the **discriminant**. It has its own fancy name because it can tell us something special about the quadratic as a whole: the total number of possible solutions to the equation. Once you plug in your a, b, and c values, look under the square root.

Discriminant	# of real solutions
Positive	Two
Equal to Zero	One
Negative	None

When do you need to know this? Rarely, and only in one specific case. If the question asks you **how many real solutions** a problem has, then simply plug-in and read the discriminant.

451

EXAMPLE 2

$$6x^2 + 18x - 13$$

How many real solutions does the above equation have?

A) 0
B) 1
C) 2
D) Infinitely many

SOLUTION

We want to know about the solutions of a quadratic equation. Our usual first step is to **try factoring**, but that doesn't work well here. Looking at the question, we see that we only care about how many solutions there are – we don't actually need to FIND those solutions. To do this, we need to read the discriminant. We don't even need to write out the whole formula! We can just focus on the $b^2 - 4ac$:

①	rewrite equation	$6x^2 + 18x - 13$
②	determine a, b, and c	$a = 6, b = 18, c = -13$
③	write discriminant	$b^2 - 4ac$
④	plug-in values	$(18)^2 - 4(6)(-13)$

Now, we COULD multiply this all out, but all we really care about is whether it's going to be positive, negative, or equal to zero, which we can figure out by focusing on the signs. We can see that we have a big, positive number (18^2) minus a negative number (–13). Since the minus sign and the negative sign will cancel, we'll end up with a big, **positive** number.

$$18^2 + 4(6)(13) > 0$$

When the discriminant is positive, we know there are TWO real solutions. So our answer is C!

C

Remainder Theorem

One last thing the SAT expects you to memorize is a little something called the **remainder theorem**. This topic, at most, will get tested only once. Here's how it works:

Remainder Theorem

If k is the result when a is plugged into a polynomial, then dividing the polynomial by (x − a) gives a remainder of k.

What does it mean? Let's look at an example. Consider the polynomial:

$$x^2 - 5x + 6$$

Let's try plugging 1 in for *x* to this polynomial and see what we get:

$$(1)^2 - 5(1) + 6 = \text{?}$$
$$1 - 5 + 6 = \text{?}$$
$$-4 + 6 = 2$$

Plugging in 1 for *x* gives us a result of 2. The remainder theorem tells us then that if we divide the polynomial by (x − 1), we'll get a remainder of 2. That's it! You don't need to know WHY this is the case, just that it IS the case. Let's look at an example to see how obvious the SAT is when they want to test this theorem:

EXAMPLE 3

For a polynomial $q(x)$, the value of $q(7)$ is 12. Which of the following must be true about $q(x)$?

A) $x - 19$ is a factor of $q(x)$.
B) $x - 12$ is a factor of $q(x)$.
C) The remainder when $q(x)$ is divided by $x - 7$ is 12.
D) The remainder when $q(x)$ is divided by $x - 12$ is 7.

SOLUTION

Not very subtle, are they? We see "remainder" in the answer choices, so it's a pretty good bet that this problem wants us to apply the remainder theorem.

When it says that $q(7) = 12$, it means that if you plug 7 in for x in the polynomial (whatever it is), you get a result of 12. The remainder theorem tells us then that if we divide the polynomial by $(x - 7)$, we'll have a **remainder of 12**.

C

Practice Problems

Use your new skills to answer each question.

1

Which of the following is a solution to the equation $x^2 + 3x - 2 = 0$?

$$x = \frac{-3 \pm \sqrt{(-3)^2 - 4(1)(-2)}}{2}$$

A) 17

B) $-3 + \sqrt{17}$

C) $-3 + \frac{\sqrt{17}}{2}$

D) $-\frac{3}{2} + \frac{\sqrt{17}}{2}$ ⟵ (circled)

2

How many solutions does the equation $x^2 + 4x + 4 = 0$ have?

A) 0

B) 1

C) 2 ⟵ (circled)

D) There is not enough information given.

$(x+2)(x+2)$

1 solution

$b^2 - 4ac$

3

How many solutions does the equation $3x^3 + 5x^2 + x = 0$ have?

A) 1

B) 2

C) 3 ⟵ (circled)

D) There is not enough information given.

4

What is the remainder when the polynomial $x^4 + 3x^2 - 5x + 7$ is divided by $(x + 2)$?

A) 1

B) −2

C) 25

D) 45 ⟵ (circled)

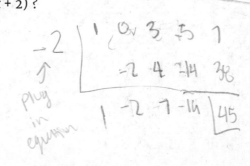

-2 ↑ plug in equation

$1 \quad 0 \quad 3 \quad -5 \quad 7$

$\quad -2 \quad 4 \quad -14 \quad 38$

$1 \quad -2 \quad 7 \quad -14 \quad \boxed{45}$

5

What are the solutions to $-3x^2 + 9x + 7 = 0$?

A) $\dfrac{-9 \pm \sqrt{165}}{6}$

B) $-\dfrac{3}{2} \pm \dfrac{\sqrt{165}}{6}$

C) $\dfrac{3}{2} \pm \dfrac{\sqrt{165}}{6}$

D) There are no real solutions.

$$x = \frac{-9 \pm \sqrt{(9)^2 - 4(-3)(7)}}{2(-3)}$$

6

For a polynomial $q(x)$, the value of $q(-3)$ is 4. Which of the following must be true about $q(x)$?

A) $x - 7$ is a factor of $q(x)$
B) $x - 4$ is a factor of $q(x)$
C) The remainder when $q(x)$ is divided by $x - 3$ is 4.
D) The remainder when $q(x)$ is divided by $x + 3$ is 4.

7

$$x^2 + 2sx = t + 2$$

In the quadratic equation above, s and t are constants. What are the solutions for x ?

A) $s \pm \sqrt{s^2 + t + 2}$

B) $-s \pm \sqrt{s^2 + t + 2}$

C) $-s \pm \dfrac{\sqrt{4s^2 + t + 2}}{2}$

D) $-s \pm \sqrt{4s^2 + 4t + 8}$

UNIT | Applied Factoring

Chapters

Key Skills

Recall how the slope-intercept form ($y = mx + b$) of linear equations helped us to see key information about the graph just by glancing at the equation.

For *quadratic* functions, like parabolas, there are **three different forms** to memorize! First, we'll learn what those forms are. Next, we'll use our factoring skills to manipulate equations until they are in the form we want. Finally, we'll investigate the connection between graphs, intercepts, and solutions to equations.

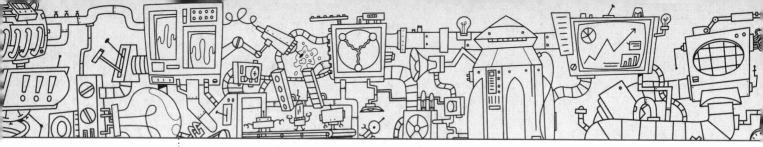

Transformers

In this chapter, we'll look at the graphs of parabolic functions.

In the *Basic Algebra* chapter, we learned that we can rearrange an algebraic equation as long as we make **balanced changes** to each side. Then, in the *Equation of a Line* chapter, we used that skill to rearrange a linear equation to get it into the slope-intercept form. This lets us see key things about the line's graph.

In this chapter, we'll learn how we can use what we know about *factoring* to rearrange a quadratic equation to get it into one of three specific forms: the **standard** form, the **vertex** form, and the **x-intercept** form. Each form helps us in different ways. Let's look at each form and see what good stuff each one tells us about the parabola.

The Three Forms

Before we dive into the specifics of each form, let's make a handy-dandy cheat sheet that shows the three forms and what manipulations we make to turn one form into another:

TIP

No need to worry if you don't know what "complete the square" means; it's an advanced trick that we'll learn later in this very chapter.

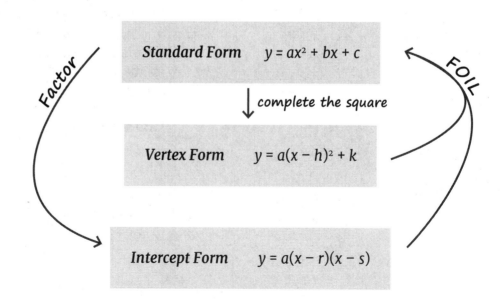

Factor

Standard Form $y = ax^2 + bx + c$

complete the square

Vertex Form $y = a(x - h)^2 + k$

FOIL

Intercept Form $y = a(x - r)(x - s)$

Direction

When a, the coefficient of x^2, is positive, the parabola opens upward. When a is negative, it opens downward.

Spread

The larger a gets, the skinnier the parabola gets. This is because the **rate of change** of y is greater for each increase in x.

Vertex (n.)

The lowest point in an upward-facing parabola, or the highest point in a downward-facing parabola.

Standard Form

In the last chapter, we talked about the quadratic formula and how it can be used to find the solutions of any equation of the form $ax^2 + bx + c = 0$. If we set this equal to y rather than 0, we get the **standard form** of the general parabola:

> **Standard Form** $y = ax^2 + bx + c$

What cool stuff does the standard form give us? As we've seen, it lets us use the quadratic formula (or our factoring skills) to find the equation's solutions. In addition, a, the coefficient of x, tells us the **direction** and **spread** of the parabola (see sidebar). It's also our "home base." We can manipulate this form to get either the vertex form or the intercept form.

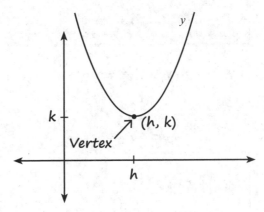

Vertex Form

A pretty important thing about a parabola is the location of its **vertex**. Any parabola can be manipulated into a form where we can read this straight from the equation. Fittingly, this form is called the **vertex form**:

> **Vertex Form** $y = a(x - h)^2 + k$

When you have the equation in this form, the coordinates of the vertex are at (h, k). So, for example, a parabola with the equation $y = (x - 2)^2 + 3$ would have a vertex at point **(2, 3)**.

PORTAL

To get from the standard form to the intercept form, we use **factoring**.

For a refresher on factoring basics, turn back to page 410.

BONUS

For any equation in vertex form, write down the coordinates of its vertex. For any in the intercept form, write down its x-intercepts.

We won't have any way of knowing that you did it, but we're working hard on that technology. Promise.

Intercept Form

Any parabola that intersects the *x*-axis (not all do!) can be written in a form that easily lets us see **where** those intersections occur:

Intercept Form	$y = a(x - r)(x - s)$

In this form, the x-intercepts happen at **(*r*, 0)** and **(*s*, 0)**. So, for example, a parabola with the equation y = 2(x – 4)(x + 5) would have x-intercepts at **(4, 0)** and **(–5, 0)**. To transform the standard form to the intercept form, we simply **factor** the polynomial.

Check the column that correctly identifies each equation's form.

Equation	Standard	Vertex	Intercept
1. $y = (x + 3)(x - 4)$			✔
2. $y = x^2 + 2x - 15$	✓		
3. $y = 3(x + 3)^2 - 10$		✓	
4. $y = 3x^2 + 12$	✓		
5. $y = \frac{1}{2}(x - 1)(x - 2)$			✓
6. $y = (x - 5)^2 - 99$		✓	

Answers: 1) Intercept (–3, 0), (4, 0) **2)** Standard **3)** Vertex (–3, –10)
4) Standard **5)** Intercept (1, 0), (2, 0) **6)** Vertex (5, –99)

EXAMPLE 1

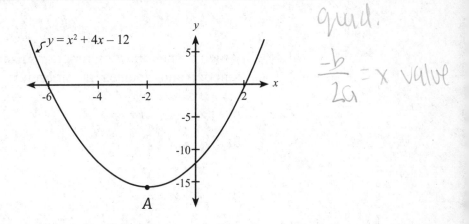

Which of the following is an equivalent form of the equation of the graph shown in the xy-plane above from which the coordinates of vertex A can be identified as constants in the equation?

A) $y = (x + 6)(x - 2)$

B) $y = (x - 6)(x + 2)$

C) $y = (x + 2)^2 - 16$

D) $y = x(x + 4) - 12$

SOLUTION

We know we are looking for a version of the equation that directly tells us the vertex. This means we are looking for the vertex form:

Vertex Form $y = a(x - h)^2 + k$

The *only* answer choice that fits this form is **choice C**.

Choice C $y = 1(x + 2)^2 - 16$

If this is indeed the correct vertex form, then we'd expect the vertex to be at (h, k), which here is $(-2, -16)$. Looking at the graph, that looks about right!

We could also double check by multiplying choice C out and seeing if we end up with the equation given in the graph:

$$(x + 2)^2 - 16 = x^2 + 4x + 4 - 16$$

$$= x^2 + 4x - 12$$

C

463

EXAMPLE 2

$$f(x) = (x - 5)(x + 1)$$

Which of the following functions has the same graph as the above function and includes its minimum value as a constant or coefficient?

A) $f(x) = (x - 2)^2 - 9$

B) $f(x) = (x + 2)^2 - 11$

C) $f(x) = x^2 - 4x - 5$

D) $f(x) = x^2 - 5$

SOLUTION

If a parabola has a "minimum value," it means the **lowest y-value** that is on the parabola. We must, then, be talking about the **vertex** of an upward-facing parabola. In other words, the question just came up with another weird way to ask:

"Which of these functions is in the correct vertex form?"

Choices C and D are in the *standard form*, and D doesn't even represent the same parabola! So we can cross those out. All we need to do now is figure out whether choice A or B is correct.

Option 1: Plug in the Vertices

If choice A is correct, then the vertex of $f(x)$ would be at **(2, –9)**. If choice B is correct, then the vertex would be at **(–2, –11)**. Let's test each choice by plugging their x-values into the original function and seeing if the machine spits out the correct y-value:

(1) *test choice A with* **(2, –9)**

$$
\begin{aligned}
f(x) &= (x - 5)(x + 1) \\
f(2) &= (2 - 5)(2 + 1) \\
f(2) &= (-3)(3) \\
f(2) &= \boxed{-9} \checkmark
\end{aligned}
$$

(2) *test choice B with* **(–2, –11)**

$$
\begin{aligned}
f(x) &= (x - 5)(x + 1) \\
f(-2) &= (-2 - 5)(-2 + 1) \\
f(-2) &= (-7)(-1) \\
f(-2) &= 7 \; ✗
\end{aligned}
$$

continue ⟶

Option 2: Eyeball the Vertex

We can use our quick-n-dirty eyeballing trick to figure out the correct vertex of this function. We were given the parabola in **intercept form**, so we know from looking at the function that the parabola crosses the *x*-axis at –1 and 5.

Since parabolas are symmetric, the *x*-coordinate of the vertex must be exactly halfway between those two points, at **$x = 2$.** This means that in vertex form, the equation must look like:

$$y = a(x - 2)^2 + k$$

..and the only choice where this is true is **choice A**.

A

Completing the Square

Ever since the Basic Algebra chapter, we've been doing quite a bit of **balancing equations**. We know that we are free to experiment by adding, subtracting, multiplying, or dividing as long as we keep the equation balanced. So, for example, we know that if we're given the equation below, we are free to add 4 to both sides if we want to:

totally fine
$$y = x^2 + 4x - 5$$
$$y + 4 = x^2 + 4x + 4 - 5$$

If we wanted to, instead of adding 4 to both sides, we could also just **add and subtract 4** from one side, which still keeps the equation unchanged:

perfectly okay
$$y = x^2 + 4x + 4 - 4 - 5$$

Before worrying about *why* you'd want to do that, make peace in your heart that it's *totally fine to do that if you want to*. Made peace? Good. As it turns out, what we just did was the first step in an extremely helpful trick called **completing the square**, which lets us factor otherwise unfactorable things and force equations *into* vertex form!

Occasionally, the SAT will insert an extra step into the problems we've worked so far. They might ask for the vertex but give you the intercept form, or vice versa. This is where your factoring skills come in! The first step is **always to get to standard form**. From there, you can factor to get intercept form, or complete the square to get vertex form.

Creating Vertex Form

Say you are given the following standard equation, and are asked to find the vertex. We'll need to transform it into vertex form:

$$\text{Standard Form} \quad y = x^2 + 8x - 2$$

$$\text{Vertex Form} \quad y = a(x - h)^2 + k$$

To get into vertex form, we will **complete the square**. To do this, we'll:

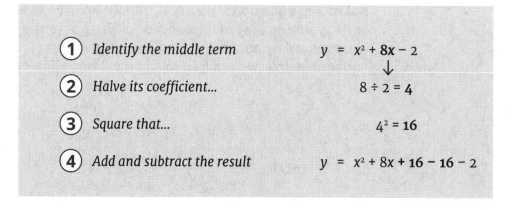

1 Identify the middle term	$y = x^2 + 8x - 2$	
2 Halve its coefficient...	$8 \div 2 = \mathbf{4}$	
3 Square that...	$4^2 = \mathbf{16}$	
4 Add and subtract the result	$y = x^2 + 8x + 16 - 16 - 2$	

By doing this, we create a group ($x^2 + 8x + 16$) that is a **perfect square**:

$$y = (x^2 + 8x + 16) - 18$$
$$\downarrow$$
$$y = (x + 4)^2 - 18$$

And, lo and behold, we have created an equation in **vertex form**! Thanks to our skillful and imaginative use of balanced manipulations and factoring, we can see that the vertex of this parabola is at **(–4, –18)**.

TIP

Remember, it's crucial to add AND subtract the same number when completing the square. If we don't, we throw off the balance of the whole equation.

EXAMPLE 3

$$y = (x - 2)(x - 10)$$

The graph of the above equation in the xy-plane is a parabola with vertex (u, v). Which of the following is equal to v ?

A) 2
B) 16
C) −2
D) −16

Handwritten work:
$$y = x^2 - 12x + 20$$
$$(x^2 - 12x + 36) + 20 - 36$$
$$(x - 6)^2 - 16$$
$$(6, -14)$$

SOLUTION

One way to solve this problem is to put the equation in vertex form. To get from intercept form to vertex form, we need to multiply it out to standard form and then **complete the square**.

(1) *rewrite equation* $(x - 2)(x - 10)$ = ?

(2) *FOIL to standard form* $(x - 2)(x - 10)$ = $x^2 - 12x + 20$

Now we can complete the square by **adding and subtracting 36**.

(3) *complete the square*
$$y = x^2 - 12x + 20$$
$$y = (x^2 - 12x + 36) - 36 + 20$$
$$y = (x - 6)^2 - 16$$

Completing the square has given us an equation in **vertex form**! Looking at the new form of the equation, we can see that our (u, v) vertex must be at **(6, −16)**. That means $v = -16$, making our answer **choice D**!

Backup Solution: Eyeball the Vertex

We can use the "Eyeball the Vertex" method here as well, though it takes an extra step. We're given the equation in **intercept form**. The equation $y = (x - 2)(x - 10)$ has solutions (x-intercepts) at $x = 2$ and $x = 10$. That means the vertex will be halfway between those points, at $x = 6$.

That gives us the x-value, but we need the y-value. But hey, we were given an equation to FIND the y-value. Just plug 6 in for x in the original equation, and the function machine will spit out −16!

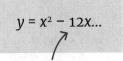

$y = x^2 - 12x...$

halve this...
...then square it.

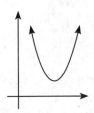

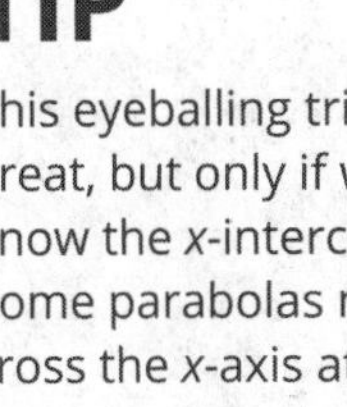

TIP

This eyeballing trick is great, but only if we know the x-intercepts. Some parabolas never cross the x-axis at all!

D

EXAMPLE 4

$$y = -x^2 - 6x - 11$$

The graph of the above equation is a parabola in the xy-plane with vertex (m, n). Which of the following is the value of $m + n$?

A) −2
B) −3
C) −5
D) −17

[handwritten:]
$(-x^2 - 6x - 9) + 9 - 11$

$-(x^2 + 6x + 9) - 9 + 11$

$-(x + 3)^2 - 2$

TIP

Remember that any variable by itself, like "x" or "w", has a hidden coefficient of 1.

Similarly, "$-x$" or "$-w$" has a hidden coefficent of −1.

SOLUTION

We can find the vertex by putting the equation in **vertex form**. The first step is to **factor out the coefficient** of the x^2 term to help us do what we gotta do:

① *rewrite equation* $\qquad y = -x^2 - 6x - 11$

② *factor out x^2 coefficient* $\qquad y = -1(x^2 + 6x + 11)$

Now we can complete the square by **adding & subtracting 9**.

③ *complete the square* $\qquad y = -1(x^2 + 6x + 9 - 9 + 11)$

$$y = -1((x + 3)^2 + 2)$$

④ *simplify to vertex form* $\qquad y = -(x + 3)^2 - 2$

Now we can see that vertex (m, n) of the parabola is at **(−3, −2)**. Just plug those values in for m and n to find our answer:

⑤ *plug-in and solve* $\qquad m + n = ?$

$$(-3) + (-2) = \boxed{-5}$$

continue →

Bonus Shortcut

Here's a fun shortcut we can use on this problem. Notice that we're given the equation of the parabola in standard form:

$$Standard\ Form \qquad y = ax^2 + bx + c$$

$$Equation \qquad y = -x^2 - 6x - 11$$

Any time you have a parabola equation in the standard form, the **x-coordinate of the vertex** will always equal:

$$x\text{-}coordinate\ of\ vertex\ = \frac{-b}{2a}$$

Which means we can just plug in our *a* and *b* values:

$$x\text{-}coordinate\ of\ vertex\ = \frac{-(-6)}{2(-1)} = \frac{6}{-2} = -3$$

We can plug in **–3** for *x* to find the *y*-coordinate of the vertex:

$$y = -(-3)^2 - 6(-3) - 11$$

$$y = -9 + 18 - 11 = -2$$

Now that we have our *m* and *n*, we just add them to get **–5.**

C

469

Equation of a Circle

Occasionally, you'll be asked about the equation of a circle. For these problems, you'll need to memorize one more formula:

The standard equation of a circle centered at (h, k) and with radius r is:

Equation of a Circle

$$(x - h)^2 + (y - k)^2 = r^2$$

Center: (h, k)   Radius: r

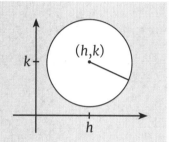

Making Connections

Ever wonder why the equation of a circle is what it is? No? Well, we'll tell you anyways. A circle is the set of points that are a fixed distance (the radius) from a single point (the center). A circle's equation is actually the same exact thing as using the **Pythagorean theorem** or the **distance formula** to find any point on that circle. We can see this if we draw it out.

Pick a point (x, y) on the circle and draw the radius connecting it to the center (h, k). Now draw a right triangle with that radius as the hypotenuse. With this picture, we can see how the equations are related:

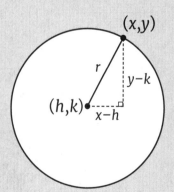

Equation of a Circle

$$(x - h)^2 + (y - k)^2 = r^2$$

Distance Formula

$$(x_1 - x_2)^2 + (y_1 - y_2)^2 = d^2$$

Pythagorean Theorem

$$a^2 + b^2 = c^2$$

EXAMPLE 5

Which of the following is the equation of a circle in the xy-plane with center (5, −4) and a radius with endpoint (2, 0) ?

A) $(x − 5)^2 + (y + 4)^2 = 25$
B) $(x + 5)^2 + (y − 4)^2 = 25$
C) $(x − 5)^2 + (y + 4)^2 = 5$
D) $(x + 5)^2 + (y − 4)^2 = 5$

SOLUTION

The first step is to plug what we know about our circle into the standard equation of a circle.

(1) *rewrite circle equation* $(x − h)^2 + (y − k)^2 = r^2$

(2) *plug in center (5, −4)* $(x − 5)^2 + (y − (−4))^2 = r^2$

     $(x − 5)^2 + (y + 4)^2 = r^2$

After plugging our given center into the equation of a circle, we can see immediately that choices B and D are out. Cross 'em off!

Now we just need to determine the radius of the circle. We aren't told how long the radius is, but we can **solve** for it! We know that point **(2, 0)** is on the circle. Let's plug that into our equation:

(3) *plug in point (2, 0)* $(2 − 5)^2 + (0 + 4)^2 = r^2$

(4) *solve for r^2* $(−3)^2 + (4)^2 = r^2$

     $9 + 16 = r^2$

     $25 = r^2$

Now be careful! It's tempting here to solve for the radius, but the equation of a circle is set equal to r^2, **not r**. Just to be safe, let's rewrite the standard equation one last time:

(5) *rewrite circle equation* $(x − h)^2 + (y − k)^2 = r^2$

(6) *plug in what we know* $(x − 5)^2 + (y + 4)^2 = 25$ **A**

EXAMPLE 6

$$x^2 + y^2 - 4x + 6y = 23$$

The above equation represents a circle in the xy-plane. What is the radius of the circle?

A) 2
B) 3
C) 6
D) 36

[handwritten work:
$x^2 - 4x + y^2 + 6y$
$x^2 - 4x + 4 - 4 + y^2 + 6y + 9$
$(x-2)^2 - 4 (y+3)^2 - 9 = 23$
$(x-2)^2 + (y+3)^2 - 13 = 23$
$+13, +13$
$(x-2)^2 + (y+3)^2 = 6$*]*

SOLUTION

Yowza! This is a tough problem, but all we need to know is **(1)** the equation of a circle, and **(2)** how to complete the square.

To figure out the radius of the circle, we'll need to **rearrange** this equation until it's in the standard equation of a circle form. To do this, we're going to need to **complete the square** *twice!* Once for x, and once for y. First, let's focus on the *x*'s.

① *rewrite equation* $\qquad\qquad x^2 + y^2 - 4x + 6y = 23$

② *gather the variables* $\qquad \underbrace{x^2 - 4x}_{1} + \underbrace{y^2 + 6y}_{2} = 23$

③ *complete the square (x)* $\qquad x^2 - 4x + 4 - 4 + y^2 + 6y = 23$

$(x - 2)^2 - 4 + y^2 + 6y = 23$

$(x - 2)^2 + y^2 + 6y = 27$

④ *complete the square (y)* $\qquad (x - 2)^2 + y^2 + 6y + 9 - 9 = 27$

$(x - 2)^2 + (y + 3)^2 - 9 = 27$

$(x - 2)^2 + (y + 3)^2 = 36$

Aha! Now that the equation is in the proper form, we can read the radius. If $r^2 = 36$, then **$r = 6$**. Choice C is the right answer!

C

Practice Problems

Use your new skills to answer each question.

1

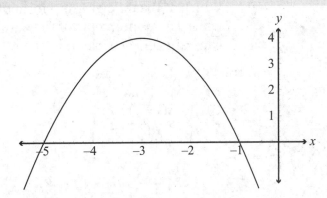

Which of the following equations could be represented by the graph above and has the coordinates of the vertex of the parabola as constants or coefficients?

A) $y = -(x + 3)^2 + 4$
B) $y = -x^2 - 6x - 5$
C) $y = (x - 1)(x - 5)$
D) $y = (x + 1)(x + 5)$

2

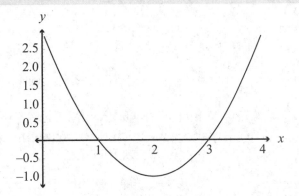

Which of the following equations could be represented by the graph above and has the x-intercepts of the graph as constants or coefficients?

A) $y = (x - 2)^2 + 15$
B) $y = x(x + 4) + 3$
C) $y = (x - 1)(x + 3)$
D) $y = (x - 1)(x - 3)$

3

$$y = x^2 - 2x - 8$$

The equation above represents a parabola in the xy-plane. Which of the following is a form of the same equation in which the x-intercepts of the parabola are displayed as constants or coefficients?

A) $y = (x + 4)(x - 2)$
B) $y = (x - 4)(x + 2)$
C) $y = x(x - 2) - 8$
D) $y + 9 = (x - 1)^2$

4

$$y = x^2 + 6x + 5$$

The equation above represents a parabola in the xy-plane. Which of the following equivalent forms of the equation displays the coordinates of the vertex of the equation as constants or coefficients?

A) $y = (x + 5)(x + 1)$
B) $y = x(x + 6) + 5$
C) $y = (x + 3)^2 - 4$
D) $y - 5 = x^2 + 6x$

5

$$f(x) = -2(x + 4)(x - 2)$$

Which of the following is an equivalent form of the function f above in which the maximum value of f appears as a constant or coefficient?

A) $f(x) = -2(x - 1)^2 + 18$
B) $f(x) = -2(x + 1)^2 + 18$
C) $f(x) = -2x^2 + 16$
D) $f(x) = -2x^2 - 4x + 16$

6

$$y = c(x^2 - 6x - 1)$$

In the quadratic equation above, c is a constant greater than zero. Which of the following is equal to the minimum value of y?

A) $-10c$
B) $-9c$
C) $8c$
D) $-c$

7

The graph of an equation in the xy-plane is a parabola with vertex $(3, -2)$, if the equation of the parabola can be written as $x^2 + bx + c$ where b and c are constants, what is the value of c?

A) -6
B) -2
C) 6
D) 7

8

$$y = c(x - 3)(x + 5)$$

In the quadratic equation above, c is a non-zero constant. The graph of the equation in the xy-plane is a parabola with vertex (u, v). Which of the following is equal to v?

A) 1
B) c
C) -16
D) $-16c$

9

Which of the following is an equation of a circle in the xy-plane with center $(1, 2)$ and a radius with endpoint $(-5, -6)$?

A) $(x - 1)^2 + (y - 2)^2 = 10$
B) $(x - 1)^2 + (y - 2)^2 = 100$
C) $(x - 1)^2 + (y + 2)^2 = 100$
D) $(x - 1)^2 + (y + 2)^2 = 64$

10

$$x^2 + 4x + y^2 - 6y = 12$$

The equation above represents a circle in the xy-plane. What is the radius of the circle?

A) $2\sqrt{3}$
B) 5
C) 12
D) 25

11

$$x + y = \sqrt{8x + 2xy - 7}$$

Which of the following is equivalent to the equation above?

A) $(x - 4)^2 + y^2 = 9$
B) $x(x - 8) + y(y - 2x) = -7$
C) $\sqrt{x + y} = 8x + 2xy - 7$
D) $-7x - 2xy + y = -7$

Zeros & Solutions

In this chapter, we take a step back and look at the connections between solutions, zeroes, and x-intercepts.

Different Names for the Same Thing

The key to mastering the SAT Math section is to not just practice different question types, but to learn the connections between similar concepts. In the polynomials chapter, we learned how we can find the **solutions** of a polynomial function by setting it equal to **zero** and factoring:

$$f(x) = x^2 + 7x + 10$$

$$x^2 + 7x + 10 = 0$$
$$(x + 2)(x + 5) = 0$$

Solutions $\quad x = -2, -5$

When we do this, we are finding the *x*-inputs that make a function machine spit out a zero. But let's think *graphically*. If we know that plugging in –2 and –5 for *x* makes f(x) equal *zero*, then that must mean that *y* is zero at those two points. In other words, the **x-intercepts** are:

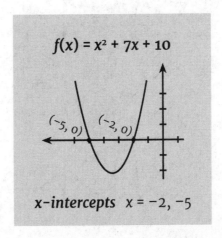

$$f(x) = x^2 + 7x + 10$$

x-intercepts $\quad x = -2, -5$

This means that, if you know the **x-intercepts** of a graph, you also know the **solutions** when you set that function equal to zero. The SAT wants you to be completely comfortable switching between these concepts, so let's get some practice!

EXAMPLE 1

If the function g has six distinct zeros, which of the following could represent the graph of g in the xy-plane?

A)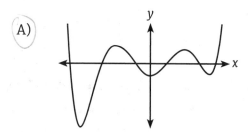

B)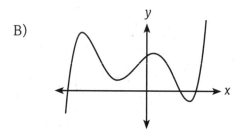

C)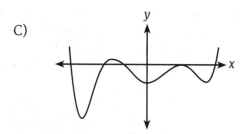

D)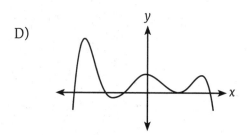

SOLUTION

Since the function has six distinct zeros, that means it **crosses the x-axis six times**. All we have to do is count how many times the graph in each answer choice crosses the x-axis.

 count x-intercepts

Choice A:
6 x-intercepts

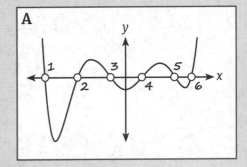

Choice B:
3 x-intercepts

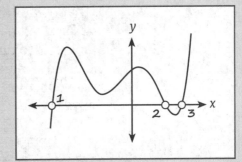

Choice C:
5 x-intercepts

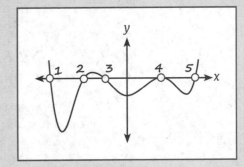

Choice D:
5 x-intercepts

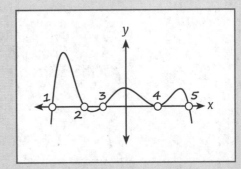

Only **choice A** has a graph that crosses the x-axis 6 times, so it could be the graph of a function with 6 solutions.

A

EXAMPLE 2

In the xy-plane, the graph of function f has x-intercepts at -5, 0, and 3. Which of the following could be the function?

A) $f(x) = (x - 5)(x + 3)$
B) $f(x) = x(x - 5)(x - 3)$
C) $f(x) = (x + 5)(x - 3)$
D) $f(x) = x(x + 5)(x - 3)$

SOLUTION

We know that x-intercepts of a function have a y-coordinate of 0. That means if we plug -5, 0, and 3 into the function **equation**, it will spit out a result of **zero**. The simplest way to solve this problem is to do just that: test each answer choice by plugging in the given x-values. If the function doesn't spit out a zero for every single one, then it's not the right equation. It turns out that only choice D works for every single value:

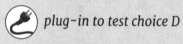 *plug-in to test choice D*

$$x(x + 5)(x - 3) = ?$$
$$0(0 + 5)(0 - 3) = 0 \checkmark$$
$$-5(-5 + 5)(-5 - 3) = 0$$
$$3(3 + 5)(3 - 3) = 0$$

SHORTCUT: Thinking with Factors

We don't *have* to trial-and-error this problem. When a function is factored out, you can **see** the solutions clearly. If the graph has an x-intercept of k, then one factor would be:

$$f(x) = (x - k)\ldots$$

That means that just knowing the x-intercepts, we can write the factors out and then compare our equation to the answer choices. If there are intercepts at 0, -5, and 3, then the factors are:

$$f(x) = (x - 0)(x - (-5))(x - 3)$$
$$f(x) = x(x + 5)(x - 3)$$

And that matches choice D! This is a great example of how we can **save time** if we understand the connection between solutions, factors, and graphs.

D

480

EXAMPLE 3

x	−5	−2	0	3	6
f(x)	10	6	4	0	2

The function f is defined by a polynomial. Some values of x with the corresponding values of $f(x)$ are shown in the table above. Which of the following must be a factor of $f(x)$?

A) $x + 3$
B) $x − 3$
C) $x − 4$
D) $x + 4$

SOLUTION

In this problem, we're not told what the equation is for f(x), but we are still asked for one of its factors. The table must be important. It gives us a series of inputs & outputs, or (x, y) pairs if you're feeling graphy. How can a point tell us a factor of the equation?

Well, every **x-intercept** of a polynomial's graph tells us one of its factors. An x-intercept is **any x input that spits out a zero** for $f(x)$. Do we see one in the table? Yes! In the fourth column:

x	−5	−2	0	**3**	6
f(x)	10	6	4	**0**	2

This tells us that when x = 3, the polynomial f(x) = 0. Which means if we factored whatever that polynomial is, one of its factors must be **(x – 3)**. So the answer is B!

B

EXAMPLE 4

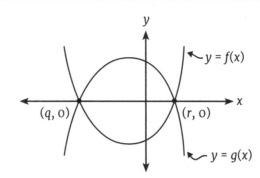

Functions f and g, defined by $f(x) = 4x^2 + 4x - 3$ and $g(x) = -4x^2 - 4x + 3$, are graphed in the xy-plane above. The graphs of f and g intersect at the points $(q, 0)$ and $(r, 0)$. What is the value of r?

A) $-\dfrac{3}{2}$

B) -3

C) $\dfrac{1}{2}$

D) 1

We know we want to find r, and we are told that (r, 0) is one of the intersections of f(x) and g(x). We could solve this by setting f(x) and g(x) equal to one another to find the points where they intersect. But let's **use the connection between x-intercepts and factors**. If we factor one of the equations, say f(x), then we'll be able to see the x-intercepts. That will look something like:

$$f(x) = 4x^2 + 4x - 3 = (\ x +\ \ )(\ \ x -\ \ )$$

We know the **coefficients** of the x's must multiply to 4, so they're either 1 and 4 or 2 and 2. The **constants** must multiply to –3, so must be –1 and 3 or 1 and –3. Playing with these combinations a bit, we find one that works:

$$f(x) = 4x^2 + 4x - 3 = (2x + 3)(2x - 1)$$

This means the two x-intercepts are at **x = 1/2** and **x = –3/2**. So which one is r? Looking at the graph, we see that r is positive, so r must equal **1/2**. Our answer is C!

C

PORTAL

This equation is a great candidate for factoring with the **box method**! For a review, turn to page 422.

EXAMPLE 5

$$h = -4.9t^2 + 80t$$

Michael is setting up for a fireworks show and needs to determine how far from his launch site the spent fireworks can safely land. He knows that t seconds after launch, the height of a particular firework is given by the above equation. He also knows that, while it is in the air, the firework travels at a rate of 13.6 m/s horizontally from the launch site. About how many meters away from the launch site will the firework remains land?

A)   13.6
B)   16.3
C)   222
D)   327

SOLUTION

We're asked to find the **distance** between where the firework was launched and where it will land. Let's draw a picture to help us:

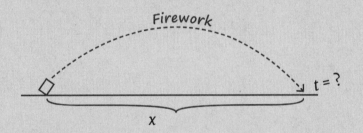

We know it travels left to right at a rate of 13.6 m/s. For this to be helpful, we need to know how long it is in the air. That's where the equation comes in! The equation has two variables: time and height. If we know one, we can find the other.

So... what is the height of the firework when it lands? That would be zero! That means if we find the zeroes of the equation we can figure out how long it was in the air:

   1   *set equal to zero* $-4.9t^2 + 80t = 0$

   2   *factor* $t(-4.9t + 80) = 0$

Now to find the values of t that would make this equation true.

continue →

TIP

Remember, distance is equal to rate times time. The total distance you drive (100 miles) is your speed (50 mph) times how long you drove (2 hours).

③ *find values of t*

$$t(-4.9t + 80) = 0$$

$$t_1 = 0$$

$$t_2 = \frac{80}{4.9} \approx 16.3$$

So there are two values of t that would make the height zero. That makes sense! The height is zero at two times: when it launches and when it lands. The launch happens at $t = 0$, so the landing must happen at $t \approx 16.3$ seconds.

To find the distance the firework traveled during that time, we multiply 16.3 seconds by the rate it travels:

④ *multiply by the rate*

$$distance = (rate)(time)$$

$$distance = (13.6 \text{ m/s})(16.3 \text{ s})$$

$$distance = \boxed{221.68 \text{ meters}}$$

Boom, problem solved!   **C**

Practice Problems

Use your new skills to answer each question.

1

The function g has roots at $x = -4$, 1, and 5. Which of the following could be the definition of g?

A) $g(x) = (x - 4)(x - 1)(x - 5)$
B) $g(x) = (x + 4)(x + 1)(x + 5)$
C) $g(x) = (x + 4)(x - 1)(x - 5)$
D) $g(x) = (x - 4)(x + 1)(x + 5)$

2

$$f(t) = -4.9t^2 + 5t + 3$$

Maureen dives into a pool from a springboard mounted 3 meters above the water. The function $f(t)$ gives her height above the water t seconds from when she jumps. After about how many seconds does she hit the water?

A) 1.4
B) 3
C) 4.9
D) 5

3

Particular values of the function g are given in the following table:

x	$g(x)$
-3	5
-1	0
0	1
2	8

Which of the following is a factor of g?

A) $(x - 1)$
B) $(x + 1)$
C) $(x - 2)$
D) $(x + 3)$

The graph of the function $f(x)$ has 3 distinct zeros. Which of the following could be the graph of $f(x)$?

A)

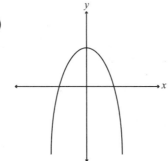

B)

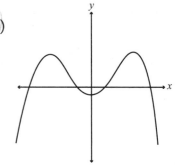

C)

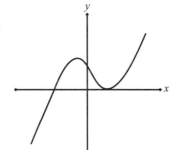

D)

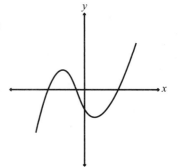

5

$$y = -16t^2 + 48t + 64$$

The equation above represents the height y, in feet, of an arrow t seconds after it was launched from the ground at a 30° angle with an initial velocity of 96 feet per second. After approximately how many seconds will the arrow hit the ground?

A) −1
B) 0
C) 1
D) 4

6

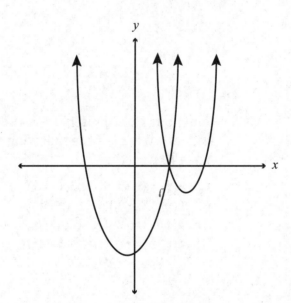

The functions f and g, defined by $f(x) = x^2 + x - 6$ and $g(x) = x^2 - 6x + 8$ are graphed in the xy-plane above. The graphs of f and g intersect at point $(a, 0)$. What is the value of a?

A) −3
B) −2
C) 2
D) 4

7

The functions f and g are defined by $f(x) = 6x^2 + x + 5$ and $g(x) = 2x^2 - 15x - 2$. For what set of x values does $f(x) + g(x) = 0$?

A) $\frac{1}{4}$ and $\frac{3}{2}$

B) $\frac{2}{3}$ and 4

C) $-\frac{1}{4}$ and $-\frac{3}{2}$

D) 2 and 3

Whats a faster way

8

Functions f and g intersect at the points $(-3, 5)$, $(2, 8)$, and $(11, -17)$. Which of the following could define the function $h(x) = f(x) - g(x)$?

A) $h(x) = (x + 3)(x - 2)(x - 11)$
B) $h(x) = (x - 5)(x - 8)(x + 17)$
C) $h(x) = (x + 2)(x - 6)(x + 6)$
D) $h(x) = (x - 3)(x + 2)(x + 11)$

UNIT

Systems of Equations

Chapters

Key Skills

In this chapter, we'll learn how to work with systems of equations. We will use strategies like **stack n' smash** and **substitution** to solve for variables, and study the connection between equations, their solutions, and their graphs.

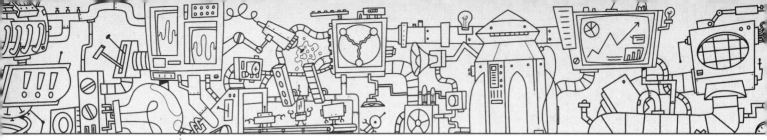

Solving Systems

a.k.a. "Finding a point we can all agree upon."

Systems of Equations

Often, you will come across problems that have multiple equations with multiple variables. For example:

$$x + y = 12$$
$$2x + 10y = 40$$

Intersections

The solutions for a system of equations are also the *points* where the graphs of the equations **intersect**. We'll be looking at systems and graphs in the next chapter.

We call this group a **system of equations**, and they show up all the time on both the calculator and non-calculator sections of the test. **Solving** systems of equations means finding which values for the variables make both equations in the system true *at the same time*. In other words, what can you plug in for *x* and *y* to make both equations work out? For example, the solutions to the system above are **_x_ = 10** and **_y_ = 2**:

$$(10) + (2) = 12$$
$$2(10) + 10(2) = 40$$

Solving Systems of Equations

To solve a system of equations, we will need to **combine** the equations into a single equation in a way that makes one of the variables disappear. Then we can solve for that variable. There are two main techniques that we can use to combine equations: **Stack & Smash** and **Substitution.**

Stack & Smash

Sometimes, the systems of equations are set up in a way that we can literally combine them by adding or subtracting the entire equations. Whenever you see one variable that has the **same coefficient** in each equation, you can add (or subtract) each corresponding piece of the equation to make that variable disappear. For example:

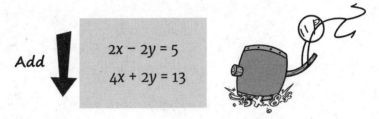

Add

$$2x - 2y = 5$$
$$4x + 2y = 13$$

If we "smash" the top equation into the bottom equation, the $2y$ and $-2y$ cancel, leaving us with:

$$6x = 18$$

From here, we can easily solve for x, and then plug that value into one of the original equations to find y. Sometimes, smashing things helps.

Stack & Smash (Advanced)

In more advanced problems, the systems are good candidates for stacking & smashing, but need a little work first. You'll need to make balanced manipulations to one equation to make smashing as effective as possible. For example:

$$2a + 3b = 12$$
$$-4a - 8b = 40$$

Divide WHOLE equation by 2

Neither a nor b has the same coefficient in each equation, but we can force it! If we **multiply** the top equation by 2, or **divide** the bottom equation by 2, we'll be set up for a smashing good time!

Balance

Remember, you are free to experiment with the equation. Just remember to **keep it balanced!**

Substitution

Other times, a more subtle approach is best. When you have one equation with an easily-isolated variable, it can be best to solve using **substitution**. Just look for x or y with a coefficient of 1. For example:

$$x - y = 2$$
$$3x + 2y = 26$$

Notice how easy it is to get x or y alone in the top equation? Let's try using that to our advantage. If we add y to both sides of the top equation, we get "x = y + 2". We can **substitute** that for x in the bottom equation:

Plug in new "name" for x →

$$3(y + 2) + 2y = 26$$
$$3y + 6 + 2y = 26$$
$$5y = 20$$

From here, we can solve for y, and plug that value back into either equation to find x. Boom! Problem solved. Remember, you can pretty much always use substitution if it helps you solve an algebra problem; just be sure to carefullly write out each step.

PORTAL

To see the FIRST time we used this joke, turn to the Basic Algebra chapter on page 345!

EXAMPLE 1

$$x - 2y = -31$$
$$x + 3y = 59$$

(handwritten: $-5y = -90$)

What is the value of x in the solution of the system of equations given above?

(handwritten: $\dfrac{-5y = -90}{-5}$ $y = 18$)

(handwritten: $x - 2y = 31$ $x = 5$)

SOLUTION

Option 1: Stack & Smash

Looking at these two equations, we see that x has the same coefficient, 1, in both equations. This means that if we **subtract** the equations, the **x's will disappear**.

1 *stack equations*

$$x - 2y = -31$$
$$-\quad x + 3y = 59$$

2 *subtract*

$$x - 2y - x - 3y = -31 - 59$$

3 *simplify*

$$-5y = -90$$

4 *solve for y*

$$y = \boxed{18}$$

We're not done yet! We were asked to **solve for x**, not y. But we can simply **plug-in 18 for y** in either equation to find x:

5 *plug-in 18 for y*

$$x - 2y = -31$$

$$x - 2(18) = -31$$

5 *solve for x*

$$x - 36 = -31$$

$$x = \boxed{5}$$

continue →

Option 2: Solve & Substitute

Let's pick an equation to solve for one of the variables. We can easily **solve the first equation for x** by adding 2y to each side:

(1) *solve for x in first equation*

$$x - 2y = -31$$

$$x = -31 + 2y$$

Now we can **substitute** (–31 + 2y) for x in the second equation:

(2) *substitute*

$$x + 3y = 59$$

$$(-31 + 2y) + 3y = 59$$

$$-31 + 5y = 59$$

(3) *solve for y*

$$5y = 90$$

$$y = \boxed{18}$$

Once again, once we find that **y = 18**, we're almost done. We just need to **substitute** that into one of the equations and solve for x. This time, for the heck of it, let's use the second equation:

(5) *plug-in 18 for y*

$$x + 3y = 59$$

$$x + 3(18) = 59$$

(5) *solve for x*

$$x + 54 = 59$$

$$x = \boxed{5}$$

EXAMPLE 2

$$3x - 2y = -54$$
$$5x + 4y = -68$$

If (x, y) is the solution to the system of equations above, what is the value of y ?

$6x - 4y = -108$
$5x + 4y = -68$
_____
$11x = -176$
$x = -16$

$5(-16) + 4y = -68$
$y = 3$

SOLUTION

The first thing to notice is that we are solving a system of equations. The coefficients of x are 3 and 5... it will be difficult making these add or subtract in a way that clears the x's, so let's look at y.

The coefficients of y in the two equations are –2 and 4. That has potential! Do you see why? If we **multiply the top equation by 2**, then we set up the equations for a clean **stack & add** maneuver:

① *multiply first equation by 2*

$$2(3x - 2y = -54)$$
$$5x + 4y = -68$$

$$6x - 4y = -108$$
$$5x + 4y = -68$$

② *add equations*

$$6x - 4y = -108$$
$$+\ \ 5x + 4y = -68$$
_____
$$11x = -176$$

③ *solve for x*

$$x = \boxed{-16}$$

④ *substitute –16 for x*

$$5(-16) + 4y = -68$$

$$-80 + 4y = -68$$

⑤ *solve for y*

$$4y = 12$$

$$y = ③$$

497

EXAMPLE 3

$$x + 2y = -11$$
$$5x + y = 8$$

If (x, y) is a solution to the system of equations above, what is the value of $2x + y$?

SOLUTION

This question asks for 2x + y rather than just x or y. Usually, when the SAT asks you for an expression like this (rather than just *x* or *y*), there is some tricky or clever way to find the answer without fully solving for all the variables.

Let's keep "2x + y" in mind and try **adding** the two equations:

1 *keep "2x + y" in mind*

2 *add equations*

$$\begin{aligned} x + 2y &= -11 \\ +\quad 5x + y &= 8 \\ \hline 6x + 3y &= -3 \end{aligned}$$

Notice anything familiar about the result? Hidden inside it is the very same expression we were asked to find:

3 *simplify* $\qquad\qquad 3(2x + y) = -3$

4 *solve for 2x + y* $\qquad\qquad 2x + y = \boxed{-1}$

Of course, you don't have to see this shortcut. You can **always** solve systems of equations the old-fashioned way by Solving & Substituting. Remember: algebra is just a tool you use to reach your goal!. As long as you **keep things balanced**, you're free to manipulate as you see fit!

EXAMPLE 4

$$\frac{x+1}{y-1} = 1$$

$$3(y + 2) = x$$

If (x, y) is a solution to the system of equations above, what is the value of y ?

[handwritten: $x = y - 2$, $x = 3(y+2)$, $3y + 6 = y - 2$, $2y = 8$, $y = -4$]

SOLUTION

Since we see two equations with the same two variables, we know we're in systems of equations land. First things first: let's clean up that fraction in the first equation:

(1) *clear fraction*

$$\frac{x+1}{y-1} = 1$$

$$x + 1 = y - 1$$

(2) *simplify*

$$\boxed{x = y - 2}$$

That's better! Let's look at our newly cleaned system.

$$x = y - 2$$

$$3(y + 2) = x$$

Well whaddya know! Now we have two equations that are solved for x. That means we can just set them equal to each other and solve for *y*.

(3) *set equal*

$$3(y + 2) = y - 2$$

(4) *solve for y*

$$3y + 6 = y - 2$$

$$2y = -8$$

$$y = \boxed{-4}$$

Practice Problems

Use your new skills to answer each question.

....

1

$$4x + 5y = -19$$
$$2\ (y - 2x = -15)$$

What is the solution (x, y) to the system of equations above?

A) $(-6, 1)$
B) $(4, -7)$
C) $(3, -7)$
D) $(5, -2)$

$4x + 5y = -19$
$-4x - 2y = -30$
_____
$3y = 49$
3

2

$$x + 3y = 27$$
$$3x + 2y = 11$$

What is the solution (x, y) to the system of equations above?

A) $(0, 9)$
B) $(-1, 7)$
C) $(-3, 10)$
D) $(1, 18)$

3

$$5x + 7y = 2$$
$$2x + 3y = 0$$

In the system of equations above, what is the value of $x + y$?

A) -1
B) 0
C) 1
D) 2

4

$$4x + 8y = -32$$
$$7x - 3y = 29$$

In the system of equations above, what is the solution (x, y) ?

A) $(2, -5)$
B) $(-2, -3)$
C) $(-2, 5)$
D) $(-13, 2)$

5

$$3x - 5y = 11$$
$$-2x + 4y = -13$$

In the system of equations above, what is the value of $x - y$?

A) -4
B) -2
C) 2
D) 4

6

$$ax - by = -2$$
$$6x - 4y = 4$$

In the system of equations above, a and b are constants and x and y are variables. If the system of equations has exactly one solution, what can $\frac{a}{b}$ NOT equal?

A) $-\frac{3}{2}$

B) $-\frac{2}{3}$

C) $\frac{2}{3}$

D) $\frac{3}{2}$

7

$$f(x) = -x + 4$$
$$g(x) = 3(x + 2)^2 - 4$$

How many solutions does the system above have?

A) 0
B) 1
C) 2
D) 3

8

$$3x - 7y = 35$$
$$x - y = 9$$

What is x when the system given above is satisfied?

9

If the product of a and b is 50% more than the sum of a and b, what is the value of $\frac{1}{a} + \frac{1}{b}$?

A) $\frac{2}{3}$

B) $\frac{3}{2}$

C) $\frac{1}{5}$

D) $\frac{1}{2}$

10

$$a = 4800 - 6t$$
$$b = 5400 - 8t$$

In the system of equations above, a and b represent the distance, in meters, two marathon runners are from the finish line after running for four hours and t seconds. How far will runner a be from the finish line when runner b passes her?

A) 200 meters
B) 300 meters
C) 1000 meters
D) 3000 meters

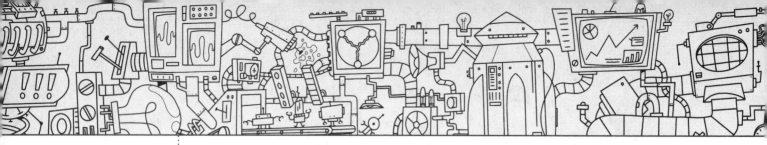

Spotting Solutions

In the previous chapter, we looked at how we can use algebra to discover the solutions to a system of equations. In this section, we will learn about how you can SEE solutions by looking at the graph of a function.

NOTE

When we talk about the **graph of a function** we are talking specifically about the line, parabola, or curve itself, not the entire coordinate system around it.

Solutions to an Equation

You can think of the graph of an equation as simply a **helpful picture** showing every (x,y) pair that makes an equation true. If we see that point (2, 5) is on the graph of $y = 2x + 1$, then we can be sure that plugging 2 in for x in the equation will spit out a y-value of 5. And that will be true for every point we know is on the line. In other words, **points on the line *are* the solutions**.

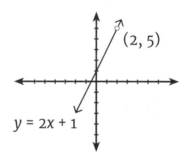

Solutions to a System of Equations

When we talk about the solutions to a **system** of equations, we are looking for an (x, y) pair that makes *both* equations true. In other words, we're looking for **the point where the graphs intersect**.

In this graph, we can see that the solution to the system of equations is x = 0 and y = 1. Try it, it works! Don't you wish *all* systems came with graphs?

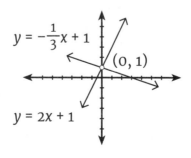

INTERACTIVE EXAMPLE

The function $f(x) = x^5 - 3x^4 - 5x^3 + 15x^2 + 4x - 17$ is graphed in the xy-plane below. Now we're going to ask a bunch of questions about it!

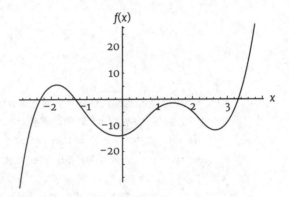

Q1) How many solutions are there to the equation $f(x) = 0$?

S1) The solutions to $f(x) = 0$ are the values of x where the y-value is **zero**. In other words, we're looking for the x-intercepts. That means the *number* of solutions is the *number* of x-intercepts. Simply counting them tells us that there are **3 solutions** to $f(x) = 0$.

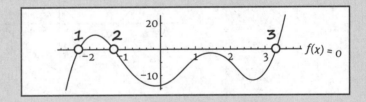

Q2) How many solutions are there to the equation $f(x) = -10$?

S2) This problem is *very* similar to the previous problem. When we were looking for solutions to $f(x) = 0$, we were looking for where the graph crossed the horizontal line at $y = 0$. That means that, here, we want to know how many times the graph crosses a horizontal line at **$y = -10$**. If we draw that line, we see there are **5 solutions** to $f(x) = -10$.

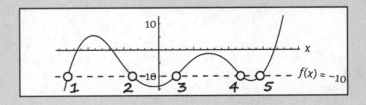

505

Q3) If *k* is a constant such that the equation $f(x) = k$ has 3 real solutions, which of the following *could* be the value of k?

A) 20
B) 5
C) −20
D) −40

S3) In the previous question, we wanted to know how many solutions there are for $f(x) = -5$. So, we drew the line y = −5 and counted. This question is essentially asking the same thing, only backwards: where can we draw a horizontal line that crosses the graph of $f(x)$ exactly 3 times? They give us four possible options, so we just need to graph and check each one. You can take it from here:

Use the graph to find where $f(x)$ has 3 solutions:

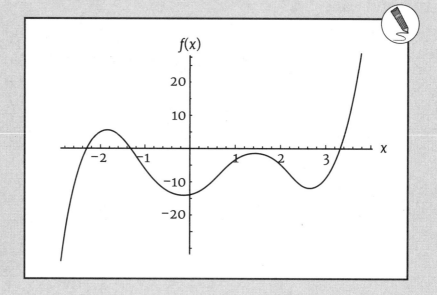

Answer to Q3: 5 (Choice B)

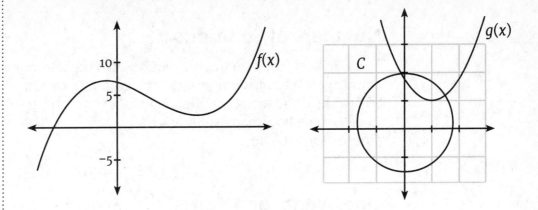

✏️ **Use the above graphs** to count the number of solutions.

How many solutions are there to...	# of Solutions
1. $f(x) = -3$	*1*
2. $f(x) = 5$	
3. $f(x) = 0$	
4. $f(x) = 10$	
5. $g(x) = 0$	
6. $g(x) = 1$	
7. $g(x) = 3$	
8. The system with circle C and line $y = 0$	
9. The system with circle C and line $y = 2$	
10. The system with circle C and $g(x)$	

Answers: 1) 1 **2)** 3 **3)** 1 **4)** 1 **5)** 0 **6)** 1 **7)** 2 **8)** 2 **9)** 1 **10)** 2

Numbers of Solutions

As we've seen, the number of solutions can be determined simply by **counting intersection points** on the graph. Occasionally, however, the SAT will give you a system of equations and not the graphs, and ask you to determine how many solutions the system has. So let's think about the different possibilities.

One, None, or a Ton

With a pair of lines, it turns out there are **three possibilities**, and it all depends on the the *slopes* of the lines.

One solution: When two lines have *different slopes*, they have one point of intersection and the system has one solution.

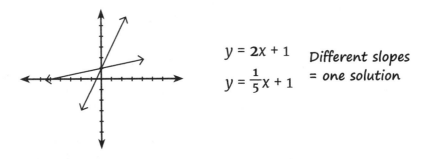

$$y = 2x + 1$$
$$y = \frac{1}{5}x + 1$$

Different slopes = one solution

No solutions: When two lines have the *same slope* and different *y*-intercepts, they are **parallel** and never intersect. Thus, the system has no solutions.

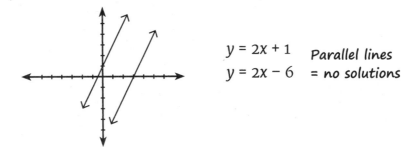

$$y = 2x + 1$$
$$y = 2x - 6$$

Parallel lines = no solutions

Infinite solutions: When two lines are actually the **same exact line**, then the system has infinitely many solutions. In this situation, you're given a system that appears to be two separate equations. But when you put the equations into slope-intercept form, you end up with identical equations.

NOTE

The "∞" symbol means "infinite".

 Identify the # of solutions to each system by writing "1", "0", or "∞".

System of Equations	# of Solutions
1. $f(x) = \frac{3}{4}x + 7$ and $g(x) = -\frac{3}{4}x + 7$	
2. $f(x) = 2x + 3$ and $g(x) = 2x + 7$	
3. $f(x) = \frac{2}{3}x + 3$ and $g(x) = \frac{4}{6}x - 4$	
4. $3x + 4y = 16$ and $-6x + 8y = 2$	
5. $y = -2x + 3$ and $6x + 3y = 9$	
6. $5x + 7y = 2$ and $3x - 4y = -13$	

Answers: **1)** 1 **2)** 0 **3)** 0 **4)** 1 **5)** ∞ **6)** 1

EXAMPLE 1

$$ax + by = 15$$
$$4x + 3y = 75$$

In the system of equations above, a and b are constants. If the system has infinitely many solutions, what is the value of $\frac{a}{b}$?

SOLUTION

Option 1: Stack & Solve

If the system has infinitely many solutions, then these equations must be **exactly the same**, other than some balanced changes that don't alter the graph of the line. Our job, then, is to reverse engineer those balanced changes. Since these equations look pretty similar to one another, we might try a hand at **stacking.**

Notice that $75 = 15 \times 5$. This gives us a good idea of where to start:

(1) *multiply top equation by 5*
$$5(ax + by = 15)$$
$$4x + 3y = 75$$

$$5ax + 5by = 75$$
$$4x + 3y = 75$$

Now we can use **pattern matching** to determine that **5a = 4** and **5b = 3**. Then we can solve for our answer:

(2) *pattern matching*
$$5a = 4$$
$$5b = 3$$

(3) *solve for $\frac{a}{b}$*
$$\frac{a}{b} = \frac{5a}{5b} = \boxed{\frac{4}{3}}$$

continue →

All is one

This is yet **another** opportunity to stop and reflect on the connectivity of all things algebra.

Slope, solutions, factors, functions, graphs, ... they're all connected!

Option 2: Thinking with Slope

If there are infinitely many solutions, then these "overlapping" lines must have the **exact same slope**. We can use that! Let's put the equations in slope-intercept form, and **match their slopes**.

1 *rewrite equations*

$$ax + by = 15$$
$$4x + 3y = 75$$

2 *slope-intercept form*

$$by = -ax + 15$$
$$3y = -4x + 75$$

$$y = -\frac{a}{b}x + \frac{15}{b}$$

$$y = -\frac{4}{3}x + 25$$

Behold, the power of thinking with slope! By putting both equations in **y = mx + b** form, and knowing that their slopes must be identical, we can easily see our answer.

3 *pattern match*

$$\frac{a}{b} = \boxed{\frac{4}{3}}$$

EXAMPLE 2

$$7x - ry = -17$$
$$-3x - 2y = 13$$

In the system of equations above, r is a constant and x and y are variables. For what value of r will the system have no solutions?

A) $-\frac{7}{3}$

B) $-\frac{14}{3}$

C) $\frac{14}{3}$

D) $\frac{3}{14}$

SOLUTION

The question asks us to find a value of r so that the system has no solutions. If a system of lines has no solutions, then we must be dealing with parallel lines. And what do we know about parallel lines? They have the **exact same slope**. So let's start by getting these lines into the slope-intercept form.

① *rewrite equations*

$$7x - ry = -17$$
$$-3x - 2y = 13$$

② *change to $y = mx + b$ form*

$$-ry = -7x - 17$$
$$-2y = 3x + 13$$

$$y = \frac{7}{r}x + \frac{17}{r}$$

$$y = -\frac{3}{2}x - \frac{13}{2}$$

③ *set slopes equal to each other*

$$\frac{7}{r} = -\frac{3}{2}$$

④ *cross multiply*

$$3r = -14$$

⑤ *solve for r*

$$r = \boxed{-\frac{14}{3}}$$

PORTAL

If you need a refresher on parallel lines and slope, turn to page 386.

Practice Problems

Use your new skills to answer each question.

1

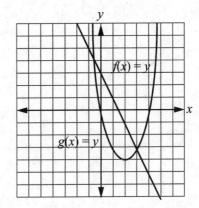

The graphs of $f(x)$ and $g(x)$ are shown above. If the point (u, v) is a solution of the system, which of the following could be u ?

A) −3
B) 0
C) 1.5
D) 3

2

$$2x + 3y = 5$$
$$3x + 2y = 0$$

How many solutions does the system above have?

A) 0
B) 1
C) Infinitely many
D) There is not enough information

3

$$y = 5x + 4$$
$$6x - y = -1$$

Which of the following is a solution to the system given above?

A) (−3, −11)
B) (1, 9)
C) (3, 19)
D) (4, 24)

4

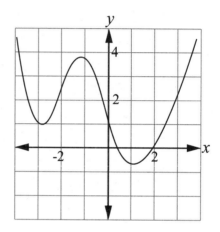

The graph of $f(x)$ is shown above. How many solutions does the equation $f(x) = 3$ have?

5

$$y = -\frac{2}{5}x + 7$$
$$5y + 2x = 35$$

How many solutions are there to the system of equations given above?

A) 0

B) 1

C) Infinitely many

D) There is not enough information given.

6

If $f(x) = 3x - 4$ and there is no solution to the system consisting of $f(x)$ and $g(x)$, which of the following could be $g(x)$?

A) $g(x) = -\frac{1}{3}x + 4$

B) $g(x) = x - 12$

C) $g(x) = 3x^2 - 4$

D) $g(x) = x^2$

7

$$y = u$$
$$y = 2x^2 + v$$

In the system of equations above, u and v are constants. For which of the following values of u and v does the system of equations have exactly two real solutions?

A) $u = 2, v = 3$

B) $u = -2, v = -2$

C) $u = 4, v = 1$

D) $u = 0, v = 2$

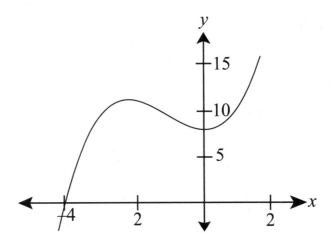

The function $f(x) = x^3 + 3x^2 - x + 7$ is graphed above. If k is a constant and $f(x) = k$ has 3 real solutions, which of the following could be k?

A) 0
B) 6
C) 10
D) 15

Systems of Inequalities

a.k.a. "Just shade above or below the line, depending on the inequality sign."

Graphing Inequalities

In this chapter, we are going to talk about linear inequalities – which are basically just line equations with an inequality sign instead of an equals sign. The graphs, however, look a bit different.

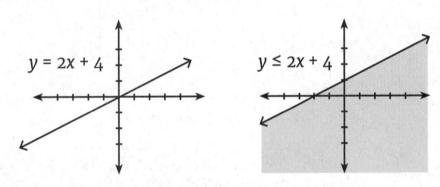

We saw last chapter that when we talk about a linear equation, such as $y = 2x + 4$, the **solutions** of the equation are xy-pairs that make the equation true. When we collect and plot every point that makes $y = 2x + 4$ true, we get a line.

But what happens when we swap the "=" sign for a "≤" sign? How is the graph of $y \leq 2x + 4$ different? First, since the sign means less than *or equal to*, every point that made the equation true before *still* makes this inequality true. So we can start by drawing in the line $y = 2x + 4$. However, for each x-coordinate, we also need to count **every single y-value** that is less than (below) the line. To show this graphically, we just shade the part of the *xy*-plane that contains the solutions.

NOTE

If we were graphing

$y < 2x + 4$

...we would draw the line as **dashed** as if to say "Hey, please don't count the points on the line."

517

Solving Systems of Inequalities

When we are looking to **solve** a system of inequalities, we are still looking for the points where the solutions intersect. So far, this has just been individual points. But when we are working with inequalities, we are looking for the regions where the shading (a.k.a., *solutions*) overlap.

INTERACTIVE EXAMPLE

Use the graph below to answer the following questions.

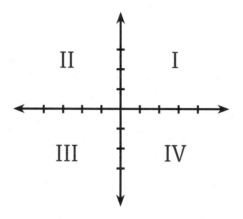

Q1) Graph the inequality $y \geq -2x + 3$.

S1) Start by graphing the line $y \geq -2x + 3$, which we know must have a y-intercept at (0, 3) and a slope of –2. Then it's time to shade. Since it is **greater than** or equal to, we want to **shade above the line**.

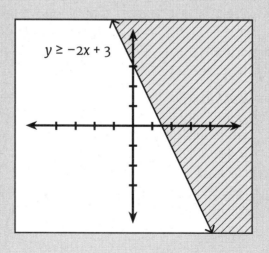

$y \geq -2x + 3$

Q2) Graph the inequality $y < \frac{1}{2}x + 1$.

S2) Start by graphing the line $y < \frac{1}{2}x + 1$, which we know must have a y-intercept at (0, 1) and a slope of $\frac{1}{2}$. However, since the sign does not include "or equal to", we should draw a *dotted line*. Since it is **less than**, we want to **shade *below*** this line.

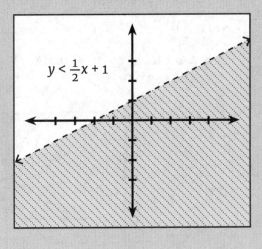

Q3) Which quadrants contain solutions of the system below?

$$y \geq -2x + 3$$
$$y < \frac{1}{2}x + 1$$

S3) To find the solutions, we want to graph both inequalities on the same axes and look **only where the shaded regions overlap**.

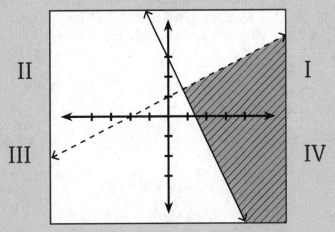

The overlap region contains all the solutions that work for *both* inequalities in the system. The region is in **quadrants I and IV.**

EXAMPLE 2

$$y \geq x + 1$$
$$y \geq -x + 3$$

In the xy-plane, if a point with coordinates (a, b) is a solution to the system of inequalities above, what is the minimum possible value of b ?

SOLUTION

We are looking for a solution to a pair of inequalities, so let's **graph** each one.

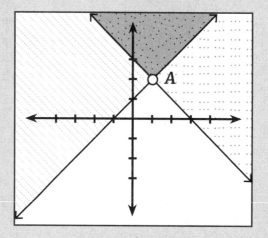

We are asked to find the **minimum possible value** for b, which we're told is our y-coordinate. That means we need the y-value at the lowest shared point in the overlap region, which we've marked as point A in our graph.

Notice that point A is just the point where the two lines **intersect**. As always, we can find an intersection point by setting the two equations equal to one another:

① *set equal to each other* $\qquad$ $x + 1 = -x + 3$

② *solve for x* $\qquad$ $2x = 2$

$\qquad\qquad\qquad\qquad\qquad$ $x = 1$

③ *plug in 1 for x* $\qquad$ $y = x + 1$

$\qquad\qquad\qquad\qquad\qquad$ $y \geq 1 + 1 = ②$

EXAMPLE 3

$$y < ax + 1$$
$$y > x + b$$

In the xy-plane, if $(1,1)$ is a solution to the system of inequalities above, which of the following relationships between a and b must be true?

A) $b = a$
B) $|a| > |b|$
C) $b > a$
D) $a > b$

SOLUTION

Our *usual* first step when presented with a system of inequalities (sketch out a graph) won't work here; there are too many unknowns. On the other hand, we are told that point $(1,1)$ is a solution. Let's plug that point into the equations and see what we learn from it:

1 *rewrite equations*

$$y < ax + 1$$
$$y > x + b$$

2 *plug in $(1, 1)$*

$$1 < a + 1$$
$$1 > 1 + b$$

3 *simplify*

$$0 < a$$
$$0 > b$$

4 *combine inequalities*

$$b < 0 < a$$

So a (which is positive) *must* be greater than b (which is negative). That means **our answer is D.**

TIP

NEVER FORGET:
If you are given a **point**, you can plug that x and y value into the equation to solve for unknown variables.

It's a classic trick.

Practice Problems

Use your new skills to answer each question!

1

$$2y - m > 3x$$
$$3y + n > 2x$$

The origin in the *xy*-plane is a solution to the system of inequalities above. Which of the following must be true?

A) *m* is greater than zero.
B) *n* is greater than *m*.
C) *m* is greater than *n*.
D) *m* is equal to −*n*.

2

If Gertie wants to get promoted to the role of project manager at her company, she must work a total of at least 4,000 hours between the two projects she has been assigned, and she must bring in a total of at least $500,000 between the two projects. Gertie predicts she will bring in $100 in revenue for each hour she spends on project *a* and $150 in revenue for each hour she spends on project *b*. Which set of inequalities represents the work Gertie would have to complete in order to receive her promotion? Let *x* represent the number of hours spent on project *a* and *y* represent the number of hours spent on project *b*.

A) $100x + 150y \geq 500,000$

   $x + y \geq 4,000$

B) $\dfrac{x}{100} + \dfrac{x}{150} \geq 500,000$

   $x + y \geq 4,000$

C) $100x + 150y \geq 4,000$

   $x + y \geq 500,000$

D) $x + y \geq 500,000$

   $100x + 150y \geq 500,000$

3

$$y < -x^2 + c$$
$$y > x + b$$

If $(0, 0)$ is a solution to the system of inequalities above, which of the following describes the relationship between b and c?

A) $b > c$
B) $b < c$
C) $|b| < |c|$
D) $|b| > |c|$

4

$$y \leq -x(x + 6)$$
$$y \geq x$$

In the system of inequalities above, what is the y-coordinate for the solution that has the smallest value for x?

$$y < -\frac{1}{2}x + a$$
$$y > 2x - a$$

If the value of a is 7, which of the following is a possible solution to the system of inequalities above?

A) $(2, 6)$
B) $(4, 5)$
C) $(5, 4)$
D) $(5, 3)$

If $y > -\frac{1}{4}x + a$ and $y > 3x + b$ are graphed in the xy-plane above and a and b are both positive integers, which of the following quadrants has no solutions to the system?

A) Quadrants I and II
B) Quadrants II and III
C) Quadrants III and IV
D) There are solutions in all four quadrants.

7

Estella has received either a 90 or a 100 on every spelling quiz she has taken this semester. She has also scored a 90 on at least one spelling quiz and a 100 on more than 4 spelling quizzes. Let x represent the number of spelling quizzes on which Estella has received a 90, and let y represent the number of spelling quizzes on which she has received a 100. Which of the following systems represents all the constraints that x and y must satisfy if Estella's quiz average is above a 95?

A) $x \geq 1$

$y > 4$

$\dfrac{90x + 100y}{x + y} > 95$

B) $x \geq 1$

$y > 4$

$x + y = 5$

$\dfrac{90x + 100y}{x + y} > 95$

C) $1 \leq x \leq 4$

$0 < y < 4$

$90x + 100y < 95(x + y)$

D) $x \geq 1$

$x > 4$

$x + y \geq 5$

$\dfrac{90x + 100y}{x + y} > 95$

UNIT | Modeling

Chapters

Key Skills

In this unit, we practice the **art of translation**: using math equations to model real-world contexts. This skill will not only net you a lot of points on the calculator section of the test, it will also improve your understanding of many problem types throughout this book!

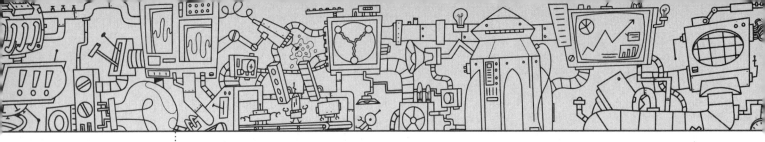

Basic Modeling

The SAT loves testing your ability to model real-world situations with algebra.

Sometimes, it's easy to forget that there is actually a POINT to all of this math. People use algebra **all the time** to learn things they didn't already know about their daily lives.

A new hire could use algebra to determine whether he'll make enough at his position to move to a better apartment; a car factory owner might use algebra to figure out how many tons of steel she needs to order for a busy month; or a college student might use algebra to tackle a major, existential question, like:

> "Wait… how many cookies did we eat last night?!"

The trick to answering such important questions is to **create an equation** using variables and constants that accurately *models* the specific situation. If you can master this skill, not only will you be a better worker, business-owner, and baker, but you'll also be able to gain a *lot* of easy points on the SAT. So let's use that last question about cookies to practice the fundamentals of **basic modeling**.

The Chocolate Chip Conundrum

Last night, you and your college roommates went on something of a cookie bender. Excited by finally having a kitchen all to yourselves, the four of you spent the evening baking and consuming chocolate chip cookies from a giant tub of cookie dough that somebody bought as a "joke" the week before. The specifics of the night are a blur when you each awaken the next morning from your respective sugar comas. A panicked disagreement breaks out over exactly how many cookies were eaten during that wild night. You decide to put an end to the debate the only way you know how: by using some good, old-fashioned algebra.

What is our Target Variable?

The first step is easy: pick a letter to represent what we're looking to find! We want to know how many cookies we ate... We could pick anything, but let's be honest, C is for Cookie (and that's good enough for me).

$$C = ?$$

"The number of cookies eaten, C, is equal to what?"

What Does it Depend On?

Now, how are we going to figure out how many cookies we ate? The key is to identify some other variable that the number of cookies depends on. We bake cookies in groups – one **tray** at a time. If we knew the number of cookies that fit on a tray AND how many trays we baked, we could figure out the number of cookies we made!

Since we don't yet know how many trays we made, let's make it a **variable**, like *t*. We know that our cookie tray comfortably fits 12 cookies at a time. If we made one tray, we'd have 12 cookies. If we made two trays, we'd have 24 cookies. In other words, the number of cookies is equal to twelve times the number of trays we baked. Let's write that in math terms:

$$C = 12t$$

"12 cookies per tray...
...times the number of trays"

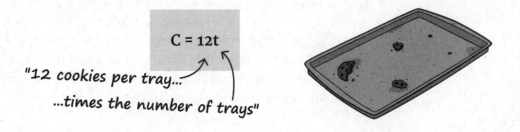

529

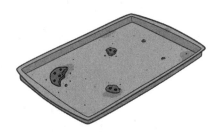

Tray Size: Coefficients & Slope

Let's think about this 12 in front of the *t* in our equation. It tells us the *rate* at which we are making cookies. What if we used a smaller sheet (or made bigger cookies) so that **only 4 fit on the tray**? To show that, we can just change the coefficient in front of *t*:

$C = 12t$	$C = 4t$
12 cookies per tray	*4 cookies per tray*

So this coefficient tells us the **rate** at which the number of cookies changes when the number of trays changes. Sound familiar? This is our rate of change, *a.k.a.* rise over run, *a.k.a.* slope, *a.k.a.* "*m*" in the equation of a line! If we graphed the two equations above, the lines would have different slopes:

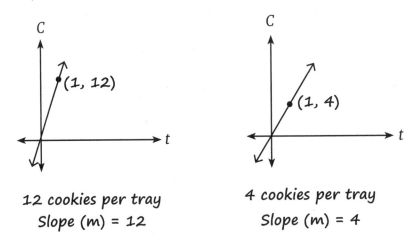

12 cookies per tray
Slope (m) = 12

4 cookies per tray
Slope (m) = 4

Labeling Points

Notice how, when we are working with a word problem, a point on the line graphs above has a real-world meaning. The horizontal axis in the graph is the number of trays, and the vertical axis is the number of cookies. That means point (1, 12) can be read (1 tray, 12 cookies), and point (1, 4) can be read (1 tray, 4 cookies). We can read equations in the same way, but we'll come back to that.

Leftovers: Constants & Intercepts

Let's get back to building our equation. Eventually, everyone agrees that you did, in fact, make regular-sized cookies such that 12 cookies fit on each tray. BUT you realize that there are **8 cookies left over** (shocking!). How can we add that information to our equation? Well, no matter how many trays of cookies were baked, we know we'll need to **subtract 8** from that total number to show how many were eaten.

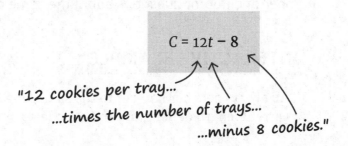

$$C = 12t - 8$$

"12 cookies per tray...

...times the number of trays...

...minus 8 cookies."

Now we've got a pretty great-looking equation of a line in the slope-intercept form. Notice that the constant we just added to model the leftovers, **– 8**, matches the "+ *b*" (intercept) part of the equation of a line. Sure enough, when we graph this cookie equation, we see that – 8 is the *y*-intercept.

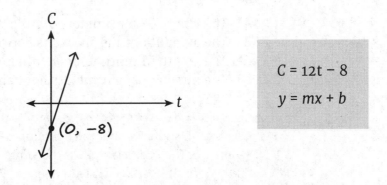

$$C = 12t - 8$$
$$y = mx + b$$

Conundrum Modeled, Cookie Crumbled

And just like that, we have modeled our cookie conundrum into a linear equation, and (bonus!) even shown how we can graph it. Now all we would have to do to determine the number of cookies eaten is figure out the number of trays baked and plug that number in for *t*.

The Art of Translation

So far, we've seen how we can go from a real-world situation to an algebraic equation. In the process, we saw how we can actually **read** that equation using the real-world context, translating the math into words:

C	$=$	12	t	$-$	8
The # of cookies	is	12 cookies per tray	times the # of trays		minus 8 cookies.

The connection between math and words might start out feeling sluggish or rusty, but once it "clicks," many questions on the SAT will instantly become *much* easier! So, let's build up some flexibility by working a number of different questions about the same context.

INTERACTIVE EXAMPLE 1

Ali always gets her hair cut to the same length. She has found that the current length of her hair can be modeled by the equation

$$l = .25w + 33$$

Where l is the length measured from the top of her head down her back in centimeters and w is the number of weeks since her latest haircut.

Q1) Which of the following is the meaning of the number .25 in the given equation?

  A) The length in centimeters of Ali's hair after a haircut.
  B) The amount of time she waits between haircuts.
  C) The length in centimeters her hair reaches before each haircut.
  D) The number of centimeters her hair grows each week.

S1) Let's start by noticing that the equation is in the slope-intercept form $y = mx + b$. The coefficient **.25** is the **slope** of the line (m). Slope (a.k.a, rise over run) shows us a rate of change. So our answer should tell us the *rate* something is *changing*. From just that information, choice D is looking good. Since l stands for the length of her hair, that's what is changing. .25 is the amount, in centimeters, that her hair is changing. And w, the number of weeks, tells us what causes l to change.

$$l = .25w + 33$$

Length of hair is .25cm per week plus 33cm.

D

Q2) Which of the following is the meaning of the number 33 in the given equation?

    A) The length in centimeters of Ali's hair after a haircut.
    B) The amount of time she waits between haircuts.
    C) The length in centimeters her hair reaches before each haircut.
    D) The number of centimeters her hair grows each week.

S2) Since w is the number of weeks since her haircut, $w = 0$ tells us how long Ali's hair is immediately after getting her hair cut. We can see this if we compare the equation $l = .25w + 33$ to the slope-intercept form $y = mx + b$. We see that the number 33 tells us the **y-intercept** of the line. That means the line crosses the y-axis at (0 weeks, 33 centimeters). In other words, when it's been 0 weeks since her hair cut, Ali's hair is 33 centimeters long.

A

Creative Exercises

The same equation could model a number of different situations. One of the best ways to get used to this idea is to try to come up with multiple contexts for the same equation. For example, for the equation below, we've come up with three plausible (if slightly odd) contexts that it could represent. We're sure that you could come up with some better ones, so on the next page you'll have an opportunity to do just that!

$$r = 4t + 5$$

"The cost of entering a raffle (r) is equal to 4 dollars per ticket (t) plus a 5 dollar bribe to the officials."

"Richard (r) drinks 5 cups of coffee a day, plus 4 cups per hour of overtime (t)."

"The length of rope (r) to pack is 5 meters plus another 4 meters for each expected snake trap (t)."

Complete the tables by coming up with contexts that might be modeled by the each equation. This is a creative exercise, so let your imagination run wild. We've come up with one of our own to get you started.

$c = 1.5d + 7$	
Context 1	The total weight, in pounds, of my Calico cat named Cali (c) is at least 7 pounds plus an additional 1.5 pounds per day off her diet (d). c = weight of cat 1.5 = pounds per day d = days off diet +7 = starting weight
Context 2	c = 1.5 = d = +7 =
Context 3	c = 1.5 = d = +7 =

$f = 1{,}000 - 13p$	
Context 1	f = −13 = p = 1,000 =
Context 2	f = −13 = p = 1,000 =
Context 3	f = −13 = p = 1,000 =

Complete the table by matching each context with the equation that best models it. We have completed the first one for you.

Match	Context	Equation
E	The profit Martha earns from a bake-sale is $5 per brownie sold, minus the $45 she spent on supplies.	A) $a = -3b + 60$
	The perceived temperature on a –6°C day drops 3°C for every additional mile per hour of wind.	B) $a = 6b + 3$
	In a psychology study, the average time it takes to finish a particular task alone is 60 minutes. Every added team member cuts that time down by 3 minutes.	C) $a = -3b - 6$
	The amount of hard drive space taken up by Ty's work project is 3mb for a single instructions file, plus 6mb per video she creates.	D) $a = 3b + 60$
	A scientist is studying the effects of a particular "diet" on a 60cm tall plant. She discovers that the plant grows 3cm every week that it is on the diet.	E̶)̶ $a = 5b - 45$

Answers: *E, C, A, B, D*

TIP

As an example, if you are given a rate in terms of gizmos (g) per widget (w), then your equation will look like:

$$g = mw + b$$

INTERACTIVE EXAMPLE 2

Morgan is following a strength training exercise plan that claims anyone following it can increase the number of consecutive pushups they can do by 13 pushups per week. Morgan can do 12 consecutive pushups before starting the plan.

Q3) Which of the following expressions gives the number of pushups Morgan should be able to do after following the plan for *t* weeks?

A) 12t + 13

B) 13t + 12

C) 13t – 12

D) (12)(13)t

S3) The number of pushups is supposed to change by a constant amount each week, so the model should be linear and look like $y = mx + b$.

- **y** stands for the thing we are interested in – the total number of pushups Morgan can do.

- **m** stands for the slope, so it's the rate at which the number of pushups Morgan can do changes each week (13 per week).

- **b** stands for the y-intercept, so the number of pushups Morgan starts out being able to do (12 pushups).

If we bring that information in, we get:

$$y = 13t + 12$$

The # of pushups Morgan can do (y) equals 13 pushups per week (t) plus 12 pushups.

B

Q4) After how many weeks will Morgan be able to do 50 consecutive pushups, rounded to the nearest tenth of a week?

A) 2

B) 2.7

C) 2.9

D) 3

S4) We want to know **when** Morgan will be able to do 50 pushups. To figure that out, we can use the formula we built in the previous questions! Since t is our time variable and y is the number of push-ups, we can set the equation equal to 50 pushups and solve for t:

$$50 \text{ pushups} = 13t + 12$$
$$38 = 13t$$
$$2.9 \text{ weeks} \approx t$$

We can check this in another way. If we start at 12 pushups and increase by 13 each week, then we can just add 13 each week and look for when we hit 50 pushups.

Week	0	1	2	3
Pushups	12	25	38	51

C

Write an equation to model each scenario in the blank provided.

Context	Model
Lucy can use a total of 1024 MB of data. Streaming a video uses 1.6 MB every minute. Model data left (d) in terms of minutes streamed (t).	$d = 1024 - 1.6t$
A taxi charges a base fare of $10.50 and an additional $.45 per mile. Model taxi fare (f) in terms of miles driven (m).	$f =$
Jose runs 2 miles to a race track, runs 6 miles per hour while he races on the track, then runs the 2 miles home. Model total miles run (m) in terms of race length in hours (h).	$m =$
Tobi the corgi has a rope that was originally comprised of 350 strings twisted together. He rips out 4 strings a day. Model strings left (s) in terms of days (d).	$s =$
Proper clown shoe length starts at 15 inches, with a half-inch added for every year the clown has been a part of the clown union. Model shoe length (c) in terms of years in the union (y).	$c =$

Answers: 1) $d = 1024 - 1.6t$ **2)** $f = .45m + 10.50$ **3)** $m = 6h + 4$ **4)** $s = 350 - 4d$ **5)** $c = 15 + .5y$

INTERACTIVE EXAMPLE 3

Luis works as a caterer. He charges a setup fee plus an additional amount for each guest expected at the event. The equation $c = 12g + 55$ gives the total amount Luis charges in dollars (c) in terms of the expected number of guests (g).

Q5) A client calls and informs Luis that there are going to be 8 more guests for an event than originally expected. How much will Luis increase the amount he charges for the event?

    A) $8
    B) $96
    C) $151
    D) $440

S5) Since c is the total cost and g is the number of guests, the number 12 in the equation (our rate of change coefficient) tells us that it costs **$12 per guest**. This means that he will charge $12 for each of the 8 additional guests. So if we simply multiply, we can find the cost:

$$12(8) = 96 \text{ dollars}$$

So it will cost $96 to fund an additional 8 guests.

B

Q6) Luis discovers that people are frequently underestimating the number of guests for events that he caters, so he decides to adjust his pricing model. In the updated model, he assumes there will be 4 more guests than the number g that the client gives him. Which of the following equations could be Luis's new model?

    A) $c = 16g + 55$
    B) $c = 12g + 59$
    C) $c = 12(g + 4) + 55$
    D) $c = 12(g - 4) + 55$

NOTE

Another possible correct answer would **distribute the 12**.

$c = 12g + 48 + 55$
$c = 12g + 103$

S6) We are told that Luis is assuming there will be **4 more guests than the number _g_** that is provided. Translating this into math means that we want to replace "_g_" with "$(g + 4)$". This gives us:

$$\text{old} \quad c = 12g + 55$$
$$\text{new} \quad c = 12(g + 4) + 55$$

So the answer is choice C.

Practice Problems

Use your new skills to answer each question.

1

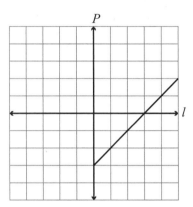

The graph above displays the total profit P, in dollars, after selling l cups of lemonade. What does the l-intercept represent in the graph?

A) The initial cost of starting a lemonade stand
B) The total cups of lemonade sold
C) The total profit the lemonade stand makes in a day
D) The cups of lemonade sold to break even

2

The total price, in dollars, that a jet-ski rental company charges a group of over five people can be calculated by the equation $10px - 24$, where $p > 5$ is the number of people in the group and x is the number of hours the group will be using the jet-skis. Which of the following is the best interpretation of the number 10 in the expression?

A) The company charges $10 per hour for each individual.
B) A maximum of 10 people can be in each group.
C) The price each member in the group will pay is $10.
D) Each member of the group will spend a maximum of 10 hours renting the jet-skis.

3

$$M = 250 - 20d$$

The equation above gives the number of miles M a tribe still has to travel before reaching its destination, where d is the number of days it has been since the tribe first left. What is the meaning of 250 in the equation?

A) The tribe must travel for 250 days.
B) The tribe must travel 250 miles every day.
C) The destination is 250 miles from the initial location.
D) The tribe travelled 250 miles the first day.

4

$$T = 45 + 15r$$

The equation above gives the number of tickets T sold, in millions, for a movie with an average movie critic rating of r, where r must be between 0 and 10. If movie theaters sold a total of 105 million tickets for a certain movie, what was the average movie critic rating of that movie?

A) 10
B) 8
C) 7
D) 4

5

$$P = 264.50 + 20m$$

Last year, Fabio bought a piggy bank to hold all of his savings. Ever since then, Fabio has been putting a fixed amount of money into his piggy bank every month. The equation above gives the amount of money P, in dollars, Fabio now has in his piggy bank after m months. If the equation was graphed in the xy-plane, with P on the y-axis and m on the x-axis, what would be the meaning of the y-intercept?

A) Fabio deposits $264.50 every month.
B) Fabio now has $264.50 in his piggy bank.
C) Fabio put $264.50 in his piggy bank the day he bought it.
D) Fabio can only put a maximum of $264.50 in his piggy bank.

6

$$S = 14 + 3.5t$$

The equation above gives the speed S of a ball, in feet per second, t seconds after it was kicked down a hill. After how many seconds will the ball be rolling down the hill at 42 feet per second?

A)   16
B)   12
C)   8
D)   4

7

Elmer works at a call center, and the number of people Elmer still needs to call on a given day can be modeled by $C = 150-20h$, where h is the number of hours Elmer has worked that day. What is the meaning of 20 in the equation?

A)   Elmer must call 20 people every day.
B)   Elmer still has 20 more people to call that day.
C)   Elmer will work 20 hours this week.
D)   Elmer calls 20 people every hour.

8

At a fast food restaurant, the price of a value meal, consisting of 30 chicken nuggets, is three times the price of a kid's meal, consisting of 8 chicken nuggets. If the price of a kid's meal is 4 dollars and the price of a value meal is n dollars, which of the following is true?

A) $\frac{n}{3} = 4$

B) $4n = 3$

C) $3n = 4$

D) $n + 4 = 3$

9

Avery and Patrick work in the telesales department of a company. Last Friday, Avery made x phone calls each hour for 6 hours and Patrick made y phone calls each hour for 8 hours. Which of the following represents the total number of phone calls Avery and Patrick made last Friday?

A) $6x + 8y$
B) $6y + 8x$
C) $48xy$
D) $14xy$

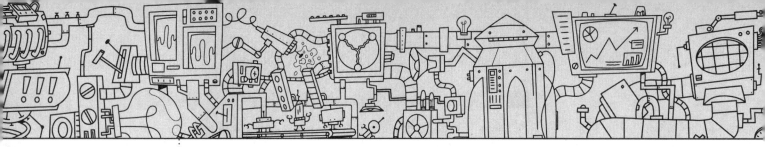

Advanced Modeling

Often, the SAT tests your modeling skills alongside other concepts.

Modeling with Graphs

In the previous chapter, we saw how our cookie model took the form of a linear equation that could easily be graphed. We saw that we could think of a "rate of change" as both the **coefficient** in the equation and as the **slope** of the line in the graph of the equation. Occasionally, the SAT will test your ability to think graphically by asking you to model with a graph rather than with an equation. Let's look at an example.

INTERACTIVE EXAMPLE

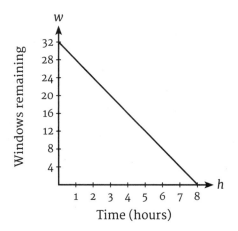

Seana has a job as a window cleaner for a particular office building. The above graph models her work on a typical day. *W* is the number of windows she has left to clean that day and *h* is the number of hours she has worked so far that day (not counting breaks).

Q1) What does the *w*–intercept in the graph represent?

    A) The total number of windows she washes in a typical day.
    B) The exact number of windows she washes every day.
    C) The number of windows she can typically wash per hour.
    D) The time it typically takes her to wash one window.

S1) To understand the *w*-intercept, we first need to understand what each axis tells us. The axis labels and the description below the graph help us out. The vertical (*w*) axis tells us the **number of windows remaining**, and the horizontal (*h*) axis tells us the **number of hours worked**. That means we could read the point (0, 32) as (0 hours, 32 windows remaining).

Since the *w*-intercept occurs where $h = 0$, we know that it must tell us the **total number of windows remaining** at the beginning of the work day. That narrows it down to A or B. The problem tells us that the graph models a *typical* day, so A is the better answer.

A

Q2) Which of the following is the best interpretation of the slope of the line?

    A) The total number of windows she washes in a typical day.
    B) The exact number of windows she washes every day.
    C) The number of windows she can typically wash per hour.
    D) The time it typically takes her to wash one window.

S2) The slope of a line is always the rate of change, so our answer needs to be a **rate**. This means we can immediately eliminate A and B. Recall that:

$$slope = \frac{change\ in\ y}{change\ in\ x}, \text{ or } \frac{change\ in\ w}{change\ in\ h}$$

This means that our answer should be in terms of windows (*w*) per hour (*h*). This corresponds with answer choice C.

C

Q3) What does the *h*–intercept in the graph represent?

    A) The number of windows she washes by the end of the day.
    B) The number of windows she washes each hour.
    C) The earliest she can finish her work.
    D) The number of hours she typically needs to finish her work.

S3) The h-intercept is the point on the line where w, the number of windows remaining to be washed, is zero. This means it is the point where she finishes her work. Since h is the number of hours she has worked, that means the h-intercept tells us the amount of hours she works before her work is finished on a typical day.

         D

PORTAL

If you need to learn or review how to solve systems of equations, turn to page 492.

Modeling with Systems of Equations

So far, the models we have looked at have all had one equation. Sometimes, situations are more complicated and it takes two (or more) equations to fully describe them. When this happens, the SAT asks you to create a **system of equations** to model the situation, and then solve the system to find the answer to a question.

EXAMPLE 1

Mary is designing a quilt that uses two different sizes of squares. The smaller squares have 5 inch sides and the larger squares have 10 inch sides. If Mary wants the finished quilt to be 60 inches by 80 inches and contain 120 total squares, how many of the smaller squares will she use?

    A) 24
    B) 48
    C) 96
    D) 100

SOLUTION

Let *s* be the number of smaller squares and *l* be the number of larger squares. Before we do anything else, let's establish our goal. We're asked to find the number of small squares, so:

 establish your goal $s = ?$

We know we need a total of **120 squares**, so let's model that:

① *write first equation*   #small + #large = #total

$$s + l = 120$$

From the side lengths, we can figure out that the small squares are 25 square inches and the larger ones are 100 square inches. We also know the finished quilt will be 60 inches by 80 inches, or **4800 square inches**. So we can show how each type of square contributes to the total area in a second equation:

② *write second equation*   (area)s + (area)l = total area

$$25s + 100l = 4800$$

And now we have a system we can use to solve for *s*!

③ *write system* $s + l = 120$

$$25s + 100l = 4800$$

It looks like **substitution** will serve us well here. If we use the first equation to get something we can plug in for *l* in the second equation, we'll be able to solve for *s*.

③ *solve for l in 1st equation* $l = 120 - s$

④ *substitute into 2nd* $25s + 100(120 - s) = 4800$

⑤ *simplify* $25s + 12{,}000 - 100s = 4800$

$$-75s = -7200$$

$s = 96$ C

547

EXAMPLE 2

A mad scientist has designed two kinds of robots that both utilize a certain kind of widget. The hopping robots, h, require 2 widgets each and the flying robots, f, require 3 widgets each. The scientist wants to produce no less than 5 of each type of robot, and at least 20 robots total. If she has a stash of 100 widgets, which of the following systems models the possible numbers of robots she can create?

A) $h = 5$
$f = 5$
$h + f < 20$
$2h + 3f = 100$

B) $h \geq 5$
$f \geq 5$
$h + f \geq 20$
$3h + 2f < 100$

C) $h > 5$
$f > 5$
$h + f = 20$
$2h + 3f = 100$

D) $h \geq 5$
$f \geq 5$
$h + f \geq 20$
$2h + 3f \leq 100$

SOLUTION

This problem asks us to *model* four different **inequalities**. Looking at the choices, we can see that getting the less than, greater than, equal to distinction will be important, so let's take it slow:

(1) *"No less than 5 of each type of robot"* $\qquad h \geq 5$
$\qquad\qquad\qquad\qquad\qquad\qquad\qquad\qquad\qquad f \geq 5$

(2) *"at least 20 robots total"* $\qquad\qquad h + f \geq 20$

Notice how already we can narrow our choices down to either choice B or choice D. The only difference between the two are the **coefficients** of h and f in the last inequality. The problem tells us that the hopping robots (h) take 2 widgets, and the flying robots (f) take 3 widgets. That means we want an equation with "$2h$" and "$3f$", so **choice D** must be correct!

D

Practice Problems

Use your new skills to answer each question.

Questions 1-2 refer to the following information:

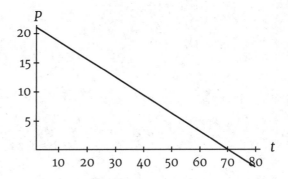

Lorraine is doing her math homework and the above graph shows the number of homework problems P she has left after working on her homework for t minutes.

1

What does the P-intercept represent?

A) The time it takes her to do one question
B) The amount of time it will take her to finish the assignment
C) The total number of homework problems she needs to complete
D) The number of problems in the section her class is currently working on

2

After how many minutes will she have finished half of her assignment?

3

The sum of four numbers is 765. The sum of the first two numbers is 25% more than the sum of the other two numbers. What is the sum of the first two numbers?

A) 170
B) 340
C) 425
D) 530

4

$$a = 1.5x + 1.50$$
$$b = 1.25x + 4.50$$

In the system of equations above, a and b represent the cost, in dollars, of buying x buffalo wings at two different restaurants. What amount of money will get you the same number of buffalo wings at both restaurants?

A) 12
B) 19.5
C) 20
D) 29.5

5

A semi-trailer truck is carrying exactly 20,000 kg of cargo consisting of 300-kg crates and 400-kg crates. If the truck is carrying eight 300-kg crates, how many 400-kg crates is the truck carrying?

6

If Julian's height h is within 4 inches of the average height, a, of an 18-year-old male, which of the following inequalities MUST be true?

I. $h + a < 4$
II. $-4 < h - a < 4$
III. $|h - a| < 4$

A) III only
B) II and III only
C) I and III only
D) I, II, and III

Questions 7-8 refer to the following information:

$$P(t) = 2t + 10$$
$$A(t) = 40 - t$$

Function $A(t)$ models the speed, in meters per second, of Aaron's car t seconds after passing a police car. Since Aaron was driving over the speed limit, the police officer sped up to Aaron's car to pull him over. Function $P(t)$ models the speed, in meters per second, of the police officer's car t seconds after Aaron passed it.

7

At 8 seconds after the police officer caught Aaron speeding, by how much had the speed of the police car changed?

A) The speed of the police car increased by 4 meters per second.
B) The speed of the police car decreased by 16 meters per second.
C) The speed of the police car decreased by 26 meters per second.
D) The speed of the police car increased by 16 meters per second.

8

After how many seconds will Aaron's car and the police car be going the same speed?

A) 10 seconds
B) 20 seconds
C) 30 seconds
D) 70 seconds

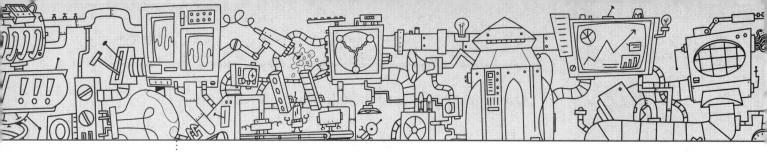

Exponential Models

The most advanced modeling problems deal with exponential growth.

So far we have been modeling **linear** situations, where one variable changes by a *constant amount* that is added (or subtracted) for every unit change in a second variable. For example, every ticket sold adds exactly $3 to the total amount raised. The *hundredth* ticket sold earns just as much as did the *first* ticket sold: three dollars.

In this chapter, we will look at a different kind of growth. For example, a population of rabbits that is *doubling* each year or a savings account that gains interest based on a *percentage* of the current balance. In these situations where something is being multiplied (or divided) by a constant factor, we need a model that shows **exponential** growth. Let's look at some examples.

Identify whether each situation is linear or exponential.

Situation	Linear or Exponential?
1. The population of mosquitos at a lake doubles every week.	
2. Jace earns $8 per hour for babysitting.	
3. A savings account earns .05% interest.	
4. A swimming pool is being filled by a hose at a rate of 6 gallons per minute.	
5. A treatment wipes out one-third of the remaining bacteria with every dose.	
6. The population of a town has been increasing by factor of 4 every 5 years.	

Answers: *See next page.*

INTERACTIVE EXAMPLE

A mad scientist has figured out how to program his robots so that they can build and program *more* robots. It takes each robot one day to make and program a new robot. The mad scientist builds three robots before turning them loose to construct an army. Since each robot makes a new robot each day, the number of robots will double each day. The following table summarizes the number of robots he has at the end of each day:

Time (days)	# of Robots	Written with Multiples	Written with Exponents
0	3	3	3
1	6	3×2	3×2^1
2	12	$3 \times 2 \times 2$	3×2^2
3	24	$3 \times 2 \times 2 \times 2$	3×2^3
4	48	$3 \times 2 \times 2 \times 2 \times 2$	3×2^4

Q1) Write an equation to model the number of robots after t days.

S1) We were told that the number of robots **doubles** each day. So we can see from the table that we get the next day's number of robots by **multiplying** by 2. This means we are dealing with *exponential growth*.

Exponents are just a shorthand for repeated multiplication. In the table, we can see how to write the number of robots using exponents. If, for example, we wanted to know how many robots he would have after **1 day**, it would be **$3 \times 2^1 = 6$** robots. To see how many robots he'd have after 2 days, it would be **$3 \times 2^2 = 12$**, and so on. So to model this growth, the number of robots after *t* days would be:

$$f(t) = 3(2)^t$$

Answers: 1) Exponential **2)** Linear **3)** Exponential **4)** Linear **5)** Exponential **6)** Exponential

In the previous example, our model follows the standard equation for exponential growth:

$$\textit{Exponential Growth:} \quad f(t) = P(r)^t$$

Where P is the **starting amount**, r is the **rate** at which it is growing (or decaying), and t is the length of time it's been growing.

When it's Tougher

The vast majority of the time all you need to know for SAT exponent problems is the standard equation above. Occasionally, on the hardest problems, you will work with time intervals that require careful calculations. Suppose our mad scientist wanted to know how many robots he has in terms of *hours* instead of days. Then, the number doesn't double when $t = 1$, it doubles when $t = 24$ (robots don't need sleep). So how could we rewrite the equation to show this?

$$f(t) = 3(2)^{\frac{t}{24}} \qquad \textit{\# of robots doubles at t = 24}$$

This way, the exponent doesn't become 1 until $t = 24$. Now, suppose he optimizes the programming so that the robots can make a new robot **every 8 hours**. This means that the first doubling occurs at $t = 8$, so the exponent needs to be 1 when $t = 8$.

$$f(t) = 3(2)^{\frac{t}{8}} \qquad \textit{\# of robots doubles at t = 8}$$

PORTAL

You can think of exponential growth as **repeated percent change**. To see more on this topic, flip to page 581.

INTERACTIVE EXAMPLE 2

Kaja opened a new savings account. She determines that if she doesn't deposit or withdraw any money, the amount of money (in dollars) in the account after t years will be modeled by the equation:

$$f(t) = 8{,}000(1.03)^t$$

Q1) What was Kaja's initial deposit?

S1) The variable, t, is in the exponent, so we know we are dealing with an exponential model. The standard form of an exponential model is:

$$f(t) = P(r)^t$$

In the standard form, the starting amount is **P**. If we compare Kaja's model to the standard model, we can see that **P = $8,000**.

$$f(t) = \mathbf{P}(r)^t$$

$$f(t) = \mathbf{8{,}000}(1.03)^t$$

Q2) What is the **interest rate** on the account?

    A) 1.03%
    B) 0.03%
    C) 3.00%
    D) 8,000%

S2) This one's a bit trickier! We want to know about the *interest* **rate**, so we want to look at **r = 1.03**. This tells us that the amount in the account at the end of one year, or $f(1)$, will be **1.03 times** the amount at the beginning of the year.

But we have to be careful. The interest is the **new money** added each year. If we were just multiplying by 1, then the money would never change. If we multiplied by 2, then the amount would double every year. So what does mutiplying by 1.03 mean? It means we're **increasing** the current balance by **3%** year.

C

555

Q3) Which of the following graphs shows the growth of the money in Kaja's account?

A)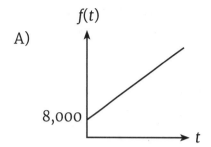

B)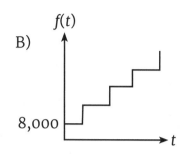

C)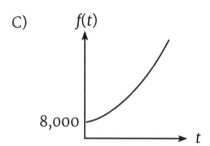

D)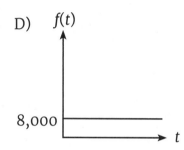

S3) Let's look at each answer choice:

Choice A shows **linear** growth, where the growth rate (slope) is constant. We are dealing with **exponential** growth, where the amount earned increases each year. This one's out.

Choice B shows a step function. This is what the graph might look like if Kaja were regularly depositing money into her account in chunks. That isn't the situation though, so we can eliminate B.

Choice C looks good - it starts at 8,000 and then grows at an increasing rate, earning more and more each year. This kind of curve looks like exponential growth. C is probably the right answer.

Choice D shows Kaja's money remaining constant – she never has more than $8,000. This is what the graph might look like if Kaja just put the money under her mattress and forgot about it.

Thus, the answer is C!

C

INTERACTIVE EXAMPLE 3

Arturo is a chemist and discovers that the rate of a particular chemical reaction is dependent on the concentration of one of the reactants. The integrated rate law states that the concentration of this reactant decreases exponentially. Arturo runs experiments and finds that 10% of the remaining reactant is converted to products each minute. He starts an experiment with 350 grams of the reactant.

Q1) Which of the following equations could Arturo use to determine the amount of reactant remaining after t minutes?

A) $f(t) = .9(350)^t$
B) $f(t) = 350(.1)^t$
C) $f(t) = 350(1.1)^t$
D) $f(t) = 350(.9)^t$

S1) The general form of an exponential equation, as we know, is

$$f(t) = P(r)^t$$

P is the starting amount, which here is **350**. This means we can immediately eliminate choice A.

r is the rate, the fraction of the initial amount that will be present when $t = 1$. Here, we know that it is **decreasing by 10%**. This means that r will be 1 – .10 = **.9**. Alternately, you know that if it is decreasing by 10% there will be 90% left, so **r = .9**. So our formula would be:

$$f(t) = 350(.9)^t$$

This matches answer choice D.

D

Q2) Rounding to the nearest gram, how much of the reactant has been converted after 10 minutes?

A) 0
B) 122
C) 228
D) 350

S2) In the previous problem, we determined the formula for the amount of reactant remaining after t minutes. Let's plug in 10 for t:

$$f(t) = 350(.9)^t$$

$$f(t) = 350(.9)^{10} = 122$$

But be careful! Rereading the question, we notice that it doesn't ask how much is **left**, it asks how much has been *converted*. Since we started with 350 and have 122 left, we can subtract to find that 350 – 122 = **228 grams** have been converted. Tricky!

So the answer is **C**.

C

Practice Problems

Use your new skills to answer each question.

Questions 1 and 2 refer to the following information:

Compounded annually: $x(1 + \frac{r}{100})^t$

Compounded quarterly: $x(1 + \frac{r}{400})^{4t}$

Compounded monthly: $x(1 + \frac{r}{1,200})^{12t}$

The equations above describe the value of three types of bank accounts t years after an initial deposit of x dollars was made with an annual interest rate of r%. Christina opened a bank account with an interest rate of 6% that is compounded annually, and she initially deposited $100 into her account.

1

What is the value, in dollars, of Christina's account after one year?

2

Christina's friend Amy opened an account that earns 6 percent interest compounded monthly. Amy also made an initial deposit of $100 into her account on the same day Christina made a deposit of $100 into her account. After 20 years, how much more money will Amy's initial deposit have earned than Christina's initial deposit? (Round your answer to the nearest cent.)

3

A 525-gram sample of an unknown substance is observed in a laboratory. Once the substance is put in a graduated cylinder filled with salt water, the substance starts to dissolve at an hourly rate of 4 percent. Which of the following functions f models the amount of dissolved substance, in grams, x hours later?

A) $f(x) = 525(0.96)^x$
B) $f(x) = 525(0.04)^x$
C) $f(x) = 525 - 525(0.96)^x$
D) $f(x) = 525 - 525(0.04)^x$

4

The population of birds in a state forest is estimated over the course of twelve years, as shown in the table below.

Year	Population
1994	200
1997	400
2000	800
2003	1,600
2006	3,200

Which of the following best describes the relationship between the year and the estimated bird population over the 12 year time period?

A) The estimated population of birds has increased linearly.
B) The estimated population of birds has decreased linearly.
C) The estimated population of birds has experienced exponential growth.
D) The estimated population of birds has experienced exponential decay.

5

Company XYZ had a poor earnings report, which resulted in its stock price of $142 dropping by 3% each day for five days after the report was released. Which of the following functions f models the company's stock price, in dollars, x days after the earnings report, where $x \leq 5$?

A) $f(x) = 142(0.97)^x$
B) $f(x) = 142(0.03)^x$
C) $f(x) = 0.97(142)^x$
D) $f(x) = 0.03(142)^x$

6

Which of the following scatterplots shows a relationship that is appropriately modeled by the equation $y = ax^b$, where both a and b are positive?

A)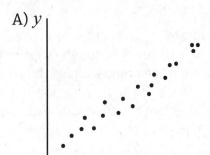

B)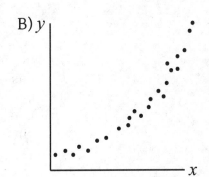

C)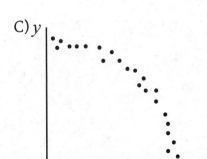

D)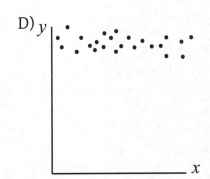

7

The population of lizards in a particular forest has increased by 8% every year due to a new wildfire preservation initiative. If there were 2,000 lizards living in the forest when the initiative was first put into place, which of the following functions f represents the number of lizards living in the forest t years after the initiative was implemented?

A) $f(t) = 2,000(.08)^t$

B) $f(t) = 2,000(1.08)^t$

C) $f(t) = 1.08(2,000)^t$

D) $f(t) = 2,000(8)^t$

8

A village located in a region that is in a severe drought has not been able to supply enough crops to its citizens. This has resulted in the population of the village decreasing by 6% every 2 years. If the current population of the village is 15,000, which of the following expressions shows the village's population t years from now?

A) $f(t) = 15,000(0.94)^{\frac{t}{2}}$

B) $f(t) = 15,000(0.94)^{2t}$

C) $f(t) = 15,000(0.06)^{\frac{t}{2}}$

D) $f(t) = 15,000(0.06)^{2t}$

9

The people in a town in Paraguay are currently trying to control the piranha population of a lake. The plan they will implement is predicted to decrease the number of piranhas by 22% every 3 years. If the current population of piranhas is 2,000, which of the following expressions shows the predicted number of piranhas in the lake t years from now?

A) $f(t) = 2{,}000(0.22)^{3t}$

B) $f(t) = 2{,}000(0.22)^{\frac{t}{3}}$

C) $f(t) = 2{,}000(0.78)^{\frac{t}{3}}$

D) $f(t) = 2{,}000(0.78)^{3t}$

10

The mayor of a city in Kansas decided to increase the city's population by giving anyone who moved to the city a free t-shirt. This initiative caused a population boom where the number of residents increased by 8% every four months. If the initial population of the city was 5,000, which of the following expressions shows the city's population y years from now?

A) $f(y) = 5{,}000(1.08)^{4y}$

B) $f(y) = 5{,}000(1.08)^{3y}$

C) $f(y) = 5{,}000(0.92)^{4y}$

D) $f(y) = 5{,}000(0.92)^{3y}$

UNIT | Data Analysis: Part 1

Chapters

Key Skills

In this unit, we dive into the Data Analysis questions that make up a large chunk of the Calculator section. We'll be looking at tables of data, finding proportions, and converting feet to inches and back again. All in the name of science!

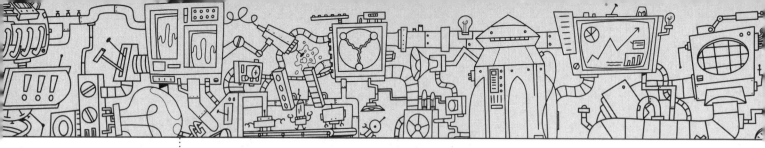

Piece over Whole

In this chapter, we'll learn how percentages and proportions are really just two sides of the same coin. In either case, we're looking at pieces of a whole.

Introduction

In the majority of Data Analysis questions (the ones with all the tables), we are asked to measure how large (or small) one group is in relation to other groups. Sometimes, we'll be given data about some piece of a population and asked to calculate a percentage. Other times, we'll be given a proportion and a population, and asked to calculate how many total individuals fall into that particular subgroup. However the question is phrased, the work is essentially the same: we're going to use percentages and proportions to measure a **piece of a whole**.

Percentages

The word percent tells us that we are looking at how many we get for every (**per-**) one hundred (**-cent**). This gives us the following equation for finding a percentage:

$$\frac{\%}{100} = \frac{piece}{whole}$$

When we are working with data on the test, we'll focus on three main components: the size of a piece, the size of the whole population, and the percentage that represents that relationship. We'll be given two of these components and asked to find the third.

EXAMPLE 1

Pooja just returned from a backpacking trip and is going through the pictures she took. Of the 375 pictures, she finds that 28% contain at least one animal. How many of her pictures do not contain an animal?

A) 72
B) 105
C) 270
D) 347

$$\frac{28}{100} = \frac{x}{375}$$
$$a = 105$$
$$375 - 105 \overline{} \quad 270$$

SOLUTION

We know that **28%** of the pictures contain an animal, and there are a total of **375 pictures**. We can use the percentage to find out exactly how many of the 375 pictures contain an animal. If **a** is the number of pictures **with** animals, then:

① *write percent formula* $\dfrac{\%}{100} = \dfrac{piece}{whole}$

② *fill in what we know* $.28 = \dfrac{a}{375}$

③ *solve for a* $.28(375) = a$

                       $105 = a$

Careful – we're not done yet! We are asked for the number of pictures **without** animals, which means we need to subtract 105 from our total:

④ *subtract 105 from total* $375 - 105 = \boxed{270}$

Bonus Solution

We could have easily skipped a step here. They told us that 28% of the pictures DO contain an animal, but asked for the number that do NOT contain an animal... which means that 28% isn't *really* our percentage. 100% – 28% = **72%**. *That's* the percentage of the whole without animals in them. This makes it simple:

① *multiply whole by percent* $(.72)(375) = \boxed{270}$

                                                  C

TIP

When working with percentages, we usually use a decimal. So instead of writing "28% of 375 pictures", we can just write:

.28(375)

It's a Trap!

Beware the traps the SAT lays in the wrong answers! If you aren't reading carefully, it would be easy to take 28% of 375 and think you are done. This gives 105, which is choice B!

Proportions

What's the difference between proportions and percentages? Not a whole lot, actually. To find the percentage, we just divide the piece over the whole fraction to get a decimal. The proportion is just that piece over whole fraction... no dividing required! In other words, percentages are decimals and proportions are fractions. That's it!

INTERACTIVE EXAMPLE

Ice Cream Sales

Mix-ins	Ice Cream Flavors				
	Vanilla	Chocolate	Strawberry	Mocha	Total
Sprinkles	3	6	8	10	27
Nuts	4	5	4	4	17
Cookie dough	6	5	4	1	16
Pretzels	9	8	2	11	30
Total	22	24	18	26	90

The *What's the Scoop?* ice cream shop ran a recent special where customers got to pick one of its four base ice cream flavors and one mix-in. The table above represents their sales during the special.

Q1) What proportion of the customers ordered strawberry with nuts?

$$4/90 = 2/45$$

S1) To build our proportion, we just need to put the **piece** (# who ordered strawberry with nuts) over the **whole** (total # of customers).

The number who ordered strawberry with nuts can be found in the second row of the strawberry column: **4 people**. The **total overall number** of customers can be found in the very bottom right of the table: **90 people**. So our proportion is:

$$\frac{piece}{whole} = \frac{4}{90} = \boxed{\frac{2}{45}}$$

Q2) What proportion of the customers that ordered pretzels as their mix-in also ordered chocolate ice cream?

$$\frac{8}{30} = \frac{4}{15}$$

S2) We have to be careful here because our "whole" is no longer ALL customers. They ask for the proportion of the number of customers that ordered pretzels **(whole)** who *also* got chocolate ice cream **(piece)**.

The total number of customers who ordered pretzels is found in the *fourth row* of the *"Total"column*: **30 people.** The number of customers who ordered both pretzels and chocolate ice cream can be found in the *fourth row* of the *"Chocolate" column*: **8 people.** Now that we've carefully determined our piece and whole, we know our proportion:

$$\frac{piece}{whole} = \frac{8}{30} = \boxed{\frac{4}{15}}$$

Percentage

If we wanted to know what **percentage** of the customers who ordered pretzels also ordered chocolate, we would just divide:

$$\frac{8}{30} \approx .27 = \mathbf{27\%}$$

Because, honestly, nobody likes fractions.

EXAMPLE 2

A mad scientist has automated the process of building his robot army. He randomly selects 3 robots to test from every 50 he produces. At this rate, how many robots will he test if he creates an army of 1000 robots?

Percentage

If you were told what **percent** of robots he tests, you could use the same process to solve the problem. 3 out of 50 is the same as 6%.

$$\frac{3}{50} = \frac{6}{100} = \frac{x}{1,000}$$

Rates of Change

Whether you use percent or proportion, you end up doing the same thing: take a rate from one population (3/50 or 6%) and multiply it by a different population.

SOLUTION

The phrase "at this rate" is often a good sign we're dealing with a proportions problem. In particular, we are given one proportion for a small group (3 robots tested out of every 50) and asked to apply it to a larger population (1000 robots). To solve, we can just set up two equal proportions – one for the small population and one for the large population. Then we can fill in what we know:

① *set up proportions* $\dfrac{piece_s}{whole_s} = \dfrac{piece_L}{whole_L}$

② *fill in what you know* $\dfrac{3 \; tested}{50 \; robots} = \dfrac{?? \; tested}{1,000 \; robots}$

Now we can see what we're solving for. Let x be the number that would be tested out of 1,000 robots.

③ *solve for x* $\dfrac{3}{50} = \dfrac{x}{1,000}$

$$\frac{3,000}{50} = x$$

$$\boxed{60} = x$$

Probability

When we use proportions to predict the likelihood of something happening, we talk in terms of **probability**. Probability questions on the SAT are simply proportion questions asked with slightly different language. You'll still be working with tables or paragraphs of data, and your job is **still** to compare the size of a "piece" with the size of the "whole" population. You'll even answer in the form of a proportion fraction or a decimal. The *only* difference is the language. Let's look at some examples.

EXAMPLE 3

	Shady Grove	Johnson Park
Swallowtails	12	6
Monarchs	18	10
Other	7	5

Kai is studying butterfly populations at two local parks. He spent an afternoon at each park catching, classifying, and releasing butterflies. The table above shows a record of all butterflies caught during the afternoon. Assuming that Kai's sample is representative of the butterfly populations in each park, what is the probability that a random butterfly caught in Shady Grove will be a swallowtail?

A) $\frac{3}{17}$

B) $\frac{7}{17}$

C) $\frac{12}{37}$

D) $\frac{28}{37}$

PORTAL

For this question, you don't need to worry about what a "representative sample" is.

However, if you're curious, check out the **Study Design** chapter on page 636 to see how the SAT will *occasionally* test this idea directly.

SOLUTION

We are asked for the probability that a butterfly caught in Shady Grove will be a swallowtail. That means our proportion will be:

$$\text{probability} = \frac{piece}{whole} = \frac{\text{\# of swallowtails in Shady Grove}}{\text{total \# of butterflies in Shady Grove}}$$

Our job then is to find the values for the numerator and the denominator using the table. First, let's grab the numerator. The # of swallowtails in Shady Grove can be found in the first row of the Shady Grove column: **12 swallowtails.** Let's fill that in:

$$\text{probability} = \frac{piece}{whole} = \frac{\text{12 swallowtails}}{\text{total \# of butterflies in Shady Grove}}$$

continue →

Now to find our denominator. We need the **total number** of tagged butterflies at Shady Grove. There is no "total" row in the table, so we'll need to add it up ourselves:

	Shady Grove	Johnson Park
Swallowtails	12	6
Monarchs	**+** 18	10
Other	**+** 7	5

Total = 37

Adding up the Shady Grove column, we get **37** for our "whole" population. That's our denominator, and it gives us an answer!

$$probability = \frac{12 \; swallowtails}{37 \; butterflies \; in \; Shady \; Grove} = \boxed{\frac{12}{37}}$$

There we have it! The probability of catching a swallowtail butterfly in Shady Grove is 12 over 37. Our answer is **C**!

C

EXAMPLE 4

	< 70%	70–90%	91–100%	Total
Teacher A	3	15	7	25
Teacher B	5	10	12	27
Total	8	25	19	52

The data in the table summarize the results of a Calculus test. There are two sections of the class, each taught by a different teacher. The number of students in each class whose score fell within a given range is recorded above. If a student is chosen at random from among those who scored a 70 or above, what is the probability that student is from Teacher A's section?

A) .25
B) .48
C) .50
D) .52

We need to determine the total **population** we are choosing the student from, and the **trait** that we're interested in.

The question says "If student is chosen at random from among those who scored a 70% or above..." so our population is **all students who scored 70 or above**. This means we need to add up all students in the "70-90%" and "91-100%" columns. Luckily, we have a "total" row that we can use.

	< 70%	70-90%	91-100%	Total
Teacher A	3	15	7	25
Teacher B	5	10	12	27
Total	8	**25**	**19**	52

$$25 + 19 = 44$$

So our population of students who scored 70% or above is **44**.

We want to find the probability that a student in this population is in Teacher A's section. To do that, we should focus on just the first row for those same two columns:

	< 70%	70-90%	91-100%	Total
Teacher A	3	**15**	**7**	25
Teacher B	5	10	12	27
Total	8	0	19	52

$$15 + 7 = 22$$

There are 22 students who scored a 70% or above in Teacher A's section. That's the "piece" with the trait we want! Now we can set up our proportion. Looking at the answer choices, we can see that we need to divide our fraction to get a decimal:

$$probability = \frac{\#\ with\ trait}{population} = \frac{22}{44} = \frac{1}{2} = \boxed{.50}$$

C

Number of STEM Bachelor's Degrees Conferred in U.S.

Major	2008	2009	2010	2011	2012	Total
Engineering	68,431	68,911	72,654	76,376	81,382	367,754
Math	15,192	15,496	16,030	17,182	18,842	82,742
Physical Sciences	22,179	22,688	23,379	24,712	26,663	119,621
Biological Sciences	79,829	82,825	86,400	90,003	95,849	434,906
Computer Science	38,476	37,994	39,589	43,072	47,384	206,515
Total	224,107	227,914	238,052	251,345	270,120	1,211,538

Pieces & Wholes

The trick to these questions is keeping track of your pieces and wholes for each problem.

Don't try to keep it all in your head! Use your pencil to take notes while you plug values into your calculator

The table above shows the number of Bachelor's degrees granted in the United States between the years 2008 and 2012 in several STEM fields. **Use the table** to answer the following questions.

Question	Answer
1. What is the probability that a randomly chosen graduate in 2009 majored in mathematics?	15496/227914
2. What is the probability that a randomly chosen engineer who graduated between 2008 and 2011 graduated in 2010?	236,072 / 941,418
3. What is the probability that a randomly chosen computer scientist who graduated during these five years graduated in 2010?	
4. What is the probability that a randomly chosen STEM graduate from these five years graduated in 2012?	
5. If a randomly chosen 2011 graduate did not major in Engineering, what is the probability that they majored in computer science?	
6. What is the probability that a randomly chosen student who graduated in 2010, 2011, or 2012 majored in either Physical or Biological Sciences?	

Answers: *See next page.*

Practice Problems

Use your new skills to answer each question.

1

36% of the seniors at Washington High School take AP Calculus. If there are 575 seniors, how many are taking AP Calculus?

A) 16
B) 36
C) 207
D) 517

2

	robins	cardinals	chickadees	blue jays
Saturday	3	7	5	7
Sunday	4	9	7	8

Loretta went bird watching one weekend and recorded the number of the four most common birds she saw in the table above. If 24% of the birds she saw were her favorite type of bird, which bird is her favorite?

A) robin
B) cardinal
C) chickadee
D) blue jay

3

$\frac{3}{4}$ of a particular library's collection is fiction and $\frac{3}{8}$ of the fiction collection is fantasy. What proportion of the library's book collection is fantasy?

A) $\frac{9}{32}$

B) $\frac{1}{2}$

C) $\frac{8}{9}$

D) $\frac{9}{8}$

4

Apples Eaten in a Week				
0	0	0	1	1
1	2	3	3	3
3	4	6	6	7
8	8	10	12	14

The table above lists the number of apples a random sample of 20 students ate in one week during their lunch period. If 2,000 students go to the school, which of the following is the best estimate for the expected number of apples that will be consumed by students at the school every week?

A) 4.6
B) 9.2
C) 920
D) 9,200

5

Results of a Math Test					
	100-90	89-80	79-70	69-60	59 and below
Attended morning review sessions	15	10	2	1	0
Did NOT attend morning review sessions	8	8	6	6	4

The table above summarizes the results of 60 high school students who took the same math test. If one of the high school students who made an 80 or higher was chosen at random, what is the probability that the student attended the morning review sessions?

A) $\frac{15}{26}$

B) $\frac{7}{18}$

C) $\frac{15}{41}$

D) $\frac{25}{41}$

Sport	Subject			Total
	Math	Reading	Writing	
Baseball	15	39	50	104
Basketball	7	32	11	50
Soccer	20	19	7	46
Total	42	90	68	200

The graph above shows the distribution of preferred subject in school and preferred sport to play for 200 people at a local high school. If a student is chosen at random, what is the probability that the student will be a soccer player whose favorite subject in school is writing?

A) 0.035
B) 0.103
C) 0.152
D) 0.255

	Likes Spam	Does NOT LIke Spam
Male	92	158
Female	8	242
Total	100	400

The owner of a local deli is considering the idea of selling spam. In order to decide if this is a good idea or not, the owner takes a survey of 500 of his customers. The results of his survey are shown in the table above. What percentage of his female customers like spam?

A) 16%
B) 8%
C) 3.2%
D) 1.6%

8

Sleeping Positions				
	Back	Stomach	Side	Total
Male	18	15	7	40
Female	2	12	25	40
Total	20	27	33	80

The table above summarizes the results of 80 participants in a sleep study to see what sleeping positions were most common among males and females. Participants were categorized by the sleeping positions: sleeping on the back, sleeping on the stomach, or sleeping on one side. If a female participant is chosen at random, what is the probability that she sleeps on her side?

A) $\frac{5}{8}$

B) $\frac{25}{33}$

C) $\frac{33}{40}$

D) $\frac{7}{26}$

9

Jackson does a survey and learns that $\frac{2}{5}$ of his classmates are only children, $\frac{1}{3}$ have exactly one sibling, and the rest have two or more siblings. If 8 of his classmates have 2 or more siblings, how many are only children?

$\frac{6}{15}$ $\frac{5}{15}$ $\frac{4}{15}$ ⅜

$\frac{8}{x} = \frac{4}{15}$

30 total

⁴/₁₅ of 30 = 12

10

Aja is sorting through her beads while designing a necklace and finds that the ratio of yellow beads to green beads is 2 to 5. If she has 35 green beads, how many yellow beads does she have?

A)   10
B)   14
C)   15
D)   21

Percent Change

In this chapter, we get practice working with percentages that grow or shrink over time. There is a very specific way to reflect this in your work, and many students make errors in the process. So let's practice!

Working with Decimals

Say you learn that the price of a pair of pants (*x*) has **increased by 20%**. Let's write that in words and then translate to math:

"the new price	is equal to	the price	plus	20% of the price."
new price	=	(100%)x	+	(20%)x

$$\text{new price} = \textbf{(120\%)x} \text{ or } \boxed{\textbf{1.2x}}$$

Notice that, to show a 20% increase, we end up just **multiplying by 1.2**. This is an extremely helpful shortcut, and it works for decreases too. If you see a "20% decrease", you can write that as:

$$100\%x - 20\%x = 80\%x$$
$$1.0x - 0.2x = \textbf{0.8x}$$

TIP

This principle applies when comparing two separate quantities. "20% more" is the same thing as "20% increase."

So... if the price of *my* pants was **30% more** than the price of your pants, then my pants cost **1.3 times** the price of your pants!

 Write each percent increase or decrease **as a decimal**.

% Change	↑ 20%	↑ 18%	↓ 92%	↑ 8%	↓ 2.3%	↑ 120%
Decimal	**1.2**	1.18	.08	1.08	.97	1.22

Answers: *See next page.*

EXAMPLE 1

Kendrick challenged his friend Sherane to a sit-ups competition. They each took 1 minute to complete as many sit-ups as possible. Kendrick told Sherane how many he did and she responded that she did 15% more. If Sherane did 46 situps, how many did Kendrick do?

A) 39
B) 40
C) 53
D) 54

TIP

We could work backwards here! Since we know that Kendrick did fewer sit-ups than Sherane, we know that choices C and D can't be right.

We can then calculate 115% of A and B and see which one works out to 46.

SOLUTION

We should always start off word problems like this by translating into math. We know that Sherane did **15% more** than Kendrick. Fifteen percent MORE means 100% of Kendrick's amount **plus** another 15% of Kendrick's amount. Let's translate that:

① *Translate:* $S = 100\%K + 15\%K$

   "S did 15% more than K" $S = 1K + .15K$

                                        $S = 1.15K$

We're also told that Sherane did 46 situps. Let's plug that in for C:

② *substitute 46 for S* $46 = 1.15K$

③ *solve for K* $\dfrac{46}{1.15} = K$

                                        $\boxed{40} = K$

                                                          B

EXAMPLE 2

Jerome is an astronomer and has been studying a table of the distances of various celestial objects from Earth. He notices that the distance to the star *Pollux* is about 48.3% less than the distance to the star *Aldebaran*. If it is about 65.3 light years to *Aldebaran*, about how far, in light years, is it to *Pollux*?

A) 31.5
B) 33.8
C) 126.3
D) 135.2

SOLUTION

Per usual, we should start by practicing some **art of translation**. We are told that the distance to Pollux is about **48.3% less** than the distance to Aldebaran.

(1) Translate:

"P is 48.3% less than A"

$$P = 100\%A - 48.3\%A$$
$$P = 1A - .483A$$
$$P = .517A$$

And since the distance to Aldebaran is **65.3 light years**, we know:

(2) Substitute 65.3 for A

$$P = .517(65.3)$$
$$P = 33.76$$

B

583

Compound Percentages

Imagine that you're out shopping and see a pair of pants on a mannequin marked "$100." Next to the mannequin is a sign that says **"50% off!"**, and, upon further inspection, you discover *another* sign that says *"take an additional 50% off!"* Now, odds are you wouldn't think:

> "Sweet! Free pants!"

...and skip out of the store with the stolen goods. You'd understand intuitively that the first sign marked the pants down to about $50, and the second knocked it down to something like 20 or 30 bucks. In the "real world," this seems obvious. However, this is a common mistake students make when working with percentages on the test. Remember, you have to take each percent change one at a time:

$$50\% \text{ off } x = .5x$$

$$50\% \text{ off the } \mathbf{50\% \text{ sale price}} = .5(.5x) = .25x$$

EXAMPLE 3

Eloise bought dinner at her favorite restaurant. She brought a coupon for 15% off the total cost of the meal. A 7% sales tax was added to the discounted price and Eloise added a 20% tip on the original price of the meal. In terms of the original price p, how much did Eloise pay?

A) $1.12p$

B) $1.42p$

C) $(1.07)(.85)(1.2)p$

D) $(1.07)(.85)p + (.20)p$

SOLUTION

There's a lot going on here, so let's work through one bit at a time.

First, we're told she has a 15% coupon. This means **15% less**, which we can represent as **.85p**.

> *Discount price after coupon* = $(1 - .15)p$ = **.85p**

Next, there is a **7%** sales tax **added** to this discounted price. To increase by 7%, we can **multiply the discount price by 1.07**.

> *Discount Price + Sales Tax* = $(.85p) + .07(.85p)$ = **(1.07)(.85p)**

Then we just need to **add** the tip. We have to be careful here: it says the tip is **20% of the *original* price**, which we can represent as $(.20)p$.

> *Taxed Discount + Tip* = $(1.07)(.85p) + (.20)p$

So the answer is **D**.

TIP

If you think you have worked it out and don't immediately see your answer in the choices, don't panic! See if you can simplify or rearrange your answer to get one of the choices.

For example, here, a correct choice could even have looked like:

[(1.07)(.85) + .2]p

Calculating Percent Change

Occasionally, you'll be asked to calculate a percent change by comparing a new and old value. For example, in keeping with our stolen pants example, you might be told that the pants were originally $52 and were marked down to $13. That's a great deal! But *how* great is it? To find the **percent change** between those prices, you can use this simple formula:

$$\% \text{ Change} = \frac{|new - old|}{old} \times 100$$

$$\% \text{ Change} = \frac{|13 - 52|}{52} \times 100 = \frac{39}{52}(100) = \boxed{72\% \text{ change}}$$

One thing to watch out for when working with percent change: this does NOT mean that the new price is 72% of the original price. Since we **decreased** by 72%, that means the new price is 100% – 72% = **28%** of the original price. Remember your piece-over-whole relationships and work out each step carefully!

Use the % change formula to complete the table below.

Old Price	New Price	% Change
$200	$80	↑ $\frac{120}{200} = 60\%$
$65	$39	↑ $\frac{65-39}{65} = 40\%$
$1,000	$1,120	↓ 12%
$16	$1	93.75%
$11,235	$6,516.30	42%
$81,321	$47,166.18	↓ 42%

Answers: **1)** 60% **2)** 40% **3)** 12% **4)** 93.75% **5)** 42% **6)** 42%

Practice Problems

Use your new skills to answer each question.

....

1

Terry went shopping and bought 5 T-shirts and 2 sweaters. The price of a sweater is 30 percent more expensive than that of a T-shirt, and Terry paid a total of $121.60. What was the price of a sweater?

A) $16.00
B) $19.00
C) $20.80
D) $24.70

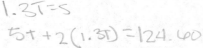

$1.3T = S$

$5t + 2(1.3T) = 124.60$

2

Five friends buy concert tickets together because the band is having a promotion where, for every four tickets purchased, the fifth ticket will be discounted by $10. The group of friends splits the cost of the 5 tickets equally such that each paid $38. What percent discount did each friend receive?

A) 5%
B) 10%
C) 15%
D) 25%

$4x + (x-10)$ $5x - 10 = 5 \cdot 38$

$5x - 10 = 190$

$+10 \quad +10$

$x \; \$40$

$\frac{95}{100} = \frac{38}{40}$

or

$\frac{5}{100} \quad \frac{2}{40}$

$4 \sqrt{\frac{38}{5}}$

$\frac{190}{}$

$5\sqrt{200}$

3

Kyle, Claire, and Fabio all went to the same bakery together and bought pumpkin spice pastries. Kyle paid the full price for his pastry, Claire used a coupon for $1 off her pastry, and Fabio used a coupon for 20 percent off his pastry. If Kyle, Claire, and Fabio paid a total of $10.20 for the three pastries, how much did Kyle pay for his pastry?

A) $3.00
B) $3.20
C) $3.30
D) $4.00

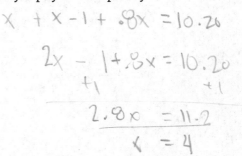

$x + x - 1 + .8x = 10.20$

$2x - 1 + .8x = 10.20$

$\quad +1 \qquad\qquad +1$

$2.8x = 11.2$

$x = 4$

4

Eliza is doing a chemistry experiment and finds that the actual weight of the product is 15% less than the predicted weight. If she expected to get 150 grams of product, how much did she actually get?

150

127.5

5

Bryant is looking at his power bill. He sees that in May when the weather was mild it was $48 and in July when he ran the AC a lot it was $178. What was the percent increase in his bill from May to July?

A) 2.7%
B) 3.7%
C) 270%
D) 370%

6

A triangle's base was increased by 15%. If its area is increased by 38%, what percent was the height of the triangle increased by?

target
$\frac{1}{2}bh \rightarrow \frac{1}{2}(1.15b)(h+x) = (1.38)\frac{1}{2}bh$

$1.15h + 1.15x = 1.38h$
$-1.15h \qquad -1.15h$

$1.15x = .23h$
$.23$

$x = \frac{1}{5}h$

20%

7

If a circle's circumference is decreased by 12%, what percent is the diameter decreased by?

A) $2\sqrt{3}$ %
B) 6%
C) 12%
D) 24%

588

Unit Conversions

In this chapter, we learn to use proportions to convert one unit into another.

Focus on Units

Word problems, by their nature, tend to be filled with units. Whether we're talking about pounds of hamburgers or how many miles someone ran after eating hamburgers, units are usually just labels for the variables in our math equations. Occasionally, however, the test-writers will **tell** you values in one unit (like miles) but then **ask** for an answer in a different unit (like feet).

The good news is that every time the test-writers do this, they **underline** the changed units! Plus, you'll always be given a **proportion** that you can use to convert your answer into the new units. Let's see that in action.

EXAMPLE 1

A 1.5 pound batch of fudge is poured into a 6 inch × 8 inch pan and allowed to cool. It is then cut into one-inch squares. What is the weight, in <u>ounces</u>, of each square? (1 pound = 16 ounces)

A) $\frac{1}{2}$

B) $\frac{1}{3}$

C) 1

D) 6

TIP

Convert your units at the very beginning of the problem whenever possible.

SOLUTION

We are asked for the weight in ounces, but we're given a weight in pounds. Let's start by converting the units so we don't forget later. Since we currently have pounds and want ounces, we need to divide by the number of pounds and multiply by the number of ounces:

① *convert units* $\qquad (1.5 \ \text{pounds}) \times \dfrac{16 \ ounces}{1 \ pound} = \textbf{24 ounces}$

This means we have a **total of 24 ounces** of fudge. We're asked to determine how many ounces a 1-inch square weighs, so let's think about how many squares there are:

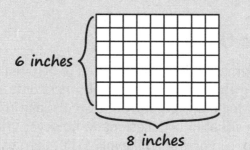

6 inches × 8 inches
= 48 square inches

So our **24 ounces** of fudge get cut up into **48 squares**. To find out how much each square weighs, we just do the math equivalent of chopping up fudge: dividing!

② *divide* $\qquad \dfrac{24 \ ounces}{48 \ squares} = \boxed{\dfrac{1}{2}}$

A

EXAMPLE 2

The average flight speed of a particular gryphon is 78 km/hr. At this rate, which of the following is closest to the distance, in kilometers, the gryphon can travel in 13 <u>minutes</u>?

A) 6
B) 17
C) 360
D) 1,014

You might see this problem and recall that:

$$distance = rate \times time$$

The only problem is that the time unit in the given rate (km/hr) is not the same as the unit we are asked about (minutes)! Since the rate is already in hours, let's just convert 13 minutes into hours. There are 60 minutes in an hour, so:

$$13 \text{ minutes} \times \frac{1 \text{ hour}}{60 \text{ minutes}} = \frac{13}{60} \text{ hr}$$

So we know that the gryphon flies 78km per hour, and we want to know how far it would get in $\frac{13}{60}$ of an hour:

$$\frac{13}{60} \text{ hr} \times \frac{78km}{1 \text{ hr}} = \boxed{16.9 \text{ km}}$$

BONUS: Estimation

In the midst of all this hardcore math genius that we've got going on, it can be easy to forget that sometimes "just sorta estimating" can often work wonders. Take this problem for example...

13 minutes is a little under a quarter of an hour. Which means the gryphon will fly *about* a quarter of the distance it would fly in an hour. We know it flies 78km in an hour, so...

$$78 \div 4 = \textbf{19.5}$$

The only answer that's close to that number is **Choice B**, 17km. Behold, the power of estimating!

B

TIP

You could also convert speed into km/min, and then multiply by 13.

EXAMPLE 3

Number of tablespoons per ounce of butter	2
Number of teaspoons per tablespoons	3
Number of ounces per pound	16
Number of tablespoons per cup	16
Number of tablespoons per pound of butter	32
Number of grams per ounce	28.3
Number of grams of flour per cup	120

Latisha is planning to make a batch of cookies. The recipe calls for 1 and a half cups of butter. She has a 1 pound block of butter and a scale that can give weight in either ounces or grams. To the nearest gram, how many <u>grams</u> of butter should she weigh out for her cookies?

A)   12
B)   180
C)   340
D)   1,440

SOLUTION

This problem gives us a whole table full of conversion factors, so we are going to have to pick out which ones we need. Let's start by identifying what we know and what we want.

1.5 cups butter = **?? grams** butter

We need to use some information from the table to connect cups with grams. "Cups" only shows up in two rows, and the last one is about flour, not butter. We can convert cups to tablespoons, so let's go ahead and set that up:

① convert cups to tbsp

$$(1.5 \text{ cups}) \times \frac{16 \text{ tbsp}}{1 \text{ cup}} = 24 \text{ tbsp}$$

Progress! Now, it'd be great to know how many grams are in a tablespoon, but we don't have that. But we CAN get to grams in two steps... do you see how?

continue →

We DO have ounces per tablespoon and grams per ounces in the table. If we convert tablespoons to ounces and then ounces to grams, we're golden!

② convert tbsp to ounces

$$(24 \ \cancel{tbsp}) \times \frac{1 \ ounce}{2 \ \cancel{tbsp}} = \textbf{12 ounces}$$

③ convert ounces to grams

$$(12 \ \cancel{ounces}) \times \frac{28.3 \ grams}{1 \ \cancel{ounce}} = \textbf{340 grams}$$

There we go! Apparently, there are 340 grams in a cup and a half of butter. Good to know!

Just to recap, let's see the whole conversion written out:

$$1.5 \ cups \cdot \frac{16 \ tbsp}{1 \ cup} \cdot \frac{1 \ ounce}{2 \ tbsp} \cdot \frac{28.3 \ grams}{1 \ ounce} = \boxed{340 \ grams}$$

C

EXAMPLE 4

The *shaku*, a Japanese unit of length, is approximately equal to 30.3 cm. The *koku* is a Japanese unit of volume equal to 10 cubic *shaku*. Approximately how many <u>cubic meters</u> is one *koku* ? (100 cm = 1 meter)

A) 0.278
B) 3.03
C) 3.58
D) 278.00

SOLUTION

There are two interesting things about this problem. First, it has units you probably aren't used to seeing. No problem, we can just use unit conversion! Second, it works with both lengths *and* volumes. We'll deal with that shortly.

We know we want to get from *koku* to **cubic meters**. The only thing we know about *koku* is that there are 1 *koku* for every 10 cubic *shaku*, so let's start there:

$$1 \; koku \cdot \frac{10 \; shaku^3}{1 \; koku} \; ... \; ? \; meters^3$$

Now, how can we get from cubic *shaku* to cubic meters? We know that 1 *shaku* = 30.3 cm, which means that 1 cubic *shaku* is $(30.3)^3$ cubic centimeters. Let's add that to our unit conversion train:

$$1 \; koku \cdot \frac{10 \; shaku^3}{1 \; koku} \cdot \frac{(30.3)^3 \; cm^3}{1 \; shaku^3} \; ... \; ? \; meters^3$$

So far we've converted koku to cubic shaku to cubic centimeters. Now we need to convert cubic centimeters to cubic meters. We know that 1m = 100cm, which means that 1 cubic meter = $(100)^3$ cubic centimeters. If we add that, we finish the link!

$$1 \; koku \cdot \frac{10 \; shaku^3}{1 \; koku} \cdot \frac{(30.3)^3 \; cm^3}{1 \; shaku^3} \cdot \frac{1 \; meter^3}{(100)^3 \; cm^3} = ? \; meters^3$$

To put this into our calculator, we can type:

$$(1 \cdot 10 \cdot (30.3)^3) \div 100^3 = \boxed{.278 \; meters^3}$$

A

594

Practice Problems

Use your new skills to answer each question.

1

Virginia is laying out a path using 10 inch square paving tiles. If the path is 15 feet long, how many tiles will she need to complete it? (12 inches = 1 foot)

A) $\frac{3}{2}$

B) 8

C) 18

D) 180

2

A Martian year is about equal to 1 year, 320 days, and 18 hours in Earth terms. About how many Earth hours is one Martian year? (1 Earth year = 365 days)

A) 7,698
B) 12,330
C) 16,440
D) 16,458

3

As lava flows and cools, the radius of a particular volcanic island is growing at an average rate of 0.75 inches per hour. Given that there are 12 inches per foot, how many days will it take for the island's radius to grow by 3.5 feet?

A) 2.33
B) 4.67
C) 31.75
D) 42

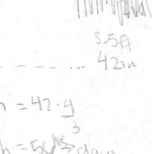

4

If *w* weeks and 3 days is equal to 66 days, what is the value of *w*?

$7w + 3 = 66$

$w = 9$

5

An apple pie recipe calls for six apples. If each apple weighs about $\frac{1}{2}$ pound and the pie is cut into 7 slices, about how many <u>ounces</u> of apple are in each slice? (1 pound = 16 ounces)

A) 0.29
B) 1.7
C) 4.6
D) 6.8

6

Jaron's favorite yarn comes in 50 gram balls. He uses two balls and knits a scarf that is 18 cm by 150 cm. If he uses 3 balls of yarn and knits a scarf that is 25 cm wide, how long will it be?

A) 54
B) 108
C) 162
D) 2,700

7

The UK Weights and Measures Act of 1835 defined a stone as 14 lbs and a hundredweight as 4 stone. If someone weighs two hundredweight, 1 stone, and 6 pounds, what is their weight in <u>pounds</u>?

UNIT | Data Analysis: Part 2

Chapters

Key Skills

In this unit, we get to become scientists ourselves. We'll be discussing "good" and "bad" study design, as well as how to make conclusions based on data using basic statistics like mean, median, and range.

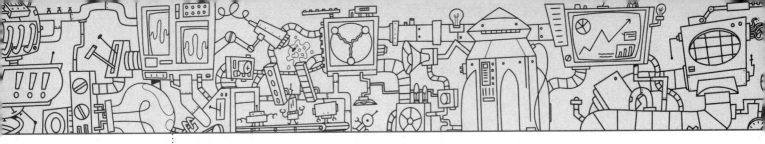

Basic Statistics

*A **statistic** is a number that provides information about a set of data. In this chapter, we look at several commonly used statistics, what they tell us, and how they differ.*

The Height of Boredom

Let's imagine that, midway through your SAT exam, you become overwhelmed with either (1) boredom or (2) the desire to organize a real, honest-to-goodness scientific study of the heights of all 21 people in the room. After a persuasive speech, you convince the students and moderator to pause the test and form a line. One-by-one, you measure their heights (in inches, since you're in America) and record your findings in the table below:

Height (in inches)						
66	65	55	66	59	60	61
54	65	55	62	65	63	66
66	71	58	68	70	71	66

So you finish filling out the table. What now? How tall, on average, were the students in the room? Were people similar in height, or not? What **conclusions** can we draw about the heights of the students in that room? To answer these (extremely) pressing questions, let's look at the statistics most commonly covered on the SAT.

Measures of Central Tendency

The statistics you're likely most familiar with are called measures of central tendency. That's a fancy way of saying statistics that describe a data set by focusing on its center in various ways.

Middleman

If we had an even number of students, then nobody would be standing directly in the middle. In that case, the median is the **average of the two students in the middle.**

- The **median** is the simplest measure of central tendency. When the data is arranged in numerical order, the median is the number smack-dab in the center. If we lined up each of our 21 students from shortest to tallest, the 11th student would have 10 people in front of her and 10 people behind her. Her height, 65 inches, is our median!

Height (in inches)						
54	55	55	58	59	60	61
62	63	65	(65)	65	66	66
66	66	66	68	70	71	71

- The **mode** of a data set is the number that occurs most frequently. We *could* simply look at the table and count the number of times the same height shows up. Or we could be fancy and do pretty much the same thing using a histogram:

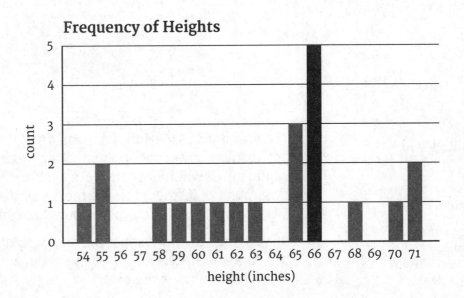

Frequency of Heights

The most common height is **66 inches**, so that's our mode!

NOTE

The mean (63.57) is lower than the median (65). This is because the shortest students are farther from the median than the tallest students.

- The **mean** is the average of the data set. To find the mean of a set of data, we add up all of the values in the set and divide by the number of values. Let's find the average height for our study. We already know there are 21 values in the set, so we just need to find the sum and divide:

$$\text{Mean} = \frac{\text{sum of terms}}{\text{\# of terms}} = \frac{54 + 55 + \ldots + 71 + 71}{21} = \boxed{63.57 \text{ inches}}$$

Measures of Spread

Measures of spread describe how similar or varied the set of observed values are. Two measures of spread that show up on the test are range and standard deviation.

- The **range** of a set of data is the difference between the largest and smallest values. A large range suggests that the data set is spread out, while a small range suggests that it is highly concentrated. In our data set, the shortest person has a height of 54 inches and the tallest has a height of 71 inches, so the range is:

$$\text{Range} = 71 - 54 = \boxed{17 \text{ inches}}$$

deviate (v.)

The verb "to deviate" means to stray or swerve from a primary path.

So it makes sense that small "deviations" mean the data is tightly clustered, while large deviations mean it's all over the place.

- The **standard deviation** is a measure of the average distance between any given data point and the mean. In our study, it would tell us whether there were a lot of different heights in the classroom, or if students were mostly similar in height. Luckily, the SAT doesn't require you to compute the standard deviation.

All you need to know is that the standard deviation is **small** when the data are clustered around the mean and **large** when they are spread far from the mean.

Boxplots

A boxplot is a way to visualize five different statistics in a given data set, including: ① the minimum value, ② the 25th percentile, ③ the median, ④ the 75th percentile, and ⑤ the maximum value.

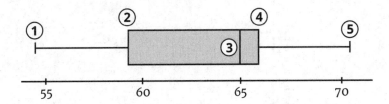

This boxplot tells us that the minimum value is just below 55, the 25th percentile is just below 60, the median is right at 65, the 75th percentile is about 66, and the maximum value is just above 70.

INTERACTIVE EXAMPLE

Number of cars washed								
Time	9–10	10–11	11–12	12–1	1–2	2–3	3–4	4–5
Saturday	3	5	7	8	6	4	6	5
Sunday	2	3	2	10	5	5	3	5

To raise funds for their high school e-sports team, a number of students held a weekend carwash. They washed cars each day, starting at 9 a.m. and going until 5 p.m. The above table lists the number of cars that were washed during each hour. Use the data in the table to answer the questions below.

Q1) Finish the following histogram to accurately represent the data.

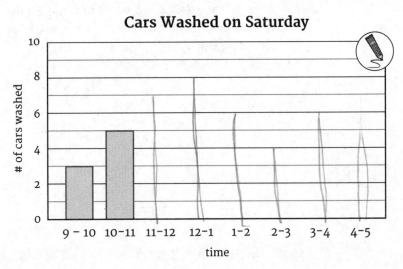

TIP

The *x*-axis on this dot plot lists the possible # of cars washed each hour. The number of dots above each possibility is just a count of the number of times that # shows up in the table.

Here, we see no 0's or 1's in the table for Sunday, so there are **no dots** above them. We see "2" twice, so there are **two dots**, etc.

Q2) Finish the following dot plot to accurately represent the data:

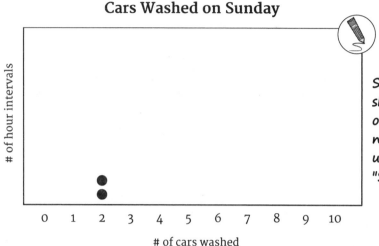

Cars Washed on Sunday

Stack dots to show the # of times each number shows up in the "Sunday" row

Q3) What was the median number of cars washed per hour on Saturday?

≈ 5.5

S3) Since we are looking for the **median**, we need to put the data for Saturday in numerical order. Fill in the blanks below, starting with the smallest number and ending with the largest:

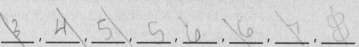

3 , 4 , 5 , 5 , 6 , 6 , 7 , 8

How many data points are there? _8_

Since there are an **even** number of data points, we need to average the two middle terms to find our median. In other words, we need a number that is directly between the two numbers in the middle of the list. If they are the same number, then it's just that number!

Median: _5.5_

Answer: *S3) List = 3, 4, 5, 5, 6, 6, 7, 8   Data points = 8   Median = 5.5*

Q4) What was the **mean** number of cars washed per hour on Sunday?

S4) To find the mean number of cars washed on **Sunday**, we take the data from the appropriate row of the table (or from the dot plot we made earlier), find the sum, and then divide by the total number of data points. Fill in the blanks below to find the mean:

$$Mean = \frac{sum\ of\ terms}{\#\ of\ terms} = \underline{\hspace{3cm}} = \underline{5 \times 25}$$

Q5) Which day had the wider **range** of cars washed per hour?

S5) The range is the largest value minus the smallest value. Fill in the blanks below to find the range for each day:

$$Range = Largest - Smallest$$

Saturday = _____ – _____ = __5__

Sunday = _____ – _____ = __6__

So the wider range is on which day? ____Sunday____

Answer: 4) Mean = $\frac{35}{8}$ = 4.375

5) Saturday = 8 – 3 = 5   Sunday = 10 – 2 = 8   wider range = Sunday

Q6) Which day do you think has the larger **standard deviation**?

S6) The standard deviation is a measure of the spread of the data set. So we need to determine which day's data are **more spread out**.

On both days, the data is fairly clustered EXCEPT for the hour where they washed **10 cars on Sunday**. This data point will significantly increase the standard deviation on Sunday.

Practice Problems

Use your new skills to answer each question.

1

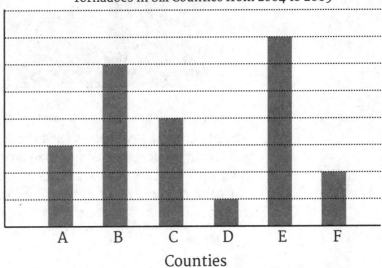

Tornadoes in Six Counties from 2004 to 2005

Counties

The number of tornadoes in 6 counties from 2004 to 2005 is shown in the graph above. If the total number of tornadoes from 2004 to 2005 is 2,300, how many tornadoes did County E have in that time period?

A) 7
B) 70
C) 700
D) 7,000

607

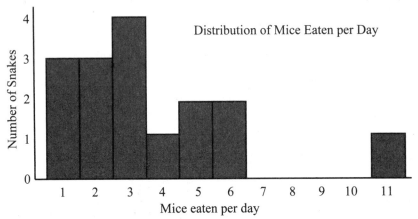

The bar graph above shows the number of mice eaten per day by snakes of the viperidae family observed in the jungle. The outlier who ate 11 mice was found to be of the colubris family, not of the viperid family. Which will change the most if the outlier is removed from the data?

A) Mode
B) Mean
C) Median
D) They will all change by the same amount.

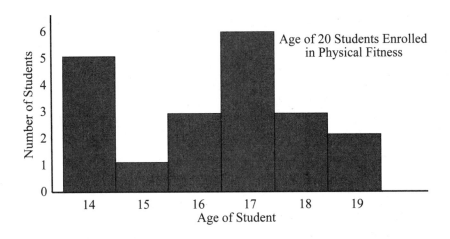

3

Based on the histogram above, of the following, what is the closest to the average (arithmetic mean) age of the students in the Physical Fitness class?

A) 14
B) 15
C) 16
D) 17

4

An accountant of a Fortune 500 company found that the mean salary of an employee in the company was $84,302 and the median salary of an employee in the company was $55,000. Which of the following situations could explain the difference between the mean and the median salaries of employees in the company?

A) The salaries of employees are all very similar.

B) Most salaries of employees in the company are between $55,000 and $84,302.

C) There are a few employee salaries that are much higher than the rest.

D) There are a few employee salaries that are much lower than the rest.

5

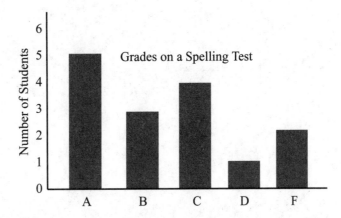

Grades on a Spelling Test

Based on the bar graph above, what is the median grade a student received on the spelling test?

A) A

B) B

C) C

D) D

Team A		Team B		Team C		Team D	
Player 1	20	Player 1	5	Player 1	25	Player 1	5
Player 2	20	Player 2	10	Player 2	30	Player 2	5
Player 3	25	Player 3	15	Player 3	35	Player 3	25
Player 4	30	Player 4	20	Player 4	35	Player 4	35
Player 5	30	Player 5	25	Player 5	45	Player 5	45

The table above shows the average number of points scored per game by the players of four teams. Based on this data, which team has the largest standard deviation in number of points per player per game?

A) Team A
B) Team B
C) Team C
D) Team D

7

Top 10 Home Run Hitters of All Time			
Baseball Player	Number of Home Runs	Baseball Players	Number of Home Runs
1. Barry Bonds	762	6. Ken Griffey	630
2. Hank Aaron	755	7. Jim Thome	612
3. Babe Ruth	714	8. Sammy Sosa	609
4. Alex Rodriguez	687	9. Frank Robinson	586
5. Willie Mays	660	10. Mark McGwire	583

The table above lists the number of home runs of the top ten home run hitters of all time. According to the table, what was the mean number of home runs of the baseball players listed above? (Round your answer to the nearest home run.)

659.8

≈ 660

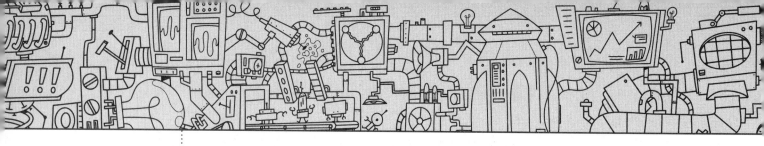

Trend-spotting

*It's time to learn yet another way to think about **slope**. In this chapter, we are going to look at how we use slope to interpret trends in data.*

PORTAL

For a refresher on the basics of slope, turn to page 378.

In this section, we will be talking a lot about slope. This time, our focus isn't on calculating slope, but rather interpreting slope. We'll ask questions like: where does the graph increase? Where does it stay constant? Where is the graph decreasing most quickly?

Generally vs. Strictly

We say that a graph (or data set) is **strictly** increasing if every data point is larger than the previous with no exceptions. In other words, straight uphill with no breaks in between! If the graph (or data) has an overall upward trend but also has a few plateaus or small dips, we can say it is **generally** increasing.

Strictly Increasing

Always rising!

Generally Increasing

Dips :(

INTERACTIVE EXAMPLE

The graph below shows the elevation of a loop trail, with trail distances measured clockwise from the trail head.

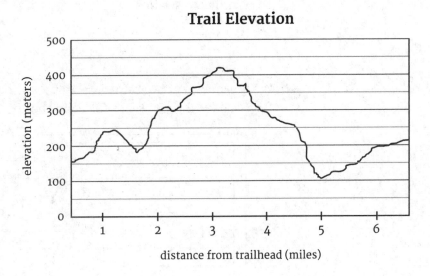

Trail Elevation

Q1) Over which of the following intervals is the trail generally increasing in elevation?

A) .5 miles to 1.5 miles
B) 1.5 miles to 3 miles
C) 3 miles to 4 miles
D) 4 miles to 5 miles

S1) Let's look at what happens for each of the listed intervals:

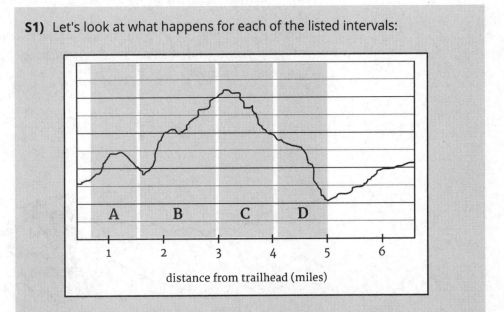

Choice A is up and down, and choices C and D are *decreasing*. Only **choice B** is generally increasing.

B

Q2) Over which of the following intervals is the trail strictly decreasing?

    A) .5 miles to 1.5 miles
    B) 1.5 miles to 3 miles
    C) 3 miles to 4 miles
    D) 4 miles to 5 miles

S2) We are looking at the same intervals as before. Since we are looking for decrease this time, let's focus on choices C and D:

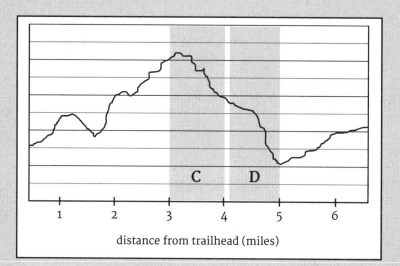

distance from trailhead (miles)

Let's look at choice C. From 3 to 4 miles, the trail is mostly going down in elevation, but it starts by going up a bit, and plateaus briefly midway down. That's generally decreasing, but not strictly.

Choice D, on the other hand, shows a **strictly decreasing** trend. It doesn't go down at a constant rate, but there are no moments of plateau or increase.

                                              D

Q3) How many miles along the trail does a hiker reach the maximum elevation?

A) 1.2

B) 3.1

C) 5

D) 430

S3) Since the *y*-axis is elevation, we need to find the tallest point on the graph. The question asks us to report "how many miles along the trail" this peak happens, so we need to find the *x*-coordinate.

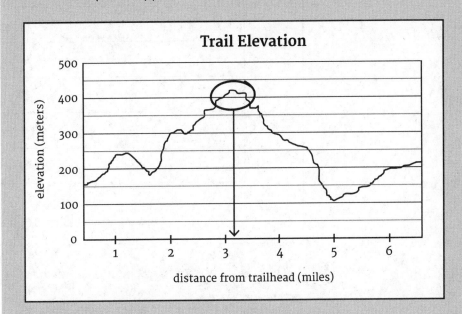

The peak happens a little past **3 miles**, so the answer is B!   B

Q4) What is the significance of the *y*-intercept in this graph?

    A) The trail starts at an elevation of 0 meters.

    B) The trail never crosses the *x*-axis, so it never gets to sea level.

    C) The trail's lowest point has an elevation of about 155 meters.

    D) The trailhead has an elevation of about 155 meters.

S4) Let's look at the *y*-intercept and see what we learn:

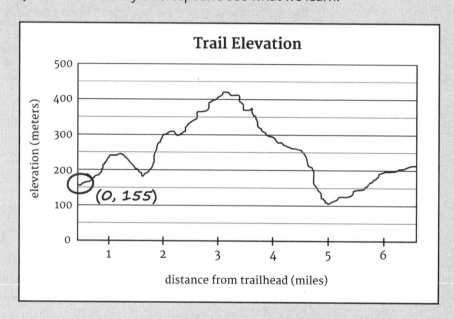

The coordinates of the point are somewhere around:

$$y\text{-intercept} = (0, 155)$$

Now we just need to interpret this in context using the axis labels. Let's **write in the labels** for the *x* and *y* coordinate:

$$y\text{-intercept} = (0 \text{ miles from trailhead}, 155 \text{ meters elevation})$$

Aha! Just labeling *x* and *y* does most of the interpretation for us! The *y*-intercept tells us that if you're standing at the trailhead, you are at 155 meters elevation. That's exactly what **choice D** says!

D

Q5) What is the elevation difference between the highest and lowest points on the trail?

A) 110
B) 280
C) 330
D) 430

S5) To find the elevation difference, we first need to find the min and max elevations on the graph.

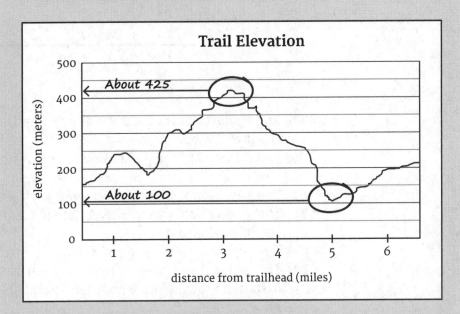

So the max elevation is around 425 meters, and the min elevation is around 100 meters. Now we just need to find the difference:

$$425 - 100 = 325 \ meters$$

The choice that is closest to our estimate is **choice C**.   C

EXAMPLE 2

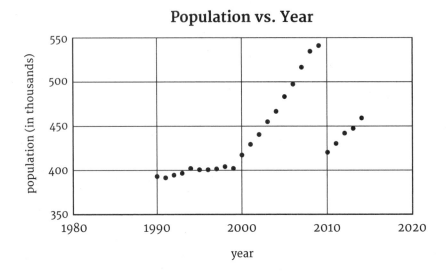

The graph above shows the population of Atlanta, GA each year from 1990 to 2014. Based on the graph, which of the following best describes the general trend of the population over this time period?

A) The population generally increased each year since 1990.
B) The population was relatively steady until 2000, after which it steadily increased.
C) The population changed unpredictably, so there is no general trend.
D) The population stayed fairly steady between 1990 and 2000, when it started growing quickly. It fell sharply in 2010 before starting to grow again.

SOLUTION

Let's test each answer choice with the graph. Only the correct choice will accurately describe the trends we see.

A) There was a a huge drop in 2010, so it's not true that the population generally increased.

B) The statement here is only true up until 2010, not 1990-2014.

C) There were two points where the behavior changed, but there are clear trends in each decade.

D) **Yes!** This answer identifies the three different regions of the graph and appropriately describes each of them.

D

Slope & Relationships

The great thing about graphs and other visualizations is that they allow us to see **relationships** between variables. In the previous example, the graph showed us the relationship between time and the population of Atlanta. When we described the trends in that graph, we were describing the **direction** and **strength** of that relationship.

Let's say we were curious whether adding a new "miracle" fertilizer will correlate ('have a relationship') with the size of a plant. If adding more fertilizer made the plant grow, we'd say there was a **positive** relationship. If adding more fertilizer made the plant shrink, then we'd say there was a **negative** relationship. If adding more and more fertilizer did zilch for the plant, then we'd say there was **no relationship**.

Positive   Negative   None

Finally, we use the words **strong** and **weak** to describe how tight the connection is between the two variables. If every application of miracle grow caused a proportional growth spurt (or shrinkage), we'd say there was a strong relationship. If instead the growth spurts were less predictable, we'd say there was a weak relationship.

PORTAL

To see how slope comes up algebraically, check out the Equation of a Line chapter on page 378.

MAKING CONNECTIONS

Notice that we use the exact same words (*positive* & *negative*) to describe **relationships** as we do to describe **slope**. That's because slope, relationships, and rates are all getting at the same idea: how much does changing *one* variable (x) affect a different variable (y) ?

When you have an equation with a large, positive slope, like:

$$y = 50x + 2$$

..then changing x even from 1 to 2 has a **positive** impact on y. Another way to phrase that is to say "x and y have a **positive relationship**."

Now that we know the connection between slope and relationships, let's look at examples of what different correlations look like **graphically**.

Positive Relationships

When variables have a **positive** relationship, they increase together.

Negative Relationships

In a **negative** relationship, one variable decreases when the other increases.

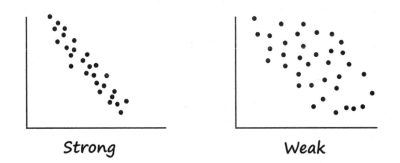

No Relationship

When there is no relationship between the variables, you'll see a straight horizontal or vertical line, or a seemingly random spread of data points.

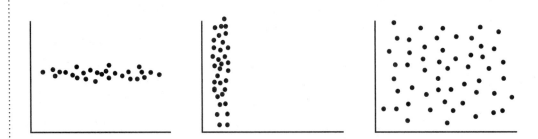

EXAMPLE 3

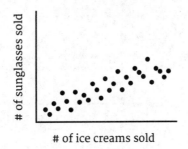

A stand on the beach sells, among other things, both ice cream and sunglasses. Each data point in the above graph represents the sales for one day during the summer. Which of the following best describes the relationship between the sales of ice cream and sunglasses?

A) A strong, negative association
B) A strong, positive association
C) A weak, positive association
D) No association

SOLUTION

When we look at the graph, we see that the data is tightly clustered, so the association is definitely **strong**. That points to A or B. Now... is it a positive or negative association?

As the sales of ice cream generally increase, so do the sales of sunglasses. This means they have a **positive** relationship. The answer choice that gets this right is choice B.

B

Practice Problems

Use your new skills to answer each question.

1

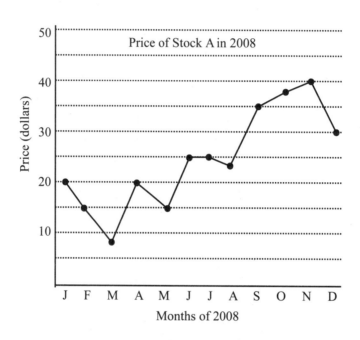

The price of a stock was recorded on the first day of every month of 2008. Based on the graph, which of the following gives a two month interval in which the price of the stock increased and then decreased?

A) February to April
B) June to August
C) September to November
D) October to December

2

Phoebe is a professional photographer who hiked to a waterfall in order to take some pictures for her next art show. The graph below shows the speed at which she hiked during her trip to and from the waterfall. During which interval did Phoebe stop to take pictures of the waterfall?

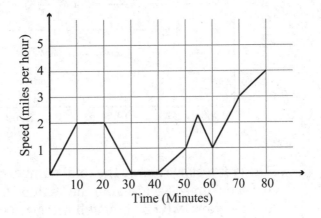

A) Between 10 and 20 minutes
B) Between 30 and 40 minutes
C) Between 50 and 60 minutes
D) Between 60 and 70 minutes

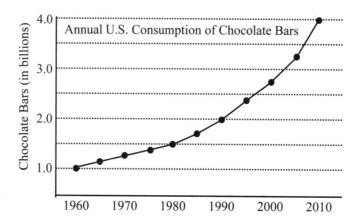

3

The graph above shows the total number of chocolate bars consumed each year in the United States. Based on the graph, which of the following best describes the relationship between the chocolate bar consumption growth from 1960 to 1980 and the growth from 1990 to 2010?

A) From 1960 to 1980, the chocolate bar consumption growth was linear, whereas from 1990 to 2010, the growth was exponential.

B) From 1960 to 1980, the chocolate bar consumption growth was exponential, whereas from 1990 to 2010, the growth was linear.

C) The chocolate bar consumption growth was exponential for both time periods.

D) The chocolate bar consumption growth was linear for both time periods.

4

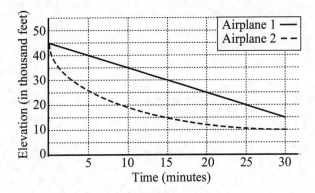

The elevation of two airplanes is shown in the graph above. Which of the following statements correctly compares the average rate at which the elevation of the two airplanes changed?

A) From 0 to 15 minutes, the rate of change in elevation of Airplane 1 is greater than that of Airplane 2, whereas from 20 to 30 minutes, the rate of change in elevation of Airplane 2 is greater than that of Airplane 1.

B) From 0 to 15 minutes, the rate of change in elevation of Airplane 1 is less than that of Airplane 2, whereas from 20 to 30 minutes, the rate of change in elevation of Airplane 2 is less than that of Airplane 1.

C) In every 5-minute interval, the magnitude of the rate of change in elevation of Airplane 1 is greater than that of Airplane 2.

D) In every 5-minute interval, the magnitude of the rate of change in elevation of Airplane 1 is less than that of Airplane 2.

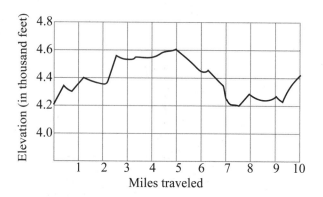

Kari went on a hiking trip, and the graph above shows Kari's elevation while hiking on the trail. Over which interval did Kari experience the largest change in elevation?

A)   From mile 1 to mile 3
B)   From mile 2 to mile 4
C)   From mile 5 to mile 7
D)   From mile 7 to mile 10

6

Which of the following graphs best shows a strong positive association beteen x and y ?

A)

B)

C)

D)

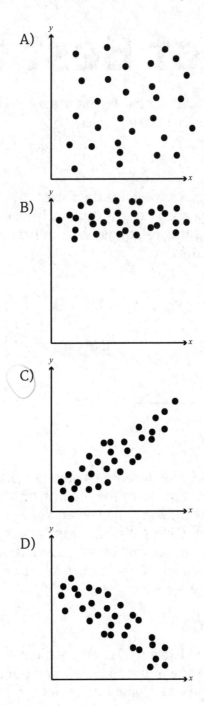

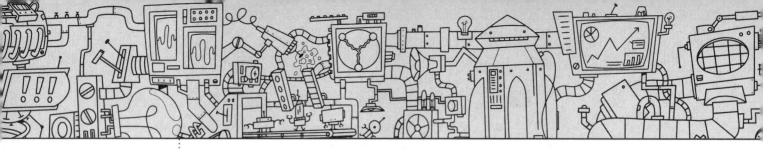

Line of Best Fit

In this chapter, we'll learn how we can use the equation of a line to describe the relationship between two variables.

At the end of the last chapter, we described the relationship between two variables by looking at some scatterplots. Notice that when you look at a scatterplot with a strong relationship, your brain automatically notices a line-like pattern in the data:

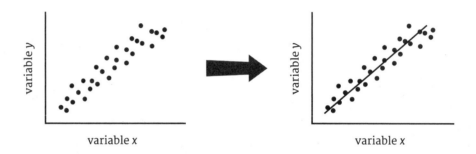

The data points **look** like they are clustered around a line. We call this invisible (but super important) line the **line of best fit** for the data. And like all lines, the line of best fit has an equation and a slope that we can use to find out interesting stuff! You won't ever need to *calculate* the line of best fit yourself, but you will be asked to use your knowledge of slope and the equation of a line to make **estimates** about the data.

Estimation Tool

A line of best fit is an extremely useful estimation tool. If we plug an *x* into the equation of the line of best fit, it will spit out a *y*-value that is **most likely** to correspond with that input. People use this statistical tool all the time. A business might use it to predict future sales based on past years' sales, or an airport might use it to predict how many travelers to expect during the summer.

The math behind all of this is simple equation-of-a-line stuff. As we've done before, we'll be working with $y = mx + b$, plugging in points, and focusing on slopes. Let's get some practice!

INTERACTIVE EXAMPLE

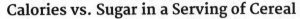

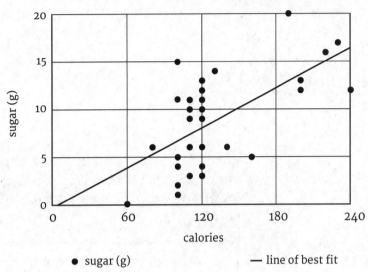

The above graph shows the number of calories and grams of sugar in a suggested serving of 30 different breakfast cereals. The line of best fit is also shown, and has the equation $y = 0.0697x - 0.335$.

Q1) According to the line of best fit, how much sugar would you expect a cereal with 180 calories per serving to have?

A) about 5 grams
B) about 8 grams
C) about 10 grams
D) about 12 grams

NOTE

Notice that even though we don't have a data point at 180 calories, we can **estimate** it using the line of best fit!

S1) This question asks us to use the line of best fit to estimate the amount of sugar per serving for a cereal with 180 calories per serving. Sugar is on the y-axis, so we want the y-value on the line of best fit at 180 calories. If we slide our finger up from 180 on the x-axis until we hit the line of best fit, we see that the line crosses somewhere between 10 and 15 on the y-axis. Only **choice D** falls in that range, so it must be our answer!

D

Q2) One cereal in the study had 0 grams of sugar per serving, as shown on the graph. For that cereal, about how much less sugar does it have than the line of best fit would predict?

A) 0
B) 2
C) 4
D) 6

S2) Step 1 is to find the data point that represents the cereal with 0 grams of sugar. Since sugar is on the *y*-axis, we are looking for a data point on the x-axis, where the *y*-coordinate is zero. That data point is at 60 calories:

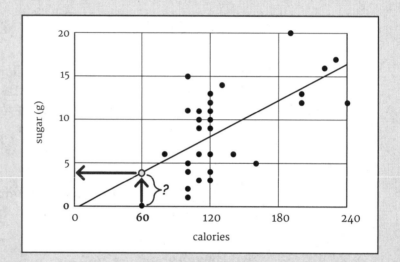

Next we need to know how much sugar the **line of best fit** predicts at **x = 60**. If we slide up to the line and check the *y*-value at that point, we see that it predicts about **4 grams** of sugar for 60 calories. To find how much less it has than was predicted, we need to subtract:

$$predicted - actual = 4 - 0 = \boxed{4}$$

Choice C is the best answer.

C

Plug in!

Remember, we can always find a point on a line if we're given the equation and a coordinate.

$0.0697x - .335 = y$
$0.0697(60) - .335 = 3.8$

Which is about 4!

Q3) Which of the following best explains how the number 0.0697 in the equation of the line of best fit relates to the scatterplot?

    A) Every cereal will have at least 0.0697 grams of sugar per serving.

    B) On average, we estimate that the amount of sugar per serving will increase by 0.0697 grams for every additional calorie per serving.

    C) A gram of sugar has 0.0697 calories.

    D) There are exactly 0.0697 grams of sugar per calorie of cereal.

S3) Let's compare the equation of the line of best fit to the standard equation of a line:

$$y = mx + b$$

$$y = 0.0697x - .335$$

This shows us that 0.0697 is the slope of the line of best fit. Slope is rise over run, or how much the *y*-axis changes for each change in the *x*-axis. In this case, that's the amount of **sugar per calorie**. Choices B and D get this idea right. However, line of best fit gives us *estimates*, NOT exact absolutes. So the answer must be choice B.

B

Use the previous graph to answer each question.

Question	Prediction
One serving of *Sweet Cuppin' Cakes* cereal has 15 grams of sugar. About how many calories does the line of best fit predict it will have?	200
If *Chunky Tree Bark* cereal contains 140 calories per serving, about how many grams of sugar does the line of best fit predict it will have?	9
If a single serving of *Chocolate Frosted Sugar Bombs* has 300 calories, how many grams of sugar does the line of best fit predict it to have?	21

Answer: Sweet Cuppin Cakes: ~220 calories
        Chunky Tree Bark: ~9.4g sugar
        Chocolate Frosted Sugar Bombs: ~20.6g sugar

Practice Problems

Use your new skills to answer each question.

1

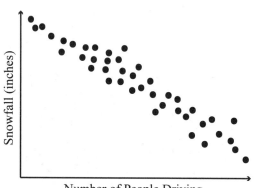

Number of People Driving

The graph above gives the number of people in Telluride, Colorado who drove each day it snowed in the city in relation to the number of inches of snowfall on that respective day. Which of the following correctly describes the correlation of the graph above?

A) Strong positive correlation
B) Strong negative correlation
C) Weak positive correlation
D) Weak negative correlation

2

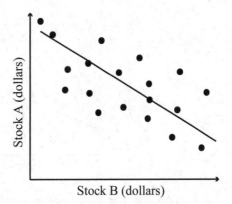

Nick has been tracking the prices, in dollars, of two stocks and recording their values in relation to one another in the graph above. If the price of Stock A drops, what will Nick's line of best fit predict Stock B will do?

A) Stock B will decrease in value.
B) Stock B will increase in value.
C) Stock B will remain at the same price.
D) A prediction cannot be determined.

3

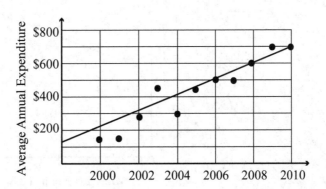

According to the line of best fit in the scatterplot above, which of the following best approximates the year in which the average annual expenditure on cellular phone services was estimated to be $300?

A) 2002
B) 2003
C) 2004
D) 2005

4

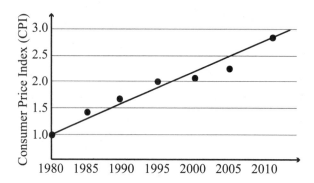

The Consumer Price Index (CPI) of the U.S. in the graph above is defined to be the ratio of the current average price of goods to the average price of goods in 1980. Which of the following conclusions is supported by the graph?

A) The initial CPI of 1980 was 1.
B) The initial CPI of 1980 was $1.
C) The CPI in 1981 was 100 percent greater than the CPI in 1980.
D) The CPI has grown by about 100% since 1980.

5

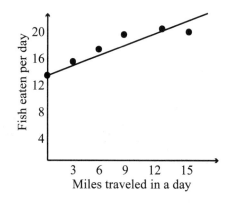

The scatterplot above gives the number of fish a grizzly bear eats in one day in relation to the number of miles the grizzly bear traveled that day. The line of best fit is also shown and has the equation $y = 0.5x + 13$. Using the line of best fit, what would be the best approximation for how many fish a bear would eat in one day if it traveled 22 miles that day?

A) 11 fish
B) 22 fish
C) 24 fish
D) 35 fish

6

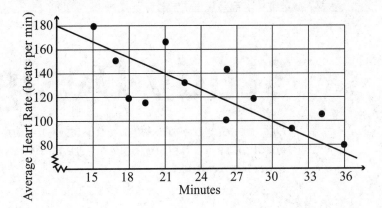

The runners of a 5K race all wore heart rate monitors. The data from each runner's heart rate monitor was then plotted against the number of minutes it took them to finish the 5K. The runner with an average heart rate of 80 beats per minute ran the 5K in how many more minutes than the time predicted by the line of best fit?

A) 1.5 minutes
B) 8.0 minutes
C) 10.0 minutes
D) 36.0 minutes

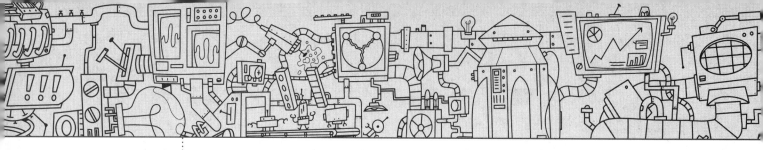

Study Design

Occasionally, the SAT will directly test your understanding of basic study design vocabulary, as well as how different factors affect the conclusions you can draw from data.

Study Vocabulary

Let's start with a review of some basic vocabulary. All studies begin with a basic question that the scientists are seeking to answer. For example, let's say we want to design a study to answer the question:

Question: Do 10th graders feel prepared for the SAT?

A **population** is the *entire* group we want to learn something about. Depending on what we're interested in, this could be "all girls in third period calculus" or "all teenagers in the United States." In our case, the population would be "all 10th graders."

A **sample** is a smaller piece of the larger population. The difference between a good sample and a bad sample rests on whether the sample is *representative* of the population. Scientists have to be very careful about how they choose their sample – if they mess this part up, then they can't really claim that their findings answer the question at hand!

Why sample?

Most of the time, it isn't practical (or possible) to survey every single member of a population (things cost money).

Luckily, we don't need to! If we are smart about it, we can study a small piece of that bigger population and still answer our question. That small piece is called a **sample**.

population

sample

What is a bad sample?

A bad sample is one that is *not* representative of the larger population. In our study, if we only surveyed 10th graders who have a copy of *Applerouth's Guide to the SAT*, then we would have picked a *bad* (not representative) sample. Can you see why?

Because... those students probably feel **more** prepared than students who do NOT have a study guide. That would cause us to overestimate how prepared ALL 10th graders feel for the SAT.

What is a good sample?

A good sample is one that *is* representative of the larger population. When it comes down to it, it's really all about **proportions**. It's okay if SOME proportion of the students we survey own a copy of *Applerouth's Guide to the SAT,* so long as it's the same proportion as in the population of all 10th graders.

If a sample is chosen **randomly** from the entire population, we usually assume it is representative. That's because, when a sample is chosen from the population at random, every individual has an equal chance of being chosen. Let's look at a couple of examples of good and bad sampling. For each example, ask yourself "Why might the bad sample affect our conclusion?"

Proportions

If 5% of all 10th graders own this book, then 5% of our sample should too. Similarly, if only 15% of 10th graders in the country go to private school, then we should make sure only 15% of our sample goes to private school.

Question: Do students at Emory University like coffee?

Population: all students at Emory University
Good Sample: random selection of all Emory students
Bad sample: all students in an 8:00 am History class.

Question: Are female students at your high school interested in adding a competitive math team?

Population: female students at your high school
Good Sample: random selection of girls in your high school
Bad sample: random selection of all U.S. high school students

Study Types

There are three main types of studies that the SAT looks at. In an **observational study**, scientists simply observe how a sample acts in its natural environment, recording what they see. In a **sample survey**, scientists recruit a sample, ask questions, and record the responses. In a **controlled experiment**, scientists carefully create a controlled environment, recruit a sample, divide it into two groups, then compare the outcomes for the two groups.

The benefit of controlled experiments over other types of studies is they allow scientists to show a *causal relationship* between variables. If you're just observing that happier people go on more walks, for example, you can't say whether being happy causes people to walk more, or vice-versa, or whether some third factor is causing both!

INTERACTIVE EXAMPLE

A team of magi-zoologists suspects that unicorns with longer horns produce rainbows with a wider spectrum of colors. To study this, the zoologists take a random sample of all captive unicorns. For each unicorn, they measure the length of its horn and take the average of the "spectrum width" of five rainbows produced by that unicorn. When they plot horn length vs. average rainbow spectrum width, they find a clear, positive association.

Q1) What type of study is this?

    A) Controlled experiment
    B) Observational study
    C) Sample survey
    D) Stratified sample

S1) The magi-zoologists are just taking measurements – not doing an experiment. So choice A is out. And they aren't asking the unicorns questions, so C is out. And "stratified sample" is a term you don't need to know that we just threw in there to sound smart. So this is an **observational study**!

B

Q2) What is the largest population of which the study's sample is representative?

    A) Unicorns with longer than average horns
    B) Only the unicorns in the sample
    C) All captive unicorns
    D) All unicorns

S2) We were told that they took a **random sample of all captive unicorns**. This means it is reasonable to assume that the sample is representative of **all captive unicorns (Choice C)**.

Since they selected randomly, we don't have to restrict our conclusions to just the several we sampled (Choice B). But... we can't say anything about wild unicorns (Choice D) from this study, because it's possible or likely that there is something fundamentally different about being in a zoo and being out in the wild.

    C

Q3) Does this study provide evidence that longer horns <u>cause</u> unicorns to make larger spectrum rainbows?

    A) Yes, it showed a positive association, so there is evidence that longer horns cause wider rainbows.
    B) Yes, but only for captive unicorns.
    C) No, the data don't show any relationship between horn length and rainbow spectrum.
    D) No, the data show a positive association but don't provide evidence for a causal relationship.

S3) The study is an observational study, so it can't say anything about a causal relationship. The data do show a positive association (also known as a "correlation"), but the scientists didn't control for any other variables that might be causing both longer horns and wider rainbow spectra.

    D

INTERACTIVE EXAMPLE 2

While collecting data for the first study, one of the zoo keepers the magi-zoologists talked to claimed that adding indigo blaze flowers to their unicorns' diets increases the spectrum range of their rainbows. The team of magi-zoologists decide to test this claim.

Q1) Which of the following studies would best allow the team to determine whether eating indigo blaze flowers increases the rainbow spectrum width of unicorns?

    A) Send a survey to the keepers of all of the unicorns from the first study asking whether they include indigo blaze flowers in their unicorn feed and then analyze it with the original data on spectrum width.

    B) Ask the keepers of all of the unicorns from the first study to add a specified quantity of indigo blaze flowers to their current feed and then test the unicorn rainbow spectrum widths again after a certain amount of time on the new diet.

    C) Randomly select a sample of unicorns and give them all the same diet and living conditions for a time and then measure the spectrum ranges of their rainbows. Then randomly divide the sample into two groups. Keep the control group on the same feed. Add a specified amount of indigo blaze flowers to the feed for the other group. Measure the spectrum ranges for both groups after a specified amount of time.

    D) Take the unicorns with the smallest spectrum and add indigo blaze flowers to their diet to see if they can get it to increase.

S1) At first, each of these choices might sound pretty reasonable. But, since we want to be able to show **causation** (eating indigo blaze flowers causes a wider spectrum range) we want a **controlled experiment**. This means we need to take a random sample and then divide it randomly into a *control group* that does not get the flowers and a *treatment group* that does. Choice C makes this careful, controlled comparison, so it's our best answer.

                                               C

Q2) The team follows the controlled experiment outlined in the answer to the previous problem. At the end of the experiment they find that the unicorns that were given the indigo blaze flowers, on average, had a significant increase in the spectrum range of their rainbows. Which of the following is an appropriate conclusion for the scientists to draw?

A) Eating indigo blaze flowers always increases the rainbow spectrum range for unicorns.

B) If a unicorn's diet does not currently include indigo blaze flowers, adding the flowers to its diet is likely to increase their rainbow spectrum range.

C) The more indigo blaze flowers a unicorn eats the wider its rainbow spectrum range will be.

D) Adding indigo blaze flowers to a unicorn's feed is the best way to increase its rainbow spectrum range.

TIP

Anytime a study design answer choice on the test uses the word **always**, it's the wrong choice.

When in doubt, be conservative about drawing conclusions from studies!

S2) Let's look at each answer choice:

A) This answer choice says something **always** happens. Statistics doesn't work in absolutes, so this can't be right.

B) This looks good! It acknowledges that the experiment was testing what happens when you add indigo blaze flowers to a diet that doesn't have any and only says that it is **likely** to increase.

C) This experiment only tested two levels - no flowers or one specific amount. It can't say anything about small amounts vs larger amounts of flowers.

D) There is no discussion of *other* methods of increasing the spectrum range, so there's no evidence that this is the *best* option.

B

Confidence Intervals & Margin of Error

The SAT, very rarely, tests the concepts of confidence intervals and margin of error. **Confidence interval** is pretty much what it sounds like: it just tells you how confident the study is in its conclusion. If the study has a 95% confidence interval, it means there is a 95% chance its conclusions are accurate. That's all you need to know for the SAT!

Margin of error lets you know how "off" the study's estimates might be. You see this all the time in polls of a politician's popularity. If a presidential candidate has a 60% approval rating with a margin of error of 2%, then it means the actual approval rating is likely somewhere between 58% and 62%. Let's see how these topics come up.

INTERACTIVE EXAMPLE 3

When applying for funding, the magi-zoologists want to discuss the public interest in their research. They take a random sample of 500 people in their nation to contact with a survey. They fail to reach 17 of the people but receive responses from the other 483. One of the questions on their survey asks "In your opinion, how important is it that we know how to enable unicorns to make the widest possible rainbows?" Options include "Not important," "Somewhat important," "Very important," and "No opinion."

When the magi-zoologists analyze the data, they find that 73% of all respondents either said "Somewhat important" or "Very important." Along with this statistic, they report a margin of error of 2.5% at the 95% confidence level.

Q3) Which of the following is most likely to be the real percentage of the population who would answer "somewhat" or "very" important?

A) 74%
B) 84%
C) 93%
D) 95%

S3) The second paragraph tells us that 73% of respondents answered "somewhat" or "very" important. Since the margin of error is 2.5%, then we can find the range for the "real" percentage by adding and subtracting 2.5 from 73. So we need an answer between 70.5% and 75.5%. The only choice that falls in that range is choice A.

A

Q4) For which of the following regions is it reasonable to assume that the survey is a representative sample?

I. The city in which the scientists live
II. The nation in which the scientists conducted the study
III. Countries neighboring the nation in which the scientists conducted the study

A) II only
B) I and II only
C) II and III only
D) None

S4) Any time you get a problem that asks you to determine which of three statements is valid, you need to go through each statement and determine whether it is correct.

Statement I: The random sample was taken from the nation as a whole. It's very possible that different cities within the country have different opinions about unicorns! Maybe the city where the scientists live is particularly Pro-Unicorn! We can't assume data for the whole country applies to one city, so we can eliminate statement I.

Statement II: The survey was given to a random sample chosen from the whole nation, so it is indeed reasonable to assume that it is a representative sample! This one's good.

Statement III: The passage indicates that only the one nation was included in the sample. Neighboring countries are a separate population, so we can't use this sample to say anything about them.

Since only statement II checks out, our answer is A.   **A**

Practice Problems

Use your new skills to answer each question.

1

In order to determine if Migraine Medication A is more effective than Migraine Medication B, a research study was conducted. From a large population of people who have recurring migraines, 600 participants were selected at random. 200 of those participating were given a placebo, 200 of those participating were given Migraine Medication A, and the last 200 participants were given Migraine Medication B. The resulting data show that participants who received Medication A experienced more relief than Medication B, and both Medications A and B worked substantially better than the placebo. Based on the results of the study, which is the following is an appropriate conclusion?

A) Migraine Medication A is the most effective migraine medication on the market.
B) People with acute migraines need only take the placebo.
C) Migraine Medication A will work for anyone who takes it.
D) Migraine Medication A is likely to give more migraine relief than Migraine Medication B.

2

Samuel owns a chain of restaurants called Sam's Salads that offer a strictly vegetarian cuisine. Samuel wants to open up a Sam's Salads in a new city, so he decides to survey 250 people who entered a local burger place in the city. Of the 250 people surveyed, 7 were vegetarians, 8 did not answer the survey, and the rest were not vegetarians. Which of the following makes it least likely that a reliable conclusion can be drawn about the percentage of vegetarians in the city?

A) The number of people who refused to respond
B) Where the survey was conducted
C) The sample size
D) The population size

3

A mad scientist is doing quality control on the automated production of his robot army. He inspects a random sample and determines that 87% of the robots are error free with a margin of error of 4% at the 95% confidence level. Which of the following is most likely to be the true percentage of robots that are error free?

A) 4%
B) 85%
C) 92%
D) 99%

4

Teresa wants to gauge interest among the senior class in having a class t-shirt, but it isn't practical for her to poll all of the seniors. Which of the following sampling methods would be best?

A) Hand out a survey in her math class
B) Set up a table in the cafeteria where students can choose to stop and fill out a survey
C) Have the counselor give her a random list of seniors to contact
D) Ask everyone on the bus she rides home

5

Cuifu is a biologist studying the panda population of China. His team has been monitoring and tagging the pandas in the Minshan Mountains in Sichuan. When he tells his family about his work, his aunt wants to know how many pandas there are in all of China. She takes the population density he has found and multiplies it by the land area of China. Will this method accurately predict the total panda population?

A) Yes, because you can use a sample to estimate the population.
B) Yes, because Cuifu's team has been studying the entire population in the Minshan Mountains.
C) No, because the sample was not taken randomly.
D) No, because we can't assume that the population in the Minshan Mountains is representative of the population across all of China.

UNIT | Geometry & Trigonometry

Chapters

Key Skills

The redesigned SAT puts much less emphasis on geometry & trigonometry. There are only a few points to be earned from these questions, though they may pull from a wide range of different topics. In this unit, we review the basic geometry & trigonometry rules that may show up.

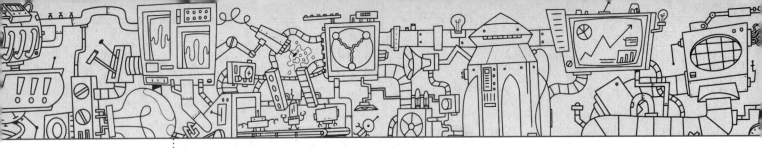

Geometry

The number of points you can earn from Geometry questions is low compared to the amount you need to know to answer any question that might come up. If you're comfortable with Geometry already, use this chapter as a refresher. If not, don't fret about learning every single rule!

The SAT math tests rarely have more than 2 or 3 Geometry questions. However, they can pull from a wide range of different topics. In this chapter, we'll do a quick review of the concepts that might show up and look at a few examples of how they are tested. You should not expect to see everything in this chapter on each test.

Hey, Thanks for the Box!

The first thing to know is that the information box they give you at the start of the math sections is *all* geometry. It doesn't have **everything** you could possibly need, but it if you are stuck - especially on a problem involving **area or volume** - remember to check back for a hint!

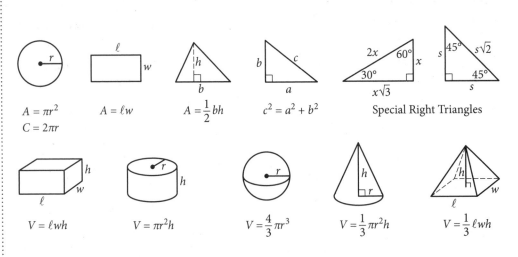

If you have this information memorized, that's great! But if you don't, you shouldn't spend time trying to shove it in your brain – after all, you'll have this on the test, and there are only a few geometry questions anyways.

TIP

If you are going to memorize *anything* in this box, we'd recommend focusing on the **special right triangles**. Often, the trick is remembering to even **look** for them in the first place.

If you're asked for an area or volume and can't remember the formula, you can simply check the box. But if you don't know to look for special right triangles, you might miss them.

Angles

First, angles can be measured in either **radians** or **degrees**.

$$180° = \pi \text{ radians}$$

Angles in a **triangle** add up to **180°**. As do angles in a **straight line**.

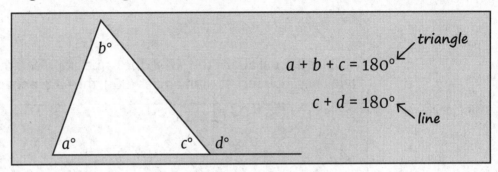

Angles in a **triangle** add up to **180°**. As do angles in a **straight line**.

This is true for ANY straight line, no matter how many angles comprise it.

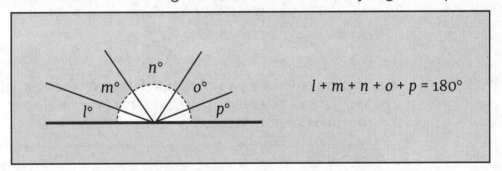

Angles in a **quadrilateral** (any 4 sided shape) add up to **360°**.

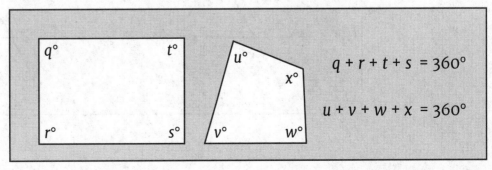

If two lines intersect, we call the angles that are opposite each other **vertical** angles. Vertical angles always have the **same angle measure**.

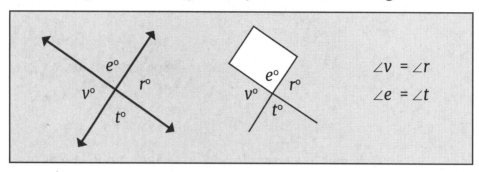

TIP

On a graph, the slopes of a line are **negative reciprocals**. For example:

$y = 3x + 4$

$y = -\dfrac{1}{3}x + 7$

The slopes of parallel lines are **identical**. For example:

$y = 2x + 13$

$y = 2x - 89$

Two lines are **parallel** if they have the same slope and thus never intersect. If two lines intersect at right angles (90°), they are **perpendicular**.

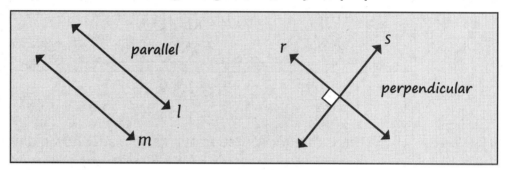

If a **line crosses a pair of parallel lines**, it creates a set of matching angles. Four angles will have the same BIG measure and four will have the same small measure.

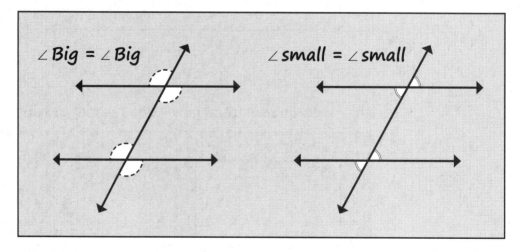

EXAMPLE 1

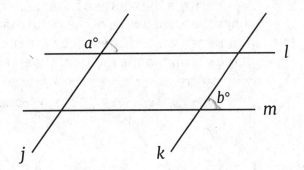

In the figure above, lines j and k are parallel, and lines l and m are parallel. If $a = 12k - 1$ and $b = 13k + 31$, then what is the value of k ?

A) 3.6
B) 6.0
C) 8.4
D) 9.0

$12k - 1 + 13k + 31 = 180$
$25k + 30 = 180$
$-30 \quad -30$
$k = 6.0$

SOLUTION

The first rule to help us out is:

① *a line crossing **parallel** lines forms 2 sets of equal angles*

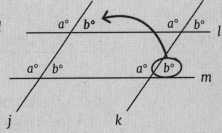

$\angle$ **Big** = $\angle$ **Big**
$\angle$ **small** = $\angle$ **small**

And since there are **180° in a line**, we know that **$a + b = 180$**. If we substitute in what we're told in the prompt, we can solve for k:

② *substitute*

$$a + b = 180$$
$$(12k - 1) + (13k + 31) = 180$$
$$25k + 30 = 180$$
$$25k = 150$$
$$\boxed{k = 6}$$

B

651

Circles

Any line from the center of a circle to its edge is a **radius**. Any line connecting two points of the circle that goes through the center is a **diameter**. Tangent lines touch the circle at only one point and are perpendicular to the radius at that point.

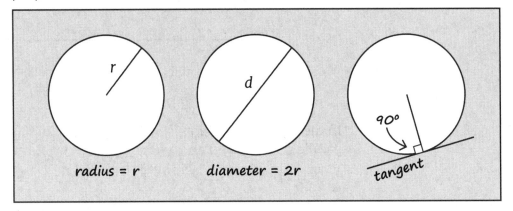

The **circumference** of a circle is equal to $2\pi r$. The **area** is equal to πr^2.

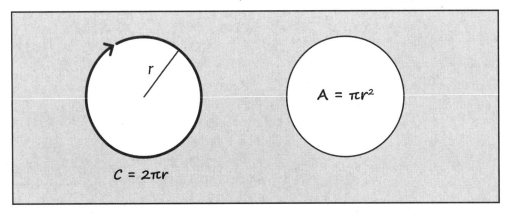

If C is the center of the circle and lines AE and BE are tangent to the circle at A and B respectively, then the measure of $\angle ACB$ is twice the measure of $\angle ADB$ and the sum of the measures of $\angle ACB$ and $\angle AEB$ is 180°.

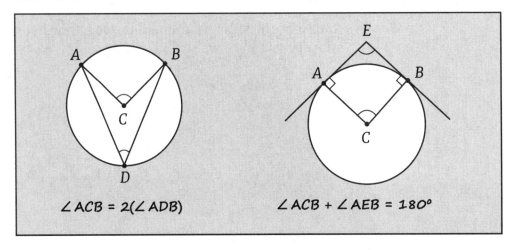

Area, Perimeter, Volume

Whenever you are given a complex shape, you can **break it up** into triangles and quadrilaterals to find its area, perimeter, or angles.

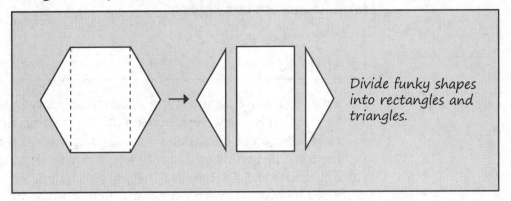

Divide funky shapes into rectangles and triangles.

Equilateral triangles have **three equal sides** and three 60 degree angles. **Isosceles** triangles have two equal sides and the angles opposite those sides are also equal.

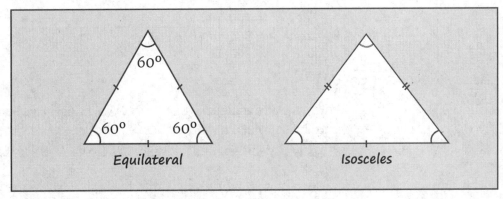

Equilateral   Isosceles

If you have a **right triangle** you can use the **pythagorean theorem**:

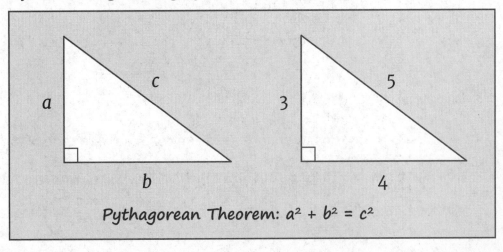

Pythagorean Theorem: $a^2 + b^2 = c^2$

TIP

There are very few integer triples small enough to come up in a right triangle. The common ratios are:

$3 : 4 : 5$
$5 : 12 : 13$

Look for any multiple of these to quickly identify right triangle lengths (e.g., **6:8:10** or **10:24:26**).

Volume

Often, the SAT will ask you to work with multiple area or volume formulas at once. Let's look at an example where remembering to **check the formula box** can be a big help.

EXAMPLE 2

Larry is at an ice cream shop and debating between two options. The first option is to get the ice cream in a cylindrical cup with a diameter of 6 inches and a height of 4 inches, completely filled and leveled off at the top. The second option is a completely filled cone with a diameter of 4 inches and a height of 6 inches, plus half of a scoop on top shaped like a hemisphere with diameter 4 inches. How many more cubic inches of ice cream would he get with the cup than with the cone?

A) $1\frac{1}{3}\pi$

B) $17\frac{1}{3}\pi$

C) $22\frac{2}{3}\pi$

D) 24π

SOLUTION

There's quite a bit going on here. We'll need to use three volume equations to answer this question, so let's check the box, copy down the formulas, and plug in the given r and h for each shape:

Cup ($r = 3$, $h = 4$)	Cone ($r = 2$, $h = 6$)	Top ($r = 2$)
$V_{cup} = \pi r^2 h$	$V_{cone} = \frac{1}{3}\pi r^2 h$	$V_{top} = \frac{1}{2}(\frac{4}{3})\pi r^3$
$V_{cup} = \pi(3)^2(4)$	$V_{cone} = \frac{1}{3}\pi(2)^2(6)$	$V_{top} = \frac{1}{2}(\frac{4}{3})\pi(2)^3$
$V_{cup} = 36\pi$	$V_{cone} = \frac{1}{3}\pi(24)$	$V_{top} = \frac{16}{3}\pi$
	$V_{cone} = 8\pi$	

So our options are a cup of 36π in^3 or a cone of $(8\pi + \frac{16}{3}\pi) = 13\frac{1}{3}\pi$.

To figure out how much more a cup is, we can subtract:

$$36\pi - 13\frac{1}{3}\pi = 22\frac{2}{3}\pi$$

C

Geometry and Proportions

The SAT often focuses on proportional ratios in circles and triangles.

$$\frac{\text{Piece}}{\text{Whole}} = \frac{\text{Angle measure}}{360°} = \frac{\text{Arc length}}{\text{Circumference}} = \frac{\text{Wedge area}}{\text{Circle area}}$$

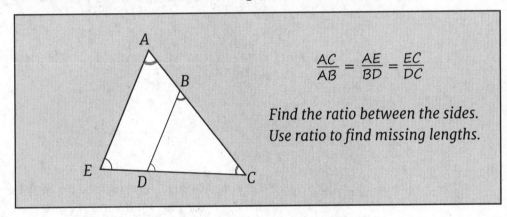

If two triangles have **equal angle measurements**, the triangles are **similar**. That means their sides lengths follow the same ratio.

$$\frac{AC}{AB} = \frac{AE}{BD} = \frac{EC}{DC}$$

Find the ratio between the sides. Use ratio to find missing lengths.

EXAMPLE 3

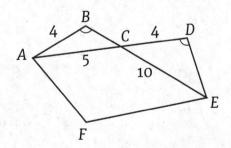

In the figure above, the measure of $\angle ABC$ is equal to the measure of $\angle CDE$. Segments $\overline{BE}$, $\overline{FE}$, and $\overline{AF}$ all have the same length. Segments $\overline{AB}$ and $\overline{CD}$ each have length 4 and segments $\overline{AC}$ and $\overline{CE}$ have lengths 5 and 10, respectively. What is the perimeter of polygon $ABCDEF$?

SOLUTION

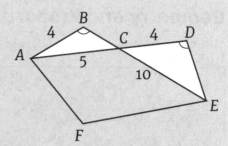

Notice that, since ∠ACB and ∠ACB are **vertical** angles, their measures are equal. This means that triangles △ABC and △CDE have **2 angles in common**, which makes them **similar triangles**.

If they are similar triangles, then their corresponding sides are proportional. We can find the fixed ratio of the triangles by comparing corresponding sides:

$$\frac{\triangle ABC}{\triangle CDE} = \frac{AC}{CD} = \frac{AB}{ED} = \frac{BC}{DC}$$

Let's plug in the lengths we know and use the proportions to help us find missing sides:

$$\frac{\triangle ABC}{\triangle CDE} = \frac{5}{10} = \frac{4}{ED} = \frac{BC}{4}$$

It looks like the sides of △CDE are **twice the length** of corresponding sides of △ABC. That must mean that $\overline{ED} = 8$ and $\overline{BC} = 2$. Let's draw those into our figure:

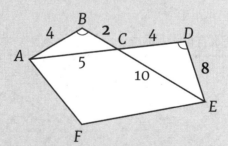

To find the full perimeter of ABCDEF, we just need to find side lengths for $\overline{AF}$ and $\overline{FE}$. So what do we know about those sides? They are **equal** to side $\overline{BE}$. Since we now know that $\overline{BE} = 12$, we know the $\overline{AF} = 12$ and $\overline{FE} = 12$. If we add all of the sides on the perimeter, we get:

$$perimeter = AB + BC + CD + DE + EF + AF$$

$$perimeter = 4 + 2 + 4 + 8 + 12 + 12 = \boxed{42}$$

Practice Problems

Use your new skills to answer each question.

1

A slushy stand uses dome-shaped lids that resemble a hemisphere, and the volume of a lid is $\frac{16}{3}\pi$ cubic inches. What is the diameter of the cups used for these lids?

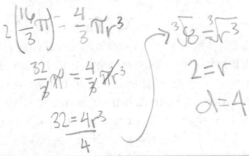

2

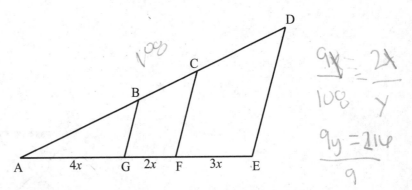

In the figure above, lines $\overline{BG}$, $\overline{FC}$, and $\overline{DE}$ are all parallel. If the length of $\overline{AD}$ is 108 inches, what is the length, in inches, of $\overline{BC}$?

A) 12
B) 24
C) 36
D) 48

3

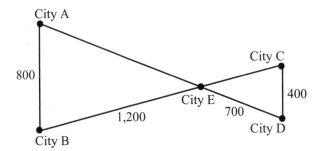

Carol took a 700-mile plane trip from City D to City E to visit Jessica, who flew 1,200 miles from City B to City E. Carol and Jessica then parted ways and traveled to Cities A and C, respectively. If the distance between City C and City D is 400 miles and the distance between City A and City B is 800 miles, how long, in miles, will Carol's plane trip be from City E to City A? (Note: $\angle ABE$ is equal to $\angle ECD$ and City E is on both line $\overline{AD}$ and line $\overline{BC}$)

4

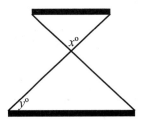

The drawing of an hourglass above can be shown as two similar isosceles triangles. What is the value of x in terms of y?

A) $x = y$

B) $x = 180 - y$

C) $x = 180 - 2y$

D) $x = \dfrac{180 - y}{2}$

5

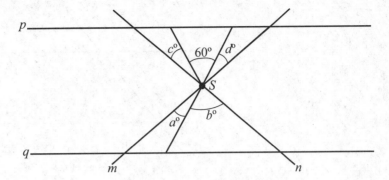

(figure not drawn to scale)

In the figure above, lines *m* and *n* intersect at point *S*, and lines *p* and *q* are parallel. If $c + d = 2a$ and $b = 80$, what is the sum of *a*, *b*, *c*, and *d* ?

A) 120
B) 140
C) 180
D) 200

6

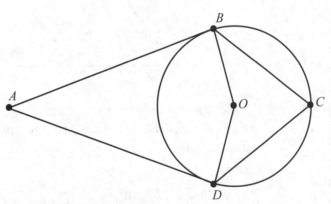

In the figure above, point *O* is the center of the circle, and line segments $\overline{AB}$ and $\overline{AD}$ are tangent to the circle at points *D* and *B* respectively. If the area of the sector formed by arc *BOD* is $\frac{5}{12}$ the area of the circle, what is the value of the measure of $\angle BAD$ added to the measure of $\angle BCD$?

A) 30°
B) 75°
C) 105°
D) 180°

7

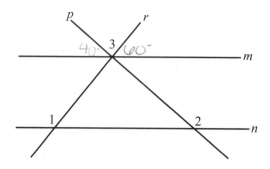

In the figure above, lines *m* and *n* are parallel. If ∠1 is 120° and ∠2 is 140°, what is the measure of ∠3 ?

A) 20°
B) 40°
C) 60°
D) 80°

8

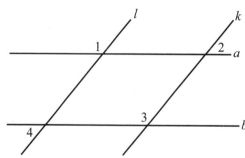

In the figure above, lines *a* and *b* are parallel, and lines *l* and *k* are parallel. What are two pairs of angles that each add up to 180° ?

A) ∠2 and ∠4, ∠1 and ∠3
B) ∠2 and ∠1, ∠4 and ∠3
C) ∠1 and ∠2, ∠4 and ∠2
D) Cannot be determined.

9

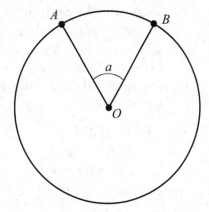

In the figure above, the circle has an area between 120 and 124 square inches, and the area of the sector formed by ∠AOB has an area between 20 and 21 square inches. What is one possible integer value of *a* ?

10

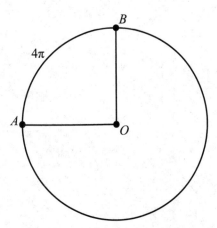

In the circle above, ∠AOB is a right angle and the length of minor arc AB is 4π inches. What is the area of the circle, in square inches?

A) 16
B) 16π
C) 64π
D) 128π

A scientist needs to fill a graduated cylinder with a diameter of 4 centimeters and a height of 6 centimeters halfway with an unknown liquid that she has stored in 6 identical test tubes. If she has to use every test tube in order to fill the graduated cylinder halfway, how many milliliters of the liquid are in each test tube? (1 milliliter is equal to 1 cubic centimeter.)

A)   2 milliliters
B) 2π milliliters
C) 4π milliliters
D) 12π milliliters

Trigonometry

Let's review the trigonometry concepts that might show up on the test.

SohCahToa

There are three key functions from trig that you need to know: sine, cosine, and tangent. On the SAT, you'll see them labelled as **sinθ**, **cosθ**, and **tanθ**, where θ is the angle of a right triangle. These functions tell us how an *angle* of a right triangle relates to the *sides* of the right triangle. To help us review what we mean by sin, cos, and tan, let's first draw and label a right triangle, focusing on one angle:

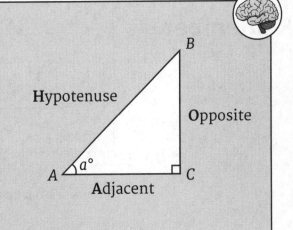

① *Draw a right triangle*

② *Focus on angle A*

③ *Label the hypotenuse*

④ *Label legs "adjacent" to A and "opposite" from A*

Important

If we were focusing on angle B instead of angle A, the sides would have different labels!

Side AC would be "opposite" angle B, and side BC would be "adjacent." The hypotenuse is always the hypotenuse.

Sine, cosine, and tangent are functions, complete with inputs and outputs. They take an **angle** of a triangle (such as angle *A* above) as an input and spit out a **fraction** which is a ratio of the different sides:

$$\text{Sin } A = \frac{Opposite}{Hypotenuse} \qquad \text{Cos } A = \frac{Adjacent}{Hypotenuse} \qquad \text{Tan } A = \frac{Opposite}{Adjacent}$$

To answer basic trig questions, you'll need to memorize these ratios. Luckily, we have "SohCahToa" to make this a simpler task. "**Soh**" reminds you that <u>S</u>ine is <u>O</u>pposite over <u>H</u>ypotenuse. "**Cah**" reminds you that <u>C</u>osine is <u>A</u>djacent over <u>H</u>ypotenuse. And "Toa", well, you get the picture!

Use SohCahToa to complete the trig function identities below.

Triangle	SohCahToa
B, 5, 4, $a°$, A, 3, C	1. $\text{Sin } A = \dfrac{\text{Opposite}}{\text{Hypotenuse}} = \dfrac{4}{5}$ 2. $\text{Cos } A = \dfrac{\text{Adjacent}}{\text{Hypotenuse}} = \underline{\quad}$ 3. $\text{Tan } A = \dfrac{\text{Opposite}}{\text{Adjacent}} = \underline{\quad}$

Now do the same thing, but **focus on angle B.**

Remember

When we change the angle we're focusing on, the side labels change too!

Triangle	SohCahToa
B, $b°$, 15, 12, A, 9, C	4. $\text{Sin } B = \dfrac{\text{Opposite}}{\text{Hypotenuse}} = \dfrac{9}{15}$ 5. $\text{Cos } B = \dfrac{\text{Adjacent}}{\text{Hypotenuse}} = \underline{\quad}$ 6. $\text{Tan } B = \dfrac{\text{Opposite}}{\text{Adjacent}} = \underline{\quad}$

Now work backwards! Use SohCahToa to **label the sides of the triangle**.

Familiar

Do these side ratios look familiar? This is one of the "special" right triangles.

Triangle	SohCahToa
B, $b°$, A, C	$\text{Sin } B = \dfrac{\text{Opposite}}{\text{Hypotenuse}} = \dfrac{13}{26}$ $\text{Cos } B = \dfrac{\text{Adjacent}}{\text{Hypotenuse}} = \dfrac{13\sqrt{3}}{26}$ $\text{Tan } B = \dfrac{\text{Opposite}}{\text{Adjacent}} = \dfrac{13}{13\sqrt{3}}$

Answers: **1)** 4/5   **2)** 3/5   **3)** 4/3   **4)** 9/15   **5)** 12/15   **6)** 9/12

Side $\overline{AB}$ = 26   Side $\overline{BC}$ = 13$\sqrt{3}$ Side $\overline{AC}$ = 13

Even More Drills!

There's no better way to solidify SohCahToa in ya' brain than to use it over and over. Complete the drill below to check your understanding.

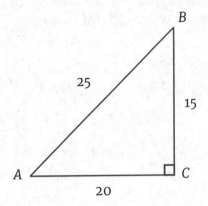

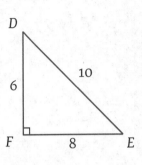

Use SohCahToa and the above triangles to complete the table.

SohCahToa	
1. $\sin(B) =$	7. $\tan(A) =$
2. $\sin(E) =$	8. $\tan(D) =$
3. $\cos(A) =$	9. $\sin(A) =$
4. $\cos(D) =$	10. $\sin(D) =$
5. $\tan(B) =$	11. $\cos(B) =$
6. $\tan(E) =$	12. $\cos(E) =$

Notice

Many of the trig ratios for triangles *ABC* and *DEF* simplify to the same fraction. Why is that?

It's because these triangles are **similar.** Though their side lengths are different, their proportions are the same.

Bonus Notice: they are both special 3-4-5 right triangles!

Answers: **1)** 20/25   **2)** 6/10   **3)** 20/25   **4)** 6/10   **5)** 20/15   **6)** 6/8
7) 15/20   **8)** 8/6   **9)** 15/25   **10)** 8/10   **11)** 15/25   **12)** 8/10

One More

Similarly, it can be helpful to remember this handy identity:

$$\sin^2(x) + \cos^2(x) = 1$$

MEMORIZE: Special Trig Identity

There is a special identity that shows up pretty regularly on the SAT, so it's worth memorizing. You don't really need to know WHY it's true, but we'll cover that in a second to help you remember it. Here is essentially the same idea written in three different ways:

$$\sin(\theta) = \cos(90 - \theta)$$
$$\cos(\alpha) = \sin(90 - \alpha)$$

$$\text{if } \sin(x) = \cos(y), \text{ then } x + y = 90$$

Just memorize that. Stare at it. *Become* it. Burn it into your brain.... Done?

Okay, now let's chat about why this is a thing. Notice that, because what's "adjacent" and what's "opposite" switch depending on which angle you focus on, **sin (A)** is equal to **cos (B)**:

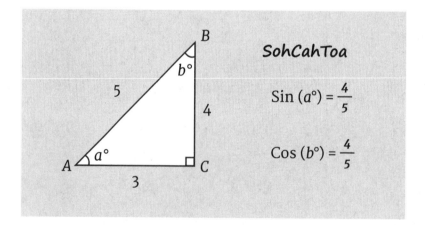

SohCahToa

$$\text{Sin}(a°) = \frac{4}{5}$$

$$\text{Cos}(b°) = \frac{4}{5}$$

Now, if all angles add up to 180°, and one angle is 90°, then the other two *must* add up to 90°. That means we could write angles A and B in a different way, solving the mystery behind that bulky thing we memorized:

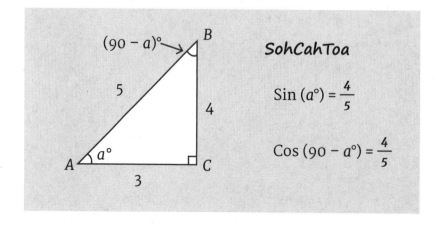

SohCahToa

$$\text{Sin}(a°) = \frac{4}{5}$$

$$\text{Cos}(90 - a°) = \frac{4}{5}$$

EXAMPLE 1

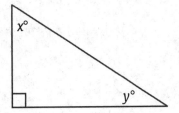

In the triangle above, sine of $x°$ = 0.6. What is cosine of $x°$?

A) 0.36
B) 0.6
C) 0.8
D) 1.66

SOLUTION

At first this problem might seem tough, but we shouldn't worry about that just yet! We see "sine" and "cosine," so we should immediately write SohCahToa:

(1) *write SohCahToa!*   **SohCahToa**

Step one done! Now, the only weirdness is that the problem uses decimals when we're used to dealing in fractions. But that's no problem, we can change 0.6 to a fraction:

(2) *write 0.6 as a fraction* $\sin(x) = 0.6 = \frac{6}{10}$

Now we're getting somewhere. We know that sine is O/H. So we can use this information to label our triangle.

(3) *label triangle*

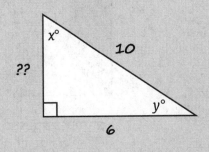

continue →

Now to find cos(x), we just need that third side. Luckily, we can use the **pythagorean theorem** to find that third side.

④ *use pythag's theorem*

$$A^2 + B^2 = C^2$$

$$6^2 + B^2 = 10^2$$

$$36 + B^2 = 100$$

$$B^2 = 64$$

$$B = 8$$

Bingo! Using the information given to us, SohCahToa, and pythagorean's theorem, we know the third side length is 8. Now to find cos(x), we just apply SohCahToa again:

⑤ *find cos(x) with "Cah"*

$$\cos(x) = \frac{8}{10} = \boxed{0.8}$$

C

Radians

Instead of degrees, we can also measure angles in **radians**. The measure of an angle in radians is the *length of the arc* it would span if it were at the center of a circle with radius 1 (often called the "unit circle"):

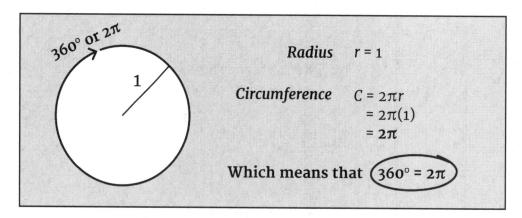

Radius $r = 1$

Circumference $C = 2\pi r$
$= 2\pi(1)$
$= 2\pi$

Which means that $360° = 2\pi$

For most questions involving radians, just remembering that **360° = 2π** will help you convert degrees to radians and vice versa.

Unit Circle

You may remember learning a good bit about the unit circle in school. It looks something like this:

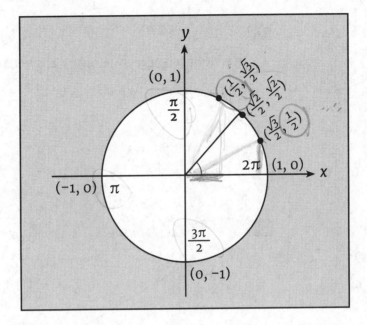

Use Special Right Triangles

Here's some good news: you don't have to memorize this unit circle for the SAT! We can find any point or angle on the unit circle if we draw a right triangle using the information we're given. As we'll see in the practice problems, there are really only two types of special triangles that come up in unit circle problems:

Drawing Triangles

If you're given a radians measurement, you can figure out the right triangle by **converting it to degrees**.

If you're given a point, then the *x* and *y* coordinates tell you the **length of the legs** of the triangle.

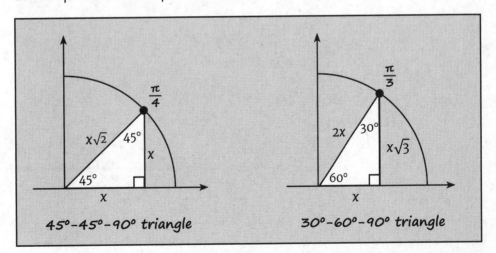

You can use these **special right triangles**, coupled with the knowledge that **360° = 2π**, to answer unit circle questions on the test. And remember, these special right triangles are given to you in the instructions box! So when in doubt, **check the box**.

Practice Problems

Use your new skills to answer each question.

1

In a right triangle, one of the angles measures $x°$ where $\sin(90° - x°) = \frac{3}{5}$. What is $\cos(x°)$?

2

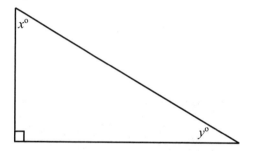

If $\cos(x°) = \frac{1}{2}$, what is the value of $\sin(y°)$?

A) $\frac{1}{2}$

B) $\frac{\sqrt{3}}{2}$

C) $\frac{\sqrt{2}}{2}$

D) $\frac{\sqrt{3}}{3}$

3

In a circle with center O, the central $\angle AOB$ has a measure of $\frac{\pi}{x}$ radians. If the area of the sector formed by angle $\angle AOB$ is one sixth the area of the circle, what is the value of x ?

4

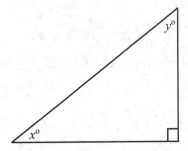

For the right triangle above, which of the following must be true?

I. $\sin(x) = \cos(x)$
II. $\sin(y) = \cos(x)$
III. $\cos(y) = \sin(x)$

A)   I
B)   I and II
C)   II and III
D)   I, II, and III

5

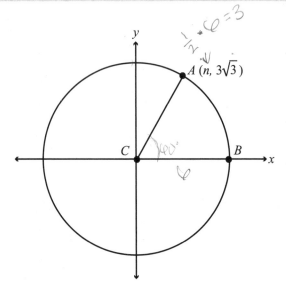

In the xy-plane above, C is the center of the circle, and the measure of $\angle ACB$ is $\frac{\pi}{3}$ radians. What is the value of n ?

6

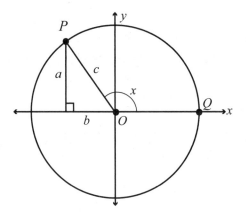

In the xy-plane above, O is the center of the circle, and the measure of $\angle POQ$ is $x°$. What is the value of $\sin(x)$?

A) $\frac{b}{c}$

B) $\frac{a}{c}$

C) $-\frac{b}{c}$

D) $-\frac{a}{c}$

Math Review

Practice Time

The following pages contain a PSAT-length math test. Section 3 should be taken **without** use of your calculator. On Section 4 you can go hog-wild with that calculator. Time yourself to get a feel for the pacing of a PSAT or SAT test. When you're ready for the real deal, take the mock test in the back of the book.

Math Review (No Calculator)
25 MINUTES, 17 QUESTIONS

This is a PSAT-length math section for practicing your new skills! Answers are in the back of the book.

DIRECTIONS

For questions 1-13, solve each problem, choose the best answer from the choices provided.
For questions 14-17, solve the problem and write your answer in the space provided.

NOTES

1. The use of a calculator **is not permitted.**
2. All variables and expressions used represent real numbers unless otherwise indicated.
3. Figures provided in this test are drawn to scale unless otherwise indicated.
4. All figures lie in a plane unless otherwise indicated.
5. Unless otherwise indicated, the domain of a given function f is the set of all real numbers x for which $f(x)$ is a real number.

REFERENCE

$A = \pi r^2$
$C = 2\pi r$

$A = \ell w$

$A = \frac{1}{2}bh$

$c^2 = a^2 + b^2$

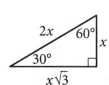

Special Right Triangles

$V = \ell wh$

$V = \pi r^2 h$

$V = \frac{4}{3}\pi r^3$

$V = \frac{1}{3}\pi r^2 h$

$V = \frac{1}{3}\ell wh$

The number of degrees of arc in a circle is 360.
The number of radians of arc in a circle is 2π
The sum of the measures in degrees of the angles of a triangle is 180.

1

If $4x + 7 = 10$, what is the value of $8x + 2$?

A) 3

B) 7

C) 8

D) 20

2

On Saturday, Car A drove m miles per hour for 7 hours and Car B drove n miles per hour for 8 hours. In terms of m and n, what was the total number of miles that Cars A and B drove on Saturday?

A) $8m + 7n$

B) $56mn$

C) $7m + 8n$

D) $15mn$

3

Phil earns $9 an hour for washing his parents' 3 cars. His parents also give him an extra $4 if he remembers to close the garage door afterwards. Which of the following expressions could be used to show how much Phil earns if he washes each car and remembers to close the garage door?

A) $9x + 4$, where x is the number of hours

B) $4x + 9$, where x is the number of hours

C) $x(9 + 3) + 4$, where x is the number of cars

D) $(4x + 9) + 3$, where x is the number of cars

CONTINUE

4

$$x + y = 0$$
$$4x - 3y = 21$$

Which ordered pair (x, y) satisfies the system of equations above?

A) (4, –3)

B) (–3,–3)

C) (–3, 3)

D) (3, –3)

5

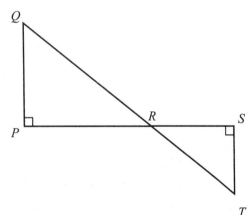

In the figure above, PQ and TS are each perpendicular to PS. If $QT = 64$ and the ratio of ST to QP is 3:5, what is the length of $\overline{RT}$?

A) 8

B) 16

C) 24

D) 40

6

Lauren is in charge of dispatching tour buses for an historic city. There are large tour buses that seat 60 people and smaller tour buses that seat 40 people. If Lauren dispatches 50 tour buses one week to pick up 2,300 people, and every bus was filled to capacity, how many large tour buses did Lauren dispatch?

A) 10

B) 15

C) 25

D) 35

7

If $\frac{x^2}{y} = 2$, what is the value of $\frac{4y}{x^2}$?

A) 2

B) 4

C) 6

D) 8

8

$$2x^2 + 11x - 21 = 0$$

If m and n are two solutions of the equation above and $m > n$, which of the following expressions is the largest?

A) $m - n$

B) $n - m$

C) $2m$

D) $-n$

9

A publishing company uses a large, industrial printer to produce copies of its current best-selling book. The printer can only print a certain number of pages before it needs to be cleaned. The number of pages that remain to be printed before the next cleaning can be modeled with the equation $P = 1500 - 7h$, where P is the number of pages remaining to be printed and h is the number of hours that the printer has been printing. What is the meaning of the value 1500 in this equation?

A) The printer will print the pages in 1500 hours

B) The printer prints at a rate of 1500 pages per day

C) The printer prints at a rate of 1500 pages per hour

D) The printer prints a total of 1500 pages each cycle

10

$$f(x) = a(x - 2)^2 + 1$$

The function f above has constant a. If $f(6) = 9$, what is the value of $f(-2)$?

A) 33

B) 16

C) 9

D) -1

677

CONTINUE

11

When line n is graphed in the standard (x, y) coordinate plane, it passes through the origin and has a slope of $\frac{2}{5}$. Which of the following is a point that lies on line n?

A) (0, 5)

B) (2, 5)

C) (5, 5)

D) (10, 4)

12

$$g(x) = 4(x^2 + 7x + 8) - 8(x + j)$$

If $g(x)$ is divisible by x, and j is a constant, what is the value of j ?

A) 4

B) 0

C) -3

D) -4

13

A parabola with equation $y = ax^2 + bx + c$ passes through the point $(-2, -3)$. If $a = \frac{1}{2}b$, then $c = ?$

A) 6

B) 3

C) −1

D) −3

14

If $\dfrac{a}{4} = b$, and $2b - 3 = 1$, what is the value of a ?

16

If $a > 1$, what is the value of $\dfrac{2a(3a)^2}{3a^3}$?

15

When $k = 2\sqrt{3}$, $4k = \sqrt{3x}$. What is the value of x ?

17

If $x - 4$ is a factor of $x^2 - 3kx + 4k$ and k is a constant, what is the value of k?

STOP

Math Review (Calculator)
45 MINUTES, 31 QUESTIONS

This is a PSAT-length math section for practicing your new skills! Answers are in the back of the book.

DIRECTIONS

For questions 1-27, solve each problem, choose the best answer from the choices provided.
For questions 28-31, solve the problem and write your answer in the space provided.

NOTES

1. The use of a calculator **is permitted.**
2. All variables and expressions used represent real numbers unless otherwise indicated.
3. Figures provided in this test are drawn to scale unless otherwise indicated.
4. All figures lie in a plane unless otherwise indicated.
5. Unless otherwise indicated, the domain of a given function f is the set of all real numbers x for which $f(x)$ is a real number.

REFERENCE

$A = \pi r^2$ $A = \ell w$ $A = \frac{1}{2}bh$ $c^2 = a^2 + b^2$ Special Right Triangles
$C = 2\pi r$

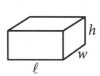

$V = \ell wh$ $V = \pi r^2 h$ $V = \frac{4}{3}\pi r^3$ $V = \frac{1}{3}\pi r^2 h$ $V = \frac{1}{3}\ell wh$

The number of degrees of arc in a circle is 360.
The number of radians of arc in a circle is 2π
The sum of the measures in degrees of the angles of a triangle is 180.

CONTINUE

1

Carissa joins a book club that charges a yearly fee of $10, as well as $0.75 per book she borrows through the club. Which of the following functions gives Carissa's cost, in dollars, for a year in which she borrows x books?

A) $C(x) = 10.75x$

B) $C(x) = 10x + 0.75$

C) $C(x) = 10 + 0.75x$

D) $C(x) = 5 + 25x$

2

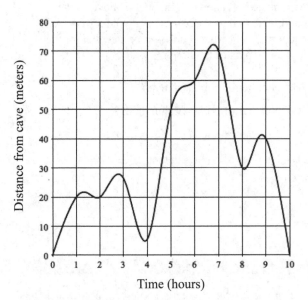

Time (hours)

A bear's distance from its cave varies as it forages its environment throughout the day. The graph above shows the bear's distance from the cave over a 10-hour period. During which period is the bear's distance from its cave strictly increasing then strictly decreasing?

A) Between 0 and 3 hours

B) Between 3 and 5 hours

C) Between 5 and 8 hours

D) Between 7 and 10 hours

3

For every 700 office chairs sold at an office furniture store, 4 are returned for minor defects. At this rate, out of the 42,000 office chairs sold per year, how many should the store expect to be returned for minor defects?

A) 200

B) 240

C) 280

D) 320

4

If $16 + 2x$ is 7 more than 15, what is the value of $4x$?

A) 3

B) 6

C) 12

D) 28

681

CONTINUE

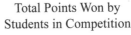

Questions 5-6 refer to the following information.

The number of millimeters a sunflower grows in one month is directly proportional to the number of gallons of water the sunflower receives in that month. A sunflower will grow 90 millimeters in one month if its receives 6 gallons of water.

5

How many millimeters will a sunflower grow in one month if it receives 15 gallons of water?

A) 540

B) 270

C) 225

D) 180

6

A gardener plants her sunflower seeds in nutrient-deficient soil, which causes a 34% decrease in the growth of the sunflowers. How many millimeters do her sunflowers grow in one month if she gives the sunflowers 6 gallons of water?

A) 30.6

B) 59.4

C) 66

D) 77

7

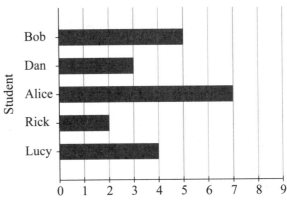

Total Points Won by Students in Competition

A competition awarded points to 5 students who participated, as shown in the graph above. If the combined total of points earned by the 5 students is equal to 2,100, what is an appropriate label for the horizontal axis of the graph?

A) Number of points (in tens)

B) Number of points (in hundreds)

C) Number of points (in thousands)

D) Number of points (in tens of thousands)

8

Samantha answered exactly 85 percent of the questions on her Biology test correctly. Which of the following could be the total number of questions on Samantha's Biology test?

A) 22

B) 20

C) 18

D) 14

CONTINUE

9

What is the slope of the line in the xy-plane that passes through the points $(-\frac{9}{2}, 2)$ and $(-\frac{1}{2}, 7)$?

A) -1

B) $-\frac{4}{5}$

C) 1

D) $\frac{5}{4}$

10

Which of the following values for x is NOT a solution of the inequality $2x + 3 \leq 5x + 9$?

A) -3

B) -2

C) -1

D) 0

11

In a certain board game, each player starts out with 90 tokens and can only gain more by rolling "doubles", which earns the player m additional tokens. Abigail avoids losing any tokens, and rolls doubles 12 times during the game. If she finishes with 162 tokens, what is the value of m?

A) 2

B) 5

C) 6

D) 10

12

	Juniors	Seniors	Total
Basketball	23	8	31
Lacrosse	26	29	55
Soccer	17	22	39
None	20	45	65
Total	86	102	190

The junior and senior class at a high school was given a survey asking what sport they planned on playing that year. The survey data was collected and compiled into the table above. Which of the following categories accounts for approximately 9 percent of the entire population surveyed?

A) Juniors planning to play lacrosse

B) Juniors planning to play soccer

C) Seniors planning to play lacrosse

D) Seniors planning to play basketball

13

$$231 - 11x = y$$

A new grocery store is giving a free T-shirt to a certain number of lucky customers each day, while supplies last. The equation above can be used to model the number of T-shirts, y, left to be given away x days after the promotion began. What does it mean that $(21,0)$ is a solution to this equation?

A) The store gives away 21 T-shirts each day.

B) The store has a total of 21 T-shirts to give away.

C) After 11 days, the store will have 21 T-shirts left to give away.

D) It will take 21 days to give away the store's supply of T-shirts.

CONTINUE

14

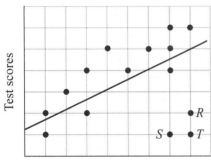

A teacher wants to show her students the relationship between the number of hours spent studying and test scores. She plots the results of 15 students' most recent test scores in the graph above. She then discovers that students R, S, and T studied for the wrong test and, as a result, should not have been considered in the data. If she removes these three scores and redraws the graph, how will the graph's line of best fit change?

A)   Its slope will decrease

B)   Its slope will increase

C)   Its slope will stay the same

D)   The line will be unaffected by the change

15

Kiki and Thomas ran a two-day fundraiser where they sold pies and cookies. On the first day, they sold 80 pies and 120 cookies. On the second day, however, they sold 30 percent fewer pies and 40 percent fewer cookies. By what percentage did the total volume of baked goods sold decline from the first day to the second?

A)   10

B)   35

C)   36

D)   70

16

$$y > x + s$$
$$y < -x + t$$

In the xy-plane, (0, 0) is a solution to the system of inequalities above. Which of the following relationships between s and t must be true?

A) $s > t$

B) $s < t$

C) $|s| > |t|$

D) $s = -t$

17

A concession stand sells hot dogs for $3.75 each and soda for $1.50 each. In one day, the stand sells a combined total of 123 hot dogs and sodas, earning $378 from the sales. How many hot dogs were sold that day?

A)   83

B)   86

C)   93

D)   102

CONTINUE

18

	Group A	Group B	Total
None	42	57	99
1 to 3	93	82	175
4 or more	65	61	126
Total	200	200	400

A nutritionist recruited two distinct populations to participate in a survey. One group (Group A) consisted of 200 people who regularly eat breakfast; the other (Group B) consisted of 200 people who usually skip breakfast. Each person was asked to report their daily intake of servings of fruits and vegetables, and the results were recorded in the table above. If a person is chosen at random from among those who eat at least 1 serving of fruits and vegetables, what is the probability that the person belonged to Group B?

A) $\dfrac{61}{200}$

B) $\dfrac{143}{200}$

C) $\dfrac{143}{301}$

D) $\dfrac{301}{400}$

19

Shakir is a manager who is evaluating the productivity of two employees. Based on his study, he concludes that Employee A, on average, completes 25% more assignments than Employee B does. If Employee A completes 85 assignments, about how many assignments will Employee B complete?

A) 63

B) 68

C) 106

D) 110

20

Researchers conducted a survey of the salaries for graphic designers with similar amounts of experience and education. They found that the mean salary was $45,000 and the median salary was $60,000. Which of the following situations could explain the difference between the mean and median salaries?

A) The designers all earn the same salary.

B) Many designers earn salaries between $45,00 and $60,000.

C) A few designers earn much more than the rest.

D) A few designers earn much less than the rest.

21

Susan estimates that she will have to study x hours for her finals next week, where $x > 40$. The goal is for the estimate to be within 4 hours of the time it will actually take her to study. If Susan meets her goal and it takes her y hours to complete all of her studying, which of the following inequalities represents the relationship between the estimated time and the actual studying time?

A) $x + y < 4$

B) $y > x + 4$

C) $y < x - 4$

D) $-4 < x - y < 4$

CONTINUE

Questions 22-24 refer to the following table.

Estimated Annual Budget for Sectors of the U.S. Federal Budget from 2016 to 2019

Sector	Year			
	2016	2017	2018	2019
Pensions	1,012	1,062	1,118	1,188
Health Care	1,107	1,134	1,175	1,273
Education	119	130	139	147
Defense	852	840	823	835
Welfare	393	402	402	414
Transportation	99	104	107	108

The table above lists the estimated annual budget, in millions of dollars, for each of six different sectors of the U.S. Federal Budget from 2016 to 2019.

22

Which of the following best approximates the average rate of change in the estimated annual budget for pensions from 2017 to 2019?

A) $50 million per year

B) $63 million per year

C) $126 million per year

D) $176 million per year

23

Of the following, which program's ratio of its 2016 to its 2019 estimated budget is closest to the health care sector's ratio of its 2016 budget to its 2019 budget?

A) Pensions

B) Education

C) Defense

D) Welfare

24

Which of the following graphs could represent the estimated change in the welfare budget over the years 2016 to 2019, inclusive ?

A)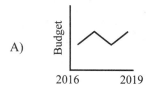

B)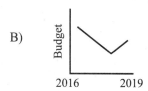

C)

D)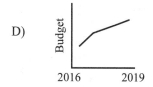

CONTINUE

25

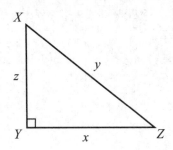

In right triangle *XYZ* above, sin *Z* is equal to which of the following?

A) $\dfrac{x}{y}$

B) $\dfrac{z}{y}$

C) $\dfrac{z}{x}$

D) $\dfrac{y}{z}$

26

A painter is making a rectangular canvas for a large-scale painting. The canvas has a length that is 8 feet less than twice its width. What is the perimeter, in feet, of the canvas if the area is 570 square feet?

A) 74

B) 80

C) 98

D) 104

27

$$h = -4.9t^2 + 16t$$

For a science project, Mark built a slingshot contraption that launches a sphere straight up into the air. He then built the equation above to show the approximate height, *h*, in meters, of the sphere *t* seconds after it is launched from the slingshot with an initial velocity of 16 meters per second. After approximately how many seconds will the sphere hit the ground?

A) 2.0

B) 2.7

C) 3.3

D) 4.0

CONTINUE

28

Earl can string at least 8 guitars per hour and at most 16 guitars per hour. Based on this information, what is a possible amount of time, in hours, that it could take Earl to string 56 guitars?

29

A local magnet school wishes to obtain a 5:2 student-to-teacher ratio. The school currently has 50 teachers on staff for a population of 180 students. The school expects the total student population to increase by 40 next year. How many additional teachers must the school add next year to reach its target ratio?

30

A college professor assigns a class of 105 students a group project to be completed in groups of 3 or 4. If each group of students has either 3 or 4 students and there will be 31 groups, how many of the students will work in a group of 3 students?

31

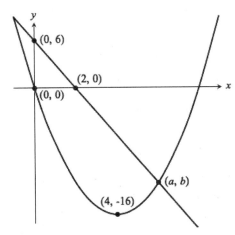

In the xy-plane above, (a, b) are the coordinates of one of the points of intersection of the graphs of a linear function and a quadratic function. If the graph of the quadratic function has its vertex at (4, -16), what is the value of a?

STOP

688

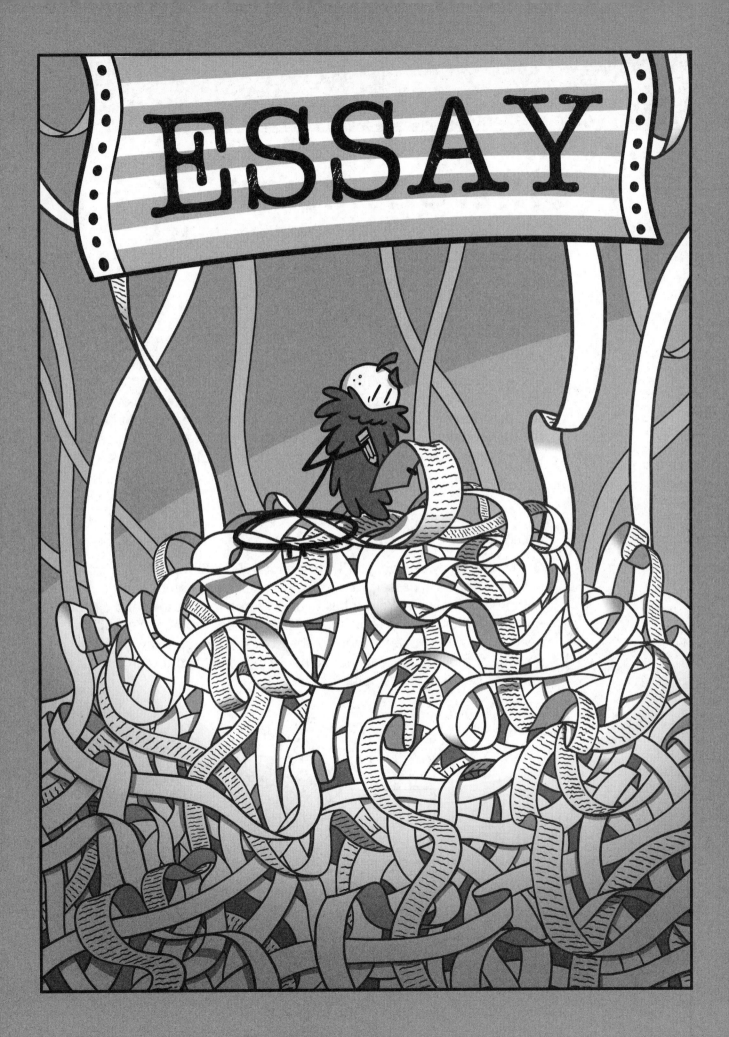

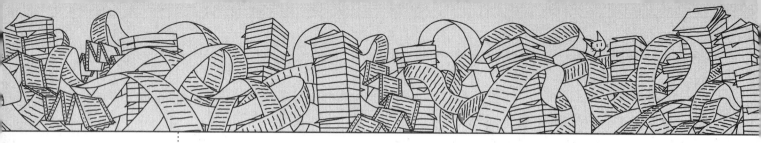

Introduction

Get your nitty gritty details about the SAT essay here!

The Practical Stuff

The essay on the SAT is an optional 50 minute section given at the end of the test. To take the test with the essay, you must choose the "SAT with essay" option when you register. There is an additional fee to cover the cost of processing and grading the essays. Some colleges do not require the essay section, but many do. Each college's website or admissions office should let you know whether or not they require the SAT essay.

How to Ace the Essay

On the SAT essay section, you'll find a short (600-700 words) persuasive passage—that is, a passage that tries to persuade the reader of the author's point of view. Your job is to understand the passage and explain how the author develops and supports his or her argument. You will need to read the passage carefully, then construct your essay detailing how the author argues. You should not respond with your opinion, but only discuss the author's opinion.

TIP

If you're taking the SAT more than once, you don't need to register for the essay every time! Once you're satisfied with your score, you can take the regular 4 sections and then skip out early!

692

Grading

The SAT essay has three subscores: Reading, Analysis, and Writing, each on a scale from 1 to 4. Two graders, working independently from each other, grade your essay and the final score is the sum of the two scores for each category. The Essay score does not affect any other score on the test.

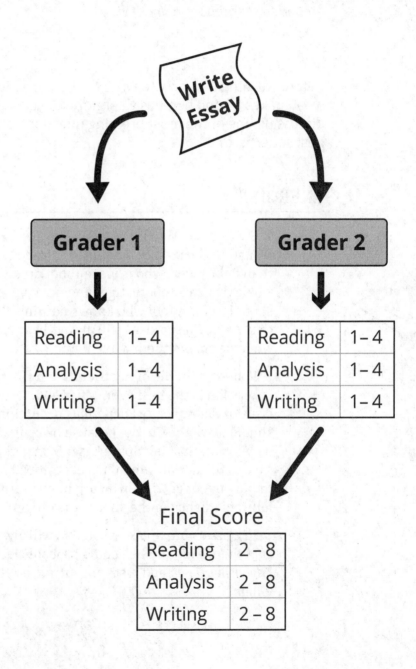

Persuasive Argument

*A persuasive essay tries to—you guessed it—***persuade*** the reader to come around to the author's point of view.*

Before we jump into how to write the essay, it's important to think about what makes a good persuasive argument. Let's look at a persuasive essay discussing one of the most pressing questions of our time: who is the best superhero?

EXERCISE 1

Space Laser Man is the best superhero ever created! He can fly and his kicks shoot out lasers. Space Laser Man is way better than Robo Tiger, who is just a robot dressed up as a tiger. Who would design a robotic tiger and not give it the ability to fly and shoot lasers? A fool who knows nothing about the real world, that's who! Laser kicks will always beat metal claws, especially when he shoots them while flying.

I polled a couple of my friends and they all agree that Space Laser Man is the best ever. My friend, Aaron, who has every issue of *United Justice Friendship Co-op*, thinks Space Laser Man should leave the Co-op, because he could defeat more villains by himself. Instead, Space Laser Man gets distracted having to save Nautical Nate when he gets trapped in a uranium powered fishing net or getting in an argument with Mr. Minutia over who left their dishes in the sink at the Co-op.

In conclusion, Space Laser Man will always be the greatest superhero ever and he should probably leave the *United Justice Friendship Co-op* and just concentrate on firing laser kicks at villains.

Q1 **Is this a persuasive argument?** _____

> It's certainly an argument, but it's not a very persuasive one. I can tell that the author believes that Space Laser Man is the best superhero, but I'm definitely not persuaded.

Q2 **What makes the argument persuasive or not persuasive?**

_____

_____

_____

> This essay doesn't contain many facts to support the author's theory that Space Laser Man is the best superhero. It focuses a lot on the **what**, but not a lot on the **why**. Why is shooting lasers so much better than being a robot? Why are laser kicks better than metal claws?

Without evidence, I don't think I can trust the author's argument. The author's "friend Aaron" may be an expert on superheroes, but he may be just a random guy! Why should I take his word on this topic? This essay is full of opinions, but very short on persuasion.

Next let's look at another essay that addresses the same topic.

EXERCISE 2

Who is the greatest superhero of all time? It's an intriguing question for fans of superheroes and has led to a diversity of opinions. Unfortunately, analyzing fans' opinions in mass often feels like looking for subtlety in the chattering howls of hungry hyenas. Rather than attempting to determine subjective "greatness," analyzing a superhero's popularity can lead to quantifiable metrics. Dr. Cadenhead, a professor at the Lilburn College of Fantasy Arts, has determined a method to track superhero preferences over time by analyzing the frequency of something he calls "hashtags" in social media.

Cadenhead's findings revealed an unexpected trend: Space Laser Man has skyrocketed in popularity over the last three years. In 1997, Space Laser Man ranked 316th in superhero popularity according to Cadenhead's findings. By 2014, Space Laser Man had broken into the top 20! While Space Laser Man trails behind many legendary superheroes— Robo Tiger, The Indestructible Thud, and Goose Kid—there has been a tangible rise in Space Laser Man's popularity.

What could account for Space Laser Man's rise in appeal? The best way to understand the trend is to investigate his fans. By and large, Space Laser Man appeals to adolescent males, especially those with limited social experience. His primary superpowers, laser-kicks and flying, represent a fight-or-flight binary that makes it easy to process potential danger. His lack of romantic subplot means that his fans can enjoy his adventures without having to navigate stories with complex interpersonal narratives.

According to researchers at the Comic Book Institute of North America, 40% of superhero fans are males between the ages of 13 and 22. These fans are the primary consumers of Space Laser Man's stories of good and evil, and the the number of sales—$39 million in the last fiscal quarter alone—prove that Space Laser

Man is undisputably popular. However, if his popularity will continue or if his die-hard base will grow up and move to more mature narratives remains to be seen.

TIP

Subjective arguments are based on opinions and are open to interpretation.

Objective arguments, like you'll see on the SAT, are based on facts and evidence.

Q1   **Is this a persuasive argument?** _____

This is a great argument! The author isn't trying to argue that Space Laser Man is subjectively better than other superheroes; instead, she's arguing that Space Laser Man is a very popular superhero.

Q2   **What makes it persuasive or not persuasive?**

_____

_____

_____

One word: **evidence**. The author backs up her claims with facts, numbers, research, data, the works! This essay still tells us what Space Laser Man does (laser kicks and flying), but also explains **why** that is important to the argument (the fight-or-flight binary is appealing, making him very popular). The author cites reputable sources: Dr. Cadenhead is an expert with evidence to back up his claims, and the Comic Book Institute of North America sounds very prestigious. After reading this essay, I am persuaded that Space Laser Man is a very popular superhero.

The good news is the SAT essay will only use quality pieces of writing, so you will not have to pick apart a bad argument. However, by analyzing a weak argument and a strong argument, you can start to notice what makes an essay persuasive, and therefore, effective.

Essay Foundations

a.k.a. the basics of writing a great essay!

Without a proper foundation, the Eiffel Tower would look a lot more like the Leaning Tower of Pisa, and your essay scores will lean a lot closer to a 2 than to a 8. Here are 8 tips that will get you on your way to a great essay score!

1 ACTIVELY READ THE PASSAGE

The essay section is also a reading test and you'll need to focus your argument around the content given in the passage. Reading is the crucial first step!

2 USE QUOTES EFFECTIVELY

Quote the essay to show that you understand the content and structure of the author's argument. But don't pad your essay with unnecessarily long quotes!

3 BE WELL-ORGANIZED

Structure, structure, structure. Make sure you have a clear introduction, a few strong body paragraphs, and a tight conclusion.

4 BE FOCUSED AND ON TOPIC

Stick to the passage and don't get side-tracked expressing your own opinions.

5 **TRANSITION SMOOTHLY BETWEEN PARAGRAPHS**

The flow of your essay is important; use good segues and transitions that lead from one paragraph or example to the next.

6 **DEMONSTRATE SKILLFUL USE OF VOCABULARY**

Instead of writing "this shows that..." break out a more advanced synonym: "the author's quote demonstrates/clarifies/exemplifies..."

7 **USE A VARIETY OF SENTENCE STRUCTURES**

Simple sentences lead to bored graders, so spice things up with complex sentences in a variety of styles.

8 **WRITE MORE, NOT LESS**

The test booklet give you 4 pages, so be sure to use as much as you can. Longer essays show more effort.

Reading Score

Did you understand the passage? Can you summarize the author's argument?

Skip to the Instructions!

Every SAT essay has the same structure: reading instructions (these are always the same), then the essay, then the writing instructions. Your first step is to **skip to the writing instructions**.

As you read the passage below, consider how Brianna Schemanke witz uses

- evidence, such as facts
- reasoning t
- stylistic or p
  to emotion,

Adapted from Brian   nkewitz, "Paleoclimatology and Some Dangers." Originally p   lished September 32, 2015.

1   The developing field of paleoclimatology is sending scientists to some of the harshest environments on the globe to research the climates of past epochs. These research projects have revealed vast variations in Earth's climate, including glacial periods when much of the Earth was covered in ice, and interglacial periods when temperatures warmed up and the polar ice caps shrunk. By gathering and refining data about what Ear   was like thousands or even millions of years ago, scientists can   better calculations about what Earth's climate will be like in the   They can also better understand the complex mechanisms that t   climate changes in the past, and build better m   l   understan   climate trends. Right now, they   ial quest   what is the exact relationship b   increased temperatures?

2   The evidence is encoded in many ways: microscopic dust and soot, even the var   (These striations show the changes thr   rk bands

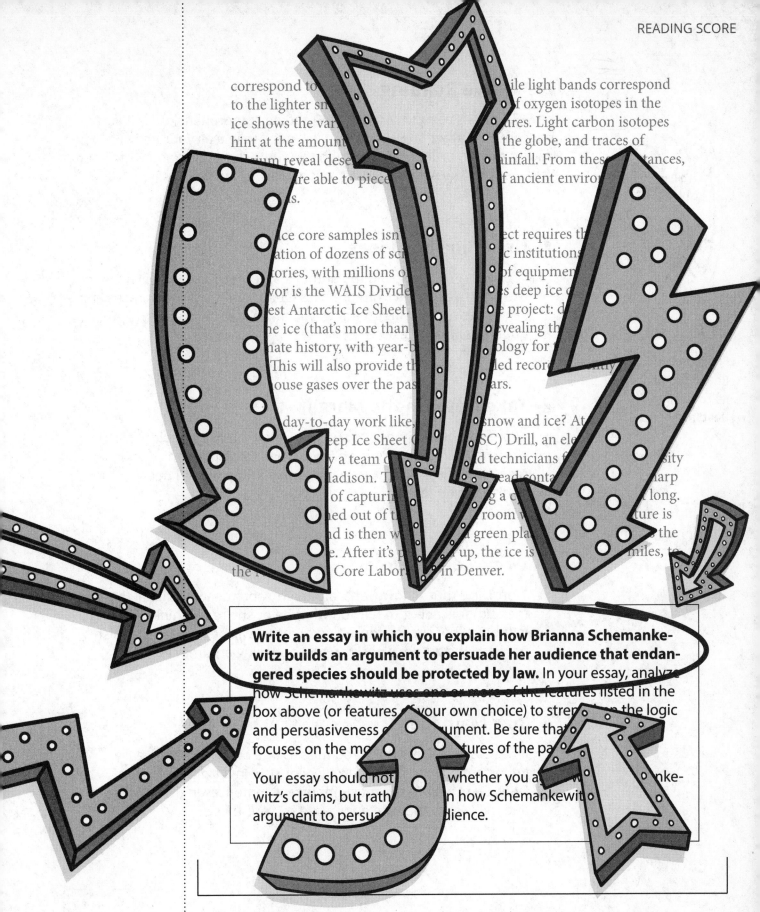

correspond to ... ...ile light bands correspond to the lighter sm... ...of oxygen isotopes in the ice shows the var... ...tures. Light carbon isotopes hint at the amoun... ...the globe, and traces of ...ium reveal dese... ...ininfall. From thes... ...tances, ...re able to piece... ...of ancient enviro...

...ice core samples isn... ...ect requires th... ...ation of dozens of sc... ...ic institutions... ...tories, with millions o... ...of equipmen... ...or is the WAIS Divide... ...s deep ice... ...est Antarctic Ice Sheet. ...e project: d... ...he ice (that's more than... ...vealing th... ...nate history, with year-b... ...ology for... ...This will also provide th... ...led record... ...ouse gases over the pas... ...ars.

...day-to-day work like, ...snow and ice? At... ...eep Ice Sheet (... ...SC) Drill, an ele... ...y a team o... ...d technicians f... ...sity ...adison. T... ...ead conta... ...arp ...of capturi... ...g a c... ...long. ...ned out of t... ...room... ...ture is ...d is then w... ...green pla... ...the ...e. After it's p... ...up, the ice is... ...miles, t... the ... ...Core Labor... in Denver.

Write an essay in which you explain how Brianna Schemanke-witz builds an argument to persuade her audience that endangered species should be protected by law. In your essay, analyze how Schemankewitz uses one or more of the features listed in the box above (or features of your own choice) to strengthen the logic and persuasiveness of... ...ument. Be sure that... focuses on the mo... ...tures of the pa...

Your essay should not... ...whether you a... ...nke-witz's claims, but rath... ...n how Schemankewit... argument to persua... ...dience.

Here the test writers tell you the author's argument! **This is super useful to know in the beginning**, so be sure to read this first. This will help you to identify main ideas and key examples from the very start.

PORTAL

For more Active Reading practice, go to p. 38 in the Reading section.

Use Active Reading

The SAT Essay is as much about your reading comprehension as it is about your essay writing ability. You will need to use all your Active Reading skills in order to understand the author's position and write your essay. Let's review Active Reading as it applies to the SAT essay!

1 Underline Key Ideas

Your essay must explain the author's argument, so you will need to use effective quotes from the passage. Underlining key phrases and sentences on your first reading will make it easier to find helpful quotes as you write.

2 Take Notes in the Margin

Your response will need to summarize the author's positions, so write notes in the margin while you read to help organize your response. In essence, your paragraph summaries will become the outline of your essay!

3 Circle Logic Words

Words like "but," "however," "although," and "despite" signal that the author is about to tell you what he or she really thinks. Getting in the habit of circling these "logic words" will help you distinguish between the author's position and opposing arguments.

4 Star Main Ideas

If the essay graders think you missed one of the author's really important points, they will likely deduct points from your score. Draw stars next to the most important sentences in the passage and make sure they are addressed by your thesis.

MAXIMIZING YOUR SCORE

- **Read the writing instructions to find the main idea**

- **Use active reading to understand the author's argument**
  The easiest way to lose points is to misunderstand the passage. Take the time to underline and write margin notes to quickly check your understanding as you read.

- **Use the whole essay**
  A response that focuses on one or two paragraphs will make the graders think you did not read the entire essay. Be sure to discuss important elements in the beginning, middle, and end of the essay.

- **Focus on the Author**
  Sadly, the SAT graders are not interested in your opinion! Make sure that you express the author's position and do not filter that position through your own feelings.

Analysis Score

How did the author persuade you of his or her argument? What persuasive elements were used, and what was the effect on the reader?

The analysis score reflects your ability to explain how the author develops his or her ideas. The majority of your essay will be dedicated to this analysis, so this score is extremely important! To ace the analysis, your job is to:

(1) Show how the author builds an argument with stylistic and persuasive elements

Hard data? Quotes from experts? Fancy metaphors? All these and more can help build an argument.

(2) Explain how those elements affect and persuade the audience

Remember, the SAT wants you to move beyond what and into why. Why does the author quote an expert? How does it persuade the audience?

On the following pages, you'll find a list of elements an author can use to build an argument. Let's review these elements so you can spot them easily and label them correctly.

TIP

No author will use everything (or even most things) on this list! When you're writing your essay, focus on the 3-4 elements the author uses most frequently and most persuasively.

Common Stylistic and Persuasive Elements

Facts and Rhetoric

Empirical Evidence	
How to spot it	Empirical evidence is just a fancy word for using statistics and studies. When you see data and percentages, that's empirical evidence.
Example	*Southern Delaware has gradually become the oral hygiene capital of the nation. A 2013 study by Truex and Findlay found that 38% of Southern Delaware middle-schoolers plan to pursue a career in dentistry.*
Why it's used	Showing that scientific studies agree with the author's beliefs can be very persuasive evidence.
Quote from an Expert	
How to spot it	This is when an author cites another expert. Look for quotes from folks with fancy titles.
Example	*"Despite the availability of downloadable and streamable music, vinyl records have surged in popularity," says Artie Newhouse, owner of The Vinyl Countdown in Locust Grove, GA.*
Why it's used	These quotes show that other smart people agree with the author.
Personal Experience and Anecdotes	
How to spot it	An anecdote is whenever the author starts talking about a personal experience and how that experience affected him or her.
Example	*I came to understand the environmental importance of Northwest Minnesota during a college geology field trip to the region.*
Why it's used	They show that their opinion is not purely theoretical, but based in real-life experiences.

TIP

Turn homework into SAT practice in a flash!

Practice looking for persuasive and stylistic elements in everything you read.

Rhetorical Question

How to spot it	A rhetorical question is a question that the author intends to answer.
Example	*Why would anyone study the life cycles of lobsters? My interest developed through a summer internship on a Portland, Maine fishing boat.*
Why it's used	Rhetorical questions allow the author to introduce a topic in a way that allows for greater exploration.

Counter Argument/Antithesis

How to spot it	This is when the author acknowledges an opposing viewpoint. Look for logic words like "however" and "but" after a counter argument to find the author's position.
Example	*Many self-proclaimed "experts" believe that it is only a matter of time before someone captures a living Sasquatch.*
Why it's used	Counter arguments can strengthen the author's own argument because the author can now directly dispute the other side's claims.

Hypothetical Example

How to spot it	The author will use words like "suppose," "imagine," or "if" to indicate the example is what could happen.
Example	*Suppose that the wooly mammoth had survived the last Ice Age. Its effect on the contemporary North American ecosystem would be dramatic.*
Why it's used	Hypothetical examples allow an author to explore future consequences of current actions.

Juxtaposition

How to spot it	Just look for two examples that the author compares and contrasts.
Example	*While Chihuahuas and Golden Retrievers are both popular dog breeds in America, their differences allow them to excel in different living environments.*
Why it's used	A juxtaposition allows for the author to analyze two sides of an argument and possibly reach a consensus.

Satire	
How to spot it	Look for the author saying the opposite of his or her point. Often times the author will place a word or phrase in quotation marks to emphasize its sarcastic use.
Example	*With multiple ethics violations and a string of shady land deals under his belt, the Governor exemplifies the "career" politician.*
Why it's used	Satire allows the author to express contempt for something but also use humor to keep the reader engaged.

Emotional Appeal and Figurative Language

Pathos/Appeal to Emotion	
How to spot it	Look for language meant to make the reader experience an emotion.
Example	*Children in underfunded orphanages subsist off of paltry meals of barely nutritious food wishing everyday for some kind of comfort and salvation.*
Why it's used	If the author can affect our emotions, then we are more likely to be persuaded.
Sensory Detail	
How to spot it	The author will describe an experience by referring to senses like sight, hearing, or touch.
Example	*A walk on the beach always calms me; the sand massages in between my toes, the salty sea air envelopes my nostrils, and the ocean itself keeps a steady rhythm as each wave cascades on the shoreline.*
Why it's used	Sensory details help a reader to imagine a situation and place him or herself in the example.
Personification	
How to spot it	If an author starts giving non-humans human emotions, then you know it is personification.
Example	*My car loves ethanol-based fuel as ethanol makes it hum a happy tune as it cruises down the road.*
Why it's used	Personification helps readers to identify with non-humans.

Metaphor

How to spot it	Look for figurative language that describes something with the qualities of another thing.
Example	*The cruel Arctic wind slapped me across the face.*
Why it's used	A metaphor helps the reader to make a connection or understand a situation in a new way.

Simile

How to spot it	If you see figurative language that uses "like" or "as" to create a comparison, you have found a simile.
Example	*During an Olympic decathlon, athletes must run like gazelles, leap like kangaroos, and throw like chimpanzees.*
Why it's used	A simile, like a metaphor, can help the reader to see a topic or situation in a new way.

Allusion

How to spot it	When the author indirectly references a famous story or historical event.
Example	*Standing against a Goliath, the small town's residents knew they needed to consolidate their efforts in order to preserve their historic downtown from outside developers.*
Why it's used	Allusions relate a topic to a well-known cultural reference and in doing so, help the topic feel more significant to the reader.

Metonymy

How to spot it	If the author uses an associated object to represent the actual subject, then you are looking at metonymy.
Example	*The Oval Office made a statement today that reflects an important shift in the allocation of international aid.*
Why it's used	Metonymy allows authors to vary their word choice rather than using the proper name all the time.

Synecdoche	
How to spot it	When the name of a part represents the whole thing, you have a synecdoche.
Example	*The hands of labor reached an accord with the suits in management.*
Why it's used	A synecdoche can draw emphasis to a particular quality of a subject.

Let's review the second superhero essay from earlier in this chapter. **Circle and label any persuasive and/or stylistic elements you see.**

Who is the greatest superhero of all time? It's an intriguing question for fans of superheroes and has led to a diversity of opinions. Unfortunately, analyzing fans' opinions in mass often feels like looking for subtlety in the chattering howls of hungry hyenas. Rather than attempting to determine subjective "greatness," analyzing a superhero's popularity can lead to quantifiable metrics. Dr. Cadenhead, a professor at the Lilburn College of Fantasy Arts, has determined a method to track superhero preferences over time by analyzing the frequency of something he calls "hashtags" in social media.

Cadenhead's findings revealed an unexpected trend: Space Laser Man has skyrocketed in popularity over the last three years. In 1997, Space Laser Man ranked 316th in superhero popularity according to Cadenhead's findings. By 2014, Space Laser Man had broken into the top 20! While Space Laser Man trails behind many legendary superheroes—Robo Tiger, The Indestructible Thud, and Goose Kid—there has been a tangible rise in Space Laser Man's popularity.

What could account for Space Laser Man's rise in appeal? The best way to understand the trend is to investigate his fans. By and far, Space Laser Man appeals to adolescent males, especially those with limited social experience. His primary superpowers, laser-kicks and flying, represent a fight-or-flight binary that makes it easy to process potential danger. His lack of romantic subplot means that his fans can enjoy his adventures without having to navigate stories with complex interpersonal narratives.

According to researchers at the Comic Book Institute of North America, 40% of superhero fans are males between the ages of 13 and 22. These fans are the primary consumers of Space Laser Man's stories of good and evil, and the the number of sales—$39 million is the last fiscal quarter alone—prove that Space Laser Man is undisputably popular. However, if his popularity will continue or if his die-hard base will grow up and move to more mature narratives remains to be seen.

Answers:

rhetorical question
Who is the greatest superhero of all time? It's an intriguing question for fans of superheroes and has led to a diversity of opinions. Unfortunately, analyzing fans' opinions in mass often feels like looking for subtlety in the *metaphor* chattering howls of *antithesis* hungry hyenas. Rather than attempting to determine subjective "greatness," analyzing a superhero's popularity can lead to quantifiable metrics. Dr. Cadenhead, a professor at the Lilburn College of Fantasy Arts, has determined a method to track superhero preferences over time by analyzing the frequency of something he calls "hashtags" in social media.

expert opinion

Cadenhead's findings revealed an unexpected trend: Space Laser Man has skyrocketed in popularity over the last three years. In 1997, Space Laser Man ranked 316th in superhero popularity according to Cadenhead's findings. By 2014, Space Laser Man had broken into the top 20! While Space Laser Man trails behind many legendary superheroes—Robo Tiger, The Indestructible Thud, and Goose Kid—there has been a tangible rise in Space Laser Man's popularity.

empirical evidence [bracket annotation for: "In 1997, Space Laser Man ranked 316th in superhero popularity according to Cadenhead's findings. By 2014, Space Laser Man had broken into the top 20!"]

rhetorical question

What could account for Space Laser Man's rise in appeal? The best way to understand the trend is to investigate his fans. By and far, Space Laser Man appeals to adolescent males, especially those with limited social experience. His primary superpowers, laser-kicks and flying, represent a fight-or-flight binary that makes it easy to process potential danger. His lack of romantic subplot means that his fans can enjoy his adventures without having to navigate stories with complex interpersonal narratives.

citing experts

According to researchers at the Comic Book Institute of North America, 40% of superhero fans are males between the ages of 13 and 22. These fans are the primary consumers of Space Laser Man's stories of good and evil, and the the number of sales—$39 million is the last fiscal quarter alone—prove that Space Laser Man is undisputably popular. However, if his popularity will continue or if his die-hard base will grow up and move to more mature narratives remains to be seen.

empirical evidence [annotation for: "40% of superhero fans are males between the ages of 13 and 22" and "$39 million is the last fiscal quarter alone"]

Author's Tone

A great way to increase the analysis score is to address the author's tone. You can focus on a specific example or paragraph, and/or address the overall tone. A discussion of the author's tone allows you to analyze specific word choices and contextualize the persuasive elements used.

Let's look at some examples:

EXAMPLE 1

When evaluating the long-term impact of hydraulic fracturing, commonly referred to as "fracking," we should not blend knee-jerk anxieties with a smattering of facts. Neither banning a process outright nor allowing unrestricted resource extraction is a sensible plan. We cannot allow the conflicting desires of economy and ecology to wage war against the realities of statistics and specific data.

Circle all the words that describe the tone of the passage:

Objective	Impassioned	Empathetic	Analytical
Measured	Confrontational	Decisive	Emotional

The author wants to evaluate both sides and reach a consensus between "economy and ecology," which would be best described as **Analytical** and **Measured**. The author also makes definitive statements about what cannot be done, and uses strong language like "knee-jerk anxieties" and "wage war." These words create an **Impassioned** and **Decisive** tone.

EXAMPLE 2

Imagine the majesty of the Northern California redwood forests. Visualize the sunlight peeking in between the towering sequoias. Inhale the crisp scent of pine needles. This is a timeless experience that needs to be treasured and curated. Now, think about your own time on this earth, and then imagine how much time a sequoia has experienced. To think that humans can happily chop down a thousand year old tree for some lumber is the most tragic manifestation of shortsightedness.

Circle all the words that describe the tone of the passage:

Objective	Impassioned	Empathetic	Analytical
Measured	Confrontational	Decisive	Emotional

This author wants you to feel the same way she does, asking you to imagine and feel the scenery. This pull on emotions creates an **Impassioned**, **Empathetic**, and **Emotional** tone.

Using Quotes Effectively: Keep 'em short!

The graders know you can pad out a paper with lengthy quotes, so an effective response will use quotes to further and support the analysis. They expect you to back up quotes from the essay with some sweet interpretations. **You must always offer your analysis of any quote you use!**

For example, instead of writing this:

In the essay, the author states "that 80% of deciduous trees in Northwestern Idaho have a parasitic infection," which is true.

You could offer this analysis:

When the author states "that 80% of deciduous trees in Northwestern Idaho have a parasitic infection," she backs up her previous concerns with a statistic that helps the reader to envision the scope of the epidemic.

713

TIP

Never quote entire sentences! Instead, combine short quotes with your own paraphrases. You can usually narrow down the meat of the quote to a few words.

Instead of this:

When the author says, "that humans can happily chop down a thousand year old tree for some lumber is the most tragic manifestation of shortsightedness," it shows that the author dislikes cutting down trees.

You could write:

The author uses the sense of time to persuade the reader; for example, when he states that cutting down a redwood tree, "is the most tragic manifestation of shortsightedness." The author needs for the reader to ponder the long term consequences of logging, so using the word "shortsightedness" frames the discussion in a larger, and longer, conversation.

Anyone can string together a series of quotes, so make sure that you give appropriate context and analysis for your quotes.

MAXIMIZING YOUR SCORE

- **Specifically describe the author's devices and tone**
  A great way to show mastery of the essay is to label the devices that the author uses. This shows a deep understanding of the rhetoric of writing and will help frame your analysis.

- **Explain every quote used in your paper**
  Any quote you use needs to explained. Quotes from the passage must be integral to your analysis.

- **Explain rather than rephrase**
  The graders are on the lookout for the student who just rewrites the given essay. Make sure the grader knows that you not only comprehend the author's argument, but also understand how the author persuades the reader.

Writing Score

Is your essay well-organized? Do you use interesting vocabulary and varied sentence structures?

Organization

The easiest way to improve your writing score is to organize your essay. You need a clear introduction that presents both the topic and the author's opinion. Each body paragraph should be focused on a specific part of the passage, which could be a specific quote, paragraph, or persuasive device. Finally, you will need a conclusion that will tie all your paragraphs together.

Introduction

The graders like the first paragraph in your response to address the author's topic before digging into the thesis. A strong introduction will not jump right into this thesis, but rather will start with the broad picture, then focus in on the author's point. Let's look at an author's thesis and a possible introduction:

EXAMPLE 1

The government needs to enact stronger restrictions on logging in the Pacific Northwest in order to protect a variety of endangered bird species.

There is great disagreement about how the United States uses its natural resource. Society needs raw materials to sustain and grow, yet we all acknowledge that irreversible damage to ecosystems should be avoided. The author takes a clear stance on the side of ecology, but limits his scope to the timber-rich forests of the Pacific Northwest. Through the use of metaphors, personal narrative, and governmental agency provided statistics, the author argues that logging restrictions are necessary to maintain avian diversity in the Pacific Northwest.

What makes this an effective introduction?

_____

_____

_____

_____

_____

SOLUTION

Let's look at what this response does that sets it up for success.

There is great disagreement about how the United States uses its natural resource. Society needs raw materials to sustain and grow, yet we all acknowledge that irreversible damage to ecosystems should be avoided.

The first sentence addresses the big picture: industry versus environment.

The author takes a clear stance on the side of ecology, but limits his scope to the timber-rich forests of the Pacific Northwest.

This sentence shifts the focus from a broad concern to the narrow focus of the author.

Through the use of metaphors, personal narrative, and governmental agency provided statistics, the author argues that logging restrictions are necessary to maintain avian diversity in the Pacific Northwest.

The last sentence addresses the author's thesis and also lists the devices the author uses. Now the grader knows what the student response will analyze in the following paragraphs: metaphors, personal narrative, and statistics.

Body Paragraphs

The body paragraphs will need to be specific to your passage, so there is not one template that will work every time. Here are some questions that can help you to organize your body paragraphs.

- **Does the author have a different focus in each paragraph?**
  If yes, then it would make sense to analyze the order of topic and how paragraphs move from one topic to the next.

- **Does the author use several devices again and again in the essay?**
  If yes, then you could focus one of your paragraphs on each device.

Each body paragraph should:

- Use short quotes and rephrasing to highlight a persuasive element
- Explain how the element supports the author's main argument
- Explain the effect of the element on the reader

Structure of a body paragraph:

- Transition: make sure that you smoothly move from each of your paragraphs
- Topic sentence: this lets the reader know the focal point of the paragraph
- Evidence: here you can use use short quotes and provide analysis
- Thesis: always conclude by relating the evidence back to your thesis

Conclusion

Your conclusion must be a separate paragraph that sums up your essay. Any essay without a conclusion will automatically lose points for being incomplete. Your conclusion should restate your thesis and summarize the main point of each of your body paragraphs.

Effective Writing

Big words are great, but a couple of four-syllabus gargantuans in your paper will not impress the reader, especially if the words are used incorrectly. Thankfully, there are some tips that will help you to pick the right words for your paper.

- **Avoid first person**
  The reason you should avoid a first person perspective (sentences with I as the subject) is that your focus should be on the author's point of view, not your perception of the issue. Remember that the graders do not want to read your opinion on the topic; you need to stick to what the author does in his or her essay. The easiest way to stay on task in your response is to avoid first person sentences.

- **Use precise language**
  It's easy to fall into a trap of using vague words and familiar phrases. Instead of writing "he is worried about its impact," try writing "Dr. Acula expresses concern about the spread of garlic in American cuisine, as exposure to garlic can negatively affect citizens that share his background."

- **Use a variety of sentences**
  Reading short, choppy sentences becomes tiring. Try to diversify your writing style by creating complex sentences that develop and distinguish your ideas. Here are some ways to vary your sentences beyond the same old "Subject predicate object" song-and-dance.

Semicolon
Our good buddy from the writing section can really spice up your writing; just remember that a semicolon must connect two independent clauses.

Write your own example of a sentence with a semicolon:

_____

Prepositional phrases
In the front of a sentence, a prepositional phrase can add context before the reader discovers the subject of the sentence.

Write your own example of a sentence with a prepositional phrase:

_____

Appositive

The appositive—**a description of the subject offset by commas or hyphens**—can allow the writer to add valuable detail within a sentence.

Write your own example of a sentence with an appositive:

_____

MAXIMIZING YOUR SCORE

- **Organize your essay**
  Make sure that you have an introduction, body paragraphs, and a conclusion.

- **In the introduction, address the topic before you address the author's opinion**
  Your introduction should state the overarching topic and then use that discussion to frame the author's argument.

- **Use effective language**
  Avoid first person sentence and vague pronouns. Use specific vocabulary and complex sentences to express your analysis.

Essay Walkthrough

In this chapter, you'll practice actively reading an argument and then test your understanding by grading some sample essays.

Now let's get some practice! Actively read the passage below, noting all the persuasive elements as you go. You can check your work on the next page.

As you read the passage below, consider how Nigel Winterbottom uses

- evidence, such as facts or examples, to support claims.
- reasoning to develop ideas and to connect claims and evidence.
- stylistic or persuasive elements, such as word choice or appeals to emotion, to add power to the ideas expressed.

Adapted from Dr. Nigel Winterbottom, "Writing through the ages."
© 2015 by Ermahgerd College.

1   In many ways, we live in an astounding age where our ability to communicate seems endless. With a few taps and swipes, we can send our thoughts across the world, delivered to millions, if not billions, of people in the blink of the eye.

2   It would seem that we live in a time that has perfected communication, but perhaps we have traded ease for quality. Are our "tweets," "e-mails," "texts," and "posts" better than the writings from earlier generations? To answer that question, we should look at the differences in how we write. In the past, letters from family and friends would be cherished; hours would be spent organizing ideas and selecting words. Writers placed emphasis on the quality of calligraphy and saw their handwriting as a means of artistic expression. Depending on the physical distance, a letter could take months to arrive, so a writer had to focus on what was important, not just an immediate reaction to the current situation. Writing letters also had a tangible cost in terms of postage and materials, especially before the advent of mass-produced paper and refillable pens. The end result was a body of writing significantly more impactful than a misspelled, acronym-heavy text message.

3   Beyond informal writings between individuals, there was also a shift in published work. Around 1500, book publishing in Europe took a great leap forward with the advent of the printing press. Previously, books were transcribed by hand; with the printing press, another key role in the publishing world, the editor, came into prominence. Before a page could be published, someone would need to overlook the writer's work and check for possible errors. The editor would eventually serve an essential role of revision before the author's ideas could reach the public. The relationship between the writer and editor can be paramount to the success of the book. John Green, author of many popular young-adult novels including *The Fault in Our Stars*, readily acknowledges the impact his editor, Julie Strauss-Gabel, has on his writing, going as far as to say, "I've never written a book without Julie. I wouldn't know how to do it." Now, thanks to the immediacy of blogs and print-on-demand publishers, many authors can circumvent the keen eye of the editor and inflict their half-baked creations on the world. Writing should not be a transcript of our thoughts, but rather a perfection of our ideas, and oftentimes, the sage wisdom of a seasoned editor is needed to help trim the gristle.

4   Some may say that we are in the golden age of literacy. Indeed, a study of nationwide literacy rates conducted by the National Assessment of Education Sciences shows a marked increase in literacy over the last 100 years with only 0.06% of the adult population categorized as "functionally illiterate." While I applaud the progress, I am often appalled at the execution. According to Pew Research Center, 28% of American adults do not read a single book in a year, and it shows in their writing. Today's society demands literacy for gainful, sustained employment, but the same society undervalues literary depth. A "bookworm" continues to be a derisive term and the "Internet," which once mandated literacy for its use has gradually chipped away at the need for literacy. As the Internet has evolved, it has pushed away from writing to other modes of communication. Blogs and forums have made way for photo and video sharing services. Perhaps most telling is the rise in popularity of "emojis," icons used to represent concepts. These are more similar to hieroglyphics than English composition and reflect a complete break from the mechanics of sentences. While emojis can capture a simple emotion and events, they cannot express complex ideas. Is there an emoji capable of expressing ambivalence?

5   Certainly we cannot collectively shelve our computers and phones to take up the quill and inkpot of our forefathers, because at best it would merely be a defiant act of nostalgia. A better approach is to embrace the writing acumen of our ancestors and continue to write works of quality and insight regardless of the medium. Then, we can use our current interconnectivity to its maximum effect.

> Write an essay in which you explain how Nigel Winterbottom builds an argument to persuade his audience that we should be concerned about the contemporary quality of writing. In your essay, analyze how Winterbottom uses one or more of the features listed in the box above (or features of your own choice) to strengthen the logic and persuasiveness of his argument. Be sure that your analysis focuses on the most relevant features of the passage.
>
> Your essay should not explain whether you agree with Winterbottom's claims, but rather explain how Winterbottom builds an argument to persuade his audience.

① Read the instructions to determine the author's main idea.

> Write an essay in which you explain how Nigel Winterbottom builds an argument to persuade his audience that **we should be concerned about the contemporary quality of writing.** In your essay, analyze how Winterbottom uses one or more of the features listed in the box above (or features of your own choice) to strengthen the logic and persuasiveness of his argument. Be sure that your analysis focuses on the most relevant features of the passage.
>
> Your essay should not explain whether you agree with Winterbottom's claims, but rather explain how Winterbottom builds an argument to persuade his audience.

② Actively Read the Passage

counter argument

1 In many ways, we live in an <u>astounding age</u> where <u>our ability to communicate seems endless.</u> With a few taps and swipes, <u>we can send our thoughts across the world</u>, delivered to millions, if not billions, of people in the blink of the eye.

rhetorical question

 2 It would seem that we live in a time that has perfected communication, (but) perhaps <u>we have traded ease for quality.</u> Are our "tweets," "e-mails," "texts," and "posts" better than the writings from earlier generations? To answer that question, <u>we should look at the differences in how we write.</u> In

the past, letters from family and friends would be cherished; hours would be spent organizing ideas and selecting words. Writers placed emphasis on the quality of calligraphy and saw their handwriting as a means of artistic expression. Depending on the physical distance, a letter could take months to arrive, so a writer had to focus on what was important, not just an immediate reaction to the current situation. Writing letters also had a tangible cost in terms of postage and materials, especially before the advent of mass-produced paper and refillable pens. The end result was a body of writing significantly more impactful than a misspelled, acronym-heavy text message.

juxtaposition between then and now

✦

3   Beyond informal writings between individuals, there was also a shift in published work. Around 1500, book publishing in Europe took a great leap forward with the advent of the printing press. Previously, books were transcribed by hand; with the printing press, another key role in the publishing world, the editor, came into prominence. Before a page could be published, someone would need to overlook the writer's work and check for possible errors. The editor would eventually serve an essential role of revision before the author's ideas could reach the public. The relationship between the writer and editor can be paramount to the success of the book. John Green, author of many popular young-adult novels including *The Fault in Our Stars*, readily acknowledges the impact his editor, Julie Strauss-Gabel, has on his writing, going as far as to say, "I've never written a book without Julie. I wouldn't know how to do it." Now, thanks to the immediacy of blogs and print-on-demand publishers, many authors can circumvent the keen eye of the editor and inflict their half-baked creations on the world. Writing should not be a transcript of our thoughts, but rather a perfection of our ideas, and oftentimes, the sage wisdom of a seasoned editor is needed to help trim the gristle. *metaphor*

transition to new topic

historical reference

quote from an expert

synecdoche

metaphor

counter argument

4   Some may say that we are in the golden age of literacy. Indeed, a study of nationwide literacy rates conducted by the National Assessment of Education Sciences shows a marked increase in literacy over the last 100 years with only 0.06% of the adult population categorized as "functionally illiterate." While I applaud the progress, I am often appalled at the execution. According to Pew Research Center, 28% of American adults do not read a single book in a year, and it shows in their writing. Today's society demands literacy for gainful, sustained employment, but the same society undervalues literary depth. A "bookworm" continues to be a derisive term and the "Internet," which once mandated literacy for its use has gradually chipped away at the need for literacy. As the Internet has evolved, it has pushed away from writing to other modes of

empirical counter-evidence

✦

empirical evidence

communication. Blogs and forums have made way for photo and video sharing services. Perhaps most telling is the rise in popularity of "emojis," icons used to represent concepts. These are more <u>similar to hieroglyphics than English composition</u> and reflect a complete break from the mechanics of sentences. While emojis can capture a simple emotion and events, they cannot express complex ideas. Is there an emoji capable of expressing ambivalence?

juxtaposition

5 Certainly we cannot collectively shelve our computers and phones to take up the quill and inkpot of our forefathers, because at best it would merely be a defiant act of nostalgia. <u>A better approach is to embrace the writing acumen of our ancestors and continue to write works of quality and insight regardless of the medium.</u> Then, we can use our current interconnectivity to its maximum effect.

③ Outline your Response

Introduction:

- The topic: how writing has changed because of technology.
- The author's position: writing has gotten easier to create and publish, but not necessarily better.
- How the author persuades the reader: juxtaposition, counter argument, word choice, and historical evidence

Body paragraphs:

- Plan the order of the paragraphs.
- Determine when to use quotes.

Conclusion:

- Restate your thesis

④ Write your Essay!

Let's take some time to evaluate some responses to Dr. Winterbottom's essay. Below, you'll find 4 students' responses to the passage. Give the responses scores in all 3 categories:

READING: Does the essay explain the author's argument?

ANALYSIS: Does the essay explain how the argument persuades the reader?

WRITING: Is the essay well-organized and well-written?

EXAMPLE 1

I think the author does not like most writing. He says "It would seem that we live in a time that has perfected communication, but perhaps we have traded ease for quality." Writing is pretty easy write now as I can just have my phone write up what I say. I think the author likes old books, because he used printting presses and John Green, I haven't read John Green book, so I don't know if they are any good.

The author picks on emojis, which is kinda funny. I like to use emojis in texts but some times I confuse my mom. I guess the author and my mom are kinda the same. He says that emojis are "similar to hieroglyphics" which I sorta guess is true.

The passage ends with saying "A better approach is to embrace the writing acumen of our ancestors and continue to write works of quality and insight regardless of the medium. Then, we can use our current interconnectivity to its maximum effect." I thought that this was a good ending and persuaded the audience.

How would you score this essay?

Reading (from 1 to 4) _____

Analysis (from 1 to 4) _____

Writing (from 1 to 4) _____

SOLUTION

Reading (from 1 to 4) **1**

This response misses the main point of the author's argument: the quality of writing today is in trouble. It almost gets close at one point ("Writing is pretty easy right now", "the author likes old books") but then veers away again. The response also misses the point of the supporting examples dealing with John Green and emojis.

Analysis (from 1 to 4) **1**

The response includes quotes, but makes no connection between the quotes and the argument.

Writing (from 1 to 4) **1**

No thesis, no body paragraphs, no organization! There are several run-on sentences and plenty of informal language that is too casual for an academic analysis. The passage has common spelling and grammatical mistakes that confuse the meaning.

EXAMPLE 2

Dr. Winterbottom is concerned with the current quality of writing. He feels that writing has gotten easier but not better. To persuade his audience, Dr. Winterbottom uses a lot of different examples to show how writing has changed, but not necessarily for the better.

The essay begins by Winterbottom discussing the progress made in creating and publishing writing, which some call "an astounding age." However, the second paragraph reveals that Winterbottom disagrees, saying that "we have traded ease for quality." He then uses some historical examples to show how much care was placed on writing earlier. He emphasizes the quality, craftsmanship, and expense that went into writing a letter long ago.

The next paragraph discusses published writing and brings up the idea that an editor is useful to make better writing. Here, Winterbottom uses a quote to show how a successful writer relies on an editor.

In the next paragraph, Winterbottom thinks about whether we are more or less literate. He uses some data to show that literacy rates are high but responds by saying "while I applaud the progress, I am often appalled at the execution," mentioning that 28% of American adults didn't read a book last year. He is concerned that we are writing simpler and simpler and using emojis the same way the Egyptians used hieroglyphics. While this works for simple ideas, like happiness, emojis cannot show complex emotions. The essay ends by not suggesting that we abandon technology, but use it to "write works of quality and insight regardless of the medium."

How would you score this essay?

Reading (from 1 to 4) _____

Analysis (from 1 to 4) _____

Writing (from 1 to 4) _____

SOLUTION

Reading (from 1 to 4) **2**

The essay focuses on the author's main argument and identifies supporting details, but either misinterprets the significance of those details (emoji/hieroglyphic link) or fails to connect them to the larger point (yes, letters were expensive, but what did that lead to?). It includes a few brief quotes, but they are not integrated very effectively.

Analysis (from 1 to 4) **1**

The response does not address the main task of the assignment: analyzing the argument. It spends most of the time restating the author's argument rather than analyzing literary and rhetorical elements used in the essay.

Writing (from 1 to 4) **2**

The essay has a thesis in a brief and effective introduction and few grammar/syntax errors. However, it lacks a conclusion and uses mainly basic sentence structures.

EXAMPLE 3

Throughout the passage, we can see that author, Nigel Winterbottom, has a concern with the quality of contemporary writing. Winterbottom uses historical juxtaposition, contemporary evidence, and word choice to persuade the audience to agree with him that writing used to mean more, that we ignore the importance of editing, and we are moving away from written communication.

Winterbottom first starts with the counter-argument before offering his own opinion that "we have traded ease for quality." He then juxtaposes older forms of writing that required more skill and effort. Winterbottom clearly prefers these writings, opposed to current emails and texts. He emphasizes this slide in quality by referring to them as "misspelled, acronym-heavy text message" as opposed to a letter from long ago written in calligraphy.

Winterbottom's next key point is how important the editor is towards creating quality writing. Again, he starts with a historical juxtaposition, but this time he refers to the early era of the printing press. He shows how important editing is now by including a quote by John Green, who attributes much of his literary success to his editor Julie Strauss-Gabel. Unfortunately for Winterbottom, most writers now do not use an editor, thanks to the ease of online publishing. Winterbottom concludes this paragraph by offering his insight that "writing should not be a transcript of our thoughts, but rather a perfection of our ideas," which nicely sums up his belief that the quality of writing is important.

Winterbottom's third point relates directly to literacy and its perceived decline. He uses contemporary evidence, in terms of overall literacy rates, but then finds fault in this study by cleverly stating " while I applaud the progress, I am often appalled at the execution," as 28% of Americans didn't read a book last year. This line nicely shows how Winterbottom is concerned with the quality of writing, rather than a simple definition of literate versus illiterate. He argues that we are experiencing a lapse in quality as emojis take over written communication. Winterbottom specifically uses the word "ambivalence," the state of mixed emotions, to show how limiting emojis can be.

Winterbottom's persuasive passage used enough juxtaposition, evidence, and careful word choice to not only make readers to evaluate the current state of writing, but also provoke readers to take action to make sure that their own writing works to counteract this trend.

How would you score this essay?

Reading (from 1 to 4) _____

Analysis (from 1 to 4) _____

Writing (from 1 to 4) _____

SOLUTION

Reading (from 1 to 4) **4**

The response effectively summarizes both the author's main point and the ways it is supported throughout the essay. It effectively uses quotes and direct references to support interpretation of the author's opinions.

Analysis (from 1 to 4) **3**

The response lists several literary elements used by the author and begins to describe how they are used, but strays somewhere in the middle and begins recapping the argument rather than analyzing it. The third point in the thesis (word choice) is never addressed in the body paragraphs.

Writing (from 1 to 4) **3**

There are a few grammatical errors, but the essay does use some complex sentence structures. The thesis is clear and the paragraphs are fairly well-organized. The writing is straightforward and easy to understand.

EXAMPLE 4

Writing will continually evolve from generation to generation as words and grammatical conventions fall out of favor. Dr. Nigel Winterbottom understands this, but he shows great concern towards the direction current writing has gone. Winterbottom not only persuades his audience that writing is heading towards decline, but he also valiantly fights against this trend with skillful refutation of counter arguments, expert language choices, and historical juxtapositions.

Winterbottom uses a counter argument to introduce the essay, offering a positive account of our "astounding age" and our ability to create and share information. Yet, Winterbottom then asks if our fast-paced " 'tweets,' 'e-mails,' 'texts,' and 'posts' " are better than the laborious writing process of history. He juxtaposes the present writing style of "misspelled, acronym-heavy texts" with the past's "emphasis on the quality" of writing. This stark contrast forces the reader to consider whether this contemporary writing style has lost that emphasis on quality in the pursuit of convenience. This juxtaposition is essential to Winterbottom's argument, since he wants to prescribe a course of action, "to embrace the writing acumen of our ancestors and continue to write works of quality and insight," without coming across as stodgy and off-puttingly retro.

In the third paragraph, Winterbottom extends his use of historical juxtaposition, this time comparing the editors of early printed materials to the editor-less blogs and forums of today. Winterbottom then chooses to quote an expert, the author John Green, to support the assertion that the editor offers "an essential role of revision" that is missing in much of today's writing. By using a popular author that many in his audience would know, Winterbottom builds the reader's confidence in his assertions. Had he chosen a more pretentious writer, the quote would be less effective and would reinforce the fallacy that Winterbottom wishes for writers to return to the "quill and the inkpot."

Winterbottom continues to use counter argument to persuade the audience that the current state of writing is troubling. In the fourth paragraph, Winterbottom references the fact that 0.06% of adults are "functionally illiterate." He then quickly reframes the argument, pointing out the empirical evidence that annually, 28% of American adults "do not read a single book." This counter argument shows that the illiteracy rate may be low, but that data point cannot express the depth of literacy that Winterbottom feels is becoming lost. Winterbottom then returns to a historical juxtaposition, but delves deeper into the past, alluding to ancient Egyptian hieroglyphics as a precursor to today's emojis. Winterbottom chooses one word, "ambivalence," to describe an emotion that cannot be expressed with a cartoon-faced emoji. His word choice is excellent, because ambivalence expresses his feelings about the current state of writing. He solidifies this opinion in the final paragraph by arguing we should not "shelve our computers," but instead "write works of quality and insight regardless of the medium." Despite all of the dire proclamations, Winterbottom believes we are still capable of great writing; the conclusion leaves the reader feeling hopeful and inspired, rather than wallowing in negativity.

As a whole, Winterbottom's essay accomplishes an impressive feat: it addresses the current lackluster quality of writing while also being an example of clever and precise writing. Winterbottom leads us through centuries of writing, yet never lets us get lost along the way so that by the end, the audience is inspired to continue the tradition of excellent writing.

How would you score this essay?

Reading (from 1 to 4) _____

Analysis (from 1 to 4) _____

Writing (from 1 to 4) _____

SOLUTION

Reading (from 1 to 4) – 4

The response grasps not only the author's main point, but also the more subtle elements of it. All quotes and examples are given with correct interpretation of the author's intentions and are directly connected to the structure of the larger argument.

Analysis (from 1 to 4) – 4

The response gives not only concrete elements of rhetorical technique, but also more abstract and subtextual dynamics used by the author to persuade readers. It also addresses the effect of those elements on the reader.

Writing (from 1 to 4) – 4

There are very few errors and the essay presents everything in a fluent style, with a complexity of structure at both the sentence and paragraph levels. The response has a clear and logical organization supporting a strong thesis.

Practice Essays

Now it's your turn! Practice writing your own essays with the given prompts.

Practice Makes Perfect

Over the next several pages, you will have the opportunity to write 4 practice essays. Each essay will be based on a passage modeled after those on the official test.

If possible, space out your practice; put at least a day or two between essays. This will give you time to reread your own essay with a critical eye and make plans for improvement. If you can, get feedback from others on your essay.

Focus on Improvement

As you work your way through this section, make sure you're practicing the key skills that we've covered so far. And remember your steps:

(1) Read the instructions to determine the author's main idea

(2) Actively read the passage, marking persuasive elements

(3) Outline your response; write a clear thesis and choose quotes for your body paragraphs

(4) Write your Essay!

As you read the passage below, consider how Mercedes Breckenridge uses

- evidence, such as facts or examples, to support claims.
- reasoning to develop ideas and to connect claims and evidence.
- stylistic or persuasive elements, such as word choice or appeals to emotion, to add power to the ideas expressed.

Adapted from Mercedes Breckenridge, "Composting: Turning Garbage into Gold."

1 As every gardener knows, nothing compares to a loamy shovelful of rich, dark soil, loaded with nutrients and teeming with fat, happy earthworms. And the best way to achieve this sublime soil? A heaping layer of decaying organic matter, also known as compost. While dumping fertilizers might offer fast short-term results, in the long term there's no substitute for compost.

2 To many, the art of composting seems counterintuitive, and perhaps even a bit off-putting. Why would someone want to collect a lot of smelly garbage? (A healthy compost pile thrives on organic matter as eclectic as used coffee grounds and broken egg shells, rotting banana peels and old scraps of lettuce, and grass clippings from the freshly mowed lawn.) It's certainly *easier* to just throw all that away.

3 But turning too quickly to the trash service has negative effects. The Environmental Protection Agency reports that food scraps represent 20 to 30 percent of Americans' trash. in 2012, that equaled approximately 35 million tons of food waste—the majority of it headed straight to a landfill. And landfills may be the single largest emitters of toxic methane gas, a major culprit behind harmful climate change.

4 Instead, those 35 million tons of food waste could be making a big difference to your garden, your bank account, and the environment of planet Earth.

5 Good compost starts with four main ingredients: organic material, water (rain will do, or you can add your own), friendly bacteria, and oxygen. "Brown" matter like dead leaves is rich in carbon, and "green" stuff like lawn clippings is rich in nitrogen; both are essential elements in healthy soil, and should be balanced one to one. Meanwhile, the bacteria and oxygen work together to process and decompose the material into compost.

6 Along with carbon and nitrogen, the finished compost is filled with recycled nutrients— the essential minerals like phosphorous and potassium that all help green stuff thrive. Plants grown in nutrient-rich soil don't just grow faster and healthier; they also produce more nutritious fruit and vegetables, bringing a better meal to your plate.

7 Adding compost to the soil also enhances its texture, turning it into a dense, crumbly soil called loam, well-aerated with oxygen pockets and moisture channels. This high-quality soil is called humus, and it's more resistant to soil erosion and better able to retain oxygen, water, and nutrients. In fact, a five percent increase in organic material in the soil

quadruples water retention, which means less watering… a *lot* less watering. That much less watering means a lower water bill, for sure, and is also a big help in areas with water shortages due to dry seasons and droughts. With drought increasing in communities all over the world, this is a big deal.

8 Along with money saved on your water bill, there are other cost benefits too. You won't have to buy commercial fertilizers, and if you pay by volume for trash pick-up, you can also save a lot on your garbage service. Plus, the healthy bacteria and microbes in compost will increase your garden's resistance to disease and pests, increasing crop yield and saving money that might otherwise be spent on pesticides.

9 With all of composting's obvious benefits, a number of beloved celebrities and famous figures are jumping on the bandwagon and spreading the word. Their numbers include Kristen Bell, Julia Roberts (she spoke eloquently on the topic to Oprah, who also composts!), and Jason Mraz, who composts on his own farm. Even the White House has three compost bins!

10 In 2013, the *Washington Post* reported on composting's growing popularity across the nation, writing, "Increasingly, local governments, entrepreneurs, and community activists are experimenting with composting." They cited an impressive 170 composting programs throughout the country, up from twenty just eight years previously. Cutting-edge metropolises like San Francisco and New York City, along with small but forward-thinking towns, are expanding their composting programs and making it easier than ever for residents to turn their old, smelly food scraps into "black gold": valuable compost.

11 Ready to try your own hand at composting? It's shockingly easy. All you need to begin is a large bucket with a tightly closing lid, or better yet, a bin positioned in a sunny spot in the yard. Add leftover food scraps (vegetarian preferred) and yard clippings like grass and leaves. When the stuff is well-decomposed, spread on a garden plot, add to landscaping, or scoop into indoor plants like flowers and herbs. Voila: you're a smart gardener—and a steward of planet Earth.

Write an essay in which you explain how Mercedes Breckenridge builds an argument to persuade her audience that they should start composting. In your essay, analyze how Breckenridge uses one or more of the features listed in the box above (or features of your own choice) to strengthen the logic and persuasiveness of her argument. Be sure that your analysis focuses on the most relevant features of the passage.

Your essay should not explain whether you agree with Breckenridge's claims, but rather explain how Breckenridge builds an argument to persuade her audience.

IMPORTANT: **DON'T WRITE OUTSIDE THE BORDER.**

PLANNING PAGE   You may plan your essay in the unlined planning space below, but use only the lined pages following this one to write your essay. Any work on this planning page will not be scored.

Use next 4 pages for your ESSAY ⟶

BEGIN YOUR ESSAY HERE.

You may continue on the next page.

DO NOT WRITE OUTSIDE OF THE BOX.

You may continue on the next page.

DO NOT WRITE OUTSIDE OF THE BOX.

You may continue on the next page.

DO NOT WRITE OUTSIDE OF THE BOX.

STOP

As you read the passage below, consider how Stewart Topor uses

- evidence, such as facts or examples, to support claims.
- reasoning to develop ideas and to connect claims and evidence.
- stylistic or persuasive elements, such as word choice or appeals to emotion, to add power to the ideas expressed.

Adapted from Stewart Topor, "Stop buying into the 'busyness' narrative, and start using the time you have."

1   We've all heard the news: Americans are busier than ever, perhaps the busiest people in human history. We're over-scheduled, over-booked and overworked, spending every waking hour rushing from appointment to appointment, rarely getting a moment's peace or a full night's sleep. Ask a friend how they're doing lately, and the typical answer is: "Busy." Or occasionally, "Slammed." Sometimes, "Everything's crazy over here."

2   The narrative that Americans are overwhelmingly busy has taken hold as unassailable fact. But is it actually true? The answer may surprise you.

3   Since 1961, the University of Oxford's Centre for Time Use Research has been conducting extensive, detailed research into how people spend their time. This research is collected via time-use diaries—which are exactly what they sound like. Participants log their activities from day to day, hour to hour. These time-use diaries have been gathered in nearly 40 countries over the course of 50 years, and represent around 850,000 days logged.

4   Sociologist and time-use scholar John Robinson has worked extensively with these diaries. Robinson says that, while people report extreme busyness, the numbers don't really add up. Despite the widely accepted narrative that we're busier than ever before, the average number of work hours per week has not actually gone up significantly since the 1980s.

5   This conclusion is supported by the US Bureau of Labor Statistics, which gathers data on how Americans spend their time. According to the 2014 American Time Use Survey numbers, employed people logged an average of 7.8 hours per workday—a manageable 39 hours per work week, nothing like the excessive fifty-, sixty-, or eighty-hour workweeks so often claimed. On an average day, 96 percent of people found time for leisure activities like watching TV, playing a sport, or hanging with friends. In fact, the average leisure time was a generous 5.3 hours a day. And participants slept an average of 8.8 hours a night, a perfectly healthy amount.

6   The unavoidable conclusion is that people are prone to exaggerating the number of hours they work, and underestimating the amount of sleep they get or time they have to relax. Perhaps this is due to a negative cognitive bias: people are more likely to remember the bad days over the good, emphasizing the sleepless night rather than the restful one, and

the long, harried day at the office rather than the Friday they left early. They're more likely to think of an overworked Wednesday than a lazy Sunday as "a typical day," even though both days happen only once a week. Another factor is the desire people have to *seem* busy, with its connotations of being hard-working, ambitious, high-impact, and perhaps irreplaceable. In today's tough economy, that impulse makes sense; the best way to secure your spot in your workplace is to give the impression that you're doing the work of two individuals, perhaps three. On the other hand, someone who never seems overworked might be the first to get a pink slip if layoffs arrive.

7   Whatever the cause, time-use diaries show that the hyperbole around work hours is quantifiable. The average person overstates their working hours by five to ten percent. And the people who claim to work the most exaggerate the most; instead of being the hardest workers, they're the biggest fibbers. People who thought they worked 75 hours a week overestimated by as much as 50 percent. "One study tracking people's estimated and actual workweeks found that those claiming to work 70, 80 or more hours were logging less than 60," writes time-use expert Laura Vanderkam in the *Wall Street Journal*.

8   A successful author, Vanderkam has published several books exploring the discrepancy between the hours we have and the hours we *think* we have. She argues that we have a lot more time than we think; we just need to take advantage of it. Her conviction grew out of her own experience. In that same 2012 *Wall Street Journal* article, she writes, "What I thought was a 60-hour workweek wasn't even close." After keeping a time diary, she began to understand where her time really went — and put it to much better use.

9   These findings suggest that as much as anything else, "busyness" is a state of mind. We have more time than we think we do, and acknowledging that fact can enable us to lead more enjoyable lives, with less stress and greater focus. So next time you're tempted to lament how busy you are, take a step back. Instead, focus on all the time you do have — and figure out how you can better use those hours in a way that's productive and fulfilling.

Write an essay in which you explain how Stewart Topor builds an argument to persuade his audience that people are less busy than they realize. In your essay, analyze how Topor uses one or more of the features listed in the box above (or features of your own choice) to strengthen the logic and persuasiveness of his argument. Be sure that your analysis focuses on the most relevant features of the passage.

Your essay should not explain whether you agree with Topor's claims, but rather explain how Topor builds an argument to persuade his audience.

IMPORTANT: **DON'T WRITE OUTSIDE THE BORDER.**

PLANNING PAGE You may plan your essay in the unlined planning space below, but use only the lined pages following this one to write your essay. Any work on this planning page will not be scored.

Use next 4 pages for your ESSAY ⟶

BEGIN YOUR ESSAY HERE.

You may continue on the next page.

DO NOT WRITE OUTSIDE OF THE BOX.

You may continue on the next page.

DO NOT WRITE OUTSIDE OF THE BOX.

You may continue on the next page.

DO NOT WRITE OUTSIDE OF THE BOX.

STOP

As you read the passage below, consider how P. W. Curtstein uses

- evidence, such as facts or examples, to support claims.
- reasoning to develop ideas and to connect claims and evidence.
- stylistic or persuasive elements, such as word choice or appeals to emotion, to add power to the ideas expressed.

Adapted from P. W. Curtstein, "Don't Fear Nanotech. Embrace It… and Fund It."

1 Nanotechnology may represent doomsday in fear-mongering sci-fi thrillers or clickbait-style news headlines. Perhaps it's not surprising; history has shown that humanity often irrationally fears what it doesn't understand, and nanotech is one of the most mind-bending new technologies around. But despite its esoteric nature, nanotech is something that humans will master, not the other way around. And B-rate movies aside, "nanotech gone wild" is no more realistic a threat to human civilization than dinosaur outbreaks or robots from the future. In fact, nanotech offers amazing benefits. Instead of fearing this fascinating technology, we should embrace it.

2 The U.S. government understood this early, and in 2000, began pouring funding into nanotech research and development. Thanks to this support, nanotech has made amazing leaps and bounds in the past fifteen years; according to the federal National Nanotechnology Initiative, 800 products relying on nanoscale elements are already on the market. A few examples: computer chip elements that have helped shrink computers from room-sized giants to pocket-sized smart phones; "hydrophobic" coating on textiles that repels liquids to stop stains; and carbon nanotubes used to add durability to items ranging from tennis rackets to space rockets.

3 Why does nanotech hold such promise?

4 To understand the answer to this question, you must grasp how mind-bogglingly small the nanoscale truly is. There's the microscale, which covers things we call "microscopic": bacteria, viruses, cells. Then, smaller than that, there's the nanoscale. A strand of hair is about 100 thousand nanometers wide. Nanotech elements are typically less than 100 nanometers. So when we talk about nanotech, we're talking about elements about 1/1000 the width of a human hair.

5 When matter is reduced to this scale, it expresses different properties, and undergoes different processes. It can become stronger, lighter, more durable, and better at conducting electrical signals. Things that seem like magic at the human scale become totally feasible at the nanoscale.

6 As a result, nanotechnology represents a new world—with astonishing possibilities on the horizon. For example, a high-speed nanomotor recently designed at the University of Texas at Austin. This motor is 500 times smaller than a grain of salt, and could travel inside the human body to administer insulin or destroy cancer cells.

7   Nanotechnology is already transforming medicine. Doctors can inject nanoparticles into the human body to detect bacteria, viruses, tumors, or the presence of Alzheimer's disease. Nanoparticles can be programmed to deliver a drug payload directly to a single cell, enabling extremely targeted pharmaceutical treatments. Medical advances like these could one day save the life of someone you love… even your own.

8   Another horizon is manufacturing. One recent example is graphene: a material made from a single layer of carbon atoms assembled hexagonally. At one atom wide, it's so thin it's essentially two-dimensional. Graphene is flexible, transparent, and light, but thanks to the unbreakable bonds between carbon atoms, it's also very strong—207 times stronger than steel. A "magic" material like this can revolutionize technological devices from cellphones to solar cells. And it's already under development in next-generation water filtration systems, which will turn salty ocean water into potable fresh water, or remove toxins to make contaminated water safe to drink.

9   Finally, nanotechnology will change computing forever. According to renowned computer scientist Ralph Merkle, "Nanotechnology will let us build computers that are incredibly powerful. We'll have more power in the volume of a sugar cube than exists in the entire world today." Imagine a computer smaller than an ant, and you get the idea. The next step is turning single molecules into processing units.

10 Nanotechnology can work marvels that seem like miracles: curing diseases from inside the body… turning brackish and polluted water into life-giving sustenance on the spot… creating artificial blood cells, bionic implants, and replacement limbs… crafting body armor that's light as cotton but bullet-proof…the list goes on. Jay West, senior director for Chemical Products and Technology at the American Chemistry Council, calls nanotechnology "an enabling science," saying "innovations in nanotechnology are already improving our society in areas such as healthcare, energy efficiency, environmental remediation, and even national security."

11 The naysayers on nanotechnology may not be *completely* wrong: every new technology undoubtedly comes with risks. But new technologies have also improved the world in countless tangible ways. People live longer, healthier lives; many diseases have been eradicated; across the globe, we're better educated, better connected, and better fed than ever been before.

12 Nanotechnology will allow us to continue that trend from the twentieth century into the twenty-first. Support funding for nanotechnology research and development—and support the making of a better world.

Write an essay in you explain how P. W. Curtstein builds an argument to persuade her audience that we need to embrace the potential of nanotechnology. In your essay, analyze how Curtstein uses one or more of the features listed in the box above (or features of your own choice) to strengthen the logic and persuasiveness of his argument. Be sure that your analysis focuses on the most relevant features of the passage.

Your essay should not explain whether you agree with Curtstein's claims, but rather explain how Curtstein builds an argument to persuade his audience.

IMPORTANT: **DON'T WRITE OUTSIDE THE BORDER.**

PLANNING PAGE You may plan your essay in the unlined planning space below, but use only the lined pages following this one to write your essay. Any work on this planning page will not be scored.

Use next 4 pages for your ESSAY ⟶

DO NOT WRITE OUTSIDE OF THE BOX.

You may continue on the next page.

DO NOT WRITE OUTSIDE OF THE BOX.

You may continue on the next page.

DO NOT WRITE OUTSIDE OF THE BOX.

STOP

As you read the passage below, consider how Kurt Stolid uses

- evidence, such as facts or examples, to support claims.

- reasoning to develop ideas and to connect claims and evidence.

- stylistic or persuasive elements, such as word choice or appeals to emotion, to add power to the ideas expressed.

Adapted from Kurt Stolid, "Brainstorming is Bad for Business. Do This Instead."

1   Imagine this: you're a team leader, and you've been tasked with generating creative ideas, whether for an innovative product, an inventive marketing campaign, or a resourceful solution to an industry problem. Chances are, your first thought will be to call all your team members to the table for a brainstorming session. But according to innovation experts, you might want to think again.

2   The concept of brainstorming was first advanced in the 1950s by advertising agency executive Alex Osborn. He defined his technique with four key rules: First, generate as many ideas as possible. Second, focus particularly on ideas that are original and off-the-wall. Third, mash-up ideas to combine and refine. Fourth, no criticizing! There are no stupid ideas at the brainstorming table.

3   As the old saying goes, "Two heads are better than one," and Osborn was convinced that his creative employees would perform better as a team.

4   On the surface, it makes sense. "Brainstorming seems like an ideal technique, a feel-good way to boost productivity," Jonah Lehrer wrote in a 2012 *New Yorker* titled "Groupthink." "But there is a problem with brainstorming. It doesn't work."

5   In 2015, Tomas Chamorro-Premuzic advanced a similar view in the *Harvard Business Review*. "After six decades of independent scientific research, there is very little evidence for the idea that brainstorming produces more or better ideas than the same number of individuals would produce working independently. In fact, a great deal of evidence indicates that brainstorming actually harms creative performance."

6   But why? To understand the downsides of brainstorming, let's go back to that hypothetical meeting you've called with your team. You've got a team member—we'll call him Bob—who's popular with the group (he always brings the best donuts). Bob is confident and outgoing, so when the team meets around the table, it's natural for Bob to supply the first idea. It's also natural for everyone else to respond positively… and that can influence the rest of the discussion. But unfortunately, Bob isn't the best creative thinker on the team—he's just the best at arguing for his own ideas.

7   Conversely, your team member Lucy is an extremely creative person. She's a careful, methodical thinker who's great at coming up with state-of-the-art solutions, but she's also shy and introverted, and it takes her a while to formulate her idea to the point where she feels comfortable sharing it with the group. By that point, everyone else around the table is already feeling comfortable with Bob's plan… and Lucy isn't the type to argue passionately for her own position.

8   The problem is clear: Bob isn't actually the best at coming up with ideas, he's merely the best at expressing them.

9   There are a number of group dynamics like this one that hamper the productivity of group brainstorming session. For one thing, the first ideas often predict the rest of the conversation—even though first ideas are typically the least original and most clichéd. For another, discussing ideas in front of a group often creates a "herd mentality"—people feel pressured to go with the flow and conform to the team, so instead of really quirky thoughts getting a chance to thrive, people tend to stick with what's safe and familiar. A third problem: freeloaders. Not everyone wants to do the hard work of generating creative ideas, so some people will inevitably piggyback onto others' contributions. Sometimes, that's not even conscious: hearing someone's idea before you get a chance to formulate your own can curtail your own creative process, and push your thought process in an already-trod direction.

10   So, next time you find yourself working with a group, consider some alternatives to the traditional brainstorming process. Ask the quieter folks in your group to weigh in; don't make them fight to communicate their ideas (which may be stellar!). Rather than outlawing criticism, encourage constructive criticism, which helps get everyone engaged and pushes people beyond the familiarity of the first idea.

11   Or, if you want to shake things up even more, get together to establish your shared goal, and then stage a "break-out session" where each individual comes up with three to five ideas on their own. Then, when you return to the table, each person can take a turn sharing their best idea with the group. An approach like this actually elicits the best creative thinking that each person has to offer—while still taking advantage of the power of collective problem-solving.shortages due to dry seasons and droughts. With drought increasing in communities all over the world, this is a big deal.

Write an essay in which you explain how Kurt Stolid builds an argument to persuade his audience that brainstorming does not produce effective results. In your essay, analyze how Stolid uses one or more of the features listed in the box above (or features of your own choice) to strengthen the logic and persuasiveness of his argument. Be sure that your analysis focuses on the most relevant features of the passage.

Your essay should not explain whether you agree with Stolid's claims, but rather explain how Stolid builds an argument to persuade his audience.

IMPORTANT: **DON'T WRITE OUTSIDE THE BORDER.**

PLANNING PAGE You may plan your essay in the unlined planning space below, but use only the lined pages following this one to write your essay. Any work on this planning page will not be scored.

Use next 4 pages for your ESSAY ⟶

BEGIN YOUR ESSAY HERE.

You may continue on the next page.

DO NOT WRITE OUTSIDE OF THE BOX.

You may continue on the next page.

DO NOT WRITE OUTSIDE OF THE BOX.

You may continue on the next page.

DO NOT WRITE OUTSIDE OF THE BOX.

STOP

BEYOND

THE

CONTENT

Beyond the Content

In this chapter, you'll learn how to master mental component of the SAT.

To fully prepare for the SAT, you need to accomplish 3 goals:

1. Understand the **structure and format** of the SAT

2. Master the **content** assessed on all sections of the test

3. Master the **test-taking skills** needed to thrive in a 4-hour, pressured testing environment

TIP

The final component, test-taking skills, is generally the most neglected aspect of test preparation, and for many students, it is the most important.

Are you a good test-taker?

Whether you believe that you are a good test-taker or a bad test-taker, that **belief** will impact your score on the SAT. In fact, your self-appraisal of your ability is a better predictor of how you will do on the SAT than your **actual** level of ability!

It doesn't matter how good you are in reality; if you repeatedly tell yourself that you are not going to do well on this test, you can override your actual abilities and sabotage your performance. And conversely, **if you believe you will succeed on the SAT, this belief will improve your performance!** Thoughts are powerful things!

Natural Test Takers

Some of you may fall under the category of natural test takers. You don't mind standardized tests. You actually kind of like them and have found a way to **treat them like a game**. You set challenging goals for yourself and work hard to achieve them. And more than likely, you are actively engaging in a lot of behaviors, both consciously and subconsciously, which are helping you to succeed!

Everybody Else

The majority of people have a different relationship with standardized tests than do the natural test takers. Most students don't love the SAT, though they eventually learn how to work with it and succeed on it. Some students get nervous or a little stressed when they have to sit for an SAT Other students feel **eternally cursed** when it comes to the SAT or any standardized test. They believe that no matter how much they prepare, they will never do well.

Does bad testing karma really exist? Is there no hope for these students?

Negative Beliefs about Testing

If you feel karmically challenged by the SAT, it's important that you examine the *origins* of your negative beliefs. When did you start to believe that you were "bad at testing?"

Are you focusing on a few isolated instances of poor performance? Are you **ignoring** instances of **strong performance?** Are you really **always** bad at testing in every possible context?

If you can locate a single success in your testing past, you can work with it and begin to build from it.

Watch your words: your mind is listening

When it comes to making global statements about your testing abilities, be careful not to sell yourself short. Rather than saying, "I am miserable at testing," shift and rephrase the statement.

> "I used to struggle with testing, but now
> I'm open to the **possibility** of doing better."

Your mind likes to be consistent, and it tends to back up your words with actions. Optimists score higher; don't close the door on what's possible!

Conquering Anxiety

Test anxiety stems from a potentially useful thought: "Hey, this test counts. I need to do well." When this thought becomes invested with too much energy, however, it starts to hurt your score.

Fight or Flight

When you are stressed about an upcoming test, your body reacts in the same way it would to an actual physical threat. These two thoughts cause the *same exact chemicals* to surge through your body:

"Ahh! A **test**!"   and   "Ahh! A **lion**!"

When those stress hormones hit your bloodstream, your muscles begin to tense, your heart rate and respiratory rate change, and your breathing may become increasingly shallow. With less oxygen going to your brain, **you start to lose focus.** Distracted, you no longer think or process information as clearly, and your working memory becomes impaired.

This increases your chances of escaping a lion... but significantly lowers your chances of acing the SAT!

Helpful Anxiety

A **low** level of anxiety is actually **useful** because it drives you to prepare for and stay focused during the SAT. There is a tipping point where things shift from good to bad.

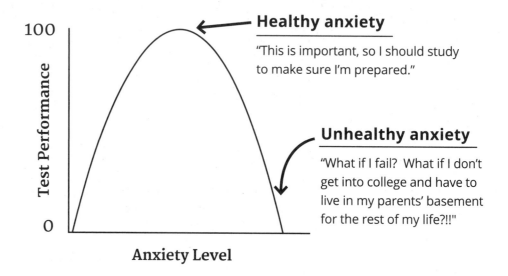

Healthy anxiety

"This is important, so I should study to make sure I'm prepared."

Unhealthy anxiety

"What if I fail? What if I don't get into college and have to live in my parents' basement for the rest of my life?!!"

The simple graph above illustrates the continuum of anxiety and its impact on performance. What it tells us is that **some** anxiety is good; too much is harmful. We want to reach the optimal point so we have just the right amount of anxiety.

Mentally Addressing Anxiety

So what can you do about anxiety? There are several strategies to address heightened anxiety. We each have a number of voices inside of our heads (some of us have more voices than others) that provide a running commentary on life. Some of these voices are negative, but others are positive and encouraging. Learning to manage your own inner-dialogue and focus on the positive voices is one of the keys to succeeding on the SAT.

Listening to Your Inner Coach

When it comes to inner dialogue, most good test-takers have a major resource on their side: their inner coach. For most students, their inner coach is actually a composite figure, created from pieces of their favorite coaches, teachers or mentors who are rooting for them to succeed.

Your inner coach can help you relax or get focused before and during the test by sending you supportive messages.

Pre-game: "You're ready. Go in relaxed. You can knock this out."

Game Time: "You're doing great. It's only one question, don't worry about it. Let it go. Relax… you can do this."

It's not difficult to imagine how receiveing these kinds of positive messages could help you remain focused and centered during the SAT. Having a supportive inner dialogue helps you keep yourself paced, calm, and focused. What an advantage!

If your inner voice isn't this positive yet, that's okay! It's something we can change with some practice. The first step is to recognize your anxiety. The next step is to conquer it! On the next page, we'll look at how a negative voice can impact your performance.

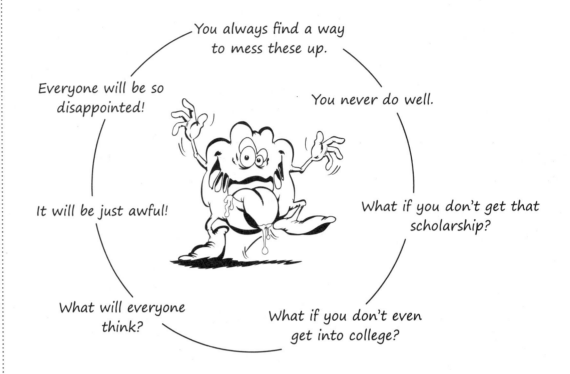

Your Inner Anxiety Monster

For other students who have not yet tapped into their inner coach, another creature may appear instead: **the anxiety monster**. The monster feeds on fear and is continually scanning the environment for potential catastrophes. He causes negative statements that cause more negative statements, raising anxiety and dropping performance.

> Do not let the monster run rampant in your inner dialogue!

If you don't deal with the monster directly and **confront** these negative statements, you run the risk of being influenced by them. If you allow yourself to focus your energy on thoughts of failure, your mind may subconsciously begin to turn these thoughts into reality.

Naming the Monster

If you can give your monster a name, you can deal with him more easily and address him directly. Though you will know the right name for your monster, for now, we'll call him Rupert.

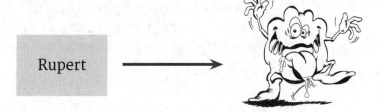

Rupert ⟶

It's important to remember that Rupert actually works *for* you (though he's not the world's best employee), and he is taking up space in your head. If you stop feeding Rupert energy and attention, he will disappear.

Taming the Monster

If you are about to take the SAT and Rupert is stoking the fire of anxiety, bringing up those negative thoughts, address him directly. At this point you may banish Rupert to a deserted island and let him entertain himself while you go in there and rock the SAT.

"Listen, buddy. I've had enough. I'm ready for this test. I'm **done** listening to your negative statements."

Reinforcing Positive Messages

A positive message might not banish Rupert on the first pass. You need to hear it about 20 times before you'll start to believe it. So reinforce! Leave yourself an encouraging note on your refrigerator. Put up a sticky note on your bathroom mirror. Some students have even been helped by recording a short 5 minute audio track on their voicemail, iPod, or smart phone reminding themselves to stay positive.

"You're ready for this. You've worked hard. You can rock this test."

Mix this message in with your favorite songs and positively rock out on the way to the test. In the right frame of mind, you'll get your best score.

Focus on your breath

Just as you can address anxiety by shifting your thoughts and your inner dialogue, you can also address anxiety by making subtle physical adjustments.

The quickest way to shift from anxiety to relaxation is through **breathing**. It is physically impossible to breathe in a deep and relaxed manner and simultaneously feel intense anxiety.

1 Take deep breaths

Deep breaths should come from your diaphragm, not your chest. When you breathe deeply, your stomach should go out (think of the Buddha). If your shoulders rise while you are inhaling, you are breathing from your chest rather than your diaphragm. **Think Buddha.**

2 Slow things down

Count to 3 during the inhalation, pause at the peak of the breath and then count to 3 during the exhalation: this will begin to automatically relax your entire body.

3 Practice breathing while counting backwards

Count backwards from 10 to 1, silently in your head, breathing slowly and deeply from your diaphragm with every count. 10....9....8....7.... With each breath, imagine yourself becoming more and more relaxed.

4 Sigh deeply or make yourself yawn

Yawning is like pressing a reset button in your brain. Yawning has many beneficial effects and can actually help you increase your level of focus and energy.

Use a physical trigger to relax

You can use a physical cue or trigger to bring yourself to a more relaxed state. Create a link between a simple movement and a state of relaxation. Make the movement— start to relax!

1 Choose a cue

You can associate a specific cue with starting to relax. Pick one that works for you or simply make up your own. Here are a few examples:

- squeezing three fingers together three times
- tapping your knee slowly three times
- putting one hand on top of the other

2 Get relaxed

Once you've officially started to relax with your cue, it's time for calm:

- Close your eyes
- Take 3 deep breaths
- Feel your body become more relaxed
- Tense your muscles, hold for a full breath, and then release
- Take 3 more deep breaths using the 3 count:

> Breathe in. Hold. Breathe Out.
> 1   2   3

3 Link 'em up

Perform your chosen trigger in this relaxed state, and create a mental association between the physical motion and a state of deep relaxation. You will need to do this a few times to create a stronger association.

4 Cue the relaxation during the test

During the test, whenever you feel anxiety coming on, perform your cue to activate your relaxed state. Take deep breaths, and begin to relax.

Test Day Anxiety

Physically sitting down and taking the test can trigger anxiety in a lot of students. Let's think about good practices at specific moments during the test.

Open your test booklets to page one.

You may begin.

You have 5 minutes remaining.

When the Test Begins

Some students become nervous the moment the test begins. They hear the proctor say, "You have 55 minutes... open your test booklet and begin." They hear the sound of turning pages fill the room, and they start to sweat. When the proctor says "begin," **pause** and **take a moment for yourself.** Once you're centered and calm, turn the page and begin.

At the Five-Minute Warning

Some students lose their cool at the 5-minute warning. They panic and start to rush, even when they are on track to finish in time. In their rush, they are frequently more careless.

When you hear the 5-minute warning, **pause** and **take a moment for yourself.** Once you're centered and calm, make any necessary adjustments, prioritize the remaining questions, and get back to the test.

When You Miss a Problem

Some students start to feel stressed when they just **know** they missed that last problem. They worry so much about that missed point that they have trouble concentrating on the next several questions. They get hung up on one little point, and make that missed question feel like a disaster:

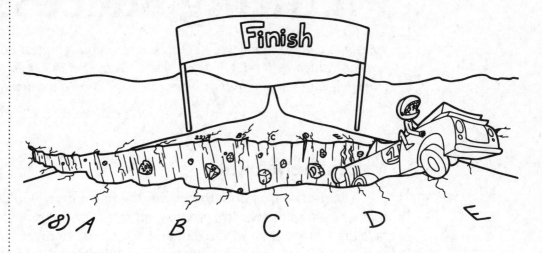

...but it's not! You don't need to get every single question right to get a great score! A missed problem is just a **speedbump** on the way to your best score yet. Remember this if you start to feel worried after a tough problem.

Keep your cool, keep perspective, and keep your eyes on the finish line!

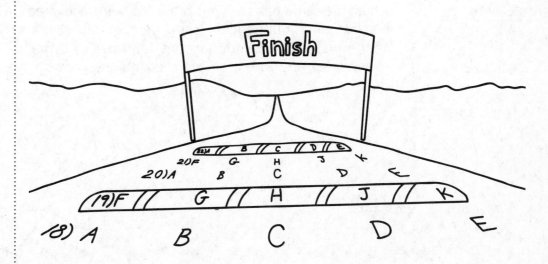

Picturing Success

Your imagination can be your greatest ally or your greatest obstacle when you are confronted with a high-stakes test such as the SAT. If you are not actively engaging your imagination, you are missing out on a tremendous opportunity.

Mental Rehearsal

If you want to learn about the power of imagination, you need look no further than to the world's greatest athletes. These individuals must face high stress situations again and again, and to prepare themselves, they tap into the power of **creative visualization.** Just ask Kobe Bryant, Michael Phelps, Maria Sharapova, or Tiger Woods. These and many other of the world's greatest athletes practice and rehearse mentally, visualizing their desired outcomes long before they walk onto their respective fields of play.

Why is mental rehearsal helpful? Why do the top performers on the planet spend hours and hours imagining desired outcomes rather than spending more time practicing on the playing field? They do so because the brain has a hard time distinguishing between **imagined** reality and **actual** reality. Whether you are imagining an action or performing that action, the same parts of your brain are being activated. When you imagine lifting your hand the same parts of the brain are triggered as when you actually lift your hand. Vividly imagine taking a test or actually take the test, and your brain will respond identically.

Rewiring your brain

If you can vividly imagine an event, engage your senses and emotions, and reinforce it through repetition, your brain will begin to treat the event like it is **real** rather than imagined.

This is huge!

When you walk into a testing situation, your brain will scan the environment to relate the current situation to past experiences and determine how to respond. If your memory of testing is marked predominantly by anxiety and disappointment, walking into the test room will cause anxiety, again reinforcing this negative cycle!

But with guided imagery and visualization, you can **break that cycle!** You actually have the power to create a new "script" for your brain to follow when you confront new testing situations. Even if you have no positive memories of past testing events, by simply **imagining a positive testing experience** you can override those bad memories.

In effect, you are **rewiring your brain** by creating a new neural pathway for your brain to follow!

Creative Visualization

On the next few pages, we'll walk through an example of how simply imagining the many details of success on the SAT can increase your confidence and reduce anxiety.

Creating a new script

To establish a new, positive "memory," we'll need to be as detailed as possible so your brain will buy it. We'll walk through an abbreviated version of the 20-minute script that we have used with students for the last decade. First **read the script.** Then, once you feel familiar with the content, close your eyes and imagine the whole scenario playing out, with **you** as the star.

Imagine yourself waking up the morning of the SAT. You turn off your alarm and get out of bed. You do your morning routine—breakfast, shower, brush teeth. (Imagine all the specific details of your personal routine in the order you would do them.) You begin to feel more and more awake and alert.

You feel good, relaxed and ready for the task ahead of you. You grab your backpack with your admission ticket, ID, pencils, calculator, water and snacks. As you drive to the test center, you begin to mentally prepare yourself. "I'm ready for this test; I'm going to go in there and knock this out." (Use whatever message feels right for you, in language you would use.) You arrive at the test center.

Before you open the car door, you pause for a moment and take a deep breath as you look in the rearview mirror: "I've worked hard, and I'm ready for this," you tell yourself. And you believe it. You walk into the school and get in the registration line. You show your ID and admission ticket and make your way to your testing room. You see the people in the room. Some are fidgety; others are relaxed; some are totally zoned out. Hear the sound of people rustling around in their seats.

Now find your seat. After you put away your things and get settled in, visualize yourself feeling ready, and relaxed. The proctor asks you to clear your desk and begins to pass out materials. See yourself bubbling-in all the preliminary info: name, date of birth, testing site, etc. Imagine the feel of the pencil in your hand, the motion of marking the bubbles on the Scantron sheet.

The proctor announces the beginning of the first section. "Open your test booklets to Page 1. You have 65 minutes to complete the Reading section. Begin." Everyone else in the room quickly opens their booklets to begin. You pause for a moment. You take a deep breath. You are feeling ready, so you pick up your pencil and turn to the first page of the test.

You move through the Reading section, remembering the strategies you have practiced so many times before. You mark up your passages with active reading, use throwaways and evidence to find right answers, and you remember all the steps of your EBQ strategy. The proctor calls time. Pencils down. You feel confident that you did well on this first section. "Now we are going to open our test booklets to section 2. You will have 35 minutes to copmlete the Writing section. You cannot turn to any other section of the test. You may begin."

You turn the page and approach the first problem, remembering the rules you have practiced so many times before. You feel relaxed. You choose your answer and move on to the next one. One by one, you work your way through all the problems; you answer them when you can, and guess and move on if they're too tough. You feel confident and know that you are tracking for your best score ever on this test.

Imagine your ten minute break. You walk outside, feeling good. You're over halfway to the finish line. Just 25 minutes for Math–No Calc, and then another 55 for Math–Calc. You eat your snack, recenter yourself, and head back in for the last two sections.

You move through the last two sections confidently, watching the clock and skillfully managing the amount of time you spend on each question. You are feeling good and know this is the best test you've ever taken.

Now take a few moments and visualize the score you want to achieve on the SAT. Imagine the number very clearly and hold it in your head. Now move forward in time. Imagine yourself going online or going to the mailbox to find the letter that contains your official score. See your score report, and visualize the goal you set for yourself directly next to your name. Really see it. You've accomplished your goal. All your hard work paid off! Feel the emotions that come with that. It's party time.

Once you have created this vision and filled it with details that work for you, repeat it every few days. Students who have used this technique and tapped into the power of their imaginations have made massive score gains on the SAT! Try this out for yourself and see how it works for you.

Practical Tips

Let's get practical! What small details will help you succeed?

The Final Week Before the SAT

In the last week before the SAT, continue to review your materials. Take a practice test to work on timing. You cannot cram for the SAT, but you want to keep the momentum going in the days leading up to the test.

Two Days Before the SAT

The Thursday night before the SAT is a very important night. A good night's sleep **Thursday** will have an enormous impact on your level of energy and ability to focus on **Saturday**. The effects of a poor night's sleep generally hit you the hardest **two days later**. So get to bed early Thursday and give yourself a full 7 to 8 hours of sleep.

The Day Before the SAT

- Light review: walk through a practice test you've completed and go over your notes.

- Mentally walk through the SAT. Rehearse every step of the process and reinforce what you want to happen in the morning.

- Keep your thoughts positive. You're ready. You've worked hard. Tomorrow you are going to do your absolute best.

- Be sure you get 7-8 hours of sleep.

- Set your alarm clock! Use the alarm on your cell phone as a backup.

- Pack the following materials in a bag that you can grab in the morning before you go to the test.

The Day Before the SAT (continued)

- Pack the following materials in a bag that you can grab in the morning before you go to the test.

1. Your SAT Admission **Ticket**

2. An acceptable (not expired) **photo ID**

3. Printed directions to the test center

4. 3-4 sharpened No. 2 **pencils** (pens and mechanical pencils are not allowed)

5. A graphing **calculator** with **fresh batteries** (make sure you check, and bring spare batteries if you have them)

6. A **watch** to keep track of time. In some testing centers, the clock will be behind you, or the room will not have a clock. Your proctor may or may not give you 5-minute warnings.

7. Bottle of **water**

8. **Snacks**: fruit and snack bars are great for the short breaks

The Morning of the Test

- Wake up early

- Eat a healthy **breakfast**

- Dress in comfortable clothes and in layers. Test rooms may be cold or hot; layers give you options.

- **Leave early** for the testing site. Give yourself plenty of time for traffic or other potential delays, especially if you've never been to the testing location before.

Before the Test, Prime your Brain for Success

You really do have a 1-track mind. The 24 hours before your test, saturate your brain with thoughts and images of success. Get that mental pathway "primed," or turned on.

Think about Einstein. Think about smart people. Research shows that if you think about great problem solvers and people you admire, you awaken potentials within yourself. By thinking about Einstein before the test, you act more like Einstein when it counts!

During the Test Administration

- Don't be thrown off by the energy of others. Stay in your zone. You've worked hard; you're prepared. Stay focused on your optimal performance.

- Bubble-in your Scantron sheet carefully. Some students transfer answers one test-page at a time rather than question-by-question. This can save a few minutes, eliminating much of the time spent going back and forth between the test booklet and the answer sheet.

- Pace yourself. Use your watch to regulate your timing.

- Use your break. Drink some water and eat a snack. You will need fluids and some extra fuel to keep you going between 8:00 am and 12:00 pm. Take this time to refocus: "You're doing great...only two more sections left."

- Be your own cheerleader. Be your own coach. Use self-talk to keep yourself engaged and focused. It's a long test. It helps to have some encouragement.

After the Test

Congratulations! Now go out and play! You deserve it!

General Test-taking Mantras

 Write **EVERYTHING** down

 Stay POSITIVE and **focus on success**

Think for yourself before looking at the answer choices

 The **clock is your ally**: use the clock to pace yourself

Be your own coach: keep yourself in the game

A **point is a point**: don't get stuck on any one problem

Take deep breaths when you need to **recenter yourself**

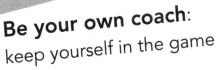

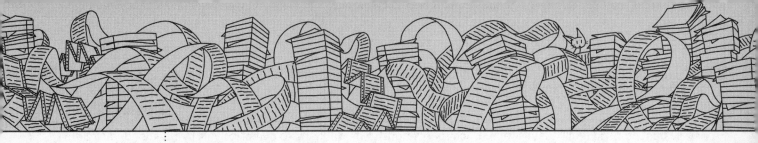

Practice Test

There's nothing like timed practice to help you prepare for the SAT.

It's a Matter of Time

The practice test to follow will allow you to practice your pacing, flex your new skills, and get more comfortable taking a complete SAT. The test simulates the difficulty, language, and timing of the official test. Take this opportunity to time yourself, taking short, 10-minute breaks between sections. To take the full test, you should reserve **3.5 hours**.

After the test, you'll find instructions on how to obtain an estimated score. Use this score to identify the best areas on which to focus your studies in the coming weeks.

TEST BREAKDOWN		
Section	Time Limit	Questions
Reading	65 minutes	52 questions
Writing	35 minutes	44 questions
Math – No Calculator	25 minutes	20 questions
Math – Calculator	55 minutes	38 questions

Mock SAT
Answer Sheet

A pencil must be used to fill out this form. Each mark needs to be dark and to completely fill in the intended circle. Do not write anywhere outside of the boxes provided to you. Completely erase any errors or stray marks. Filling out this answer sheet properly will ensure accurate score reporting.

Last Name

First Name

Today's Date

◯ Jan	0	0	0	0
◯ Feb	1	1	1	1
◯ Mar	2	2		2
◯ Apr	3	3		3
◯ May		4		4
◯ Jun		5		5
◯ Jul		6		6
◯ Aug		7		7
◯ Sep		8		8
◯ Oct		9		9
◯ Nov				
◯ Dec				

Test Form

◯ Practice Test #1
◯ Practice Test #2
◯ Practice Test #3
◯ Practice Test #4

HS Grad Year

I agree to refrain from any activity that may be considered cheating as described to me by the proctor. I confirm that the information I provide on this page and the next is accurate (to the best of my understanding). I will take this mock exam as seriously as an official exam.

_____   _____

Your Signature   Today's Date

Student Account Information:

Fill out your Applerouth ID or
enter a four-digit PIN that you can use to receive
your graded score report online.

Then fill out the Event Code.

See your confirmation email for details,
or ask your proctor for assistance.

Applerouth ID

or

PIN

Event Code

Parent Contact Information:

Please provide us with contact information for your (primary) parent or guardian so that we can
return your scores to you after this mock has been graded.

Parent/Guardian Last Name

Parent/Guardian First Name

Parent/Guardian Phone

Parent/Guardian Email

SECTION 1

1 Ⓐ Ⓑ Ⓒ Ⓓ	14 Ⓐ Ⓑ Ⓒ Ⓓ	27 Ⓐ Ⓑ Ⓒ Ⓓ	40 Ⓐ Ⓑ Ⓒ Ⓓ
2 Ⓐ Ⓑ Ⓒ Ⓓ	15 Ⓐ Ⓑ Ⓒ Ⓓ	28 Ⓐ Ⓑ Ⓒ Ⓓ	41 Ⓐ Ⓑ Ⓒ Ⓓ
3 Ⓐ Ⓑ Ⓒ Ⓓ	16 Ⓐ Ⓑ Ⓒ Ⓓ	29 Ⓐ Ⓑ Ⓒ Ⓓ	42 Ⓐ Ⓑ Ⓒ Ⓓ
4 Ⓐ Ⓑ Ⓒ Ⓓ	17 Ⓐ Ⓑ Ⓒ Ⓓ	30 Ⓐ Ⓑ Ⓒ Ⓓ	43 Ⓐ Ⓑ Ⓒ Ⓓ
5 Ⓐ Ⓑ Ⓒ Ⓓ	18 Ⓐ Ⓑ Ⓒ Ⓓ	31 Ⓐ Ⓑ Ⓒ Ⓓ	44 Ⓐ Ⓑ Ⓒ Ⓓ
6 Ⓐ Ⓑ Ⓒ Ⓓ	19 Ⓐ Ⓑ Ⓒ Ⓓ	32 Ⓐ Ⓑ Ⓒ Ⓓ	45 Ⓐ Ⓑ Ⓒ Ⓓ
7 Ⓐ Ⓑ Ⓒ Ⓓ	20 Ⓐ Ⓑ Ⓒ Ⓓ	33 Ⓐ Ⓑ Ⓒ Ⓓ	46 Ⓐ Ⓑ Ⓒ Ⓓ
8 Ⓐ Ⓑ Ⓒ Ⓓ	21 Ⓐ Ⓑ Ⓒ Ⓓ	34 Ⓐ Ⓑ Ⓒ Ⓓ	47 Ⓐ Ⓑ Ⓒ Ⓓ
9 Ⓐ Ⓑ Ⓒ Ⓓ	22 Ⓐ Ⓑ Ⓒ Ⓓ	35 Ⓐ Ⓑ Ⓒ Ⓓ	48 Ⓐ Ⓑ Ⓒ Ⓓ
10 Ⓐ Ⓑ Ⓒ Ⓓ	23 Ⓐ Ⓑ Ⓒ Ⓓ	36 Ⓐ Ⓑ Ⓒ Ⓓ	49 Ⓐ Ⓑ Ⓒ Ⓓ
11 Ⓐ Ⓑ Ⓒ Ⓓ	24 Ⓐ Ⓑ Ⓒ Ⓓ	37 Ⓐ Ⓑ Ⓒ Ⓓ	50 Ⓐ Ⓑ Ⓒ Ⓓ
12 Ⓐ Ⓑ Ⓒ Ⓓ	25 Ⓐ Ⓑ Ⓒ Ⓓ	38 Ⓐ Ⓑ Ⓒ Ⓓ	51 Ⓐ Ⓑ Ⓒ Ⓓ
13 Ⓐ Ⓑ Ⓒ Ⓓ	26 Ⓐ Ⓑ Ⓒ Ⓓ	39 Ⓐ Ⓑ Ⓒ Ⓓ	52 Ⓐ Ⓑ Ⓒ Ⓓ

SECTION 2

1 Ⓐ Ⓑ Ⓒ Ⓓ	12 Ⓐ Ⓑ Ⓒ Ⓓ	23 Ⓐ Ⓑ Ⓒ Ⓓ	34 Ⓐ Ⓑ Ⓒ Ⓓ
2 Ⓐ Ⓑ Ⓒ Ⓓ	13 Ⓐ Ⓑ Ⓒ Ⓓ	24 Ⓐ Ⓑ Ⓒ Ⓓ	35 Ⓐ Ⓑ Ⓒ Ⓓ
3 Ⓐ Ⓑ Ⓒ Ⓓ	14 Ⓐ Ⓑ Ⓒ Ⓓ	25 Ⓐ Ⓑ Ⓒ Ⓓ	36 Ⓐ Ⓑ Ⓒ Ⓓ
4 Ⓐ Ⓑ Ⓒ Ⓓ	15 Ⓐ Ⓑ Ⓒ Ⓓ	26 Ⓐ Ⓑ Ⓒ Ⓓ	37 Ⓐ Ⓑ Ⓒ Ⓓ
5 Ⓐ Ⓑ Ⓒ Ⓓ	16 Ⓐ Ⓑ Ⓒ Ⓓ	27 Ⓐ Ⓑ Ⓒ Ⓓ	38 Ⓐ Ⓑ Ⓒ Ⓓ
6 Ⓐ Ⓑ Ⓒ Ⓓ	17 Ⓐ Ⓑ Ⓒ Ⓓ	28 Ⓐ Ⓑ Ⓒ Ⓓ	39 Ⓐ Ⓑ Ⓒ Ⓓ
7 Ⓐ Ⓑ Ⓒ Ⓓ	18 Ⓐ Ⓑ Ⓒ Ⓓ	29 Ⓐ Ⓑ Ⓒ Ⓓ	40 Ⓐ Ⓑ Ⓒ Ⓓ
8 Ⓐ Ⓑ Ⓒ Ⓓ	19 Ⓐ Ⓑ Ⓒ Ⓓ	30 Ⓐ Ⓑ Ⓒ Ⓓ	41 Ⓐ Ⓑ Ⓒ Ⓓ
9 Ⓐ Ⓑ Ⓒ Ⓓ	20 Ⓐ Ⓑ Ⓒ Ⓓ	31 Ⓐ Ⓑ Ⓒ Ⓓ	42 Ⓐ Ⓑ Ⓒ Ⓓ
10 Ⓐ Ⓑ Ⓒ Ⓓ	21 Ⓐ Ⓑ Ⓒ Ⓓ	32 Ⓐ Ⓑ Ⓒ Ⓓ	43 Ⓐ Ⓑ Ⓒ Ⓓ
11 Ⓐ Ⓑ Ⓒ Ⓓ	22 Ⓐ Ⓑ Ⓒ Ⓓ	33 Ⓐ Ⓑ Ⓒ Ⓓ	44 Ⓐ Ⓑ Ⓒ Ⓓ

SECTION 3

1 Ⓐ Ⓑ Ⓒ Ⓓ	6 Ⓐ Ⓑ Ⓒ Ⓓ	11 Ⓐ Ⓑ Ⓒ Ⓓ
2 Ⓐ Ⓑ Ⓒ Ⓓ	7 Ⓐ Ⓑ Ⓒ Ⓓ	12 Ⓐ Ⓑ Ⓒ Ⓓ
3 Ⓐ Ⓑ Ⓒ Ⓓ	8 Ⓐ Ⓑ Ⓒ Ⓓ	13 Ⓐ Ⓑ Ⓒ Ⓓ
4 Ⓐ Ⓑ Ⓒ Ⓓ	9 Ⓐ Ⓑ Ⓒ Ⓓ	14 Ⓐ Ⓑ Ⓒ Ⓓ
5 Ⓐ Ⓑ Ⓒ Ⓓ	10 Ⓐ Ⓑ Ⓒ Ⓓ	15 Ⓐ Ⓑ Ⓒ Ⓓ

Grid in this section as directed in SECTION 3 of your exam booklet.

Only answers that are bubbled-in will be scored.

16 **17** **18** **19** **20**

(Grid-in response boxes, each with columns of bubbles 0–9 and a fraction bar and decimal point.)

SECTION 4

1. Ⓐ Ⓑ Ⓒ Ⓓ
2. Ⓐ Ⓑ Ⓒ Ⓓ
3. Ⓐ Ⓑ Ⓒ Ⓓ
4. Ⓐ Ⓑ Ⓒ Ⓓ
5. Ⓐ Ⓑ Ⓒ Ⓓ
6. Ⓐ Ⓑ Ⓒ Ⓓ
7. Ⓐ Ⓑ Ⓒ Ⓓ
8. Ⓐ Ⓑ Ⓒ Ⓓ

9. Ⓐ Ⓑ Ⓒ Ⓓ
10. Ⓐ Ⓑ Ⓒ Ⓓ
11. Ⓐ Ⓑ Ⓒ Ⓓ
12. Ⓐ Ⓑ Ⓒ Ⓓ
13. Ⓐ Ⓑ Ⓒ Ⓓ
14. Ⓐ Ⓑ Ⓒ Ⓓ
15. Ⓐ Ⓑ Ⓒ Ⓓ
16. Ⓐ Ⓑ Ⓒ Ⓓ

17. Ⓐ Ⓑ Ⓒ Ⓓ
18. Ⓐ Ⓑ Ⓒ Ⓓ
19. Ⓐ Ⓑ Ⓒ Ⓓ
20. Ⓐ Ⓑ Ⓒ Ⓓ
21. Ⓐ Ⓑ Ⓒ Ⓓ
22. Ⓐ Ⓑ Ⓒ Ⓓ
23. Ⓐ Ⓑ Ⓒ Ⓓ
24. Ⓐ Ⓑ Ⓒ Ⓓ

25. Ⓐ Ⓑ Ⓒ Ⓓ
26. Ⓐ Ⓑ Ⓒ Ⓓ
27. Ⓐ Ⓑ Ⓒ Ⓓ
28. Ⓐ Ⓑ Ⓒ Ⓓ
29. Ⓐ Ⓑ Ⓒ Ⓓ
30. Ⓐ Ⓑ Ⓒ Ⓓ

SAT Essay
(optional)

Form: _____

_____

_____

_____

_____

_____

_____

_____

_____

_____

_____

_____

_____

_____

_____

_____

_____

_____

_____

_____

Reading Test
65 MINUTES, 52 QUESTIONS

Turn to Section 1 of your answer sheet to answer the questions in this section.

DIRECTIONS

Each passage or pair of passages below is followed by a number of questions. After reading each passage or pair, choose the best answer to each question based on what is stated or implied in the passage or passages and in any accompanying graphics (such as a table or graph).

Questions 1-10 are based on the following passage.

This passage is adapted from Louisa May Alcott, *Work: A Story of Experience*. Originally published in 1873. In the story, Christie has just told her Aunt Betsey her plans to leave home.

Having kissed the old lady, Christie swept her work away, and sat down to write the letter which was the first step toward freedom. When it was done, she drew
Line nearer, to her friendly confidante the fire, and till late into
5 the night sat thinking tenderly of the past, bravely of the present, hopefully of the future. Twenty-one to-morrow, and her inheritance a head, a heart, a pair of hands; also the dower of most New England girls, intelligence, courage, and common sense, many practical gifts, and,
10 hidden under the reserve that soon melts in a genial atmosphere, much romance and enthusiasm, and the spirit which can rise to heroism when the great moment comes.
Christie was one of that large class of women who, moderately endowed with talents, earnest and
15 true-hearted, are driven by necessity, temperament, or principle out into the world to find support, happiness, and homes for themselves. Many turn back discouraged; more accept shadow for substance, and discover their mistake too late; the weakest lose their purpose and
20 themselves; but the strongest struggle on, and, after danger and defeat, earn at last the best success this world can give us, the possession of a brave and cheerful spirit, rich in self-knowledge, self-control, self-help. This was the real desire of Christie's heart; this was to be her lesson
25 and reward, and to this happy end she was slowly yet surely brought by the long discipline of life and labor.
Sitting alone there in the night, she tried to strengthen herself with all the good and helpful memories she could recall, before she went away to find her place in the
30 great unknown world. She thought of her mother, so like

herself, who had borne the commonplace life of home till she could bear it no longer. Then had gone away to teach, as most country girls are forced to do. Had met, loved, and married a poor gentleman, and, after a few
35 years of genuine happiness, untroubled even by much care and poverty, had followed him out of the world, leaving her little child to the protection of her brother.
Christie looked back over the long, lonely years she had spent in the old farm-house, plodding to
40 school and church, and doing her tasks with kind Aunt Betsey while a child; and slowly growing into girlhood, with a world of romance locked up in a heart hungry for love and a larger, nobler life.
She had tried to appease this hunger in many ways,
45 but found little help. Her father's old books were all she could command, and these she wore out with much reading. Inheriting his refined tastes, she found nothing to attract her in the society of the commonplace and often coarse people about her. She tried to like the
50 buxom girls whose one ambition was to "get married," and whose only subjects of conversation were "smart bonnets" and "nice dresses." She tried to believe that the admiration and regard of the bluff young farmers was worth striving for; but when one well-to-do neighbor
55 laid his acres at her feet, she found it impossible to accept for her life's companion a man whose soul was wrapped up in prize cattle and big turnips.

CONTINUE

1

Which choice best describes what happens in the passage?

A) A character flees from her home to get away from a childhood of disappointment.

B) A character reminisces about her upbringing the night before embarking on her own.

C) A character gradually admits that she has made a hasty decision.

D) A character reconsiders her choices after learning about the stories of other young women.

2

On line 7, the phrase "her inheritance a head, a heart, a pair of hands" suggests that Christie

A) had clear physical gifts inherited from her parents.

B) was predominantly neglected by her Uncle and Aunt.

C) is dependent on herself to create her own success.

D) is ill-equipped for life on her own.

3

The second paragraph serves to

A) show that Christie is one of many young women yearning for independence.

B) chastise Christie's decision to leave her Uncle and Aunt's home.

C) analyze how often young women are unable to find a successful career.

D) show how different Christie is from her Aunt.

4

Christie indicates that she considers success to be

A) independence and a home of her own.

B) a self-reliant and courageous character

C) a place in genteel society.

D) recognition of her intelligence and independence.

5

Which choice provides the best evidence for the answer to the previous question?

A) Lines 7-12 ("also … comes")

B) Lines 13-17 ("Christie … themselves")

C) Lines 20-23 ("but the … self-help")

D) Lines 47-49 ("Inheriting … about her")

6

As used on line 39, "plodding" suggests that Christie

A) had no interest in learning how to read or write.

B) has been tired of the monotony of her routine for most of her life.

C) had planned to leave the farm house for a long time.

D) lacked good judgement from ignoring the moral lessons taught to her.

7

As used on line 46 "command" most nearly means

A) control.

B) require.

C) organize.

D) recite.

8

On line 57, the passage references "prize cattle and big turnips" in order to

A) provide context about the region where the story takes place

B) characterize the concerns of a man whom Christie would have no interest in marrying.

C) juxtapose the success of some in the community with Christie's pennilessness.

D) justify Christie's lack of interest in an agricultural lifestyle.

CONTINUE

9

The passage implies that Christie's mother

A) abandoned Christie to focus on becoming a teacher.

B) met an early death.

C) no longer bothers to write to Christie.

D) made the same mistakes that Christie will make.

10

Which choice provides the best evidence for the answer to the previous question?

A) Lines 17-20 ("Many … themselves")

B) Lines 30-32 ("She thought … longer")

C) Lines 32-33 ("Then … do")

D) Lines 36-37 ("had followed … brother")

Questions 11-20 are based on the following passage.

This passage is adapted from J. Walter Weatherman, "North Dakota's Oil Boom." Originally published in 2014.

Economic booms have dramatically shaped the demographics of our nation; American history is ripe with stories of "rushes" offering quick wealth for anyone
Line brave enough to take the gamble. The California gold
5 rush of 1849 sparked migration westward and turned San Francisco and Sacramento into "boomtowns," cities that experienced rapid growth due to economic opportunity. While not all boomtowns are a byproduct of natural resources, as Las Vegas, NV and Branson,
10 MO can attest, the era of mining and drilling for prosperity has not come to an end. Just ask anyone in Williston, North Dakota, a recent example of the highs and lows of a boomtown economy.

Located in Northwest North Dakota, Williston
15 has been a sleepy farm town since its founding in 1887. It shares its name with the Williston Basin–the subterranean rock formation on which the town is located. In 2006, geologist Mike Johnson discovered the Parshall oil field within the Williston Basin,
20 uncovering a rich new petroleum reservoir. While the discovery of new oil reserves occurs periodically across the country, the Parshall oil field discovery was an ideal cure for the national energy ills of the day.

The year 2002 marked the beginning of a huge
25 spike in the price of crude oil, rocketing from an annual average of $22.50 per barrel to an annual average of $94.04 by the end of 2008. A combination of increased international demand for oil–primarily from China's own manufacturing boom–a globally
30 weak dollar, economic decline caused by the Great Recession of 2008, and instability in the Middle East led to this substantial increase in price. American oil producers saw the discovery of oil in North Dakota as a low-risk supply of prized new oil.
35 Williston and the surrounding area have seen tremendous growth in the last decade, and the state of North Dakota has reaped the economic benefits. The influx of investment has led to a billion dollar tax surplus; financial publication *24/7 Wall Street* named North Dakota
40 the "best run state in the country" in 2014. While many states have seen only gradual economic recovery after the 2008 global recession, North Dakota has the lowest unemployment rate in the nation at 2.6%. The oil industry offers high wages to anyone willing to make the move
45 and endure long hours in often extremely cold weather.

With this influx of oil workers, Williston became

CONTINUE

a boomtown whether the community desired that classification or not. The 2000 US Census poll reported the population of Williston as 12,512, showing a
50 4.7% decrease from 1990. A 2014 estimate place the population of Williston at 24,562, showing a 96% population increase. Current census data may still be inaccurately low, as it is difficult to account for workers who take contracts to work for a month at a
55 time, returning to their hometowns on their time off.

    A population explosion as dramatic as what Williston has experienced will undoubtedly lead to some negative consequences. There is a significant lack of housing to accommodate the new residents. The most obvious
60 solution–build more housing–has been problematic as construction projects would use the same pool of workers that are needed for jobs on the oil fields, which offer substantially higher wages. The solution has been temporary and minimal at best–trailers and no-frills
65 housing camps–both with shockingly steep rent.

    Another consequence of a boomtown economy is an uptick in vice and violence. After long shifts in the harsh environment of the oil fields, workers with pockets full of cash come into Williston looking for a good time and
70 an opportunity to blow off some steam. This has put a strain on the police force, which has also begun losing its workforce to the alluring salaries of the oil fields.

    No boom economy can sustain itself indefinitely, and the North Dakota oil boom shows signs of slowing
75 down. Demand for oil is not as strong as it was a few years ago, which has reduced the proliferation of new oil drills. While there are still jobs there, the wages have lowered and not everyone can find continual work. The long-term impact of the oil
80 boom is still unknown, and whether Williston will mature into a regionally significant city or fade into obscurity as a "ghost town" still remains to be seen.

Figure 1

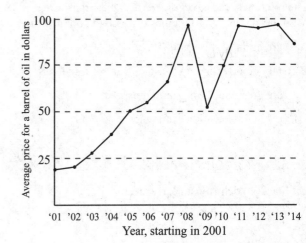

Source: U.S. Energy Information Administration

Figure 2

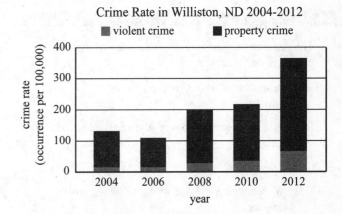

The main purpose of the passage is to

A)   provide a historical context for current economic trends.

B)   suggest reasons why boomtowns often end up as ghost towns.

C)   praise North Dakota for encouraging economic growth.

D)   present a case study of an economic rush and analyze its effects on the community.

797

12

The reference to Las Vegas, Nevada and Branson, Missouri on lines 9-10 implies that not all boomtowns

A) are initially successful.

B) rely on an economy based on natural resources.

C) are guaranteed long-term prosperity.

D) display fluctuation economies.

13

On line 20, "rich" most nearly means

A) expensive.

B) wealthy.

C) abundant.

D) intense.

14

The passage suggests that the discovery of the Parshall oil fields

A) came at a fortuitous time for the American oil industry.

B) was the largest discovery of oil in the United States.

C) ended the economic recession in North Dakota.

D) was a shock for residents of Williston, North Dakota.

15

The passage describes the jobs in the North Dakota oil fields as

A) unpleasant and demeaning.

B) seasonal and undesirable.

C) arduous and lucrative.

D) temporary and flexible.

16

Which choice provides the best evidence for the answer to the previous question?

A) Lines 20-23 ("While...day")

B) Lines 43-45 ("The oil...weather")

C) Lines 52-56 ("Current...off")

D) Lines 67-70 ("After...steam")

17

On line 34, "prized" most nearly means

A) strained.

B) valuable.

C) victorious.

D) bountiful.

18

According to Figure 2, the years 2010-2012 were characterized by

A) a sharp increase in property crime rate but a decrease in violent crime rate.

B) roughly equal growth in crime rate as had taken place between 2004 and 2010.

C) a greater increase in crime rate than had taken place between 2006 and 2008.

D) a significant decline in crime rate.

19

The author would likely attribute the increase in crime in Williston as represented in Figure 2 to

A) the rising unemployment rate.

B) the lack of proper housing.

C) the waning demand for oil.

D) the rapid population increase.

CONTINUE

20

What information discussed in the third and fourth paragraphs (lines 24-47) is represented by Figure 1?

A) The information in lines 24-27 ("The year … 2008")

B) The information in lines 32-34 ("American … oil")

C) The information in lines 35-37 ("Williston … benefits")

D) The information in lines 37-40 ("The influx … 2014")

Questions 21-31 are based on the following passage.

Passage 1 is adapted from Liza Gross, "Untapped Bounty: Sampling the Seas to Survey Microbial Biodiversity." ©2007 by Liza Gross. Passage 2 is adapted from Kira O'Day, "Gut Reaction: Pyrosequencing Provides the Poop on Distal Gut Bacteria." ©2008 Kira O'Day. Both passages discuss bacteria, a type of microbe.

Passage 1

Being invisible to the naked eye, microbes managed to escape scientific scrutiny until the mid-17th century, when Dutch scientist Antonie van Leeuwenhoek
Line invented the microscope. These cryptic organisms
5 continued to thwart scientists' efforts to probe, describe, and classify them until about 40 years ago, owing largely to similar body structures that are hard to visually differentiate and obscure body functions that make them notoriously difficult to grow in a lab.
10   Most of what we know about the biochemical diversity of microbes, however, comes from the tiny fraction that do submit to lab investigations. Not until scientists determined that they could use molecular sequences, or an organism's unique DNA code, to
15 identify species and determine their evolutionary heritage did it begin to become apparent just how diverse microbes are. We now know that microbes are the most widely distributed organisms on earth, having adapted to environments as diverse as boiling sulfur
20 pits and the human gut. Accounting for half of the world's biomass, microbes provide essential ecosystem services by cycling the mineral nutrients that support life on earth. And marine microbes remove so much carbon dioxide from the atmosphere that some scientists
25 see them as a potential solution to global warming.
      Yet even as scientists describe seemingly endless variations on the cosmopolitan microbial lifestyle, the concept of a bacterial species remains elusive. Some bacterial species (such as anthrax) appear
30 to have little genetic variation. In other species (such as *Escherichia coli*), individuals can have completely different sets of genes, challenging scientists to explain the observed diversity.
      The emerging field of environmental genomics
35 aims to capture the full measure of microbial diversity by trading the lens of the microscope for the lens of genomics. By recovering communities of microbial genes where they live (streams, oceans, even the human gut), environmental genomics avoids the need to culture
40 uncooperative organisms in labs. And by analyzing

CONTINUE

factors found in the microbes' environments, such
as pH, salinity, and water temperature, it sheds light
on the biological processes encoded in the genes.

Passage 2

The human distal gut hosts a bustling community
45 comprising thousands of different kinds of bacteria.
Fortunately, most of these intestinal residents don't
cause disease but instead play key roles in nutrition,
metabolism, pathogen resistance, and immune response
regulation. Unfortunately, these beneficial bacteria
50 are just as susceptible to the antibiotics we take to
treat disease-causing bacteria. Antibiotics drastically
alter the balance among members of different taxa*
of beneficial distal gut bacteria that have coevolved
with one another and with their human host.
55   To find out more about the changes taking place
in the gut during antibiotic treatment, researchers
extracted DNA from stool samples collected from
three healthy adults before, during, and after treatment
for five days with ciprofloxacin (a broad-spectrum
60 antibiotic that is used to treat a variety of bacterial
conditions such as infections of the lower respiratory
or urinary tracts). Ciprofloxacin was selected because
of its safety profile and the previous belief that it does
not harm the most abundant bacteria of the distal gut.
65   Researchers confirmed the presence of over 5,600
bacterial taxa in the human gut—far more taxonomic
richness than had been seen in previous investigations
of host-associated bacterial communities. They also
found that ciprofloxacin had a dramatic effect on
70 microbial communities and that the specific bacterial
taxa most strongly affected varied among the human
hosts. Ciprofloxacin treatment caused a sizeable decrease
in taxonomic richness in two of the participants,
while bacterial diversity was somewhat less strongly
75 affected in the third participant. Most members of
the bacterial community returned to pretreatment
numbers within four weeks following treatment.
    Although the effects on their gut inhabitants were
profound, none of the participants reported any changes
80 in their gut function either during or after treatment,
indicating that the tremendous diversity of the distal
gut bacterial community makes it both resilient and
functionally redundant. Notably, however, some taxa had
not recovered completely even six months later. Because
85 specific bacterial taxa are responsible for different aspects
of nutrition, metabolism, and immune response, even
seemingly minor changes in the composition of the gut
microbial community as the result of antibiotic treatment

might have long-term effects on health that could go
90 undetected in the relatively short length of the study.

* A distinct group or unit.

21

As used in line 37, "recovering" most nearly means

A) healing.

B) overcoming.

C) increasing.

D) retrieving.

22

The author of Passage 1 refers to global warming (Line
25) in order to

A) note a common misconception about an event.

B) explain a new phenomenon.

C) highlight an action's unexpected effect.

D) present a potential solution to a problem.

23

As used in line 67, "richness" most nearly means

A) abundance.

B) affluence.

C) intensity.

D) flavor.

CONTINUE ➤

24

The author of Passage 1 suggests that until recently, microbes were considered

A) detrimental.

B) mysterious.

C) controversial.

D) innovative.

25

Which choice provides the best evidence for the answer to the previous question?

A) Lines 4-9 ("These ... lab")

B) Lines 17-20 ("We ... gut")

C) Lines 20-23 ("Accounting ... earth")

D) Lines 34-37 ("The emerging ... genomics")

26

The primary finding in Passage 2 is that the antibiotic Ciprofloxacin dramatically decreases the diversity of the bacteria found in the distal gut but

A) all original taxa can be located within the host after a few weeks.

B) the functional capabilities of the gut do not change.

C) it may be unsafe for people to consume even for short periods of time.

D) its use increases a person's rate of metabolism.

27

Which choice provides the best evidence for the answer to the previous question?

A) Lines 62-64 ("Ciprofloxacin ... gut)

B) Lines 78-83 ("Although ... redundant)

C) Lines 83-84 ("Notably ... later")

D) Lines 84-90 ("Because ... study")

28

The main purpose of both passages is to

A) question the methods used to cultivate microbes.

B) discuss the prevailing knowledge regarding the diversity of microbial life.

C) describe the evolutionary relationship between microbes and humans.

D) explain the change over time in the classification of microbes.

29

Unlike the author of Passage 1, the author of Passage 2 acknowledges the

A) abundance of bacteria on Earth.

B) diversity between different taxa of bacteria.

C) harmful nature of some bacteria.

D) critical role bacteria play within their habitats.

CONTINUE

30

Which choice best describes the relationship between the two passages?

A) Passage 2 analyzes the implications of the results that are described in Passage 1.

B) Passage 2 draws alternative conclusions from the evidence presented in Passage 1.

C) Passage 2 describes a study used to investigate a particular aspect of a topic introduced in Passage 1.

D) Passage 2 summarizes the negative reactions to the questions raised in Passage 1.

31

The authors of both passages would most likely agree with which of the following statements about the current understanding of bacterial species?

A) The invention of the microscope was the most important scientific advance in discovering the microbial world.

B) Antibiotics alter the abundance and diversity of bacteria in the distal gut of humans.

C) Very few of the existing species of bacteria have been identified.

D) Traditional methods of classifying organisms based on morphology are more useful than molecular sequencing.

Questions 32-41 are based on the following passage.

This passage is adapted from James Madison, *Federalist No. 14. Objections to the Proposed Constitution From Extent of Territory Answered*. Originally published in 1787. The Federalist Papers were a series of influential articles offering opinions on creating a new government in the aftermath of the Revolutionary War.

We have seen the necessity of the Union, as our bulwark against foreign danger, as the conservator of peace among ourselves, as the guardian of our commerce
Line and other common interests, as the only substitute for
5 those military establishments which have subverted the liberties of the Old World, and as the proper antidote for the diseases of faction, which have proved fatal to other popular governments, and of which alarming symptoms have been betrayed by our own. All that remains, within
10 this branch of our inquiries, is to take notice of an objection that may be drawn from the great extent of country which the Union embraces. A few observations on this subject will be the more proper, as it is perceived that the adversaries of the new Constitution are availing
15 themselves of the prevailing prejudice with regard to the practicable sphere of republican administration, in order to supply, by imaginary difficulties, the want of those solid objections which they endeavor in vain to find.
   The error which limits republican government to a
20 narrow district has been unfolded and refuted in preceding papers. I remark here only that it seems to owe its rise and prevalence chiefly to the confounding of a republic with a democracy, applying to the former reasonings drawn from the nature of the latter. The true distinction between
25 these forms was also adverted to on a former occasion. It is, that in a democracy, the people meet and exercise the government in person; in a republic, they assemble and administer it by their representatives and agents. A democracy, consequently, will be confined to a small
30 spot. A republic may be extended over a large region.
   To this accidental source of the error may be added the artifice of some celebrated authors, whose writings have had a great share in forming the modern standard of political opinions. Being subjects either of an absolute
35 or limited monarchy, they have endeavored to heighten the advantages, or palliate the evils of those forms, by placing in comparison the vices and defects of the republican, and by citing as specimens of the latter the turbulent democracies of ancient Greece and modern
40 Italy. Under the confusion of names, it has been an easy task to transfer to a republic observations applicable to a democracy only; and among others, the observation that

CONTINUE

it can never be established but among a small number of people, living within a small compass of territory.

45   Such a fallacy may have been the less perceived, as most of the popular governments of antiquity were of the democratic species; and even in modern Europe, to which we owe the great principle of representation, no example is seen of a government wholly popular, and

50 founded, at the same time, wholly on that principle. If Europe has the merit of discovering this great mechanical power in government, by the simple agency of which the will of the largest political body may be concentered, and its force directed to any object which the public

55 good requires, America can claim the merit of making the discovery the basis of unmixed and extensive republics. It is only to be lamented that any of her citizens should wish to deprive her of the additional merit of displaying its full efficacy in the establishment of the

60 comprehensive system now under her consideration.

    As the natural limit of a democracy is that distance from the central point which will just permit the most remote citizens to assemble as often as their public functions demand, and will include no greater number

65 than can join in those functions; so the natural limit of a republic is that distance from the centre which will barely allow the representatives to meet as often as may be necessary for the administration of public affairs. Can it be said that the limits of the United States exceed this

70 distance? It will not be said by those who recollect that the Atlantic coast is the longest side of the Union, that during the term of thirteen years, the representatives of the States have been almost continually assembled, and that the members from the most distant States are not

75 chargeable with greater intermissions of attendance than those from the States in the neighborhood of Congress.

32

In the passage, Madison states that a republic can

A) be less stable than Ancient Greek democracies.

B) be less desirable than a democracy because a republic uses elected officials.

C) function properly over a great area of land.

D) be similar to the monarchies of European nations.

33

Which choice provides the best evidence for the answer to the previous question?

A) Lines 21-24 ("I remark … latter")

B) Line 30 ("A republic … region")

C) Lines 34-40 ("Being … Italy")

D) Lines 50-57 ("If Europe … republics")

34

The first sentence of the passage (lines 1-9) primarily serves to

A) address the danger of attack by other nations.

B) summarize topics previously addressed.

C) express concern over managing a complex undertaking.

D) dismiss objections that are no longer relevant.

35

As used in line 10, "branch" most nearly means

A) support.

B) outreach.

C) topic.

D) bureau.

36

"Ancient Greece and modern Italy" (lines 39-40) serve as examples

A) that show that democratic nations cannot succeed.

B) used by supporters of a traditional monarchy.

C) that inspired the desire for freedom in America.

D) to suggest that democracies can compete successfully against monarchies.

CONTINUE ▶

37

"The confusion of names" (line 40) refers to

A) the subtle differences between a democracy and a republic.

B) how different states refer to each other.

C) language differences among nations.

D) debate over geographic regions.

38

7. As used in line 44, "compass" most nearly means

A) direction.

B) path.

C) belief.

D) range.

39

Madison critiques democracy by arguing that democracies

A) restrict personal freedom.

B) often evolve into a different system.

C) have limitations of scale.

D) promote an impossible ideal.

40

Which choice provides the best evidence for the answer in the previous question?

A) Lines 19-21 ("The error ... papers")

B) Lines 24-25 ("The true ... occasion")

C) Lines 45-50 ("Such ... principle")

D) Lines 61-65 ("As ... functions")

41

The last paragraph (lines 61-76) addresses

A) the process for electing representatives.

B) the need for more frequent meetings of elected officials.

C) the practicality of assembly over a large geographic region.

D) the need for more transportation options in the interior of the country.

CONTINUE

Questions 42-52

This passage is adapted from Mary Hoff, "DNA Amplification and Detection Made Simple (Relatively)." ©2006 Public Library of Science. The passage discusses DNA amplification, the production of multiple copies of a sequence of DNA.

Twenty-three years ago, a man musing about work while driving down a California highway revolutionized molecular biology when he envisioned a technique
Line to make large numbers of copies of a piece of DNA
5 rapidly and accurately. Known as the polymerase chain reaction, or PCR, Kary Mullis' technique involves separating the double strands of a DNA fragment into single-strand templates by heating it, attaching primers that initiate the copying process, using DNA polymerase
10 to make a copy of each strand from free nucleotides floating around in the reaction mixture, detaching the primers, then repeating the cycle using the new and old strands as templates. Since its discovery in 1983, PCR has made possible a number of procedures we
15 now take for granted, such as DNA fingerprinting of crime scenes, paternity testing, and DNA-based diagnosis of hereditary and infectious diseases.

As valuable as conventional PCR is, it has limits. Heat is required to separate the DNA and cooler temperatures
20 are needed to bind the primer to the strands, so the reaction chamber must repeatedly cycle through hot and cold phases. As a result, the technique can only be performed in laboratories using sophisticated equipment.

Now Olaf Piepenburg, Niall Armes, and colleagues
25 have come up with a new approach to DNA amplification that can be carried out at a constant temperature, using only a tiny amount of DNA, without elaborate equipment. Called recombinase polymerase amplification (RPA), the technique opens the door to dramatically extending
30 the application of DNA amplification in fieldwork and in laboratories where PCR machines are not available.

RPA uses five main ingredients: a sample of the DNA to be amplified; a primer–recombinase complex, which initiates the copying process when it attaches to
35 the template; nucleotides from which to form the new strands; a polymerase, which brings them together in the right order; and single-stranded DNA-binding proteins (SSBs), which help keep the original DNA from zipping back together while the new DNA is being made. The
40 primer–recombinase complex is able to attach to the double-stranded DNA, eliminating the need to heat the mixture. After the complex is in place, it disassembles, allowing the DNA polymerase to begin synthesizing a

new strand of DNA complementary to the template, while
45 the SSBs attach to and stabilize the displaced strand. Under the right conditions—a precise milieu of process-regulating chemicals—the process automatically repeats, resulting in an exponential increase in the DNA sample.

The researchers tested the sensitivity, specificity, and
50 speed of RPA by using it to amplify three kinds of human DNA, as well as DNA from *Bacillus subtilis*. They found the technique to be rapid and accurate. However, when using RPA to detect the presence of a specific type of DNA–such as in a test for a suspect's DNA at a crime
55 scene–the primer used to disassemble the DNA strands could produce a false positive result. To counteract this, the researchers developed a detection method that causes the sample to glow in the presence of the DNA being tested for, but not in the presence of primer alone.

60 To demonstrate the usefulness of the new system, the researchers used it to test for the presence of methicillin-resistant *Staphylococcus aureus* (MRSA), a disease-causing bacterium known as a "superbug" because it is unharmed by penicillin antibiotics. They
65 found that RPA could detect a miniscule amount of the superbug: fewer than ten copies of MRSA DNA. It could also determine the presence of three different genotypes of MRSA, and distinguish them from a methicillin-sensitive *S. aureus* strain. How easy would
70 it be to apply such a test in real-life situations? The researchers demonstrated one possible approach by encapsulating the entire process in a dipstick that could be used in the field to detect the presence of a pathogen.*

*organism, such as bacterium, that causes a disease

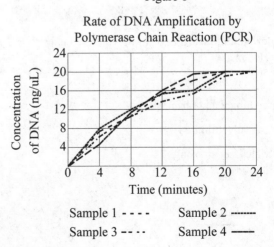

Figure 1

Rate of DNA Amplification by
Polymerase Chain Reaction (PCR)

Sample 1 - - - -   Sample 2 ---------
Sample 3 -- - ·   Sample 4 ———

CONTINUE ➡

Figure 2

Rate of DNA Amplification by
Recombinase Polymerase Amplification (RPA)

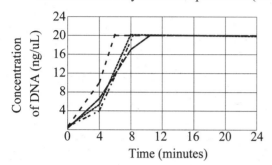

Sample 1 - - - -   Sample 2 --------
Sample 3 - - · ·   Sample 4 ———

42

The primary purpose of the passage is to

A) recount the development and application of a
    technique.

B) evaluate the research that led to a scientific
    discovery.

C) summarize the findings of a long-term research
    project.

D) explain the evolution of a branch of scientific
    study.

43

The author views the technique of polymerase chain
reaction (PCR) as

A) costly and unimportant.

B) conventional and obsolete.

C) beneficial yet limited.

D) restricted yet amusing.

44

Based on the fourth paragraph (lines 32-48), it can be
inferred that without the use of SSBs during RPA, DNA
would

A) reform its original shape.

B) acquire a new shape.

C) overheat.

D) copy itself.

45

As used in line 46, "right" most nearly means

A) reasonable.

B) conservative.

C) correct.

D) pleasing.

46

What does the author suggest about the DNA found in
Bacillus subtilis?

A) Slow and methodical RPA analysis can be
    completed on it.

B) It is different from the DNA found in humans.

C) It glows in the presence of primer.

D) It is unharmed by penicillin antibiotics.

47

What choice provides the best evidence for the answer
to the previous question?

A) Lines 49-51 ("The researchers … subtilis")

B) Lines 51-52 ("They … accurate")

C) Lines 56-59 ("To counteract … alone")

D) Lines 60-64 ("To demonstrate … antibiotics")

CONTINUE

48

The author mentions MRSA to

A) provide a real-life example for the application of a scientific tool.

B) describe the spread of an infectious disease.

C) critique a practical technology.

D) criticize Piepenburg's approach.

49

The passage implies that, unlike PCR, RPA

A) uses elaborate equipment.

B) is a multi-step process.

C) can be performed at crime scenes.

D) requires extreme temperatures.

50

Which choice provides the best evidence for the answer to the previous question?

A) Lines 7-12 ("separating … primers")

B) Lines 13-17 ("Since … diseases")

C) Lines 18-22 ("Heat … phases")

D) Lines 70-73 ("The researchers … pathogen")

51

According to Figure 2, the DNA from which sample was the first to reach a concentration of 20 ng/µL?

A) Sample 1

B) Sample 2

C) Sample 3

D) Sample 4

52

Taken together, the two figures suggest that

A) PCR amplifies DNA more quickly than does RPA.

B) PCR amplifies DNA more accurately than does RPA.

C) RPA amplifies DNA more quickly than does PCR.

D) RPA amplifies DNA more accurately than does PCR.

STOP
If you finish before time is called, you may check your work on this section only.
Do not turn to any other section.

No Test Material On This Page

Writing and Language Test
35 MINUTES, 44 QUESTIONS

Turn to Section 2 of your answer sheet to answer the questions in this section.

DIRECTIONS

Each passage below is accompanied by a number of questions. For some questions, you will consider how the passage might be revised to improve the expression of ideas. For other questions, you will consider how the passage might be edited to correct errors in sentence structure, usage, or punctuation. A passage or a question may be accompanied by one or more graphics (such as a table or graph) that you will consider as you make revising and editing decisions.

Some questions will direct you to an underlined portion of a passage. Other questions will direct you to a location in a passage or ask you to think about the passage as a whole.

After reading each passage, choose the answer to each question that most effectively improves the quality of writing in the passage or that makes the passage conform to the conventions of standard written English. Many questions include a "NO CHANGE" option. Choose that option if you think the best choice is to leave the relevant portion of the passage as it is.

Questions 1-11 are based on the following passage.

Is chocolate a health food?

The news media love stories that uncover healthy foods. People love to read about a new "superfood" that will offer a **1** multitude of health benefits. Even better are stories about secretly healthy foods. One food that has garnered a lot of praise lately is **2** chocolate, it has been touted for containing high amounts of flavonol. While its flavonol content is certainly beneficial, chocolate's other ingredients may undermine its potential as a health food.

1

Which of the following would be the best substitution for the underlined word?

A) cluster

B) variety

C) heap

D) colony

2

A) NO CHANGE

B) chocolate, which

C) chocolate; which

D) chocolate, but it

CONTINUE

Flavonols are types of antioxidants that are used in the human body to repair and rebuild cells. Cocoa powder, a primary ingredient in **3** chocolates, is especially high in flavonols, which have shown in scientific studies to increase blood flow to the brain and improve memory. The news of chocolate's new health benefits was very well-publicized, as a common "guilty pleasure" food became a healthy food overnight. There appeared to be only one catch: the health benefits were most pronounced with dark chocolates, since **4** it contains more cocoa powder than milk chocolates or white chocolates do. **5** Now it seemed health conscious people could have their cake and eat it too, as long as the cake was made with dark chocolate containing lots of flavonols!

3

A) NO CHANGE
B) chocolates is
C) chocolates, are
D) chocolates are

4

A) NO CHANGE
B) it contained
C) they contain
D) they are containing

5

The writer is considering adding the following sentence at this point:

> "Most people do not think of white chocolate as comparable to darker chocolates, but all types come from the same cocoa plant."

Should the author include this sentence?

A) Yes, because it defines a term that would otherwise puzzle readers.

B) Yes, because it shows why white chocolate is not as healthy as dark chocolate.

C) No, because it contradicts statements made later in the passage.

D) No, because it blurs the focus of the paragraph.

CONTINUE ➡

[6] Additionally for chocolate lovers, there are other health factors that must be considered when evaluating chocolate — factors that seriously detract from the health benefits. Flavonols are naturally bitter; anyone who [7] has tasted pure cocoa powder knows that it is far too bitter to be eaten by itself. Chocolate derives much of its deliciousness from its other ingredients, chiefly sugar and cocoa butter. Both contain a high calorie count, and cocoa butter is made of saturated fats that can negatively [8] affect you're cholesterol levels. Another key factor is that much of the flavonol found in cocoa powder is destroyed during the chocolate making process. In order to get a large enough dose of flavonol to make a noticeable impact, a person would have to eat seven chocolate bars a day. [9]

[6]

A) NO CHANGE

B) Happily

C) Unfortunately

D) Consequently

[7]

A) NO CHANGE

B) will be tasting

C) taste

D) tasting

[8]

A) NO CHANGE

B) effect your

C) effect ones

D) affect one's

[9]

The author wants to add a sentence that concludes the paragraph and refers to the opening of the passage. Which choice accomplishes this goal?

A) There are few people who would describe that amount of chocolate as healthy eating!

B) Anyone living with high cholesterol should search out other sources of flavonols.

C) Even the most devoted chocolate lover would balk at such a large daily consumption.

D) Kilwin's, an independent chocolatier, is currently developing a chocolate-making method to reduce the amount of flavonols lost in the process.

CONTINUE ➡

There are many other foods that contain flavonol without chocolate's high sugar and calorie count. Black tea offers the greatest amount of flavonol and has no calories, as long as no sugar is added. Onions, too, are packed with flavonol, but, like cocoa powder, they lose much of their dietary impact when cooked. **10** **11** While the nutrition of black tea has received some favorable press, it is doubtful that there will be many news stories encouraging readers to eat raw onions for their health.

Top ten foods that contain
the most flavonol per gram.

Food	Percent of total flavonols consumed (%)
Tea	
Black, brewed	32.11
Black, brewed, decaffeinated	5.70
Onion	
Boiled, drained	3.81
Raw	21.46
Apples	
Raw, with skin	7.02
Beer	
Regular	6.20
Lettuce	
Iceberg, raw	1.93
Coffee	
Brewed from grounds	1.74
Tomato	
Puree, canned	1.45
Red, ripe, raw	1.17

10

Does the table provided support the statement made in the preceding sentence?

A) Yes, because onions have more flavonol than cocoa powder.

B) Yes, because the percentage of flavonol is higher in raw onions than in cooked onions.

C) No, because black tea has more flavonol than raw onions.

D) No, because cooking onions does not change the percentage of flavonol.

11

Which of the following provides a concluding sentence that restates the main argument of the passage?

A) NO CHANGE

B) Those seeking truly healthy foods, not just those celebrated in the media, would do well to look beyond a bar of chocolate.

C) Canned tomatoes, however, have more flavonol than their raw counterparts.

D) Clearly, chocolate does not contain enough flavonol to be labeled a healthy food.

CONTINUE ➡

Questions 12-22 are based on the following passage.

Big screen sound effects

[1]

I have always enjoyed recording and manipulating sound. **12** As a boy, I had a handheld tape recorder that I would use to capture sounds, which I could then speed up, slow down, or reverse. I went to school to become an audio engineer, but I ended up working not only in the music industry, **13** but as well in the film industry. For the past decade, I have been a foley artist: a creator of sound effects.

12

The author is considering deleting the underlined sentence. Should the author do this?

A) Yes, because the sentence detracts from the focus on his current career.

B) Yes, because the passage does not mention reversed sounds again.

C) No, because the sentence shows how he got into an audio engineering program.

D) No, because the sentence provides a relevant example to support the previous sentence.

13

A) NO CHANGE

B) but additionally

C) but also

D) and also

[2]

You might think that I work on the set, making sound off-camera, but I have never gone to a film shoot. The only sound recorded during the filming is dialogue. After the film has been edited, I begin creating sound effects in my recording studio. **14** Projected on one wall, I watch scenes from the film to synch the sounds I create. The studio contains all kinds of objects useful for making sounds. I have small pieces of every type of floor imaginable and a pile of shoes with different kinds of soles. Along one side of the studio **15** is various types of doors and windows equipped with specific latches and locks. Bins containing all kinds of wood, metal, and plastic allow me to make any possible combination of scratching, bumping, **16** and scrapes.

14

A) NO CHANGE

B) I watch scenes from the film to synch the sounds I create projected on one wall.

C) Projected on one wall, the sounds I create watch scenes from the film to synch.

D) I watch scenes from the film projected on one wall to synch the sounds I create.

15

A) NO CHANGE

B) were

C) are

D) was

16

A) NO CHANGE

B) and, scrapes.

C) and scraping.

D) and, scraping.

CONTINUE

[3]

[17] The crackle of a fire may just be some crumpled cellophane. The pitter patter of rain could be dry rice sprinkled on a baking sheet. One famous movie sound [18] effect–the warm throb of a lightsaber in Star Wars, came from an unexpected discovery. The foley artist discovered that moving a microphone near a plugged-in old television [19] made a funny noise. So every time an actor swung a lightsaber, a foley artist moved a microphone around a TV!

[4]

My favorite type of film to work on is an action movie. There is nothing more fun than creating sound effects for punches and kicks. A sledgehammer blow to a 20 pound bag of flour certainly sounds like a punch to the gut. If the film needs a hit to the head, I might drop a watermelon [20] into a pile of crackers.

17

Which of the following sentences would provide the best introduction to the third paragraph?

A) All great foley artists invent new ways to make familiar sounds.

B) Many of the sound effects heard in films come from surprising sources.

C) Often times a foley artist will need to record outside of the studio.

D) The sound of fire is the most difficult sound effect to create.

18

A) NO CHANGE

B) effect: the

C) effect, the

D) effect; the

19

A) NO CHANGE

B) generated odd humming vibrations.

C) produced a unique buzzing sound.

D) created electrostatic emissions.

20

A) NO CHANGE

B) onto

C) within

D) with

[5]

While I find my job immensely rewarding, becoming a foley artist is not a straightforward career path. Some schools offer degrees in sound design, but there is no specific program for creating sound effects for films. Anyone interested in working in foley should start creating his or her own portfolio of sounds. These can be created fairly easily with a microphone and any audio recording software **21**. The best way to find work in a sound effects studio is to ask for an internship. This will give you invaluable experience, and every sound effects studio needs someone to sweep up the dry rice and smashed watermelon after a long day of recording!

The author is considering changing the period to a comma and adding the phrase "but watch out because microphones can get very expensive." Should the writer add this phrase?

A) Yes, because the phrase shows concern over the potential cost of recording equipment.

B) Yes, because the phrase would discourage readers who lack commitment to sound recording.

C) No, because the phrase is unclear about the cost of microphones.

D) No, because the phrase undermines the encouraging tone of the passage.

22

The author is considering adding the following sentence to the passage.

"The sound of a bone breaking is probably just a broken celery stalk."

This sentence would best fit in which paragraph?

A) Paragraph 2

B) Paragraph 3

C) Paragraph 4

D) Paragraph 5

CONTINUE

Questions 23-33 are based on the following passage.

Are 42 strings better than 6?

In 1984, jazz guitarist Pat Metheny contacted Canadian guitar maker Linda Manzer with an unusual request for a stringed **23** instrument: a guitar with "as many strings on it as possible." Manzer kept the standard 6-string guitar neck untouched, and instead added two smaller necks set at diagonals and several harp-like strings across the body of the guitar. The result was the Pikasso guitar, a maze of 42 overlapping strings.

[1] The name of the guitar clearly **24** evades famed Spanish modern artist Pablo Picasso. [2] Picasso was instrumental in developing **25** Cubism a type of painting that attempts to represent objects from simultaneous yet opposing points of view. [3] Early in **26** Picassos Cubist phase, he often would paint still-lifes, frequently including a guitar among the objects. [4] Picasso would often break apart the pattern of strings and frets, depicting the guitar as seen through a kaleidoscope. [5] Manzer's Pikasso guitar was envisioned as a physical recreation of one of Picasso's impossible Cubist guitars. **27**

23

A) NO CHANGE
B) instrument. A guitar
C) instrument, it was for a guitar
D) instrument; a guitar

24

A) NO CHANGE
B) provokes
C) engages
D) references

25

A) NO CHANGE
B) Cubism; a type
C) Cubism, a type
D) Cubism. Being a type

26

A) NO CHANGE
B) Picasso's Cubist phase
C) Picasso's Cubist's phase
D) Picasso Cubist's phase

27

The author is considering adding the following sentence at this point:

> This effect was created by breaking down the subject into flattened, geometric forms and depicting it from different angles.

This sentence should be placed where in Paragraph 2?

A) After sentence 1
B) After sentence 2
C) After sentence 3
D) After sentence 4

817

CONTINUE ➡

Should we call the Pikasso guitar a success? The answer is a matter of perspective and priority. The construction of the guitar is impeccable, and the very fact that an acoustic guitar made of wood can withhold that amount of string tension is extremely impressive. Manzer is clearly a skilled luthier able to build an instrument **28** that is intricate in its complexity. Whether or not the guitar is aesthetically pleasing depends on a personal preference for excess or minimalism. Should a guitar have embellishments or stick to practical essentials?

Perhaps the most important area to judge the Pikasso **29** guitar, its usability as a musical instrument, is where it disappoints the most. Pat Metheny has had over a quarter of a century to master the Pikasso guitar, yet he appears entirely uneasy when playing the 42-stringed behemoth. The guitar's cumbersome girth and width impact the natural grace of a guitar player. **30** At best, he sticks to the traditional guitar neck, ignoring the harp-like strings. At worst, Metheny's hands meander across the instrument, plucking harp strings simply because they are there.

28

A) NO CHANGE

B) of uncommon complexity.

C) that is exceedingly complicated and convoluted.

D) of shockingly surprising intricacy.

29

A) NO CHANGE

B) guitar, it's

C) guitar–it's

D) guitar–its

30

The author wants to add the following phrase to the preceding sentence, replacing the period with a comma:

> "which many beginners struggle with, even on a standard acoustic guitar."

Should the writer make this change?

A) Yes, because it adds a detail that clarifies the author's feelings about guitarists.

B) Yes, because it adds a transition between the Pikasso guitar and Methany's overall ability on guitar.

C) No, because it interrupts the flow of the paragraph with an irrelevant digression.

D) No, because it implies that Metheny is a beginner guitarist.

CONTINUE →

A sampling of Metheny's songs featuring the Pikasso guitar **31** <u>will find</u> most of them sound strikingly similar, and many of his best songs are played on a traditional acoustic guitar. Metheny brings the Pikasso guitar out on stage mostly for its theatricality, **32** <u>or</u> its musicality.

In the world of musical instruments, there will always be a desire for the unique and the exotic. The Pikasso guitar itself has been eclipsed by another Manzer creation, the 52 string Medusa guitar, which features three playable necks. **33**

31

A) NO CHANGE

B) would find

C) will reveal that

D) will be revealing

32

A) NO CHANGE

B) and

C) rather than

D) because of

33

Which of the following concluding sentences would best reflect the tone of the passage?

A) Whether or not the Medusa guitar will be more musically useful than its predecessor remains to be seen.

B) It is truly unfortunate that a talented guitar builder wastes her talents on such pointless guitars.

C) The Medusa cost over $50,000 dollars, so don't expect to see one in a guitar store anytime soon.

D) Hopefully someone soon will build a guitar with a 100 strings!

CONTINUE

Question 34-44 are based on the following passage.

Migratory patterns of American young adults

We tend to think of migration in terms of flocks of birds and herds of animals, moving from one area to another in search of resources and favorable climates. Humans migrate too, although our movements often go unnoticed [34] between the interwoven chaos of contemporary life. Immigration and emigration between countries are the easiest migrations to [35] notice, yet they involve visas and border crossing. Within a single country, migrations are less obvious, but determining who migrates and for what reasons can illuminate important social trends.

[36] Gathering accurate data on migrations is very difficult, and best left to government entities such as the United States Census. The Census takers track migration by asking the participants if they have changed cities within the last year; any person who answers yes is considered a migrant, [37] which means that they moved recently. The group that has moved the most in the last ten years has been young adults, [38] being defined by the U.S. Census as people from the age of 18 to 34.

34

A) NO CHANGE

B) out of

C) along

D) among

35

A) NO CHANGE

B) notice, since

C) notice. Because

D) notice; as

36

Which choice provides the smoothest and most effective transition between the first and second paragraphs?

A) NO CHANGE

B) The United States Census provides valuable information for researchers in many fields.

C) Using data from the United States Census, sociologists can track which categories of people move.

D) The United States Constitution mandates a Census be taken every ten years to determine how the population of the country is changing.

37

A) NO CHANGE

B) which includes people who move

C) as these are the people who have moved

D) DELETE the phrase

38

A) NO CHANGE

B) defined

C) defining

D) be defined

CONTINUE

Between 2010 and 2012, the migration rates for young adults **39** exceeded the average population's rate. Dividing up the **40** young population into three subcategories, uncovers some of the reasons for all this moving. People 18 to 26 years old accounted for nearly half of the movers in the young adult group, representing 20.8 percent of the total population movement within the country.

[1] This explains why small towns with colleges and universities **41** see the largest influx of migration, as students arrive each fall to attend the schools. [2] As University-level education becomes the cultural norm, an increasing number of young adults choose to leave their hometowns to pursue a higher education. [3] Once college is finished, the same young adults may have to relocate again in order to find employment. [4] There are multiple reasons for the young adult migration trend. **42**

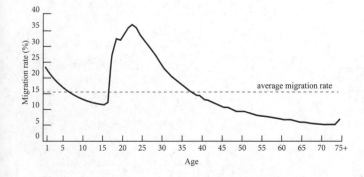

Migration Rates, 2010-2012

Which choice gives an accurate representation of the figure?

A) NO CHANGE

B) declined as age increased.

C) remained above 30%.

D) remained unchanged as age increased.

A) NO CHANGE

B) young population, into three subcategories, uncovers

C) young population into three, subcategories uncovers

D) young population into three subcategories uncovers

A) NO CHANGE

B) view

C) perceive

D) comprehend

Which of the following is the most logical order for the sentences in the third paragraph?

A) NO CHANGE

B) 2, 1, 3, 4

C) 4, 1, 2, 3

D) 4, 2, 1, 3

Another reason for so much movement within this section of the population is the change in manufacturing in the United States. A half-century ago, the "factory town" was a common phenomenon. **43** There a family could expect steady employment and benefits, with successive generations following in their parent's footsteps and taking a similar job with the primary employer. As manufacturing shifted from domestic production to imports, the job stability in factory towns disappeared as well, leading younger generations to spread their wings and look for better job opportunities. **44** Those who leave will likely never come back to their hometowns. As this generation migrates across the country, the population redistribution will likely have a long-lasting effect on the demographics of the nation, determining which cities and regions grow and prosper and which recede into history.

43

A) NO CHANGE

B) When

C) If

D) Since

44

Should the author delete the underlined sentence?

A) Yes, because it makes an unsupported claim about the future.

B) Yes, because it repeats a statement made earlier in the passage.

C) No, because it provides a specific detail that supports the main idea of the paragraph.

D) No, because it expresses the author's opinion that young adults should migrate.

STOP

If you finish before time is called, you may check your work on this section only. Do not turn to any other section.

Mathematics Test – No Calculator
25 MINUTES, 20 QUESTIONS

Turn to Section 3 of your answer sheet to answer the questions in this section.

DIRECTIONS

For questions 1-15, solve each problem, choose the best answer from the choices provided, and fill in the corresponding circle on your answer sheet. **For questions 16-20,** solve the problem and enter your answer in the grid on the answer sheet. Please refer to the directions before question 16 on how to enter you answers in the grid. You may use any available space in your test booklet for scratch work.

NOTES

1. The use of a calculator **is not permitted.**
2. All variables and expressions used represent real numbers unless otherwise indicated.
3. Figures provided in this test are drawn to scale unless otherwise indicated.
4. All figures lie in a plane unless otherwise indicated.
5. Unless otherwise indicated, the domain of a given function f is the set of all real numbers x for which $f(x)$ is a real number.

REFERENCE

$A = \pi r^2$
$C = 2\pi r$

$A = \ell w$

$A = \frac{1}{2} bh$

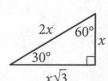

$c^2 = a^2 + b^2$

Special Right Triangles

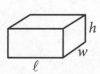

$V = \ell wh$

$V = \pi r^2 h$

$V = \frac{4}{3} \pi r^3$

$V = \frac{1}{3} \pi r^2 h$

$V = \frac{1}{3} \ell wh$

The number of degrees of arc in a circle is 360.
The number of radians of arc in a circle is 2π
The sum of the measures in degrees of the angles of a triangle is 180.

CONTINUE ▶

1

Which of the following statements is true about the equation $y = (x - 3)^2$?

A) y is always less than 3.

B) y is always greater than 3.

C) y is always greater than –2.

D) y is always greater than x.

2

n	2	3	4
$f(n)$	3	4	5
$g(n)$	4	2	6

The table above shows values of the functions f and g. What is the value of $f(g(2))$?

A) 3

B) 4

C) 5

D) 6

3

$$x + y = 9$$
$$5x + y = -19$$

According to the system of equations above, what is the value of y?

A) –7

B) 4

C) 5

D) 16

4

$$g(x) = \frac{3}{a}x - 24$$

In the function above, a is a constant. If $g(9) = 12$, what is the value of $g(3)$?

A) 12

B) –3

C) –12

D) –36

5

$$4[(x + 6)(x - 1)+10]$$

Which of the following is equivalent to the expression above?

A) $4x^2 + 5x + 16$

B) $4(x + 5)^2 + 10$

C) $4(x + 4)(x + 1)$

D) $4(x - 4)(x - 1)$

6

For what value of n will 8 equal $\frac{3-n}{3+n}$?

A) $-\frac{7}{3}$

B) $-\frac{29}{3}$

C) -3

D) $\frac{9}{2}$

7

In an effort to eat healthier, Cambry is trying to decrease her weekly consumption of candy bars, and she has decided to do this by decreasing the number of candy bars she eats each week by a constant rate. If Cambry's candy bar eating plan allows her to eat 21 candy bars during week 2 and 9 candy bars during week 5, how many candy bars will the candy bar eating plan allow Cambry to eat during week 6 ?

A)   3

B)   4

C)   5

D)   6

8

$$x = 2y$$
$$6y - 3x = 4$$

The graph of each equation above in the xy-plane is a line. Which of the following statements is true about these two lines?

A)   The slope of both lines is negative.

B)   The lines are the same.

C)   The lines are parallel.

D)   The lines are perpendicular.

CONTINUE

9

$$(m - 3)^2 = 5m + p$$

If $p = -1$, what is the solution set of the equation above?

A) $\{10, 1\}$

B) $\{10\}$

C) $\{1\}$

D) $\{-10, -1\}$

10

If $\frac{3}{x} = \frac{15}{x+16}$, what is the value of $\frac{24}{x}$?

A) 6

B) 5

C) 4

D) 3

11

$$y = x^2 + a$$
$$y = -x^2 + b$$

In the system of equations above, a and b are constants. Which of the following must be true if the system of equations has two solutions?

A) a is less than b.

B) a is greater than b.

C) a is equal to b.

D) a and b are both equal to zero.

12

On September 4, 2014, Janet and Esther started a bake sale to raise money for their high school drama department. The drama department's budget is currently $650 and their goal is to raise the budget to $900. If Janet and Esther increase the drama department's budget by $36 every day by selling baked goods, and d represents the number of days since September 4, 2014, which of the following inequalities describes the set of days d in which Janet and Esther have yet to reach their goal?

A) $900 - 36 > d$

B) $650 < 36d$

C) $900 > 36d$

D) $650 + 36d < 900$

13

The functions f and g are defined by $f(x) = 2x^2 + x - 2$ and $g(x) = -x^2 - 2x - 4$. For what set of x values does $f(x) + g(x) = 0$?

A) $\{2, 3\}$

B) $\{-2, 3\}$

C) $\{-1, -3\}$

D) $\{1, 3\}$

14

$$\frac{4-2i}{1+i}$$

If the expression above is rewritten in the form $a + bi$, where a and b are real numbers, what is the value of $a + b$?

A) -3

B) -2

C) 2

D) 4

15

$$x^2 = 2rx + \frac{d}{2}$$

In the quadratic equation above, r and d are constants. What are the solutions for x ?

A) $x = 2r \pm \dfrac{\sqrt{4r^2 + 2d}}{2}$

B) $x = 2r \pm \dfrac{\sqrt{4r^2 + 2d}}{4}$

C) $x = r \pm \dfrac{\sqrt{4r^2 + 2d}}{2}$

D) $x = r \pm \dfrac{\sqrt{4r^2 + 2d}}{4}$

CONTINUE ▶

DIRECTIONS

For questions 16-20, solve the problem and enter your answer in the grid, as described below, on the answer sheet.

1. Although not required, it is suggested that you write your answer in the boxes at the top of the columns to help you fill in the circles accurately. You will receive credit only if the circles are filled in correctly.

2. Mark no more than one circle in any column.

3. No question has a negative answer.

4. Some problems may have more than one correct answer. In such cases, grid only one answer.

5. **Mixed numbers** such as 3 ½ must be gridded as 3.5 or 7/2. (If is entered into the grid, it will be interpreted as 3½, not 3 ½.)

6. **Decimal answers:** If you obtain a decimal answer with more digits than the grid can accommodate, it may be either rounded or truncated, but it must fill the entire grid.

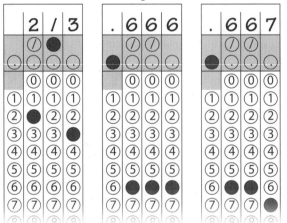

Acceptable ways to grid $\frac{2}{3}$ are:

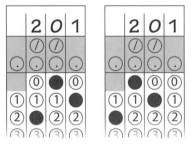

Answer: 201 – either position is correct

NOTE: You may start your answers in any column, space permitting. Columns you don't need to use should be left blank.

16

A zoo has 3 different pens, Pen A, Pen B, and Pen C, for holding animals. Pen A has half the area of that of Pen B, and Pen A has one third of the area of Pen C. If Pens A, B, and C have a combined area of 7,200 square feet, what is the area of the biggest pen?

17

The sine of one angle of a right triangle is $\frac{12}{13}$. What is the cosine of that angle?

18

$$f(x) = x^3 - cx^2 + 4x - 4c$$

In the function f above, c is a constant. How many x-intercepts does the function have?

19

$$3x + ay = 6$$
$$bx + 4y = 8$$

If the system of equations above is parallel, what is the value of ab?

20

When companies have between 100 and 500 employees, the average annual pay raise decreases at a constant rate as the number of employees in the company increases. Company X has 100 employees and the average employee raise is $1,700. Company B has 450 employees and the average employee raise is $1,200. For every 7 employees hired, how much does the annual raise decrease? Round your answer to the nearest dollar.

STOP
**If you finish before time is called, you may check your work on this section only.
Do not turn to any other section.**

No Test Material On This Page

Mathematics Test – Calculator
55 MINUTES, 38 QUESTIONS

Turn to Section 4 of your answer sheet to answer the questions in this section.

DIRECTIONS

For questions 1-30, solve each problem, choose the best answer from the choices provided, and fill in the corresponding circle on your answer sheet. **For questions 31-38**, solve the problem and enter your answer in the grid on the answer sheet. Please refer to the directions before question 16 on how to enter you answers in the grid. You may use any available space in your test booklet for scratch work.

NOTES

1. The use of a calculator **is permitted.**
2. All variables and expressions used represent real numbers unless otherwise indicated.
3. Figures provided in this test are drawn to scale unless otherwise indicated.
4. All figures lie in a plane unless otherwise indicated.
5. Unless otherwise indicated, the domain of a given function f is the set of all real numbers x for which $f(x)$ is a real number.

REFERENCE

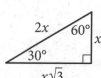

$A = \pi r^2$

$C = 2\pi r$

$A = \ell w$

$A = \frac{1}{2}bh$

$c^2 = a^2 + b^2$

Special Right Triangles

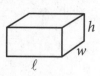

$V = \ell w h$

$V = \pi r^2 h$

$V = \frac{4}{3}\pi r^3$

$V = \frac{1}{3}\pi r^2 h$

$V = \frac{1}{3}\ell w h$

The number of degrees of arc in a circle is 360.

The number of radians of arc in a circle is 2π

The sum of the measures in degrees of the angles of a triangle is 180.

CONTINUE

1

At the beginning of each semester, an English teacher assigns each of her students a participation grade of 42. Over the course of the semester, she will award 2.5 points to a student every time the student voluntarily participates in class discussion, but the student does not receive extra points if the teacher calls on him or her to answer a question. At the end of a semester, a particular student has a participation grade of 82. How many times did she participate in class voluntarily?

A) 15

B) 16

C) 17

D) 18

2

Felix is saving up money to buy a new laptop that costs $1,400. If Felix has already saved $900, and he saves an additional $50 each week, how much money will Felix have saved w weeks from now?

A) $50 + 900w$

B) $1,400 + 50w$

C) $900 + 50w$

D) $900 - 50w$

3

Americans eat an average of 1,500 hamburgers every second. If 45% of all hamburgers are eaten in the Southeast of the United States, which of the following equations represents the total number of hamburgers x Americans in the Southeast eat in m minutes?

A) $x = \dfrac{(0.45)60m}{1,500}$

B) $x = \dfrac{(0.45)1,500m}{60}$

C) $x = (0.45)1,500(60m)$

D) $x = (0.45)1,500m + 60$

4

A member of the journalism club gives a poll to a group of high school juniors and seniors asking whether or not they had attended last weekend's varsity basketball game. Of the 25 juniors and seniors polled, 6 juniors and 10 seniors attended the game. Assuming that the results of this poll accurately reflect the decisions of the 450 juniors and seniors at the school to attend or not attend the basketball game, approximately how many juniors and seniors attended the game?

A) 200

B) 225

C) 250

D) 300

5

The force, in Newtons, exerted on an object is equal to the mass, in kilograms, of the object multiplied by the acceleration, in meters per second squared. If a force of 2 Newtons accelerates an object by 8 meters per second squared, what is the mass of the object in kilograms?

A) 16

B) 8

C) 4

D) 0.25

6

Fiona and Sebastian made a combined total of $1,000 last week waiting tables. If Fiona made 76 more dollars than Sebastian did, what fraction of the $1,000 did Sebastian make?

A) $\frac{231}{500}$

B) $\frac{49}{100}$

C) $\frac{269}{500}$

D) $\frac{58}{100}$

7

City Council Voting Preference for Town of Smithfield 2012-13							
Candidates for City Council	Age of voting population						
	18-27	28-37	38-47	48-57	58-67	68+	Total
Candidate A	43	76	79	82	36	27	343
Candidate B	36	45	54	51	19	21	226
Candidate C	8	12	9	15	18	32	94
Undecided	2	6	5	4	9	8	34
Total	89	139	147	152	82	88	697

The table above shows the voting preferences of a poll given to 697 residents of Smithfield. Polled residents had a choice of three candidates or undecided. Of the polled residents between 48 and 67 years of age, approximately what percentage favored Candidate C ?

A) 5%

B) 10%

C) 14%

D) 22%

8

The graph of a linear function f has a positive slope with intercepts $(a, 0)$ and $(0, b)$, where a and b are non-zero integers. Which of the following statements about a and b could be true?

A) $a + b = 0$

B) $a - 2b = 0$

C) $a = b$

D) $0 < a < b$

CONTINUE ▶

Questions 9-10 refer to the following information.

Year	Total population	U.S. supply of seafood	Per capita consumption of imported seafood	Per capita consumption of domestic seafood
2005	297	20,529	36.7	32.4
2006	299	20,960	38.3	31.6
2007	302	20,484	37.3	30.6
2008	305	19,252	35.9	27.3
2009	307	18,900	35.4	26.1

The table above shows the total U.S. population in millions of persons, supply of seafood in millions of pounds, and per capita consumption of imported and domestic seafood in pounds, from 2005 to 2009.

9

In 2008, the per capita consumption of imported seafood was approximately what percent greater than the per capita consumption of domestic seafood?

A) 20%

B) 25%

C) 30%

D) 45%

10

From 2006 to 2009, what was the average annual rate of decrease in the U.S. supply of seafood, in millions of pounds (Round your answer to the nearest pound)?

A) 515

B) 543

C) 687

D) 2,060

11

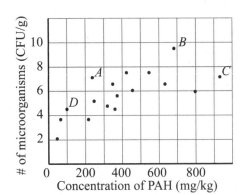

In the graph above, a study examines the number of microorganisms present in soil with varying concentrations of polycyclic aromatic hydrocarbon (PAH), a byproduct of various industrial processes. Four petri dishes listed above were exposed to various concentrations of PAH, and the number of colony-forming units (CFU) were counted after a week of incubation. For what petri dish was ratio of the number of microorganisms to the concentration of PAH the greatest?

A) A

B) B

C) C

D) D

12

x	f(x)
–5	0
–1	36
0	0
1	6
2	0

The function f is defined by a polynomial. Some values of x and $f(x)$ are shown in the table above. Which of the following could define f?

A) $(x - 5)(x + 2)$

B) $(x + 5)^2(x - 2)^3$

C) $x^2(x + 5)(x - 2)^2$

D) $x(x + 5)(x - 2)$

13

Since government officials of North Dakota allowed for an increase in the number of drilling sites for oil, the state's population is projected to increase by 19% every three years. If the population of the state is currently 700,000, which of the following expressions shows the state's population x years from now?

A) $f(x) = 700,000(0.81)^{\frac{x}{3}}$

B) $f(x) = 700,000(0.81)^{3x}$

C) $f(x) = 700,000(1.19)^{\frac{x}{3}}$

D) $f(x) = 700,000(1.19)^{3x}$

CONTINUE

Questions 14-15 refer to the following information.

A speleologist visits a particular cave on the same day every year and has been recording the lengths of a particular stalactite and the stalagmite growing up directly below it. The lengths in millimeters from several years are recorded in the table below.

Year	Stalagmite length	Stalactite length
2010	30.76	345.12
2011	30.77	345.25
2012	30.78	345.38
2013	30.79	345.51

14

If the stalactite continues to grow down from the top of the cave at the same rate, how long will it be in 2230 ?

A) 347.72

B) 373.72

C) 375.02

D) 635.02

15

The height of the cave where the stalagmite and stalactite are located is one meter. If the growth rates remain constant, in which year will the two meet? (1 meter = 1000 millimeters)?

A) 4458

B) 4940

C) 6468

D) 6949

16

16 ounces (oz)	1 pound (lb)
128 fluid ounces (fl. oz)	1 gallon (g)

One gallon of honey weighs approximately 12 pounds. If one gallon of honey is mixed into 5 gallons of water to make tea, how many <u>ounces</u> of honey will be in each 8 fluid ounce cup of the tea?

A) 1

B) 2

C) 3

D) 4

17

Which of the following is NOT a solution of the inequality $4x - 2 \geq 3x - 8$?

A) −7

B) −6

C) −5

D) −4

18

A researcher observes that an incubated bacteria colony with initial population I doubles every hour. Which of the following functions would estimate the population P of a bacteria colony after h hours of incubation?

A) $P(h) = 2Ih$

B) $P(h) = I + 2h$

C) $P(h) = (I)(2^h)$

D) $P(h) = 2$

19

Suzie can pay $7.50 for a softcover comic book and $12 for a hardcover comic book. If she spends more than $35 but less than $40 on comic books and buys at least 2 hardcover books, what is one possible number of softcover comic books that she bought?

A) 1

B) 2

C) 3

D) 4

20

A party planner has ordered a certain number of appetizers for a party. If each party attendant gets 3 appetizers, there will be 2 appetizers left over, and if each party attendant gets 4 appetizers, the planner will be short 13 appetizers. How many appetizers did the party planner order?

A) 14

B) 15

C) 45

D) 47

CONTINUE

Questions 21-22 refer to the following information.

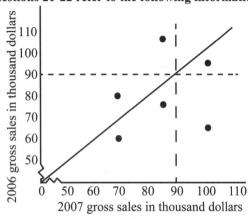

Line of profitability for 2006 ‑ ‑ ‑ ‑ ‑‑
Line of profitability for 2007 ‑‑ ‑ ‑ ‑

The scatterplot above shows the gross sales, in thousands of dollars, for six franchise restaurants in 2006 and 2007. The solid line indicates the same gross sales in 2007 as in 2006.

For how many of the restaurants did the gross sales from 2007 exceed those of 2006 ?

A) 1

B) 2

C) 3

D) 4

For the restaurant that saw the greatest decrease in gross sales from 2006 to 2007, the manager will set the goal of matching the 2007 revenue of the restaurant that saw the greatest increase in gross sales for that period. How much more will the restaurant need to make in gross sales to reach that goal?

A) $5,000

B) $10,000

C) $15,000

D) $20,000

23

A group in Everitt polled two groups of 50 people and asked their ages. In Group A the standard deviation of the ages was 7 years and in Group B the standard deviation of the ages was 13 years. Which of the following statements could be true?

A) The ages of people in Group A are closer to the average age of Group A than the ages of the people in Group B are to the average age of Group B

B) The ages of people in Group B are closer to the average age of Group B than the ages of the people in Group A are to the average age of Group A.

C) The distributions of ages in Groups A and B are about the same.

D) None of the above conclusions are valid.

24

The area of an equilateral triangle is $36\sqrt{3}$, what is the height of the triangle?

A) 6

B) $6\sqrt{3}$

C) $9\sqrt{3}$

D) $12\sqrt{3}$

25

$$g(x) = \frac{2x - 6}{3x^3 + 15x^2 + 2x + 10}$$

For what value of x is the function g above undefined if $x \le 0$?

A) -5

B) -3

C) -23

D) $-\dfrac{2}{3}$

26

A produce company sells watermelons that are advertised to weight m pounds. In order to maintain customer satisfaction, each watermelon sold cannot vary by more than 1 pound from the advertised weight. If a watermelon that weighs n pounds meets the weight standards, which of the following inequalities represents the relationship between the advertised weight and the weight n of the watermelon?

A) $-1 \le m - n \le 1$

B) $m \le n - 1$

C) $m \le 1 \le n$

D) $m + n \le 1$

27

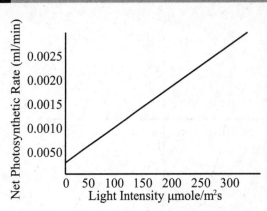

The rate at which a plant absorbs carbon dioxide and emits oxygen, called the net photosynthetic rate in milliliters per minute, is modeled for various light intensities, measured in micromoles (μmole) per square meter per second, using the equation $P = 0.00005I + 0.003$, where P represents the net photosynthetic rate, in milliliters per minute, and I represents the light intensity, in micromoles per square meter per second. Which of the following best explains the y-intercept on the graph?

A) When there is no light, a plant will emit 0.003 ml of oxygen per minute.

B) When there is no light, a plant will absorb 0.003 ml of oxygen per minute.

C) At a light intensity of 0.003 μmole, a plant emits 0.00005 ml of oxygen per minute.

D) At a light intensity of 0.00005 μmole, a plant emits 0.003 ml of oxygen per minute.

CONTINUE

28

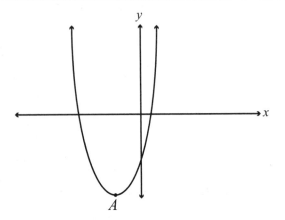

Which of the following is a form of the equation for the graph shown above from which coordinates of vertex A can be identified as constants or coefficients in the equation?

A) $y = (x + 6)(x - 2)$

B) $y = (x - 6)(x + 2)$

C) $y = (x(x + 4)) - 12$

D) $y = (x + 2)^2 - 16$

29

If the average of a and $2b$ also equals the average of b and $2c$, what is the average of a and b in terms of c ?

A) c

B) $2c$

C) $\dfrac{2c}{3}$

D) $\dfrac{1}{c}$

30

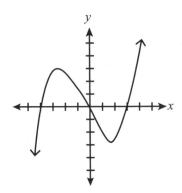

The function above, $f(x)$, has x-intercepts at -4, 0, and 3. If a is a positive constant and $f(x) = a$ has two real solutions, what is one possible value of a ?

A) −1

B) 1

C) 3

D) 4

DIRECTIONS

For questions 31-38, solve the problem and enter your answer in the grid, as described below, on the answer sheet.

1. Although not required, it is suggested that you write your answer in the boxes at the top of the columns to help you fill in the circles accurately. You will receive credit only if the circles are filled in correctly.

2. Mark no more than one circle in any column.

3. No question has a negative answer.

4. Some problems may have more than one correct answer. In such cases, grid only one answer.

5. **Mixed numbers** such as 3 ½ must be gridded as 3.5 or 7/2. (If is entered into the grid, it will be interpreted as ³¹⁄₂, not 3 ½.)

6. **Decimal answers:** If you obtain a decimal answer with more digits than the grid can accommodate, it may be either rounded or truncated, but it must fill the entire grid.

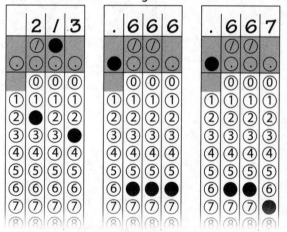

Acceptable ways to grid $\frac{2}{3}$ are:

Answer: 201 – either position is correct

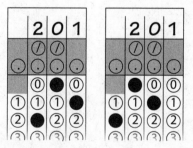

NOTE: You may start your answers in any column, space permitting. Columns you don't need to use should be left blank.

CONTINUE →

31

The mayor of Apelburg started an initiative to increase the number of trees in the city at a constant rate until there will be 80,000 trees by 2030. If the city is projected to have 64,000 trees by 2020, how many trees will be planted every two years?

32

Geoffrey can approximate the grade he will receive on a test with the equation $60 + 8h$, where $0 \leq h \leq 5$ is the number of hours Geoffrey spends studying for the test. What is the increase in Geoffrey's score for each additional hour of studying?

33

A dram is $\frac{1}{16}$ of an ounce. A dram is also approximately 1.77 grams. If there are 16 ounces to a pound, what fraction of a pound is 90 grams? (Round to the nearest thousandths place.)

34

The livestock on Darnell's farm solely consist of cows and chickens. Darnell owned 160 chickens but recently bought x more chickens. If Darnell owns 80 cows, how many chickens did Darnell buy if 20% of his farm animals are cows?

35

The period of a simple pendulum with a mass attached to a string is approximated by the equation $T = 2\pi\sqrt{\frac{L}{9.8}}$ where L is the length of the string, in meters, and T is the duration of the period, in seconds. A physicist compares two pendulums with strings of lengths 16 meters and 9 meters. What is the ratio of the period of the longer string pendulum to that of the shorter string pendulum?

36

A wedge of a circle has a central angle measure between 70° and 80°. If the area of the circle is 38 square inches, what is one possible value for the area of the wedge?

Questions 37-38 refer to the following information.

The base sales tax for the state of Georgia is 4%, with an additional local sales tax of 3%. By contrast, the base sales tax for the state of Iowa is 6%, with no additional local sales tax.

If a resident of Georgia and a resident of Iowa spent the same amount of money, including tax, for groceries, the relationship between what they paid can be modeled by the equation $(1 + G)(x) = (1 + I)(y)$, where x represents the cost of the groceries in Georgia before tax is applied, G represents the sales tax for Georgia, y represents the cost of the groceries in Iowa before tax is applied, and I represents the sales tax for Iowa.

37

What is the value of I in the equation?

38

If a resident of Georgia and a resident of Iowa each purchased $300 in groceries, including tax, how many more groceries would a resident of Iowa have been able to purchase, in dollars, not including the sales tax? Round your answer to the nearest cent.

STOP
If you finish before time is called, you may check your work on this section only.
Do not turn to any other section.

Scoring Your Test

Answers to the test can be found in the answer key on page 851.

Your raw scores (the number of questions you answered correctly) will help you calibrate how well you mastered the content in this book. Use the table on the next page to translate your raw score into to an estimated scaled score, keeping in mind that the College Board is still in the process of adjusting the scoring tables for the upcoming tests.

Scoring your Test

To score your test, first obtain your Reading, Writing, and Math raw scores by adding up correct answers in sections as indicated in the table below. Fill in the third column with your raw scores.

Section	Count # correct to find Raw Scores		My Scaled
Reading	Section 1 =	(0-52)	(10-40)
Writing	Section 2 =	(0-44)	(10-40)
Math	Sections 3 + 4 =	(0-58)	(200-800)

) Add & x10

Next, obtain your **scaled scores** for each section using your raw scores and the table on the next page. You will find a **Math score** between 200-800, a **Reading score** between 10-40, and a **Writing score** between 10-40. Add your Reading and Writing scores and multiply by 10 to get your **Evidence-Based Reading and Writing Score** between 200-800.

Your total score is found by adding your Math Score (200-800) and your Evidence-Based Reading and Writing Score (200-800).

MATH	+	READING	=	TOTAL
(200-800)		& WRITING		(400-1600)
		(200-800)		

Raw Score	Scaled Score			Raw Score	Scaled Score		
	Reading + Writing		Math		Reading + Writing		Math
0	10	10	200	30	27	30	580
1	10	10	200	31	28	31	590
2	10	10	210	32	28	31	600
3	11	11	230	33	28	32	600
4	12	12	250	34	29	32	610
5	13	13	270	35	29	33	620
6	14	14	280	36	30	33	630
7	15	15	300	37	30	34	640
8	16	16	320	38	31	35	650
9	16	16	340	39	31	36	660
10	17	17	350	40	32	37	670
11	18	18	360	41	32	37	680
12	18	18	370	42	33	38	690
13	19	19	390	43	33	39	700
14	20	19	410	44	34	40	710
15	20	20	420	45	35		710
16	21	21	430	46	35		720
17	21	22	450	47	36		730
18	22	23	460	48	37		730
19	22	23	470	49	38		740
20	23	24	480	50	39		750
21	23	24	490	51	39		750
22	23	25	500	52	40		760
23	24	26	510	53			770
24	24	26	520	54			780
25	25	27	530	55			790
26	25	27	540	56			790
27	26	28	550	57			800
28	26	29	560	58			800
29	27	29	570				

Writing

Comma Basics

1) D
2) A
3) D
4) C
5) A
6) B
7) C
8) A
9) D
10) B

All About Clauses

1) B
2) B
3) D
4) B
5) D
6) C
7) C
8) C
9) C
10) D

PP1: Dirt

1) A
2) C
3) D
4) B
5) C
6) B
7) D
8) D
9) A
10) C
11) B

Tense Switch

1) D
2) A
3) B
4) C
5) C
6) B
7) D
8) D
9) A
10) B

Subject-Verb Agreement

1) B
2) B
3) D
4) B
5) C
6) B
7) A
8) B
9) B
10) D

Pronoun Error

1) C
2) B
3) C
4) D
5) B
6) A
7) D
8) C

PP2: Comics

1) B
2) A
3) B
4) D
5) C
6) A
7) C
8) C
9) D
10) B
11) B

Possession

1) C
2) D
3) A
4) C
5) D
6) C
7) B
8) D
9) A
10) B

Parallelism

1) B
2) D
3) A
4) B
5) D
6) C
7) D
8) B
9) C
10) C

Writing

Misplaced Modifier

1) D
2) B
3) B
4) D
5) B

PP3

1) D
2) B
3) A
4) C
5) C
6) D
7) B
8) C
9) A
10) D
11) C

Redundancy

1) D
2) D
3) A
4) B
5) C
6) D
7) A
8) B

Prepositions

1) C
2) A
3) B
4) C
5) D
6) C
7) B
8) B
9) A
10) D

Vocabulary in Context

1) B
2) B
3) D
4) B
5) D

PP4

1) C
2) B
3) C
4) B
5) A
6) A
7) D
8) C
9) B
10) D
11) B

Illogical Connectors

1) D
2) D
3) D
4) C
5) B
6) D
7) D
8) C
9) D
10) A

PP5

1) C
2) A
3) D
4) B
5) B
6) D
7) C
8) B
9) A
10) D
11) A

PP6

1) A
2) C
3) B
4) B
5) B
6) B
7) A
8) C
9) B
10) A
11) D

Math

Basic Algebra

1) B
2) 5
3) C
4) C
5) B
6) D
7) C
8) D
9) C
10) A

Exponents & Algebra

1) C
2) D
3) A
4) D
5) C
6) D
7) A
8) A
9) B

Applied Algebra

1) A
2) B
3) D
4) A
5) C
6) D
7) A
8) C
9) C
10) A
11) C
12) C
13) D

Equation of a Line

1) B
2) 2/3
3) B
4) C
5) A
6) B
7) A
8) C
9) D
10) D

Function Machines

1) B
2) C
3) C
4) B
5) C
6) B
7) C
8) D
9) D
10) B

Factoring Basics

1) C
2) C
3) A
4) D
5) B
6) 4
7) D
8) B
9) A
10) 5

Pattern Matching

1) D
2) B
3) B
4) C
5) B
6) A
7) B
8) A
9) A

Advanced Factoring

1) 2
2) 3
3) 7
4) D
5) C
6) C
7) A
8) C
9) C

The Unfactorables

1) D
2) B
3) C
4) D
5) C
6) D
7) B

Math

Transformers

1) A
2) D
3) B
4) C
5) B
6) A
7) D
8) D
9) B
10) B
11) A

Zeros and Solutions

1) C
2) A
3) B
4) D
5) D
6) C
7) A
8) A

Solving Systems

1) B
2) C
3) D
4) A
5) B
6) D
7) C
8) 7
9) A
10) D

Spotting Solutions

1) D
2) B
3) C
4) 4
5) C
6) D
7) C
8) C

Systems of Inequalities

1) B
2) A
3) B
4) -7
5) C
6) C
7) A

Basic Modeling

1) D
2) A
3) C
4) D
5) C
6) C
7) D
8) A
9) A

Advanced Modeling

1) C
2) 35
3) C
4) A
5) 44
6) B
7) D
8) A

Exponential Models

1) 106
2) 10.31
3) C
4) C
5) A
6) B
7) B
8) A
9) C
10) B

Piece Over Whole

1) C
2) C
3) A
4) D
5) D
6) A
7) C
8) A
9) 12
10) B

Percent Change

1) C
2) A
3) D
4) 127.5
5) C
6) 20
7) C

Math

Unit Conversion

1) C
2) D
3) A
4) 9
5) D
6) C
7) 132

Basic Statistics

1) C
2) B
3) C
4) C
5) B
6) D
7) 660

Trend-spotting

1) D
2) B
3) A
4) B
5) C
6) C

Line of Best Fit

1) B
2) B
3) A
4) A
5) C
6) A

Study Design

1) D
2) B
3) B
4) C
5) D

Geometry

1) 4
2) B
3) 1400
4) C
5) B
6) C
7) D
8) B
9) $59 \leq x \leq 63$
10) C
11) B

Trigonometry

1) 3/5
2) A
3) 3
4) C
5) 3
6) B

Math Review (NC)

1) C
2) C
3) A
4) D
5) C
6) B
7) A
8) A
9) D
10) C

11) D
12) A
13) D
14) 8
15) 64
16) 6
17) 2

Math Review (C)

1) C
2) C
3) B
4) C
5) C
6) B
7) B
8) B
9) D
10) A
11) C
12) B
13) D
14) B
15) C
16) B
17) B
18) C
19) B
20) D
21) D
22) B
23) A
24) C
25) B
26) C
27) C
28) $3.5 \leq x \leq 7$
29) 38
30) 19
31) 6

Practice Test

Reading

1) B
2) C
3) A
4) B
5) C
6) B
7) A
8) B
9) B
10) D
11) D
12) B
13) C
14) A
15) C
16) B
17) B
18) C
19) D
20) A
21) D
22) D
23) A
24) B
25) A
26) B
27) B
28) B
29) C
30) C
31) C
32) C
33) B
34) B
35) C
36) B
37) A
38) D
39) C
40) D
41) C
42) A
43) C
44) A
45) C
46) B
47) A
48) A
49) C
50) D
51) A
52) C

Writing

1) B
2) B
3) A
4) C
5) D
6) C
7) A
8) D
9) A
10) B
11) B
12) D
13) C
14) D
15) C
16) C
17) B
18) C
19) C
20) B
21) D
22) C
23) A
24) D
25) C
26) B
27) B
28) B
29) A
30) C
31) B
32) C
33) A
34) D
35) B
36) C
37) D
38) B
39) A
40) D
41) A
42) D
43) A
44) A

Practice Test

Math No Calc

1) C
2) C
3) D
4) C
5) C
6) A
7) C
8) C
9) A
10) A
11) A
12) D
13) B
14) B
15) C
16) 3600
17) 5/13
18) 1
19) 12
20) 10

Math Calc

1) B
2) C
3) C
4) D
5) D
6) A
7) C
8) A
9) C
10) C
11) D
12) C
13) C
14) B
15) C
16) B
17) A
18) C
19) B
20) D
21) D
22) C
23) A
24) B
25) A
26) A
27) A
28) D
29) A
30) C
31) 3200
32) 8
33) 0.199
34) 160
35) 4/3
36) $7.39 \leq x \leq 8.44$
37) 0.06
38) 2.65

Citations

Passage, p. 41: Louise Walsh. "Play's the thing." University of Cambridge, originally published August 4, 2015. <www.cam.ac.uk/research/features/plays-the-thing

Passage, p. 44: McNeile, H.C. "A Question of Personality." Originally published 1921. <http://www.gutenberg.org/ebooks/49590?msg=welcome_stranger#a-question-of-personality>

Passage, p. 62: Young, Emma. "10 Mysteries of you: Superstition." New Scientist 05 Aug 2009. 09 Sept 2009. <http://www.newscientist.com/article/mg20327201.400-10-mysteries-of-you-superstition.html> Printed with permission of newscientist.com.

Passage, p. 80: Harper, Ida Husted. The Life and Work of Susan B. Anthony Vol. 1. The Bowen-Merrill Company, 1899. <https://www.gutenberg.org/files/15220/15220-h/15220-h.htm>

Passage, p. 86: Sarah Collins. "New design points a path to the 'ultimate' battery." University of Cambridge, originally published October 29, 2015. <http://www.cam.ac.uk/research/news/new-design-points-a-path-to-the-ultimate-battery>

Passage, p. 93: Hoff M (2007) "What's Behind the Spread of White Syndrome in Great Barrier Reef Corals?" PLoS Biol 5(6): e164. doi:10.1371/journal.pbio.0050164

Figure, p. 94: Xue, Y., Z. Hu, A. Kumar, V. Banzon, T. M. Smith, and N. A. Rayner, 2012: [Global oceans] Sea surface temperatures [in "State of the Climate in 2011"]. Bull. Amer. Meteor. Soc., 93 (7), S58–S62. <https://www.climate.gov/news-features/understanding-climate/state-climate-2011-sea-surface-temperature>

Passage, p. 103: Twain, Mark. A Dog's Tale. New York: Harper & Brothers, 1904.

Passage, p. 113: Stanton, Elizabeth Cady; Anthony, Susan B.; Gage, Matilda Joslyn. HIstory of Woman Suffrage, Vol. 1. Copyright 1881.

Passage, p. 124: (2004) "Natural Biodiversity Breaks Plant Yield Barriers." PLoS Biol 2(10): e331. doi:10.1371/journal.pbio.0020331

Passage, p. 130: Gross L (2006) "Math and Fossils Resolve a Debate on Dinosaur Metabolism." PLoS Biol 4(8): e255. doi:10.1371/journal.pbio.0040255

Passage 1, p. 794: Alcott, Louisa May. Work: A Story of Experience. Boston, 1901.
Figure 1, p. 797 : Information found through U.S. Energy Information Administration.
Figure 2, p. 797: Information found at <http://www.city-data.com/crime/crime-Williston-North-Dakota.html>
Passage 3, p. 799: Gross L (2007) "Untapped Bounty: Sampling the Seas to Survey Microbial Biodiversity." PLoS Biol 5(3): e85. doi:10.1371/journal.pbio.0050085
Passage 4, p. 800: O'Day K (2008) "Gut Reaction: Pyrosequencing Provides the Poop on Distal Gut Bacteria." PLoS Biol 6(11): e295. doi:10.1371/journal.pbio.0060295
Passage 5, p. 802, : Hamilton, Alexander; Jay, John; Madison, James. The Federalist Papers. Originally published in 1788. <https://www.gutenberg.org/files/1404/1404-h/1404-h.htm?
Passage 6, p. 805: Hoff M (2006) "DNA Amplification and Detection Made Simple (Relatively)." PLoS Biol 4(7): e222. doi:10.1371/journal.pbio.0040222